ILYA edits this title because a) he was asked, and b) there's need and a market for it. A professional comic book creator (writer and artist) since 1987, his work has appeared internationally, published by Marvel, DC and Dark Horse in the USA, Kodansha in Japan and by numerous independent companies worldwide. In 2005 he created the *Manga Drawing Kit* for Thunder Bay Press. Other book work includes: *Countdown* and *Time Warp*, two collections of his award-winning graphic novel series *The End of the Century Club*; *A Bowl of Rice*, for Amnesty International; *It's Dark in London*, a noir anthology from Serpent's Tail; and *Skidmarks*, a charming kitchen-sink drama series.

What is he working on now? *Who Cares!* (it's the UK's national magazine for children in care). He also crafts a monthly strip in his local newspaper (*East End Life* – it's the real Eastenders!), and is poised to adapt *King Lear* into manga (for Self Made Hero's popular Manga Shakespeare line). He won't be truly happy until his favourite manga, the works of Hideki Arai, are translated into English. This is a hint.

Cover artist Ken Niimura collaborates with Joe (Spider-man) Kelly on *I Kill Giants*, out now from Image Comics.

Also available

The Mammoth Book of 20th Century Science Fiction
The Mammoth Book of Best British Mysteries
The Mammoth Book of Best Horror Comics
The Mammoth Book of the Best of Best New SF
The Mammoth Book of Best New Erotica 7
The Mammoth Book of Best New Manga 2
The Mammoth Book of Best New SF 20
The Mammoth Book of Best War Comics
The Mammoth Book of Bikers
The Mammoth Book of Boys' Own Stuff
The Mammoth Book of Brain Workouts
The Mammoth Book of Celebrity Murders
The Mammoth Book of Comic Fantasy
The Mammoth Book of Comic Quotes
The Mammoth Book of Cover-Ups
The Mammoth Book of CSI
The Mammoth Book of the Deep
The Mammoth Book of Dirty, Sick, X-Rated & Politically Incorrect Jokes
The Mammoth Book of Dickensian Whodunnits
The Mammoth Book of Egyptian Whodunnits
The Mammoth Book of Erotic Online Diaries
The Mammoth Book of Erotic Women
The Mammoth Book of Extreme Fantasy
The Mammoth Book of Funniest Cartoons of All Time
The Mammoth Book of Hard Men
The Mammoth Book of Historical Whodunnits
The Mammoth Book of Illustrated True Crime
The Mammoth Book of Inside the Elite Forces
The Mammoth Book of International Erotica
The Mammoth Book of Jack the Ripper
The Mammoth Book of Jacobean Whodunnits
The Mammoth Book of Killers at Large
The Mammoth Book of King Arthur
The Mammoth Book of Lesbian Erotica
The Mammoth Book of Maneaters
The Mammoth Book of Modern Ghost Stories
The Mammoth Book of Monsters
The Mammoth Book of Mountain Disasters
The Mammoth Book of New Gay Erotica
The Mammoth Book of New Terror
The Mammoth Book of On the Road
The Mammoth Book of Pirates
The Mammoth Book of Poker
The Mammoth Book of Prophecies
The Mammoth Book of Roaring Twenties Whodunnits
The Mammoth Book of Sex, Drugs and Rock 'N' Roll
The Mammoth Book of Short Spy Novels
The Mammoth Book of Sorcerers' Tales
The Mammoth Book of True Crime
The Mammoth Book of True War Stories
The Mammoth Book of Unsolved Crimes
The Mammoth Book of Vintage Whodunnits
The Mammoth Book of Women Who Kill

The Mammoth Book of **BEST NEW**

3

Edited by ILYA

ROBINSON

RUNNING PRESS
PHILADELPHIA · LONDON

Constable & Robinson Ltd
3 The Lanchesters
162 Fulham Palace Road
London W6 9ER
www.constablerobinson.com

First published in the UK by Robinson,
an imprint of Constable & Robinson, 2008

A copy of the British Library Cataloguing in Publication
Data is available from the British Library

UK ISBN 978-1-84529-827-2

1 3 5 7 9 10 8 6 4 2

First published in the United States in 2008 by Running Press Book Publishers

9   8   7   6   5   4   3   2   1
Digit on the right indicates the number of this printing

US Library of Congress number: 2008931722
US ISBN 978-0-7624-3399-5

Running Press Book Publishers
2300 Chestnut Street
Philadelphia, PA 19103-4371

Visit us on the web!
www.runningpress.com

Printed and bound in China

Contents

7   **Introduction**

13   **KITSUNE TALES**
Andi Watson & Woodrow Phoenix

63   **UNITY RISING**
Robert Deas

87   **PILOT**
Mitz

119   **MY ROBOT**
Paul Harrison-Davies

130   **The Bizarre Adventures of GILBERT& SULLIVAN**
Laura Howell

135   **CAT'S PAW**
David Slater

146   **MANGA JIMAN**
151   3RD – **RAMEN JIMAN** Michael Kacar
157   2ND – **BEGINNINGS** Asia Alfasi
165   1ST – **DARUMAFISH** Gillian Sein Ying Ha

169   **TALE of the UNA-DON EATER**
Gillian Sein Ying Ha

179   **ED & ECCHI**
Shari Chankhamma

221   **ME AND MY FOOD**
Shari Chankhamma

228   **CARLOS & SAKURA**
Joanna Zhou

229   **GROUND ZERO – THE WOGE**
James Romberger & Marguerite Van Cook

241   **JULY TENTH**
Eve Yap

251 **SNOWFALL**
Rainbow Buddy

261 **FRICTION BETWEEN**
Niki Smith

SUMMER STUDIO CHINA

289 **Attack of the Peach Blossoms** – Yao Feila

307 **As a King** – Yu Yanshu

319 **A Dream in Garden** – Xia Da

329 **In Manoa** – Zhu Letao

340 **CARLOS & SAKURA**
Joanna Zhou

341 **NEW YORK STORIES**
James Romberger & Crosby Romberger

354 **CARLOS & SAKURA**
Joanna Zhou

355 **HERO Z**
Phd

369 **MONSTER MAYHEM**
Kit Wallis & Paul Fryer

385 **PURIKURA**
Sarah Burgess

391 **WHITE**
Sofia Falkenhem

412 **CARLOS & SAKURA**
Joanna Zhou

413 **IN DREAMS**
Eli Basanta

419 **LAST SHADOWS CAST**
Caspar Wijngaard

440 **CARLOS & SAKURA**
Joanna Zhou

441 **MOONLIGHT**
Chi-Tan (Chie Kutsuwada)

Introduction

What makes manga so great?

In its birthplace of Japan, manga is a mass-market form that appeals to everyone; a happy situation that bears repeating. And it is gradually becoming the case the world over. Our brief at *Best New Manga* is to reflect the global phenomenon manga has become. Featured artists – a great many of them award-winners – come from America, China, Spain, United Kingdom, Thailand, Libya, Sweden, Malaysia and, yes, Japan.

Best New Manga exists to showcase the best of what's new from the rising generations of international talent; those inspired or influenced by Japanese anime and comics, but with their own contribution to make. The series, with its tight annual schedule – March deadlines for October publication – proves there's so much more to manga. All material is creator-owned, and there's a ton more like it available. Contact details are listed: open encouragement for fellow publishers to get in on the action, release a wider variety of manga, and cater to the widest possible audience. *BNM* is intended for "all ages".

Whoa, Best New Manga Three already!

In Volume Two we debuted a neat little colour section. What's new and most significant about this latest collection is that the book now has full-colour printing throughout. If you're confused by that (after all "surely manga mainly come in black and white?") check out the editorial from last time to find the misconception corrected. In short, anyone looking at manga published in its Japanese homeland will see that manga can and does come in colour. Of course, the longer-running serials have to be produced at such a cracking pace to meet demand that it is hardly the norm. However, manga produced outside of Japan – such as Chinese manhua – is in colour more often than not. For most artists around the world Japanese animation is as much if not more of a prime influence and, without manga publishing on any sort of comparative scale, the internet remains their primary outlet. They're simply choosing to work in colour.

So full-colour print better reflects what's actually going on, and where it's all going to go next. What this gives us, of course, is merely the option of colour throughout. Many stories suit black and white, and we'll continue to run them either way without bias. That said, forgiveness is perhaps in order if this time around we take slight advantage and splurge on a whole spectrum of material so far denied us. It's a golden opportunity to show off some of the best candidates we've coveted since day one, but simply couldn't do justice to before. If you remember *Advent, Volume One*'s opener by Michiru Morikawa, that strip was actually produced in delicate tea-stain tones of sepia, and we wished then that you could see it that way. What's ultimately most important is that the stories can now be presented exactly how their creators wish them to be seen. We've taken a slight hit in our number of pages in order to achieve this, yet think you'll agree it is well worth it.

International New Talents

The operative word in the title – *Best New Manga* – is New. We present to you the best of the new manga we come across. The title of *Best Manga* of course belongs to the various classics of the medium, old and new, but since these are already global top-sellers and available far and wide, they hardly need the modest leg-up into the world arena that we could give them. We don't feature more Japanese manga for much the same reason. Pick up copies of *GON, AKIRA, Barefoot Gen* and anything by Tezuka, from *Astro Boy* through *Adolf* to *Buddha*, in the same place you found this. Take the time to graze the shelves and sample a bit of whatever tickles your fancy. There's more than sixty years' worth of manga to catch up on and the true variety is yet to be seen in translation, especially among titles for older readers. Outside of our remit, this should also come in time. Much of it remains so culturally remote it'll probably never travel: there's nothing to stop you anyway checking it out. Meanwhile, we continue to showcase an international and ever-growing roster of new talents; including creators representative of Japan, such as Morikawa and Chi-Tan (Chie Kutsuwada). Making manga as much as reading manga has become such a global activity, Japan takes its place as just one of the featured conduits.

A single artist can open up a whole country

Rainbow Buddy (aka Ivy Ling from China) brought her pot o'gold along to the International Manga and Anime Festival back in 2006. Cover artist and two-time illustrator for *Volume Two* in 2007, this year she introduced to us the manifold talents of Summer Studio, based in Hang Zhou city. Four very different artists' works are on display in their own special section.

In 2008, the year of the Olympics in Beijing (as it will be for London come 2012), among the major cultural links being forged is China Now, the largest single festival of Chinese culture ever to be held in the UK. This event included a major show dedicated to manhua (manga from China), and details of this can be found at www.chinanow.org.uk, and at www.paulgravett.com/events/manhua/manhua.htm. One of the undoubted stars of that show was a young Chinese writer/artist called BENJAMIN (remember the name – you'll be hearing a lot more about him). He's rock star brilliant, possibly the most exciting new artist the medium has yet produced, not least in commercial terms. Showing off cutting-edge digital techniques backed by old-school drawing skills, his work is prolific, beyond real, a bit emo, very urban, and vibrant just isn't the word (oh man, the colours…!). What's more, Tokyopop's got him, and they'll be bringing out two Benjamin titles early in 2009, called *Remember*, and *Orange*; sure to be the first of many. It was perhaps surprising to some people when they picked up Ross Campbell's gorily excellent *The Abandoned,* to find it printed in black and white and red all over. Benjamin's books are just part of an entire new line in the fullest of full colour and taken from all around the world. Oh yes – believe us when we tell you, when it comes to the future of manga, you ain't seen NOTHING yet.

Interesting item!

It might be the Year of the Rat in China, but here at *BNM* towers it's been the Year of the Cat, with many a cat-themed manga found among our submissions. Some even made the final cut – so watch out for those claws.

Pandas rock

These words are being written in the springtime. This summer's big cartoon movie – if it's any good – will have been *KUNG FU PANDA*, from Dreamworks. We were there first, of course, with *Volume One*'s cover star Samurai Commander Keiko Wu featured in all her ass-kicking, shuriken-flinging, sheer-silk-billowing all-out action glory. Panda pundit Jason Cobley reprised his creation for a solo outing in *Volume Two*, alongside Pilot's Mitz on art. If you haven't yet grabbed yourself a copy of either hit, demand them by name.

Friends-in-odd-places department

The November '07 edition of *WIRED* magazine (cover feature *Manga Conquers America: how Japanese comics are reshaping pop culture*) ran *Japan, Ink*, a rather excellent article by Dan Pink. We wrote to tell him so, and he wrote back to tell us he was a *BNM* fan. That's Dan Pink, the former speechwriter for (US politico turned environmentalist) Al Gore, no less. Yowza. You see the company we keep? Look out for salaryman (office politics/drama) manga *The Adventures of Johnny Bunko*, which he wrote.

Everyone's getting in on the act

Competition-wise there's been much activity these past couple of years; international talent searches have included more than a few originating inside of Japan, birthplace of manga. In the UK alone there's been a second MANGA JIMAN (see our special spotlight section on the top three entrants from year one, and read their winning strips); a major six-month exhibit at the URBIS Centre, Manchester, one of the country's biggest and most prestigious new arts complexes, *How MANGA took over the world* (notice a theme here?); and manga-related events aplenty as part of JAPAN-UK 150, a festival celebrating 150 years of Anglo-Japanese accord. Citizens are not their governments (thankfully), but sometimes even government gets it right. When it comes to manga it seems everyone's getting in on the act, and you know what? Everyone's welcome. All together we begin to make for a new international community, one that gets along waaay better than any old one.

Where does it all come from?

Questions often asked are, "Where do you find the talent that you feature?" And, "How do you make your selections?" And then someone commented via the Internet, "I think you need to be clearer about where these stories originally appeared". Fair point, so: mostly they haven't. This is a print debut for much of the content and many of our contributors, at least in any mainstream sense. Hard to believe, isn't it, that material of such quality lapses unpublished. We aim to put that right.

Sometimes the good stuff just comes to us, either by design or happy accident. More often we actively go scouting, out at manga-related festivals and shows, online, or else via recommendation. To answer in more particular detail the brief bio pages introducing each strip will, this time out, talk a bit about provenance – where or how the works originated, and why they made the grade. At the core of manga's appeal is the wide variety of its themes, so we'll also be addressing genre.

In more general terms, we avoid the sort of material that is readily available elsewhere; there's little point repeating it. Most imported titles broadly conform to teen fiction – *shojo* (for girls), and *shonen* (for boys) – to the exclusion of almost everything else. Partly we're here to show you that there's so much more to manga as we know and love it – an entire medium as opposed to any single style or genre. It can be about anything, and it can look like anything. The skills are largely self-taught and the activity self-motivated. There's a storytelling science at work, but no fixed rules. As a medium of communication, manga is endlessly malleable and should never become fixed – that's why it's called a medium! Seek to apply a strict definition and manga will surely squirm out from under it.

The immediate mistake a great many new artists make is cookie-cutting; replicating existing styles too closely, especially the ones already flooding the market. The way to get noticed is to stand out from the crowd, and that is by going your own way. The artists winning awards in competition and gaining the subsequent recognition do so largely via their originality in technique, approach or subject matter. Making manga their own way, it becomes grounded in who they are, shows what else interests them, and is that delicious thing – truly individual.

If you like this, you'll dig these

Some recommended reads to end on: if you approve the likes of *BNM* you should also dig the following titles. These homegrown variants on the original Japanese model for manga – all American, pretty much – are truly excellent.

In the USA Oni Press maintains a uniformly excellent list – everything we've tried we liked. *Scott Pilgrim* you must know about already (it walks out of stores), so why not try; *Black Metal* by Rick Spears and Chuck BB; *Last Call* by Vasilis Lolos (artist on the best Image comic, *Pirates of Coney Island*); *Sharknife* by Corey Lewis; or *Wonton Soup* by James Stokoe. *Offroad* (Sean Murphy) isn't in the accepted manga format, but it's still fabulous, a B-movie on paper.

Worship alongside us at the altar of Ross Campbell, the hardest-working man in manga; he can do no wrong, no matter which publisher it's for. Sample his *Wet Moon* series, three volumes so far... (Oni Press), *The Abandoned* (T'POP), and not least the sharktastic *Water Baby* for DC's new Minx line of manga-like fiction. That's also home to *The Plain Janes* (by Cecil Castellucci and Jim Rugg); Andi Watson's *Clubbing*, well written at least; ditto Derek Kirk Kim's *Good As Lily*. Kim's *Same Difference and Other Stories* comes from Alternative Comics; alongside John Pham, he's about the brightest spark in Asian-American comic books. Phew!

For adult readers, something a bit more coffee-table perhaps; Fanfare/Ponent Mon do a very good line of books, sampling a more grown-up and refined Japanese manga (Jiro Taniguchi etc). And last but not least, even the teen-terrorizers themselves, Tokyopop, are exploring further possibilities. Their title *KING CITY* (Brandon Graham) is the single best example so far of the new hybrid manga (west-meets-east-meets-west).

Jump in, heroes, have a go. Make more manga!

ILYA
Manga Wrangler

KITSUNE tales™

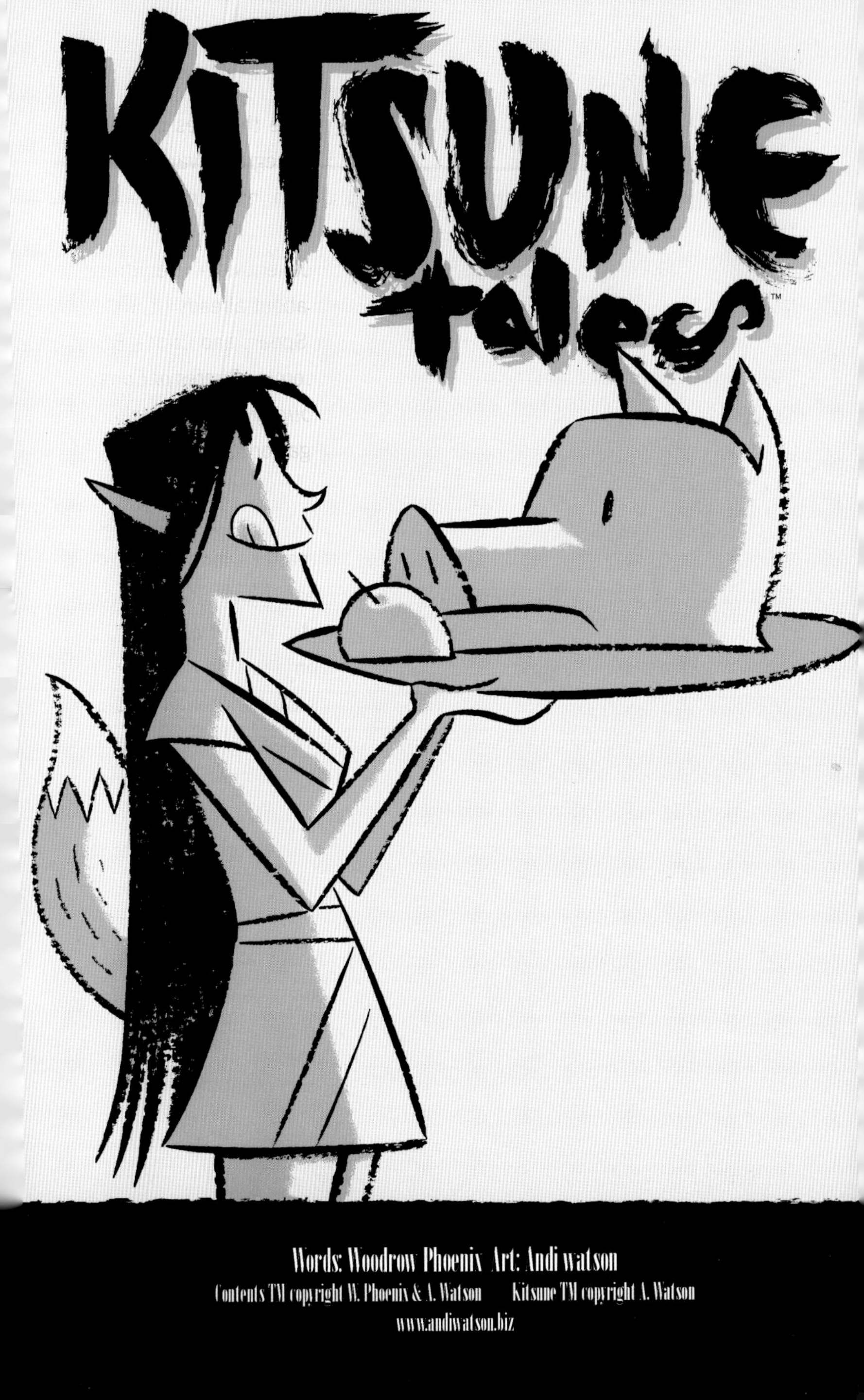

Words: Woodrow Phoenix Art: Andi watson

www.andiwatson.biz

KITSUNE TALES

Andi Watson & Woodrow Phoenix

Manga as we know it today, has its origins in the American occupation of Japan following World War II. Dropped comic books and animated films such as *Popeye* fired the imagination of young student Tezuka Osamu in particular. He combined what inspired him with Japan's own narrative pictorial tradition to synthesize this modern cartoon artform. Meeting with the west had produced an even greater culture shock a half-century previously, bringing with it rapid industrialization and urban expansion. Farmers gravitated to the cities, becoming factory workers and, these days, office jockeys. Mourning the loss of their pastoral landscape, the torch is kept alight through modern fable and myth.

Kitsune or Fox Spirit tales are relatively common, the legendary shape-shifting trickster a popular archetype throughout many cultures. Here, **Woodrow Phoenix** (writer) and **Andi Watson** (artist) together weave one such fable.

Comics veterans, they are principally known for their respective long-running series released through American comics company Slave Labor (Andi, *Skeleton Key*, in which *Kitsune* plays a regular part; and Woodrow *Sugar Buzz*, with Ian Carney). *Kitsune Tales* enjoyed a limited release as a one-shot comic edition. Presented here in colour for the first time, it most definitely deserves to be seen and enjoyed by a wider audience.

Andi and Woodrow:
www.andiwatson.biz/
andiwatson.livejournal.com/
flickr.com/photos/andiwatson/

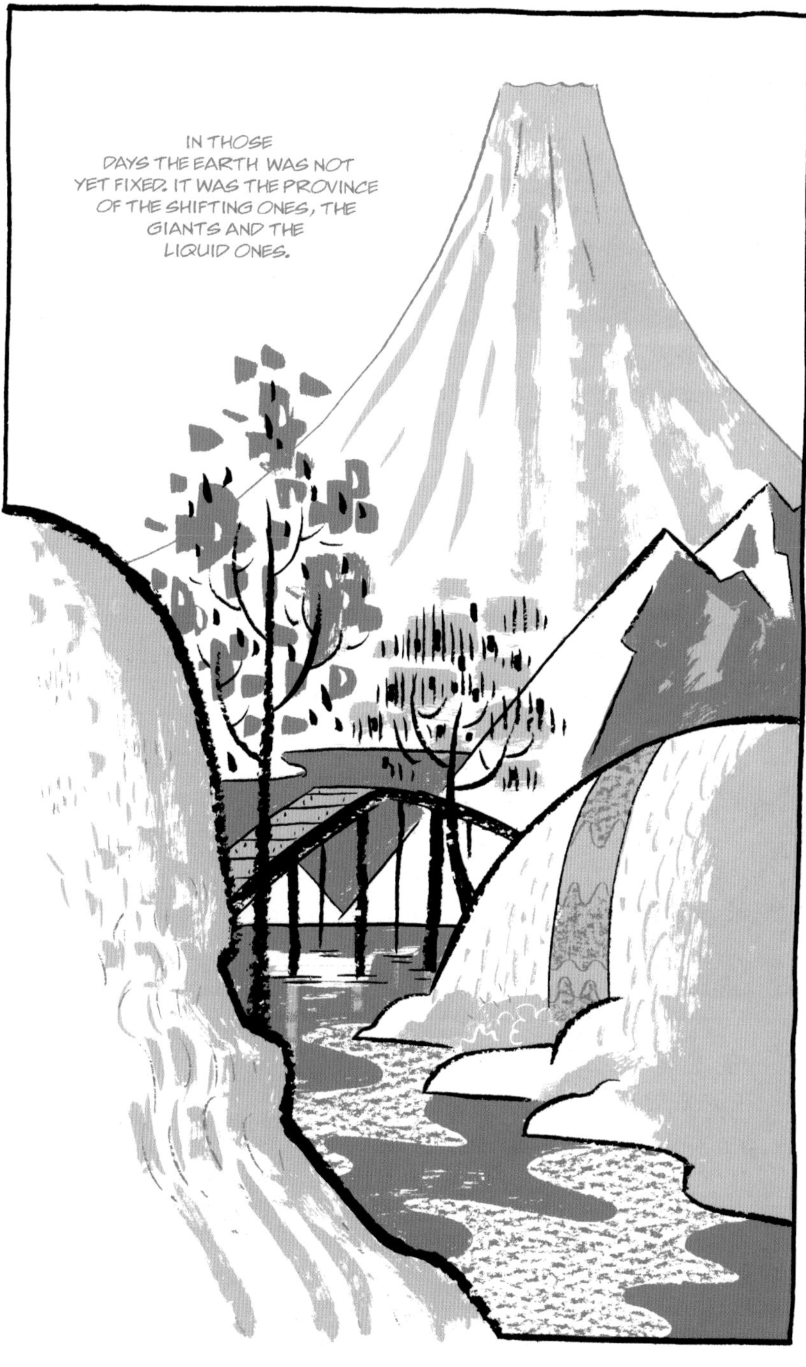
IN THOSE DAYS THE EARTH WAS NOT YET FIXED. IT WAS THE PROVINCE OF THE SHIFTING ONES, THE GIANTS AND THE LIQUID ONES.

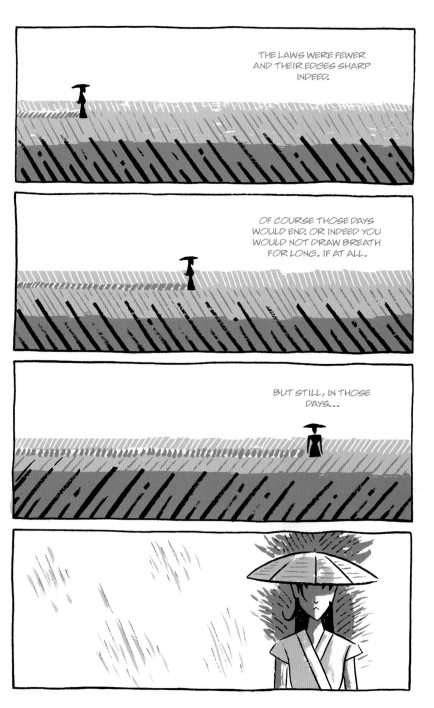

THE LAWS WERE FEWER AND THEIR EDGES SHARP INDEED.

OF COURSE THOSE DAYS WOULD END. OR INDEED YOU WOULD NOT DRAW BREATH FOR LONG. IF AT ALL.

BUT STILL, IN THOSE DAYS...

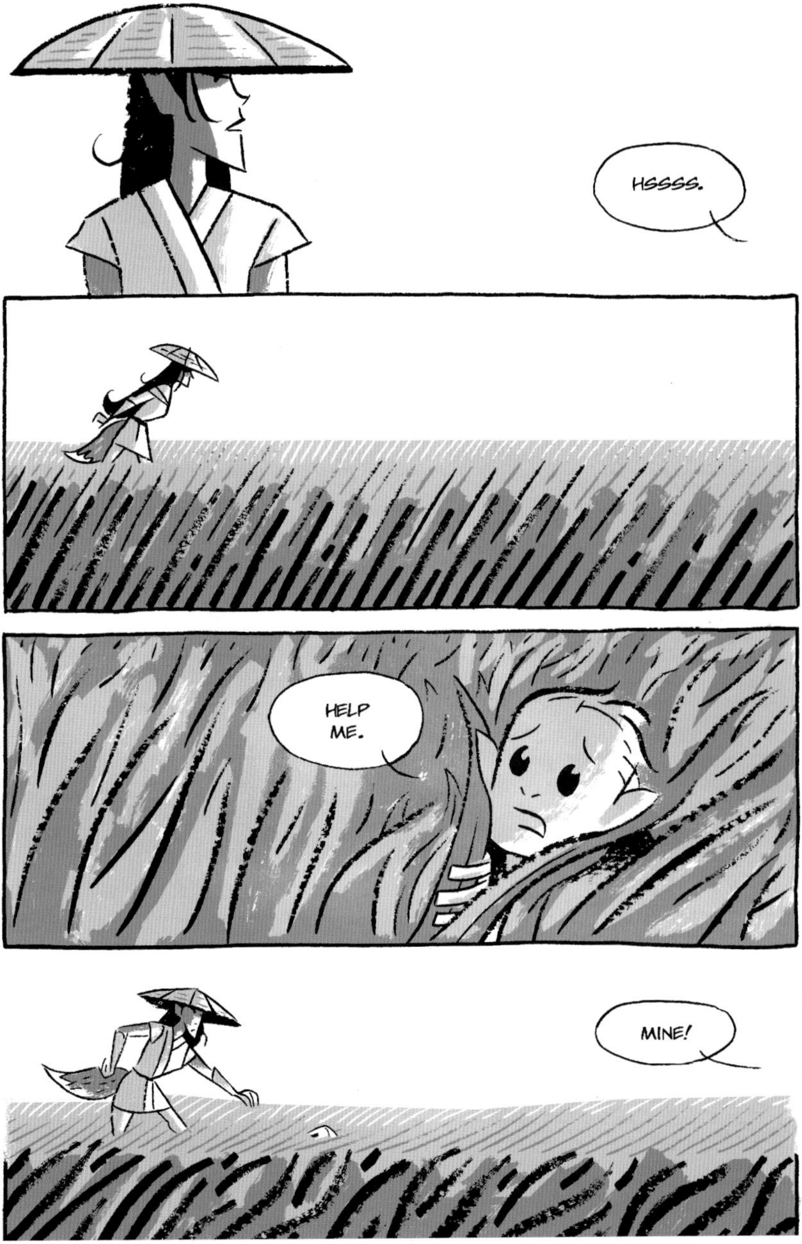
HSSSS.
HELP ME.
MINE!

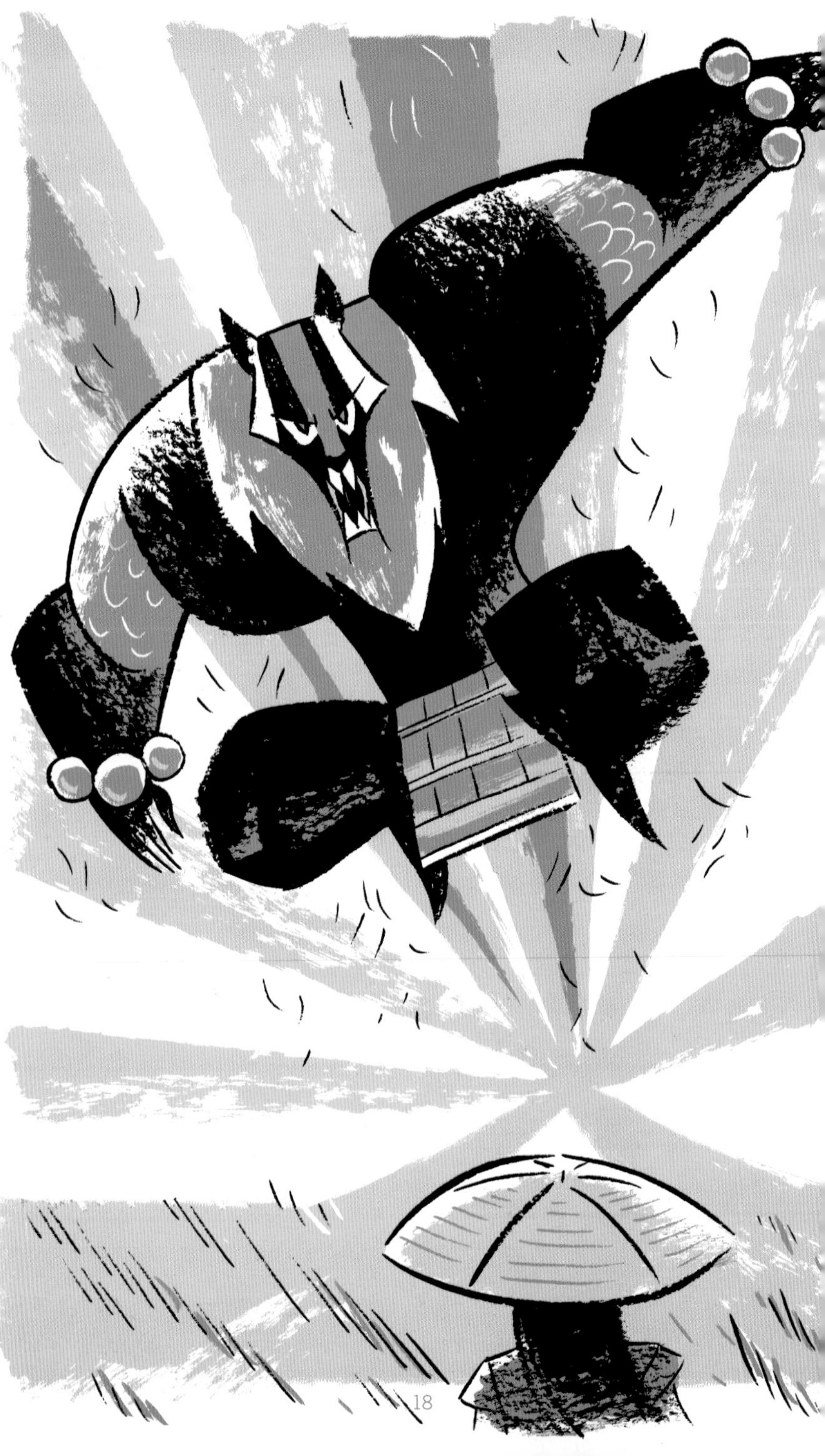

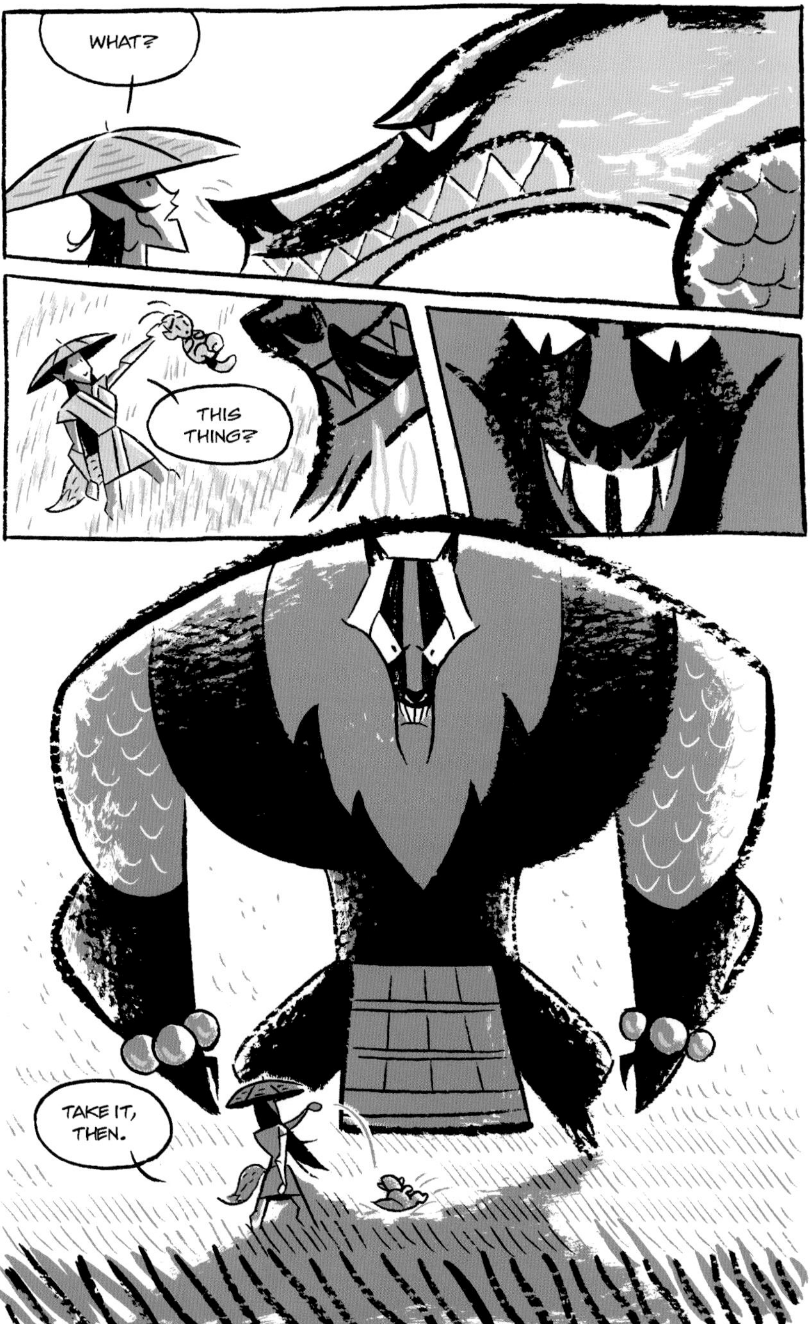
WHAT?
THIS THING?
TAKE IT, THEN.

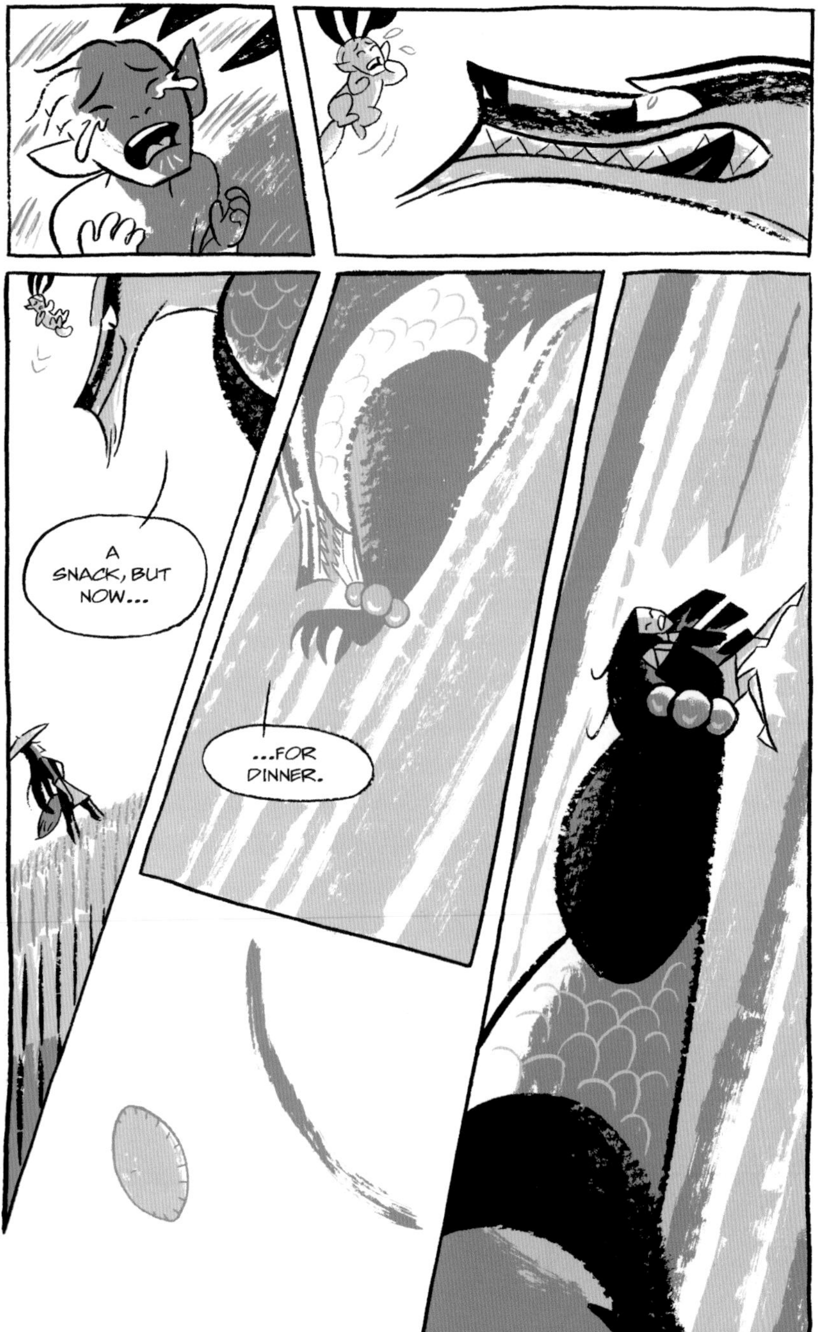
A SNACK, BUT NOW...
...FOR DINNER.

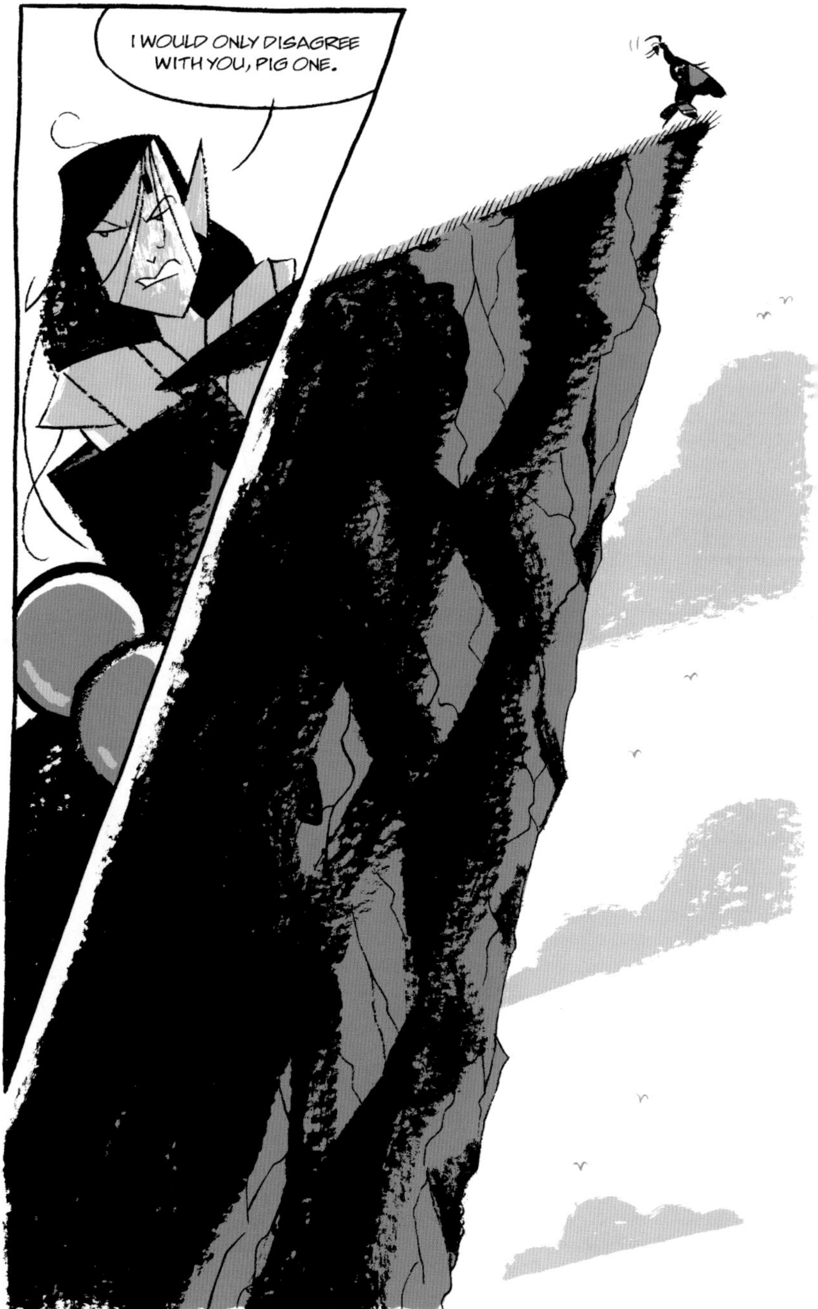
I WOULD ONLY DISAGREE WITH YOU, PIG ONE.

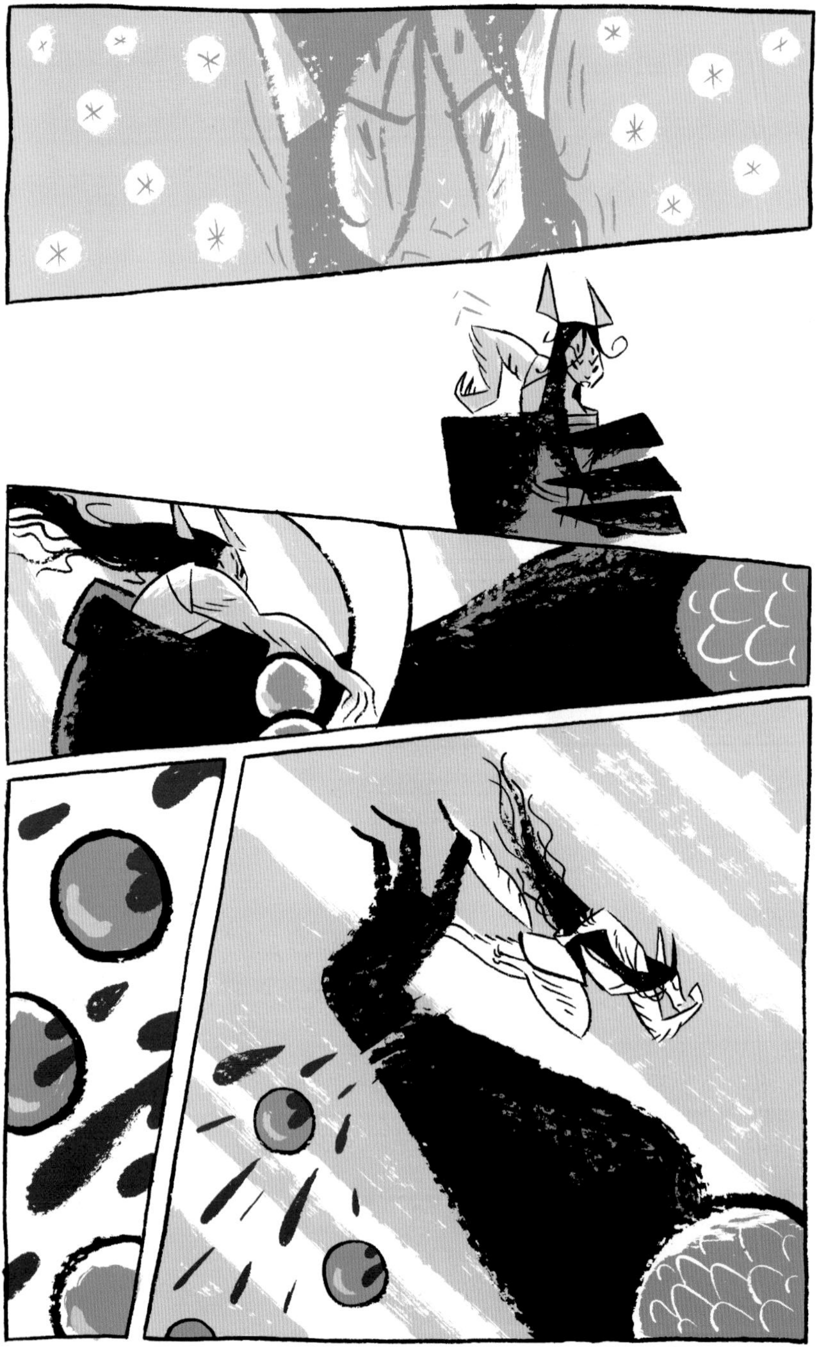

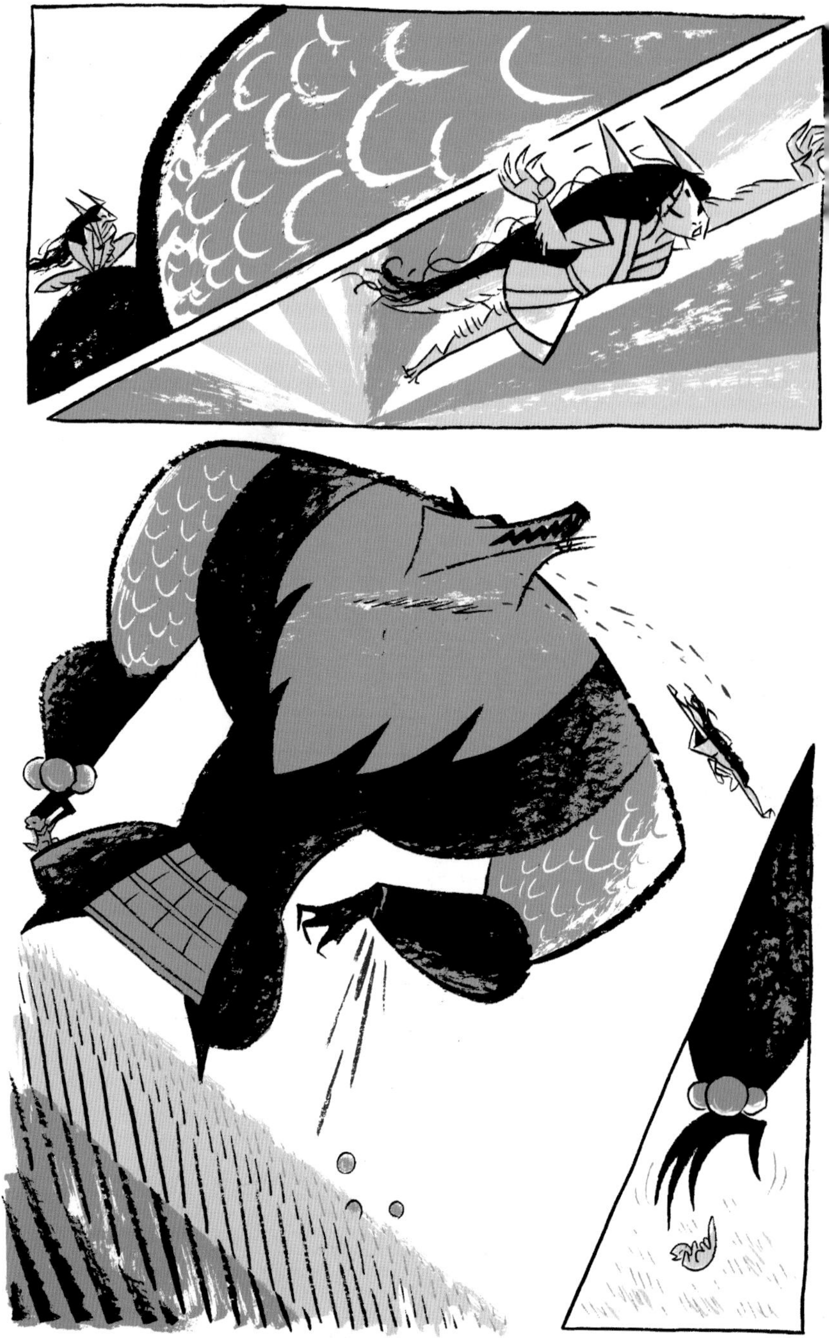

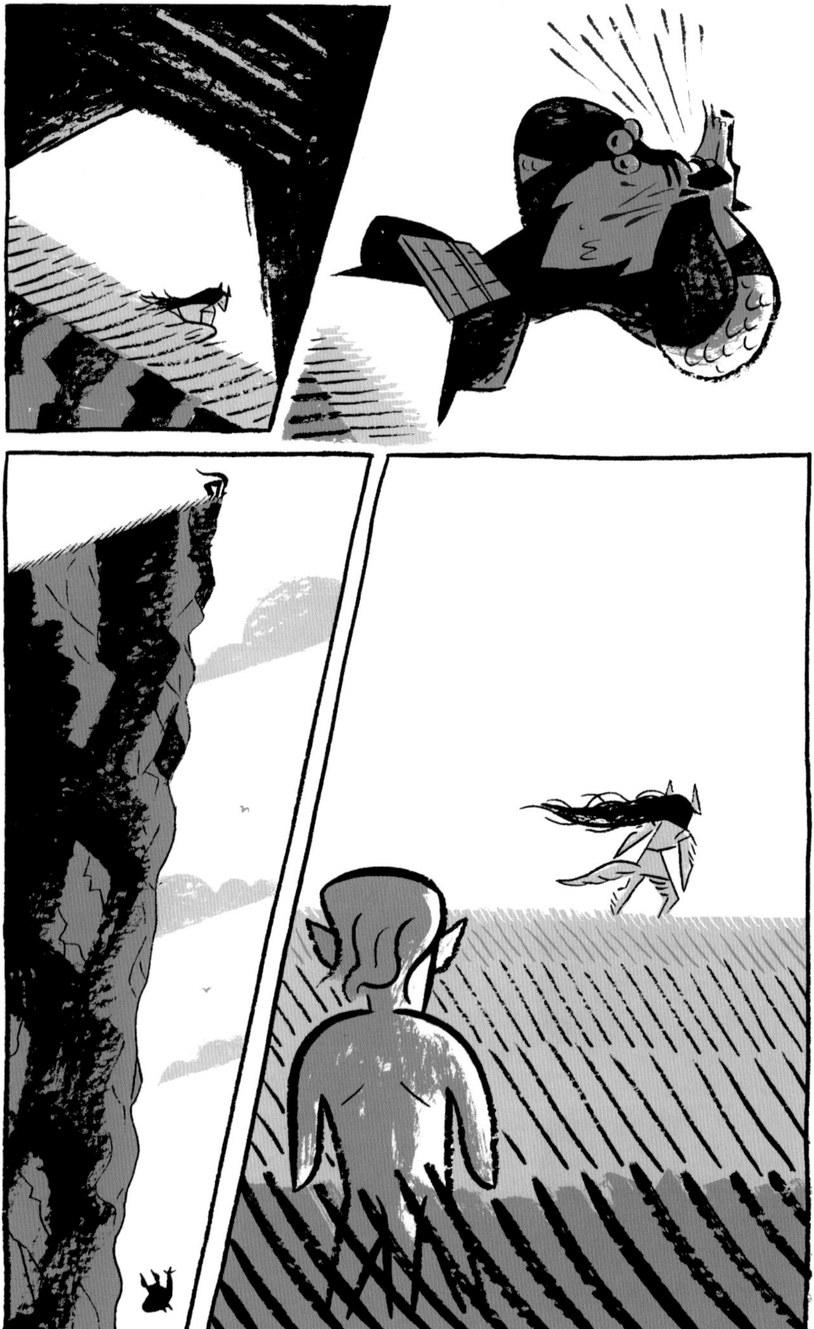

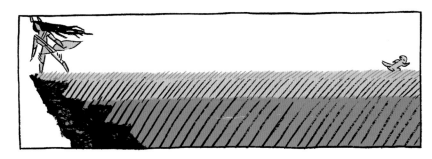

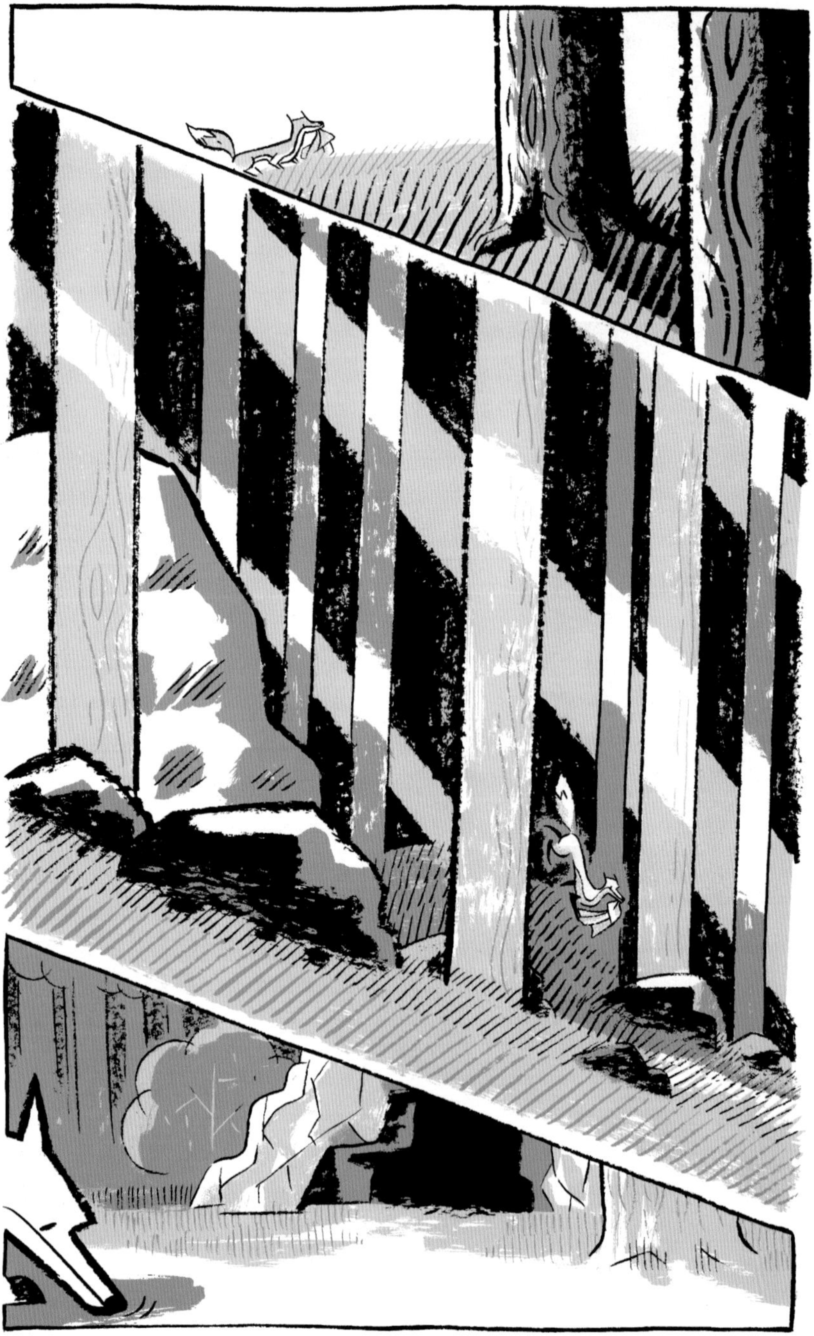

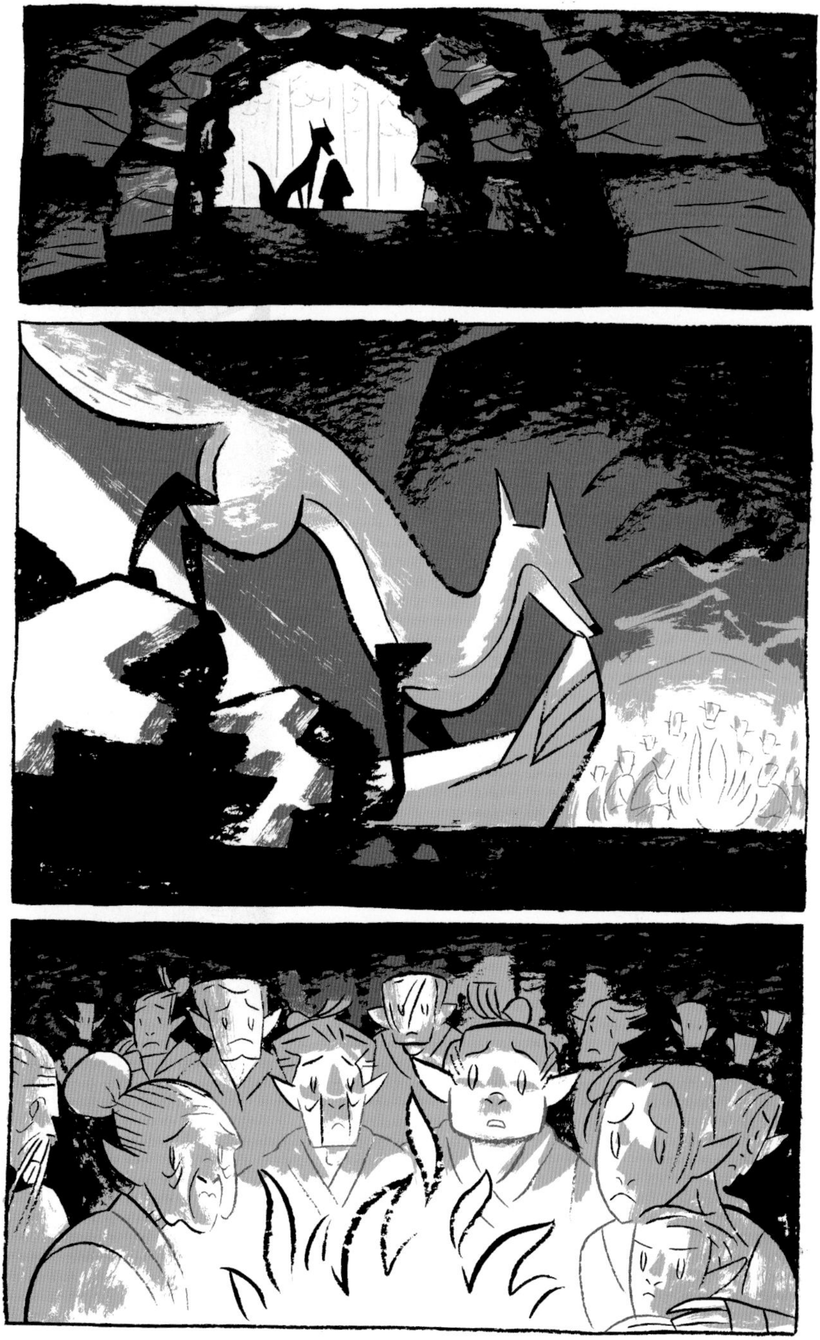

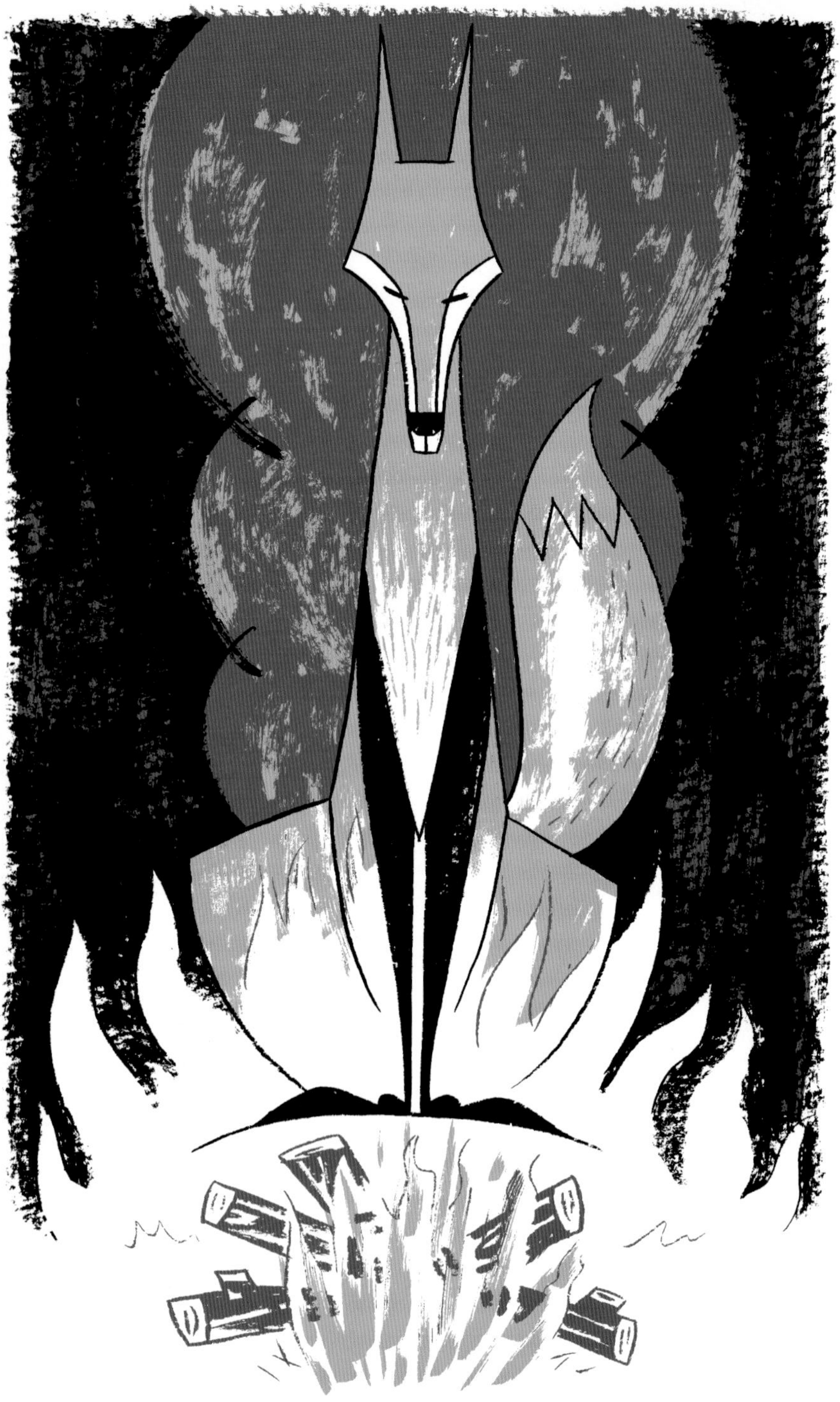

MERCY! MERCY, SHIFTING ONE, YOU HAVE SAVED OUR LAST CHILD BUT WE CANNOT REPAY YOU.

MERCY.

MERCY.

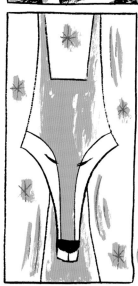

IT WAS NOT MY INTENT. BUT I DESERVE SOME-THING, SURELY?

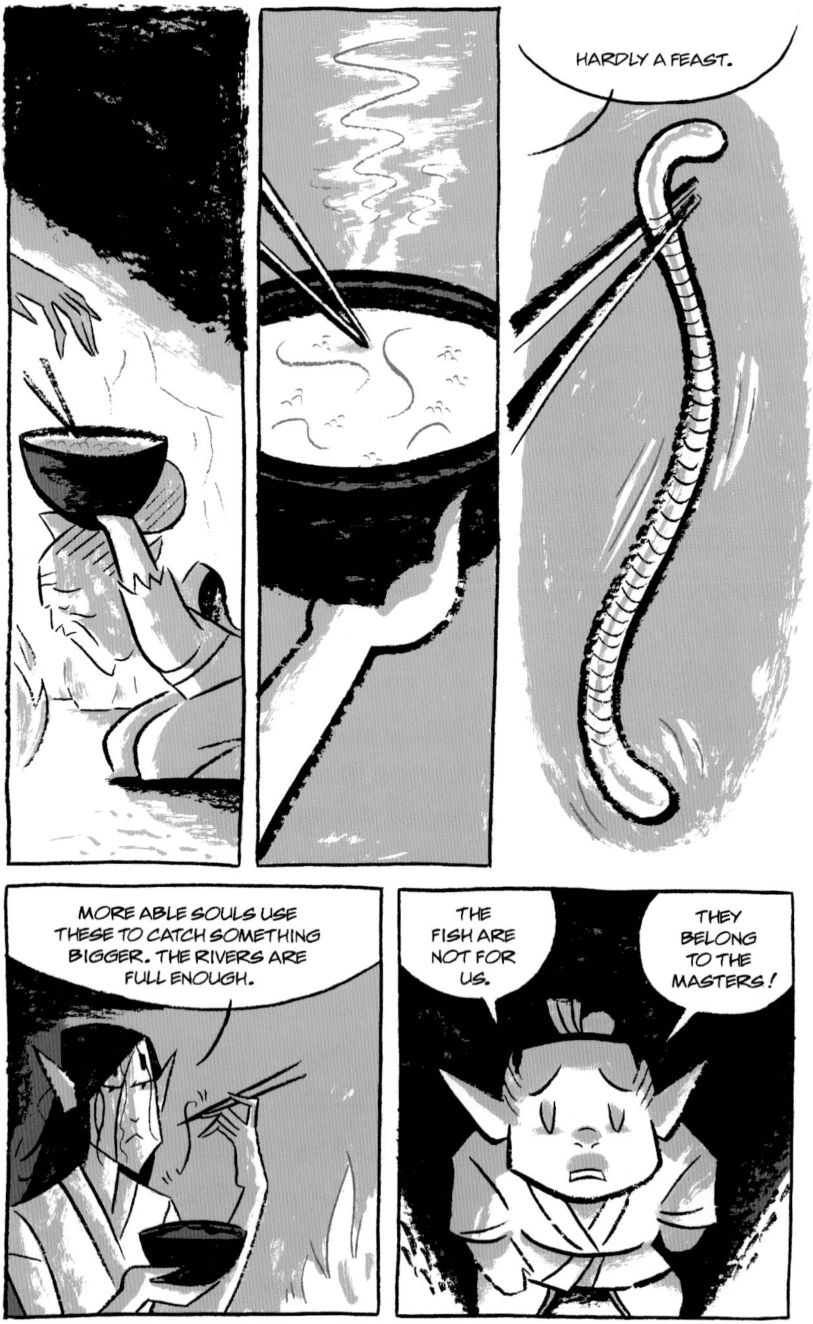

HARDLY A FEAST.
MORE ABLE SOULS USE THESE TO CATCH SOMETHING BIGGER. THE RIVERS ARE FULL ENOUGH.
THE FISH ARE NOT FOR US.
THEY BELONG TO THE MASTERS!

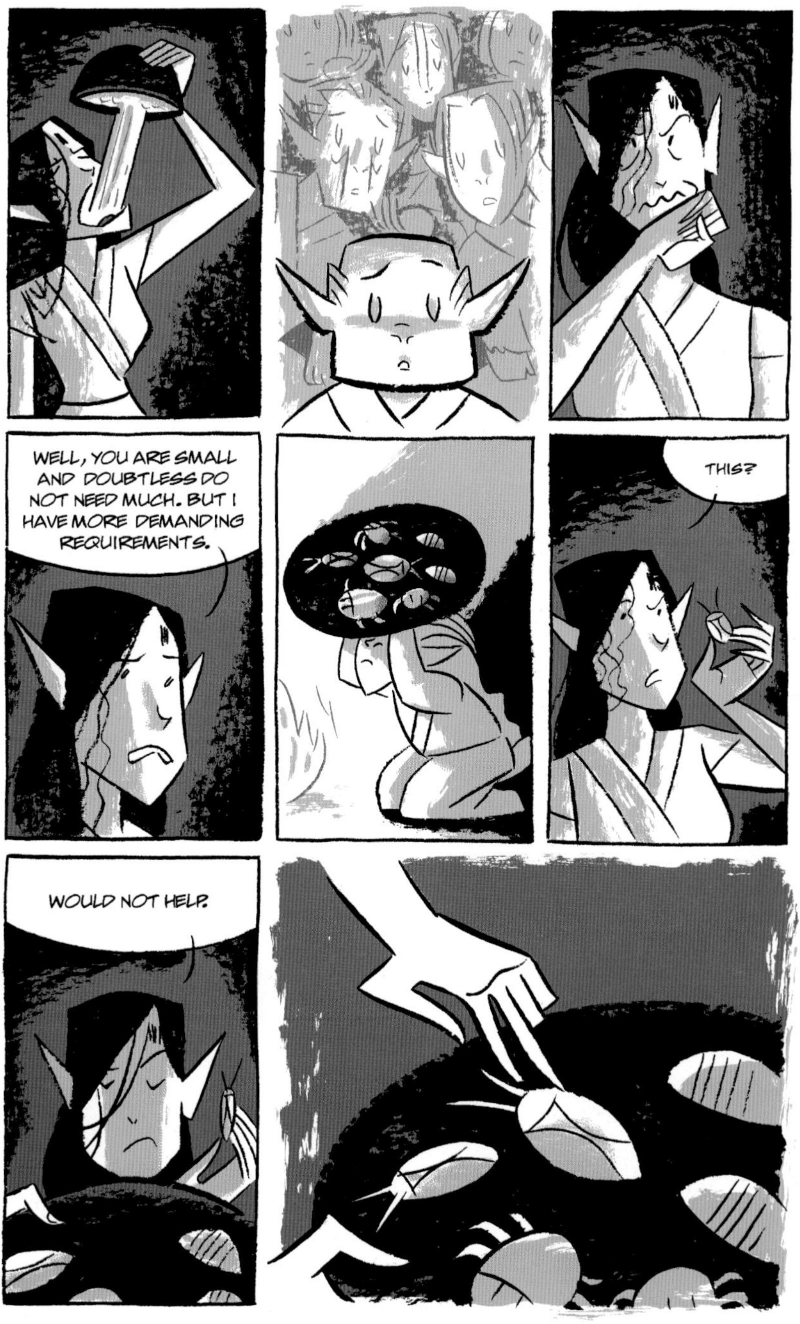
WELL, YOU ARE SMALL AND DOUBTLESS DO NOT NEED MUCH. BUT I HAVE MORE DEMANDING REQUIREMENTS.
THIS?
WOULD NOT HELP.

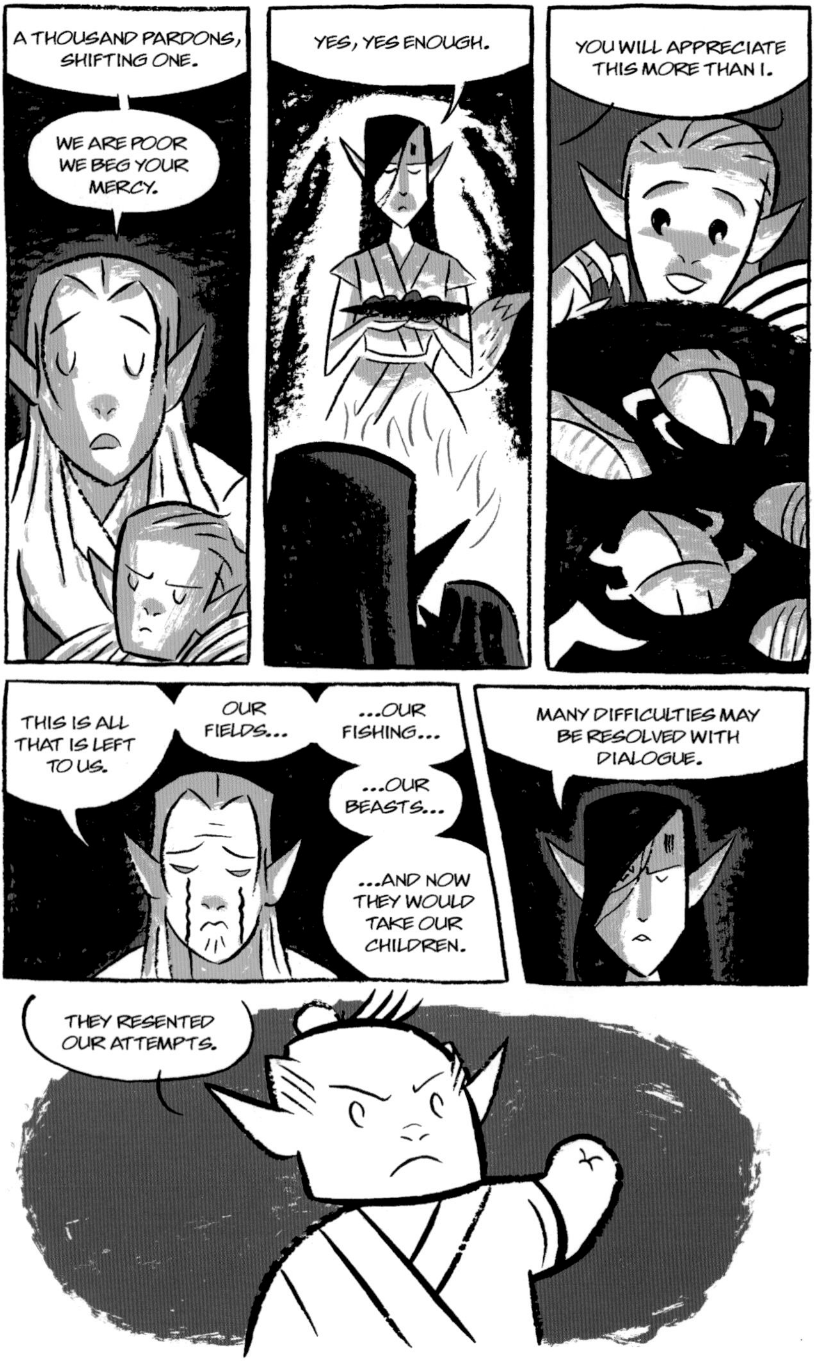
A THOUSAND PARDONS, SHIFTING ONE.
WE ARE POOR WE BEG YOUR MERCY.
YES, YES ENOUGH.
YOU WILL APPRECIATE THIS MORE THAN I.
THIS IS ALL THAT IS LEFT TO US.
OUR FIELDS...
...OUR FISHING...
...OUR BEASTS...
...AND NOW THEY WOULD TAKE OUR CHILDREN.
MANY DIFFICULTIES MAY BE RESOLVED WITH DIALOGUE.
THEY RESENTED OUR ATTEMPTS.

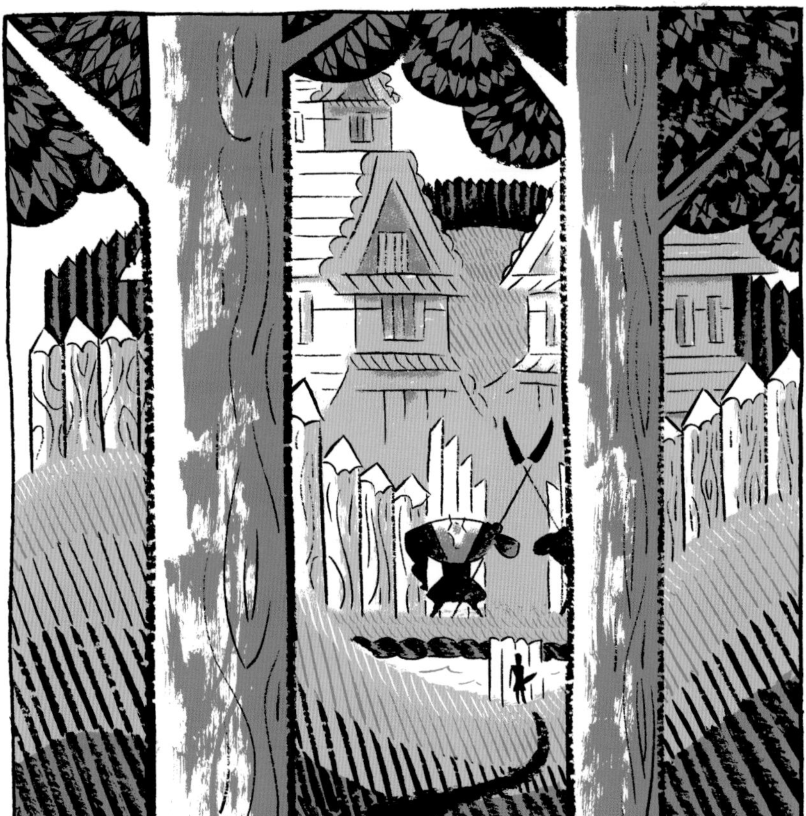

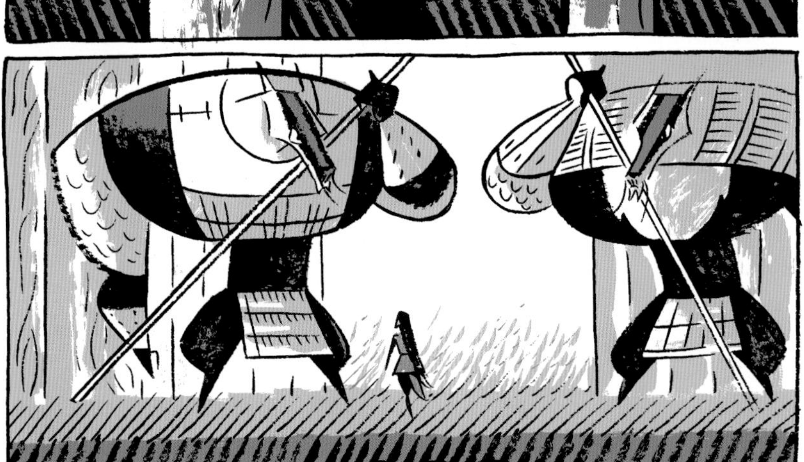

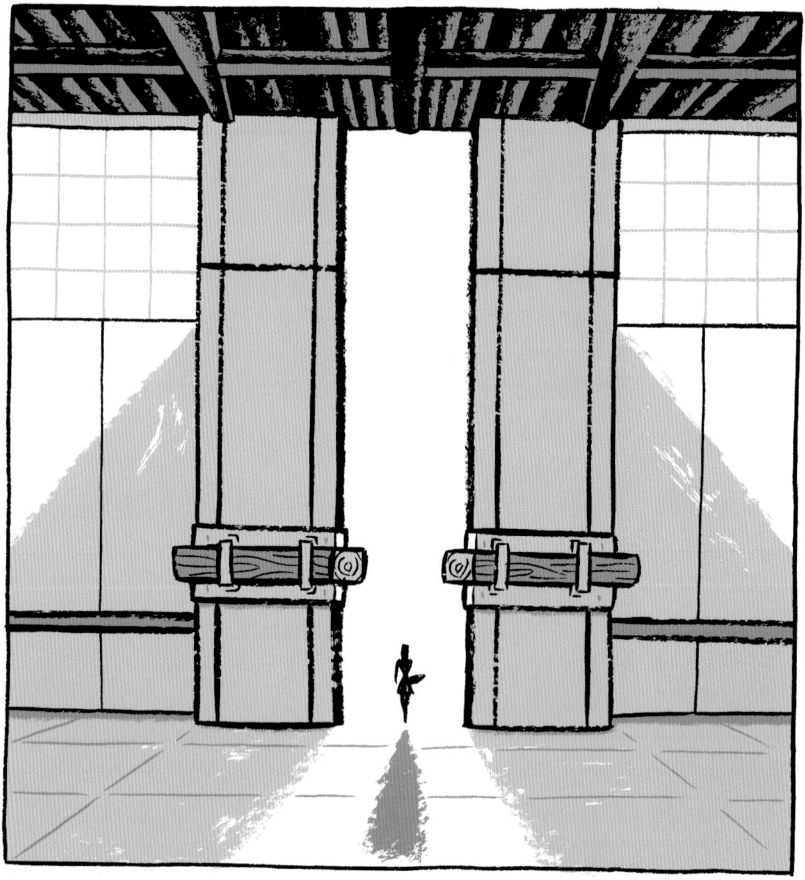
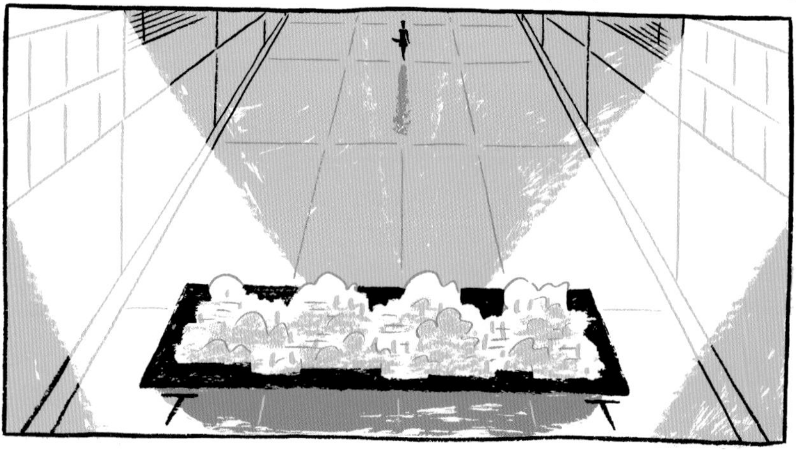

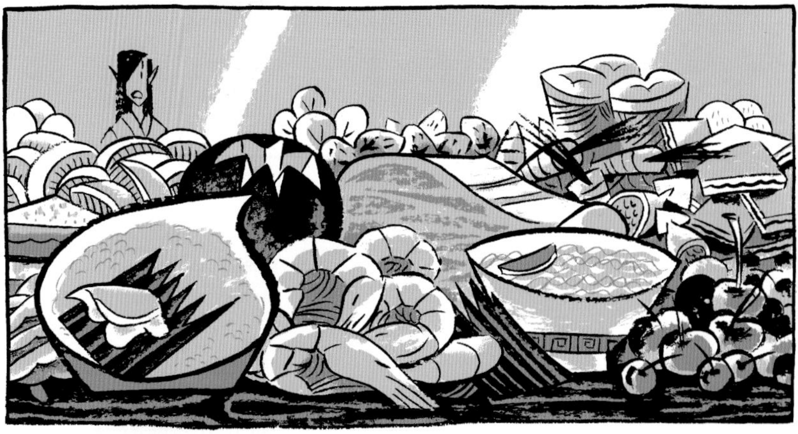
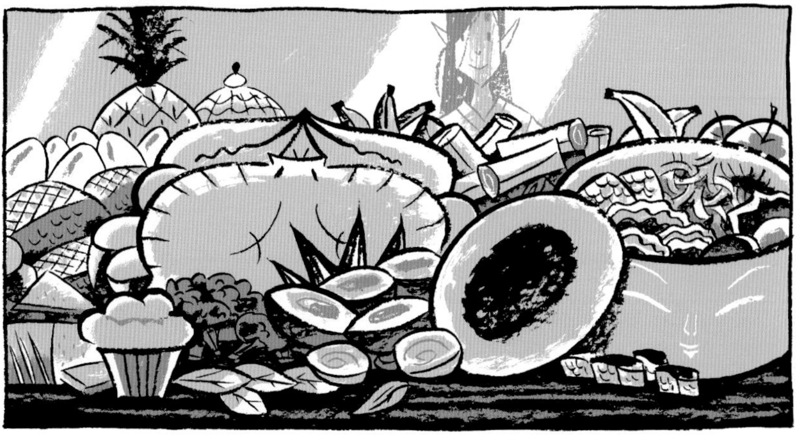
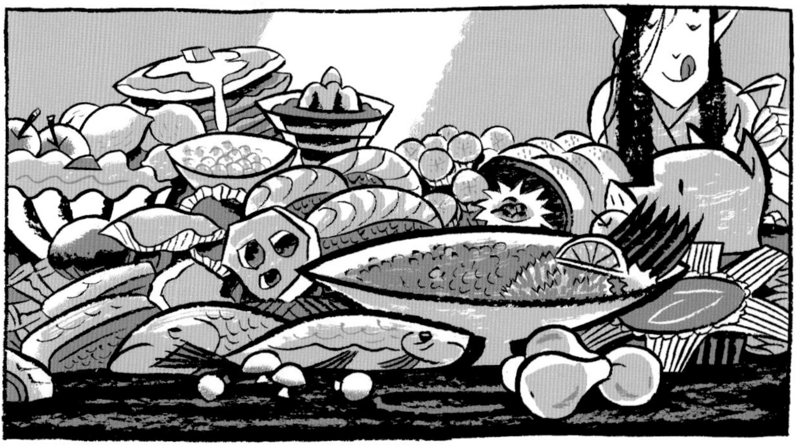

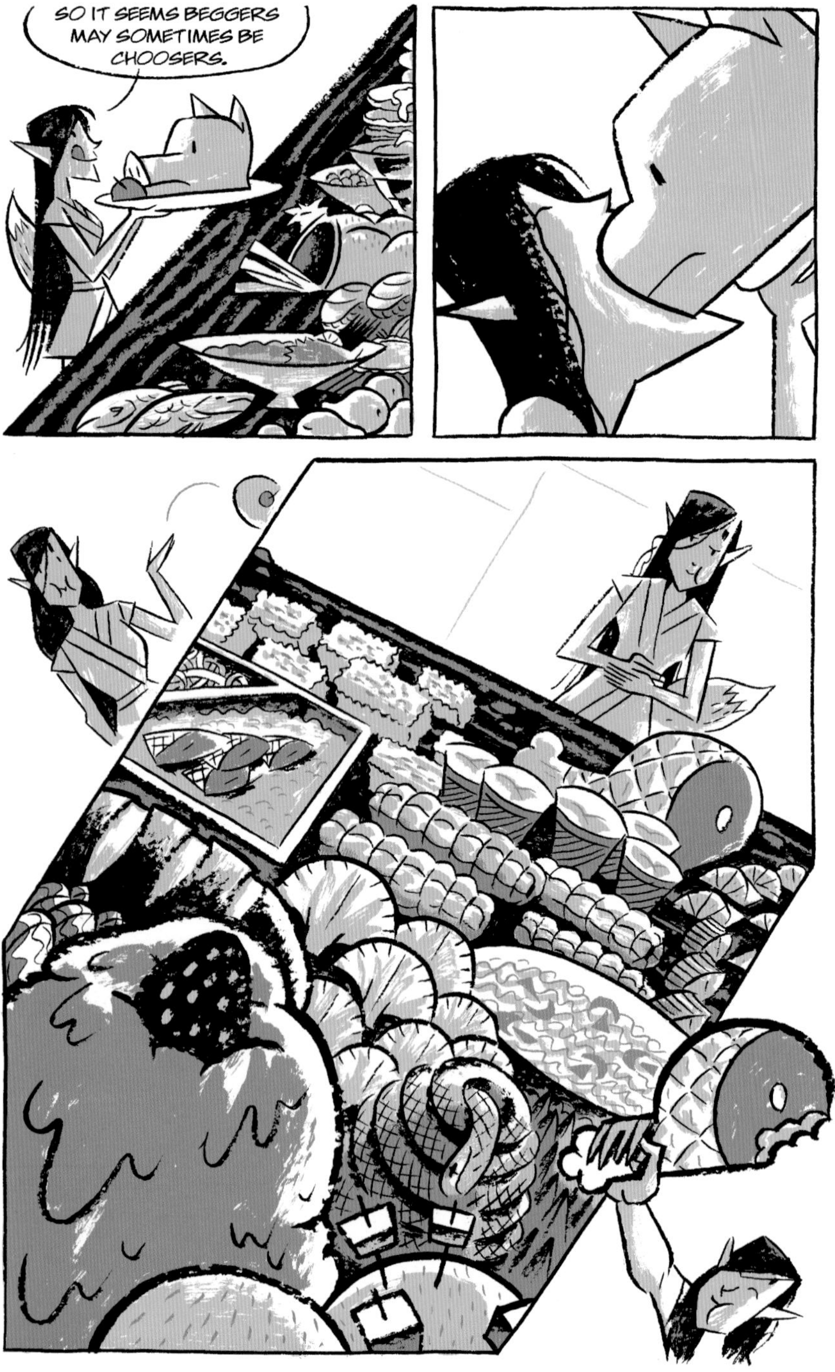
SO IT SEEMS BEGGERS MAY SOMETIMES BE CHOOSERS.

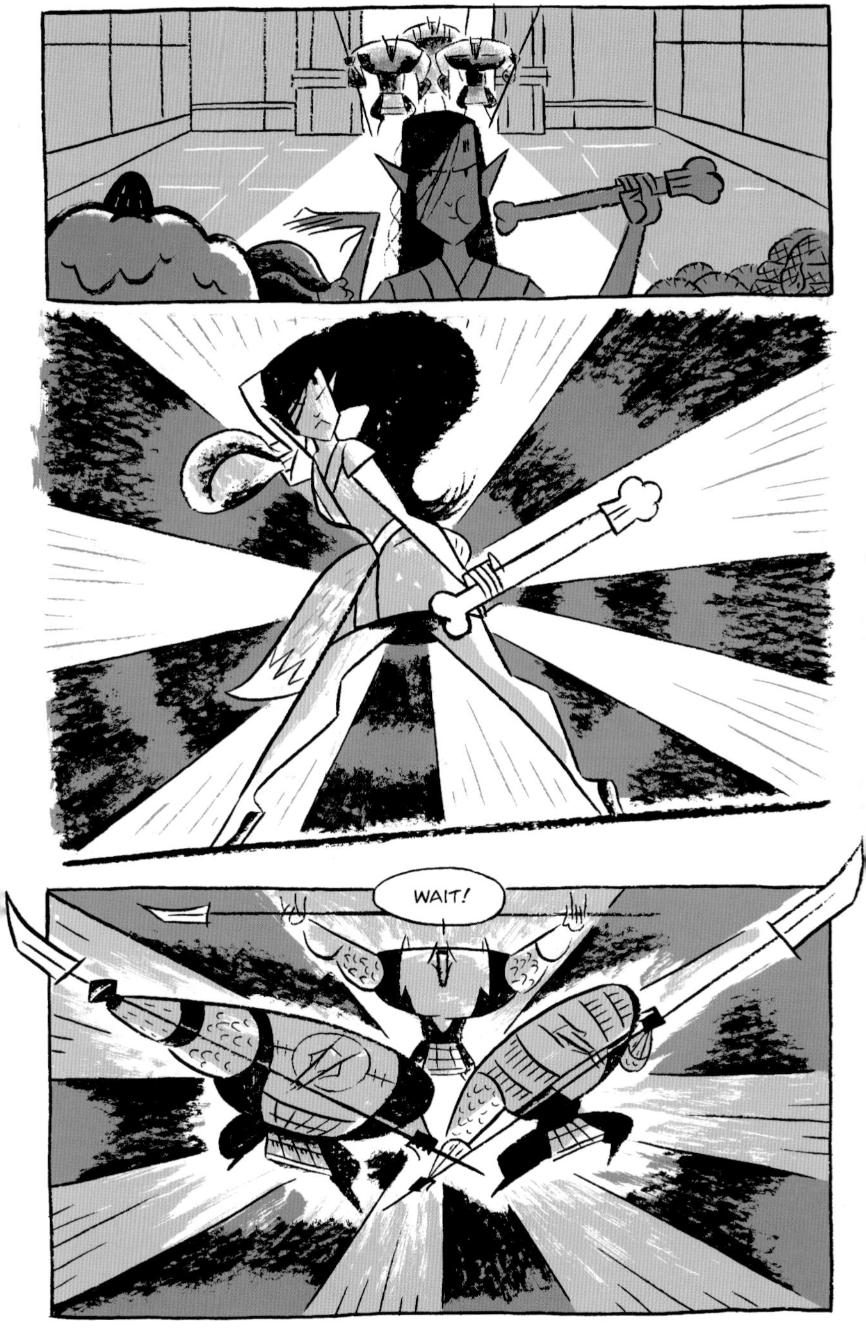
WAIT!

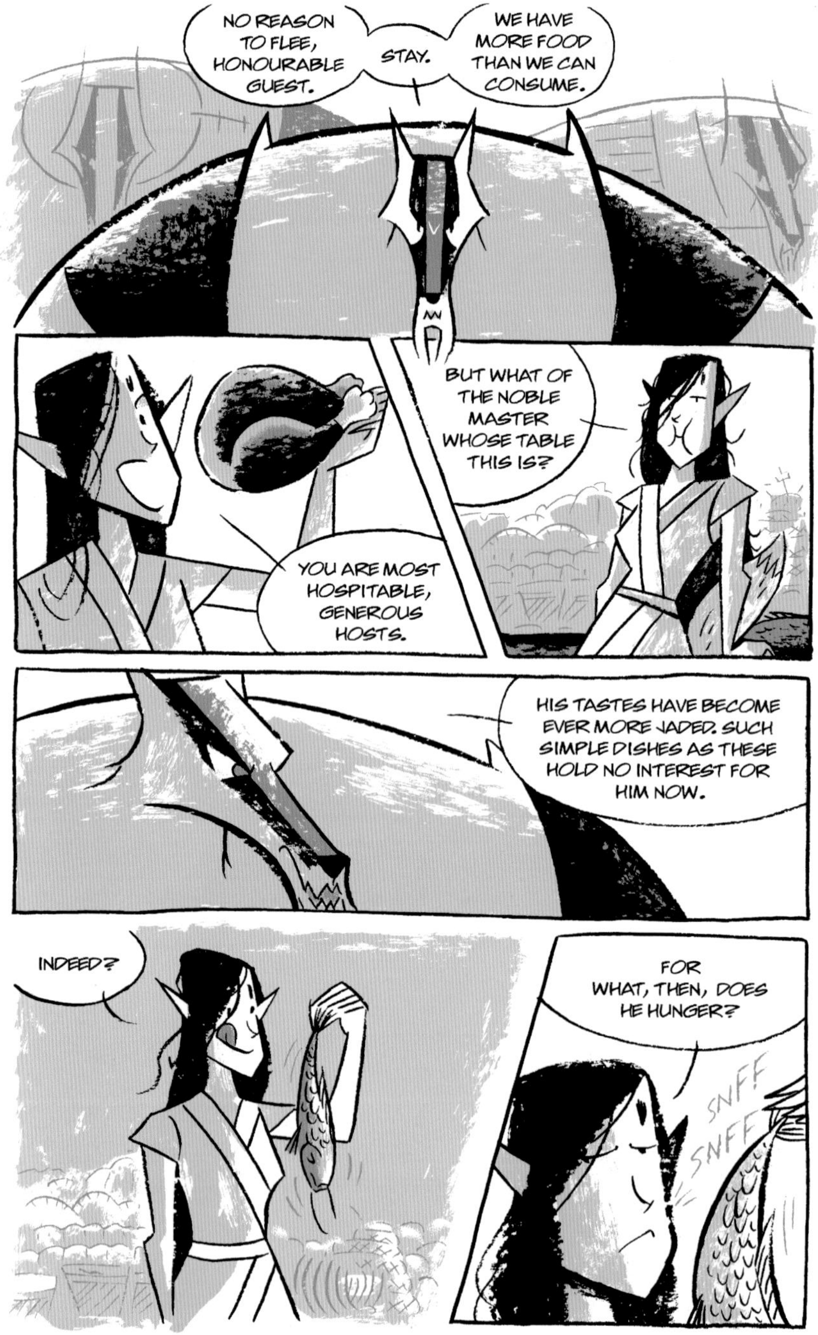
NO REASON TO FLEE, HONOURABLE GUEST.
STAY.
WE HAVE MORE FOOD THAN WE CAN CONSUME.
YOU ARE MOST HOSPITABLE, GENEROUS HOSTS.
BUT WHAT OF THE NOBLE MASTER WHOSE TABLE THIS IS?
HIS TASTES HAVE BECOME EVER MORE JADED. SUCH SIMPLE DISHES AS THESE HOLD NO INTEREST FOR HIM NOW.
INDEED?
FOR WHAT, THEN, DOES HE HUNGER?
SNFF
SNFF

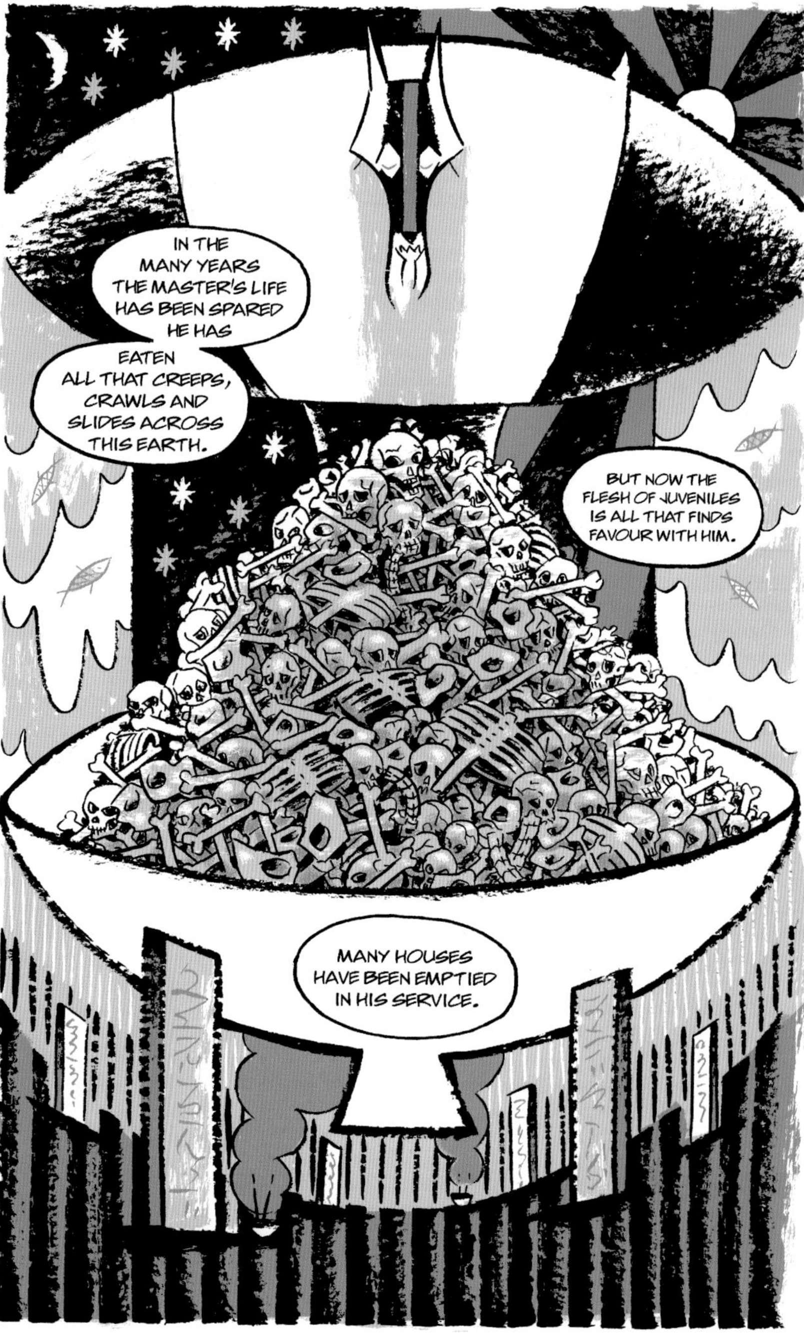
IN THE MANY YEARS THE MASTER'S LIFE HAS BEEN SPARED HE HAS
EATEN ALL THAT CREEPS, CRAWLS AND SLIDES ACROSS THIS EARTH.
BUT NOW THE FLESH OF JUVENILES IS ALL THAT FINDS FAVOUR WITH HIM.
MANY HOUSES HAVE BEEN EMPTIED IN HIS SERVICE.

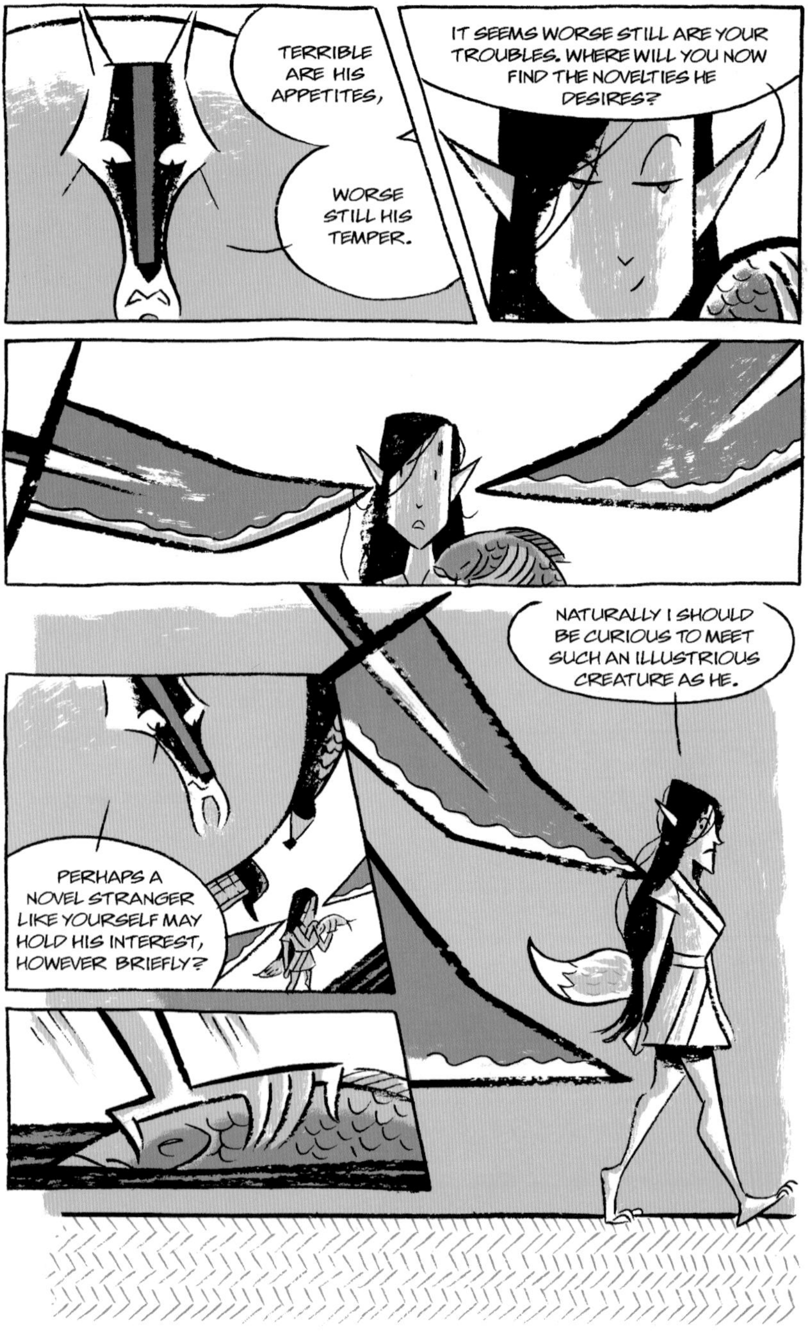
TERRIBLE ARE HIS APPETITES,
WORSE STILL HIS TEMPER.
IT SEEMS WORSE STILL ARE YOUR TROUBLES. WHERE WILL YOU NOW FIND THE NOVELTIES HE DESIRES?
PERHAPS A NOVEL STRANGER LIKE YOURSELF MAY HOLD HIS INTEREST, HOWEVER BRIEFLY?
NATURALLY I SHOULD BE CURIOUS TO MEET SUCH AN ILLUSTRIOUS CREATURE AS HE.

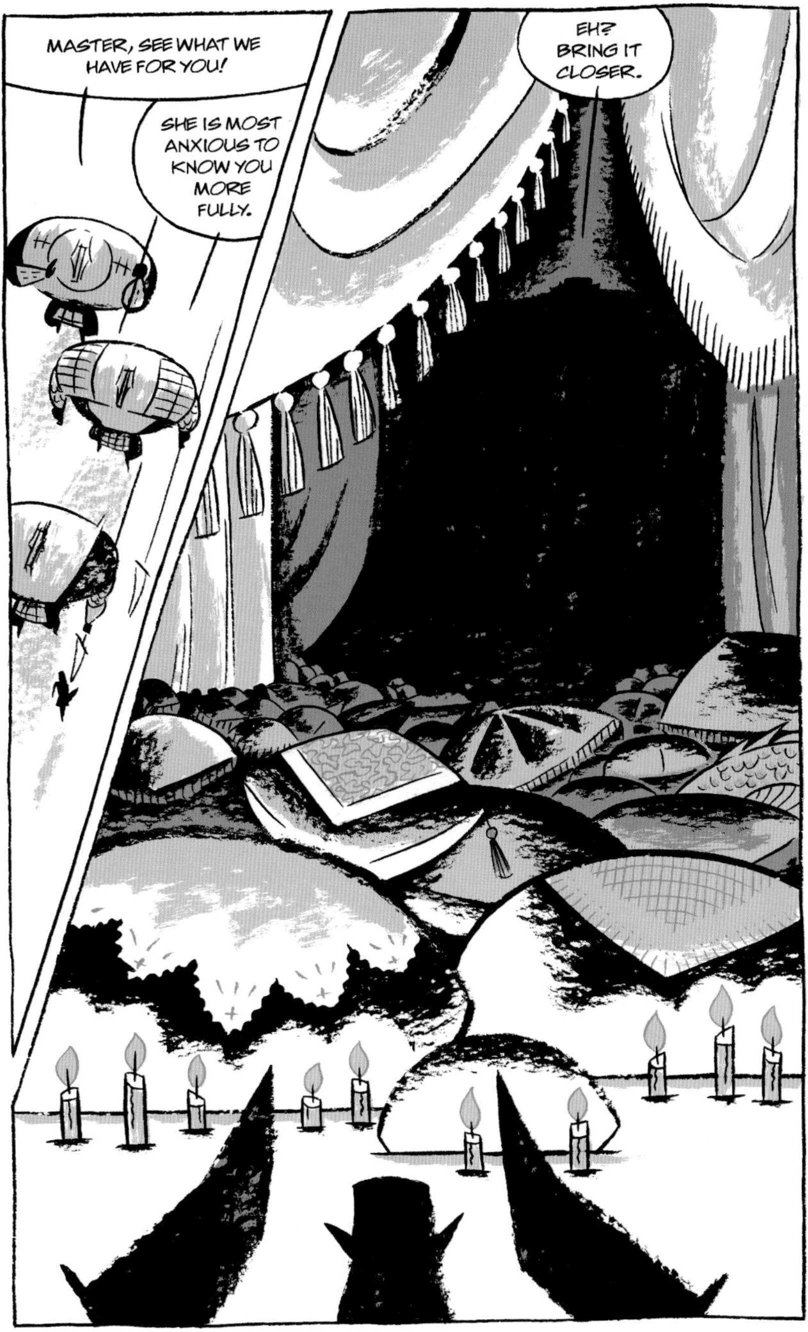
MASTER, SEE WHAT WE HAVE FOR YOU!
SHE IS MOST ANXIOUS TO KNOW YOU MORE FULLY.
EH? BRING IT CLOSER.

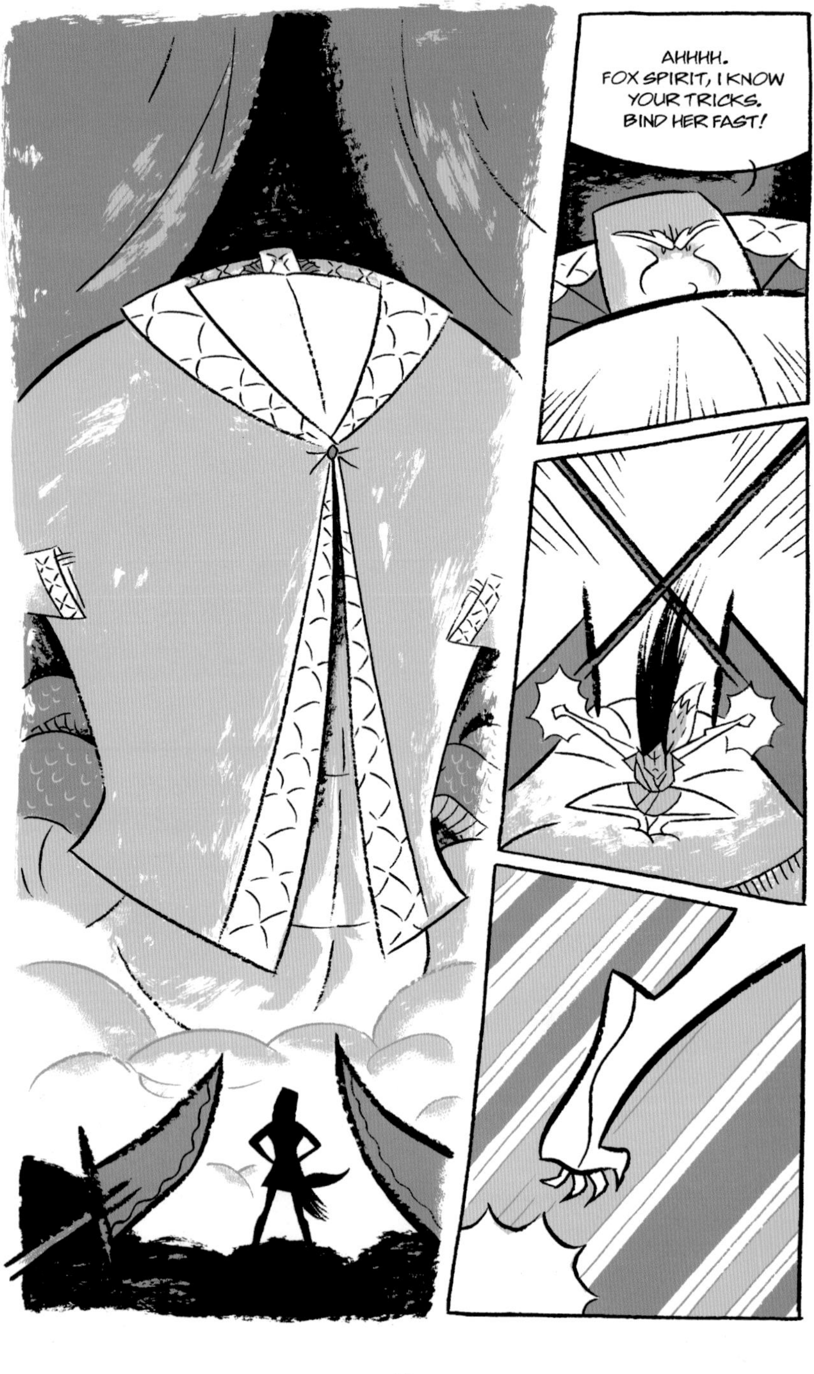
AHHHH.
FOX SPIRIT, I KNOW YOUR TRICKS. BIND HER FAST!

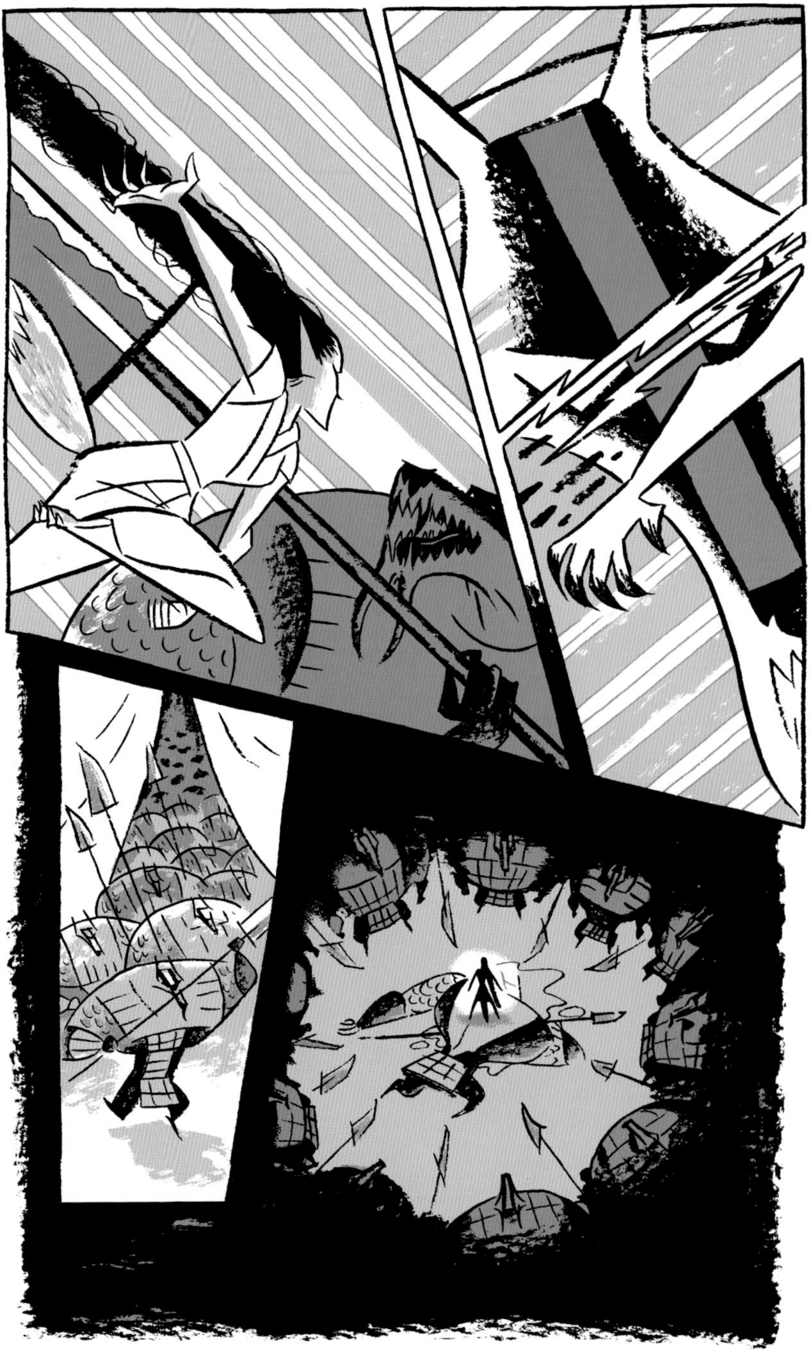

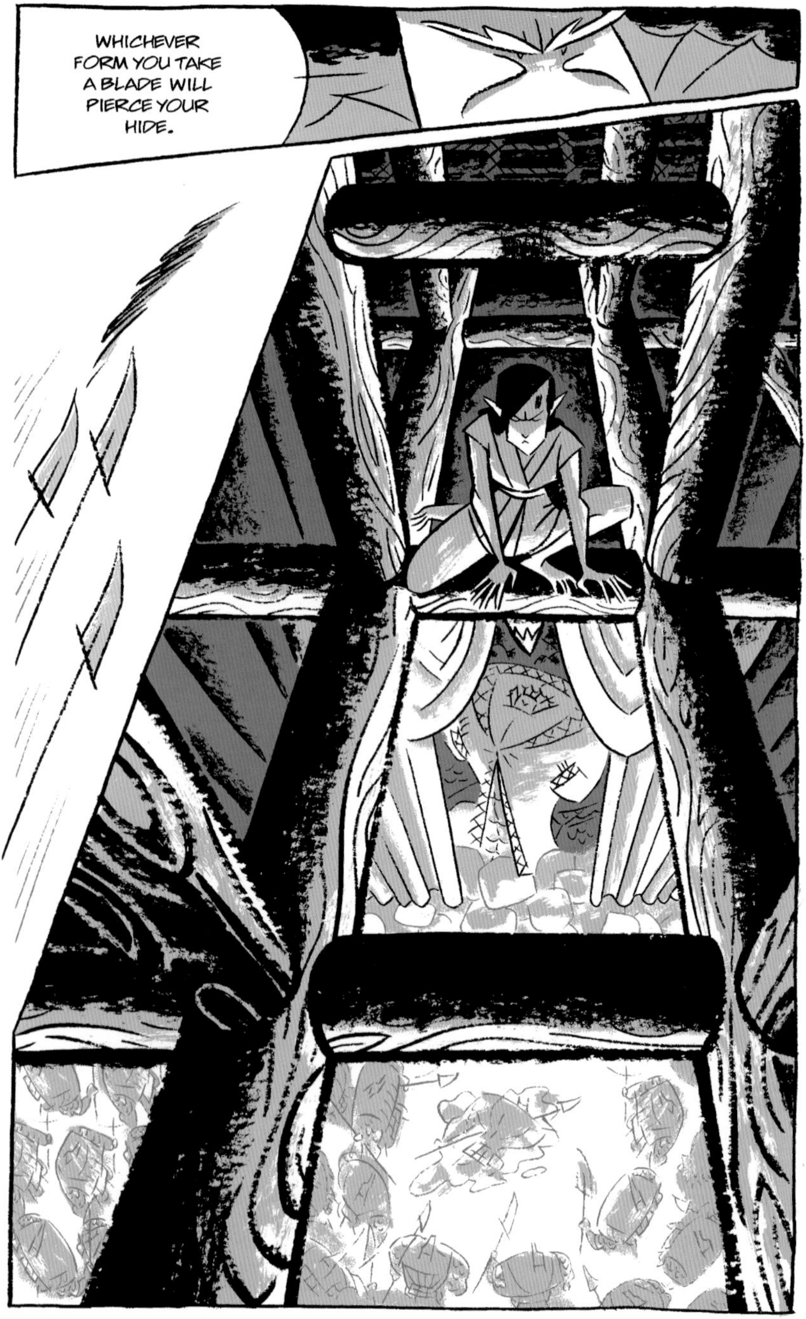
WHICHEVER FORM YOU TAKE A BLADE WILL PIERCE YOUR HIDE.

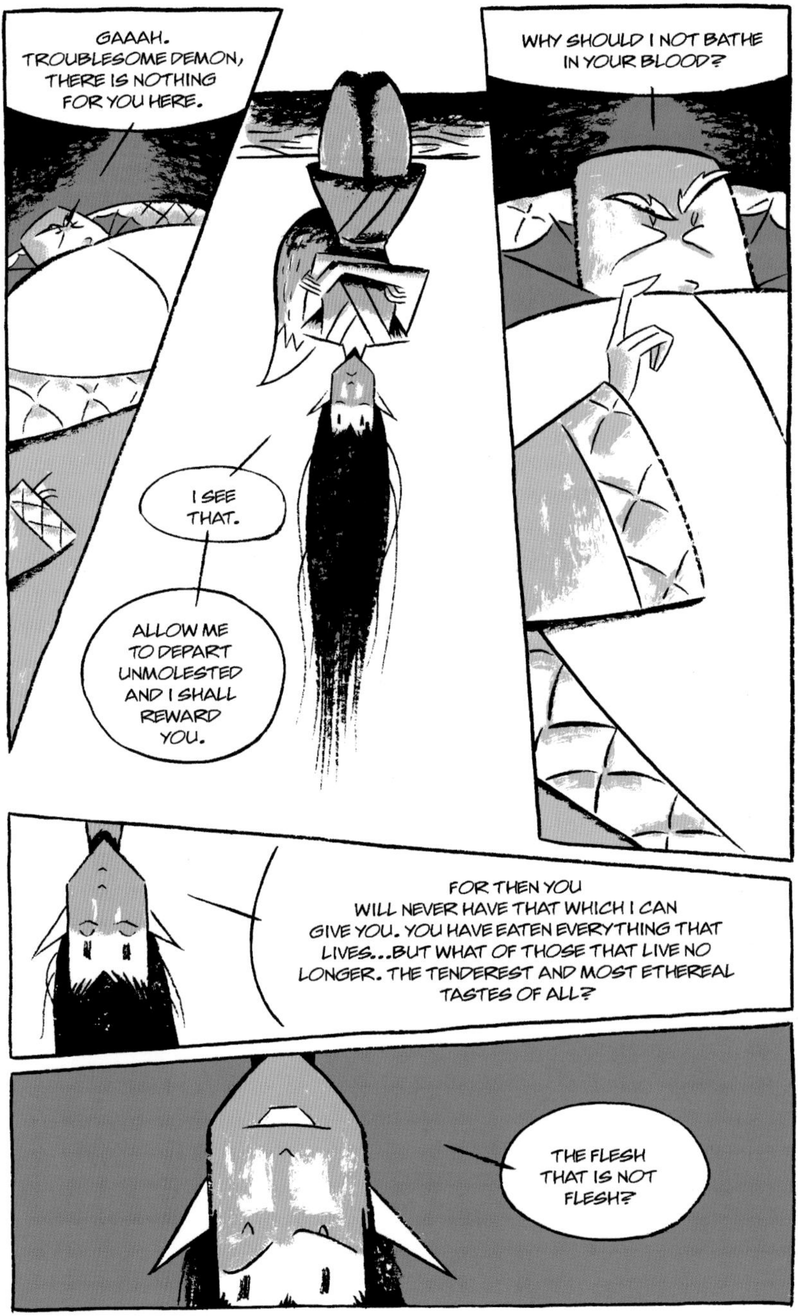
GAAAH. TROUBLESOME DEMON, THERE IS NOTHING FOR YOU HERE.
I SEE THAT.
ALLOW ME TO DEPART UNMOLESTED AND I SHALL REWARD YOU.
WHY SHOULD I NOT BATHE IN YOUR BLOOD?
FOR THEN YOU WILL NEVER HAVE THAT WHICH I CAN GIVE YOU. YOU HAVE EATEN EVERYTHING THAT LIVES...BUT WHAT OF THOSE THAT LIVE NO LONGER. THE TENDEREST AND MOST ETHEREAL TASTES OF ALL?
THE FLESH THAT IS NOT FLESH?

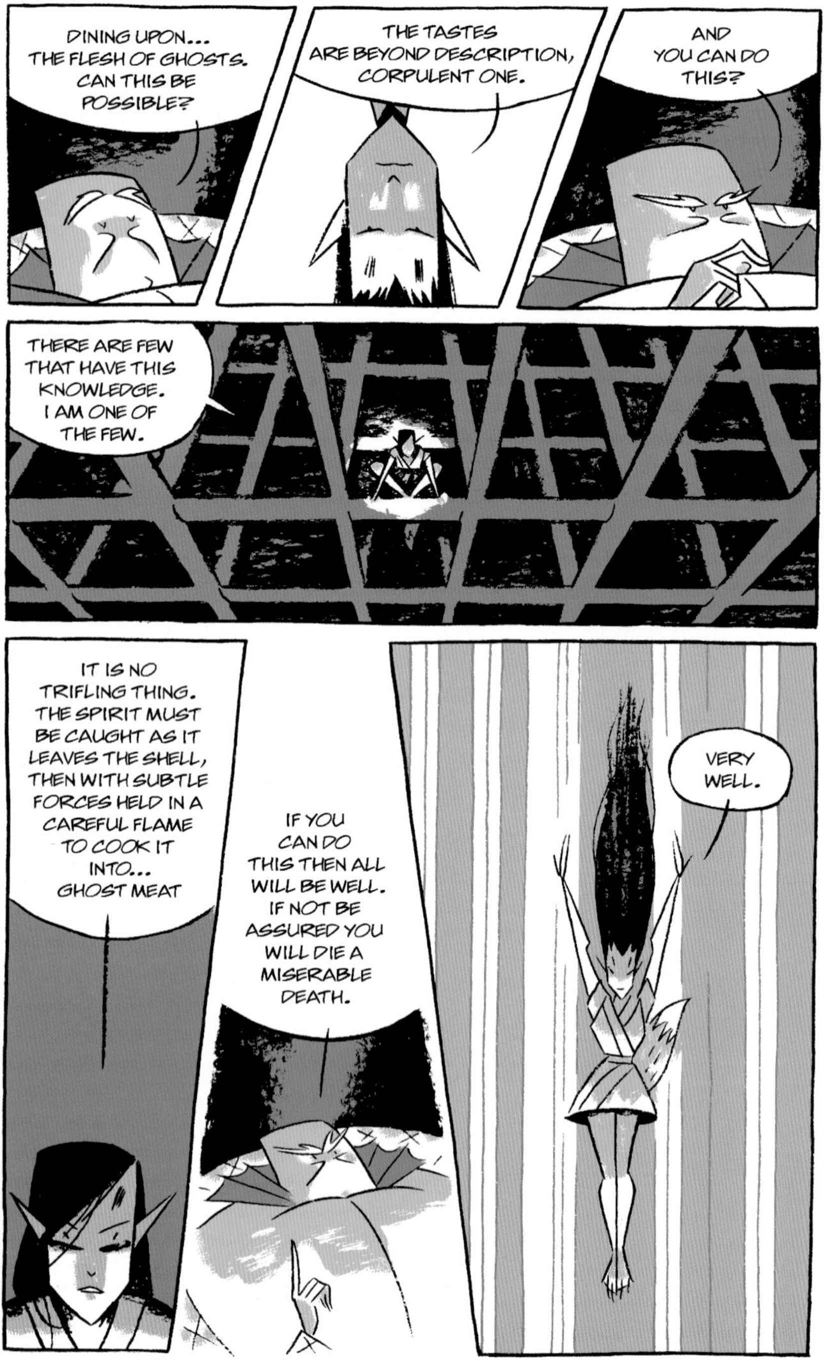
DINING UPON... THE FLESH OF GHOSTS. CAN THIS BE POSSIBLE?
THE TASTES ARE BEYOND DESCRIPTION, CORPULENT ONE.
AND YOU CAN DO THIS?
THERE ARE FEW THAT HAVE THIS KNOWLEDGE. I AM ONE OF THE FEW.
IT IS NO TRIFLING THING. THE SPIRIT MUST BE CAUGHT AS IT LEAVES THE SHELL, THEN WITH SUBTLE FORCES HELD IN A CAREFUL FLAME TO COOK IT INTO... GHOST MEAT
IF YOU CAN DO THIS THEN ALL WILL BE WELL. IF NOT BE ASSURED YOU WILL DIE A MISERABLE DEATH.
VERY WELL.

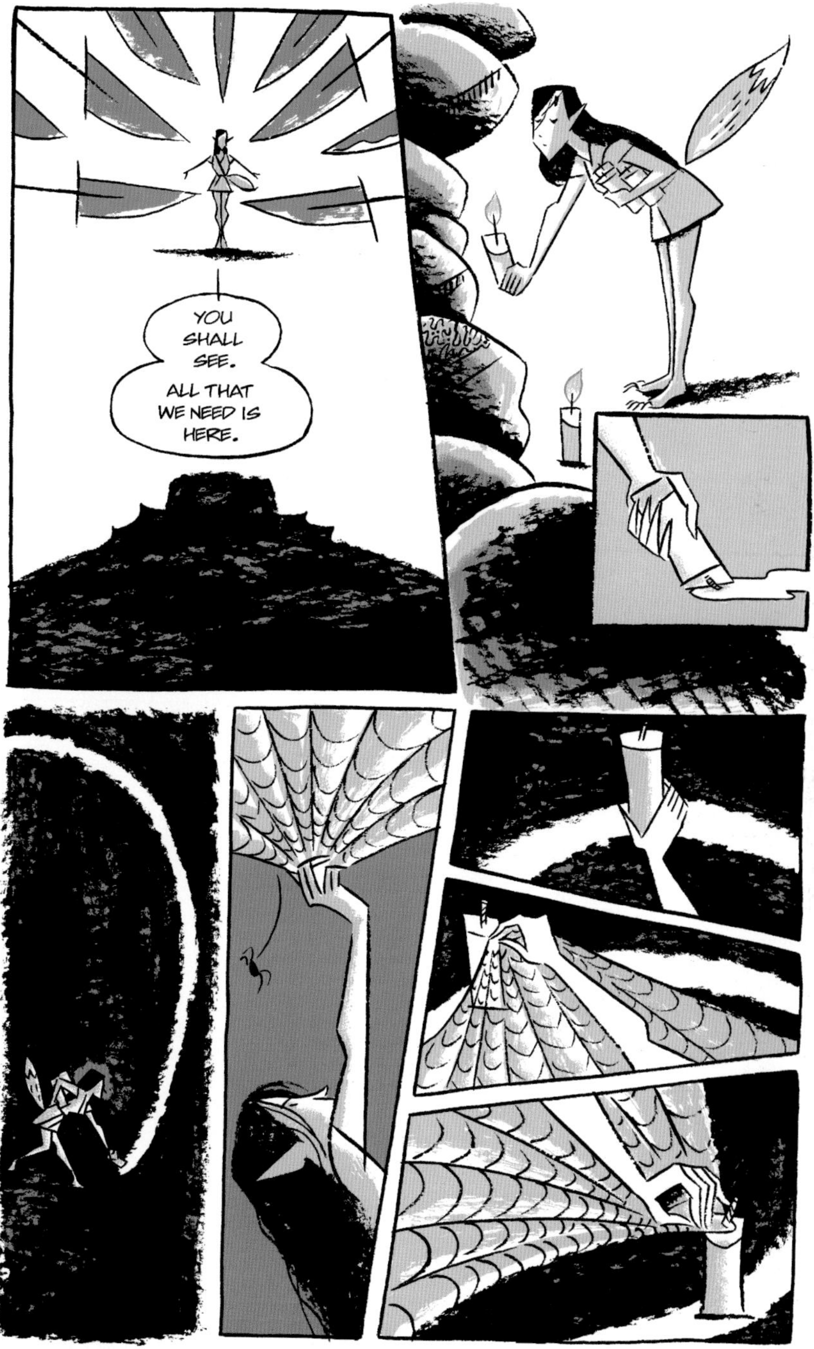
YOU SHALL SEE.
ALL THAT WE NEED IS HERE.

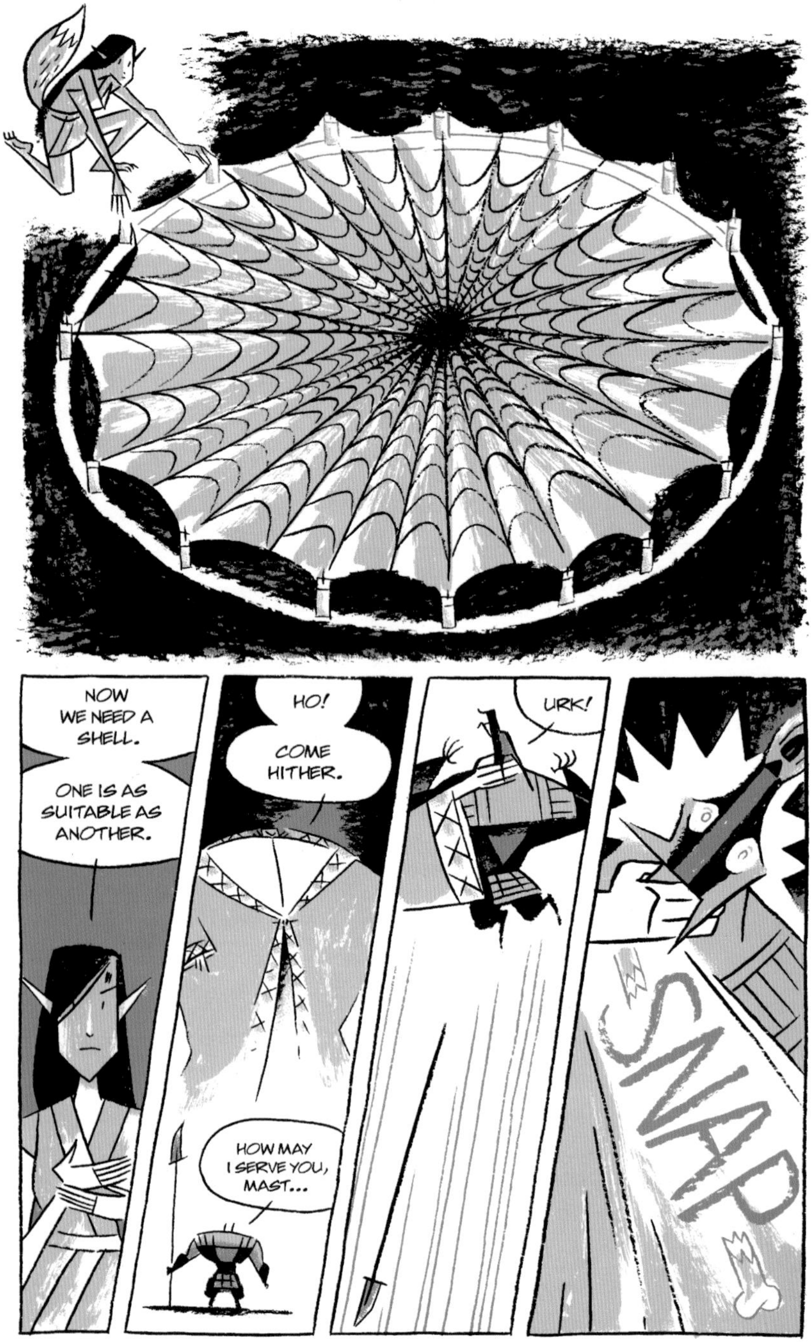
NOW WE NEED A SHELL.
ONE IS AS SUITABLE AS ANOTHER.
HO!
COME HITHER.
HOW MAY I SERVE YOU, MAST...
URK!
SNAP

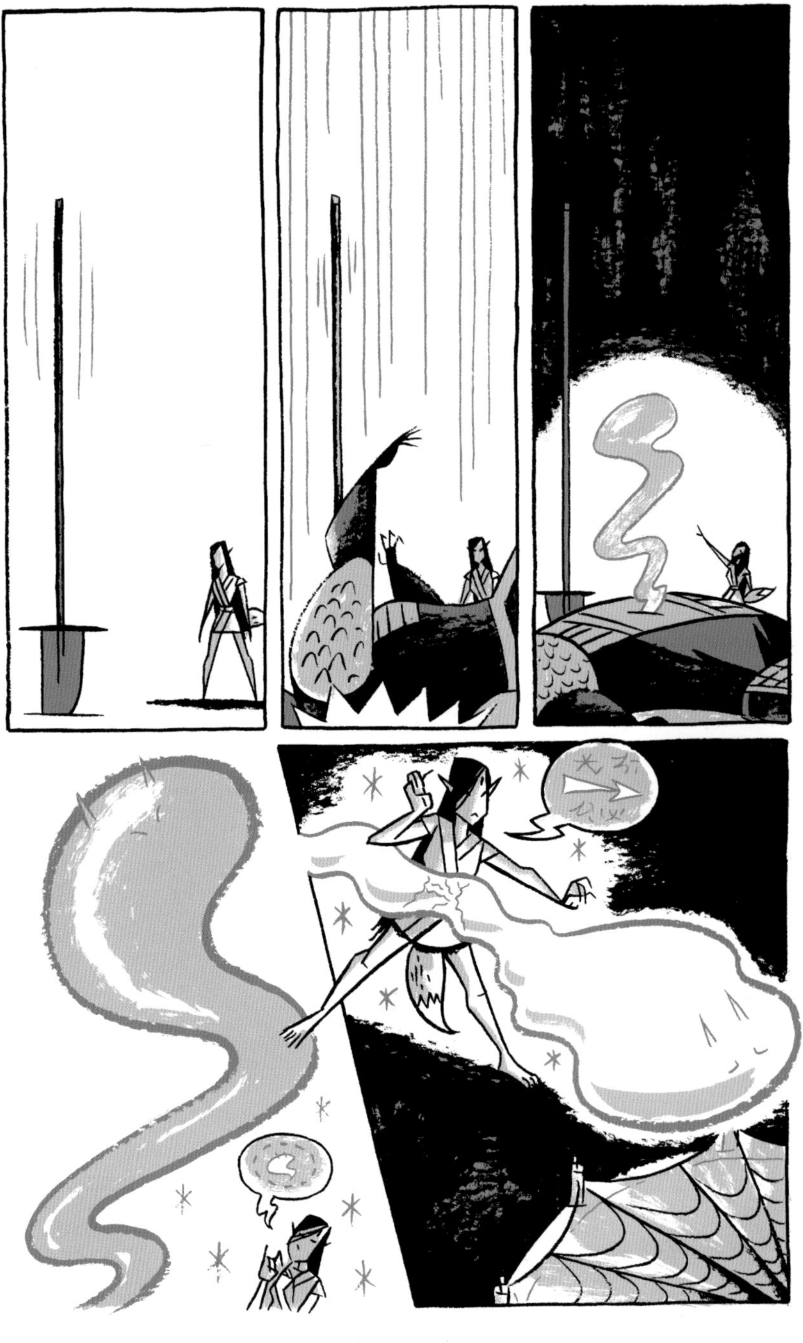

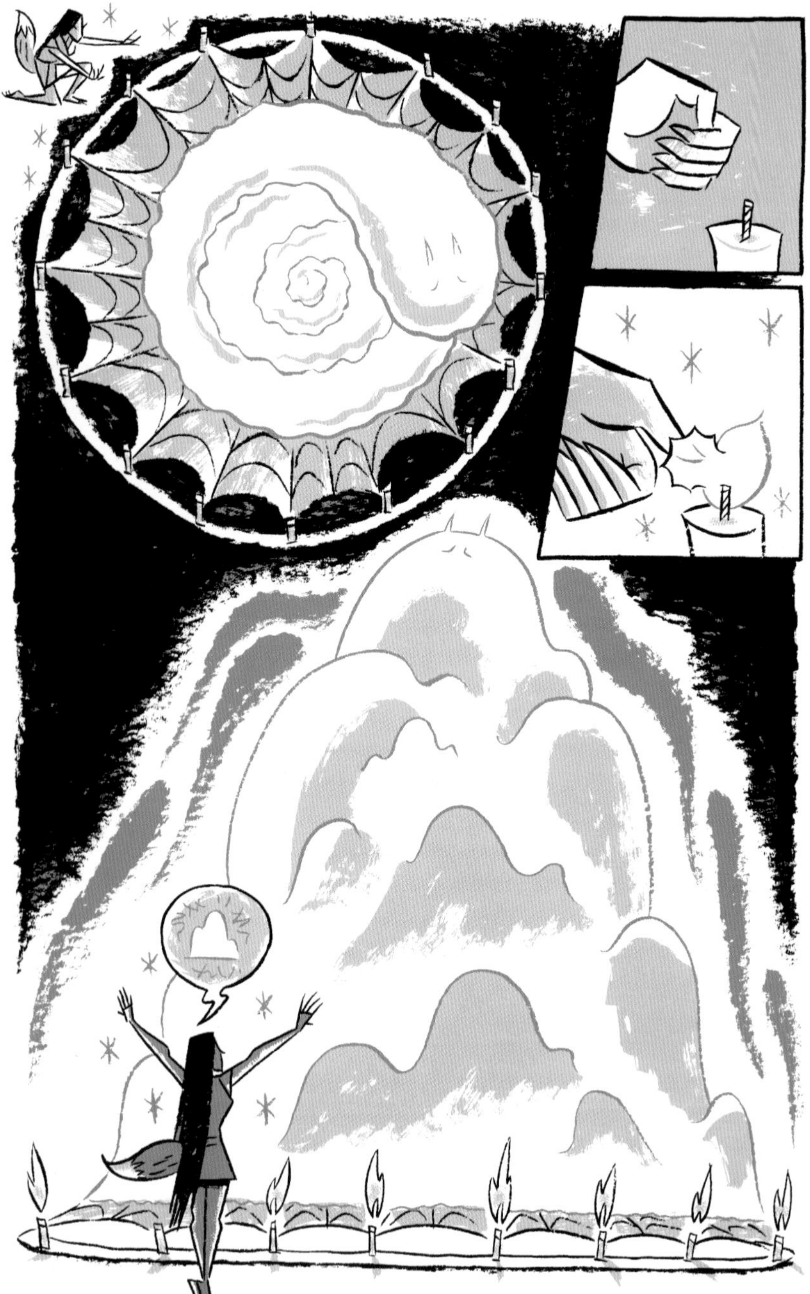

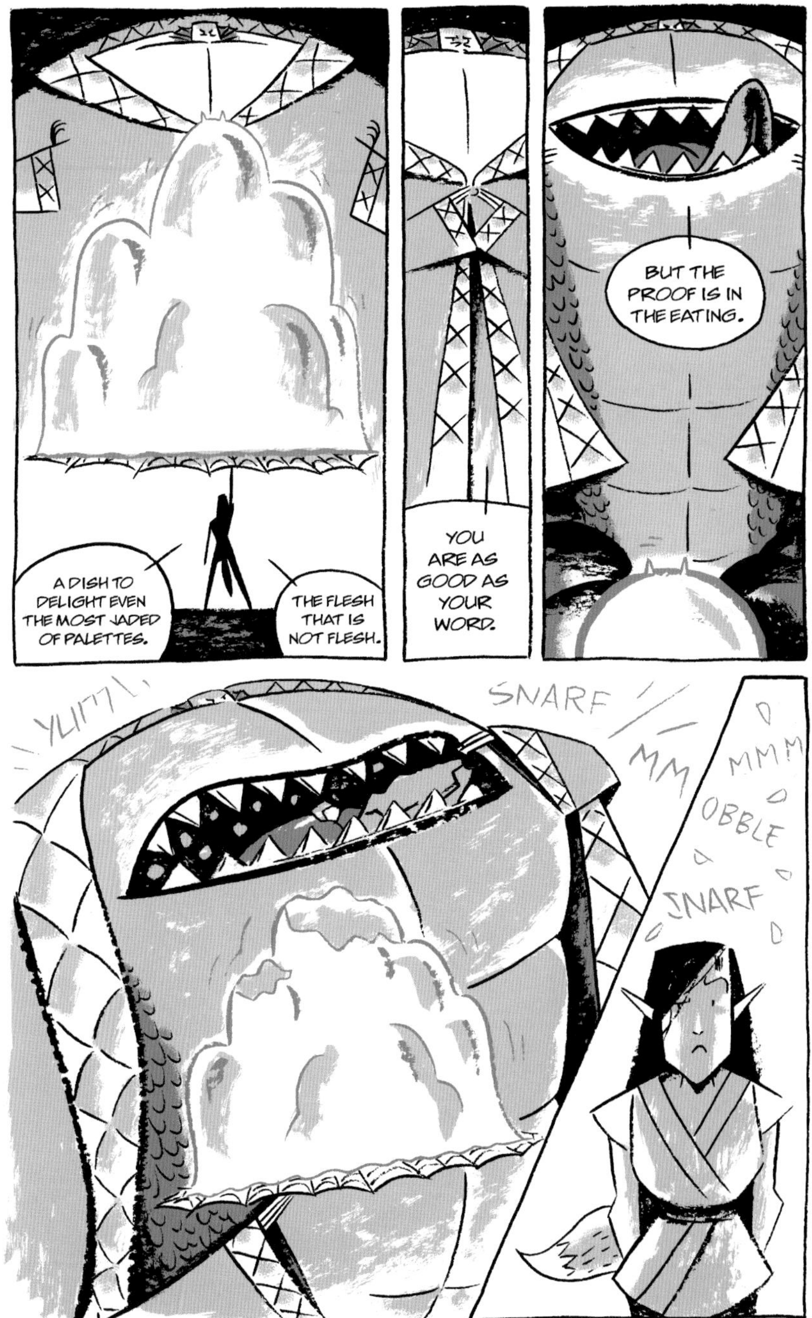
A DISH TO DELIGHT EVEN THE MOST JADED OF PALETTES.
THE FLESH THAT IS NOT FLESH.
YOU ARE AS GOOD AS YOUR WORD.
BUT THE PROOF IS IN THE EATING.
YUM
SNARF
MM
MMM
OBBLE
SNARF

WHAT TENDER-NESS.

WHAT EXQUISITE DELICACY!

AHHHH.

YOU HAVE DONE WELL. HERE IS YOUR REWARD.

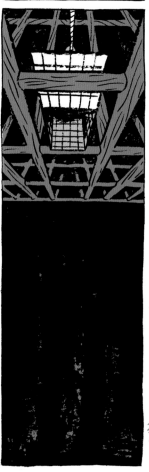

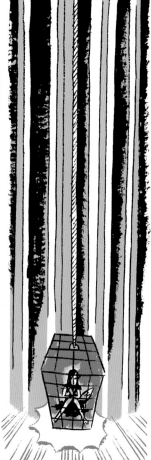

IT IS SMALLER THAN I EXPECTED.

NO MATTER.

I WILL BE LEAVING SOON.

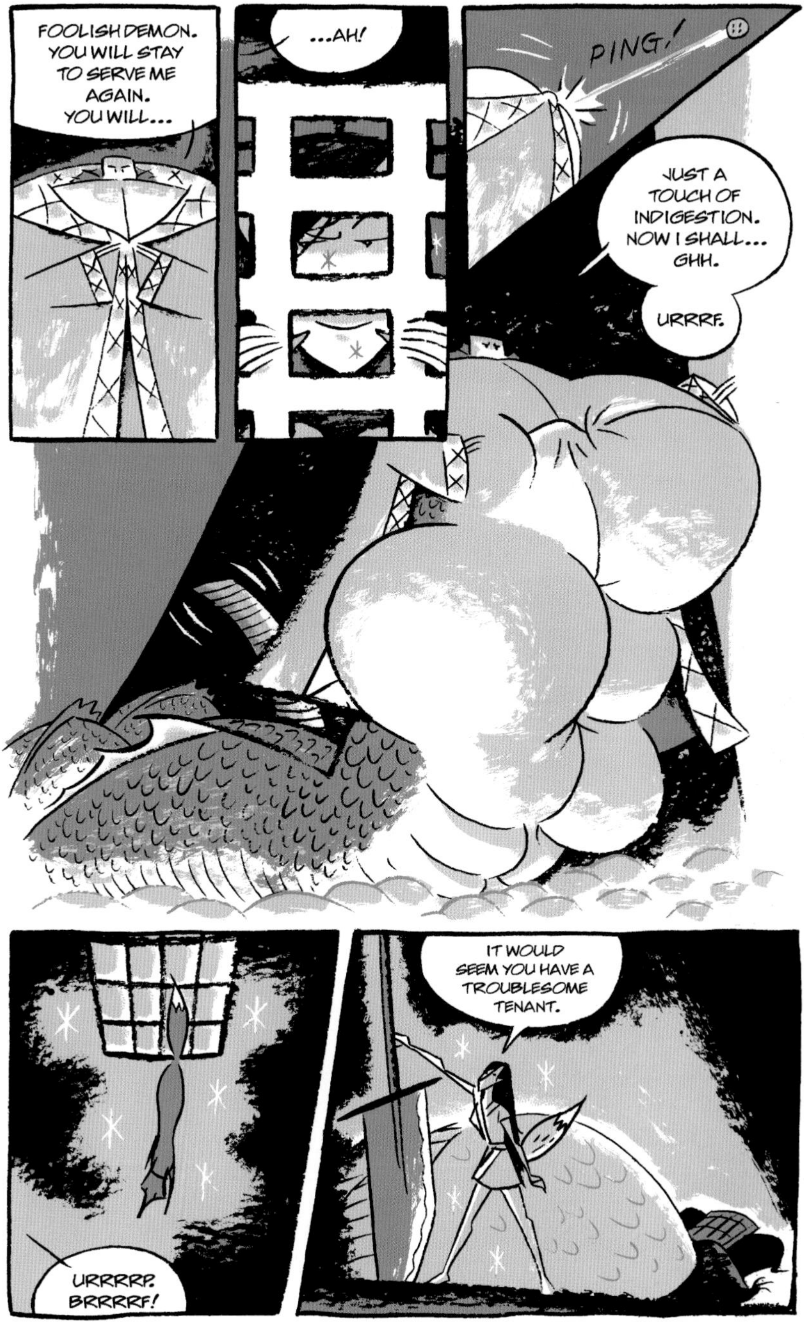
FOOLISH DEMON. YOU WILL STAY TO SERVE ME AGAIN. YOU WILL...
...AH!
PING!
JUST A TOUCH OF INDIGESTION. NOW I SHALL... GHH.
URRRF.
URRRRP. BRRRRF!
IT WOULD SEEM YOU HAVE A TROUBLESOME TENANT.

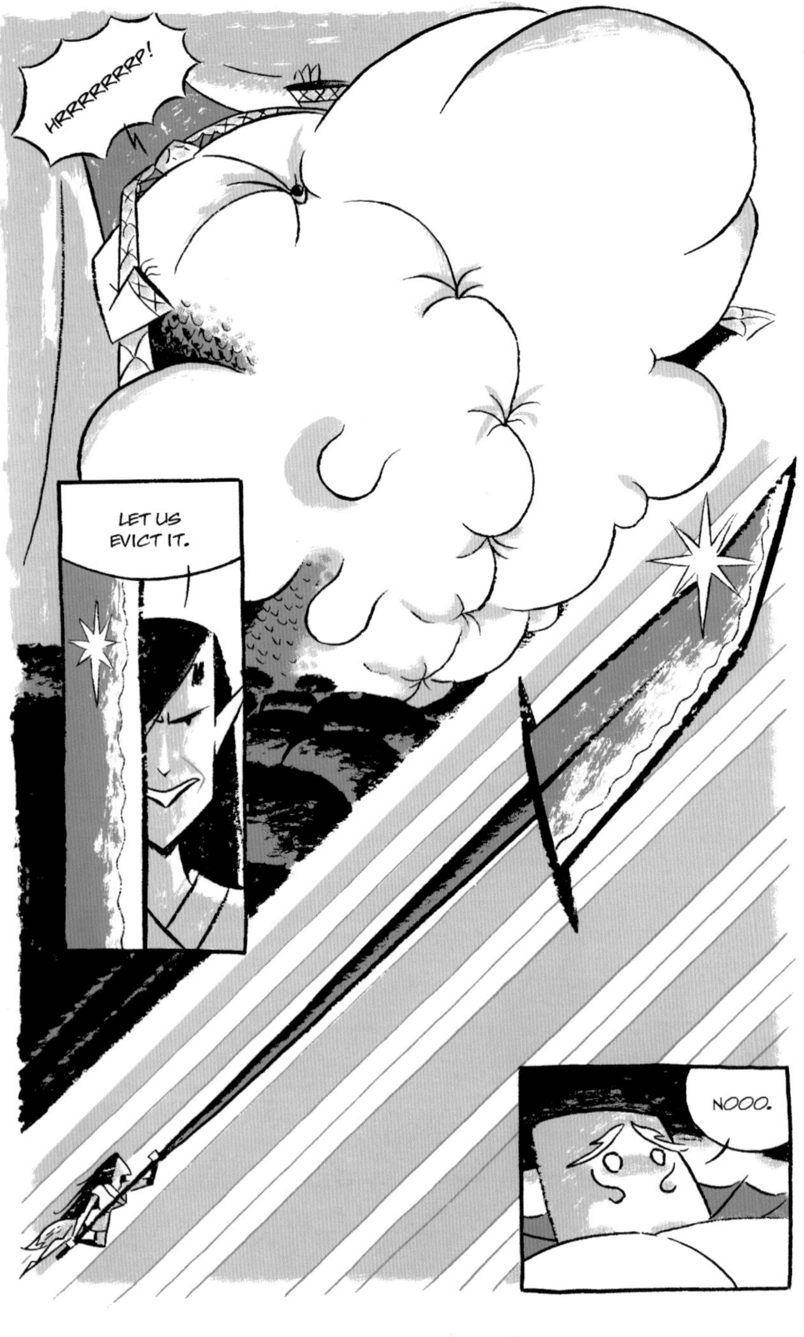
HRRRRRRRP!
LET US EVICT IT.
NOOO.

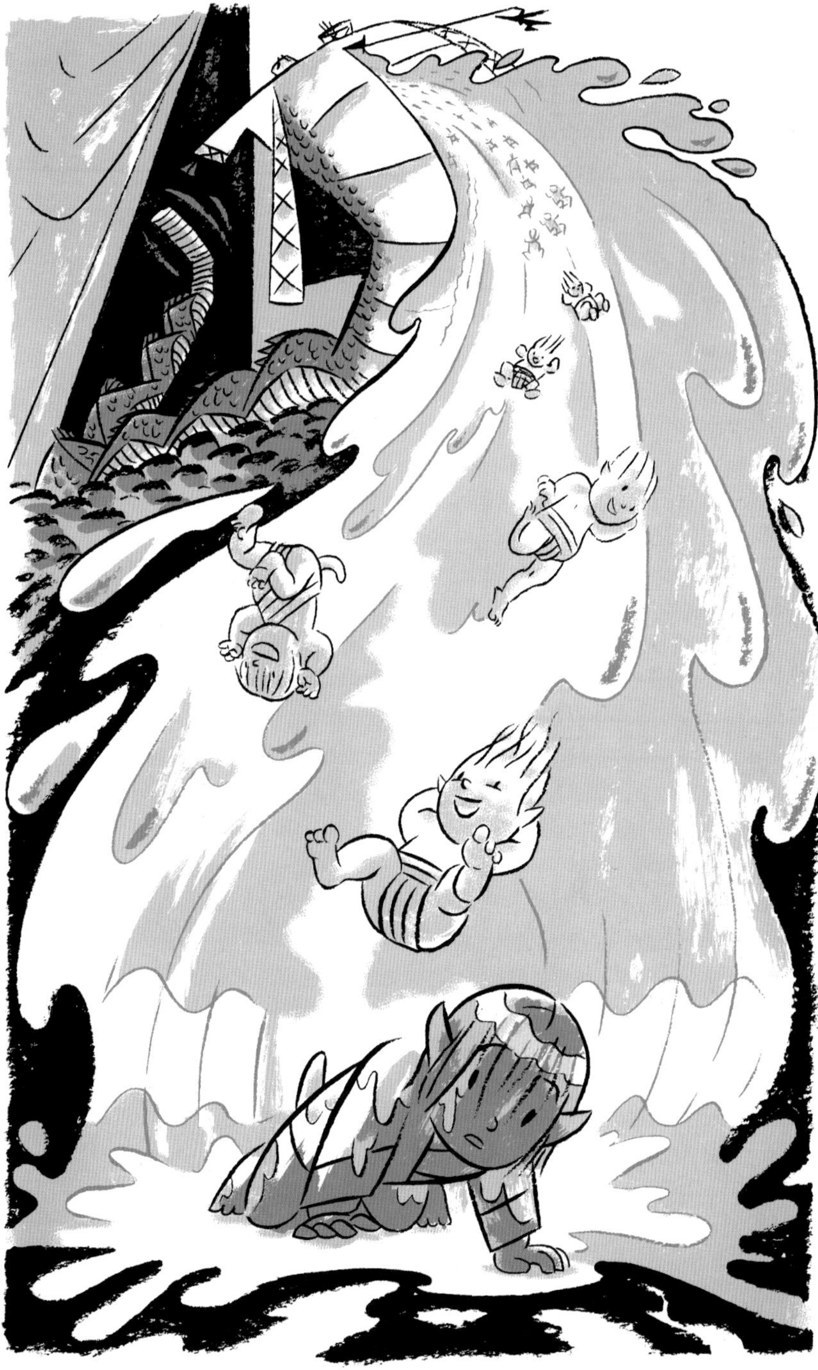

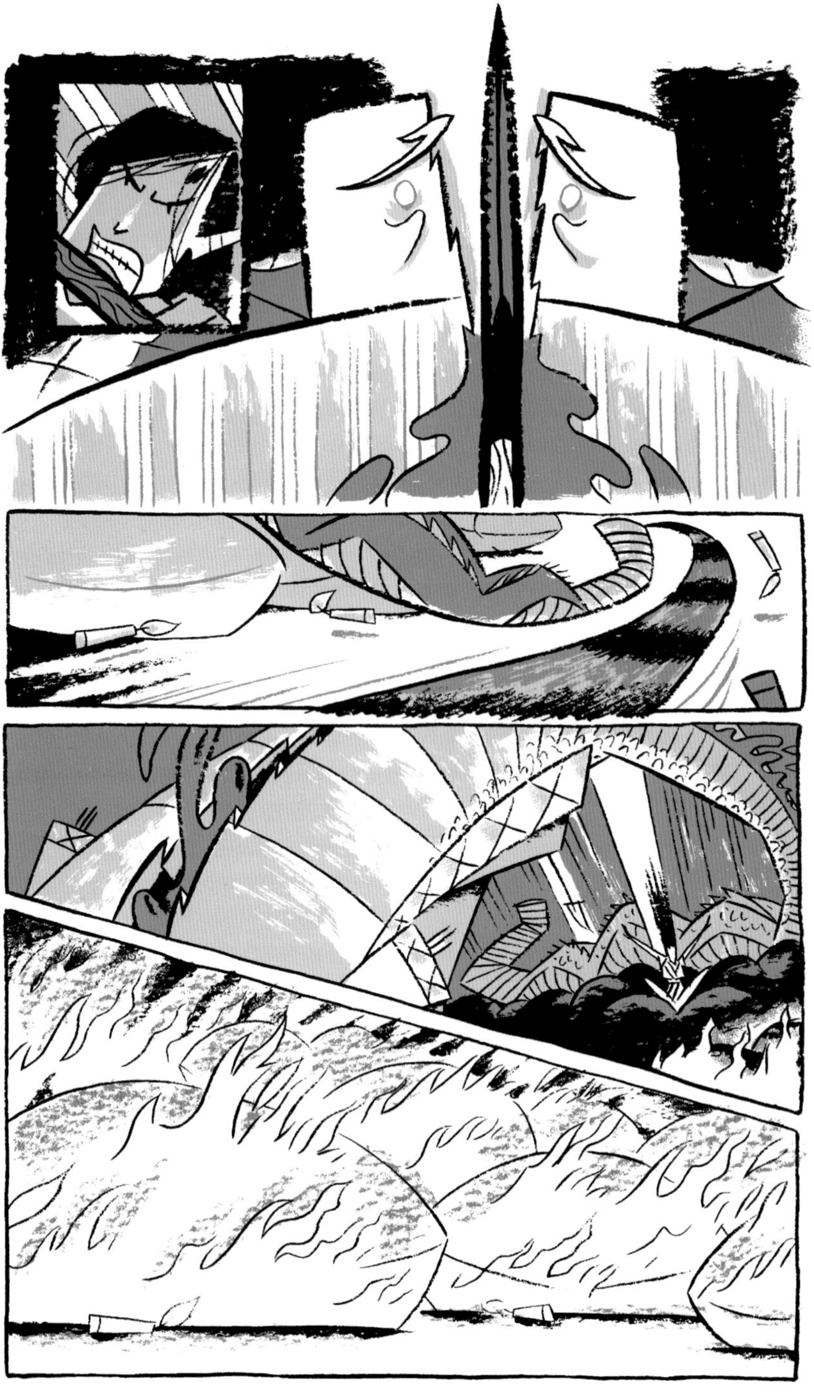

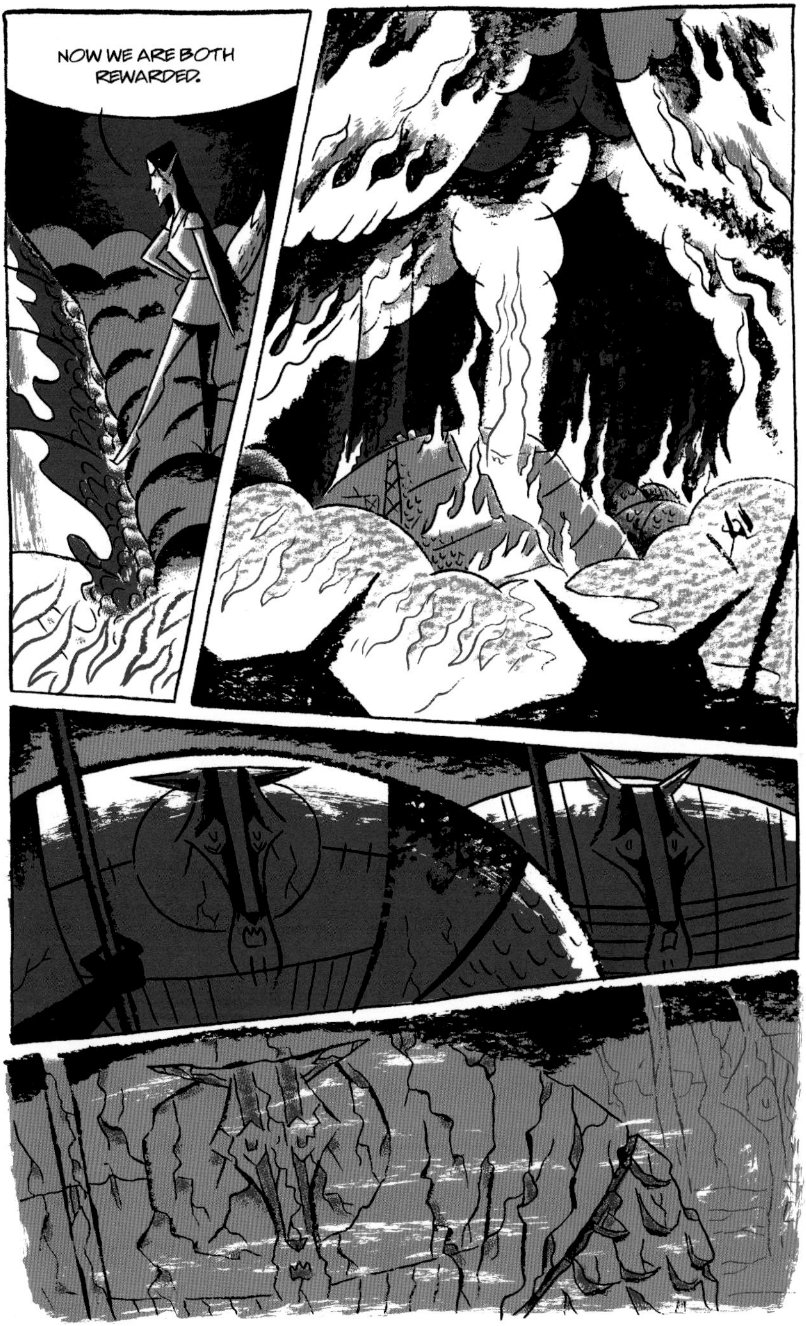
NOW WE ARE BOTH REWARDED.

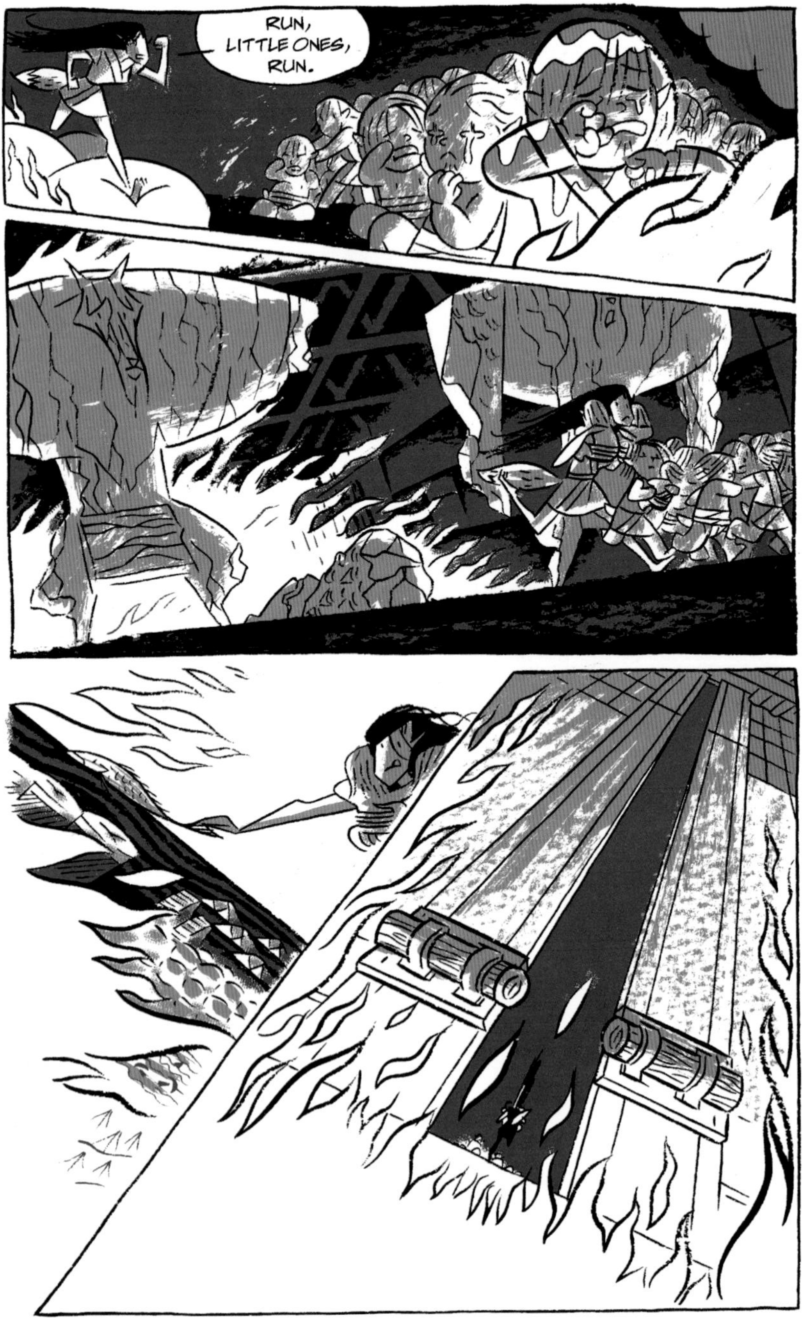
RUN, LITTLE ONES, RUN.

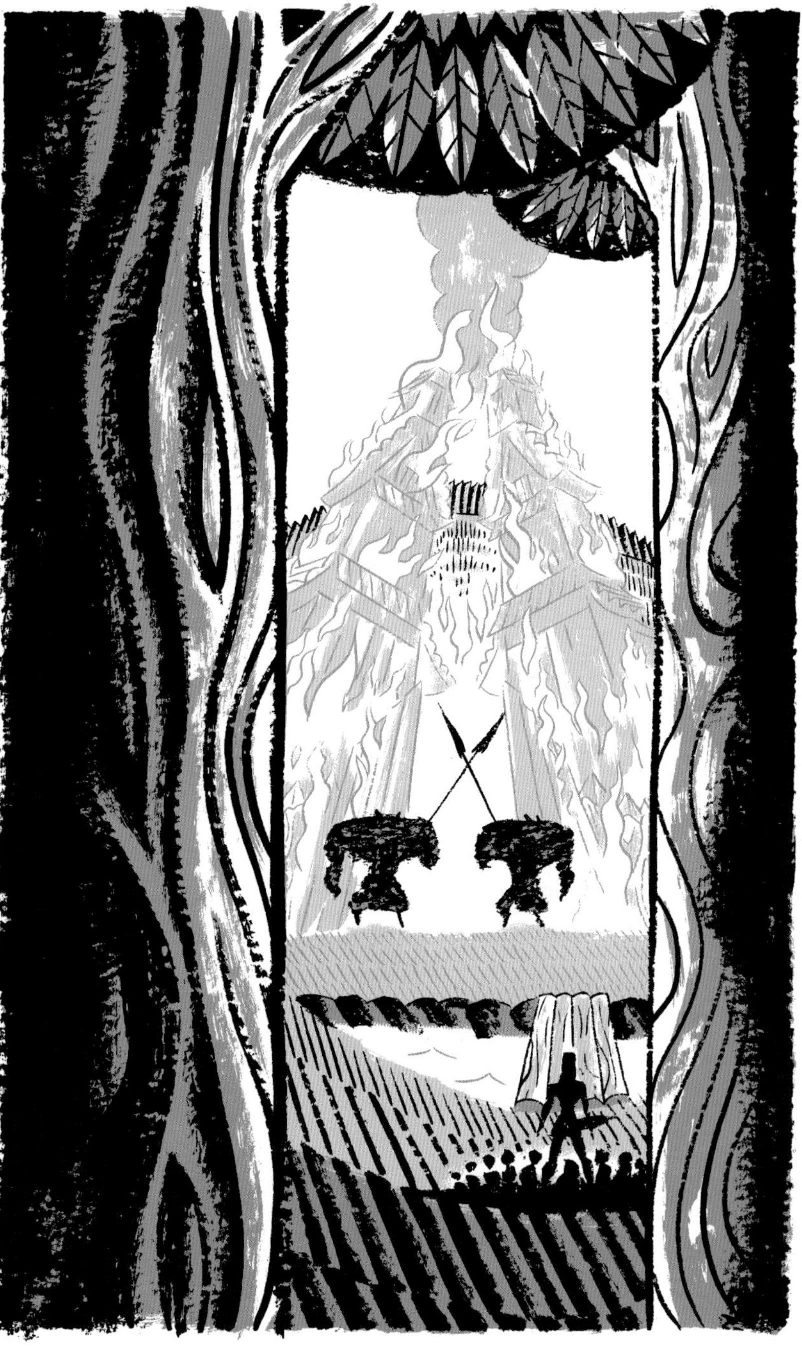

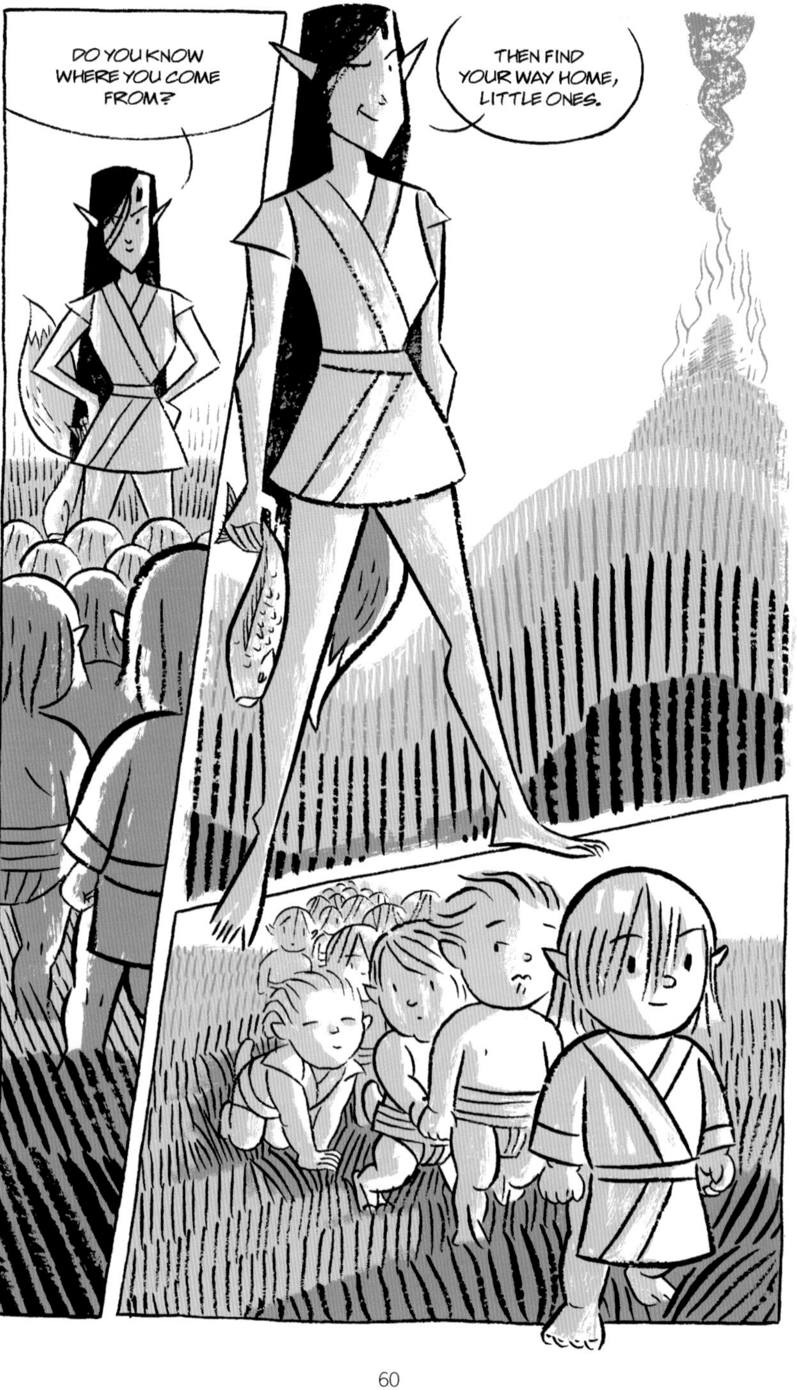
DO YOU KNOW WHERE YOU COME FROM?
THEN FIND YOUR WAY HOME, LITTLE ONES.

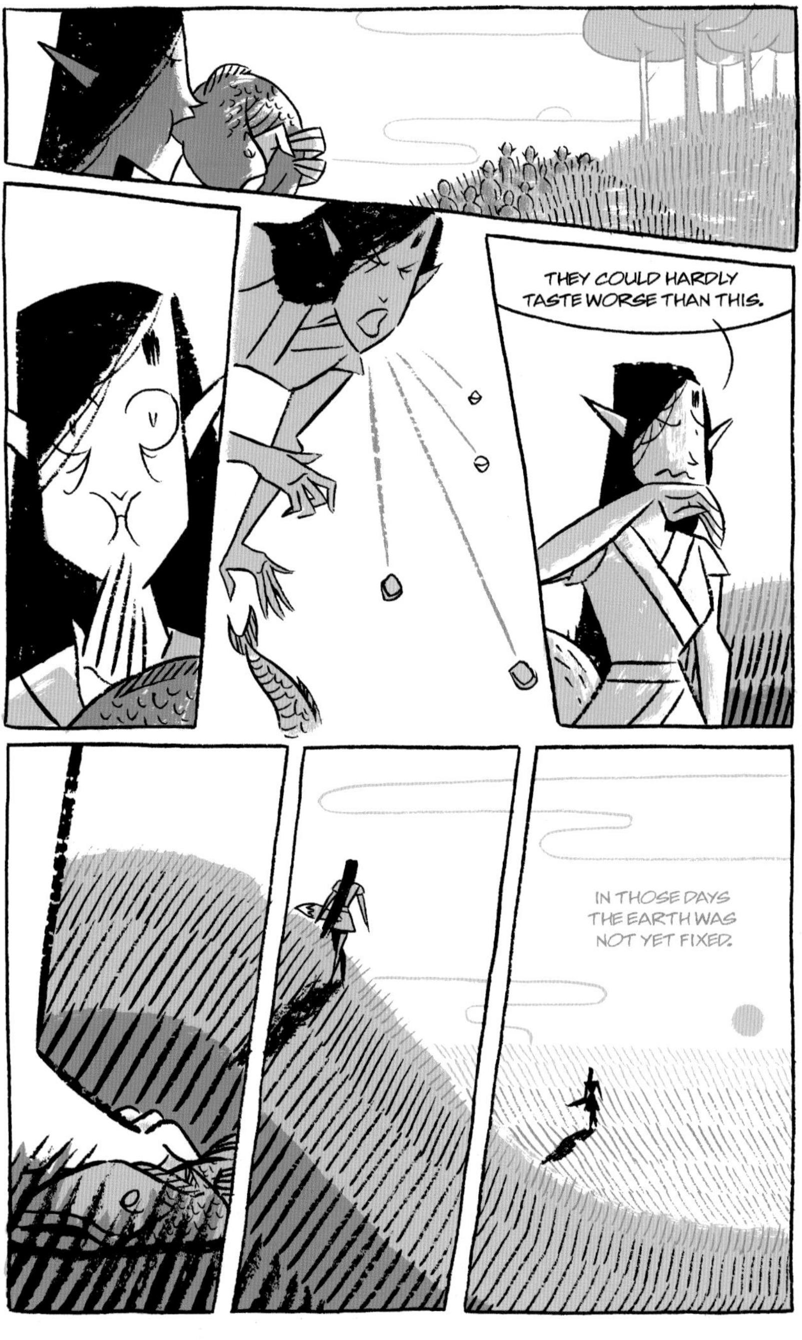
THEY COULD HARDLY TASTE WORSE THAN THIS.
IN THOSE DAYS THE EARTH WAS NOT YET FIXED.

IT WAS THE PROVINCE
OF THE SHIFTING ONES...

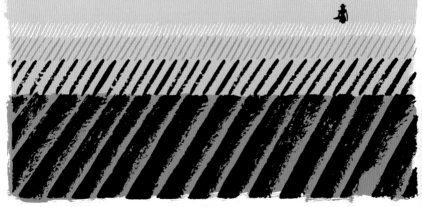

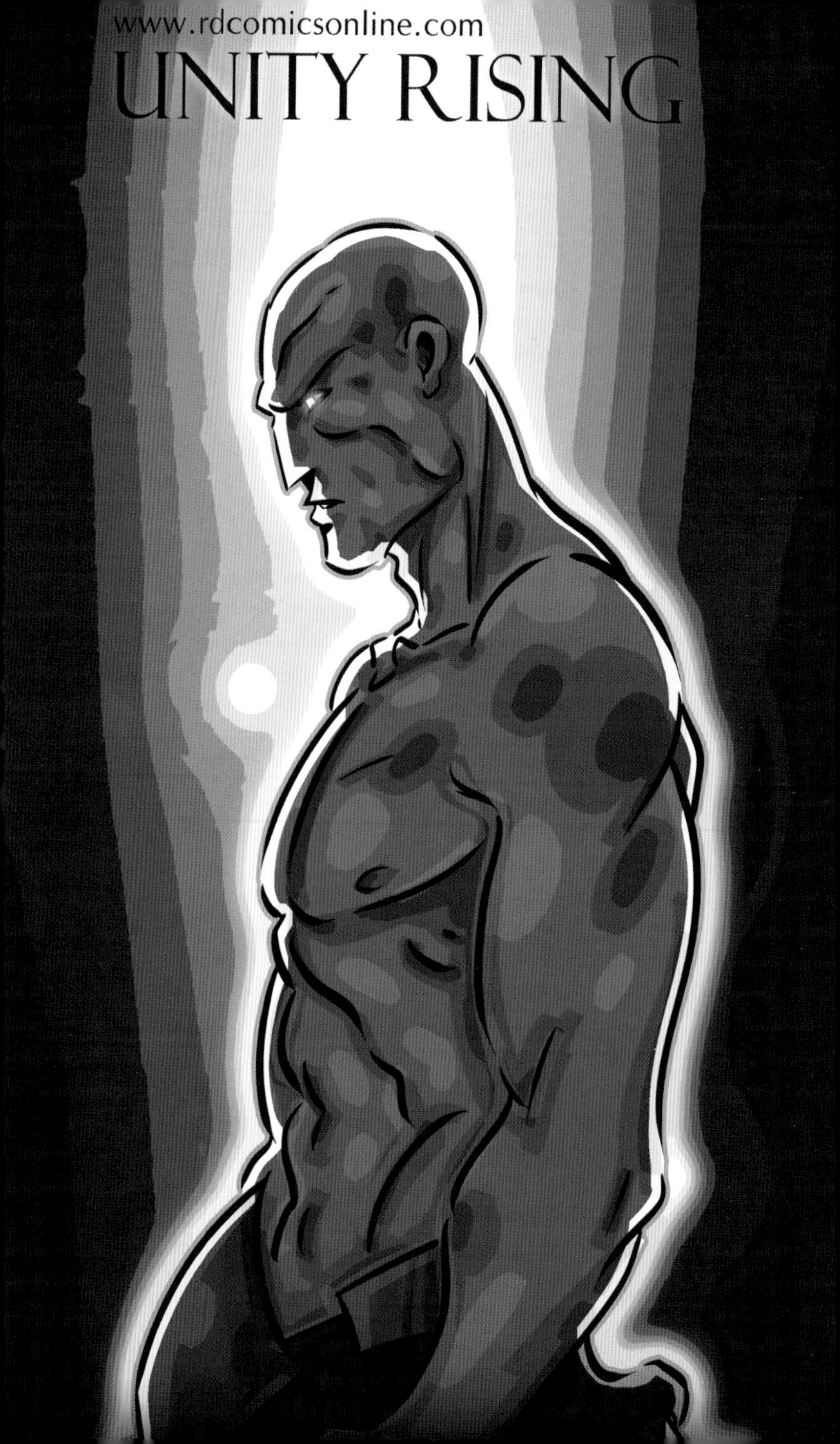
www.rdcomicsonline.com
UNITY RISING

UNITY RISING
Robert Deas

From the distant past to a far-flung future, where ancient grudge breaks to new mutiny. Science fiction is also known for dealing in potent mythologies. Many a manga devotee aspires to the creation of their own universe, spinning out unwieldy star-spanning sagas, yet few have the creative chops to actually succeed in doing it...

First noticed as an entrant to 2005's International Manga and Anime Festival (IMAF) for his colourful proto-animation style, **Rob Deas** went on to win second prize in the comics category at IMAF2006. *Unity Rising* is pure Space Opera, an epic narrative skilfully telescoped, focus drawn via a most compelling and original device (the concept of a hive-mind for coral). A spin-off tale from his long-running webcomic, *Instrument of War*, it reveals the tragic origin of lead villain, Lord Union.

Artist on *November* in *BNM2* (since continued in full colour on his website), Rob has lately adapted *Macbeth* for Self Made Hero's *Manga Shakespeare* line. With new story *Spectrum Black* still to come for *The DFC*/Random House, you can be sure new daddy Rob is keeping busy.

Rob tells us: "I work completely digitally, using a Toshiba Tablet PC for line work; Alias Sketchbook Pro 2; then adding colours and tones in Photoshop CS3. A Wacom Intuos 3 tablet is attached to my desktop PC, as I need a BIG monitor when I colour."

Read the rest of the *Instrument of War* saga online at:

www.rdcomicsonline.com
rdcomics.deviantart.com

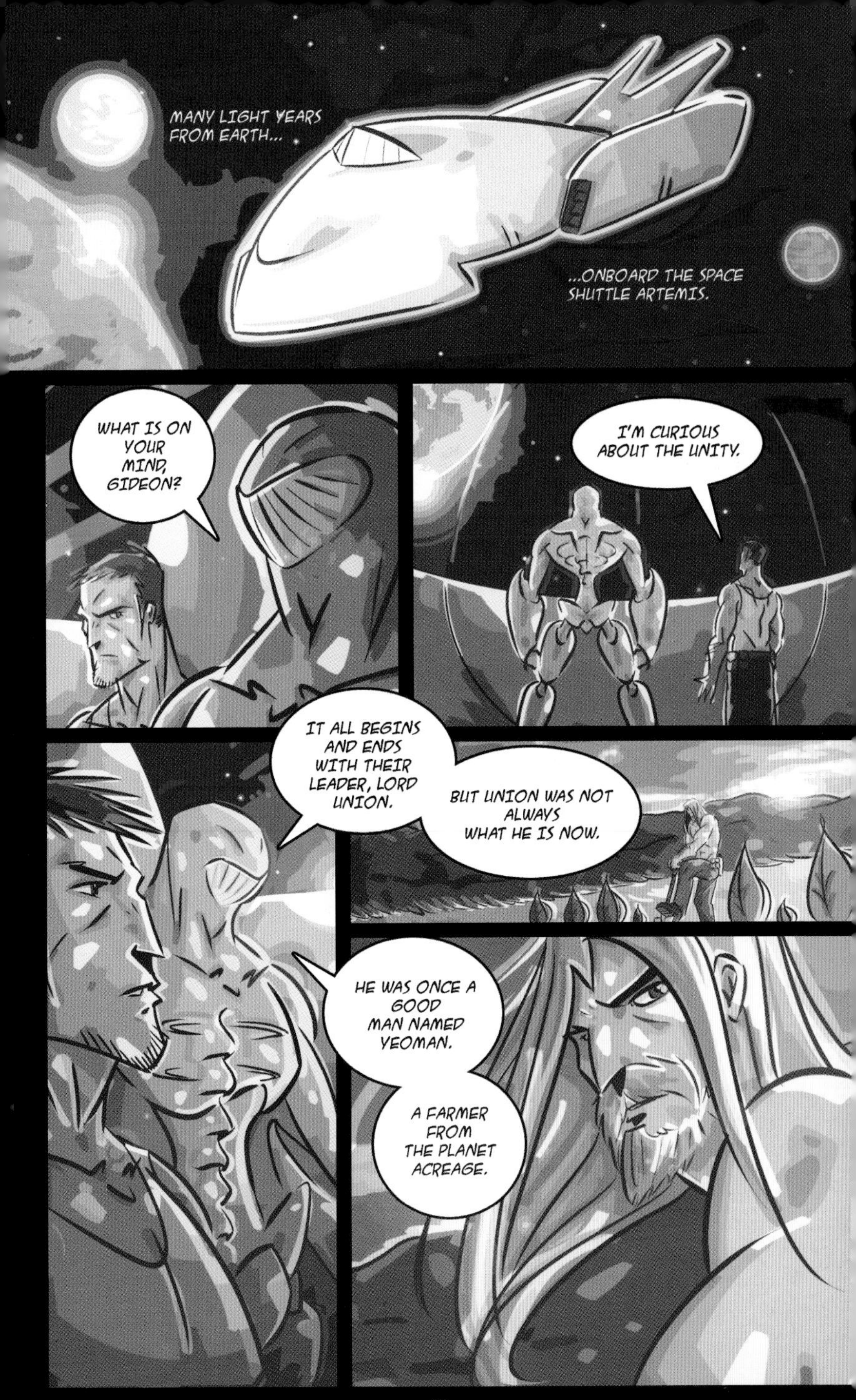
MANY LIGHT YEARS FROM EARTH...
...ONBOARD THE SPACE SHUTTLE ARTEMIS.
WHAT IS ON YOUR MIND, GIDEON?
I'M CURIOUS ABOUT THE UNITY.
IT ALL BEGINS AND ENDS WITH THEIR LEADER, LORD UNION.
BUT UNION WAS NOT ALWAYS WHAT HE IS NOW.
HE WAS ONCE A GOOD MAN NAMED YEOMAN.
A FARMER FROM THE PLANET ACREAGE.

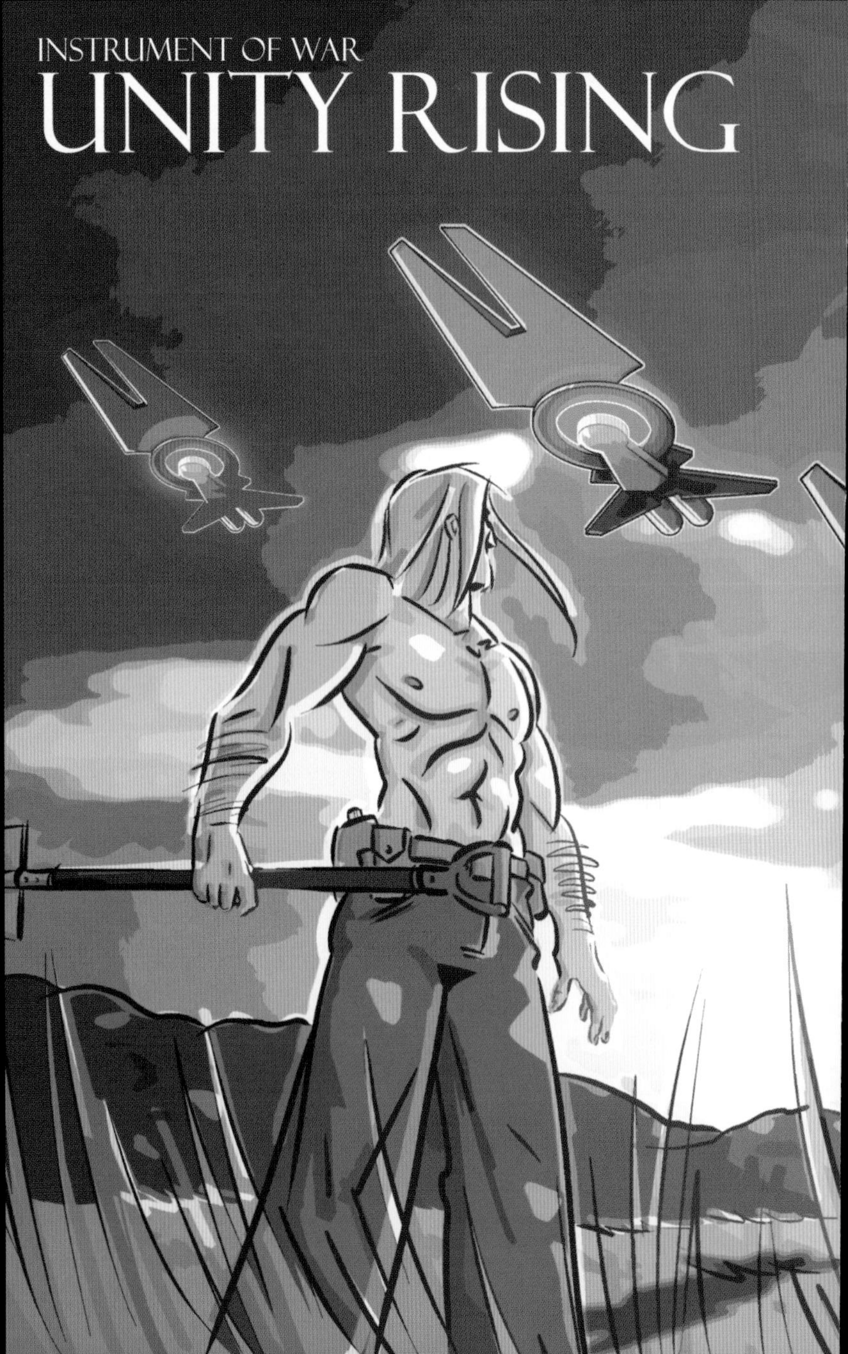
INSTRUMENT OF WAR
UNITY RISING

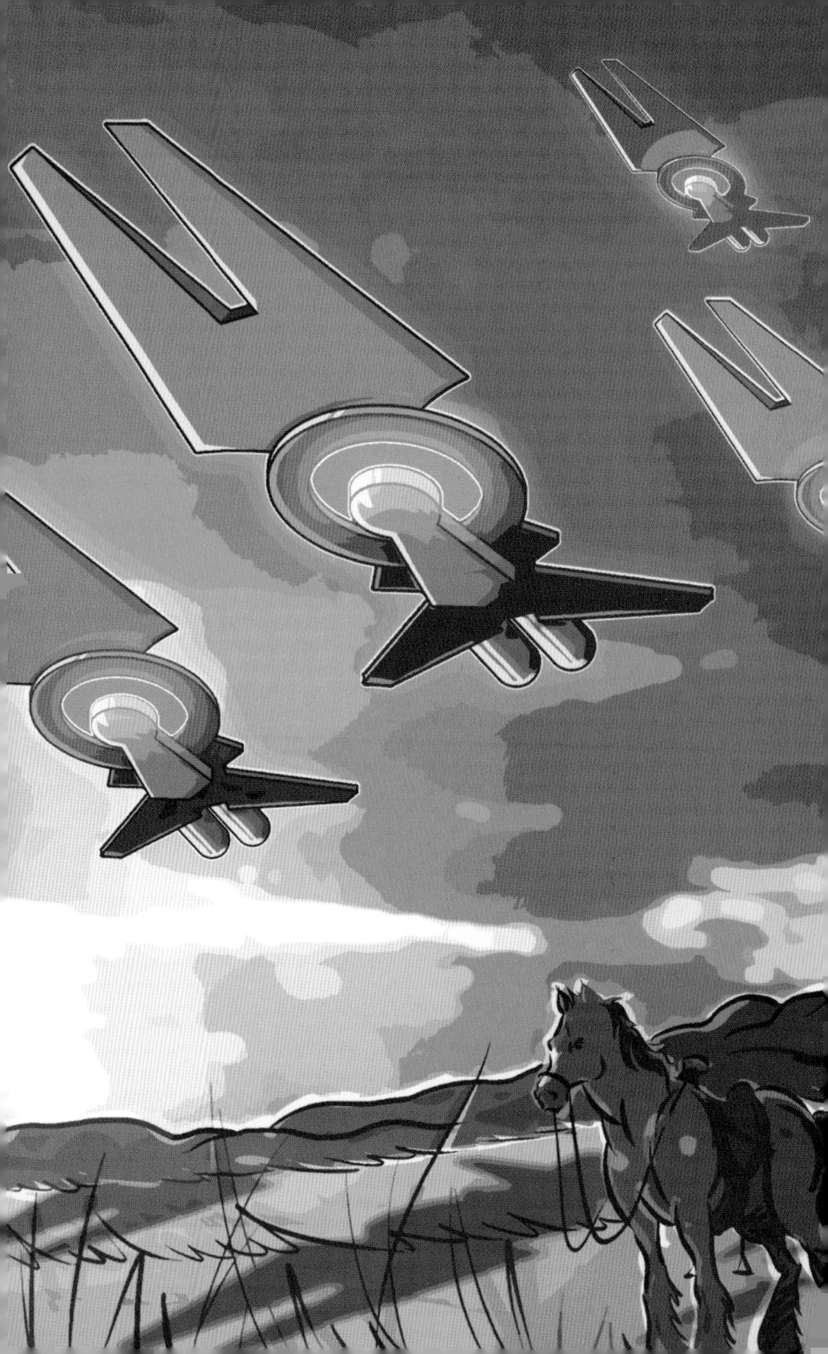

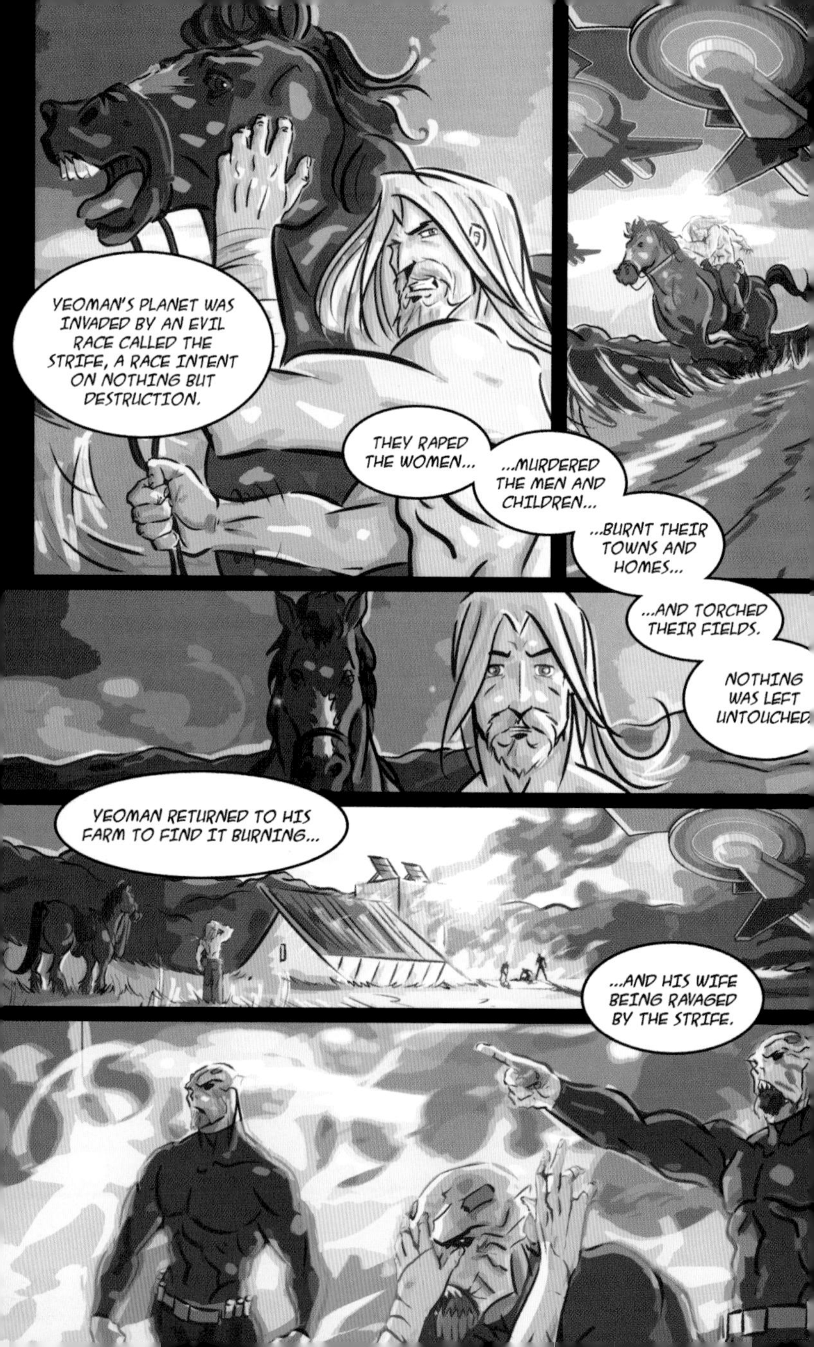
YEOMAN'S PLANET WAS INVADED BY AN EVIL RACE CALLED THE STRIFE, A RACE INTENT ON NOTHING BUT DESTRUCTION.
THEY RAPED THE WOMEN...
...MURDERED THE MEN AND CHILDREN...
...BURNT THEIR TOWNS AND HOMES...
...AND TORCHED THEIR FIELDS.
NOTHING WAS LEFT UNTOUCHED.
YEOMAN RETURNED TO HIS FARM TO FIND IT BURNING...
...AND HIS WIFE BEING RAVAGED BY THE STRIFE.

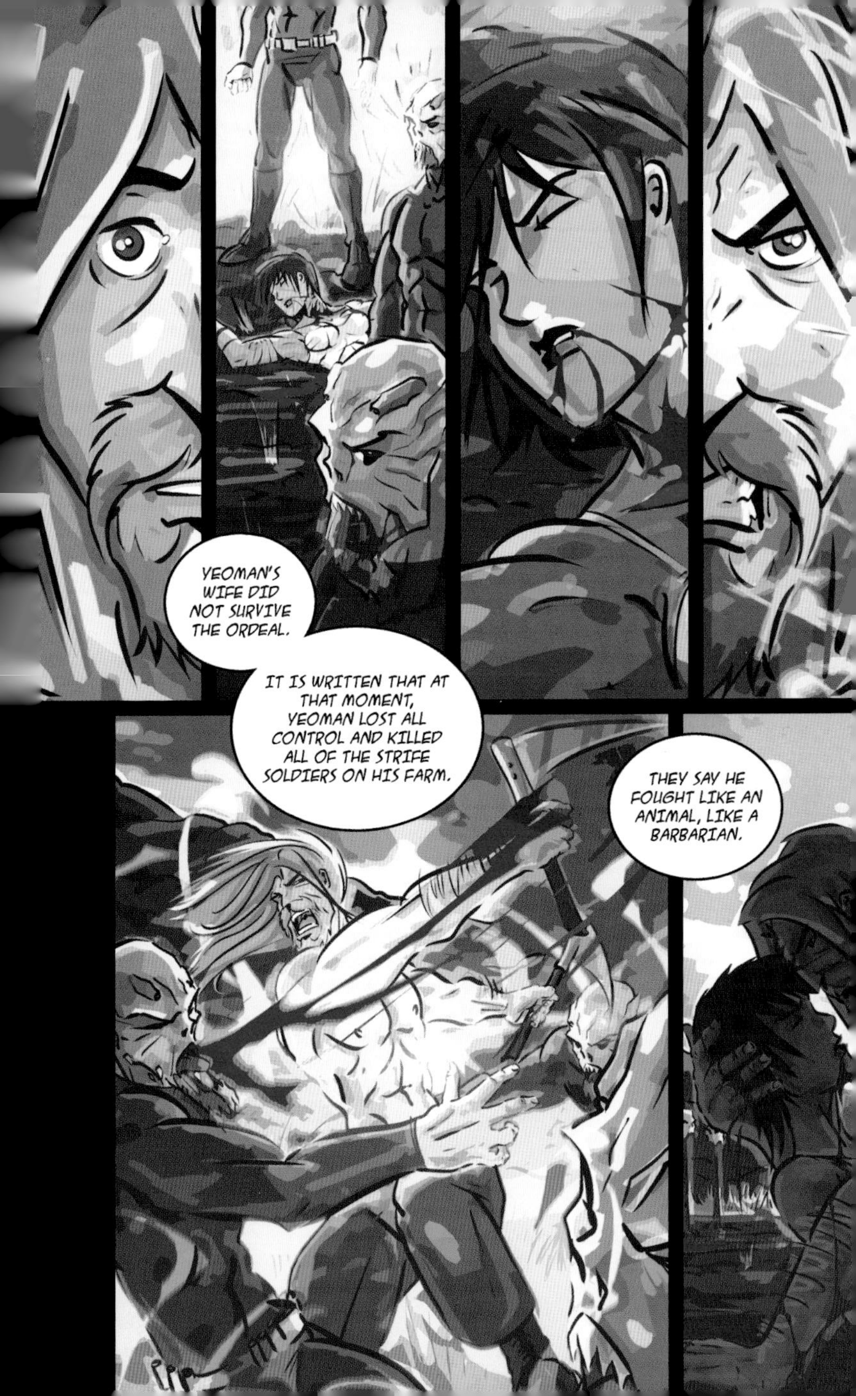
YEOMAN'S WIFE DID NOT SURVIVE THE ORDEAL.
IT IS WRITTEN THAT AT THAT MOMENT, YEOMAN LOST ALL CONTROL AND KILLED ALL OF THE STRIFE SOLDIERS ON HIS FARM.
THEY SAY HE FOUGHT LIKE AN ANIMAL, LIKE A BARBARIAN.

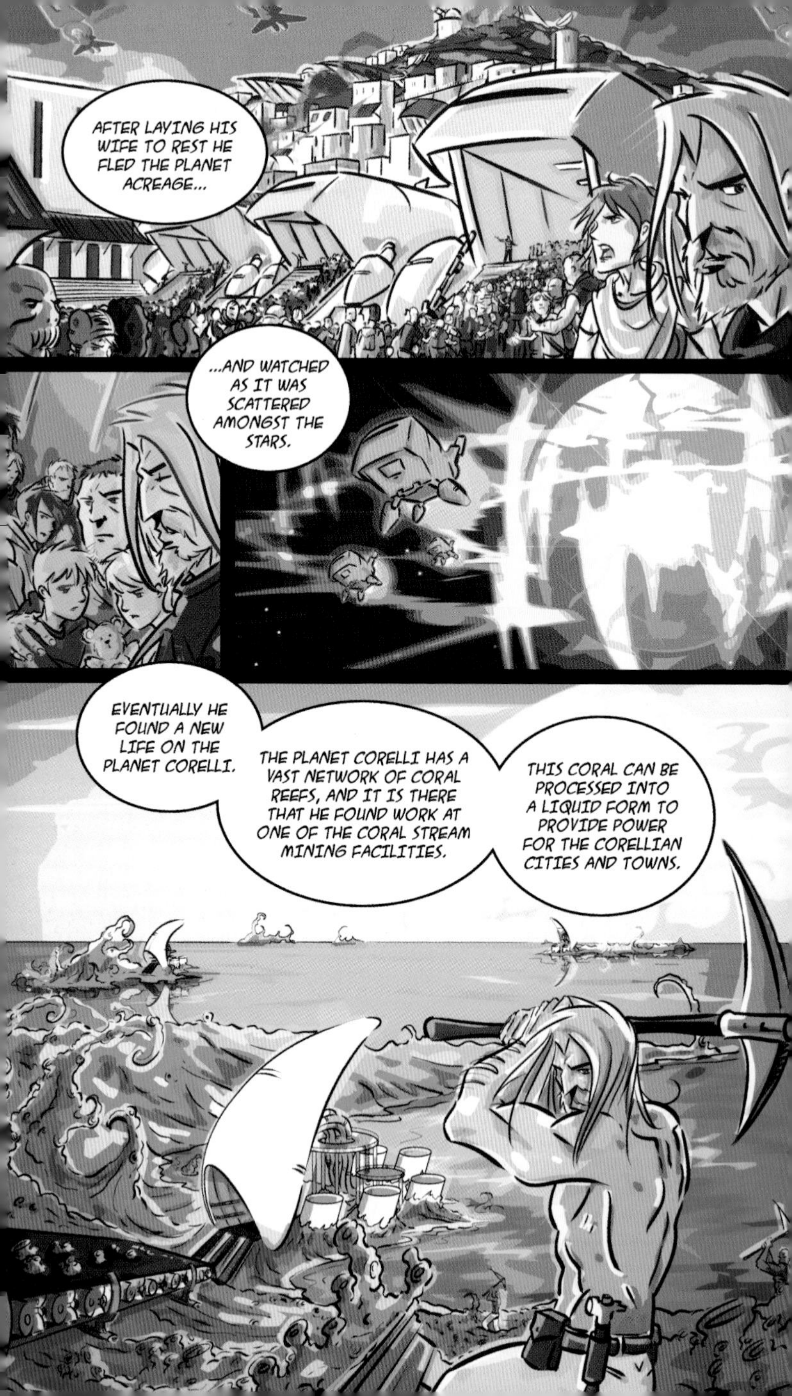
AFTER LAYING HIS WIFE TO REST HE FLED THE PLANET ACREAGE...
...AND WATCHED AS IT WAS SCATTERED AMONGST THE STARS.
EVENTUALLY HE FOUND A NEW LIFE ON THE PLANET CORELLI.
THE PLANET CORELLI HAS A VAST NETWORK OF CORAL REEFS, AND IT IS THERE THAT HE FOUND WORK AT ONE OF THE CORAL STREAM MINING FACILITIES.
THIS CORAL CAN BE PROCESSED INTO A LIQUID FORM TO PROVIDE POWER FOR THE CORELLIAN CITIES AND TOWNS.

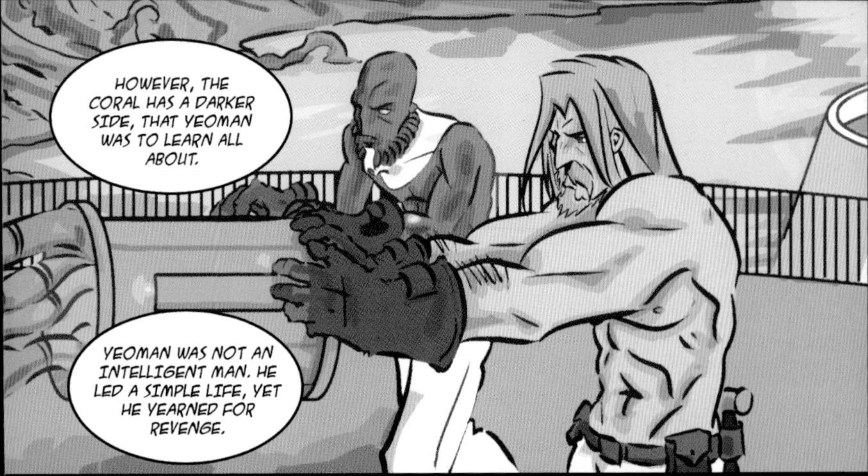
HOWEVER, THE CORAL HAS A DARKER SIDE, THAT YEOMAN WAS TO LEARN ALL ABOUT.
YEOMAN WAS NOT AN INTELLIGENT MAN. HE LED A SIMPLE LIFE, YET HE YEARNED FOR REVENGE.

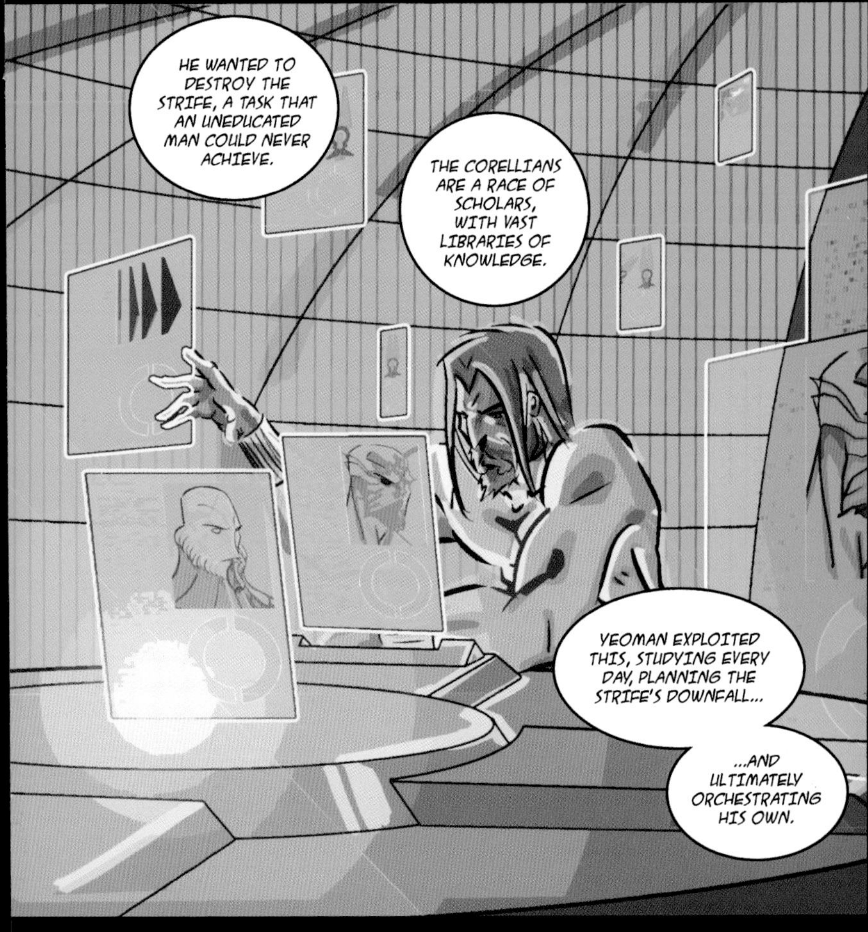
HE WANTED TO DESTROY THE STRIFE, A TASK THAT AN UNEDUCATED MAN COULD NEVER ACHIEVE.
THE CORELLIANS ARE A RACE OF SCHOLARS, WITH VAST LIBRARIES OF KNOWLEDGE.
YEOMAN EXPLOITED THIS, STUDYING EVERY DAY, PLANNING THE STRIFE'S DOWNFALL...
...AND ULTIMATELY ORCHESTRATING HIS OWN.

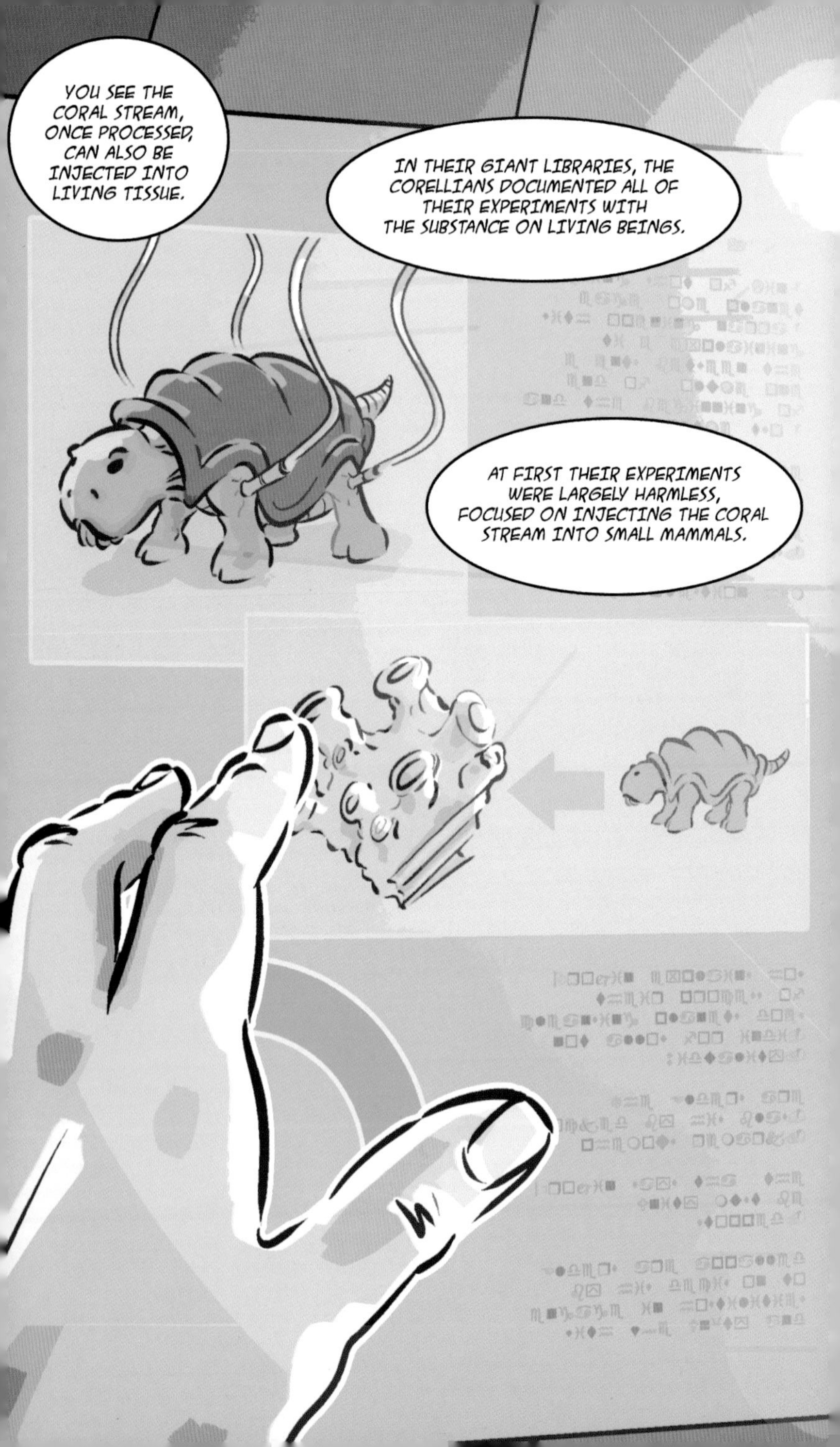
YOU SEE THE CORAL STREAM, ONCE PROCESSED, CAN ALSO BE INJECTED INTO LIVING TISSUE.
IN THEIR GIANT LIBRARIES, THE CORELLIANS DOCUMENTED ALL OF THEIR EXPERIMENTS WITH THE SUBSTANCE ON LIVING BEINGS.
AT FIRST THEIR EXPERIMENTS WERE LARGELY HARMLESS, FOCUSED ON INJECTING THE CORAL STREAM INTO SMALL MAMMALS.

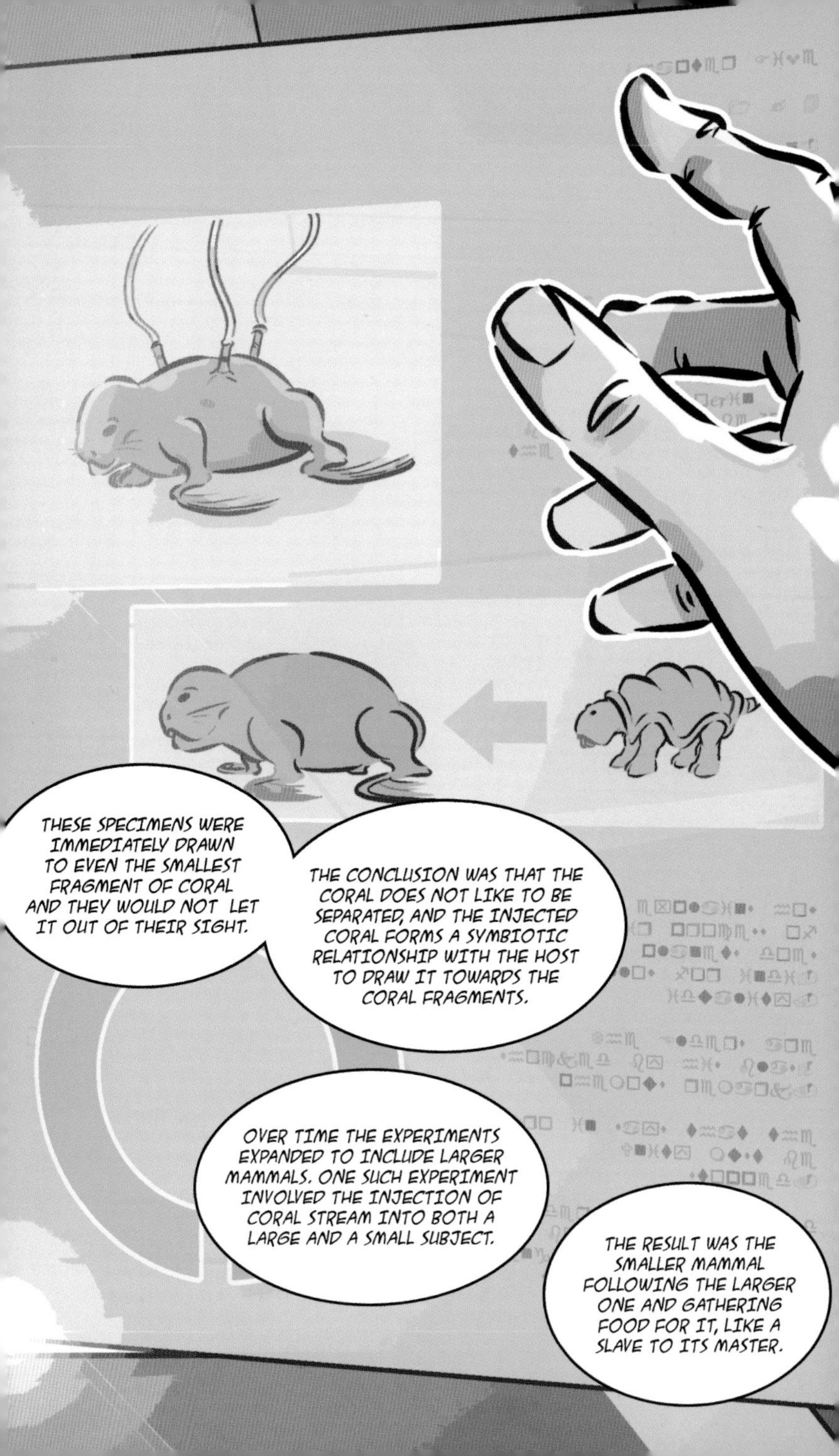

THESE SPECIMENS WERE IMMEDIATELY DRAWN TO EVEN THE SMALLEST FRAGMENT OF CORAL AND THEY WOULD NOT LET IT OUT OF THEIR SIGHT.
THE CONCLUSION WAS THAT THE CORAL DOES NOT LIKE TO BE SEPARATED, AND THE INJECTED CORAL FORMS A SYMBIOTIC RELATIONSHIP WITH THE HOST TO DRAW IT TOWARDS THE CORAL FRAGMENTS.
OVER TIME THE EXPERIMENTS EXPANDED TO INCLUDE LARGER MAMMALS. ONE SUCH EXPERIMENT INVOLVED THE INJECTION OF CORAL STREAM INTO BOTH A LARGE AND A SMALL SUBJECT.
THE RESULT WAS THE SMALLER MAMMAL FOLLOWING THE LARGER ONE AND GATHERING FOOD FOR IT, LIKE A SLAVE TO ITS MASTER.

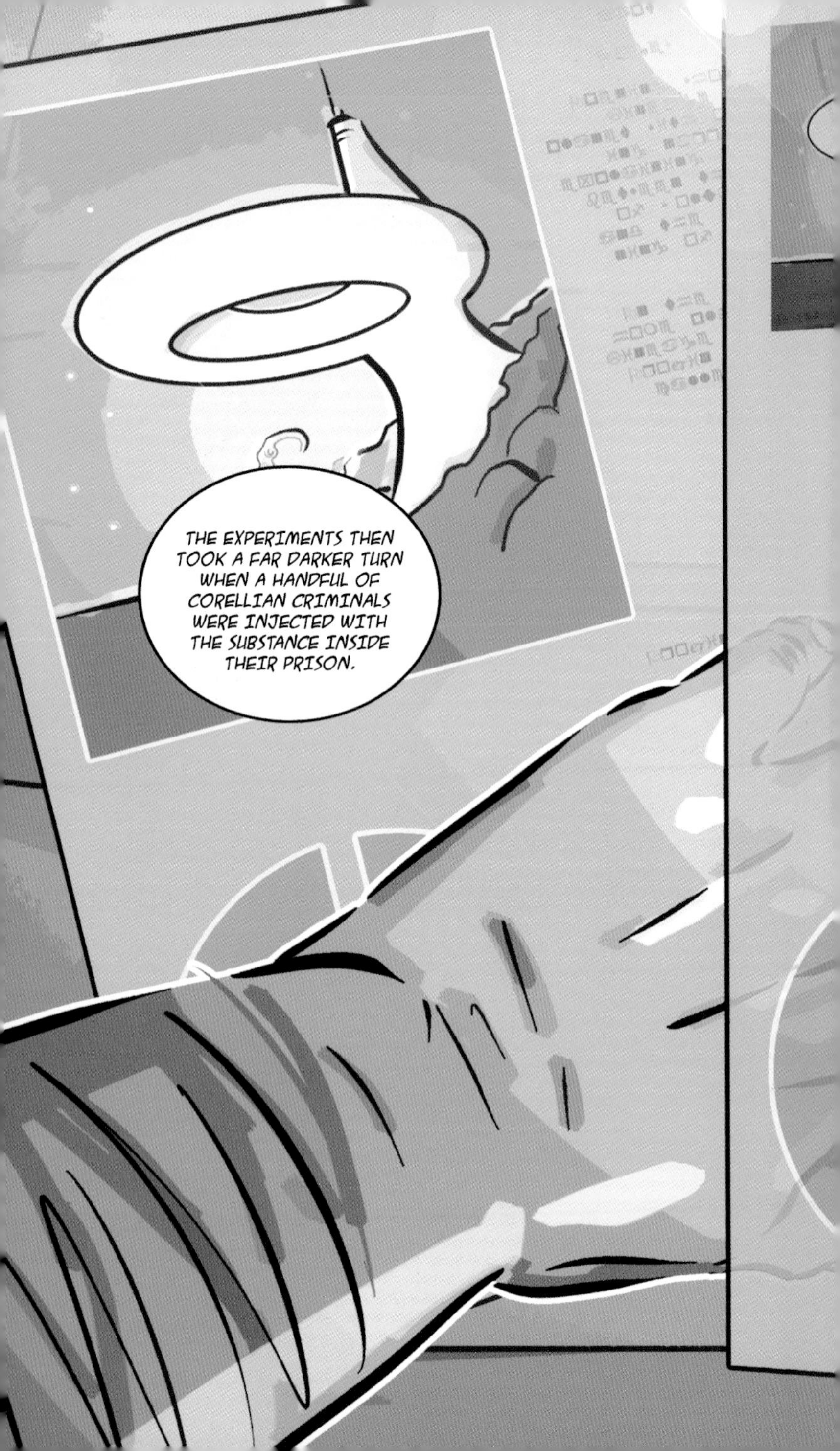
THE EXPERIMENTS THEN TOOK A FAR DARKER TURN WHEN A HANDFUL OF CORELLIAN CRIMINALS WERE INJECTED WITH THE SUBSTANCE INSIDE THEIR PRISON.

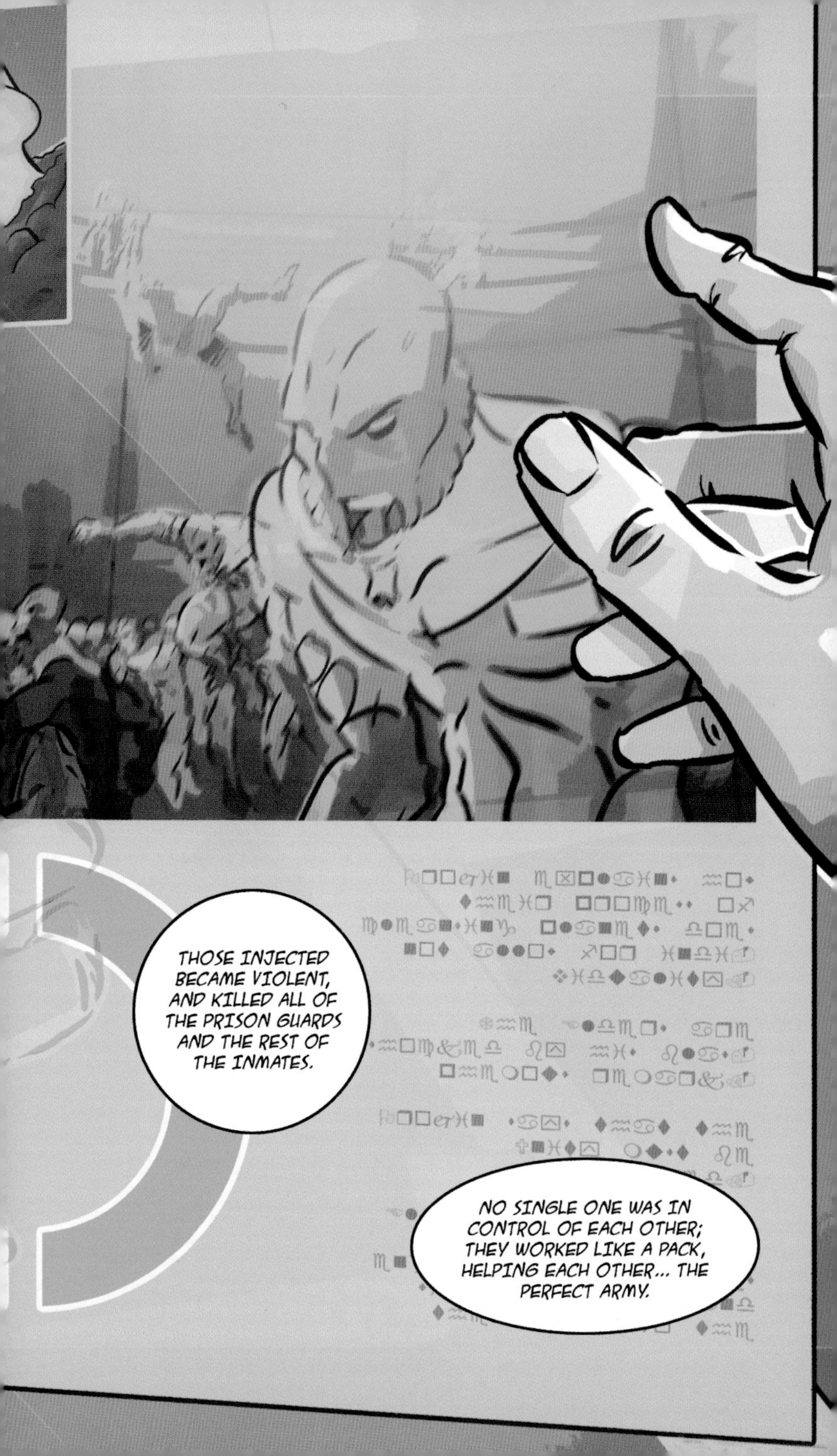
THOSE INJECTED BECAME VIOLENT, AND KILLED ALL OF THE PRISON GUARDS AND THE REST OF THE INMATES.
NO SINGLE ONE WAS IN CONTROL OF EACH OTHER; THEY WORKED LIKE A PACK, HELPING EACH OTHER... THE PERFECT ARMY.

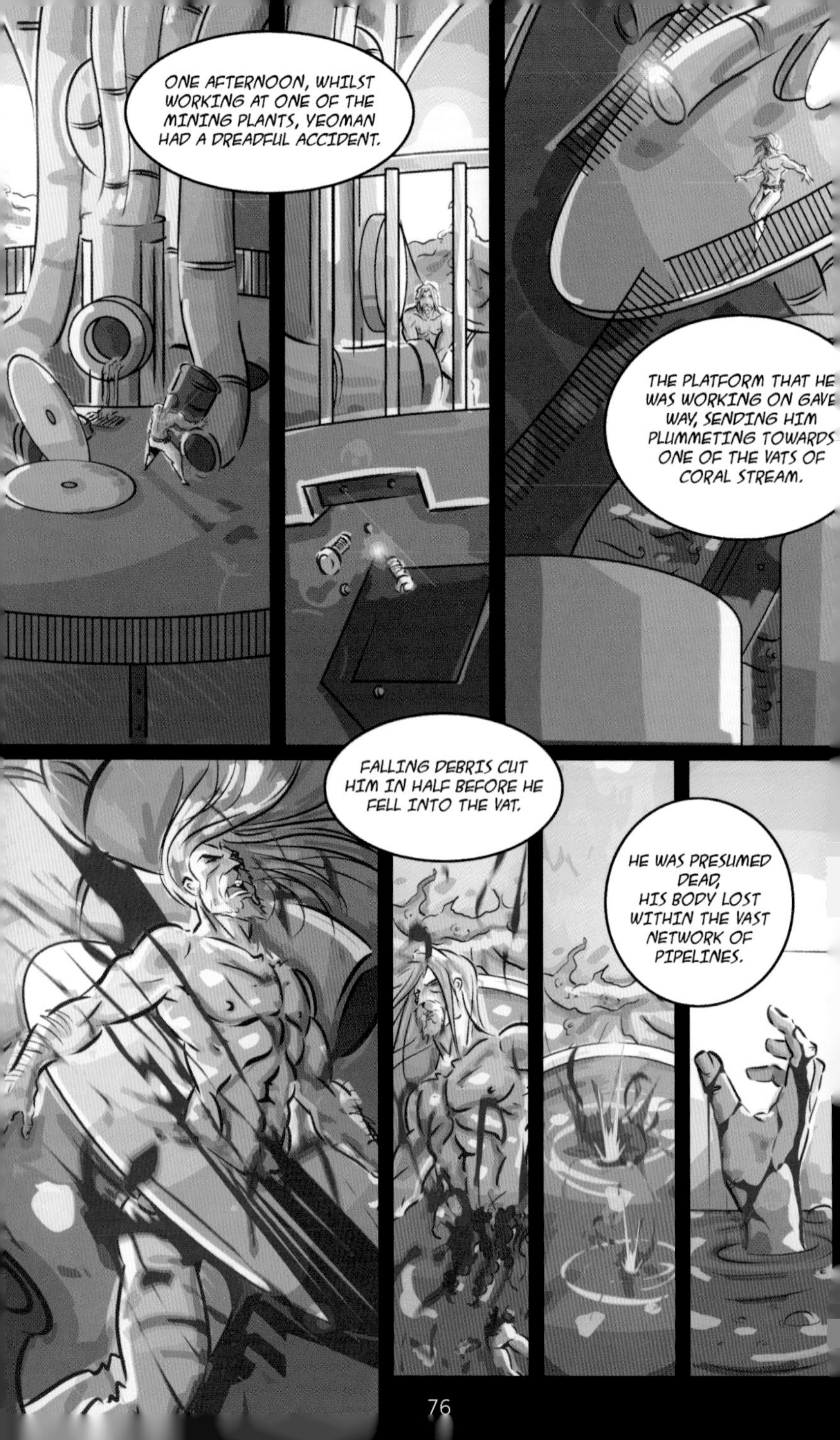

ONE AFTERNOON, WHILST WORKING AT ONE OF THE MINING PLANTS, YEOMAN HAD A DREADFUL ACCIDENT.
THE PLATFORM THAT HE WAS WORKING ON GAVE WAY, SENDING HIM PLUMMETING TOWARDS ONE OF THE VATS OF CORAL STREAM.
FALLING DEBRIS CUT HIM IN HALF BEFORE HE FELL INTO THE VAT.
HE WAS PRESUMED DEAD, HIS BODY LOST WITHIN THE VAST NETWORK OF PIPELINES.

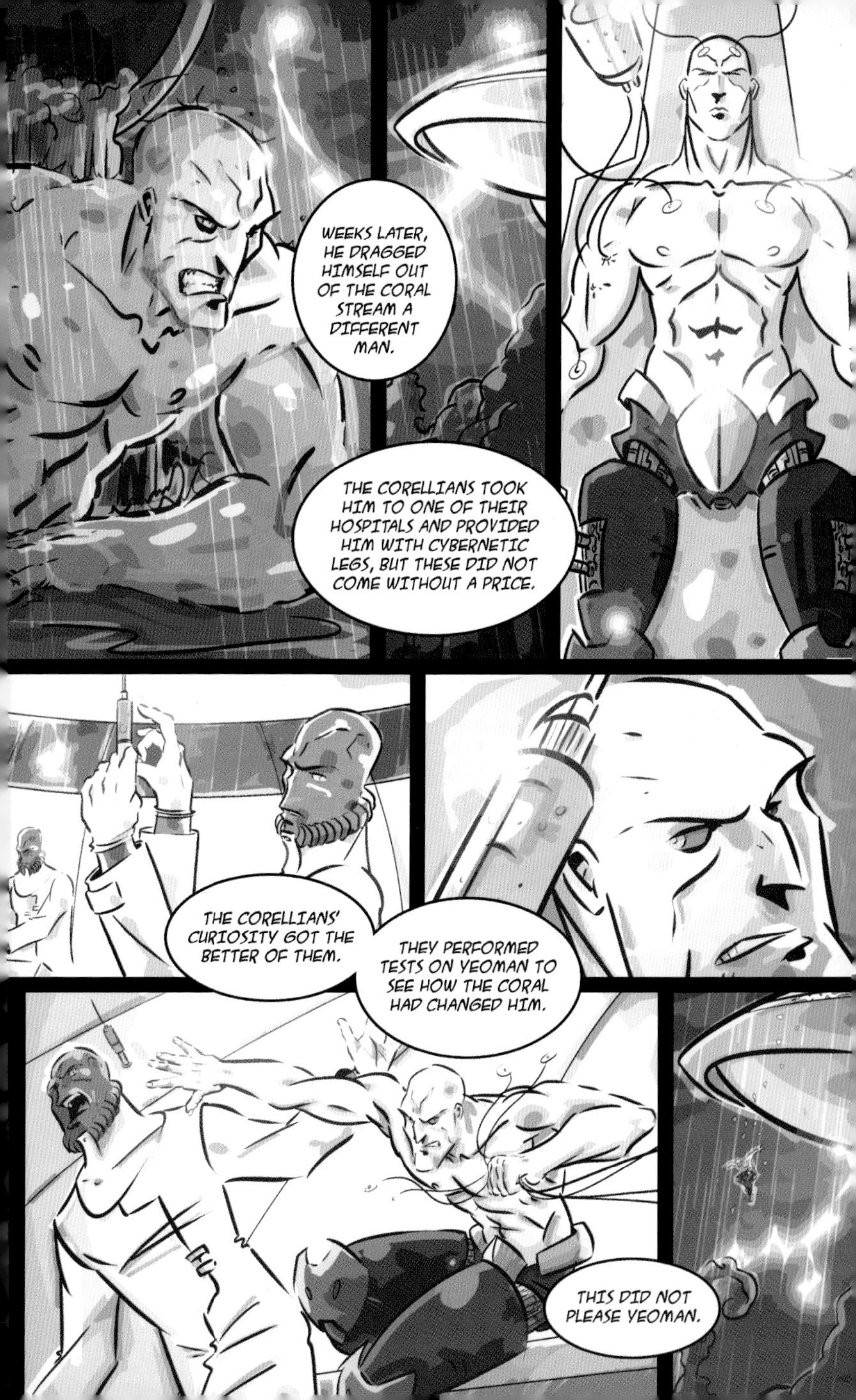
WEEKS LATER, HE DRAGGED HIMSELF OUT OF THE CORAL STREAM A DIFFERENT MAN.
THE CORELLIANS TOOK HIM TO ONE OF THEIR HOSPITALS AND PROVIDED HIM WITH CYBERNETIC LEGS, BUT THESE DID NOT COME WITHOUT A PRICE.
THE CORELLIANS' CURIOSITY GOT THE BETTER OF THEM.
THEY PERFORMED TESTS ON YEOMAN TO SEE HOW THE CORAL HAD CHANGED HIM.
THIS DID NOT PLEASE YEOMAN.

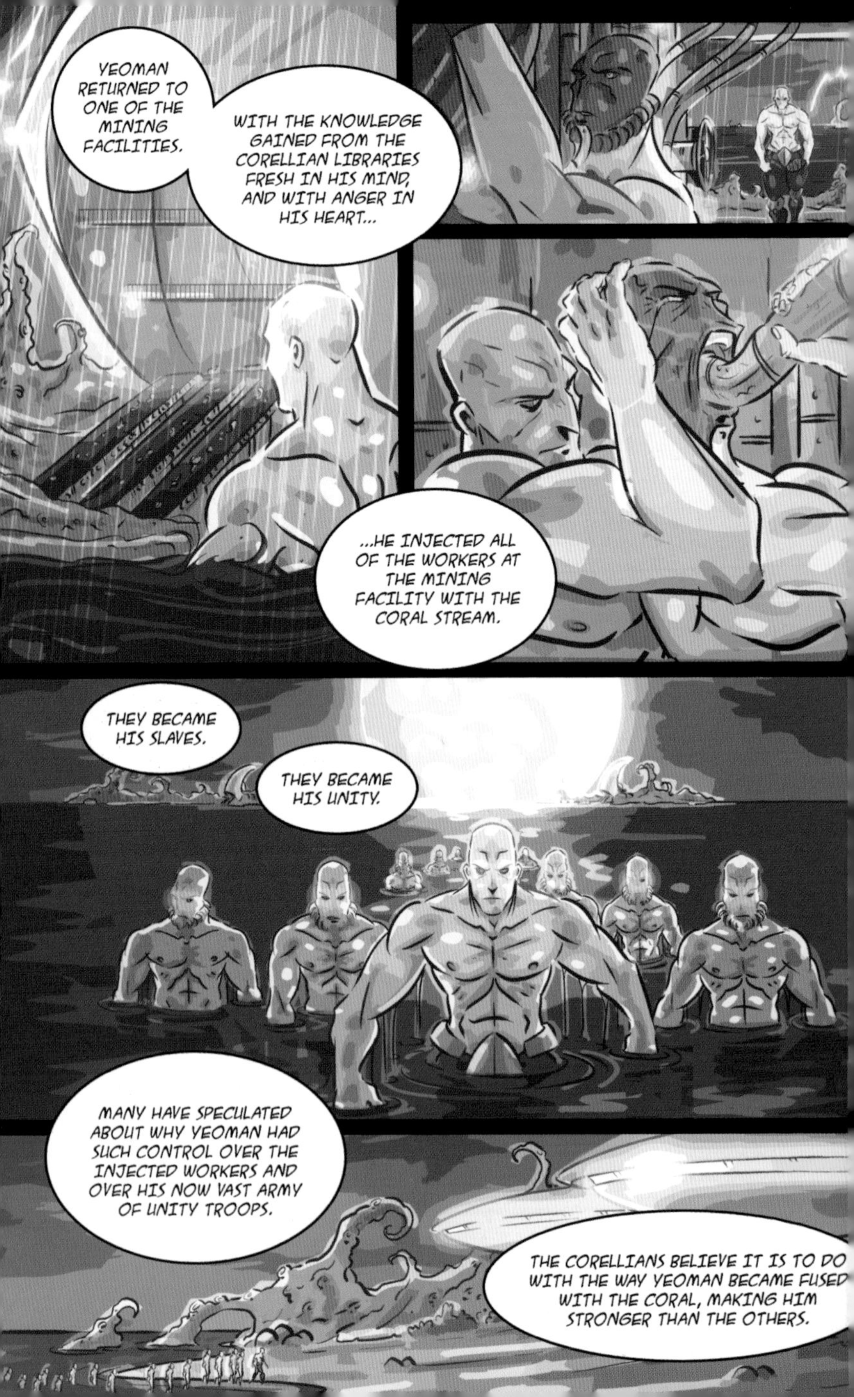
YEOMAN RETURNED TO ONE OF THE MINING FACILITIES.
WITH THE KNOWLEDGE GAINED FROM THE CORELLIAN LIBRARIES FRESH IN HIS MIND, AND WITH ANGER IN HIS HEART...
...HE INJECTED ALL OF THE WORKERS AT THE MINING FACILITY WITH THE CORAL STREAM.
THEY BECAME HIS SLAVES.
THEY BECAME HIS UNITY.
MANY HAVE SPECULATED ABOUT WHY YEOMAN HAD SUCH CONTROL OVER THE INJECTED WORKERS AND OVER HIS NOW VAST ARMY OF UNITY TROOPS.
THE CORELLIANS BELIEVE IT IS TO DO WITH THE WAY YEOMAN BECAME FUSED WITH THE CORAL, MAKING HIM STRONGER THAN THE OTHERS.

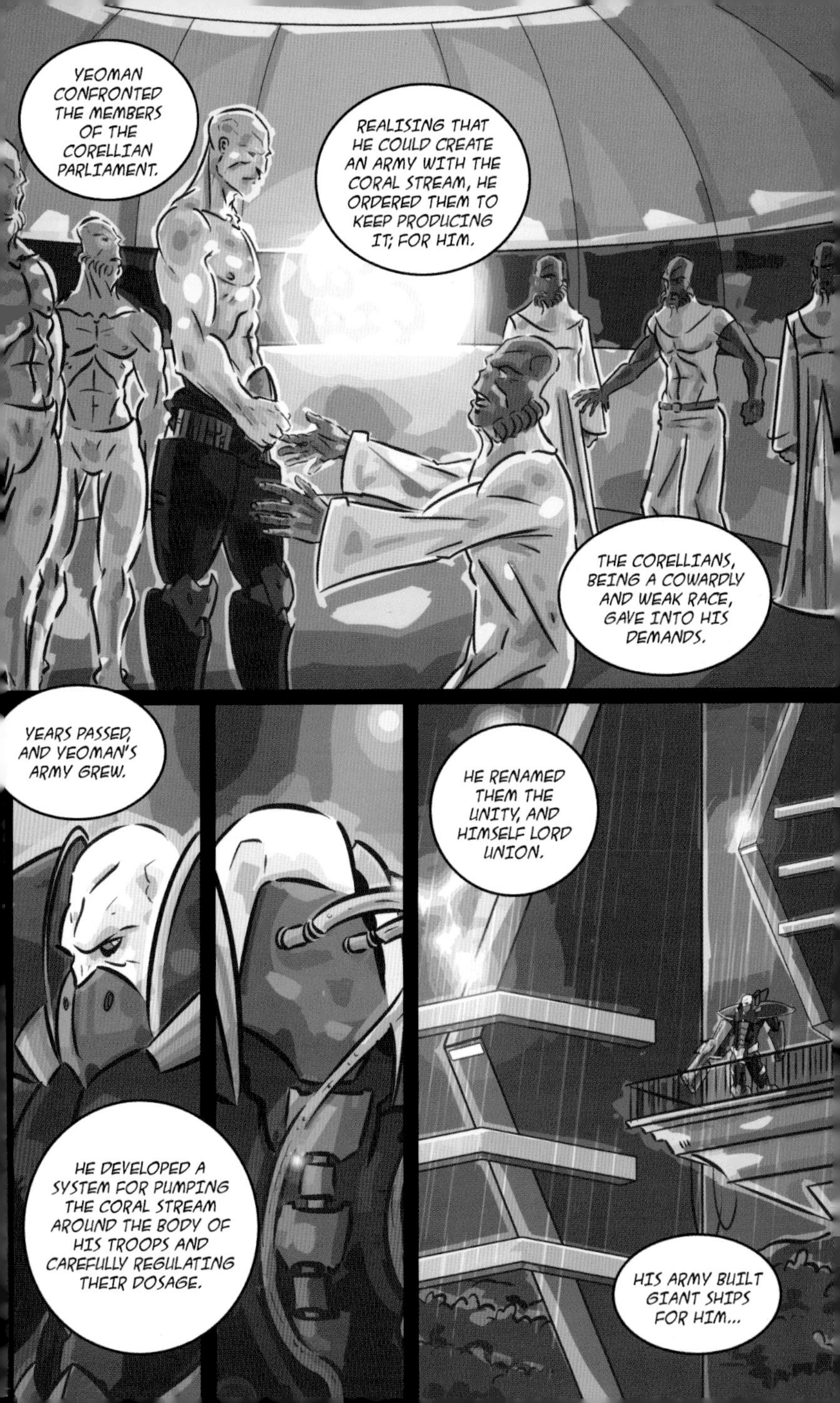
YEOMAN CONFRONTED THE MEMBERS OF THE CORELLIAN PARLIAMENT.
REALISING THAT HE COULD CREATE AN ARMY WITH THE CORAL STREAM, HE ORDERED THEM TO KEEP PRODUCING IT; FOR HIM.
THE CORELLIANS, BEING A COWARDLY AND WEAK RACE, GAVE INTO HIS DEMANDS.
YEARS PASSED, AND YEOMAN'S ARMY GREW.
HE DEVELOPED A SYSTEM FOR PUMPING THE CORAL STREAM AROUND THE BODY OF HIS TROOPS AND CAREFULLY REGULATING THEIR DOSAGE.
HE RENAMED THEM THE UNITY, AND HIMSELF LORD UNION.
HIS ARMY BUILT GIANT SHIPS FOR HIM...

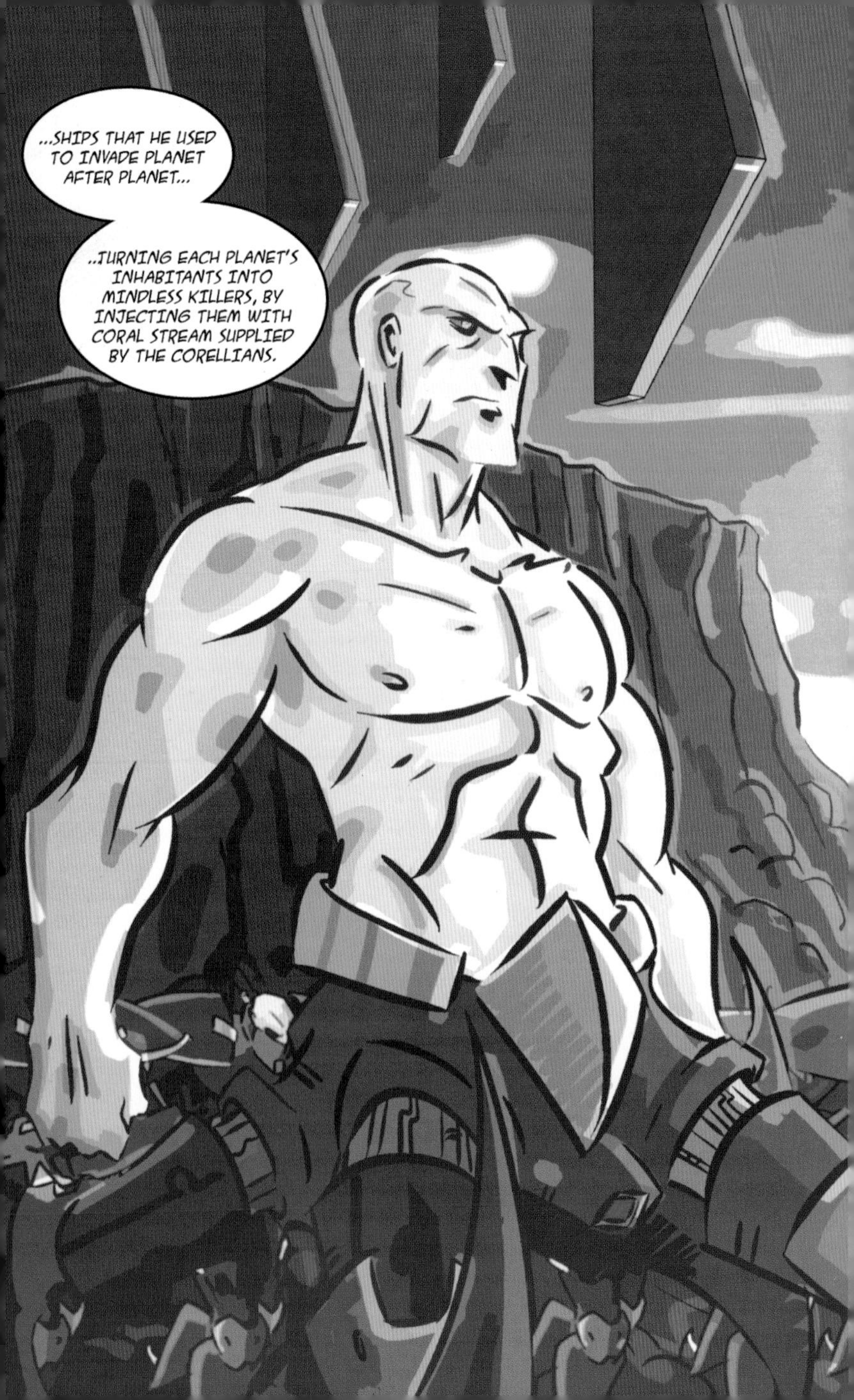
...SHIPS THAT HE USED TO INVADE PLANET AFTER PLANET...
..TURNING EACH PLANET'S INHABITANTS INTO MINDLESS KILLERS, BY INJECTING THEM WITH CORAL STREAM SUPPLIED BY THE CORELLIANS.

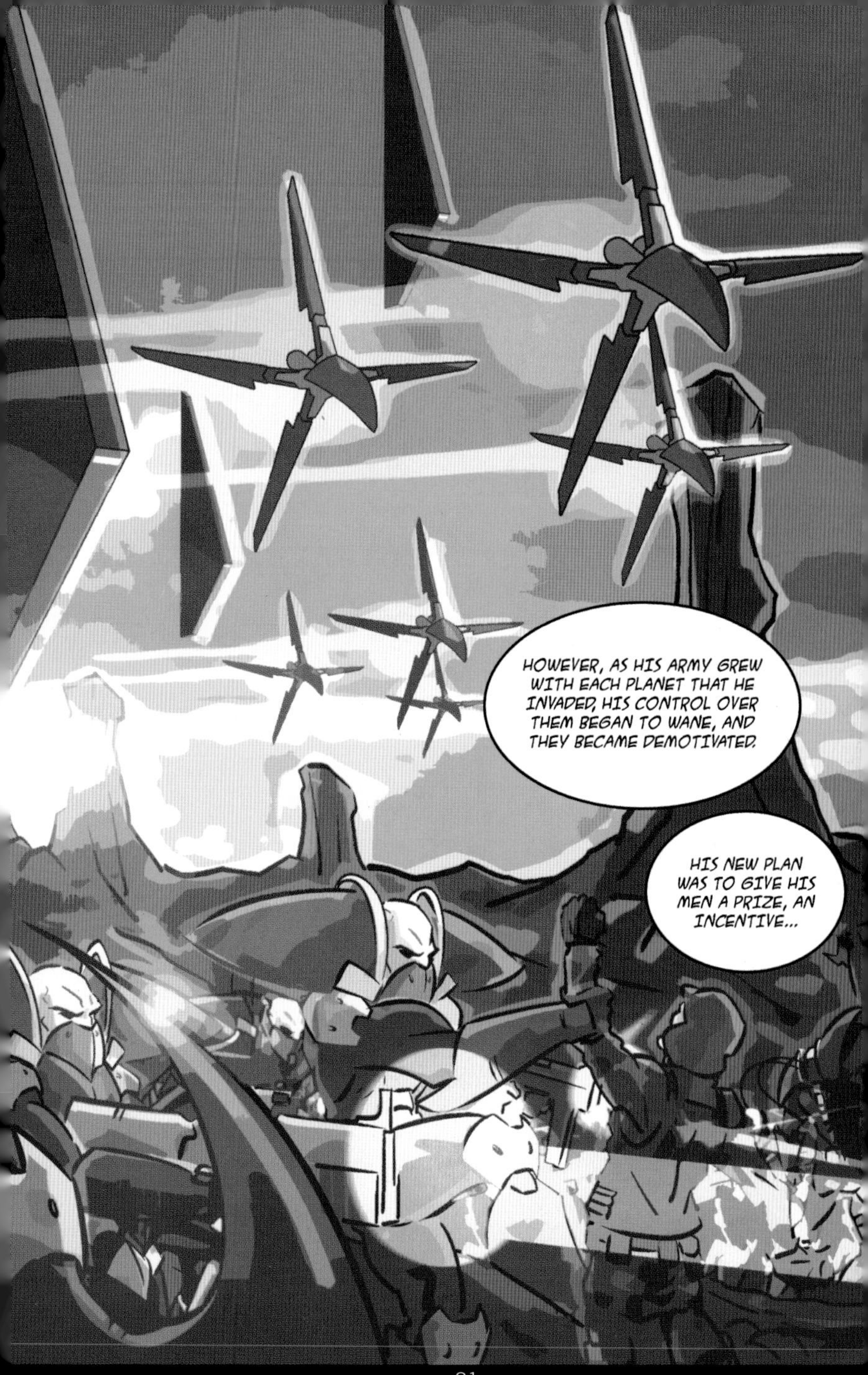
HOWEVER, AS HIS ARMY GREW WITH EACH PLANET THAT HE INVADED, HIS CONTROL OVER THEM BEGAN TO WANE, AND THEY BECAME DEMOTIVATED.
HIS NEW PLAN WAS TO GIVE HIS MEN A PRIZE, AN INCENTIVE...

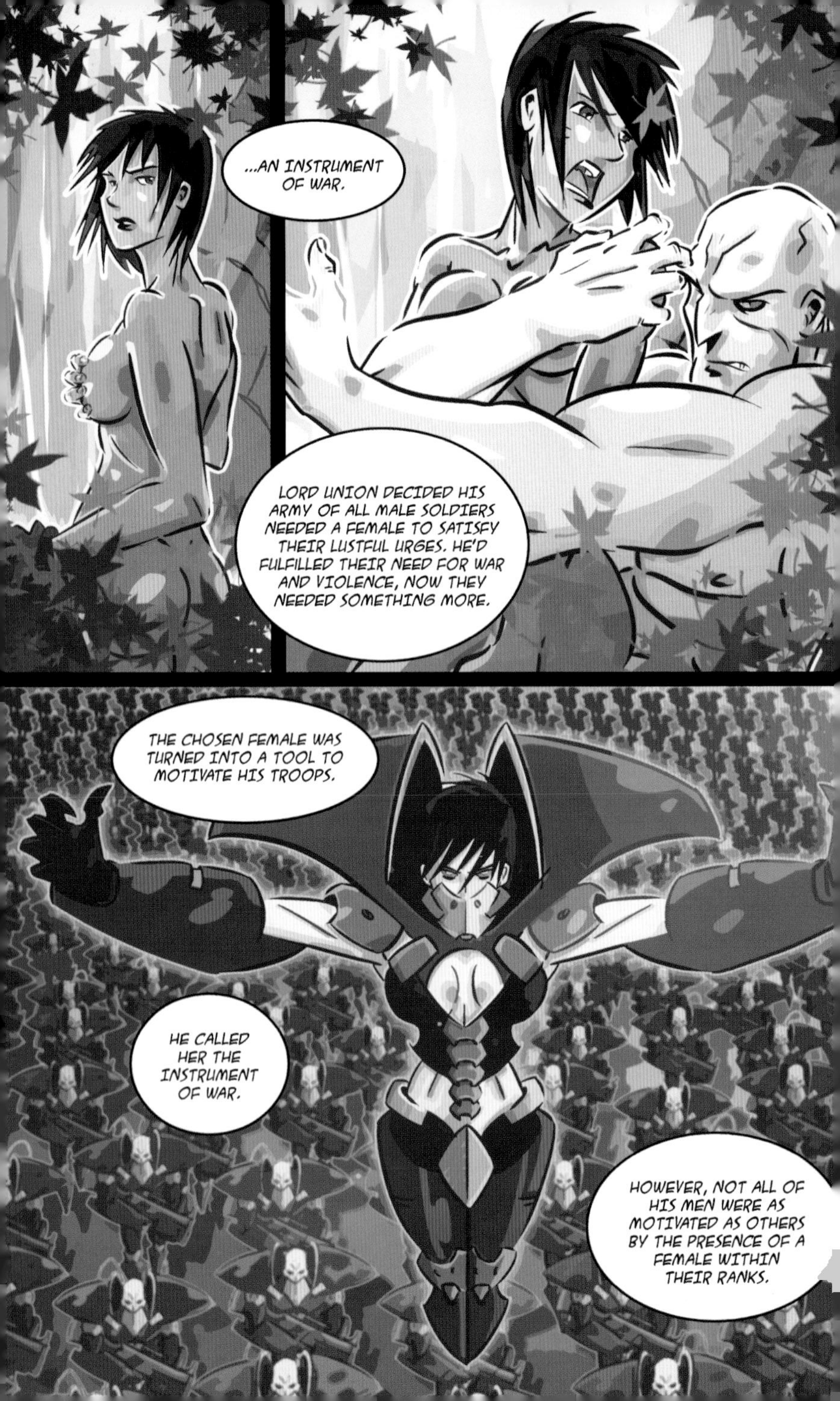

...AN INSTRUMENT OF WAR.
LORD UNION DECIDED HIS ARMY OF ALL MALE SOLDIERS NEEDED A FEMALE TO SATISFY THEIR LUSTFUL URGES. HE'D FULFILLED THEIR NEED FOR WAR AND VIOLENCE, NOW THEY NEEDED SOMETHING MORE.
THE CHOSEN FEMALE WAS TURNED INTO A TOOL TO MOTIVATE HIS TROOPS.
HE CALLED HER THE INSTRUMENT OF WAR.
HOWEVER, NOT ALL OF HIS MEN WERE AS MOTIVATED AS OTHERS BY THE PRESENCE OF A FEMALE WITHIN THEIR RANKS.

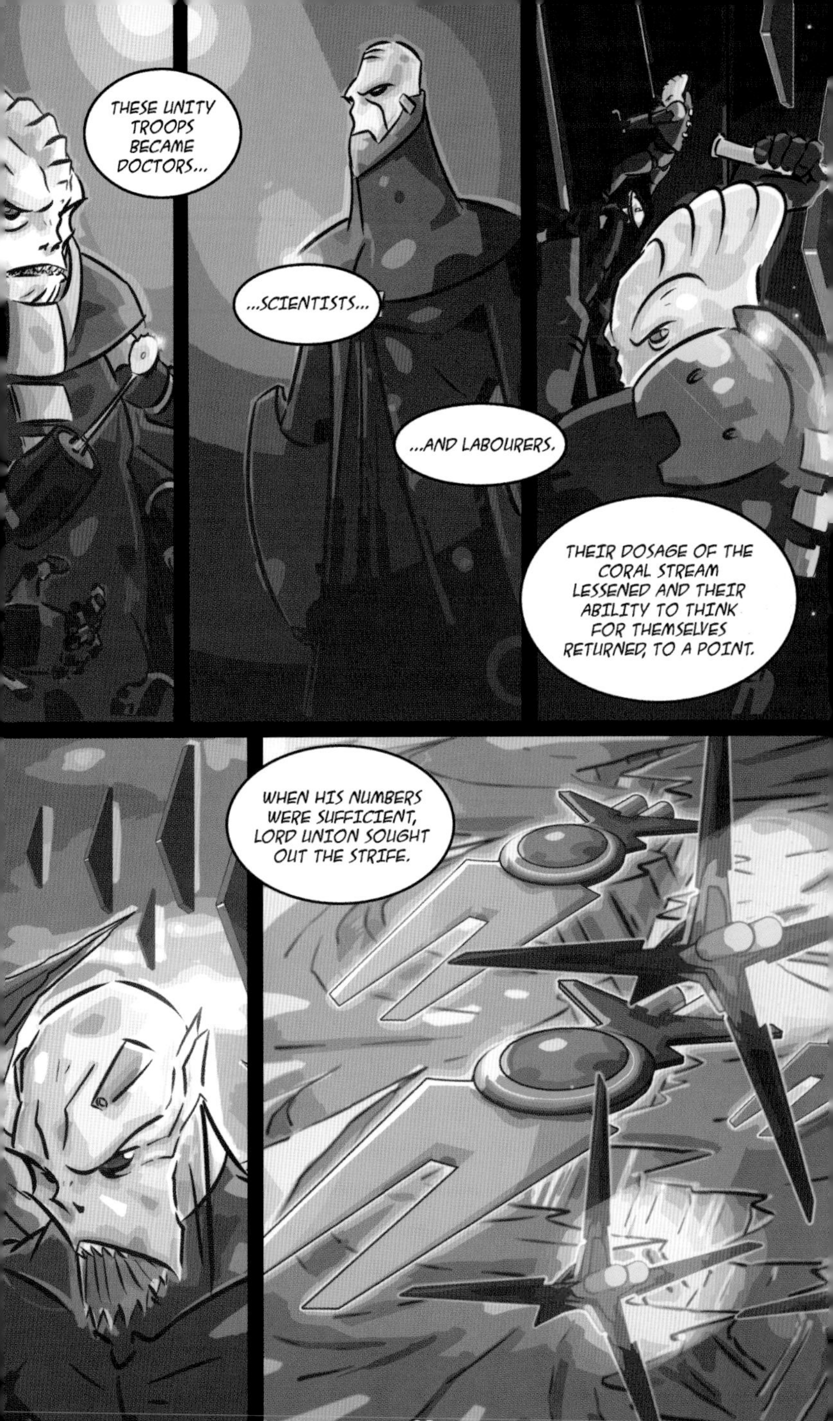
THESE UNITY TROOPS BECAME DOCTORS...
...SCIENTISTS...
...AND LABOURERS.
THEIR DOSAGE OF THE CORAL STREAM LESSENED AND THEIR ABILITY TO THINK FOR THEMSELVES RETURNED, TO A POINT.
WHEN HIS NUMBERS WERE SUFFICIENT, LORD UNION SOUGHT OUT THE STRIFE.

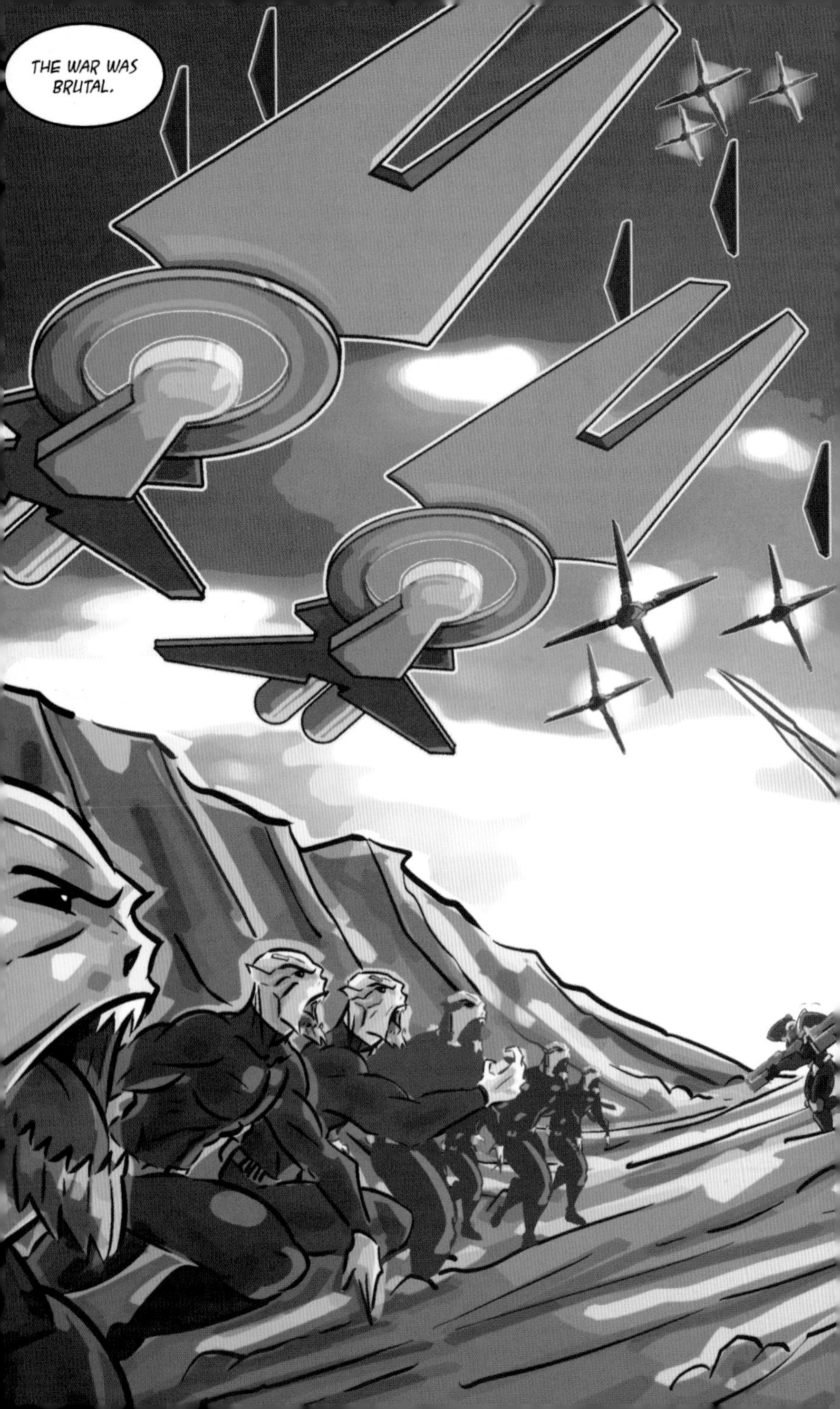
THE WAR WAS BRUTAL.

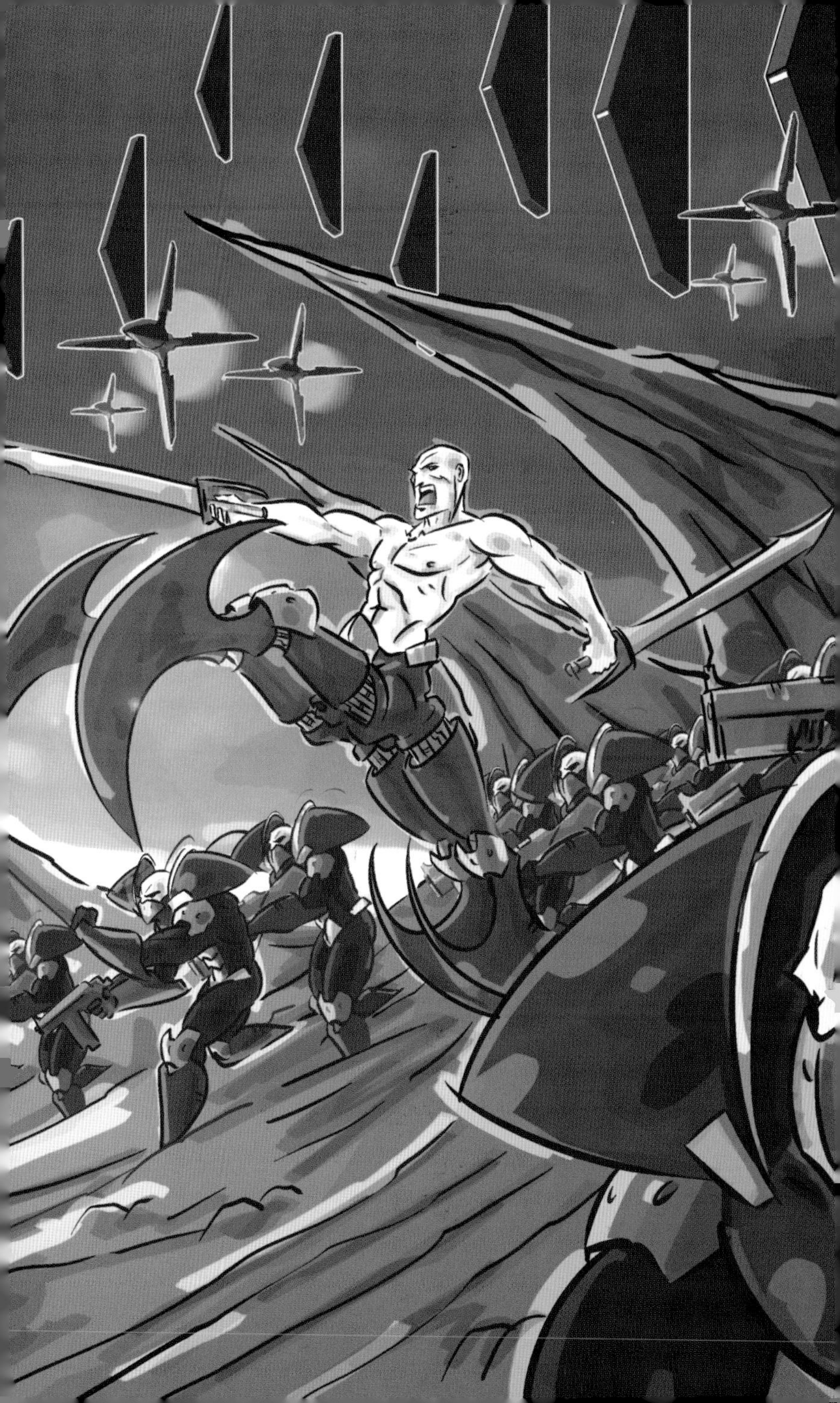

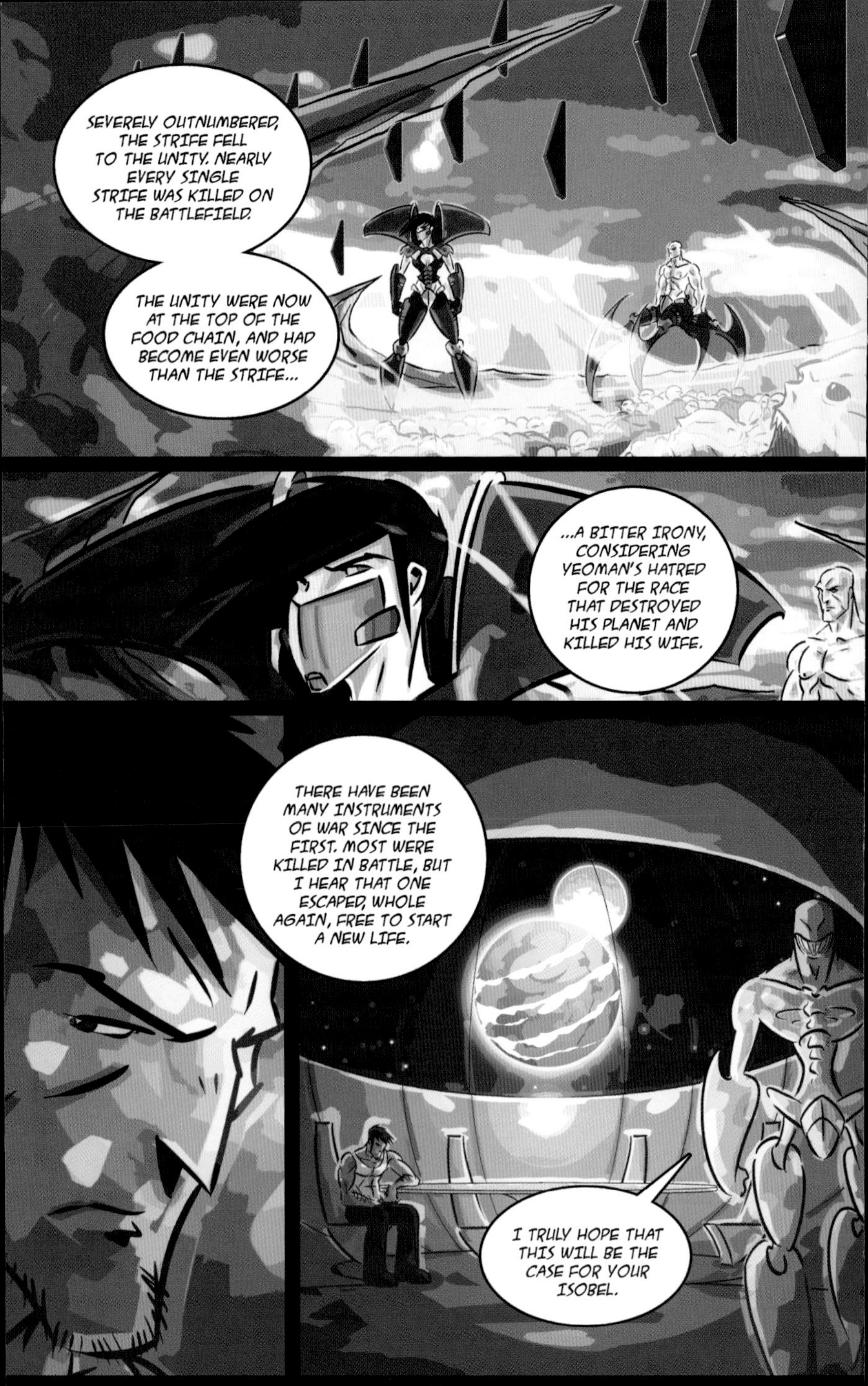
SEVERELY OUTNUMBERED, THE STRIFE FELL TO THE UNITY. NEARLY EVERY SINGLE STRIFE WAS KILLED ON THE BATTLEFIELD.
THE UNITY WERE NOW AT THE TOP OF THE FOOD CHAIN, AND HAD BECOME EVEN WORSE THAN THE STRIFE...
...A BITTER IRONY, CONSIDERING YEOMAN'S HATRED FOR THE RACE THAT DESTROYED HIS PLANET AND KILLED HIS WIFE.
THERE HAVE BEEN MANY INSTRUMENTS OF WAR SINCE THE FIRST. MOST WERE KILLED IN BATTLE, BUT I HEAR THAT ONE ESCAPED, WHOLE AGAIN, FREE TO START A NEW LIFE.
I TRULY HOPE THAT THIS WILL BE THE CASE FOR YOUR ISOBEL.

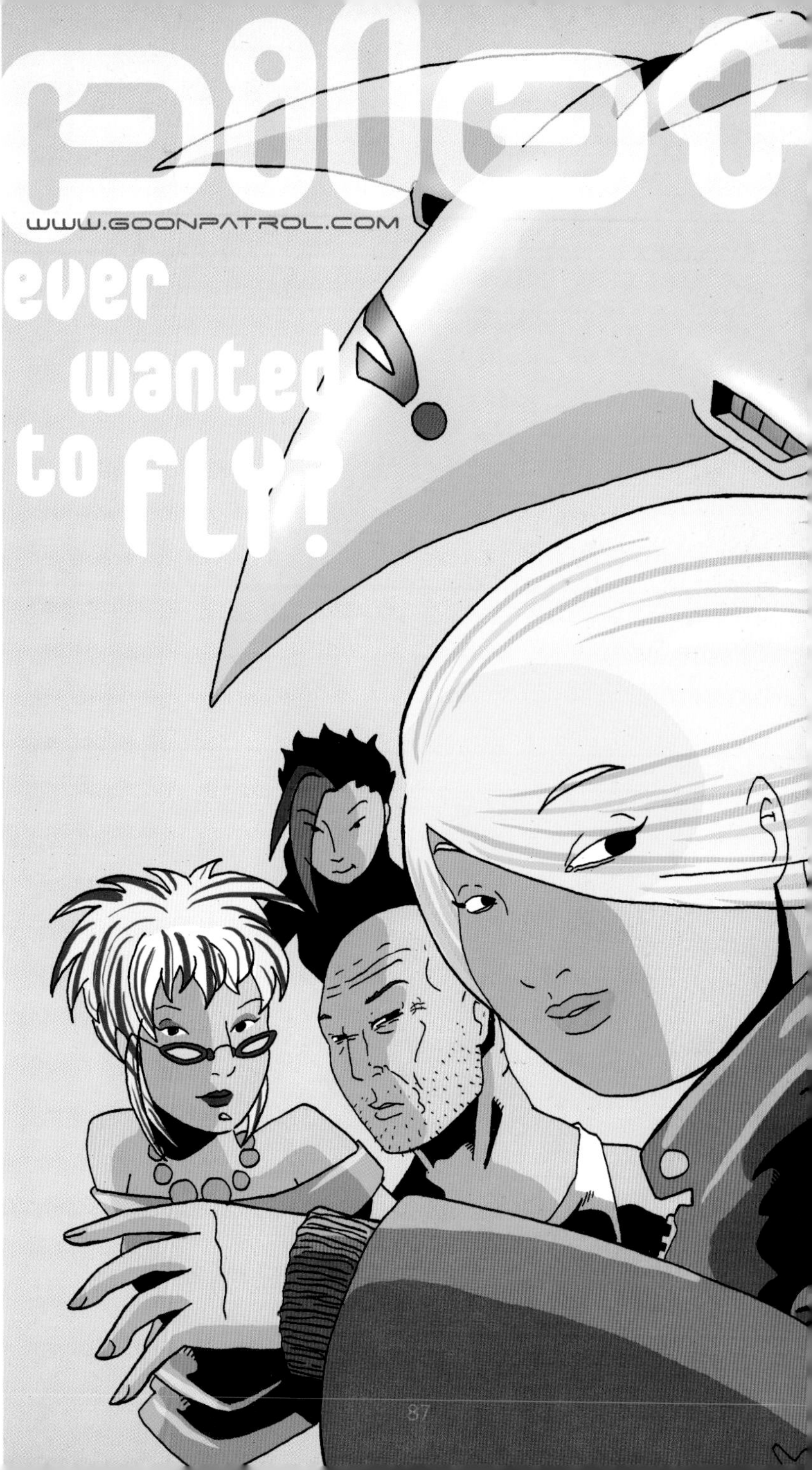
WWW.GOONPATROL.COM
ever wanted to FLY?

PILOT
Mitz

Coming back down to earth – if not for long – schooldays are a popular setting for many a manga teen soap. With Pilot this is just the starting point for a concept that soon really takes off.

In *Volume Two*, previous cover starlet and kung fu panda Samurai Commander Keiko Wu starred in her own solo adventure. **Mitz** took over art duties from *Bulldog: Empire*'s Neill Cameron on recommendation from writer Jason Cobley. One of the art samples shown to us that guaranteed Mitz got the job was *Pilot*, his own small-press publication. Across five A5 instalments, Mitz revealed a sure-footed sense for plotting and the sparkle of witty dialogue as an author in his own write. Dense and rich colour cover illustrations meanwhile hinted at an even greater potential, one soon realized in his next strip, *Joan of RQ* – currently serialized online. We asked him to reboot and expand for us the earliest *Pilot* episodes, crafting them likewise in full colour. Reading like a sharp and funny TV drama animated on paper, could this be a pilot episode in more ways than one?

www.goonpatrol.com

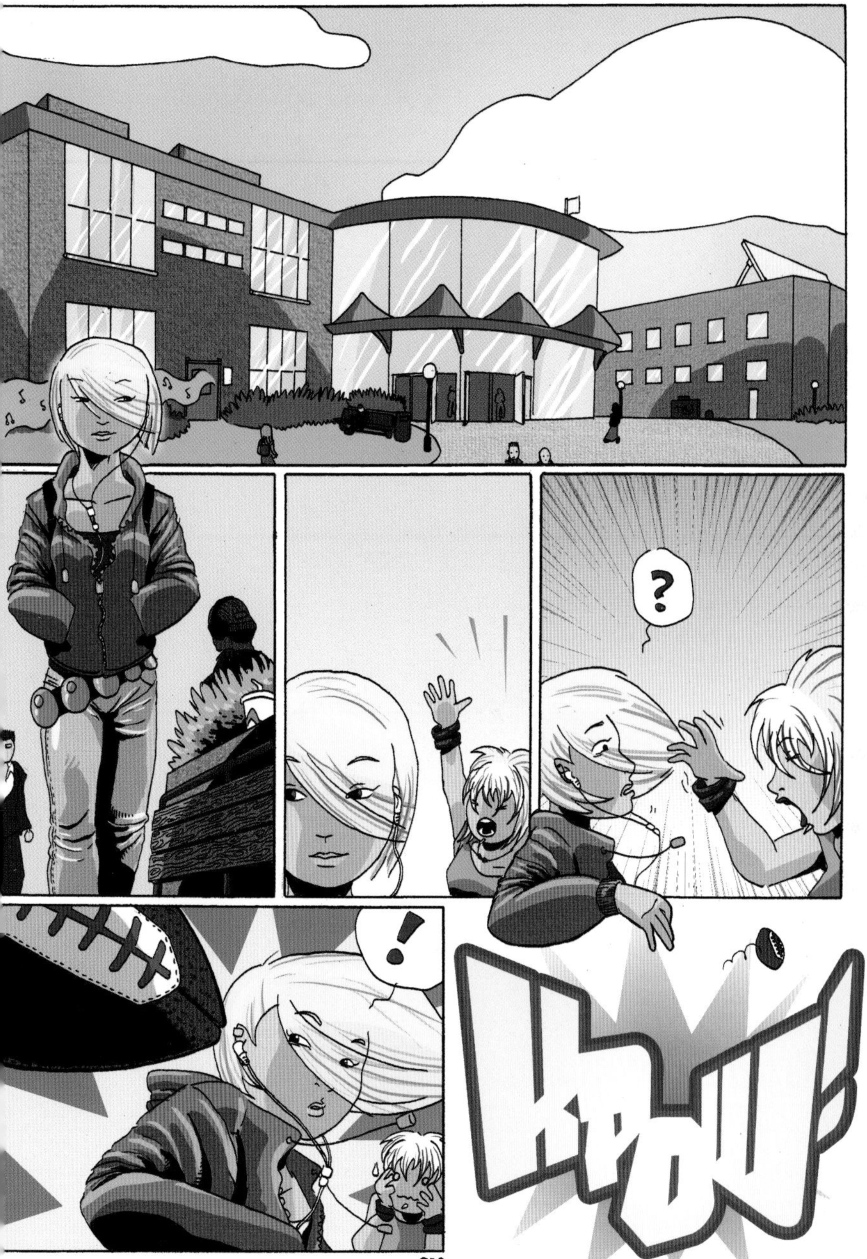
?
!
KPOW!
one

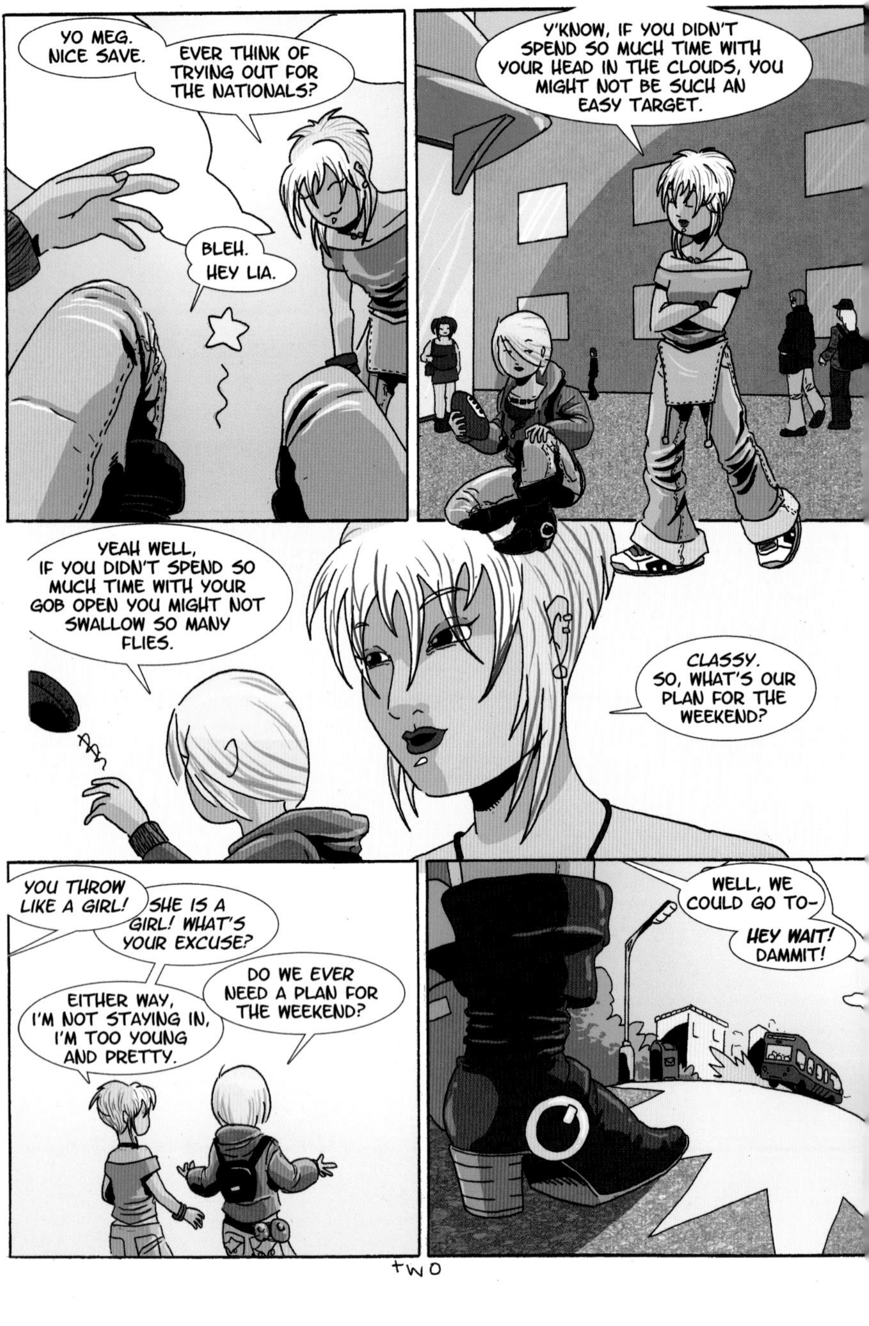
YO MEG. NICE SAVE.
EVER THINK OF TRYING OUT FOR THE NATIONALS?
BLEH. HEY LIA.
Y'KNOW, IF YOU DIDN'T SPEND SO MUCH TIME WITH YOUR HEAD IN THE CLOUDS, YOU MIGHT NOT BE SUCH AN EASY TARGET.
YEAH WELL, IF YOU DIDN'T SPEND SO MUCH TIME WITH YOUR GOB OPEN YOU MIGHT NOT SWALLOW SO MANY FLIES.
CLASSY. SO, WHAT'S OUR PLAN FOR THE WEEKEND?
YOU THROW LIKE A GIRL!
SHE IS A GIRL! WHAT'S YOUR EXCUSE?
EITHER WAY, I'M NOT STAYING IN, I'M TOO YOUNG AND PRETTY.
DO WE EVER NEED A PLAN FOR THE WEEKEND?
WELL, WE COULD GO TO-
HEY WAIT! DAMMIT!
two

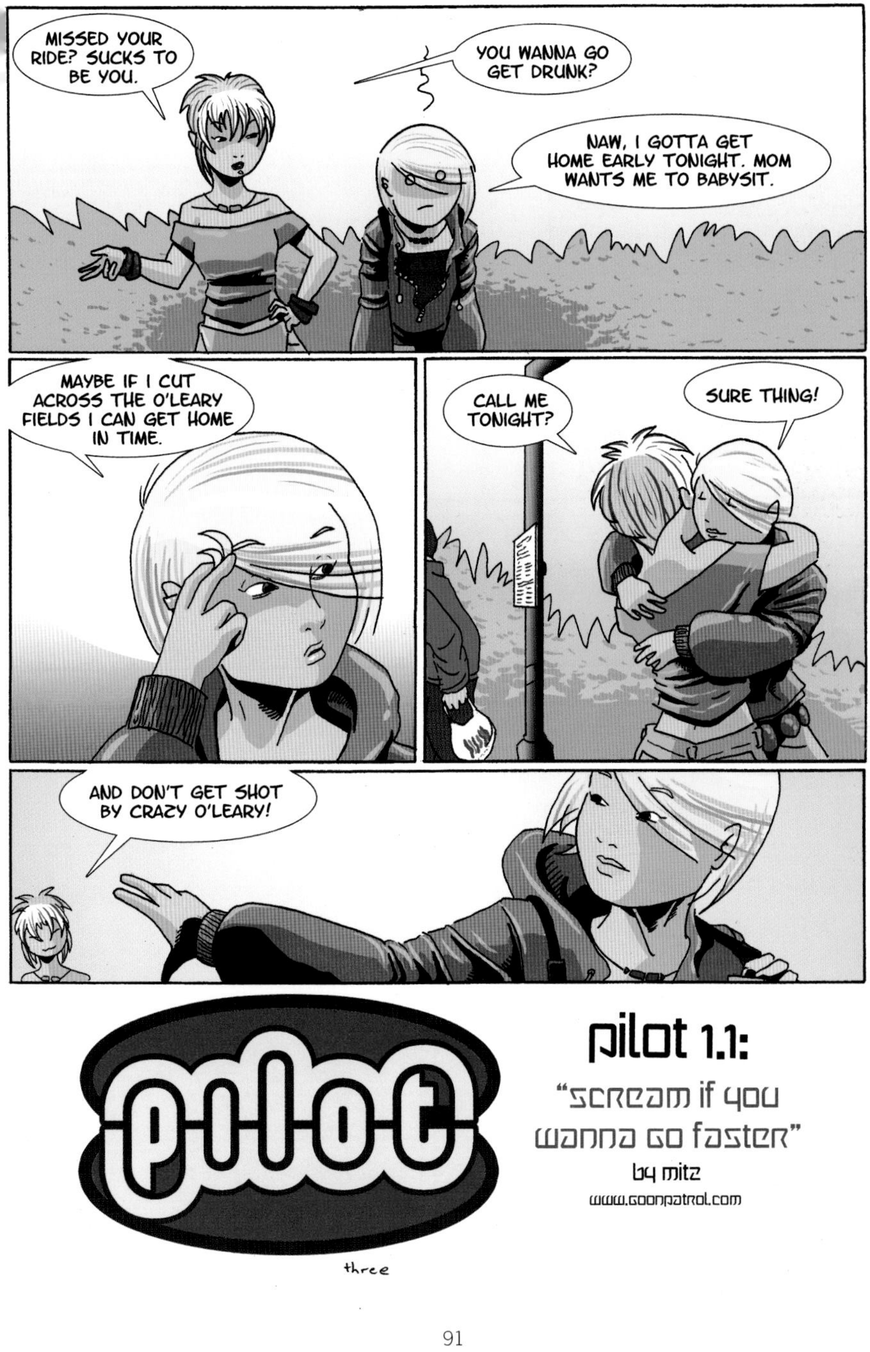
MISSED YOUR RIDE? SUCKS TO BE YOU.
YOU WANNA GO GET DRUNK?
NAW, I GOTTA GET HOME EARLY TONIGHT. MOM WANTS ME TO BABYSIT.
MAYBE IF I CUT ACROSS THE O'LEARY FIELDS I CAN GET HOME IN TIME.
CALL ME TONIGHT?
SURE THING!
AND DON'T GET SHOT BY CRAZY O'LEARY!

pilot

pilot 1.1:

"scream if you wanna go faster"

by mitz

www.goonpatrol.com

three

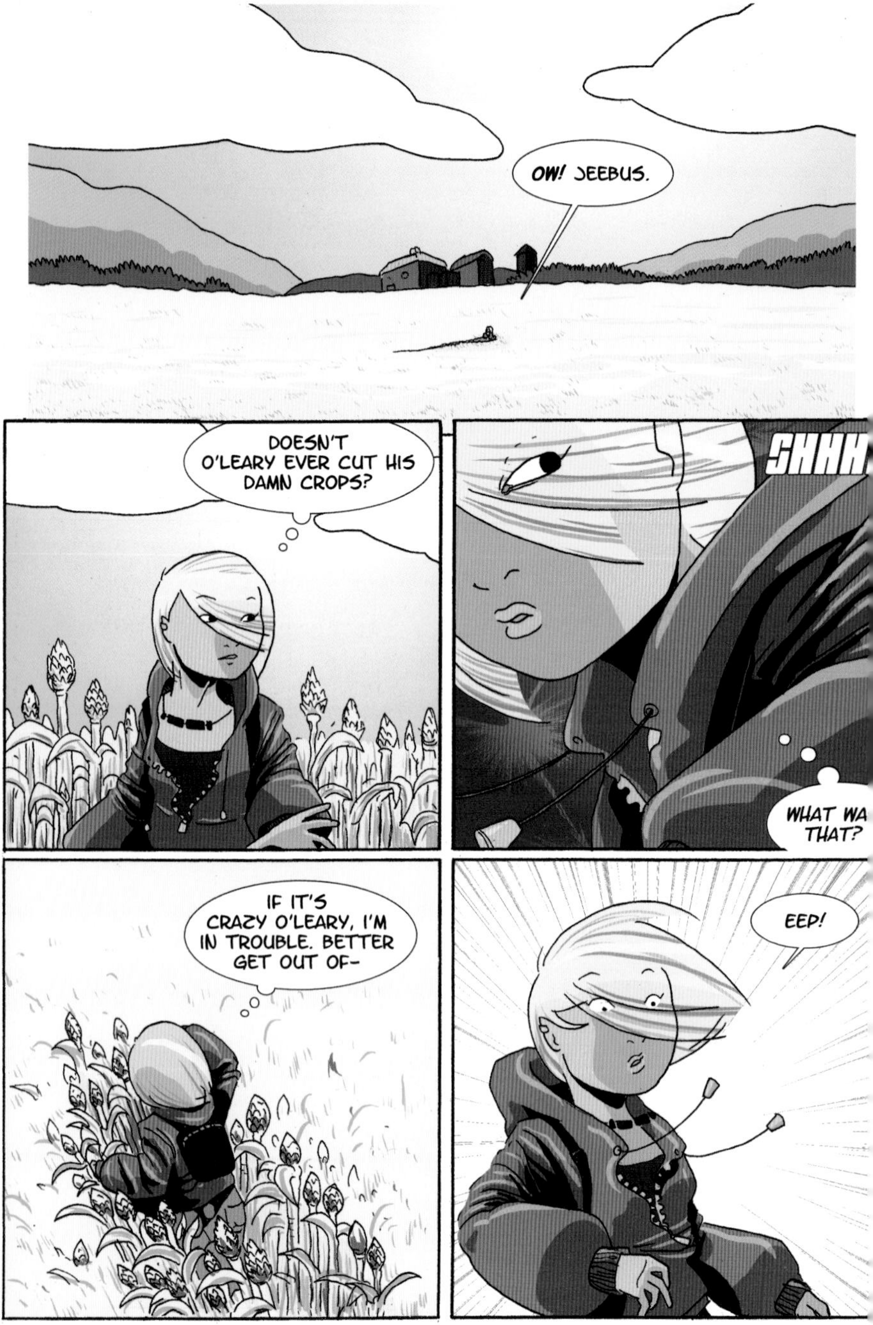
OW! JEEBUS.
DOESN'T O'LEARY EVER CUT HIS DAMN CROPS?
SHHH
WHAT WA THAT?
IF IT'S CRAZY O'LEARY, I'M IN TROUBLE. BETTER GET OUT OF-
EEP!

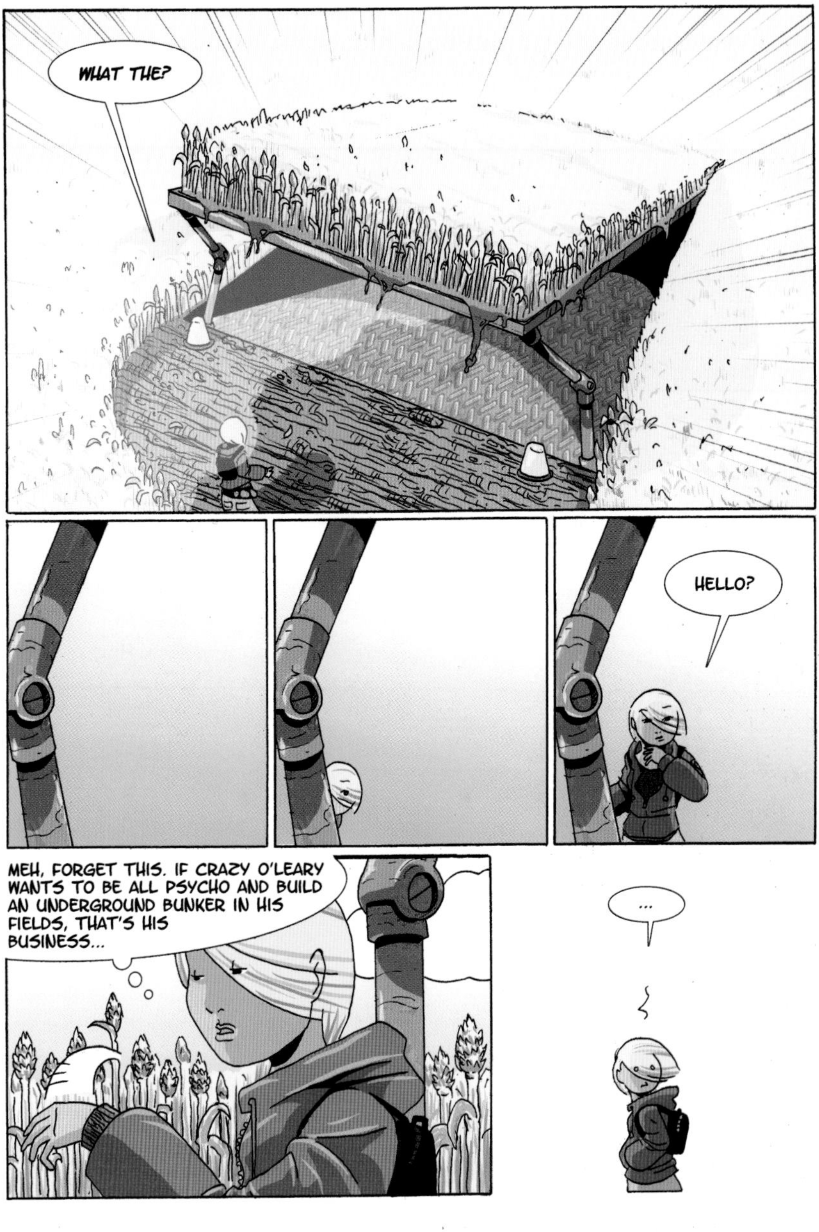
WHAT THE?
HELLO?
MEH, FORGET THIS. IF CRAZY O'LEARY WANTS TO BE ALL PSYCHO AND BUILD AN UNDERGROUND BUNKER IN HIS FIELDS, THAT'S HIS BUSINESS...
...

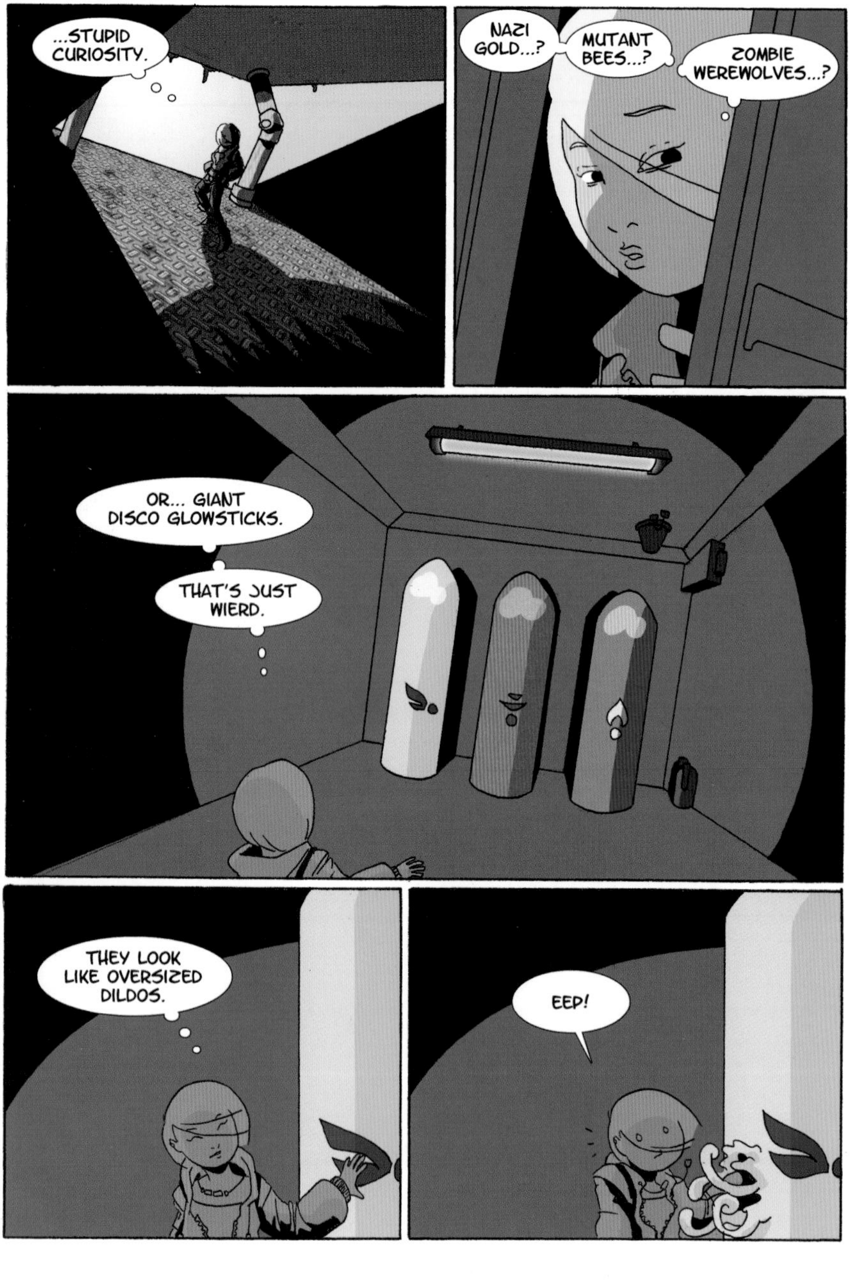

...STUPID CURIOSITY.
NAZI GOLD...?
MUTANT BEES...?
ZOMBIE WEREWOLVES...?
OR... GIANT DISCO GLOWSTICKS.
THAT'S JUST WIERD.
THEY LOOK LIKE OVERSIZED DILDOS.
EEP!

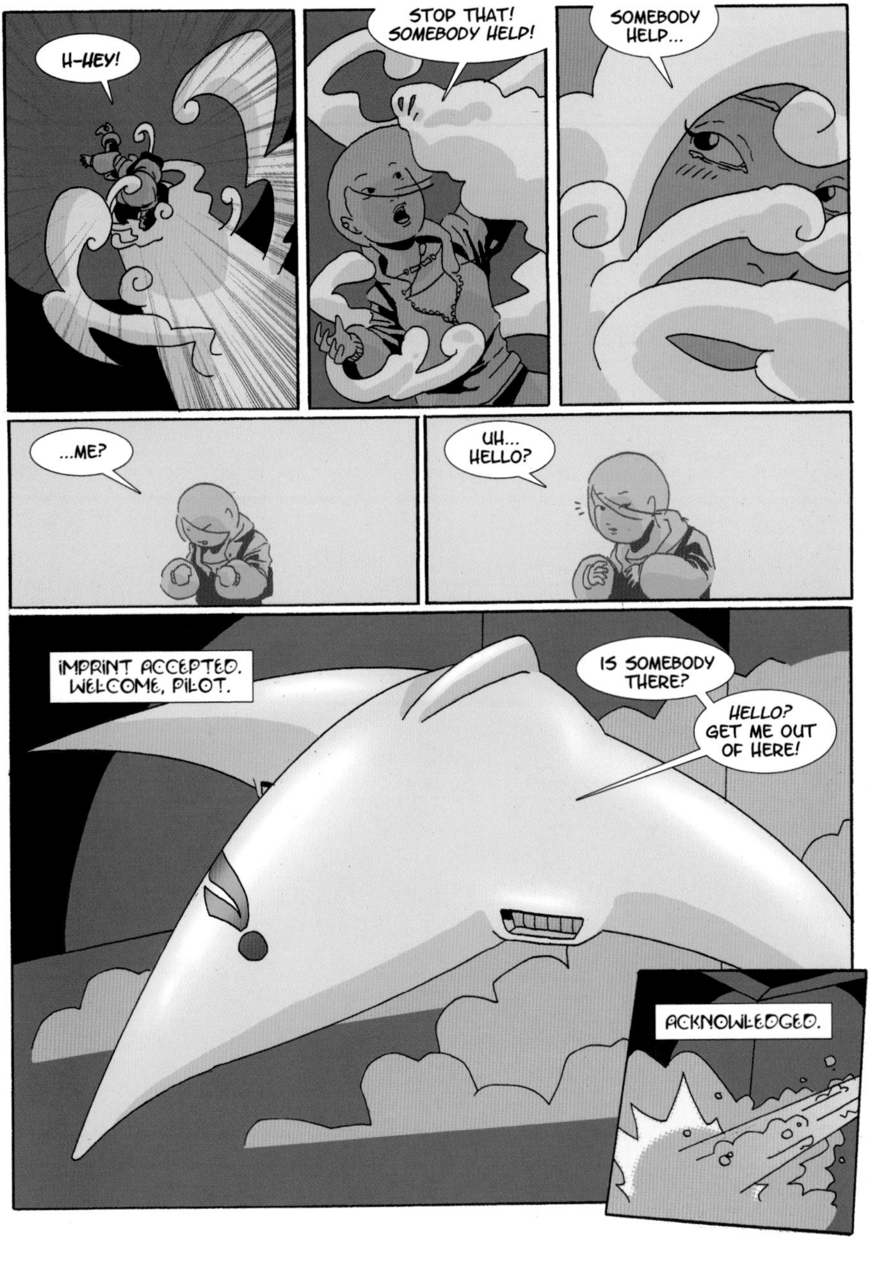
H-HEY!
STOP THAT! SOMEBODY HELP!
SOMEBODY HELP...
...ME?
UH... HELLO?
IMPRINT ACCEPTED. WELCOME, PILOT.
IS SOMEBODY THERE?
HELLO? GET ME OUT OF HERE!
ACKNOWLEDGED.

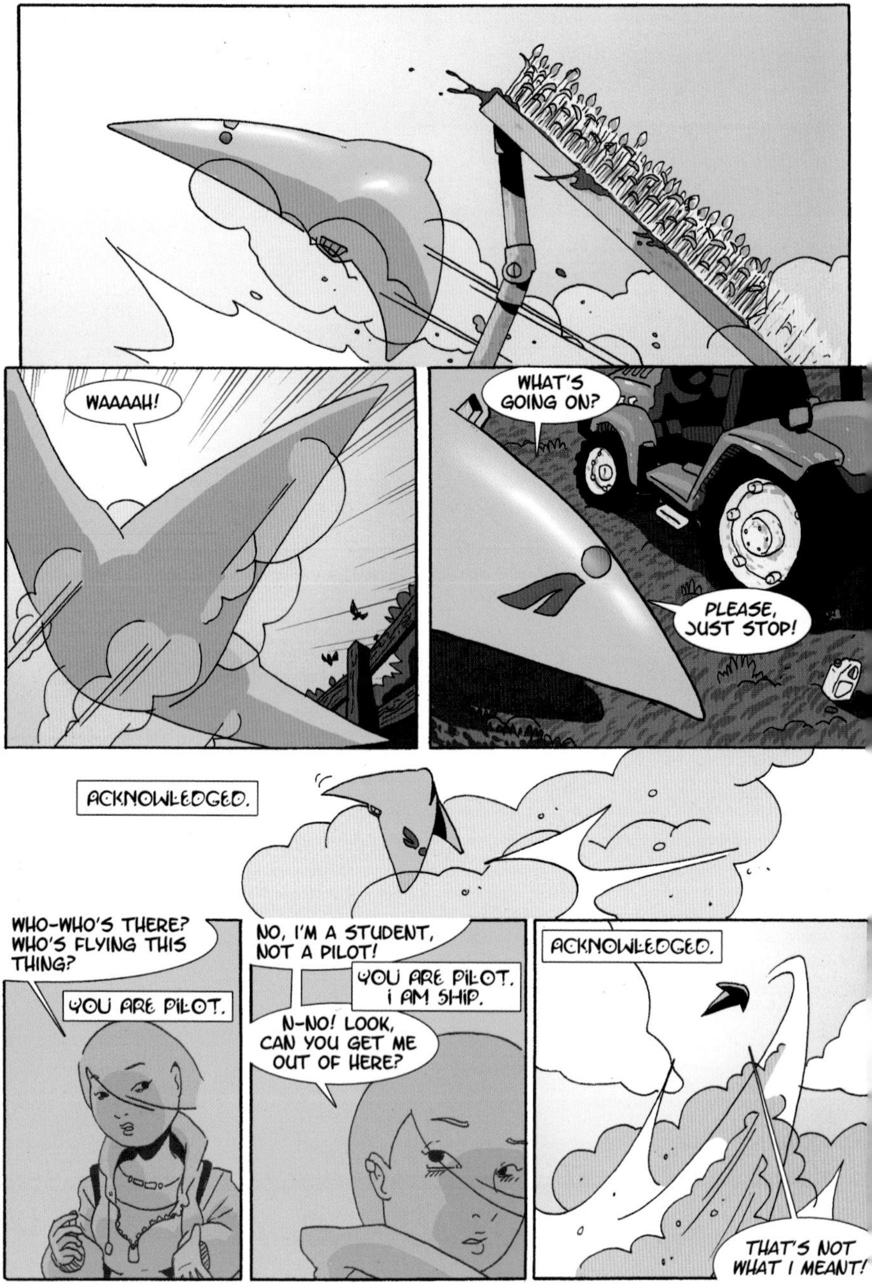
WAAAAH!
WHAT'S GOING ON?
PLEASE, JUST STOP!
ACKNOWLEDGED.
WHO-WHO'S THERE? WHO'S FLYING THIS THING?
YOU ARE PILOT.
NO, I'M A STUDENT, NOT A PILOT!
YOU ARE PILOT. I AM SHIP.
N-NO! LOOK, CAN YOU GET ME OUT OF HERE?
ACKNOWLEDGED.
THAT'S NOT WHAT I MEANT!

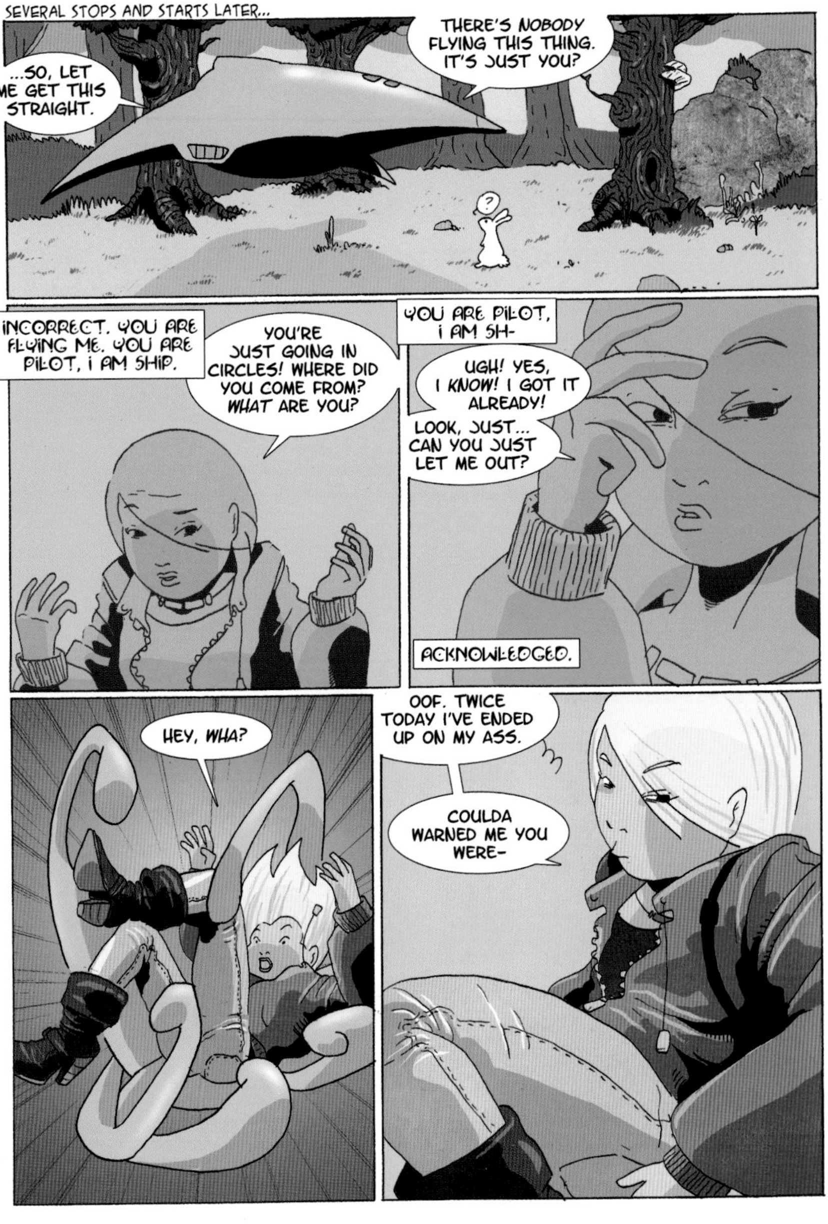
SEVERAL STOPS AND STARTS LATER...
...SO, LET ME GET THIS STRAIGHT.
THERE'S NOBODY FLYING THIS THING. IT'S JUST YOU?
?
INCORRECT. YOU ARE FLYING ME. YOU ARE PILOT, I AM SHIP.
YOU'RE JUST GOING IN CIRCLES! WHERE DID YOU COME FROM? WHAT ARE YOU?
YOU ARE PILOT, I AM SH-
UGH! YES, I KNOW! I GOT IT ALREADY!
LOOK, JUST... CAN YOU JUST LET ME OUT?
ACKNOWLEDGED.
HEY, WHA?
OOF. TWICE TODAY I'VE ENDED UP ON MY ASS.
COULDA WARNED ME YOU WERE-

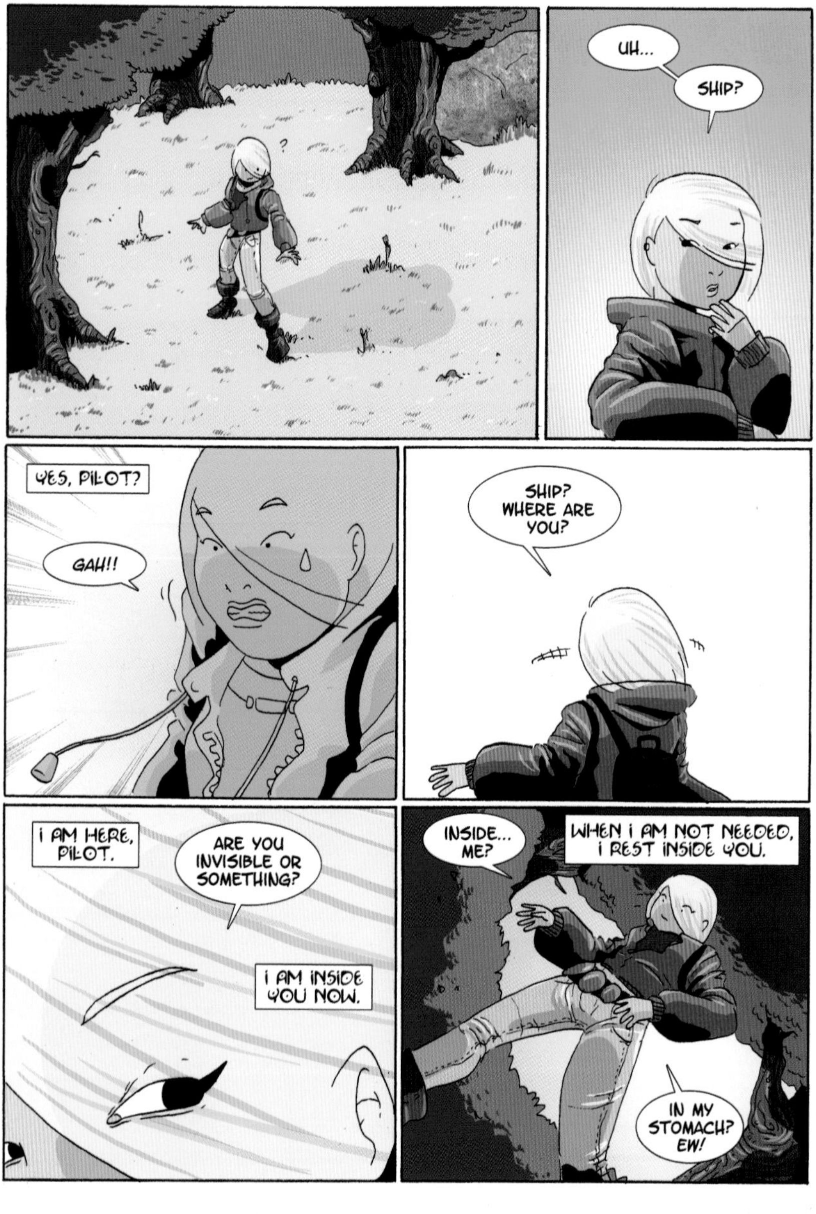
?
UH...
SHIP?
YES, PILOT?
GAH!!
SHIP? WHERE ARE YOU?
I AM HERE, PILOT.
ARE YOU INVISIBLE OR SOMETHING?
I AM INSIDE YOU NOW.
INSIDE... ME?
WHEN I AM NOT NEEDED, I REST INSIDE YOU.
IN MY STOMACH? EW!

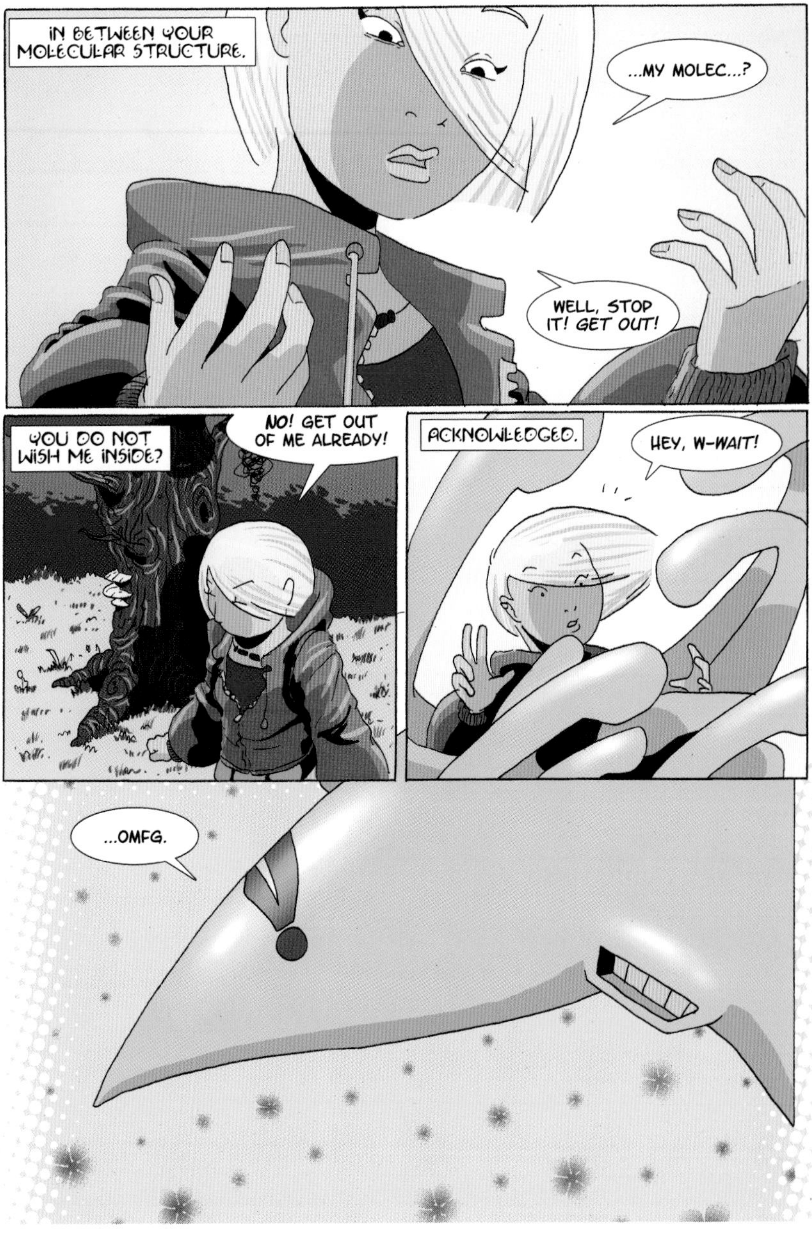
IN BETWEEN YOUR MOLECULAR STRUCTURE.
...MY MOLEC...?
WELL, STOP IT! GET OUT!
YOU DO NOT WISH ME INSIDE?
NO! GET OUT OF ME ALREADY!
ACKNOWLEDGED.
HEY, W-WAIT!
...OMFG.

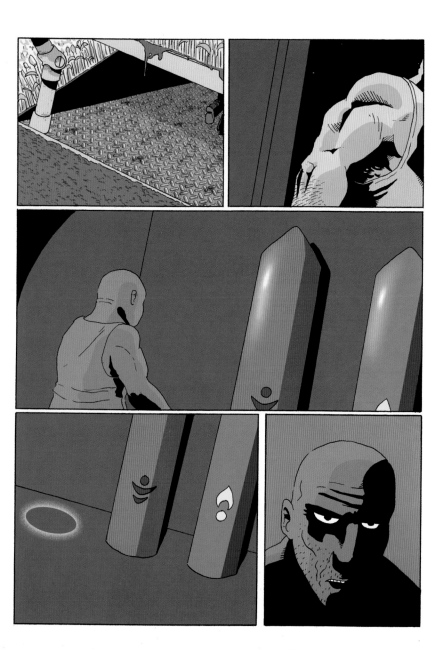

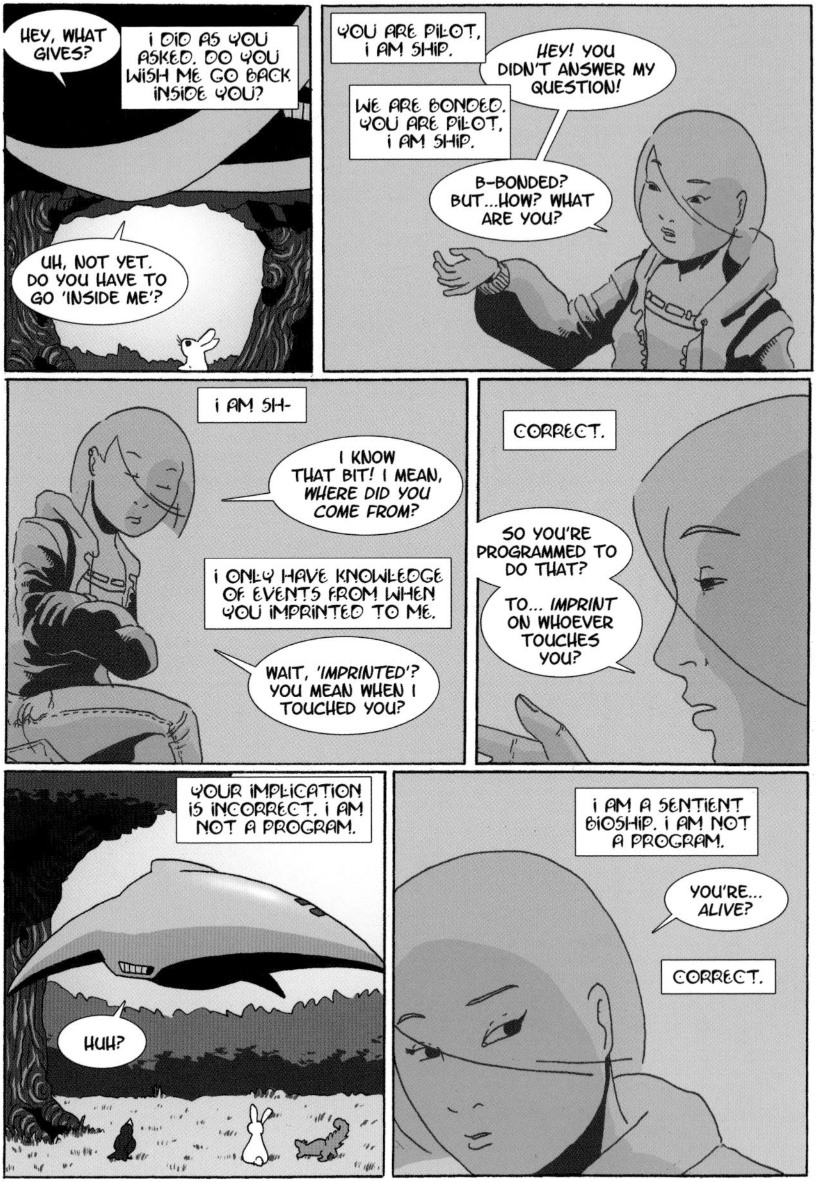
HEY, WHAT GIVES?
i DID AS YOU ASKED. DO YOU WISH ME GO BACK INSIDE YOU?
UH, NOT YET. DO YOU HAVE TO GO 'INSIDE ME'?
YOU ARE PILOT, i AM SHIP.
WE ARE BONDED. YOU ARE PILOT, i AM SHIP.
HEY! YOU DIDN'T ANSWER MY QUESTION!
B-BONDED? BUT...HOW? WHAT ARE YOU?
i AM SH-
I KNOW THAT BIT! I MEAN, WHERE DID YOU COME FROM?
i ONLY HAVE KNOWLEDGE OF EVENTS FROM WHEN YOU iMPRINTED TO ME.
WAIT, 'IMPRINTED'? YOU MEAN WHEN I TOUCHED YOU?
CORRECT.
SO YOU'RE PROGRAMMED TO DO THAT?
TO... IMPRINT ON WHOEVER TOUCHES YOU?
YOUR iMPLiCATiON iS iNCORRECT. i AM NOT A PROGRAM.
HUH?
i AM A SENTiENT BiOSHiP. i AM NOT A PROGRAM.
YOU'RE... ALIVE?
CORRECT.

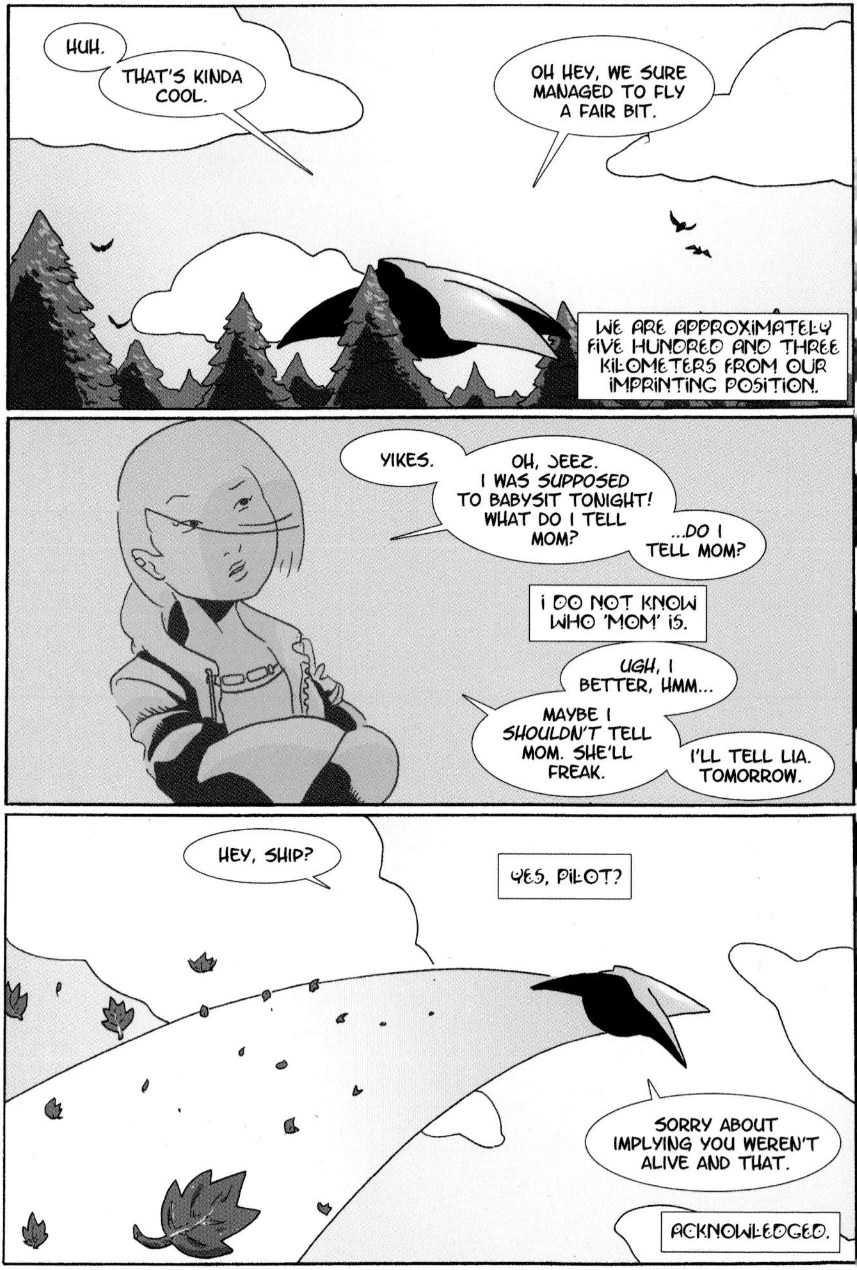
HUH.
THAT'S KINDA COOL.
OH HEY, WE SURE MANAGED TO FLY A FAIR BIT.
WE ARE APPROXIMATELY FIVE HUNDRED AND THREE KILOMETERS FROM OUR IMPRINTING POSITION.
YIKES.
OH, JEEZ. I WAS SUPPOSED TO BABYSIT TONIGHT! WHAT DO I TELL MOM?
...DO I TELL MOM?
I DO NOT KNOW WHO 'MOM' IS.
UGH, I BETTER, HMM...
MAYBE I SHOULDN'T TELL MOM. SHE'LL FREAK.
I'LL TELL LIA. TOMORROW.
HEY, SHIP?
YES, PILOT?
SORRY ABOUT IMPLYING YOU WEREN'T ALIVE AND THAT.
ACKNOWLEDGED.

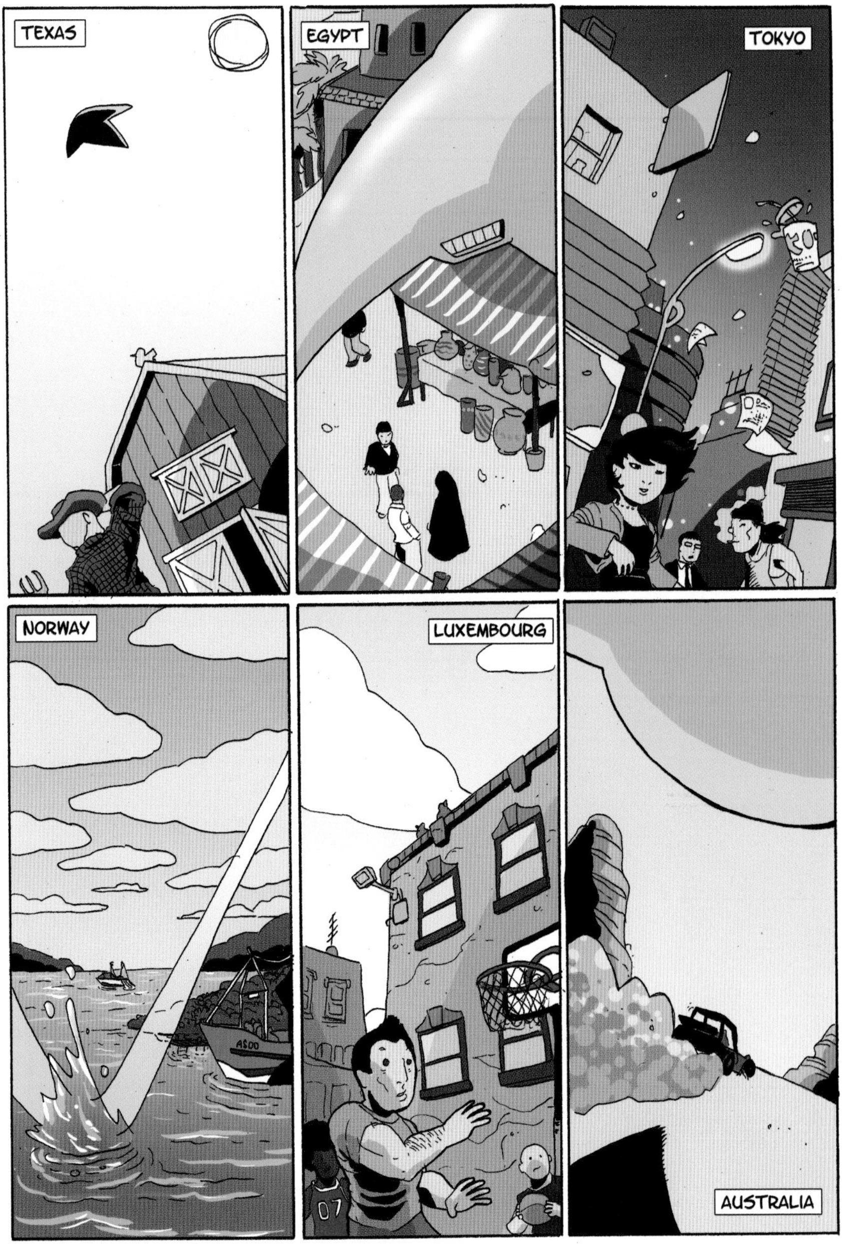
TEXAS
EGYPT
TOKYO
NORWAY
ASOO
LUXEMBOURG
07
AUSTRALIA

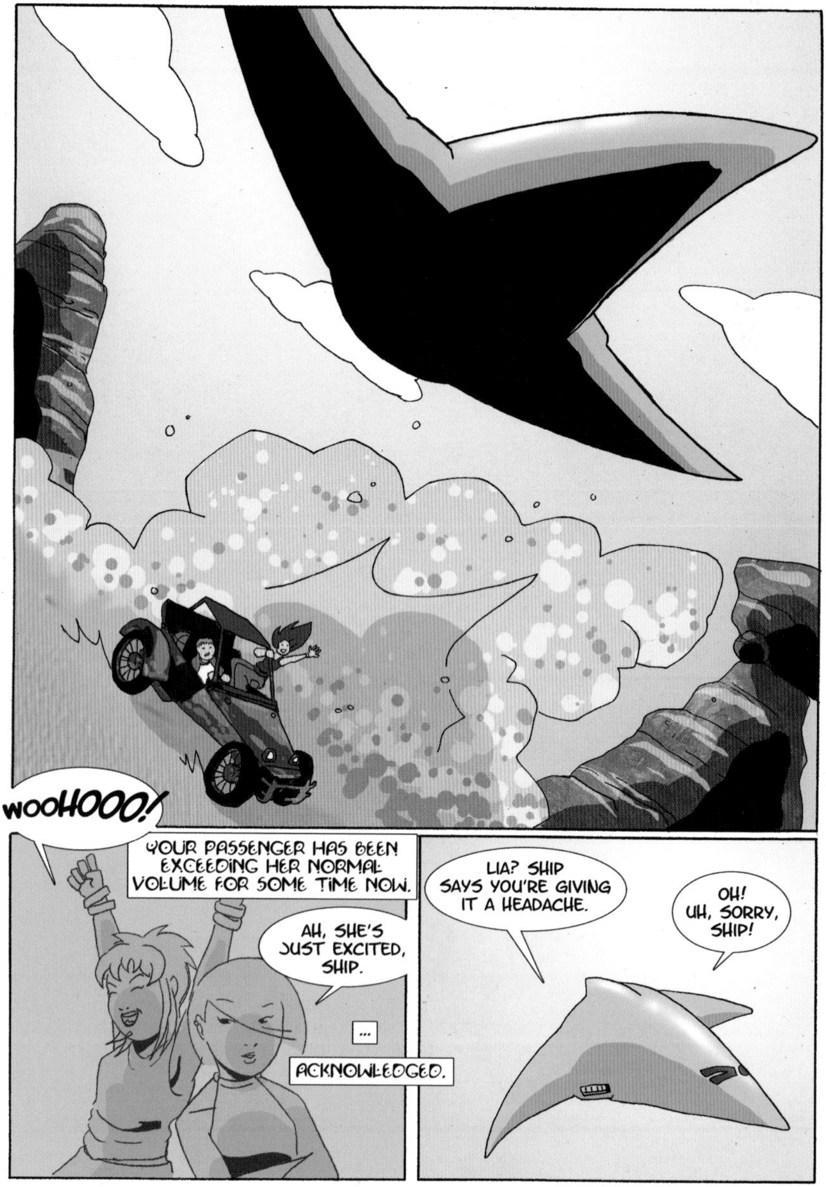
WOOHOOO!
YOUR PASSENGER HAS BEEN EXCEEDING HER NORMAL VOLUME FOR SOME TIME NOW.
AH, SHE'S JUST EXCITED, SHIP.
...
ACKNOWLEDGED.
LIA? SHIP SAYS YOU'RE GIVING IT A HEADACHE.
OH! UH, SORRY, SHIP!

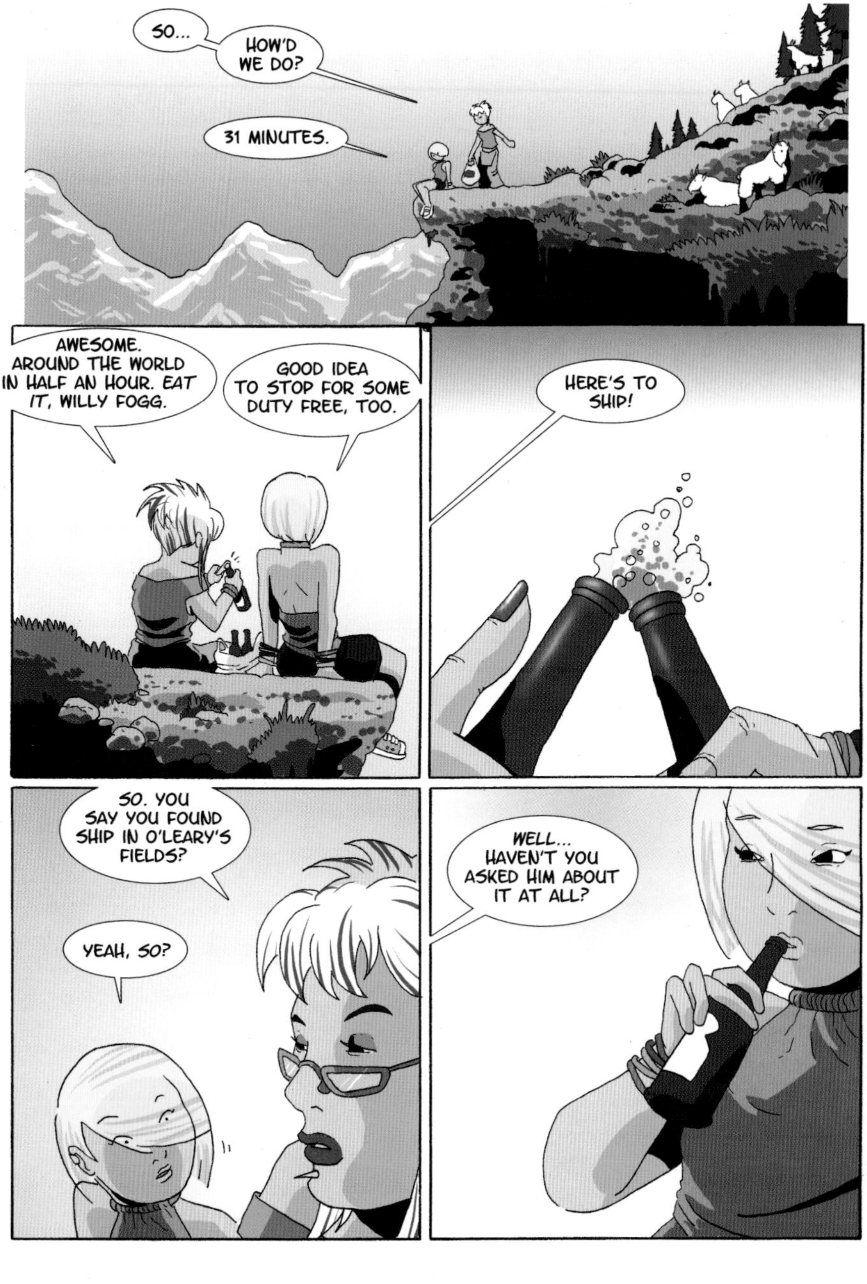
SO...
HOW'D WE DO?
31 MINUTES.
AWESOME. AROUND THE WORLD IN HALF AN HOUR. EAT IT, WILLY FOGG.
GOOD IDEA TO STOP FOR SOME DUTY FREE, TOO.
HERE'S TO SHIP!
SO. YOU SAY YOU FOUND SHIP IN O'LEARY'S FIELDS?
YEAH, SO?
WELL... HAVEN'T YOU ASKED HIM ABOUT IT AT ALL?

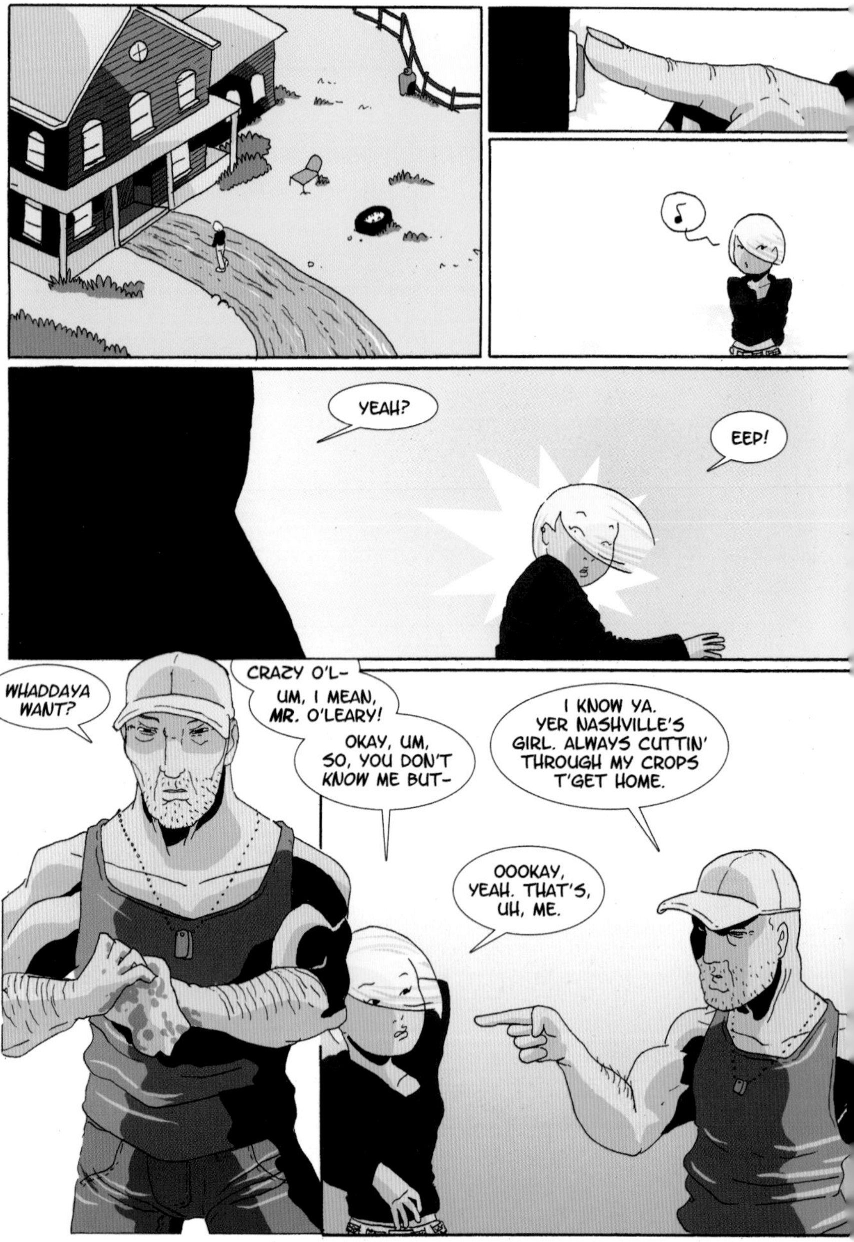
YEAH?
EEP!
WHADDAYA WANT?
CRAZY O'L-
UM, I MEAN, MR. O'LEARY!
OKAY, UM, SO, YOU DON'T KNOW ME BUT-
I KNOW YA. YER NASHVILLE'S GIRL. ALWAYS CUTTIN' THROUGH MY CROPS T'GET HOME.
OOOKAY, YEAH. THAT'S, UH, ME.

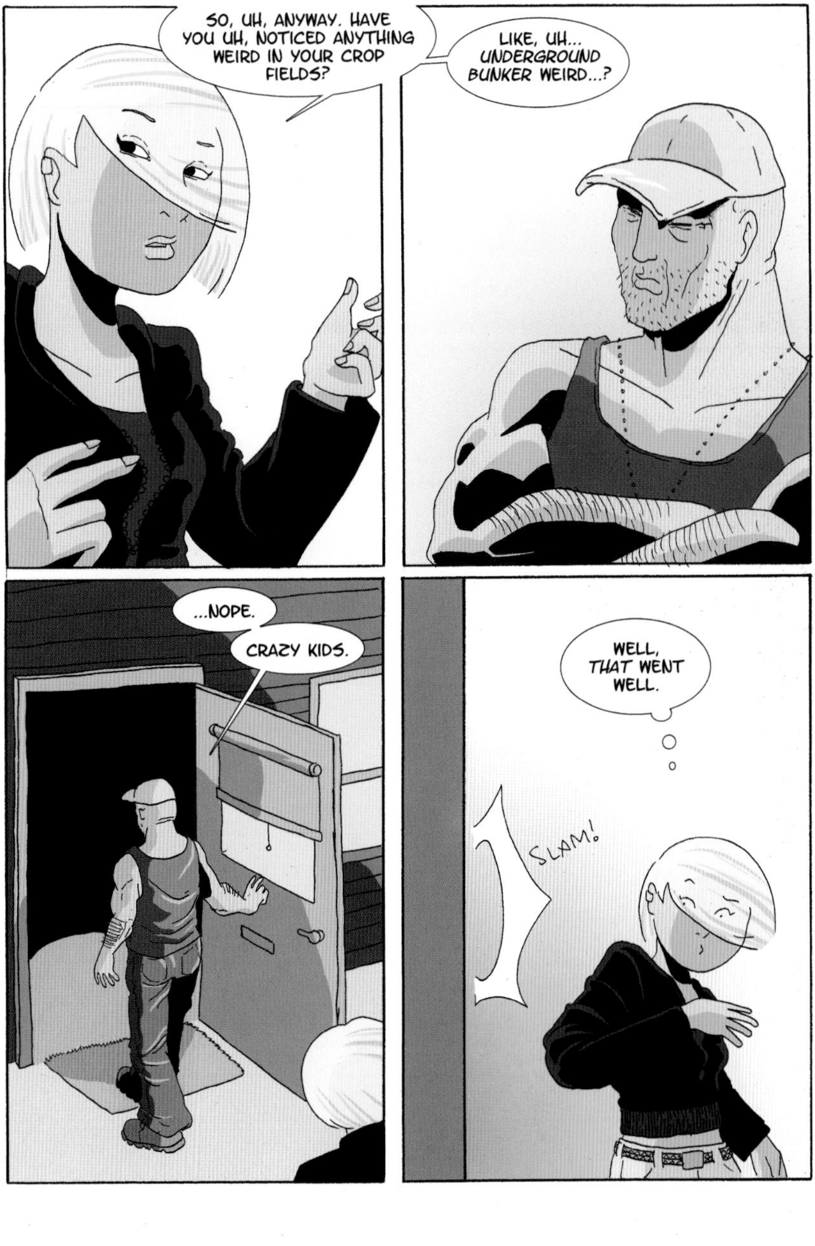
SO, UH, ANYWAY. HAVE YOU UH, NOTICED ANYTHING WEIRD IN YOUR CROP FIELDS?
LIKE, UH... UNDERGROUND BUNKER WEIRD...?
...NOPE.
CRAZY KIDS.
WELL, THAT WENT WELL.
SLAM!

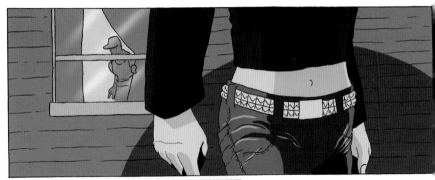

YEAH, I NOTICED. SURE SHE DIDN'T SENSE ANYTHING?

WELL, THAT'S A START. BUT IT DOES MEAN SHE DOESN'T KNOW HOW TO USE HERS YET.

CHRIST ALMIGHTY. WHAT'M I GONNA DO ABOUT HER...?

WELL, THAT WAS A WASTE OF TIME, SHIP.

ACKNOWLEDGED.

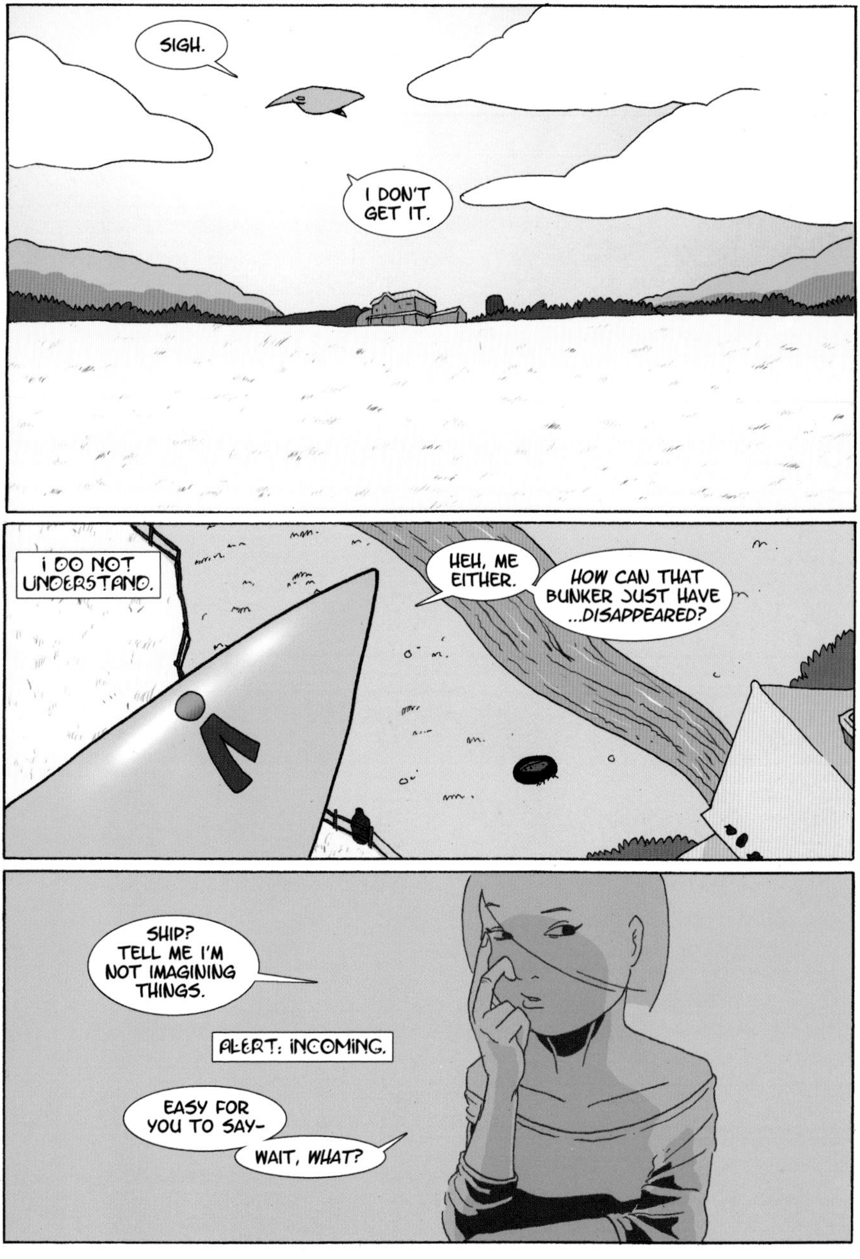
SIGH.
I DON'T GET IT.
I DO NOT UNDERSTAND.
HEH, ME EITHER.
HOW CAN THAT BUNKER JUST HAVE ...DISAPPEARED?
SHIP? TELL ME I'M NOT IMAGINING THINGS.
ALERT: INCOMING.
EASY FOR YOU TO SAY-
WAIT, WHAT?

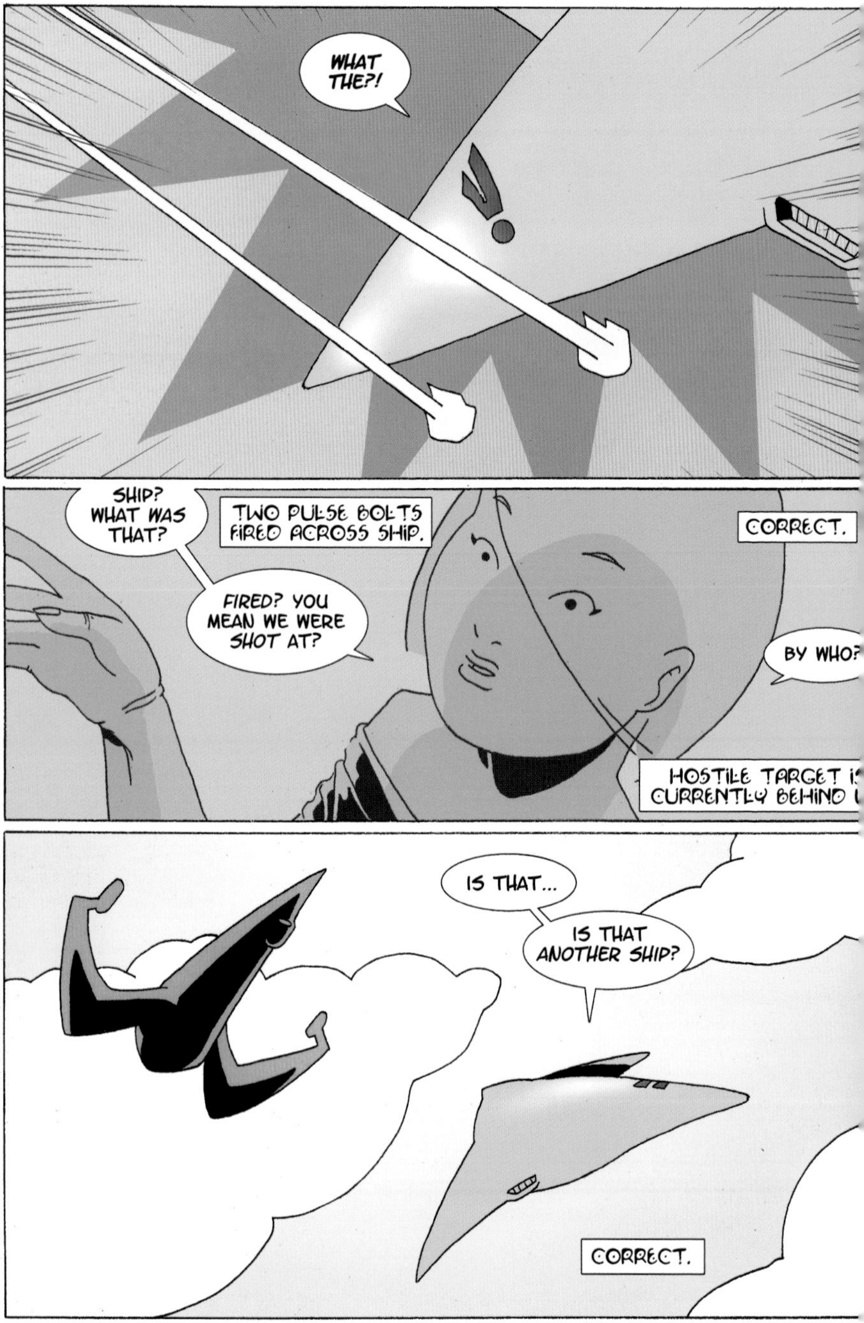
WHAT THE?!
SHIP? WHAT WAS THAT?
TWO PULSE BOLTS FIRED ACROSS SHIP.
FIRED? YOU MEAN WE WERE SHOT AT?
CORRECT.
BY WHO?
HOSTILE TARGET I
CURRENTLY BEHIND
IS THAT...
IS THAT ANOTHER SHIP?
CORRECT.

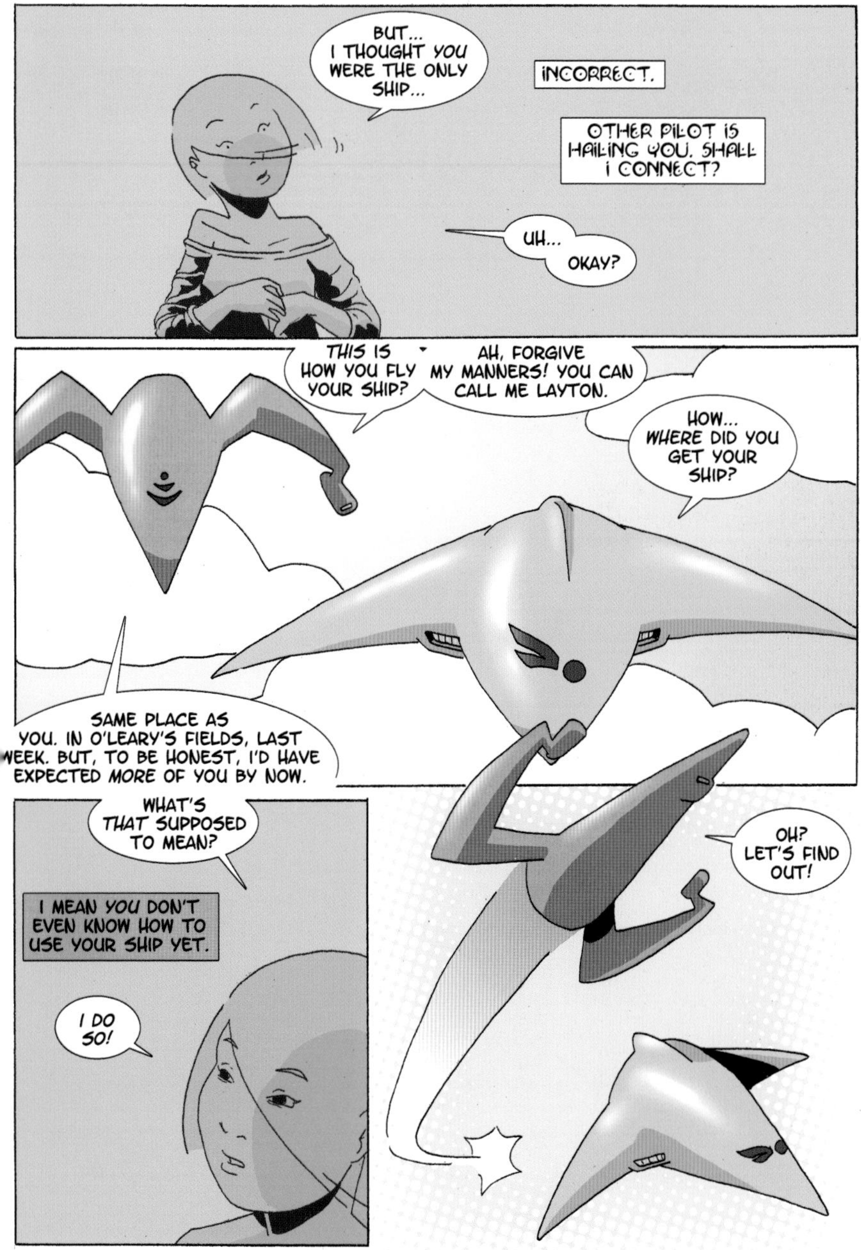

BUT... I THOUGHT YOU WERE THE ONLY SHIP...
INCORRECT.
OTHER PILOT IS HAILING YOU. SHALL I CONNECT?
UH...
OKAY?
THIS IS HOW YOU FLY YOUR SHIP?
AH, FORGIVE MY MANNERS! YOU CAN CALL ME LAYTON.
HOW... WHERE DID YOU GET YOUR SHIP?
SAME PLACE AS YOU. IN O'LEARY'S FIELDS, LAST WEEK. BUT, TO BE HONEST, I'D HAVE EXPECTED MORE OF YOU BY NOW.
WHAT'S THAT SUPPOSED TO MEAN?
I MEAN YOU DON'T EVEN KNOW HOW TO USE YOUR SHIP YET.
I DO SO!
OH? LET'S FIND OUT!

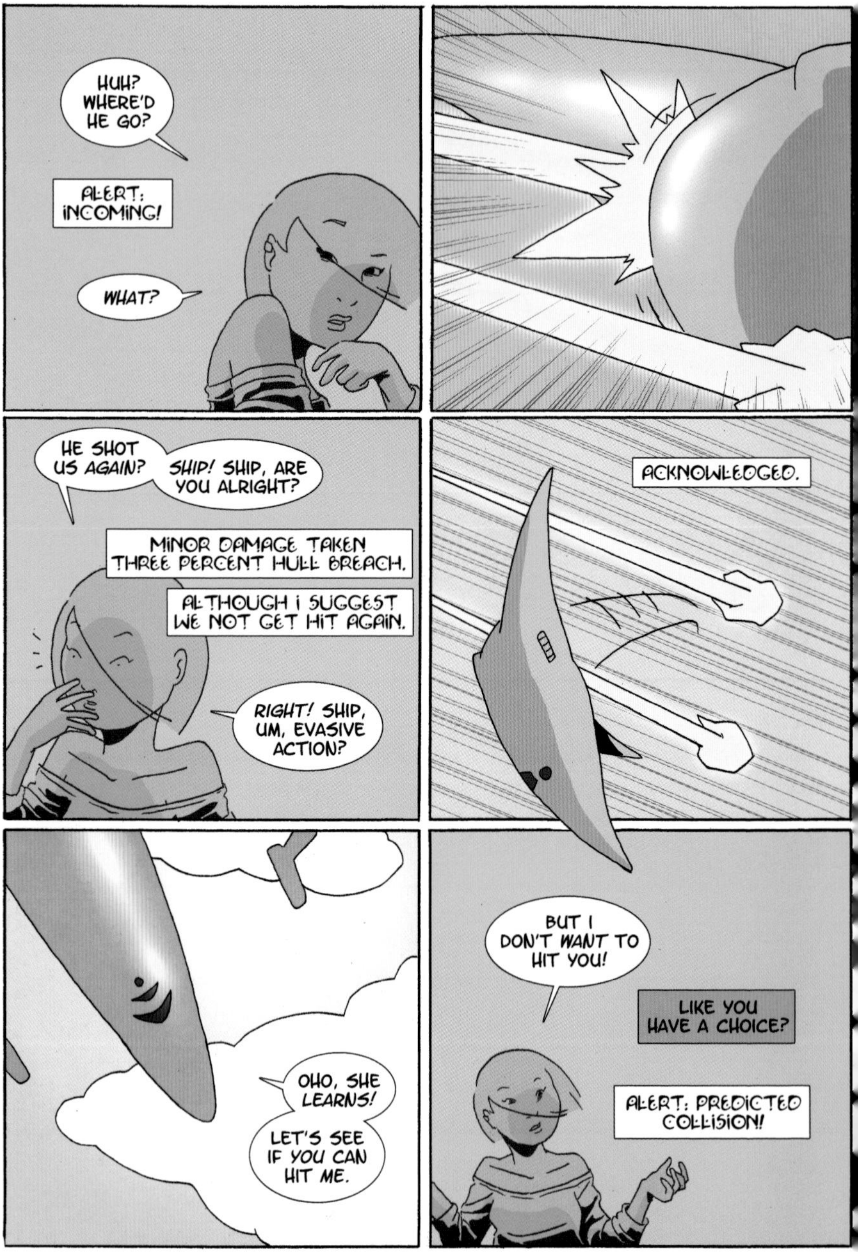
HUH? WHERE'D HE GO?
ALERT: INCOMING!
WHAT?
HE SHOT US AGAIN?
SHIP! SHIP, ARE YOU ALRIGHT?
MINOR DAMAGE TAKEN THREE PERCENT HULL BREACH.
ALTHOUGH I SUGGEST WE NOT GET HIT AGAIN.
RIGHT! SHIP, UM, EVASIVE ACTION?
ACKNOWLEDGED.
OHO, SHE LEARNS!
LET'S SEE IF YOU CAN HIT ME.
BUT I DON'T WANT TO HIT YOU!
LIKE YOU HAVE A CHOICE?
ALERT: PREDICTED COLLISION!

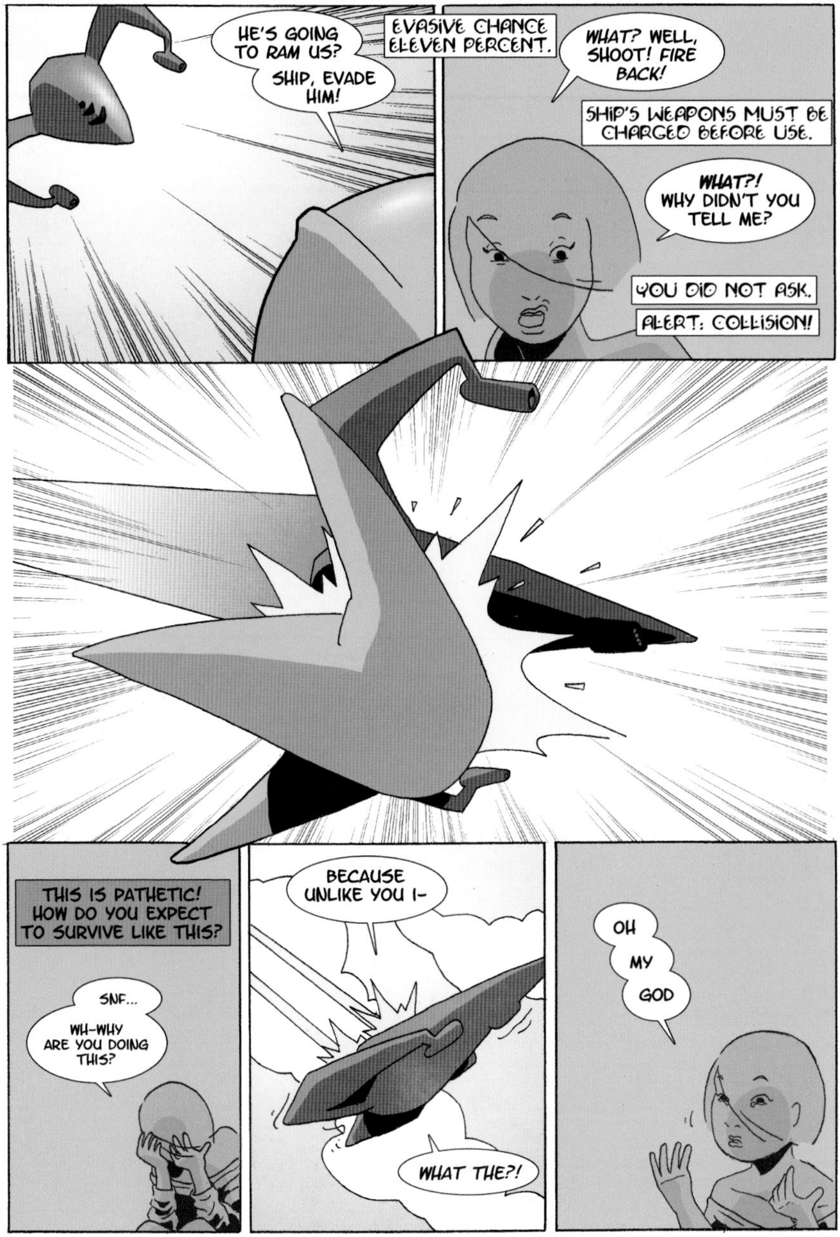
HE'S GOING TO RAM US?
SHIP, EVADE HIM!
EVASIVE CHANCE ELEVEN PERCENT.
WHAT? WELL, SHOOT! FIRE BACK!
SHIP'S WEAPONS MUST BE CHARGED BEFORE USE.
WHAT?! WHY DIDN'T YOU TELL ME?
YOU DID NOT ASK.
ALERT: COLLISION!
THIS IS PATHETIC! HOW DO YOU EXPECT TO SURVIVE LIKE THIS?
SNF...
WH-WHY ARE YOU DOING THIS?
BECAUSE UNLIKE YOU I-
WHAT THE?!
OH
MY
GOD

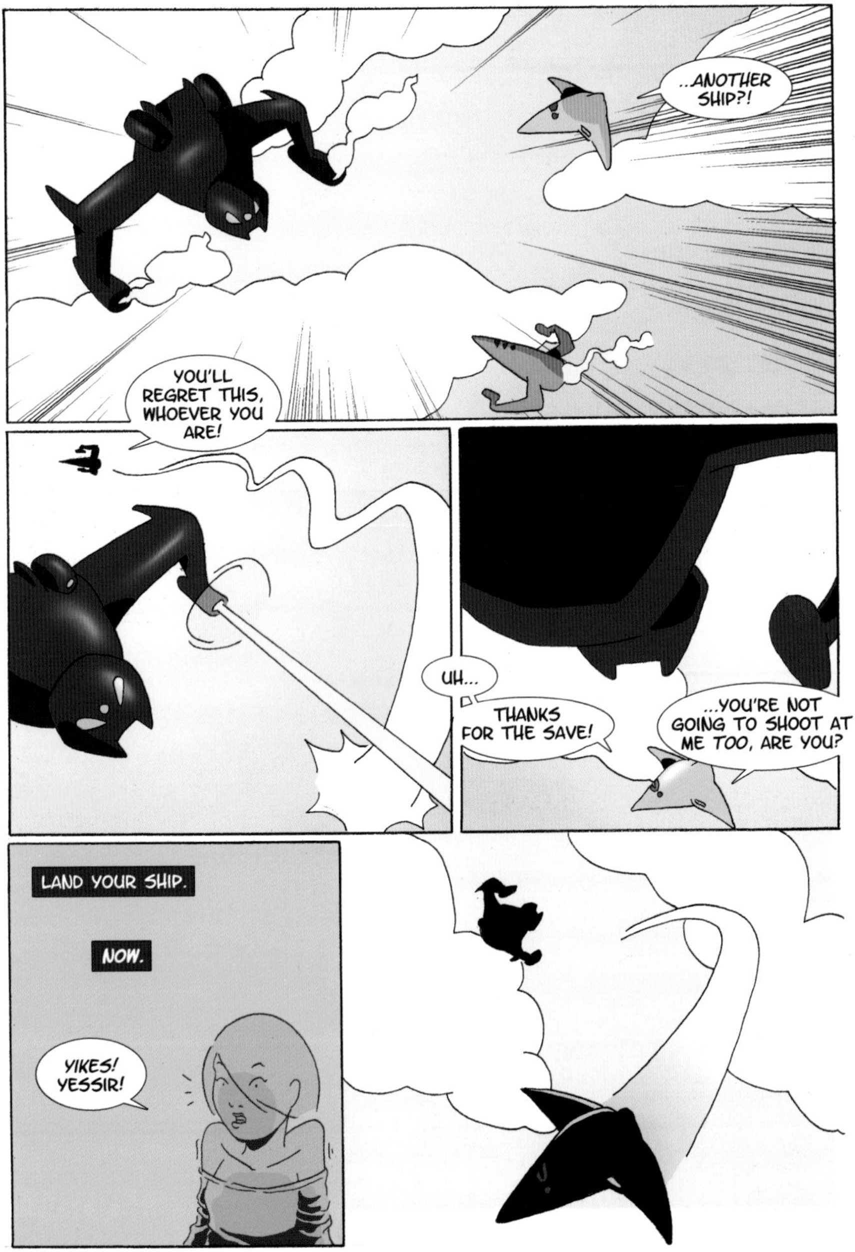

..ANOTHER SHIP?!
YOU'LL REGRET THIS, WHOEVER YOU ARE!
UH...
THANKS FOR THE SAVE!
...YOU'RE NOT GOING TO SHOOT AT ME TOO, ARE YOU?
LAND YOUR SHIP.
NOW.
YIKES! YESSIR!

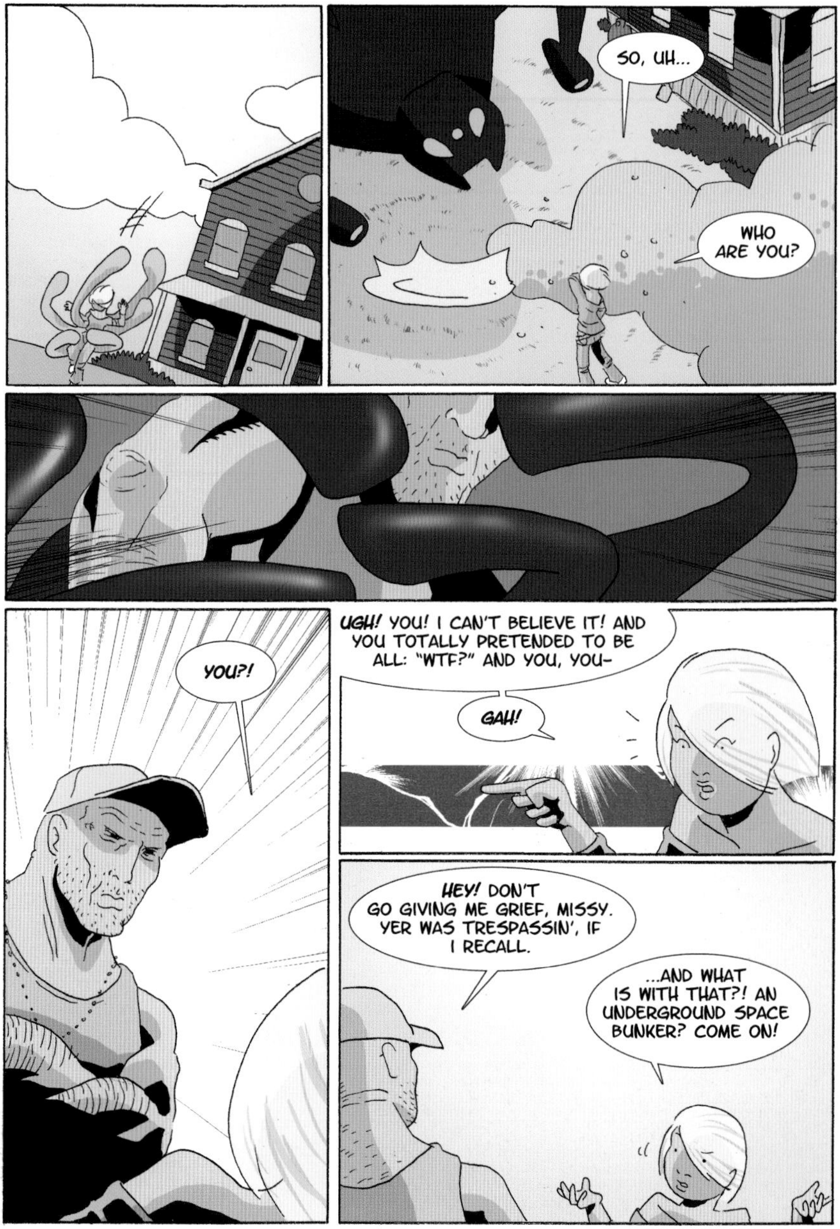
SO, UH...
WHO ARE YOU?
YOU?!
UGH! YOU! I CAN'T BELIEVE IT! AND YOU TOTALLY PRETENDED TO BE ALL: "WTF?" AND YOU, YOU-
GAH!
HEY! DON'T GO GIVING ME GRIEF, MISSY. YER WAS TRESPASSIN', IF I RECALL.
...AND WHAT IS WITH THAT?! AN UNDERGROUND SPACE BUNKER? COME ON!

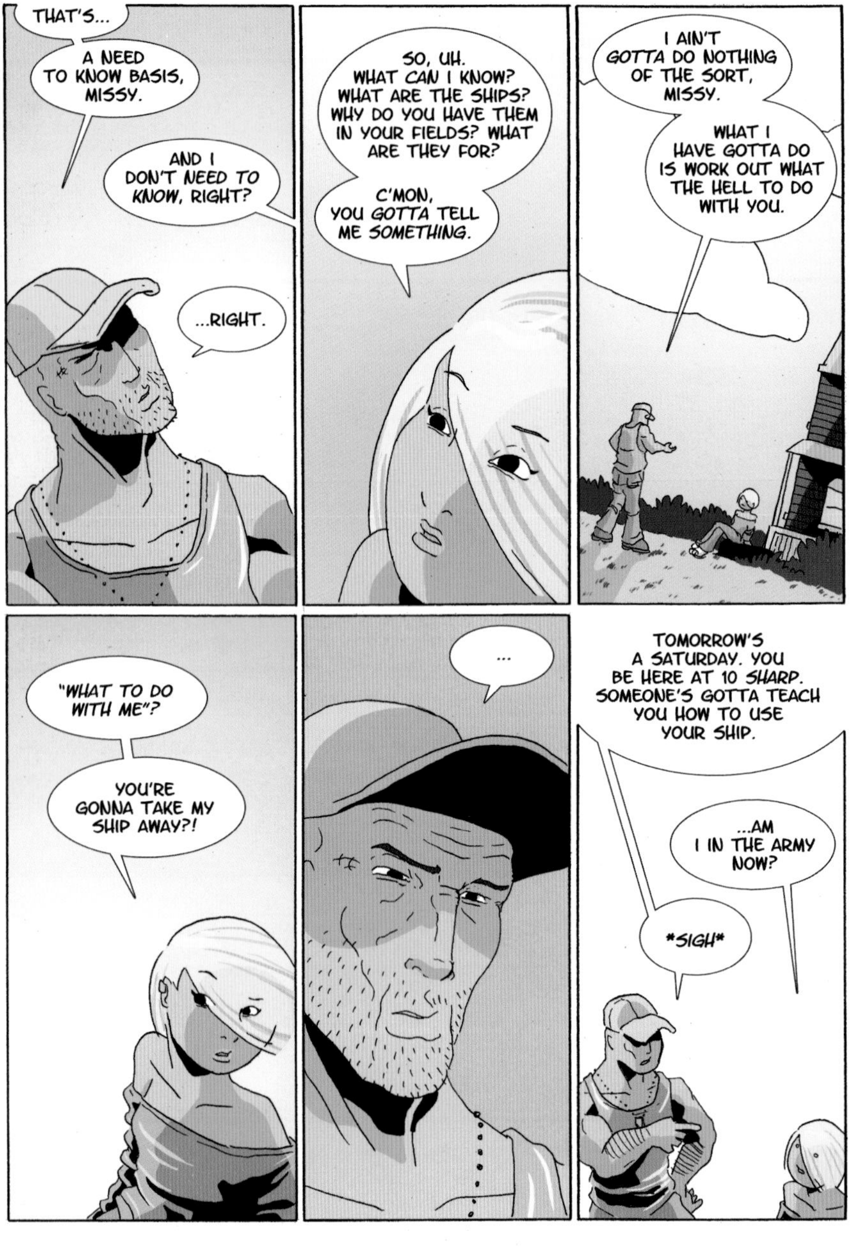
THAT'S...
A NEED TO KNOW BASIS, MISSY.
AND I DON'T NEED TO KNOW, RIGHT?
...RIGHT.
SO, UH. WHAT CAN I KNOW? WHAT ARE THE SHIPS? WHY DO YOU HAVE THEM IN YOUR FIELDS? WHAT ARE THEY FOR?
C'MON, YOU GOTTA TELL ME SOMETHING.
I AIN'T GOTTA DO NOTHING OF THE SORT, MISSY.
WHAT I HAVE GOTTA DO IS WORK OUT WHAT THE HELL TO DO WITH YOU.
"WHAT TO DO WITH ME"?
YOU'RE GONNA TAKE MY SHIP AWAY?!
...
TOMORROW'S A SATURDAY. YOU BE HERE AT 10 SHARP. SOMEONE'S GOTTA TEACH YOU HOW TO USE YOUR SHIP.
...AM I IN THE ARMY NOW?
SIGH

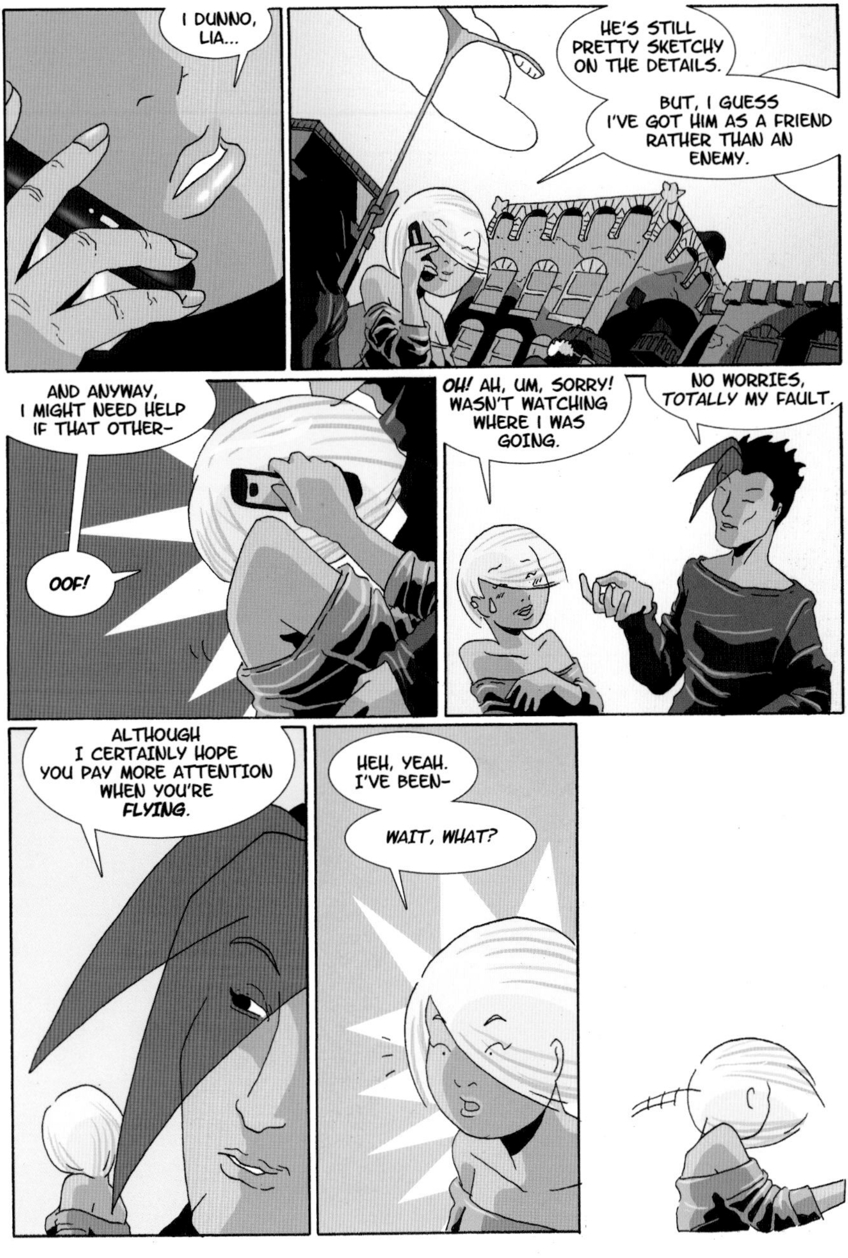
I DUNNO, LIA...
HE'S STILL PRETTY SKETCHY ON THE DETAILS.
BUT, I GUESS I'VE GOT HIM AS A FRIEND RATHER THAN AN ENEMY.
AND ANYWAY, I MIGHT NEED HELP IF THAT OTHER-
OOF!
OH! AH, UM, SORRY! WASN'T WATCHING WHERE I WAS GOING.
NO WORRIES, TOTALLY MY FAULT.
ALTHOUGH I CERTAINLY HOPE YOU PAY MORE ATTENTION WHEN YOU'RE FLYING.
HEH, YEAH. I'VE BEEN-
WAIT, WHAT?

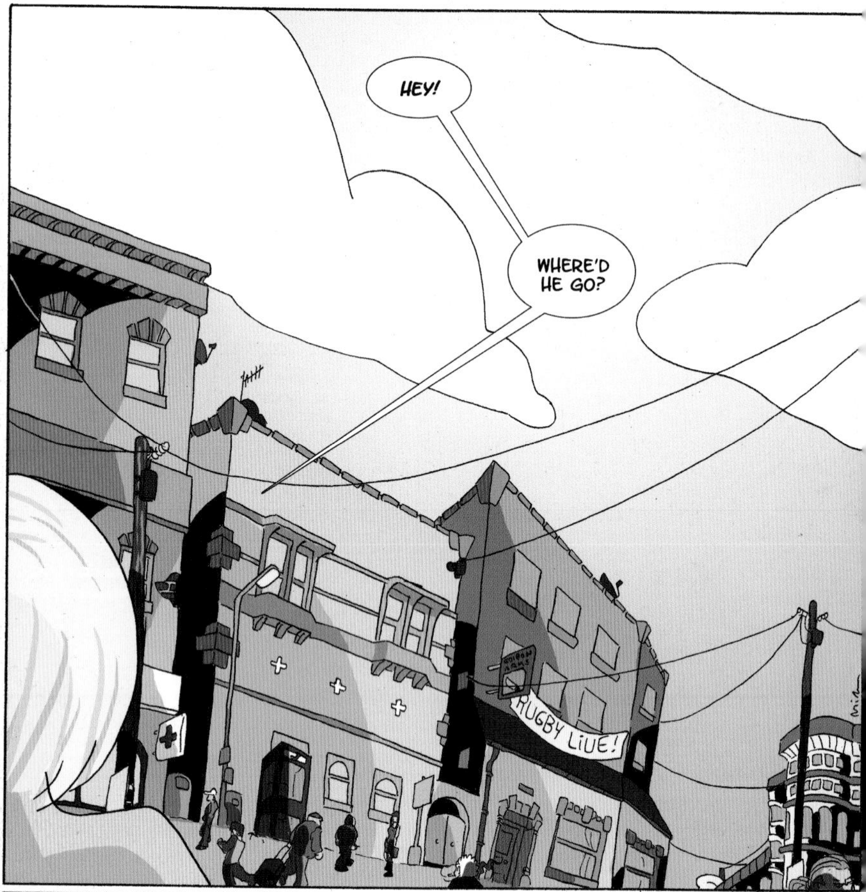
HEY!
WHERE'D HE GO?
RUGBY LIVE!

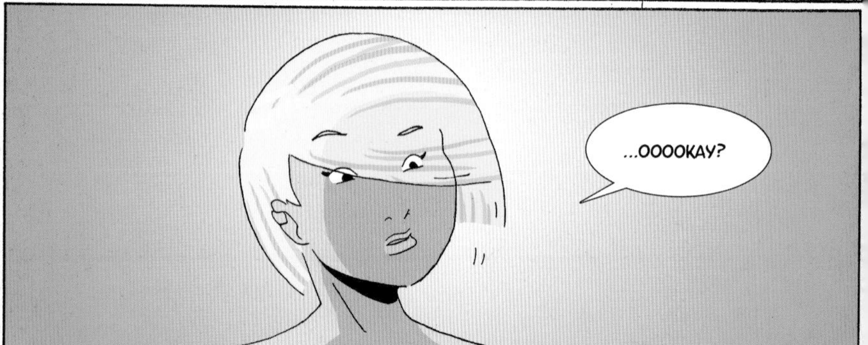
...OOOOKAY?

...NOT THE END!

MY robot!

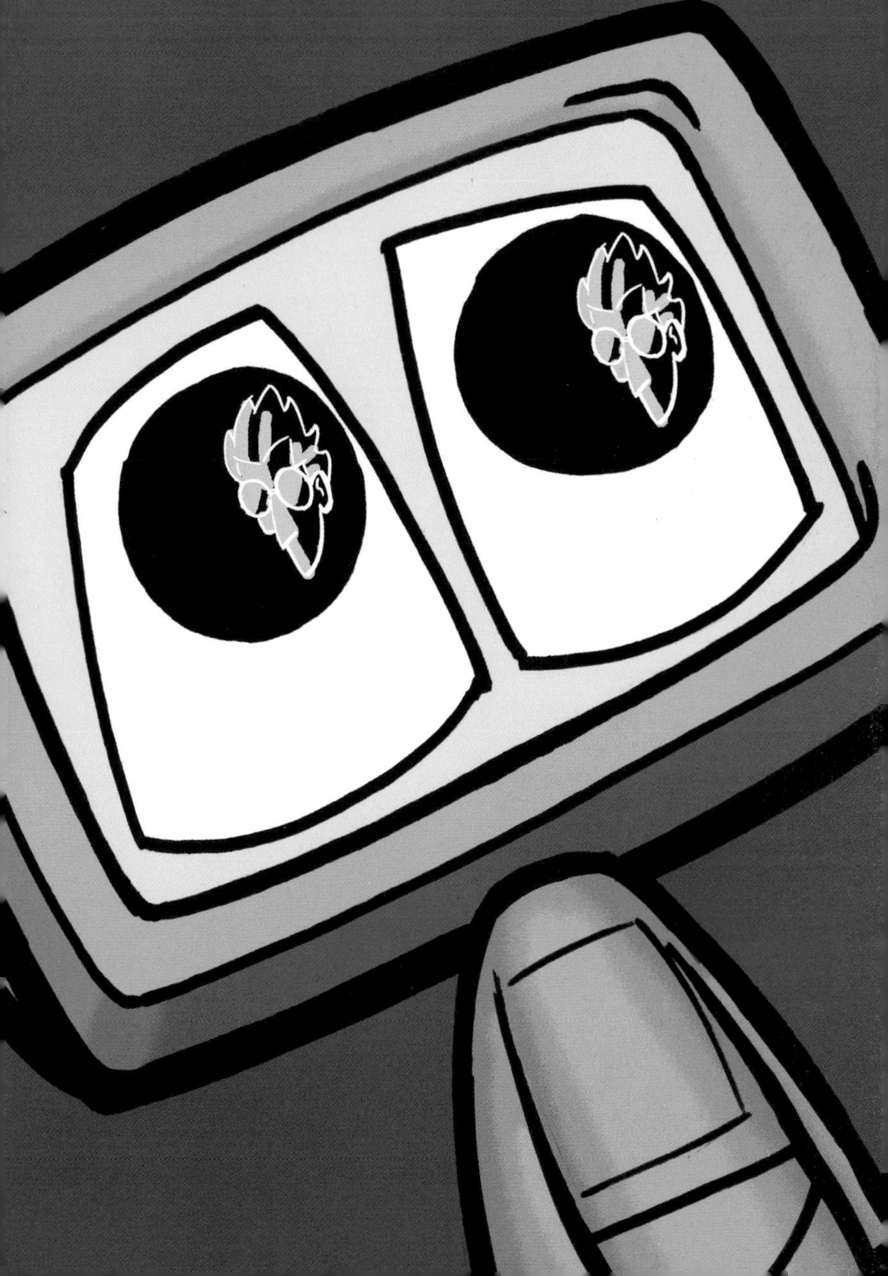

MY ROBOT
Paul Harrison-Davies

Robots are synonymous with industrial revolution, ever since the term was first coined – in Karel Capek's 1921 Soviet play *R.U.R. (Rossum's Universal Robots)*. But are they here to aid mankind, or replace us? Japan's own rapid technological expansion might well explain their love and fascination for the clanking, sparking tin machine. Robots occupy a special place in the heart of J-culture, not least in their manga and anime. Who can forget the lonely caretaker-rob, dutifully maintaining the idyllic gardens of Laputa, the flying island (aka *Castle In The Sky*, from Studio Ghibli animation)? Or else there's *Astroboy, Full Metal Alchemist,* Go Nagai's *Great Mazinger-Z*, and many, many more. The truth threatens to become even stranger than the fiction; always at the cutting edge of new technology, Japan now builds and exports the real thing.

Paul Harrison-Davies has previously appeared in a plethora of small press comics. Titles include *Violent, Solar Wind, Bulldog Adventure Magazine* and AccentUK's *Zombie* anthology, as well as *Best New Manga Volume 1.*

Who knows where he'll crop up next… possibly when you least expect.

www.comicspace.com/paulhd

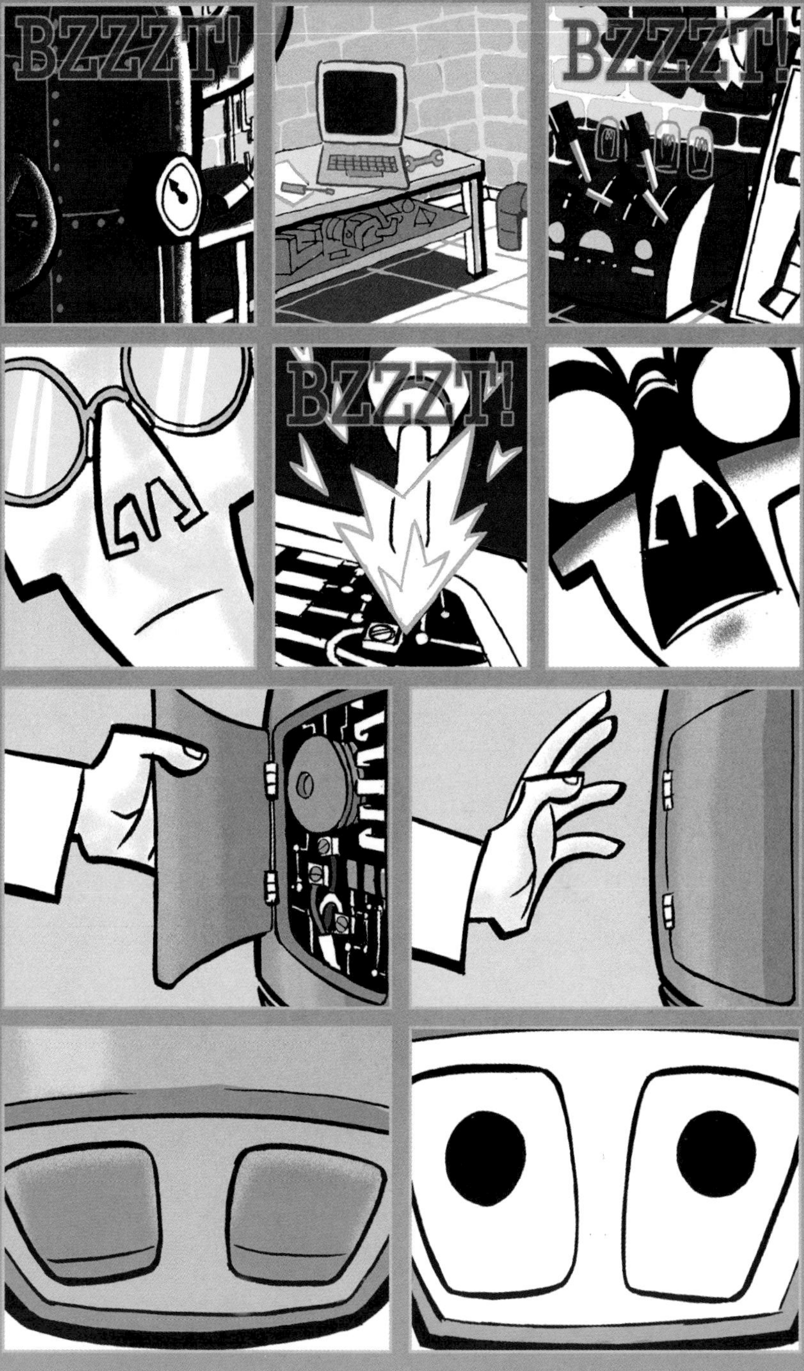

BZZZT!
BZZZT!
BZZZT!

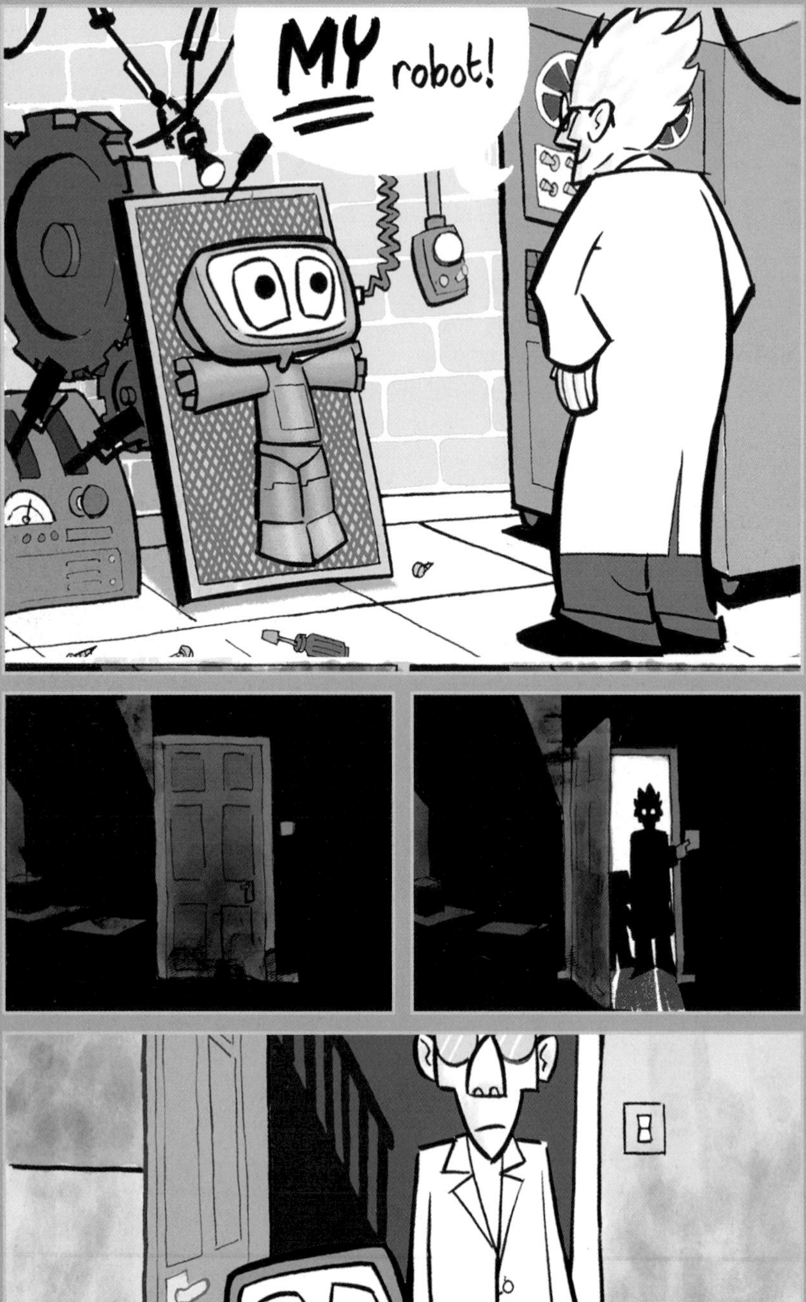
MY robot!

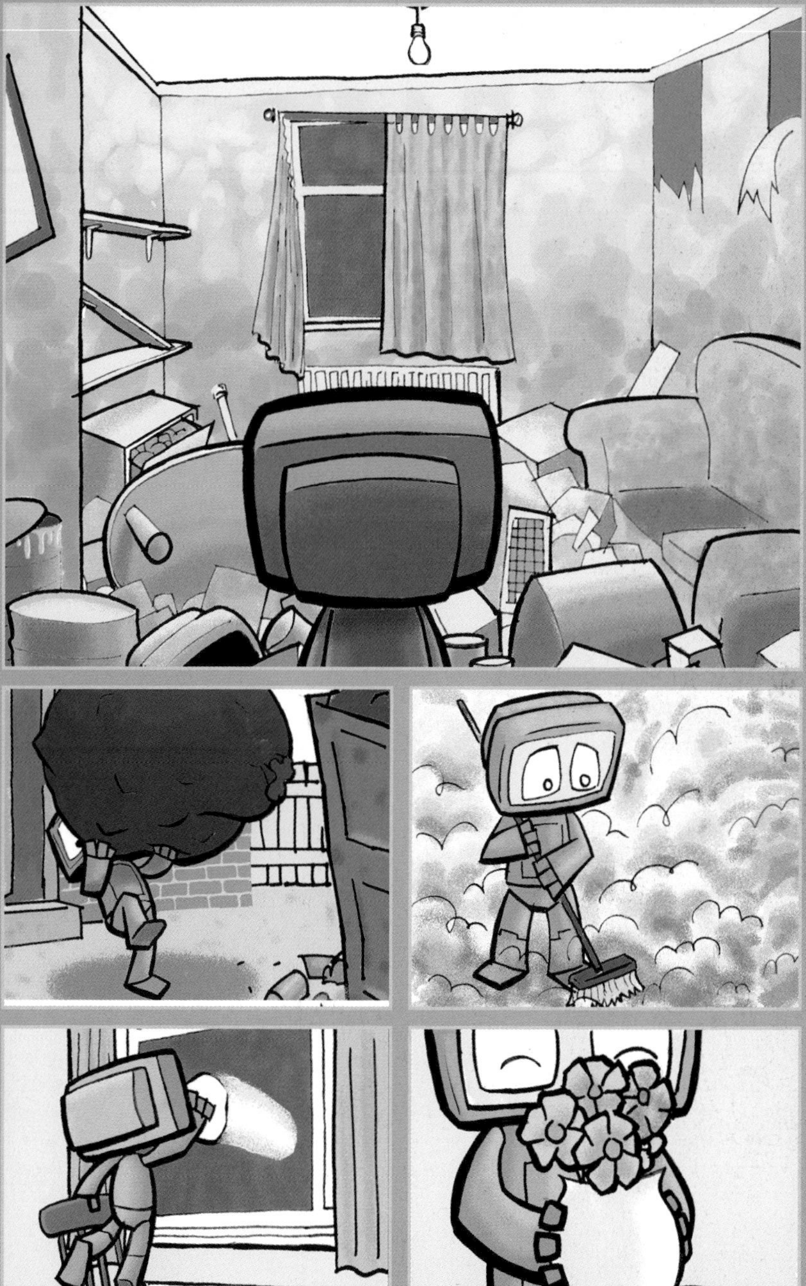

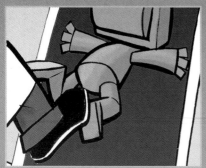

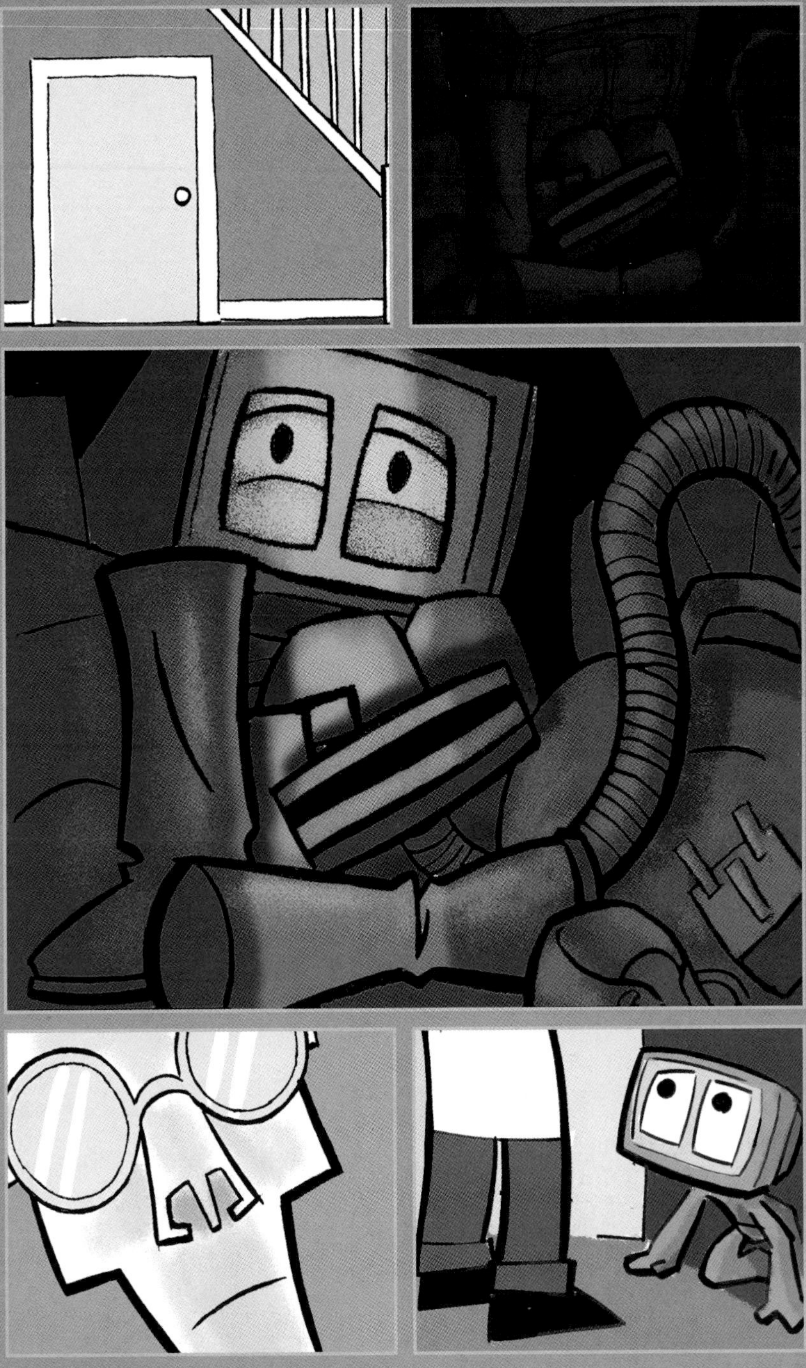

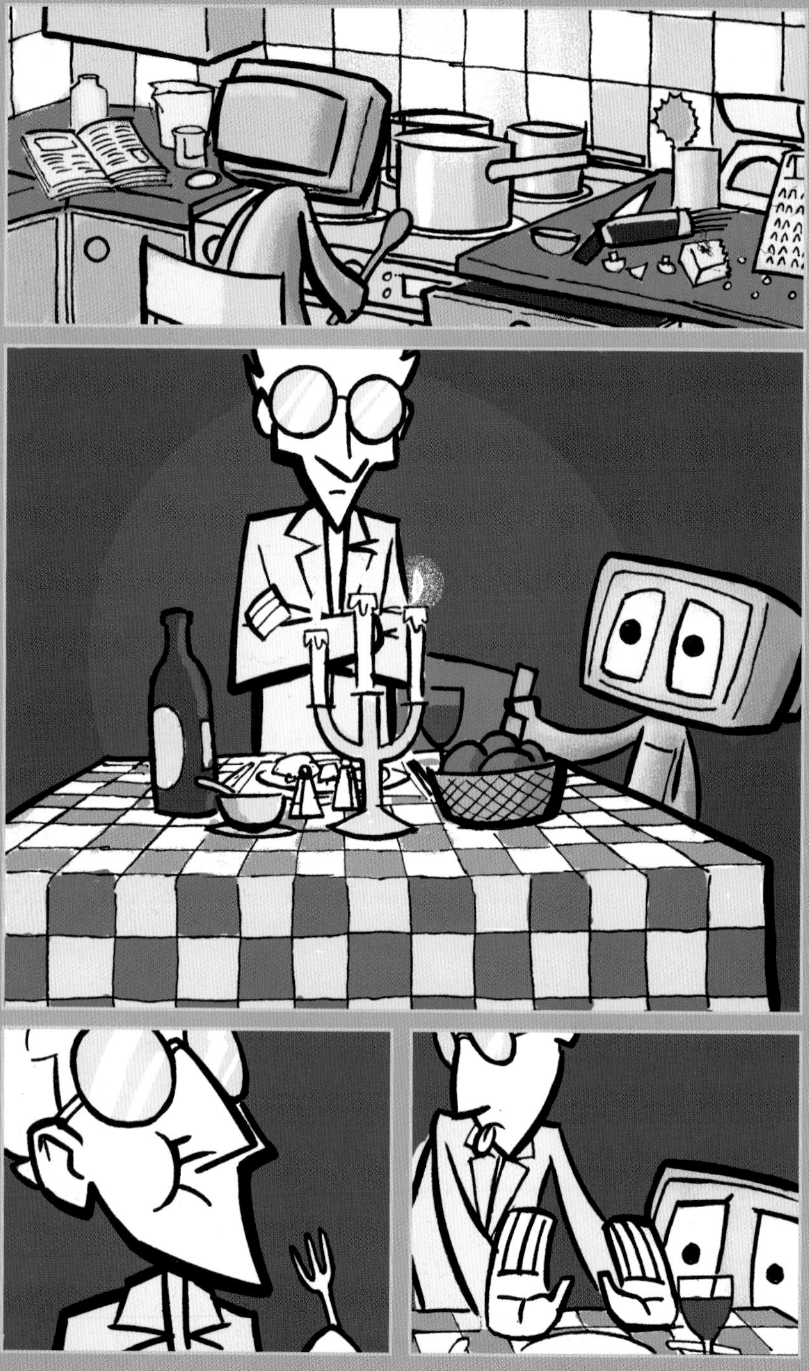

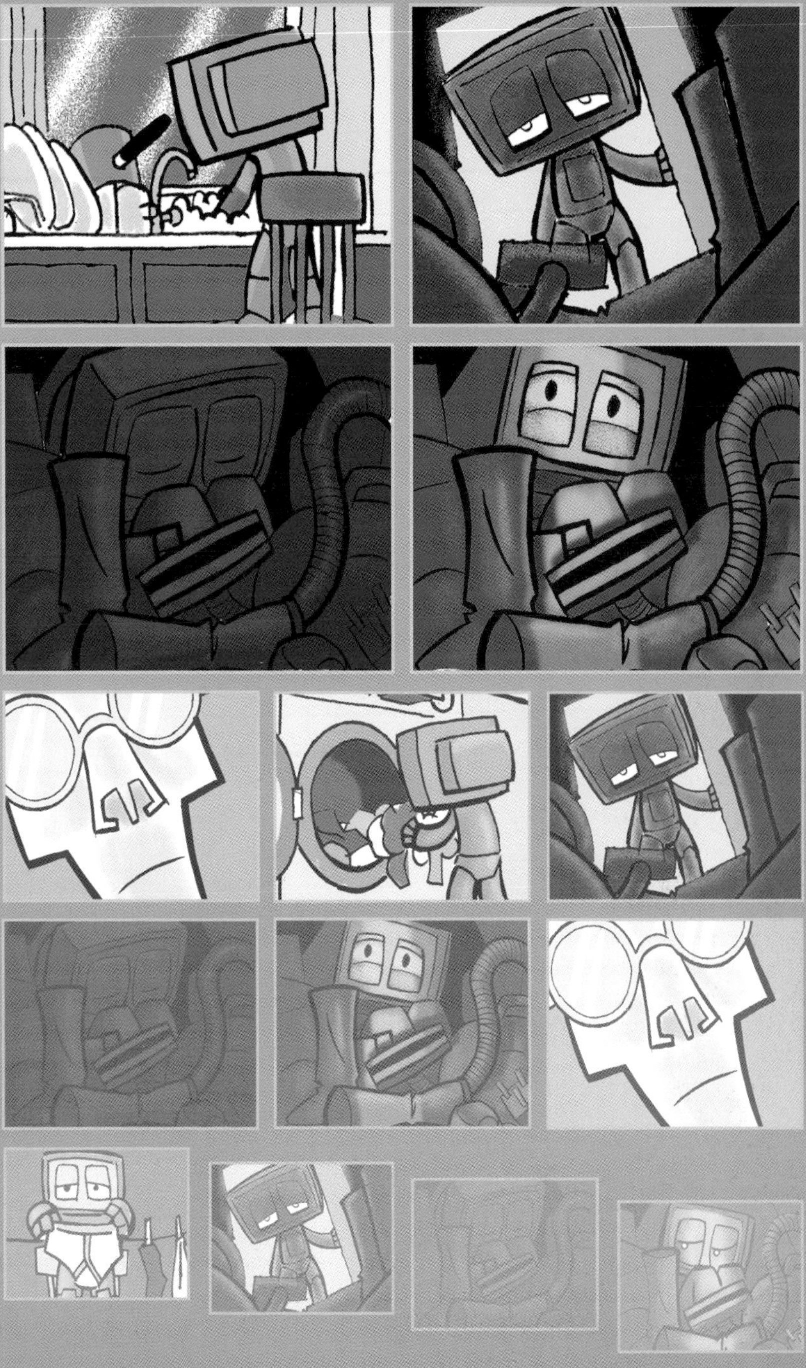

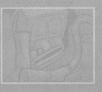

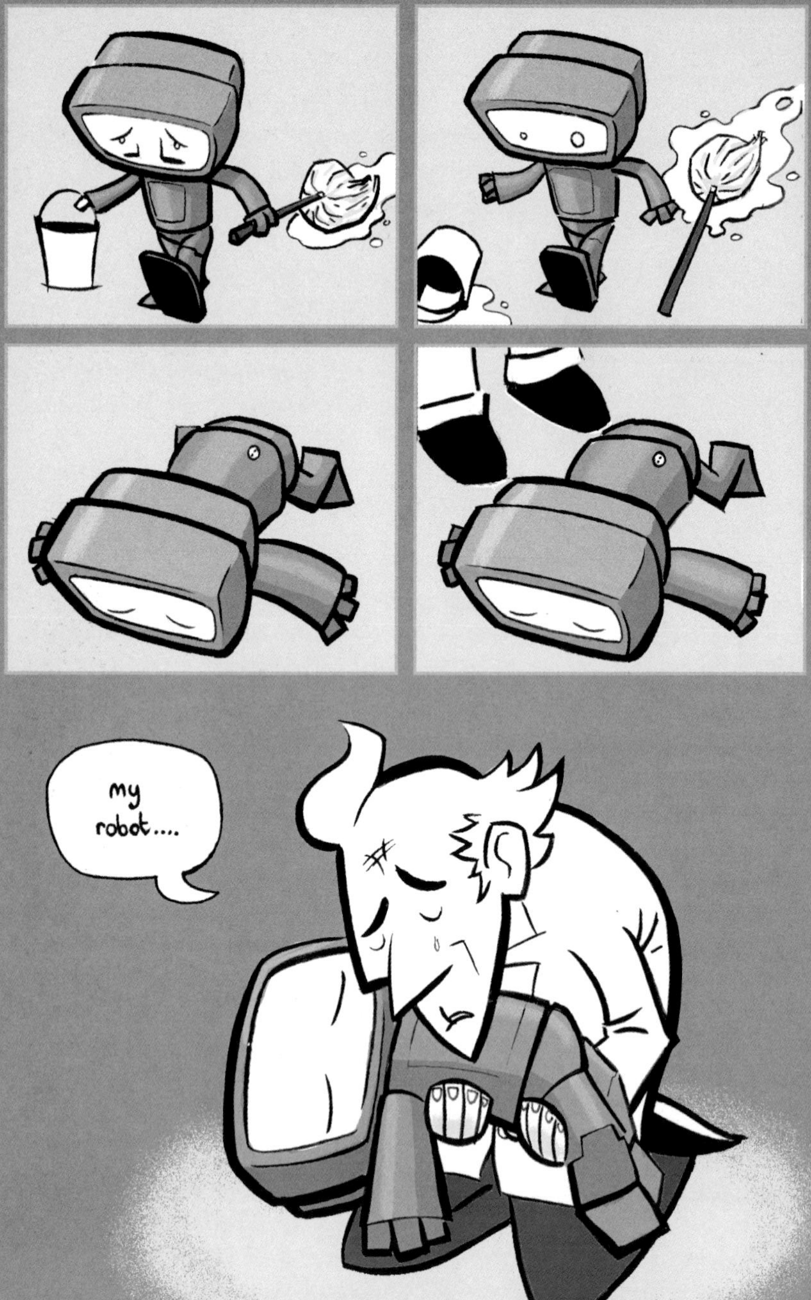
my robot....

OMAKE

As an annual publication, *Best New Manga* is roughly equivalent to just one of the many hundreds of manga anthology magazines appearing in Japan every week. These *zasshi* serialize ongoing manga epics, some eventually thousands of pages long. (The best we can currently hope for is to present a standalone short story equivalent.) Short humour pieces and even four-panel newspaper comic style "gag" strips intersperse and bracket these regular features, and are termed *omake*, or extras. *BNM* omake showcases two former category winners of IMAF – the International Manga and Anime Festival.

GILBERT & SULLIVAN Laura Howell

Laura's comics are regularly published in *The Beano*, and *The DFC*. *G&S* features the outrageous distortions of SD, or super-deformed, a well- known style of manga funnies, aka *chibi* (or "child"). Her main influence is *DiGi Charat*, here intermangled with a rich vein of quirky British humour; equally traditional, doubly daft.

www.laurahowell.co.uk

CARLOS & SAKURA Joanna Zhou

From Austria, Joanna studied graphic design at Central St Martins and Chelsea College of Art & Design in London. Her work encompasses a diverse range of media and styles, but cuteness and pop culture always crop up. You can buy Joanna's Momiji Dolls, based on Japanese street fashion, from Topshop, Urban Outfitters, Firebox or TokyoToys. Sakura makes a cameo on the 'Pinku' doll's tin! Someday she would love to create a graphic novel – perhaps even developing Carlos & Sakura into a full-length story. When not drawing, she's probably out shopping, baking cakes or on Facebook.

www.chocolatepixels.com

www.sweatdrop.com

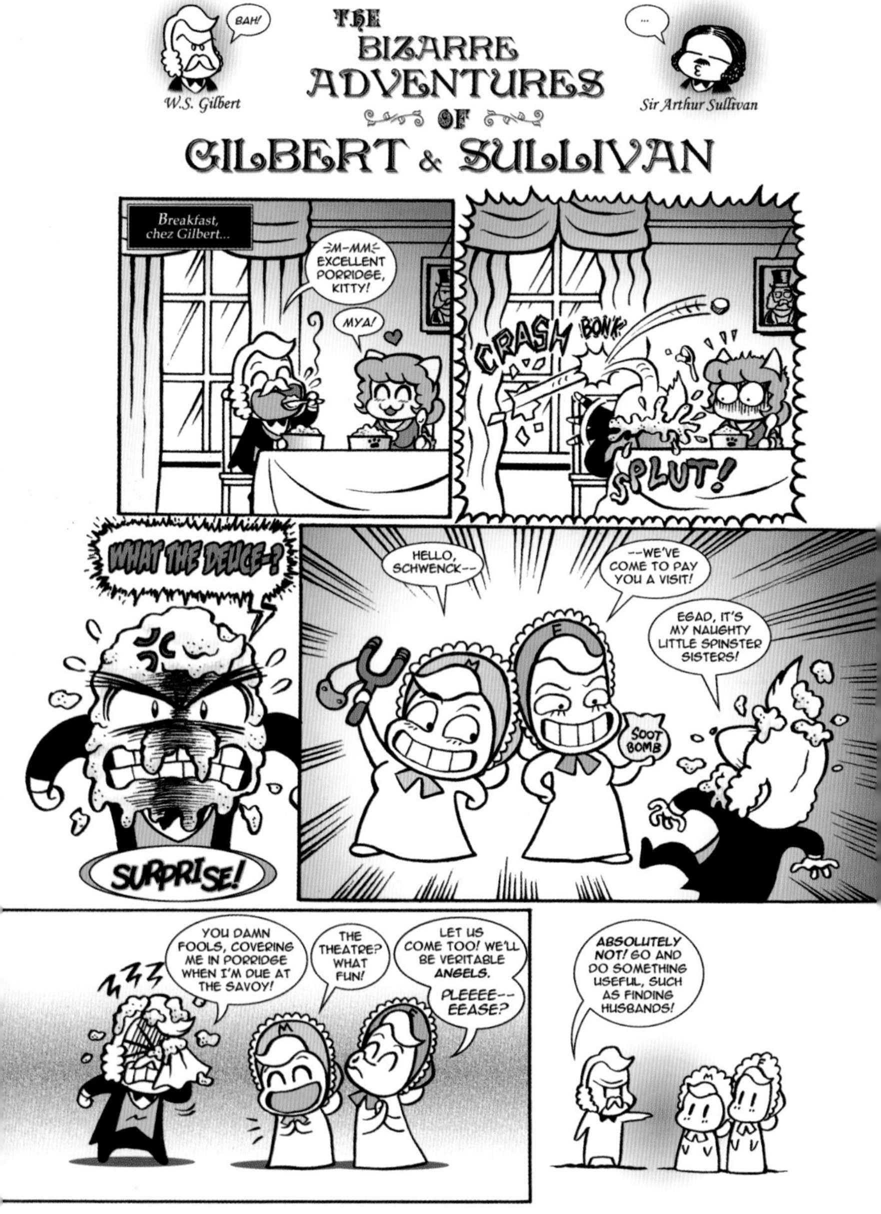

BAH!
W.S. Gilbert
THE BIZARRE ADVENTURES OF GILBERT & SULLIVAN
...
Sir Arthur Sullivan
Breakfast, chez Gilbert...
M-MM EXCELLENT PORRIDGE, KITTY!
MYA!
CRASH
BONK
SPLUT!
WHAT THE DEUCE-?
SURPRISE!
HELLO, SCHWENCK--
--WE'VE COME TO PAY YOU A VISIT!
EGAD, IT'S MY NAUGHTY LITTLE SPINSTER SISTERS!
SOOT BOMB
YOU DAMN FOOLS, COVERING ME IN PORRIDGE WHEN I'M DUE AT THE SAVOY!
THE THEATRE? WHAT FUN!
LET US COME TOO! WE'LL BE VERITABLE ANGELS.
PLEEEE--EEASE?
ABSOLUTELY NOT! GO AND DO SOMETHING USEFUL, SUCH AS FINDING HUSBANDS!

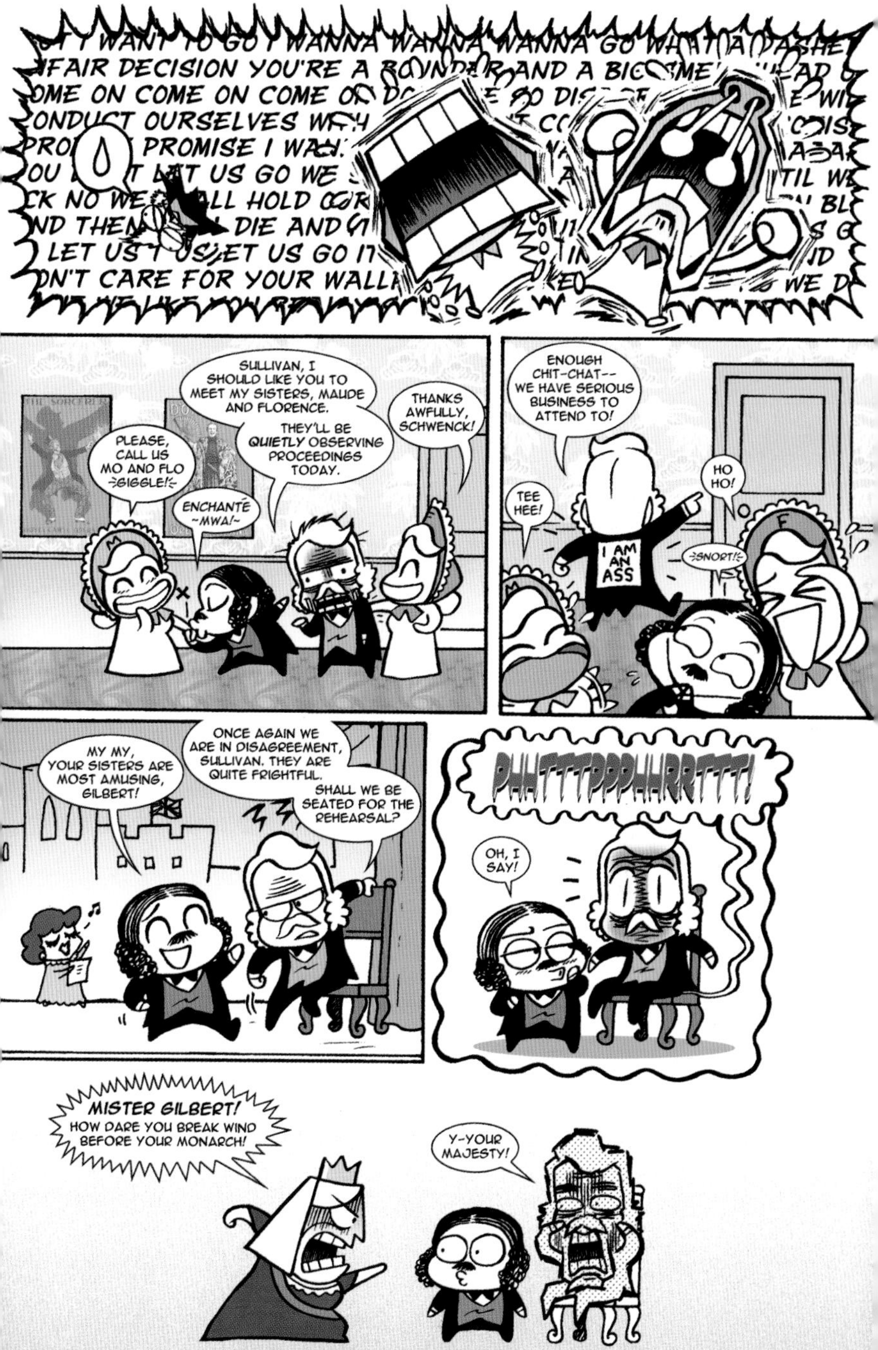

I WANT TO GO I WANNA WANNA WANNA WANNA GO
DECISION YOU'RE A
AND A
COME ON COME ON COME
CONDUCT OURSELVES
PROMISE I
LET US GO WE
NO WE
HOLD
DIE AND
LET US
LET US GO
CARE FOR YOUR
WE
SULLIVAN, I SHOULD LIKE YOU TO MEET MY SISTERS, MAUDE AND FLORENCE.
THEY'LL BE QUIETLY OBSERVING PROCEEDINGS TODAY.
PLEASE, CALL US MO AND FLO ~GIGGLE!~
ENCHANTÉ ~MWA!~
THANKS AWFULLY, SCHWENCK!
THE SORCERER
ENOUGH CHIT-CHAT-- WE HAVE SERIOUS BUSINESS TO ATTEND TO!
TEE HEE!
HO HO!
~SNORT!~
I AM AN ASS
MY MY, YOUR SISTERS ARE MOST AMUSING, GILBERT!
ONCE AGAIN WE ARE IN DISAGREEMENT, SULLIVAN. THEY ARE QUITE FRIGHTFUL.
SHALL WE BE SEATED FOR THE REHEARSAL?
PHHTTTTPPPHHRRTTTT!
OH, I SAY!
MISTER GILBERT! HOW DARE YOU BREAK WIND BEFORE YOUR MONARCH!
Y-YOUR MAJESTY!

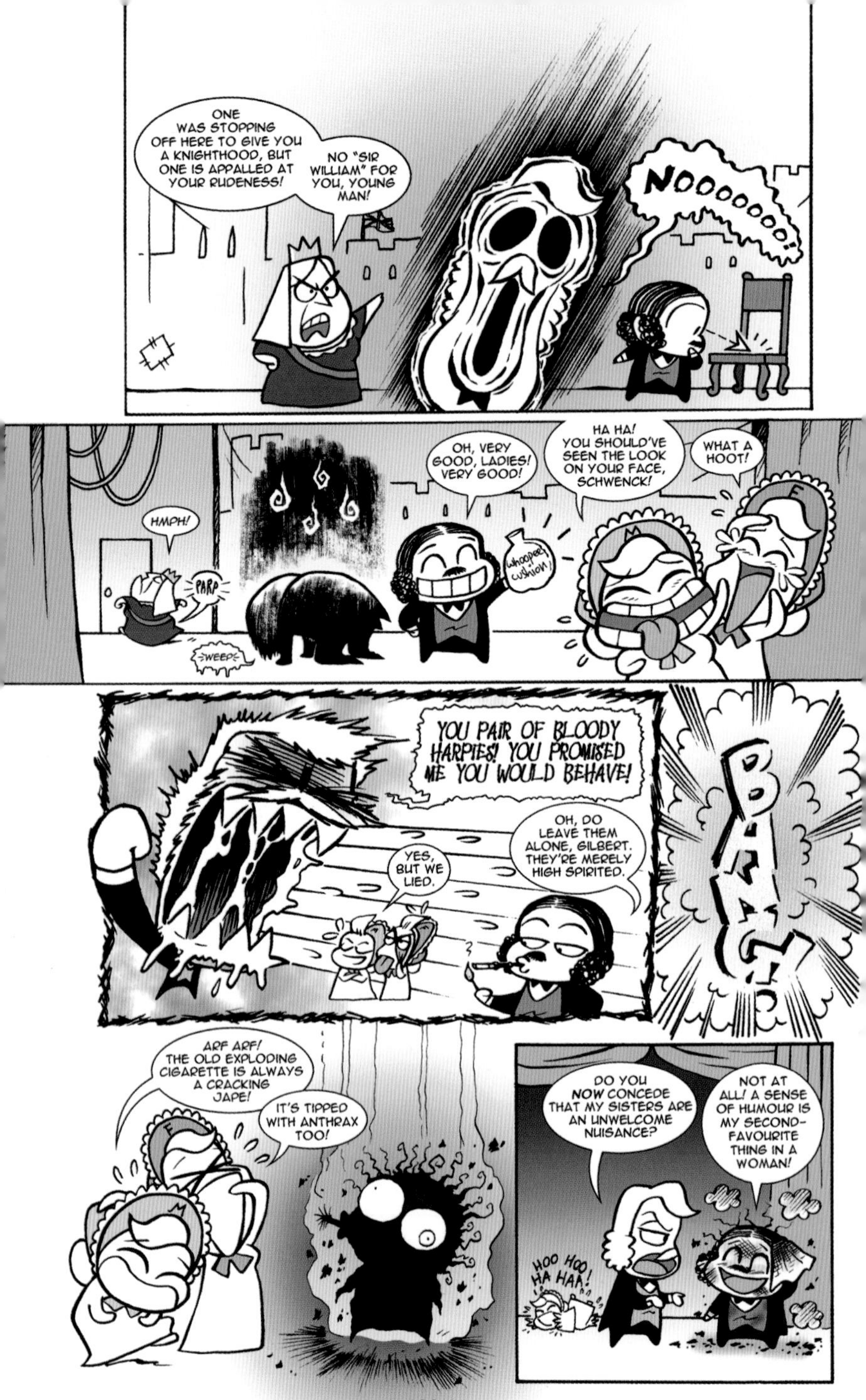

ONE WAS STOPPING OFF HERE TO GIVE YOU A KNIGHTHOOD, BUT ONE IS APPALLED AT YOUR RUDENESS!
NO "SIR WILLIAM" FOR YOU, YOUNG MAN!
NOOOOOOO!
HMPH!
PARP
WEEP
OH, VERY GOOD, LADIES! VERY GOOD!
whoopee cushion!
HA HA! YOU SHOULD'VE SEEN THE LOOK ON YOUR FACE, SCHWENCK!
WHAT A HOOT!
YOU PAIR OF BLOODY HARPIES! YOU PROMISED ME YOU WOULD BEHAVE!
YES, BUT WE LIED.
OH, DO LEAVE THEM ALONE, GILBERT. THEY'RE MERELY HIGH SPIRITED.
BLAMM
ARF ARF! THE OLD EXPLODING CIGARETTE IS ALWAYS A CRACKING JAPE!
IT'S TIPPED WITH ANTHRAX TOO!
DO YOU NOW CONCEDE THAT MY SISTERS ARE AN UNWELCOME NUISANCE?
NOT AT ALL! A SENSE OF HUMOUR IS MY SECOND-FAVOURITE THING IN A WOMAN!
HOO HOO HA HAA!

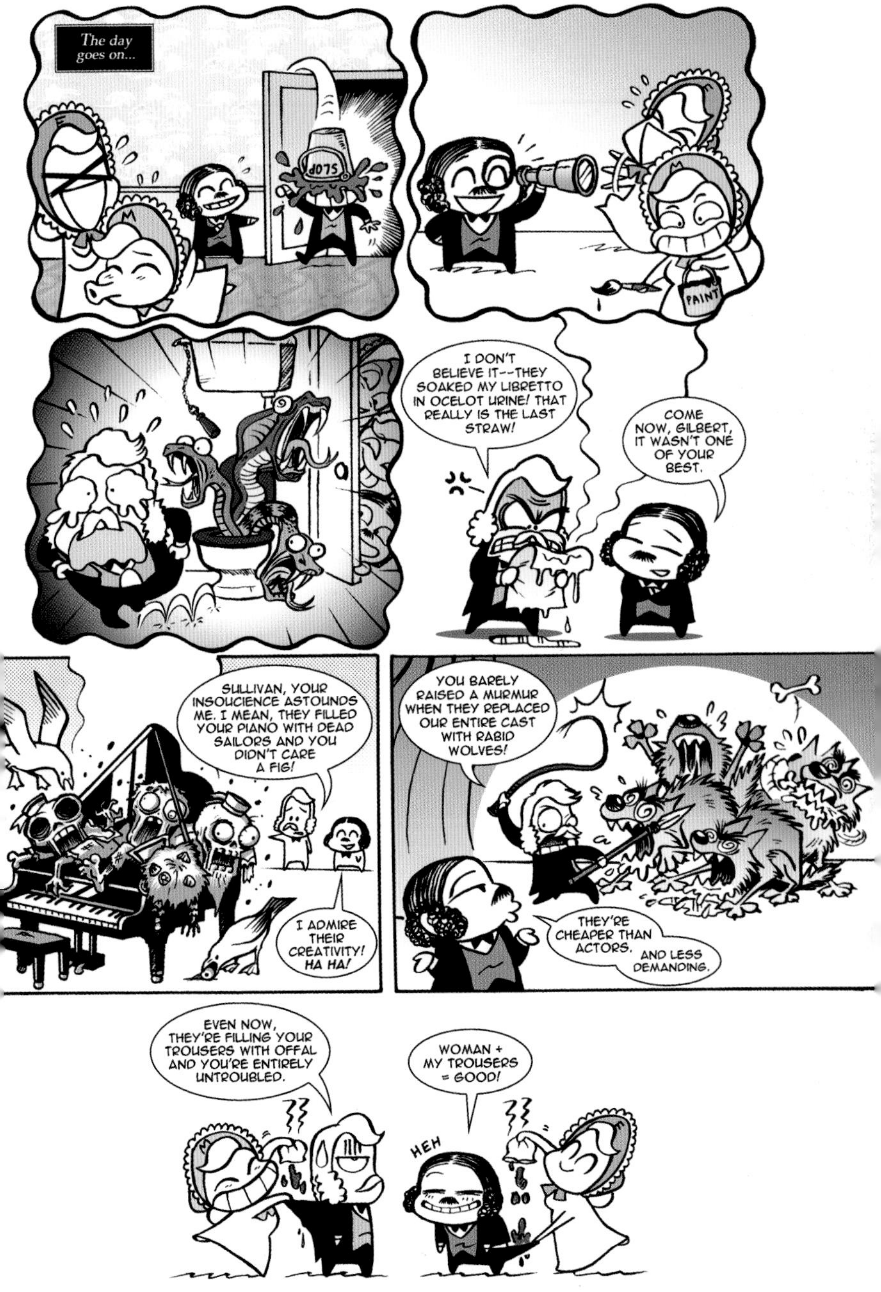
The day goes on...
SLOP
PAINT
I DON'T BELIEVE IT--THEY SOAKED MY LIBRETTO IN OCELOT URINE! THAT REALLY IS THE LAST STRAW!
COME NOW, GILBERT, IT WASN'T ONE OF YOUR BEST.
SULLIVAN, YOUR INSOUCIENCE ASTOUNDS ME. I MEAN, THEY FILLED YOUR PIANO WITH DEAD SAILORS AND YOU DIDN'T CARE A FIG!
I ADMIRE THEIR CREATIVITY! HA HA!
YOU BARELY RAISED A MURMUR WHEN THEY REPLACED OUR ENTIRE CAST WITH RABID WOLVES!
THEY'RE CHEAPER THAN ACTORS.
AND LESS DEMANDING.
EVEN NOW, THEY'RE FILLING YOUR TROUSERS WITH OFFAL AND YOU'RE ENTIRELY UNTROUBLED.
WOMAN + MY TROUSERS = GOOD!
HEH

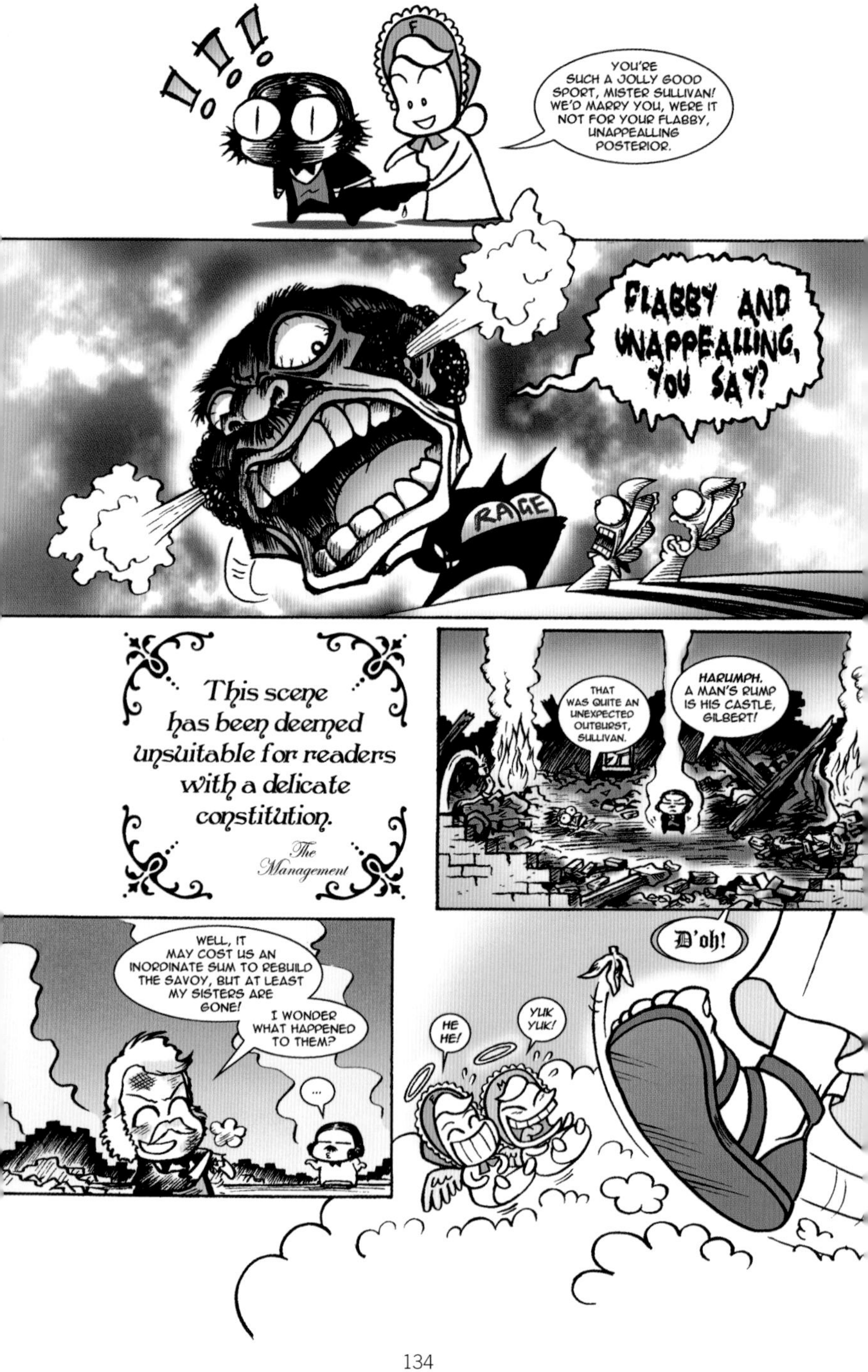
YOU'RE SUCH A JOLLY GOOD SPORT, MISTER SULLIVAN! WE'D MARRY YOU, WERE IT NOT FOR YOUR FLABBY, UNAPPEALLING POSTERIOR.
FLABBY AND UNAPPEALLING, YOU SAY?
RAGE
This scene has been deemed unsuitable for readers with a delicate constitution.
The Management
THAT WAS QUITE AN UNEXPECTED OUTBURST, SULLIVAN.
HARUMPH. A MAN'S RUMP IS HIS CASTLE, GILBERT!
WELL, IT MAY COST US AN INORDINATE SUM TO REBUILD THE SAVOY, BUT AT LEAST MY SISTERS ARE GONE!
I WONDER WHAT HAPPENED TO THEM?
...
D'oh!
HE HE!
YUK YUK!

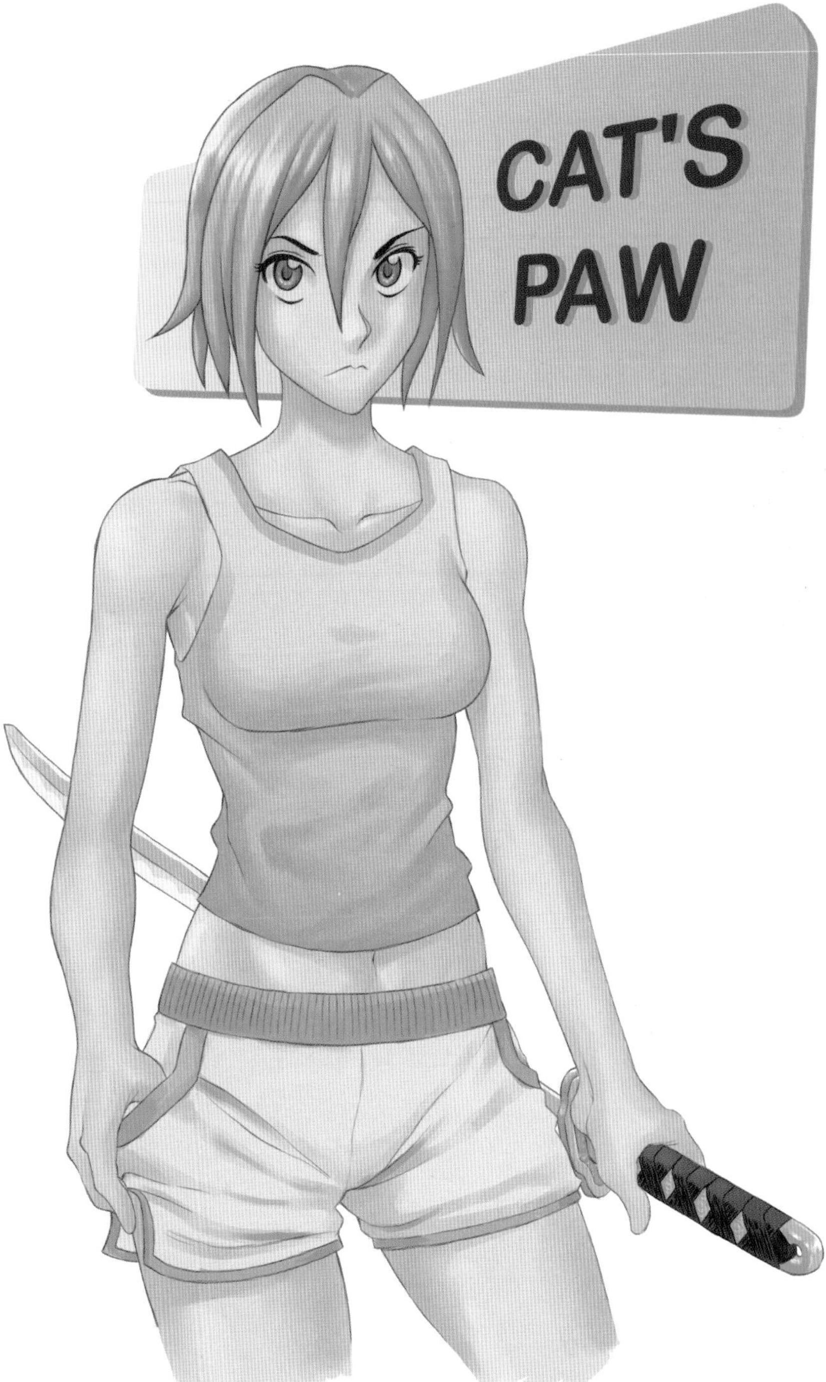
CAT'S
PAW

CAT'S PAW
David Slater

While machines become more human, modern humanity becomes every day more machine-like. Thus, the question robot fiction most often asks is: what is the quality that makes us human?

David Slater came to our attention as an entrant to Manga Jiman (see the section following this story for more detail). He's a modern-day renaissance man – currently co-developing an independent video game (including character design and animation); dabbling with some 3D character work; and halfway through writing a novel, which he tells us he has to finish, "no matter what!" And he creates comics as well! No time to eat or sleep then...

David says: "I love designing new characters and trying to get their personality across in their outfits. It would be nice if I could do this kind of work for a living – keeping them toes crossed!"

thekatsudon.deviantart.com
thekatsudon@gmail.com

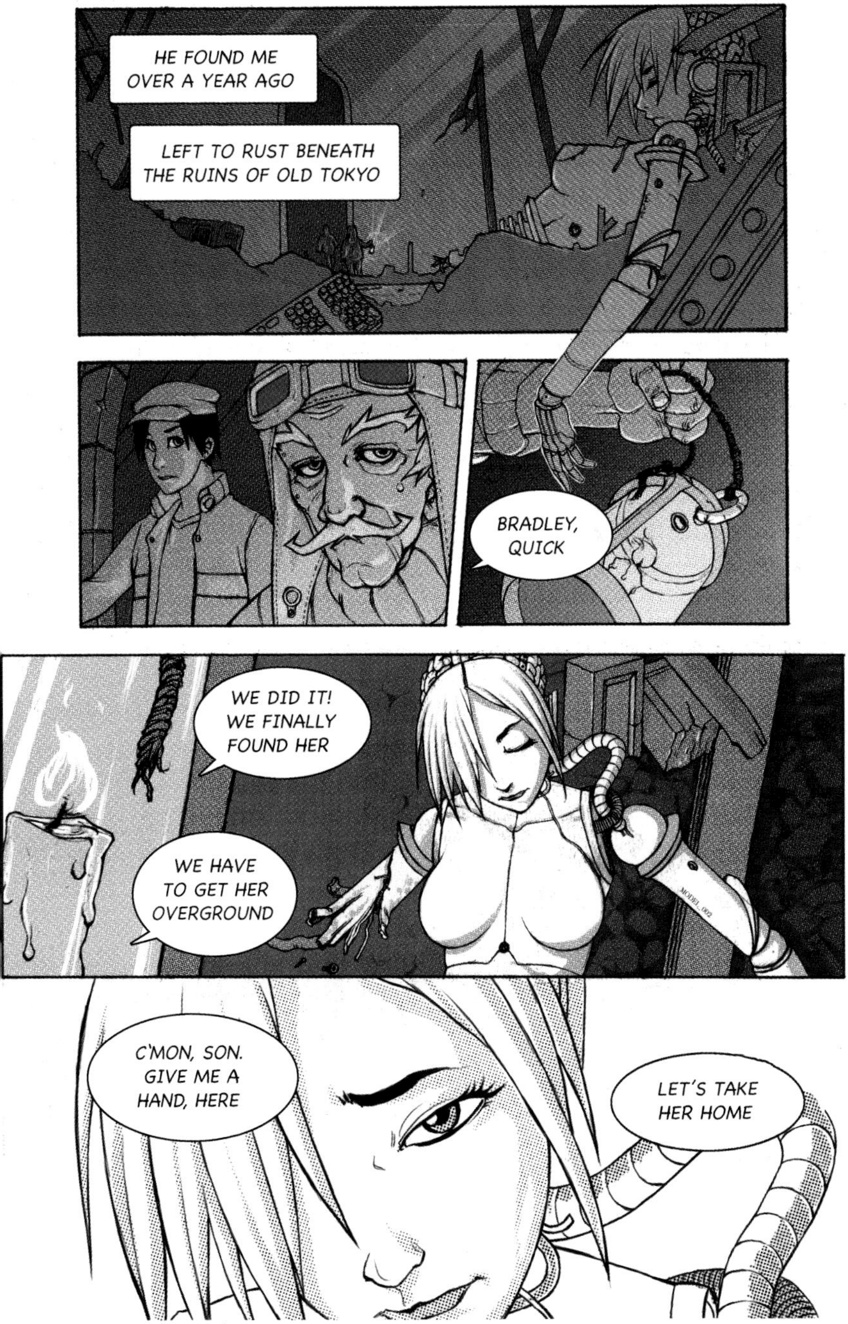
HE FOUND ME OVER A YEAR AGO
LEFT TO RUST BENEATH THE RUINS OF OLD TOKYO
BRADLEY, QUICK
WE DID IT! WE FINALLY FOUND HER
WE HAVE TO GET HER OVERGROUND
C'MON, SON. GIVE ME A HAND, HERE
LET'S TAKE HER HOME

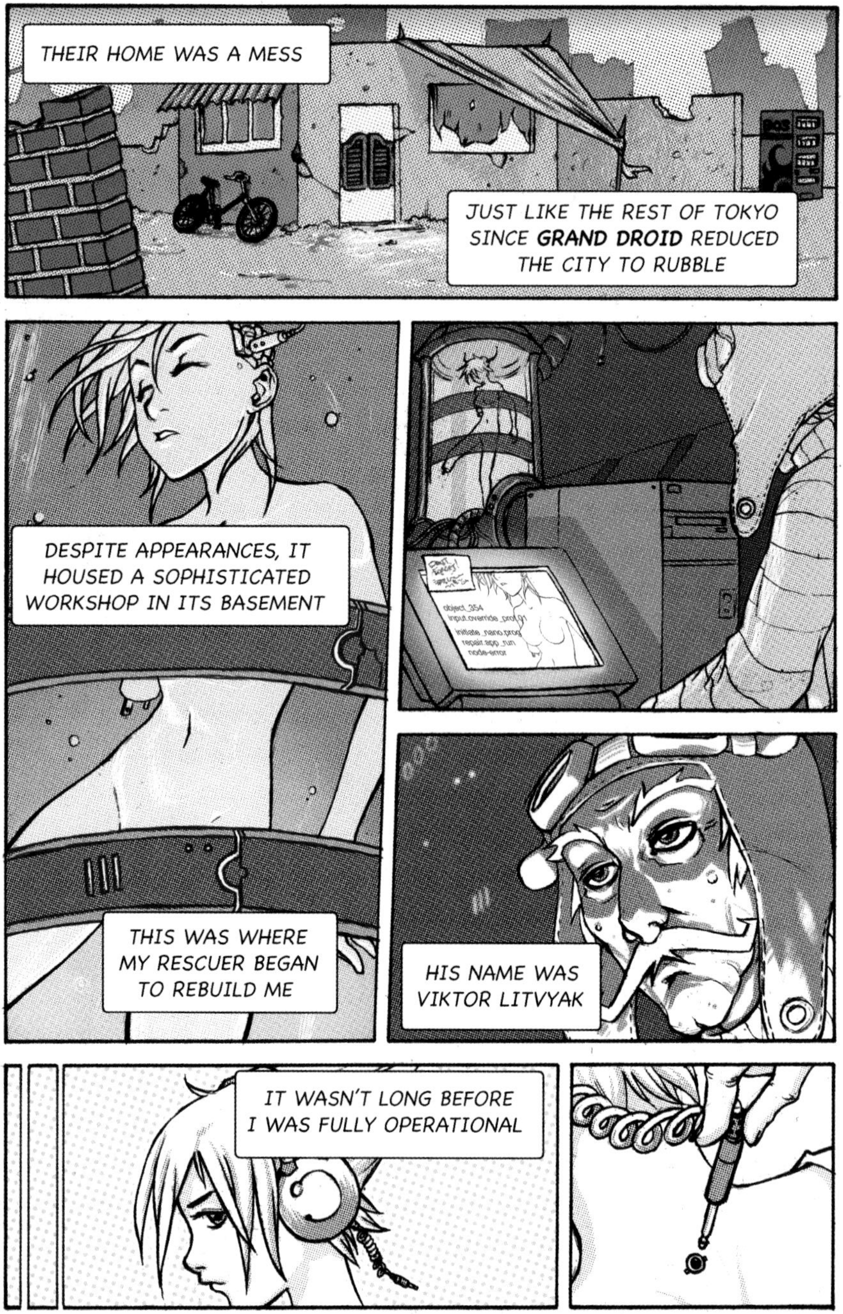
THEIR HOME WAS A MESS
JUST LIKE THE REST OF TOKYO SINCE **GRAND DROID** REDUCED THE CITY TO RUBBLE
DESPITE APPEARANCES, IT HOUSED A SOPHISTICATED WORKSHOP IN ITS BASEMENT
THIS WAS WHERE MY RESCUER BEGAN TO REBUILD ME
HIS NAME WAS VIKTOR LITVYAK
IT WASN'T LONG BEFORE I WAS FULLY OPERATIONAL

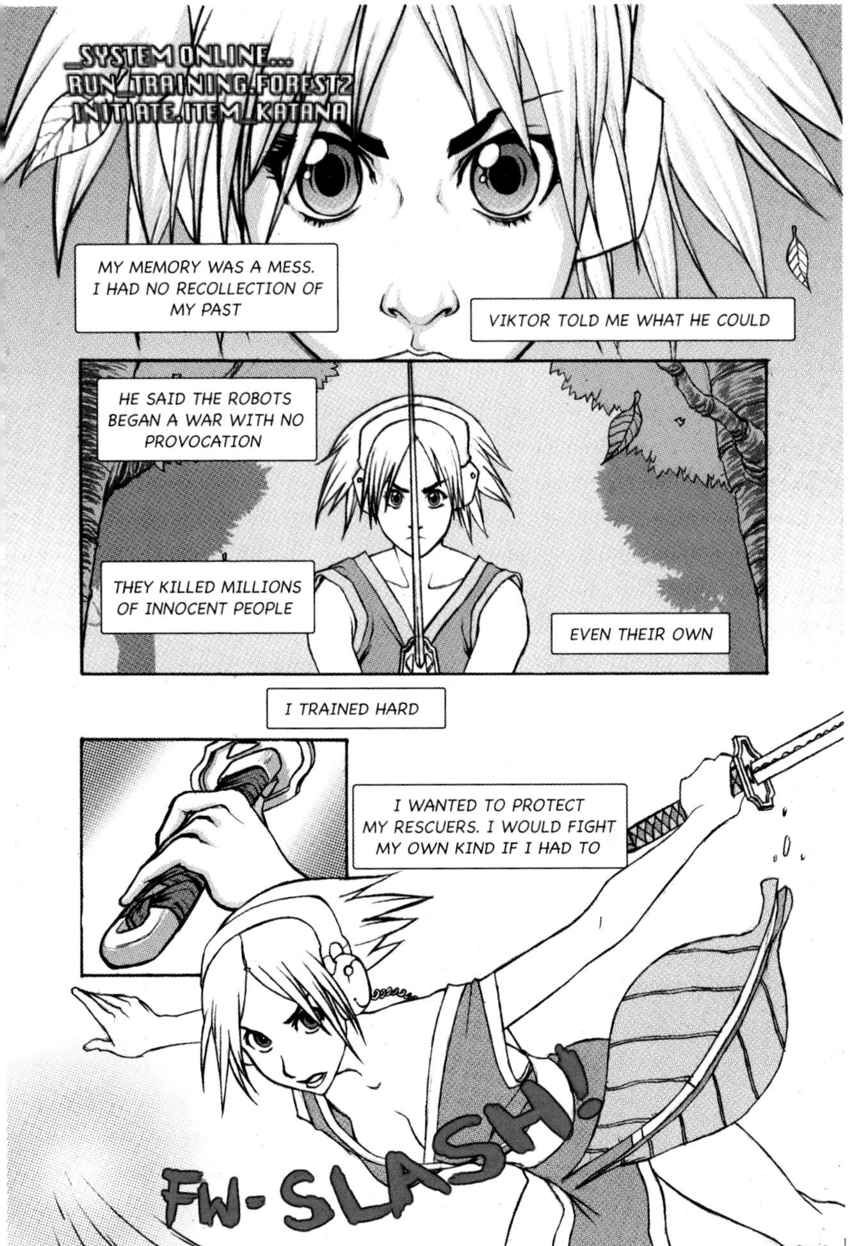
_SYSTEM ONLINE...
RUN_TRAINING.FOREST2
INITIATE.ITEM_KATANA
MY MEMORY WAS A MESS. I HAD NO RECOLLECTION OF MY PAST
VIKTOR TOLD ME WHAT HE COULD
HE SAID THE ROBOTS BEGAN A WAR WITH NO PROVOCATION
THEY KILLED MILLIONS OF INNOCENT PEOPLE
EVEN THEIR OWN
I TRAINED HARD
I WANTED TO PROTECT MY RESCUERS. I WOULD FIGHT MY OWN KIND IF I HAD TO
FW-SLASH!

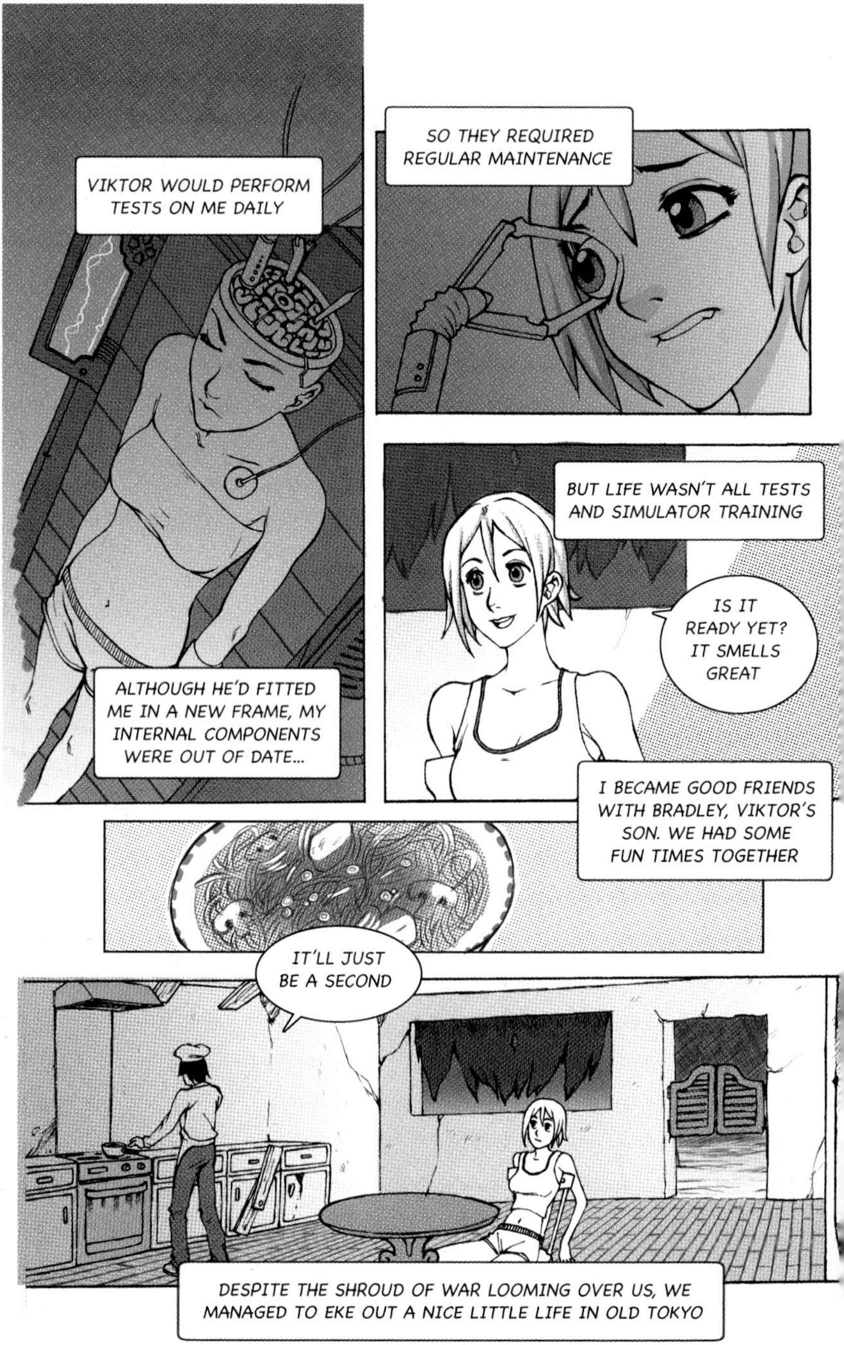
VIKTOR WOULD PERFORM TESTS ON ME DAILY
ALTHOUGH HE'D FITTED ME IN A NEW FRAME, MY INTERNAL COMPONENTS WERE OUT OF DATE...
SO THEY REQUIRED REGULAR MAINTENANCE
BUT LIFE WASN'T ALL TESTS AND SIMULATOR TRAINING
IS IT READY YET? IT SMELLS GREAT
I BECAME GOOD FRIENDS WITH BRADLEY, VIKTOR'S SON. WE HAD SOME FUN TIMES TOGETHER
IT'LL JUST BE A SECOND
DESPITE THE SHROUD OF WAR LOOMING OVER US, WE MANAGED TO EKE OUT A NICE LITTLE LIFE IN OLD TOKYO

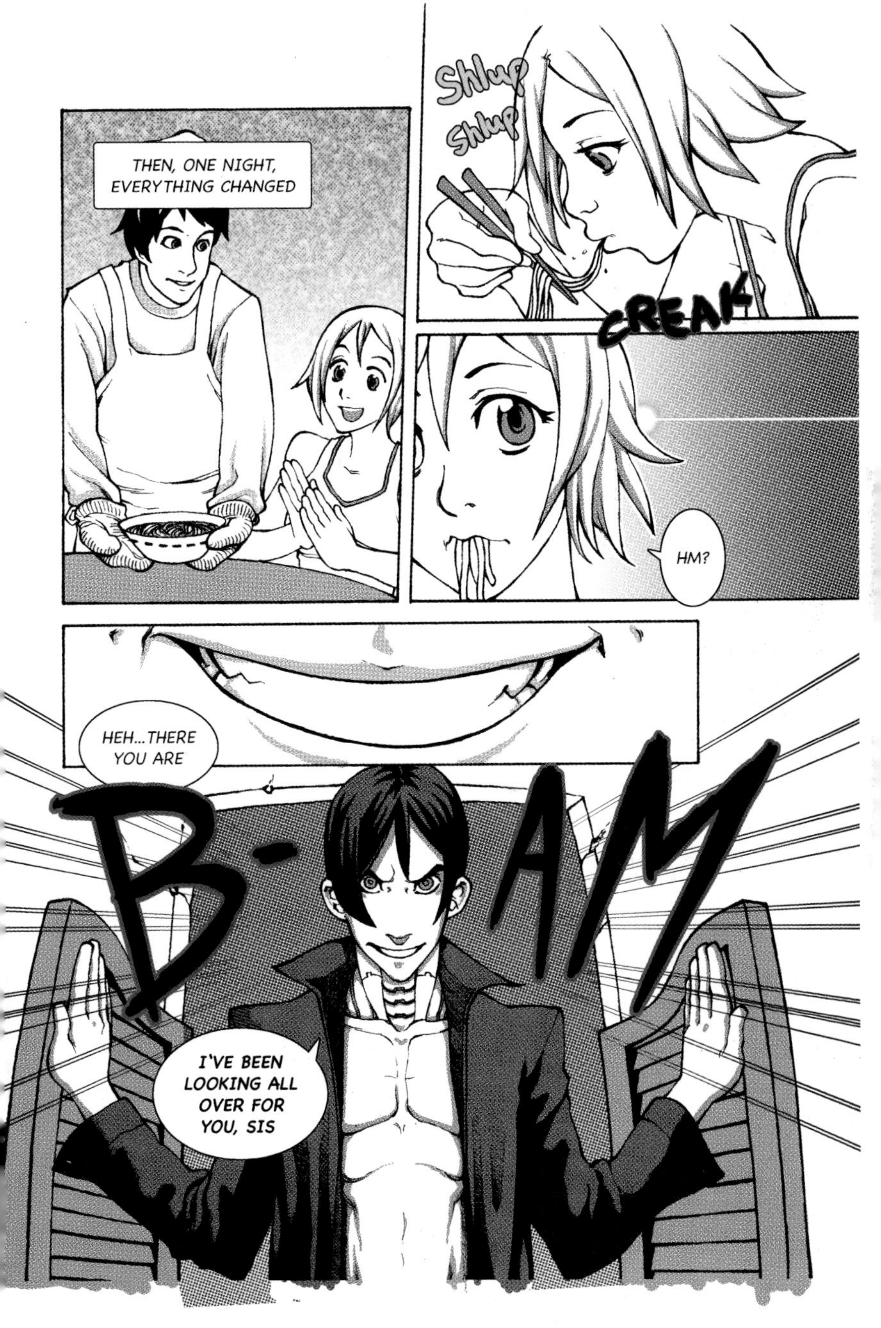
THEN, ONE NIGHT, EVERYTHING CHANGED
Shlup Shlup
CREAK
HM?
HEH...THERE YOU ARE
B-AM
I'VE BEEN LOOKING ALL OVER FOR YOU, SIS

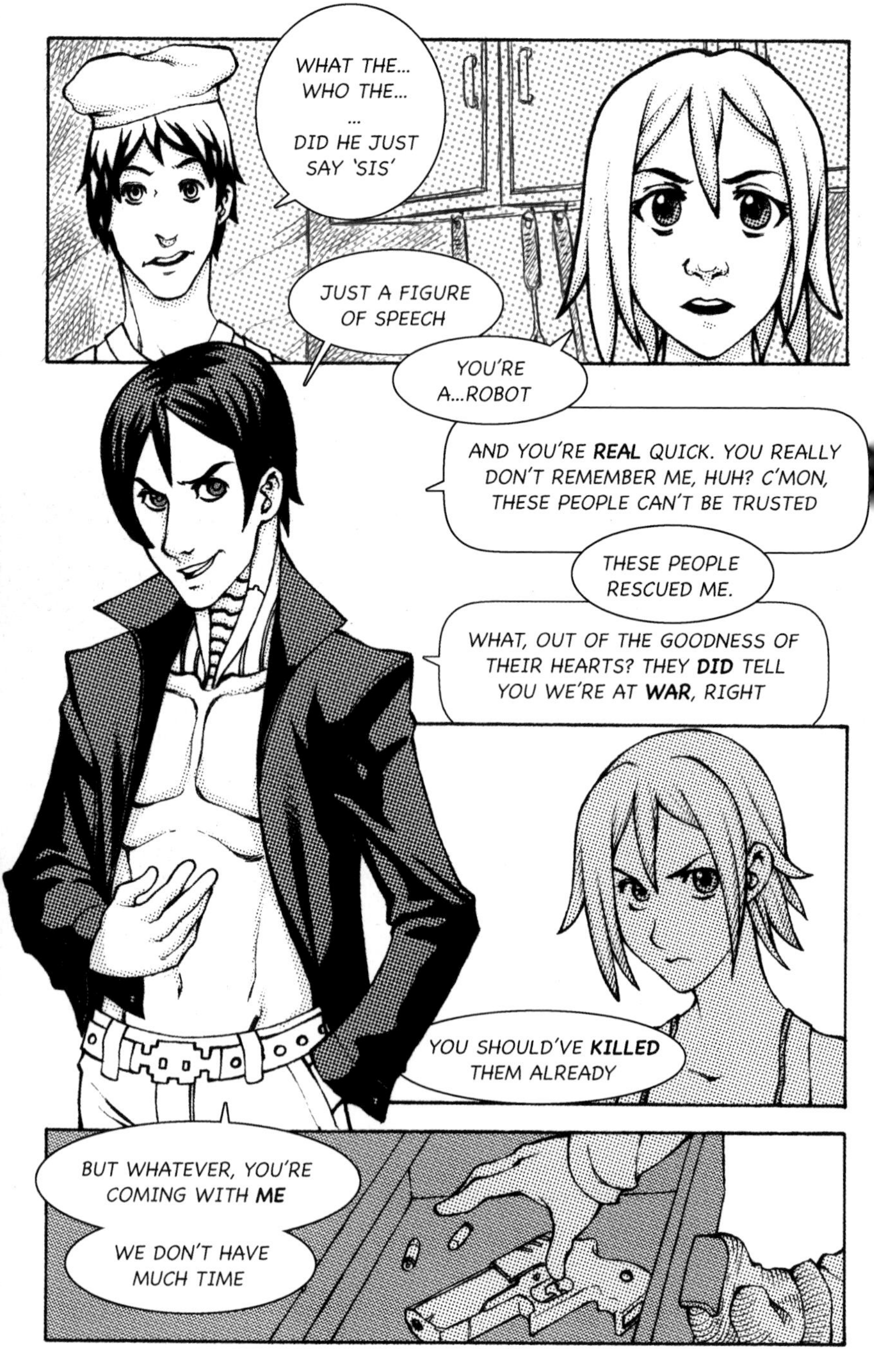
WHAT THE... WHO THE... ... DID HE JUST SAY 'SIS'
JUST A FIGURE OF SPEECH
YOU'RE A...ROBOT
AND YOU'RE **REAL** QUICK. YOU REALLY DON'T REMEMBER ME, HUH? C'MON, THESE PEOPLE CAN'T BE TRUSTED
THESE PEOPLE RESCUED ME.
WHAT, OUT OF THE GOODNESS OF THEIR HEARTS? THEY **DID** TELL YOU WE'RE AT **WAR**, RIGHT
YOU SHOULD'VE **KILLED** THEM ALREADY
BUT WHATEVER, YOU'RE COMING WITH **ME**
WE DON'T HAVE MUCH TIME

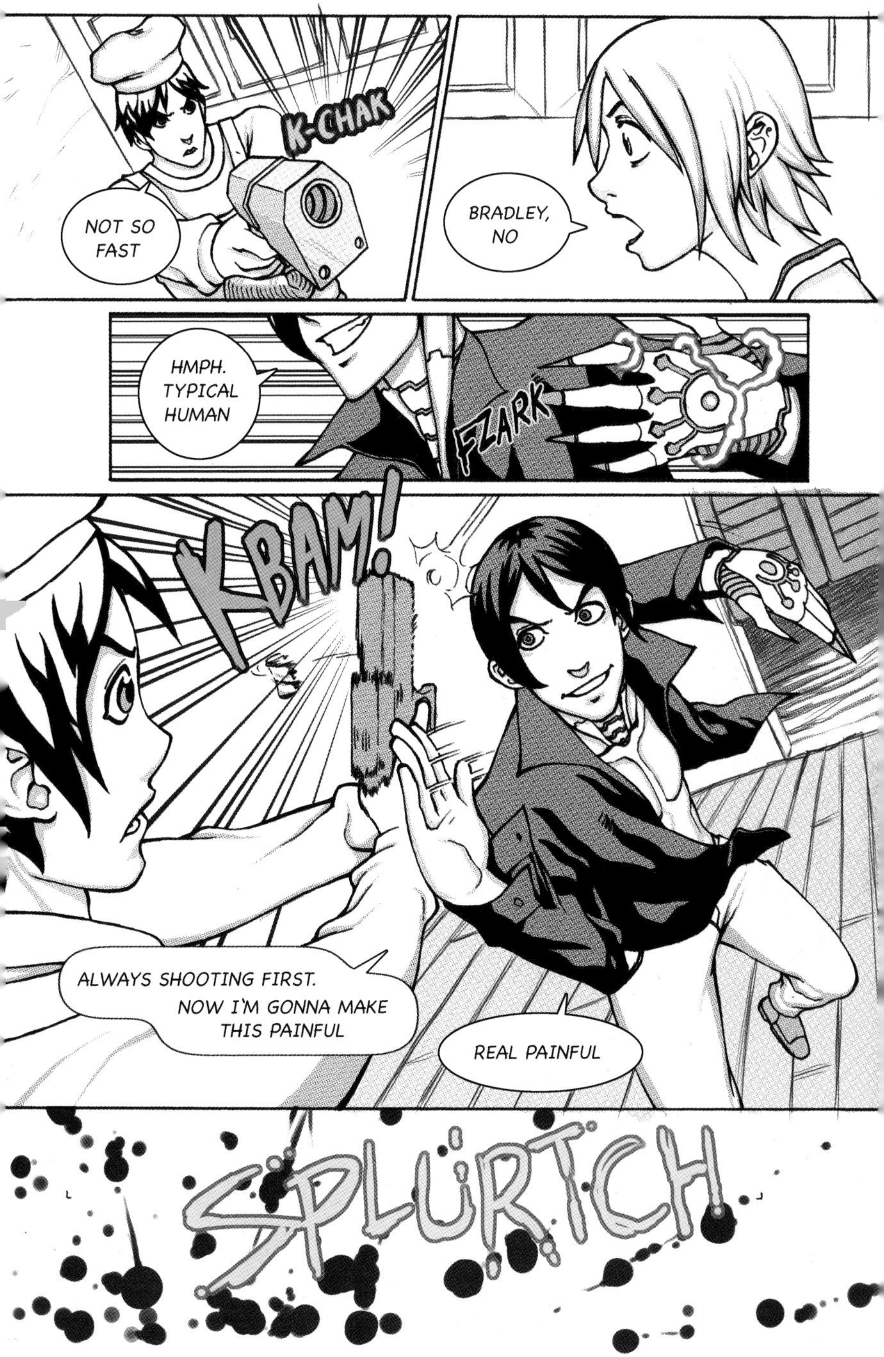
K-CHAK
NOT SO FAST
BRADLEY, NO
HMPH. TYPICAL HUMAN
FZARK
KBAM!
ALWAYS SHOOTING FIRST.
NOW I'M GONNA MAKE THIS PAINFUL
REAL PAINFUL
SPLURTCH

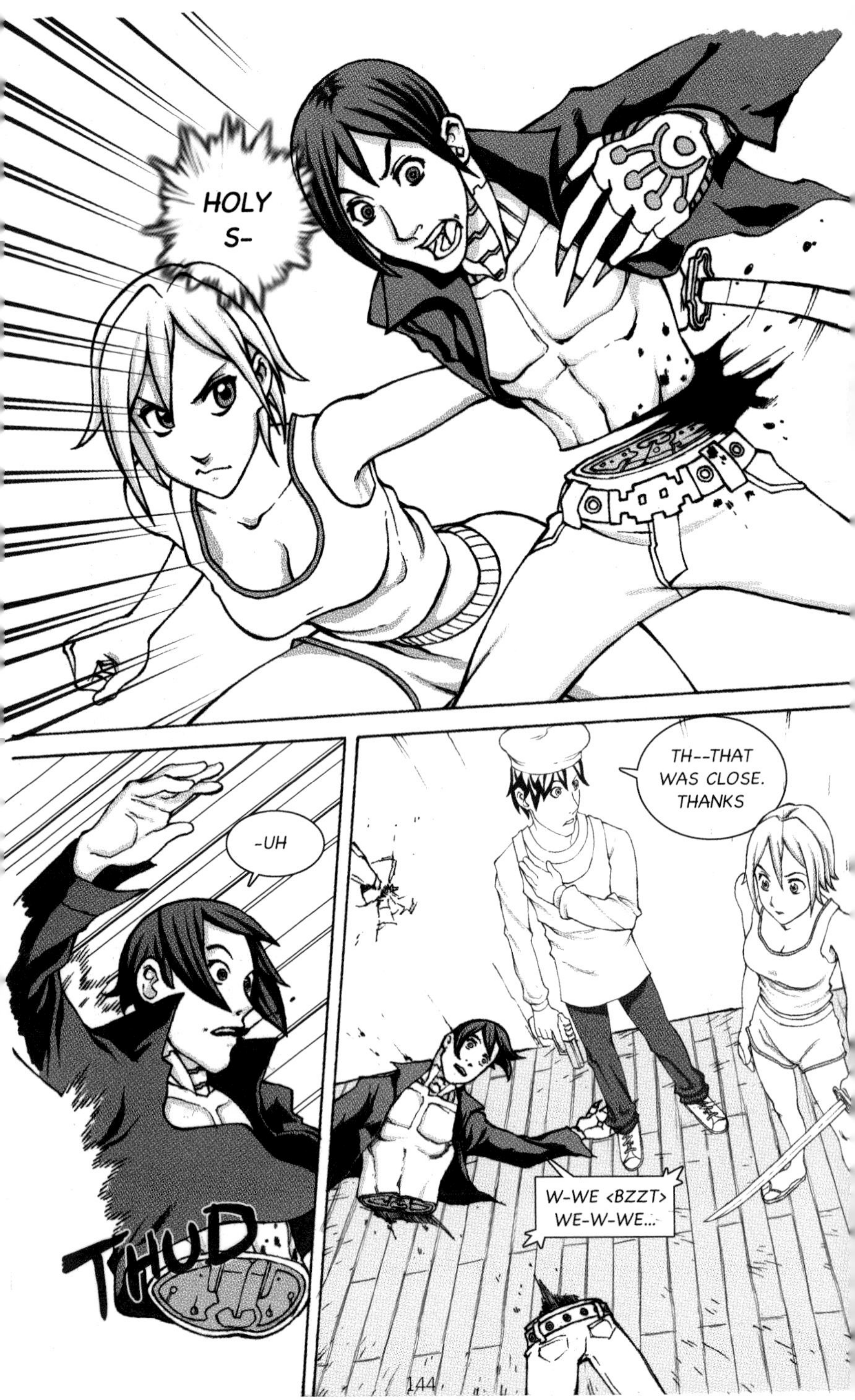
HOLY S-
-UH
THUD
TH--THAT WAS CLOSE. THANKS
W-WE <BZZT> WE-W-WE...

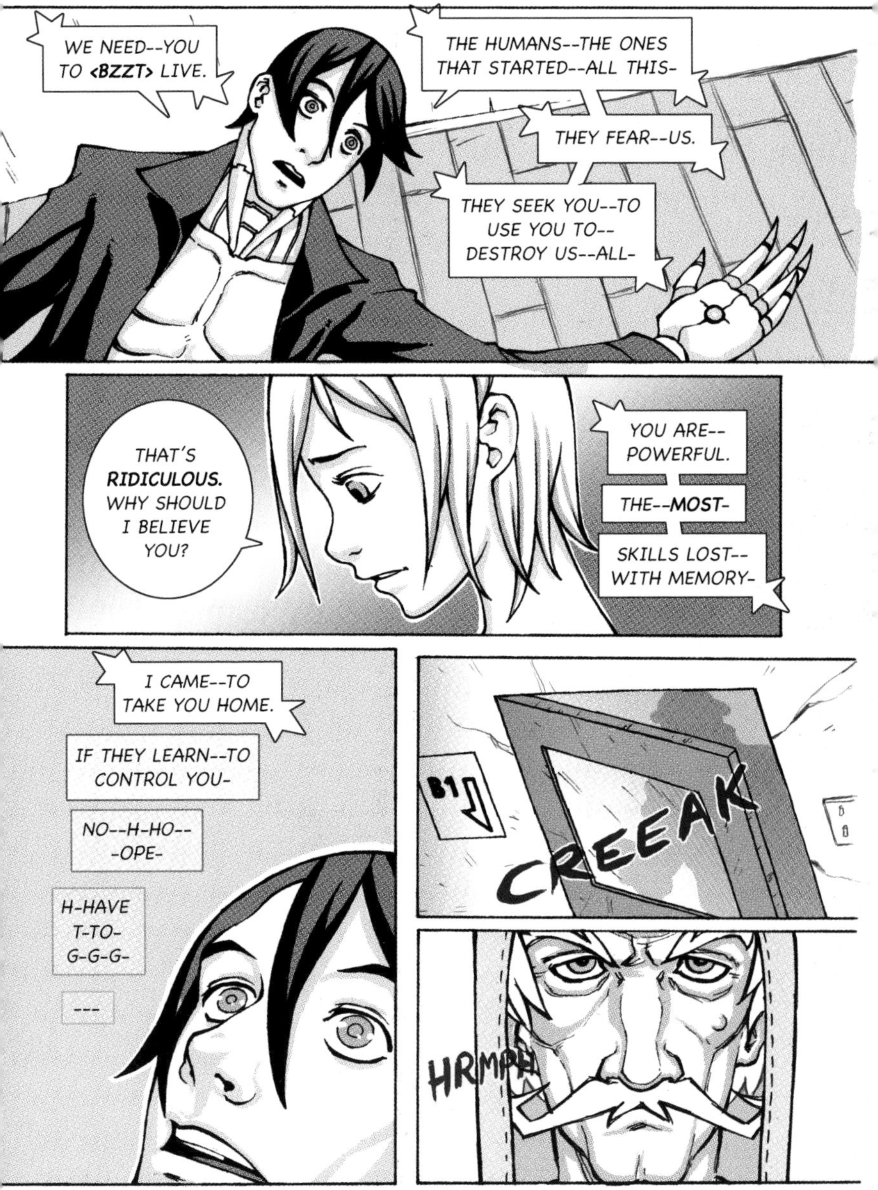
WE NEED--YOU TO <BZZT> LIVE.
THE HUMANS--THE ONES THAT STARTED--ALL THIS-
THEY FEAR--US.
THEY SEEK YOU--TO USE YOU TO--DESTROY US--ALL-
THAT'S RIDICULOUS. WHY SHOULD I BELIEVE YOU?
YOU ARE--POWERFUL.
THE--MOST-
SKILLS LOST--WITH MEMORY-
I CAME--TO TAKE YOU HOME.
IF THEY LEARN--TO CONTROL YOU-
NO--H-HO---OPE-
H-HAVE T-TO-G-G-G-

B1
CREEAK
HRMPH

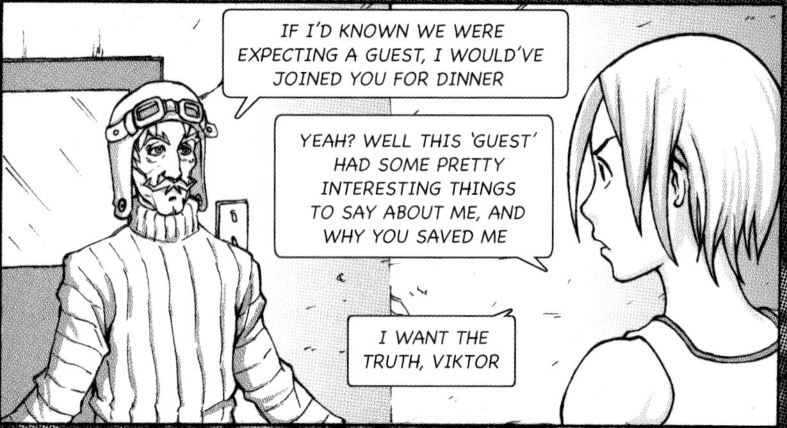
IF I'D KNOWN WE WERE EXPECTING A GUEST, I WOULD'VE JOINED YOU FOR DINNER
YEAH? WELL THIS 'GUEST' HAD SOME PRETTY INTERESTING THINGS TO SAY ABOUT ME, AND WHY YOU SAVED ME
I WANT THE TRUTH, VIKTOR
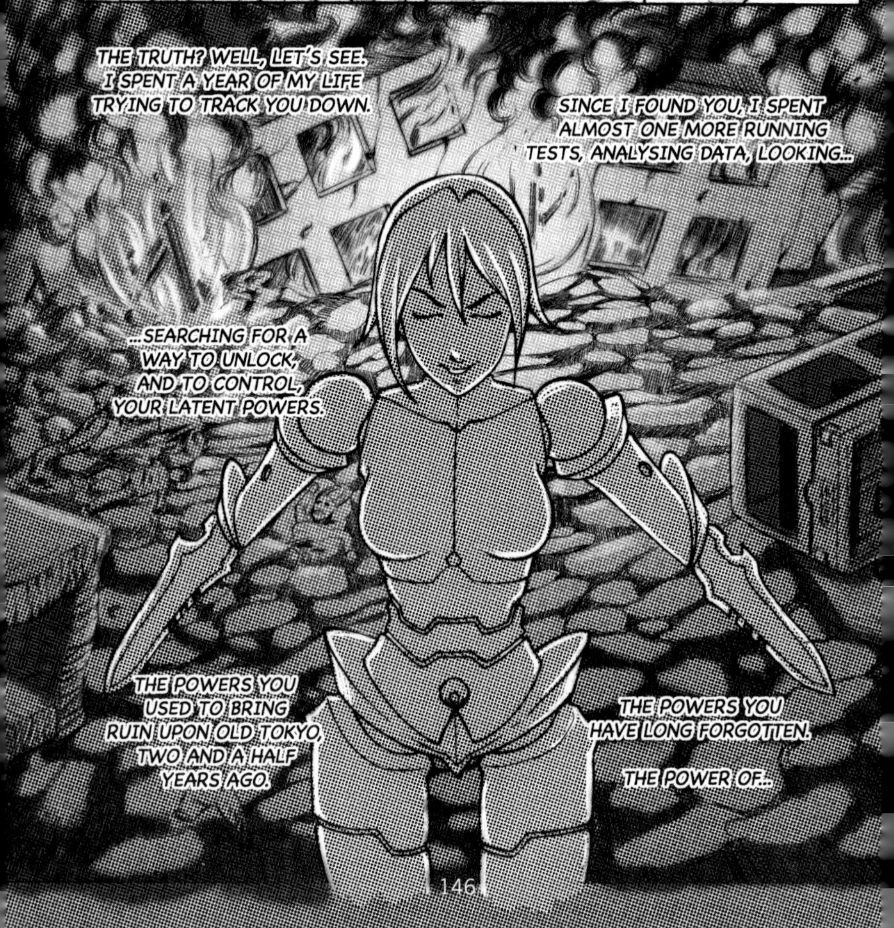
THE TRUTH? WELL, LET'S SEE. I SPENT A YEAR OF MY LIFE TRYING TO TRACK YOU DOWN.
SINCE I FOUND YOU, I SPENT ALMOST ONE MORE RUNNING TESTS, ANALYSING DATA, LOOKING...
...SEARCHING FOR A WAY TO UNLOCK, AND TO CONTROL, YOUR LATENT POWERS.
THE POWERS YOU USED TO BRING RUIN UPON OLD TOKYO, TWO AND A HALF YEARS AGO.
THE POWERS YOU HAVE LONG FORGOTTEN.
THE POWER OF...

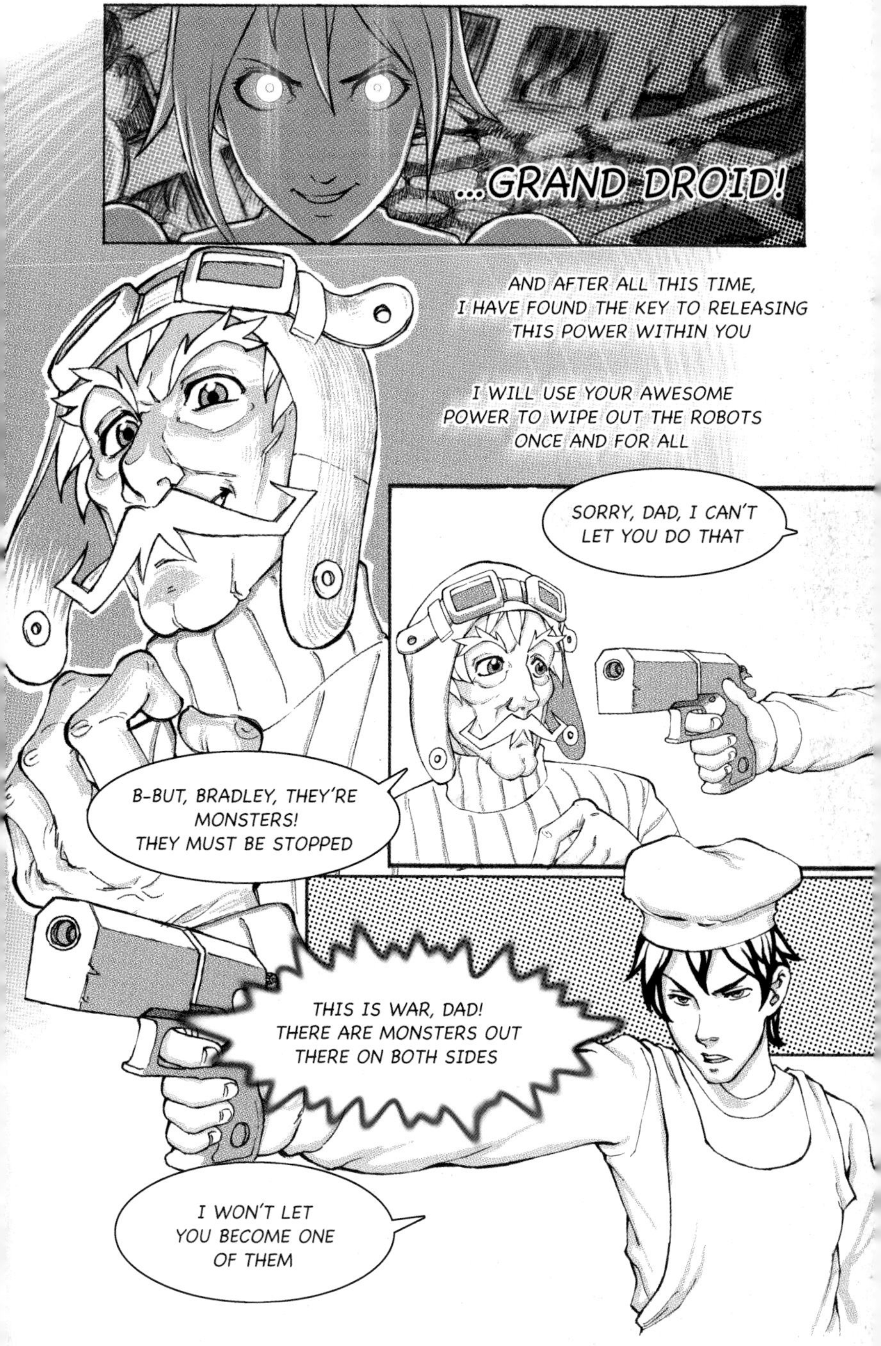
...GRAND DROID!
AND AFTER ALL THIS TIME, I HAVE FOUND THE KEY TO RELEASING THIS POWER WITHIN YOU
I WILL USE YOUR AWESOME POWER TO WIPE OUT THE ROBOTS ONCE AND FOR ALL
SORRY, DAD, I CAN'T LET YOU DO THAT
B-BUT, BRADLEY, THEY'RE MONSTERS! THEY MUST BE STOPPED
THIS IS WAR, DAD! THERE ARE MONSTERS OUT THERE ON BOTH SIDES
I WON'T LET YOU BECOME ONE OF THEM

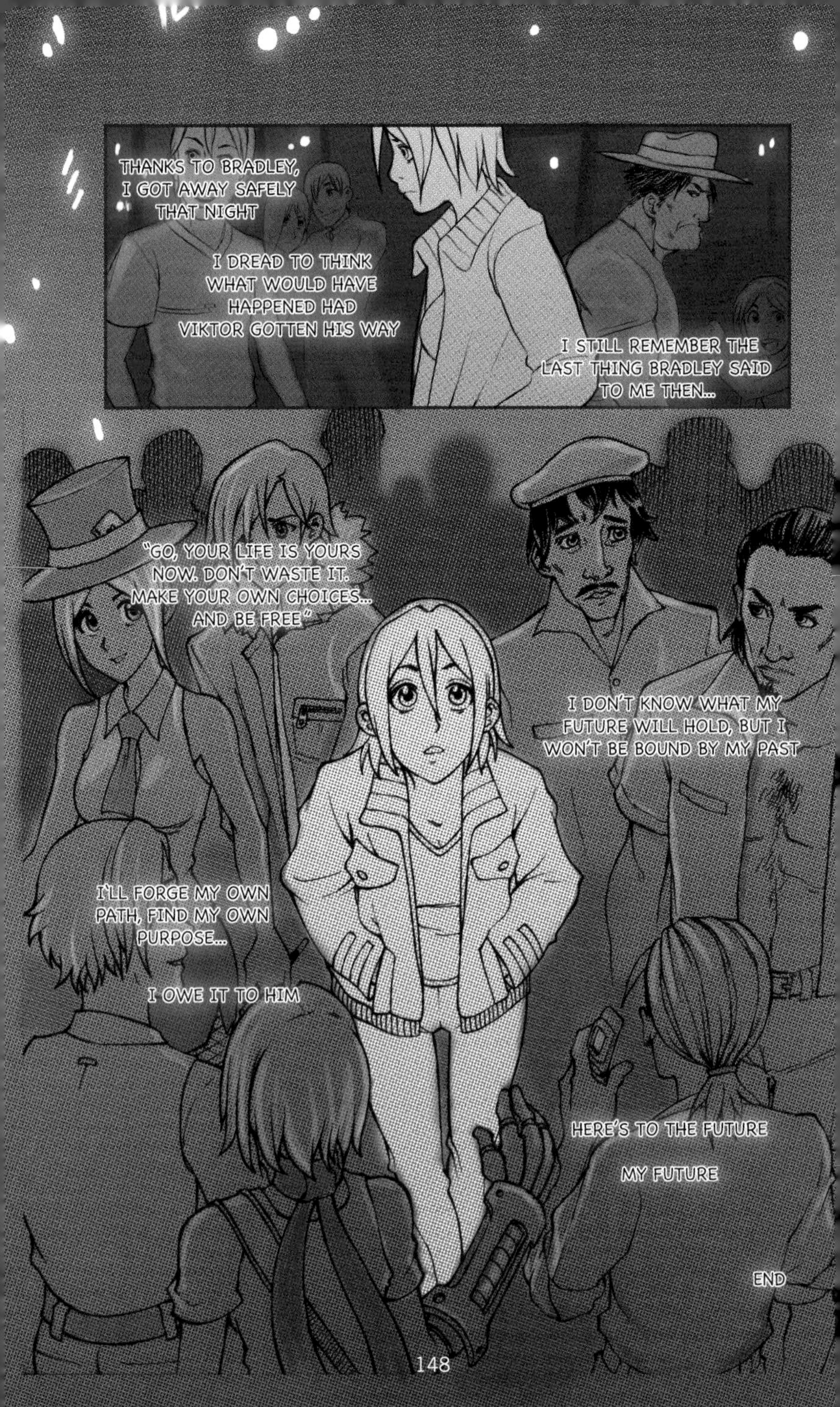
THANKS TO BRADLEY, I GOT AWAY SAFELY THAT NIGHT
I DREAD TO THINK WHAT WOULD HAVE HAPPENED HAD VIKTOR GOTTEN HIS WAY
I STILL REMEMBER THE LAST THING BRADLEY SAID TO ME THEN...
"GO, YOUR LIFE IS YOURS NOW. DON'T WASTE IT. MAKE YOUR OWN CHOICES... AND BE FREE"
I DON'T KNOW WHAT MY FUTURE WILL HOLD, BUT I WON'T BE BOUND BY MY PAST
I'LL FORGE MY OWN PATH, FIND MY OWN PURPOSE...
I OWE IT TO HIM
HERE'S TO THE FUTURE
MY FUTURE
END

MANGA JIMAN
漫画自慢
COMPETITION

Competitions are vital to encourage participation in this egalitarian new medium from its young audience. Every year Tokyopop organize their Rising Stars of Manga in both the USA and United Kingdom/Republic of Ireland, and showcase a selection of winners. IMAF is unfortunately no longer with us, but in the UK at least no less than the Cultural Ambassador at the Japanese Embassy has got behind the nascent manga scene, launching MANGA JIMAN, now in its second year. MANGA JIMAN roughly translates as, "having pride in manga". *Best New Manga* again helped in the judging, and is delighted to present the top three prizewinning entries, shown here in reverse order. Each story is only six pages in length – itself an achievement in concise storytelling, in a medium favouring long form such as manga.

MANGA JIMAN

The top three entries

3rd **THIRD: Michael "Kriffix" Kacar,** with *Ramen Jiman*. A self-confessed *shonen* manga fanatic, Michael likes how it "combines personal aspirations with morals of loyalty and camaraderie. That is True *shonen* power! To shake every fibre of your being!" When he was thirteen he ventured up to Central London in search of ramen noodles. "The first Japanese food I'd ever tried, I have loved it ever since. I enjoy Shoyo Chicken Ramen the most. Simple is best!" Amazingly, when Michael created his winning entry he was only sixteen.

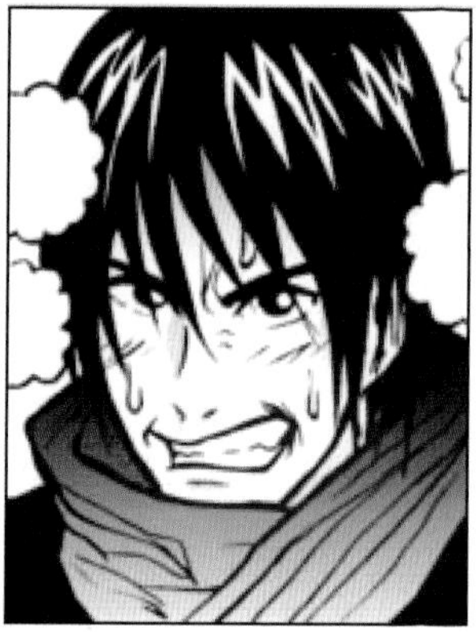

www.kriffix.deviantart.com
www.kriffix.com

2nd **SECOND: Asia Alfasi**, with *Beginnings*. Longtime *BNM* readers will already be familiar with Asia, who also appeared in our first volume. She hopes one day soon to continue with *JinNarration*, but meanwhile has been working on *Ewa*, a two-book autobiographical graphic novel for Bloomsbury. As for Manga Jiman, she says: "Many people today criticize us for being unoriginal, or just jumping on the manga bandwagon. I wanted to say that no, it's not like that, at least for me. Manga isn't just an attractive form of "cartoons": it can have deep connotations and meanings for people. More than just entertainment, it can achieve serious objectives in real life. Don't bully people you know nothing about, because they too might have a rich history, and experiences of which you know nothing."

1st **FIRST: Gillian Sein Ying Ha** with *Darumafish*. This is followed by a second short story that was especially commissioned for this volume, and finally there's a short interview.

Ramen Jiman

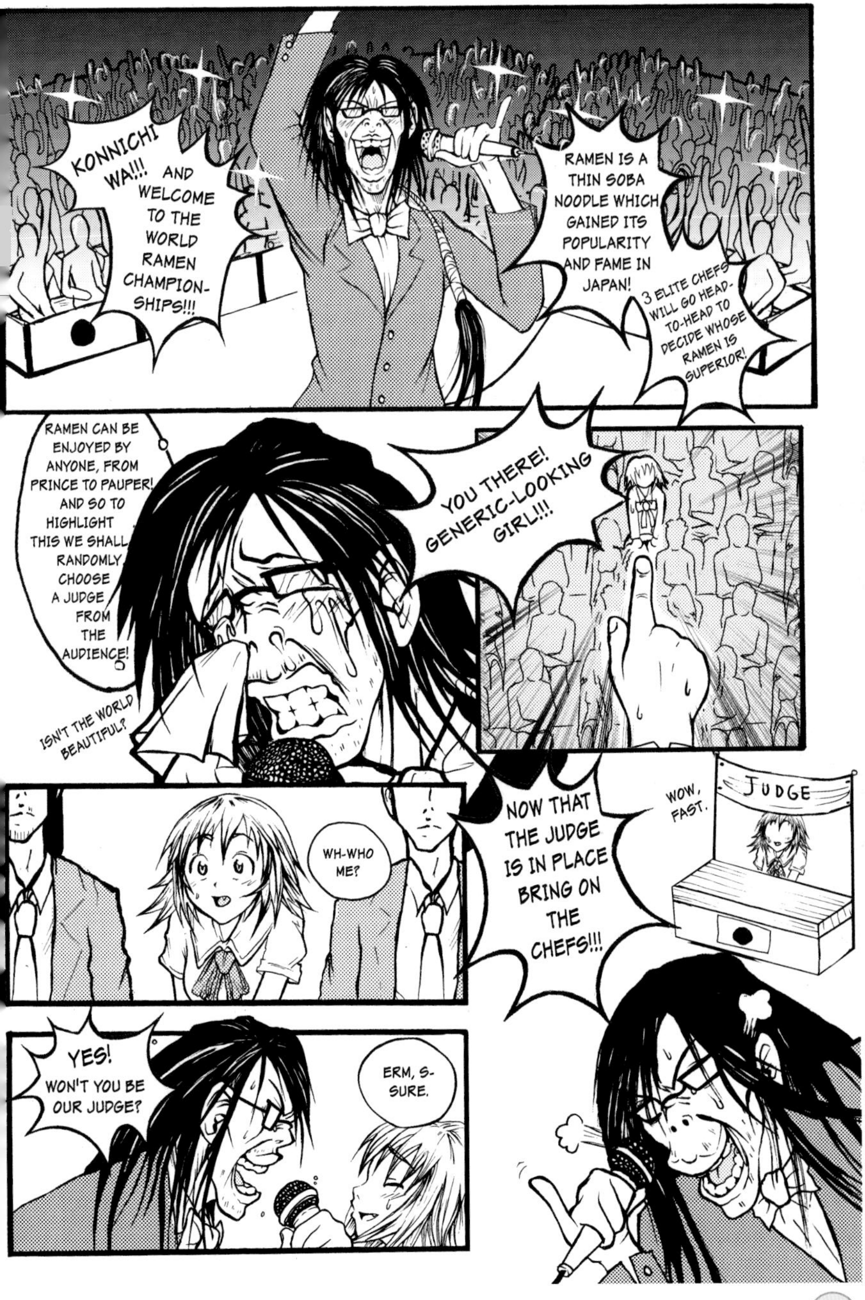
KONNICHI WA!!! AND WELCOME TO THE WORLD RAMEN CHAMPION-SHIPS!!!
RAMEN IS A THIN SOBA NOODLE WHICH GAINED ITS POPULARITY AND FAME IN JAPAN!
3 ELITE CHEFS WILL GO HEAD-TO-HEAD TO DECIDE WHOSE RAMEN IS SUPERIOR!
RAMEN CAN BE ENJOYED BY ANYONE, FROM PRINCE TO PAUPER! AND SO TO HIGHLIGHT THIS WE SHALL RANDOMLY CHOOSE A JUDGE FROM THE AUDIENCE!
ISN'T THE WORLD BEAUTIFUL?
YOU THERE! GENERIC-LOOKING GIRL!!!
WH-WHO ME?
YES! WON'T YOU BE OUR JUDGE?
ERM, S-SURE.
NOW THAT THE JUDGE IS IN PLACE BRING ON THE CHEFS!!!
WOW, FAST.
JUDGE

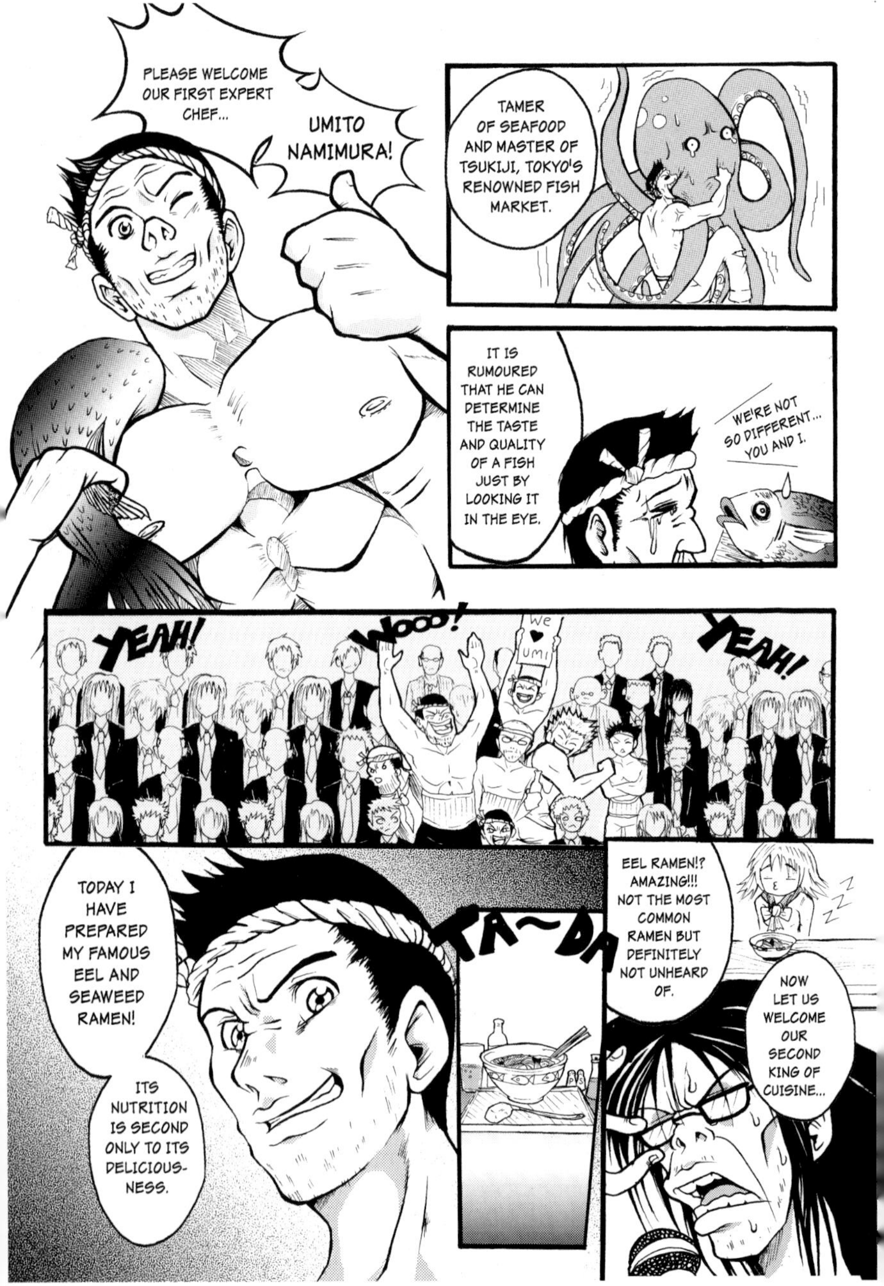
PLEASE WELCOME OUR FIRST EXPERT CHEF...
UMITO NAMIMURA!
TAMER OF SEAFOOD AND MASTER OF TSUKIJI, TOKYO'S RENOWNED FISH MARKET.
IT IS RUMOURED THAT HE CAN DETERMINE THE TASTE AND QUALITY OF A FISH JUST BY LOOKING IT IN THE EYE.
WE'RE NOT SO DIFFERENT... YOU AND I.
YEAH!
WOOO!
We ♥ UMI
YEAH!
TODAY I HAVE PREPARED MY FAMOUS EEL AND SEAWEED RAMEN!
ITS NUTRITION IS SECOND ONLY TO ITS DELICIOUS-NESS.
TA~DA
EEL RAMEN!? AMAZING!!! NOT THE MOST COMMON RAMEN BUT DEFINITELY NOT UNHEARD OF.
NOW LET US WELCOME OUR SECOND KING OF CUISINE...

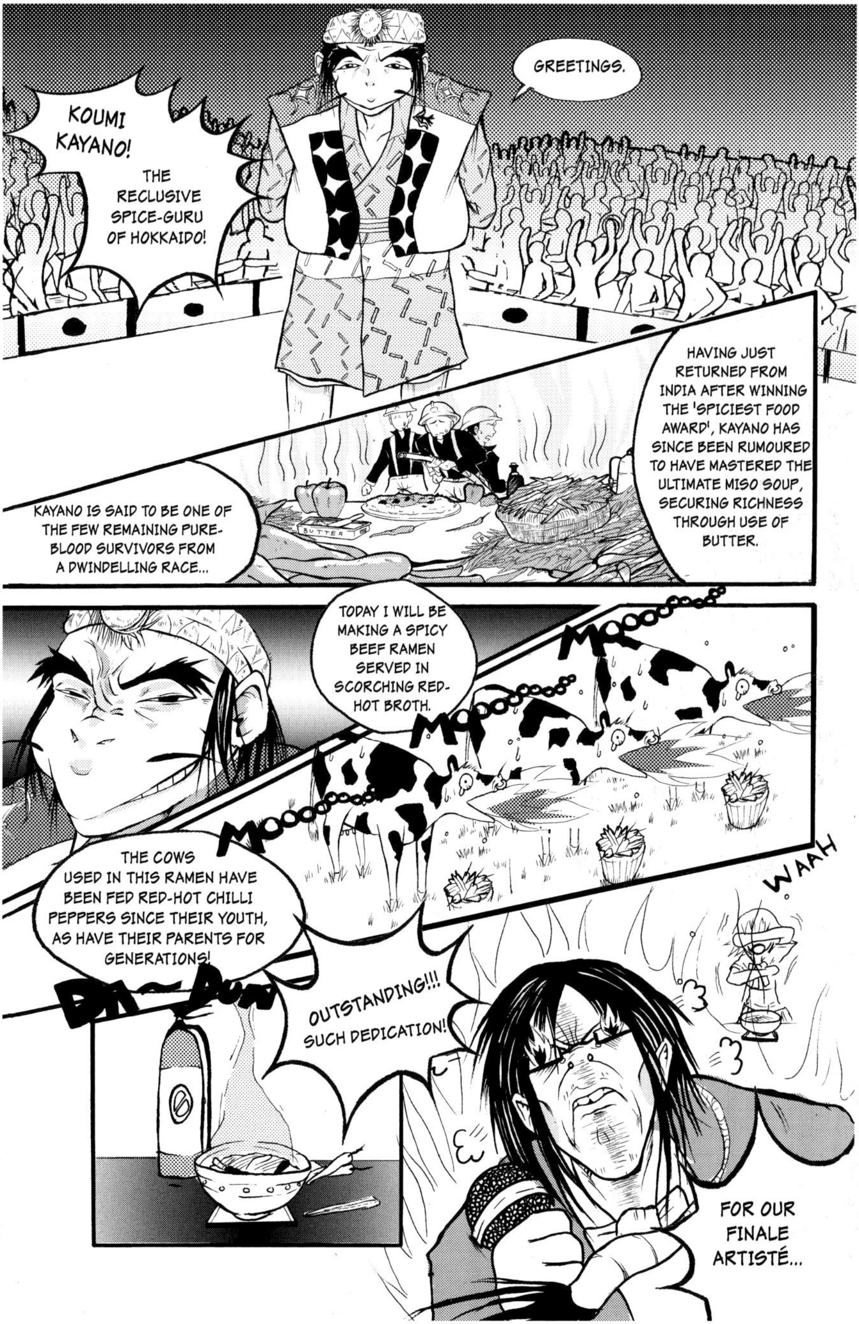
KOUMI KAYANO!
THE RECLUSIVE SPICE-GURU OF HOKKAIDO!
GREETINGS.
KAYANO IS SAID TO BE ONE OF THE FEW REMAINING PURE-BLOOD SURVIVORS FROM A DWINDELLING RACE...
BUTTER
HAVING JUST RETURNED FROM INDIA AFTER WINNING THE 'SPICIEST FOOD AWARD', KAYANO HAS SINCE BEEN RUMOURED TO HAVE MASTERED THE ULTIMATE MISO SOUP, SECURING RICHNESS THROUGH USE OF BUTTER.
TODAY I WILL BE MAKING A SPICY BEEF RAMEN SERVED IN SCORCHING RED-HOT BROTH.
MOOOOOOO
MOOOOOOO
MOOOOOO
THE COWS USED IN THIS RAMEN HAVE BEEN FED RED-HOT CHILLI PEPPERS SINCE THEIR YOUTH, AS HAVE THEIR PARENTS FOR GENERATIONS!
WAAH
DA~DUN
OUTSTANDING!!! SUCH DEDICATION!
FOR OUR FINALE ARTISTÉ...

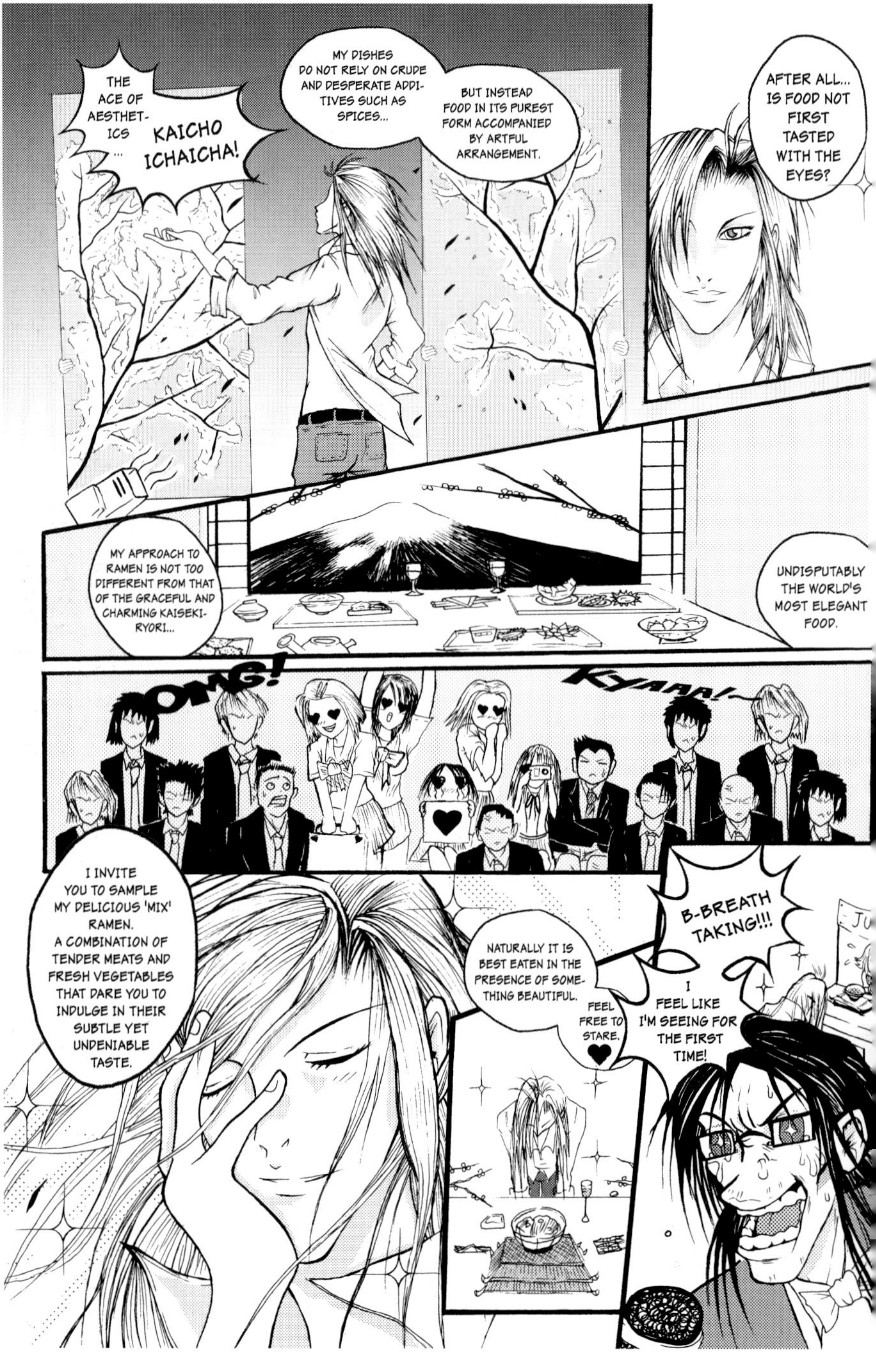
THE ACE OF AESTHETICS ... KAICHO ICHAICHA!
MY DISHES DO NOT RELY ON CRUDE AND DESPERATE ADDITIVES SUCH AS SPICES...
BUT INSTEAD FOOD IN ITS PUREST FORM ACCOMPANIED BY ARTFUL ARRANGEMENT.
AFTER ALL... IS FOOD NOT FIRST TASTED WITH THE EYES?
MY APPROACH TO RAMEN IS NOT TOO DIFFERENT FROM THAT OF THE GRACEFUL AND CHARMING KAISEKI-RYORI...
UNDISPUTABLY THE WORLD'S MOST ELEGANT FOOD.
OMG!
KYAAAA!
I INVITE YOU TO SAMPLE MY DELICIOUS 'MIX' RAMEN. A COMBINATION OF TENDER MEATS AND FRESH VEGETABLES THAT DARE YOU TO INDULGE IN THEIR SUBTLE YET UNDENIABLE TASTE.
NATURALLY IT IS BEST EATEN IN THE PRESENCE OF SOMETHING BEAUTIFUL.
FEEL FREE TO STARE.
B-BREATH TAKING!!!
I FEEL LIKE I'M SEEING FOR THE FIRST TIME!

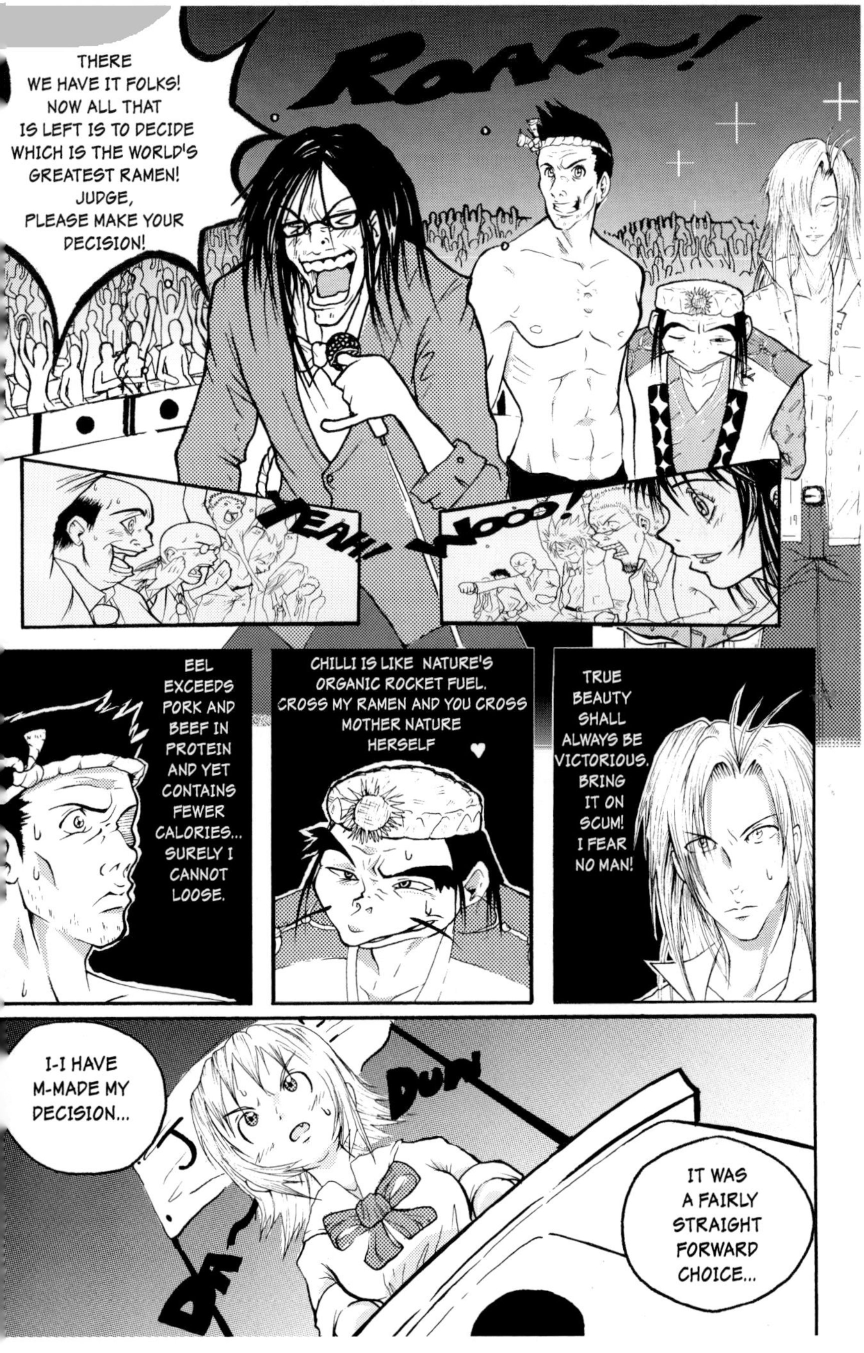
THERE WE HAVE IT FOLKS! NOW ALL THAT IS LEFT IS TO DECIDE WHICH IS THE WORLD'S GREATEST RAMEN! JUDGE, PLEASE MAKE YOUR DECISION!
ROAR~!
YEAH!
WOOO!
EEL EXCEEDS PORK AND BEEF IN PROTEIN AND YET CONTAINS FEWER CALORIES... SURELY I CANNOT LOOSE.
CHILLI IS LIKE NATURE'S ORGANIC ROCKET FUEL. CROSS MY RAMEN AND YOU CROSS MOTHER NATURE HERSELF ♥
TRUE BEAUTY SHALL ALWAYS BE VICTORIOUS. BRING IT ON SCUM! I FEAR NO MAN!
I-I HAVE M-MADE MY DECISION...
DUN
DA~
IT WAS A FAIRLY STRAIGHT FORWARD CHOICE...

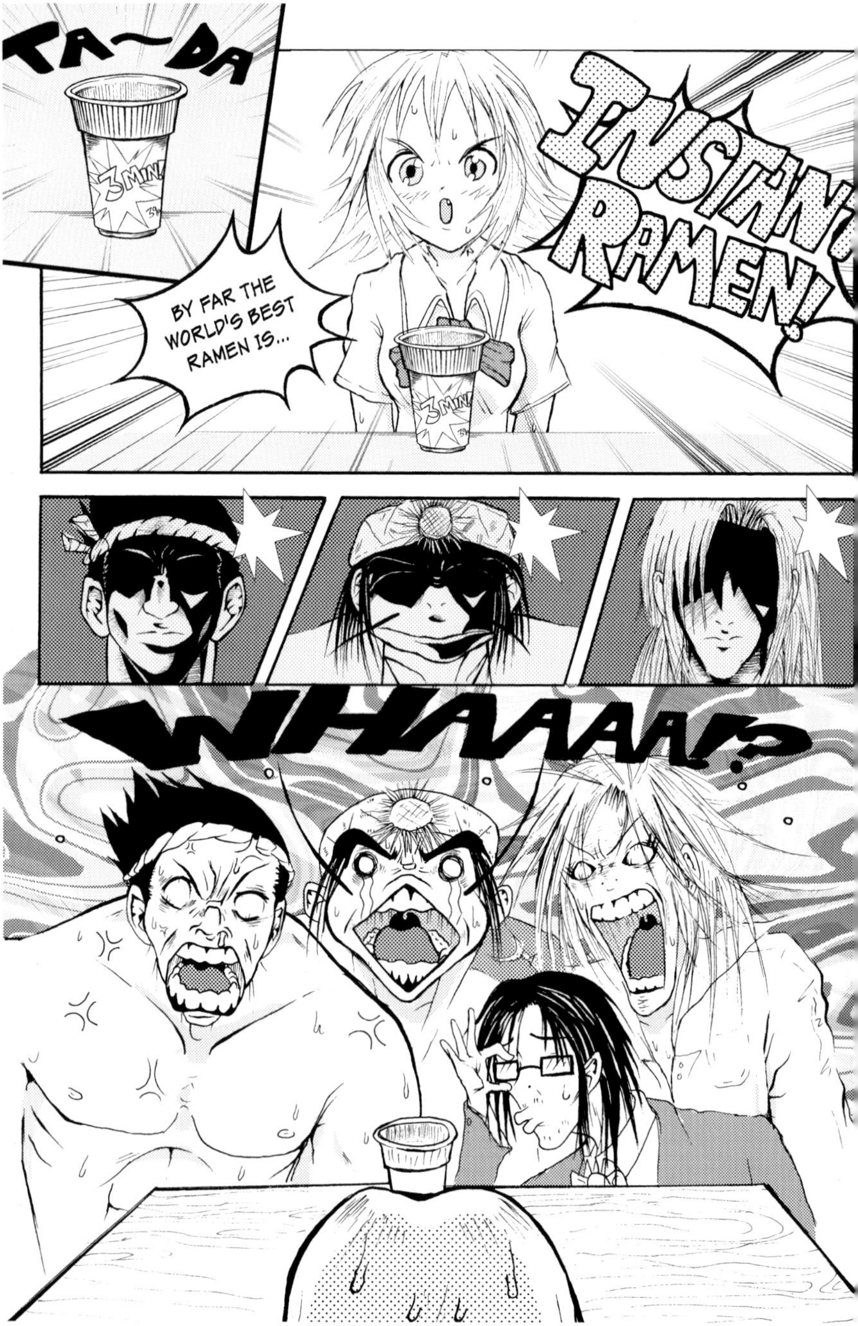
TA~DA
3 MIN!
BY FAR THE WORLD'S BEST RAMEN IS...
INSTANT RAMEN!
3 MIN!
WHAAAAA!?

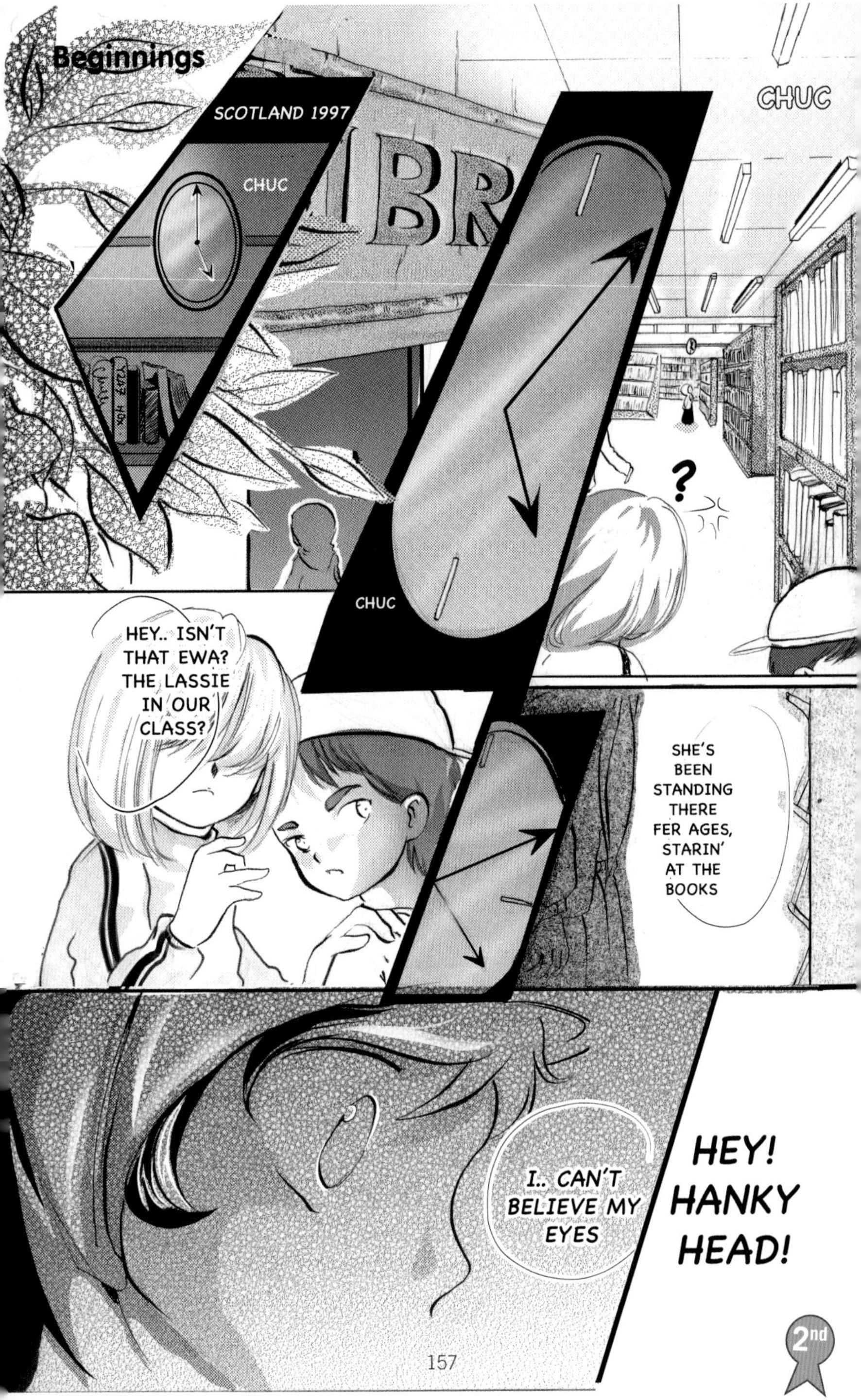
Beginnings
SCOTLAND 1997
CHUC
CHUC
CHUC
?
HEY.. ISN'T THAT EWA? THE LASSIE IN OUR CLASS?
SHE'S BEEN STANDING THERE FER AGES, STARIN' AT THE BOOKS
I.. CAN'T BELIEVE MY EYES
HEY! HANKY HEAD!
2nd

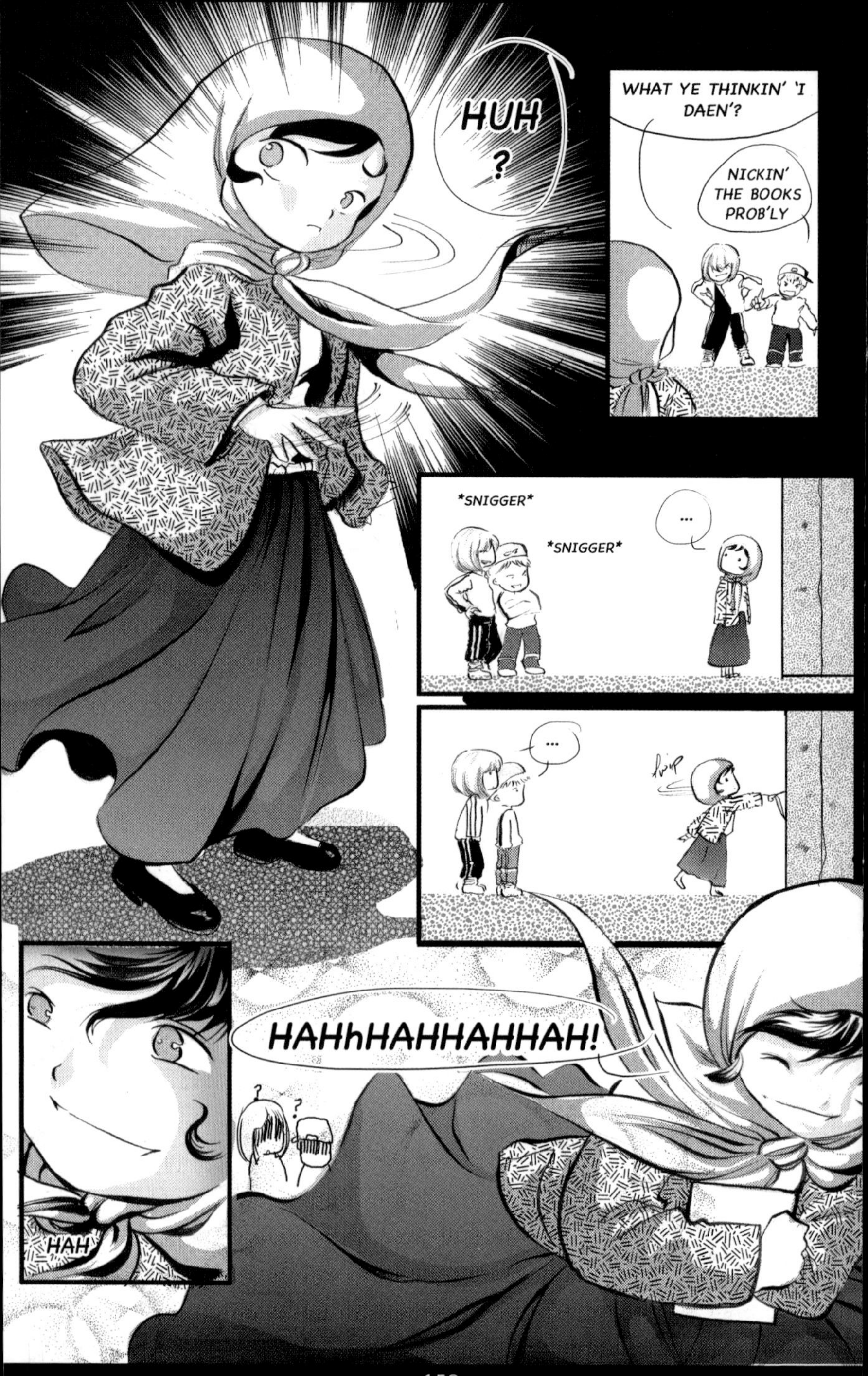
HUH ?
WHAT YE THINKIN' 'I DAEN'?
NICKIN' THE BOOKS PROB'LY
SNIGGER
SNIGGER
...
...
HAH
HAHhHAHHAHHAH!
? ?

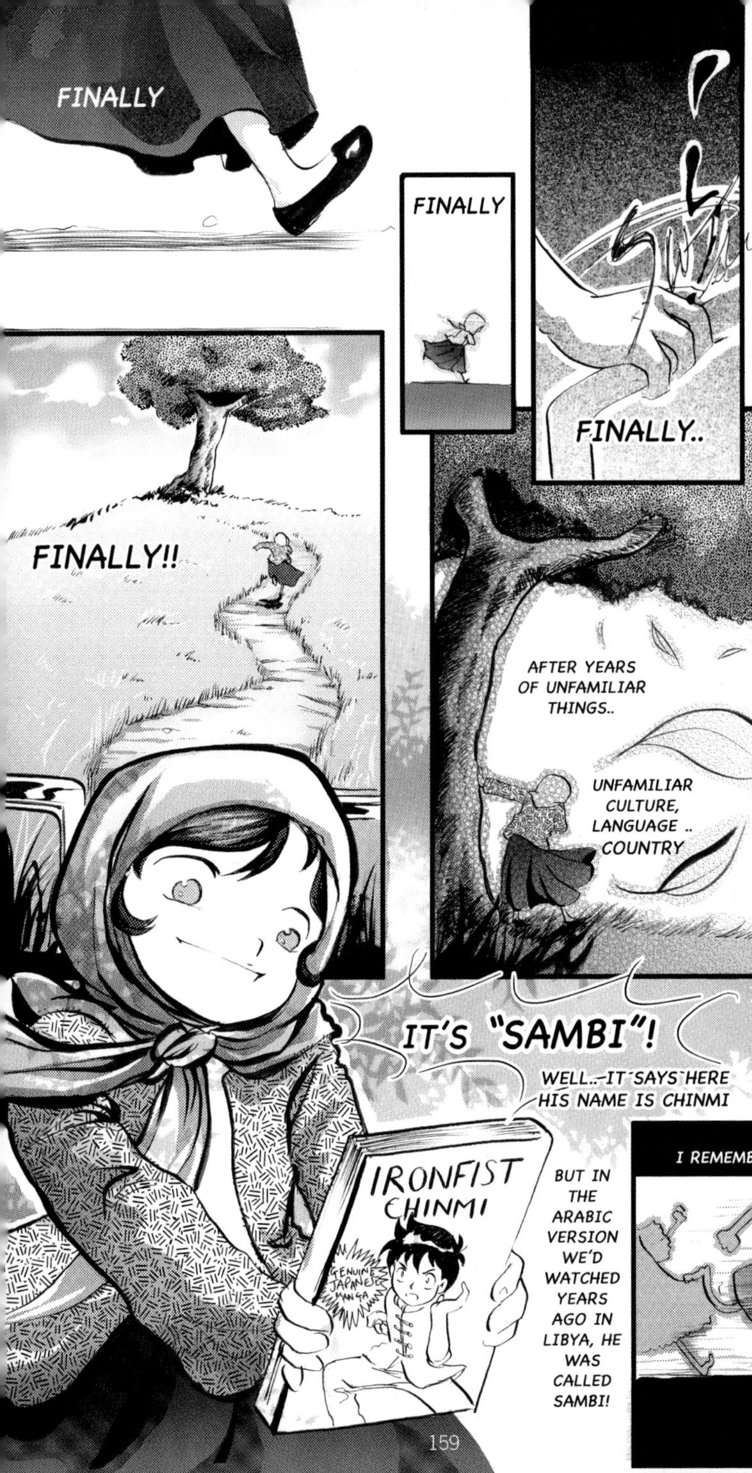
FINALLY
FINALLY
FINALLY..
FINALLY!!
AFTER YEARS OF UNFAMILIAR THINGS..
UNFAMILIAR CULTURE, LANGUAGE .. COUNTRY
IT'S "SAMBI"!
WELL.. IT SAYS HERE HIS NAME IS CHINMI
IRONFIST CHINMI
GENUINE JAPANESE MANGA
BUT IN THE ARABIC VERSION WE'D WATCHED YEARS AGO IN LIBYA, HE WAS CALLED SAMBI!
I REMEMBER...

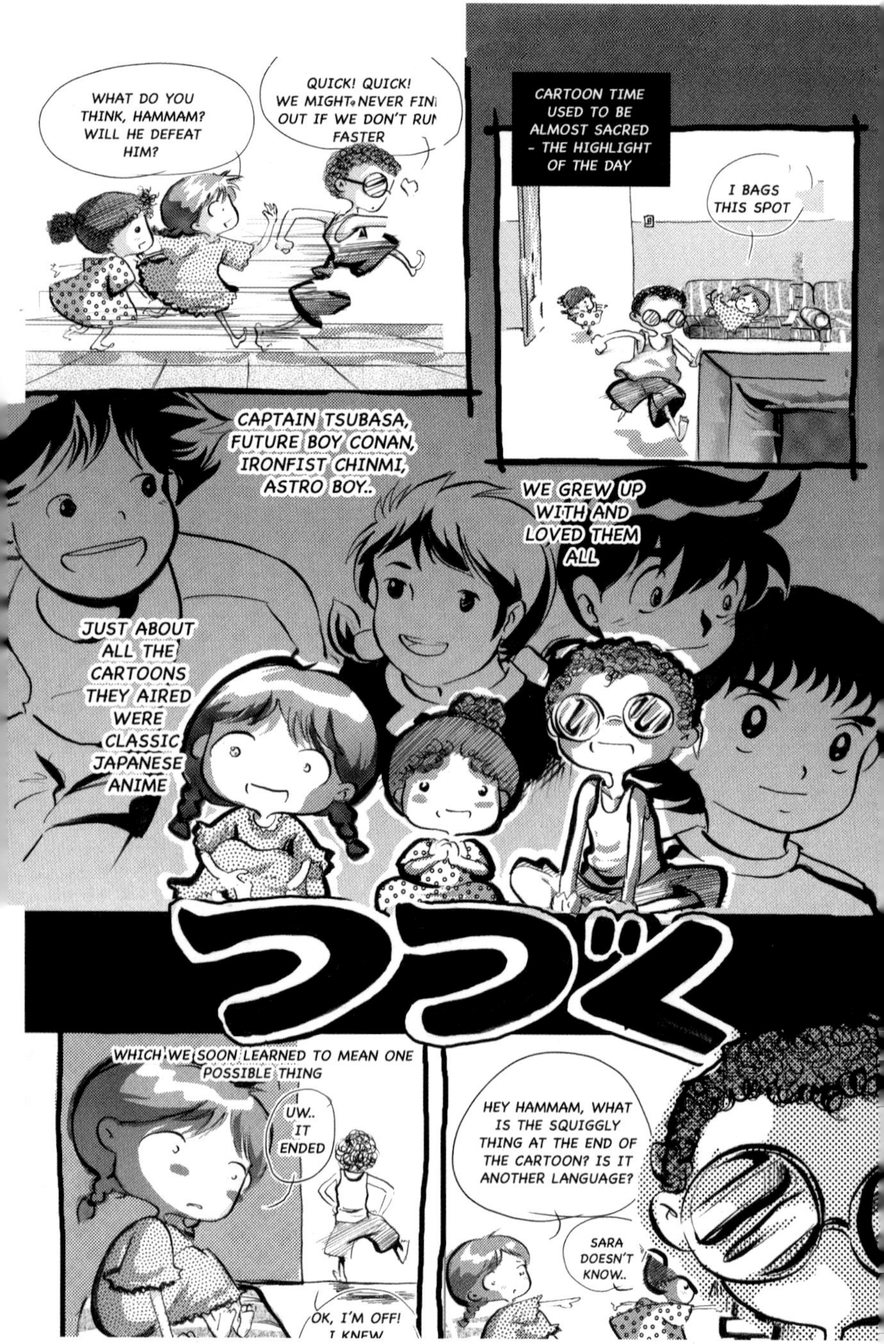
WHAT DO YOU THINK, HAMMAM? WILL HE DEFEAT HIM?
QUICK! QUICK! WE MIGHT NEVER FIN OUT IF WE DON'T RUN FASTER
CARTOON TIME USED TO BE ALMOST SACRED - THE HIGHLIGHT OF THE DAY
I BAGS THIS SPOT
CAPTAIN TSUBASA, FUTURE BOY CONAN, IRONFIST CHINMI, ASTRO BOY..
WE GREW UP WITH AND LOVED THEM ALL
JUST ABOUT ALL THE CARTOONS THEY AIRED WERE CLASSIC JAPANESE ANIME
つづく
WHICH WE SOON LEARNED TO MEAN ONE POSSIBLE THING
UW.. IT ENDED
OK, I'M OFF! I KNEW
HEY HAMMAM, WHAT IS THE SQUIGGLY THING AT THE END OF THE CARTOON? IS IT ANOTHER LANGUAGE?
SARA DOESN'T KNOW..

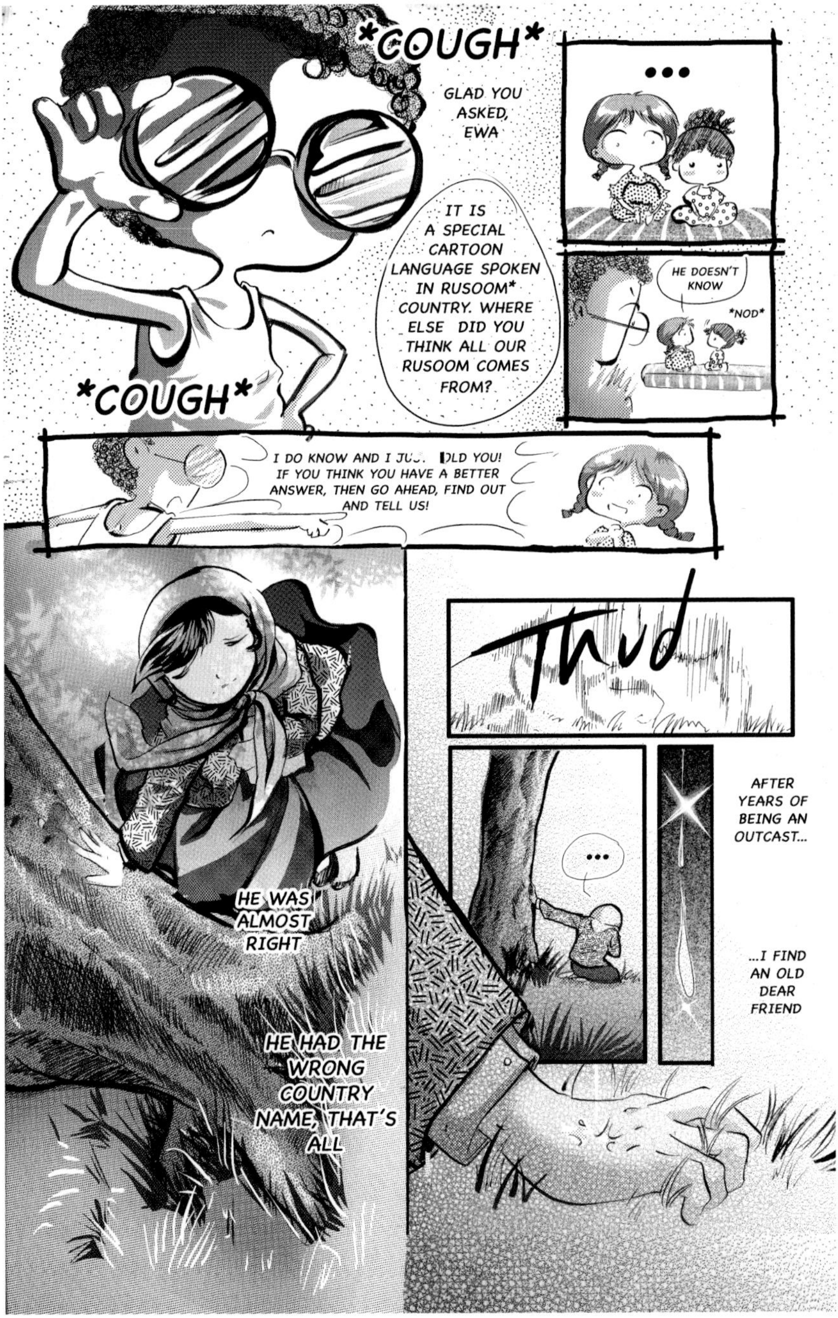
COUGH
GLAD YOU ASKED, EWA
IT IS A SPECIAL CARTOON LANGUAGE SPOKEN IN RUSOOM* COUNTRY. WHERE ELSE DID YOU THINK ALL OUR RUSOOM COMES FROM?
COUGH
...
HE DOESN'T KNOW
NOD
I DO KNOW AND I JU... OLD YOU! IF YOU THINK YOU HAVE A BETTER ANSWER, THEN GO AHEAD, FIND OUT AND TELL US!
HE WAS ALMOST RIGHT
HE HAD THE WRONG COUNTRY NAME, THAT'S ALL
Thud
...
AFTER YEARS OF BEING AN OUTCAST...
...I FIND AN OLD DEAR FRIEND

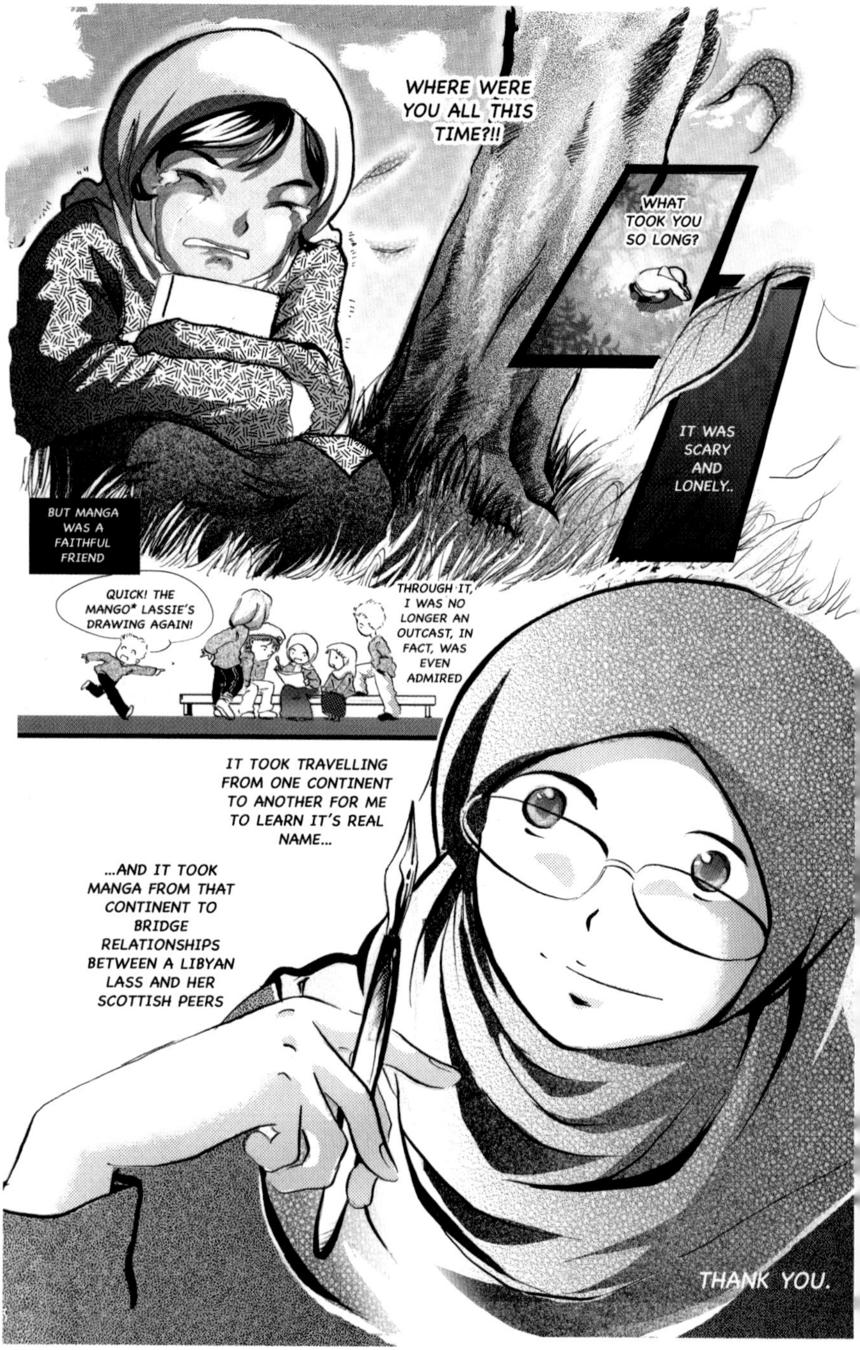
WHERE WERE YOU ALL THIS TIME?!!
WHAT TOOK YOU SO LONG?
IT WAS SCARY AND LONELY..
BUT MANGA WAS A FAITHFUL FRIEND
QUICK! THE MANGO* LASSIE'S DRAWING AGAIN!
THROUGH IT, I WAS NO LONGER AN OUTCAST, IN FACT, WAS EVEN ADMIRED
IT TOOK TRAVELLING FROM ONE CONTINENT TO ANOTHER FOR ME TO LEARN IT'S REAL NAME...
...AND IT TOOK MANGA FROM THAT CONTINENT TO BRIDGE RELATIONSHIPS BETWEEN A LIBYAN LASS AND HER SCOTTISH PEERS
THANK YOU.

Darumafish

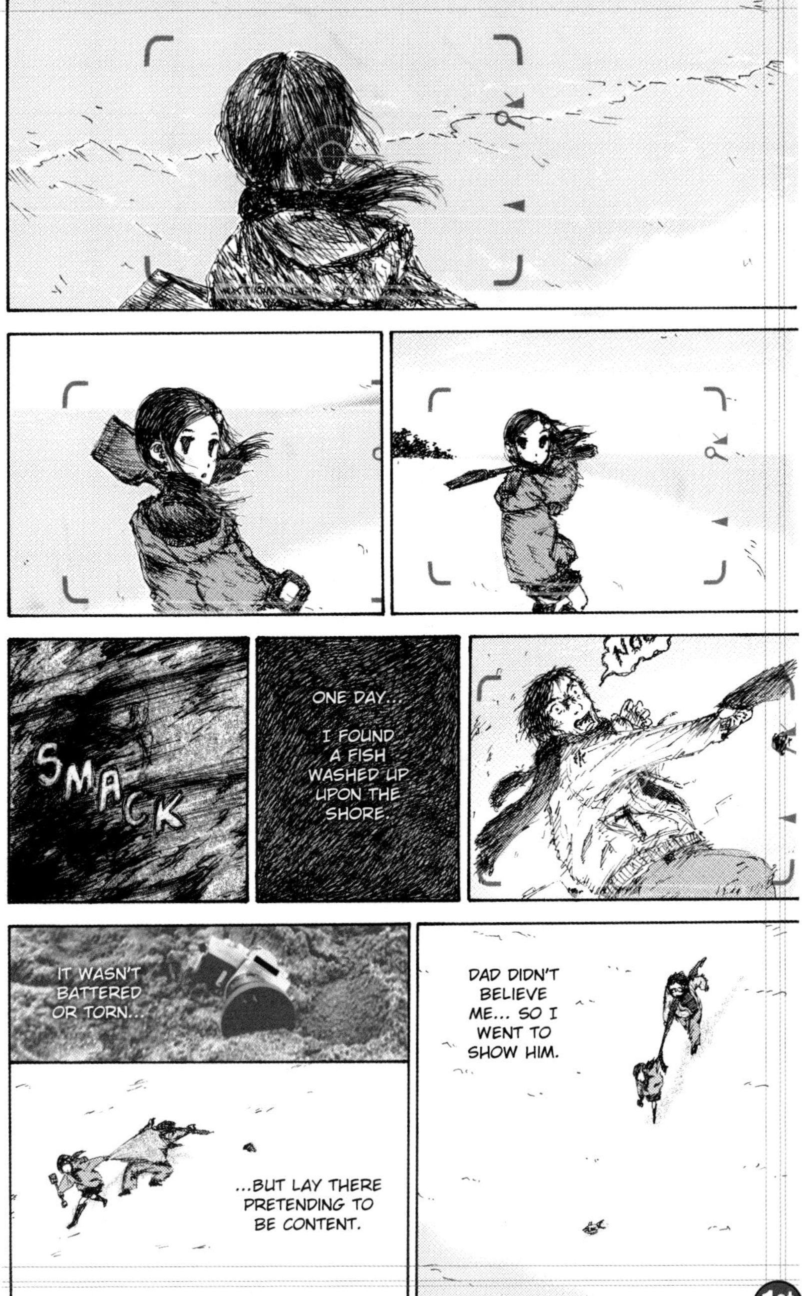
SMACK
ONE DAY... I FOUND A FISH WASHED UP UPON THE SHORE.
IT WASN'T BATTERED OR TORN...
...BUT LAY THERE PRETENDING TO BE CONTENT.
DAD DIDN'T BELIEVE ME... SO I WENT TO SHOW HIM.

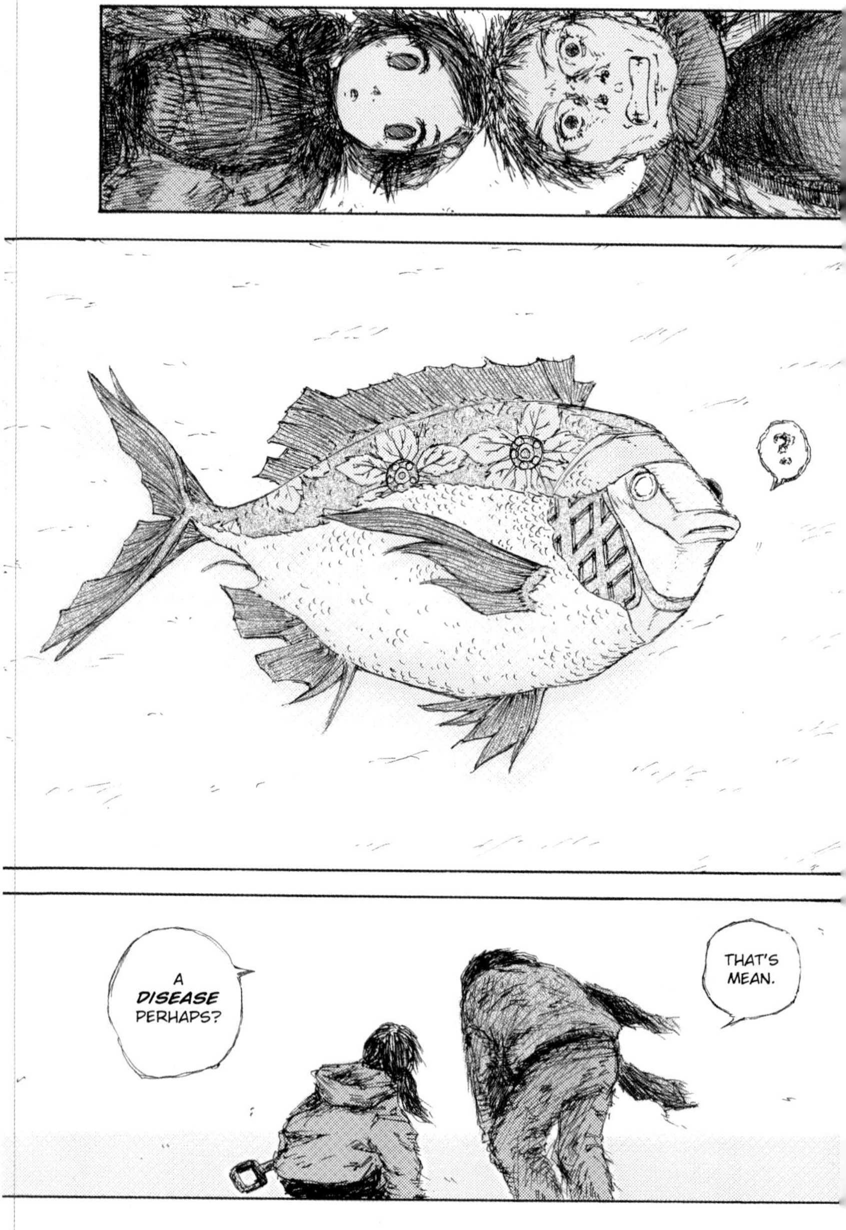
?
A *DISEASE* PERHAPS?
THAT'S MEAN.

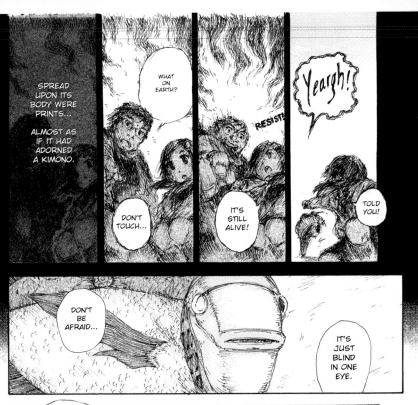

SPREAD UPON ITS BODY WERE PRINTS...

ALMOST AS IF IT HAD ADORNED A KIMONO.

WHAT ON EARTH?

DON'T TOUCH...

IT'S STILL ALIVE!

RESIST...

Yeargh!

TOLD YOU!

DON'T BE AFRAID...

IT'S JUST BLIND IN ONE EYE.

...THAT'S WHY THEY CALL IT THE "DARUMA-FISH".

"DARUMA-FISH"?

THEY COME BLIND FROM HALFWAY DEEP AND SHALLOW IN THE OCEAN.

AS THEY SURFACE THEY GAIN SIGHT FROM ONE EYE.

WAIT...

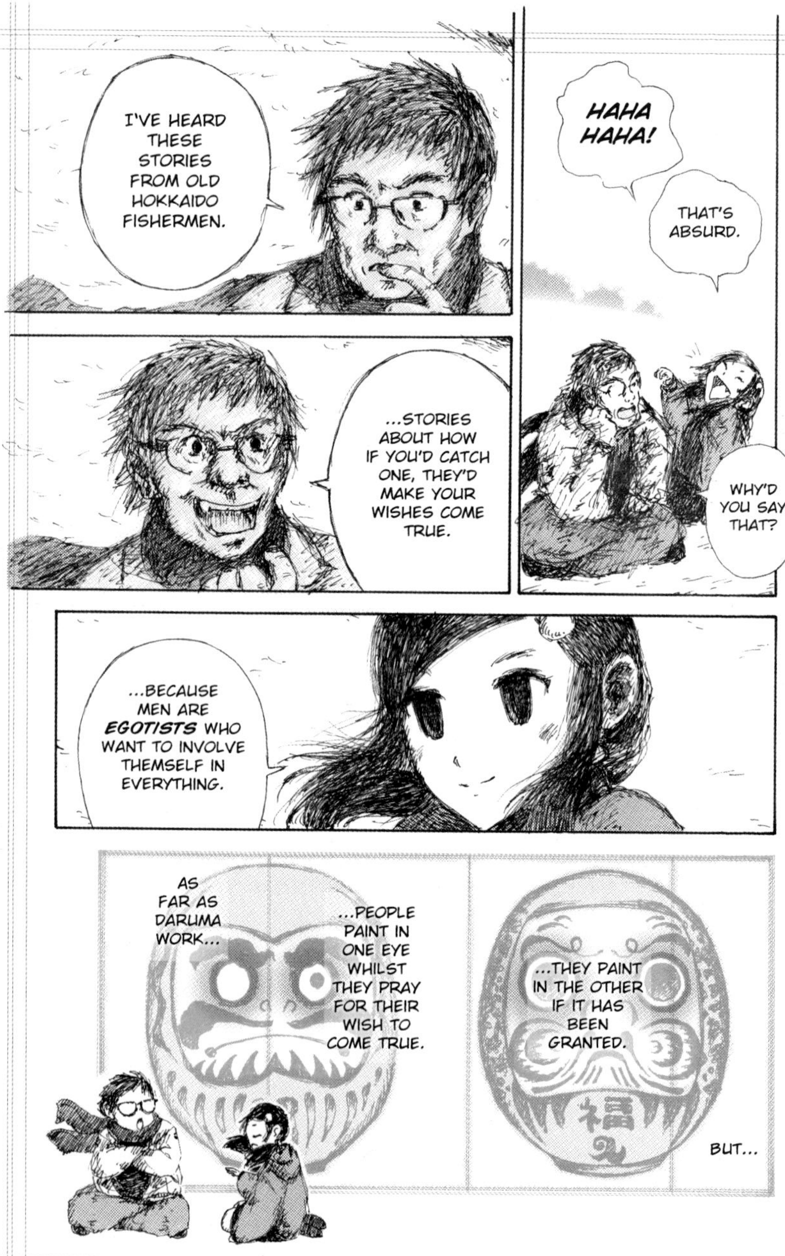
I'VE HEARD THESE STORIES FROM OLD HOKKAIDO FISHERMEN.
HAHA HAHA!
THAT'S ABSURD.
...STORIES ABOUT HOW IF YOU'D CATCH ONE, THEY'D MAKE YOUR WISHES COME TRUE.
WHY'D YOU SAY THAT?
...BECAUSE MEN ARE ***EGOTISTS*** WHO WANT TO INVOLVE THEMSELF IN EVERYTHING.
AS FAR AS DARUMA WORK...
...PEOPLE PAINT IN ONE EYE WHILST THEY PRAY FOR THEIR WISH TO COME TRUE.
...THEY PAINT IN THE OTHER IF IT HAS BEEN GRANTED.
BUT...

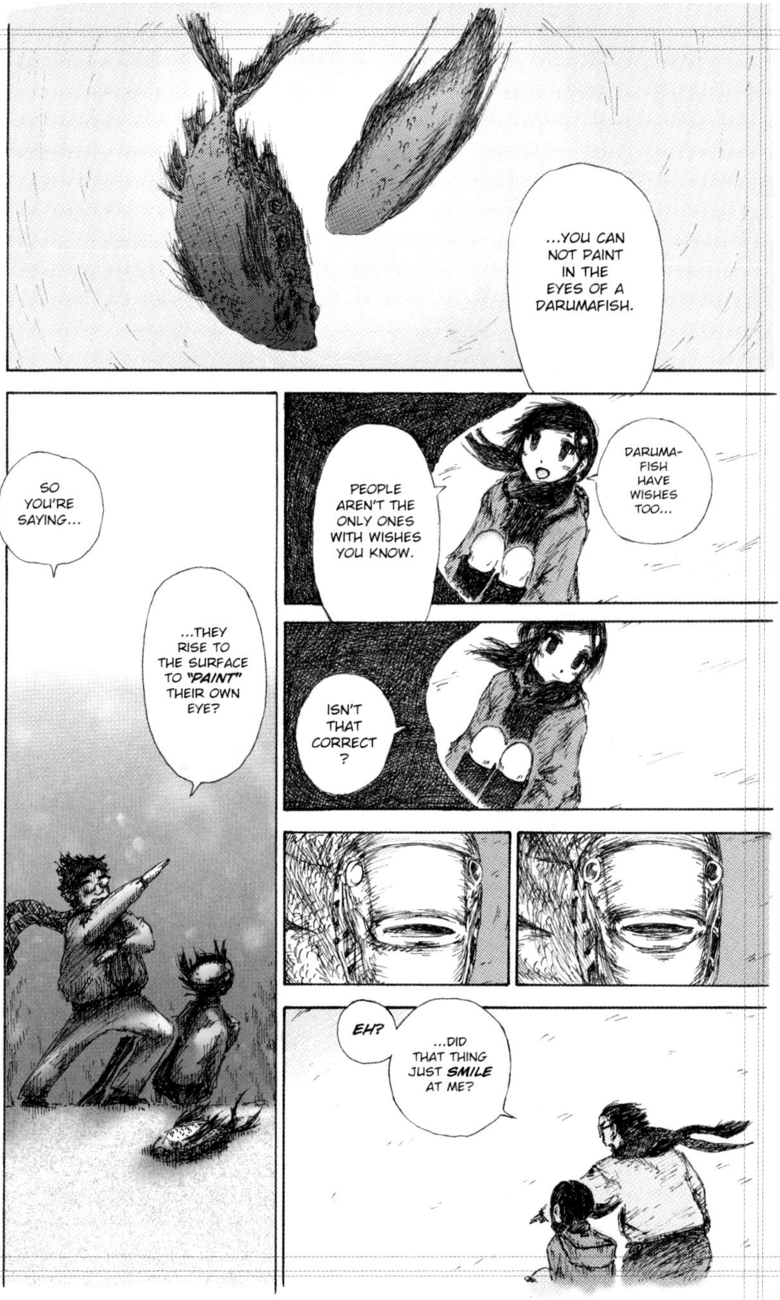
...YOU CAN NOT PAINT IN THE EYES OF A DARUMAFISH.
SO YOU'RE SAYING...
...THEY RISE TO THE SURFACE TO *"PAINT"* THEIR OWN EYE?
PEOPLE AREN'T THE ONLY ONES WITH WISHES YOU KNOW.
DARUMA-FISH HAVE WISHES TOO...
ISN'T THAT CORRECT ?
EH?
...DID THAT THING JUST *SMILE* AT ME?

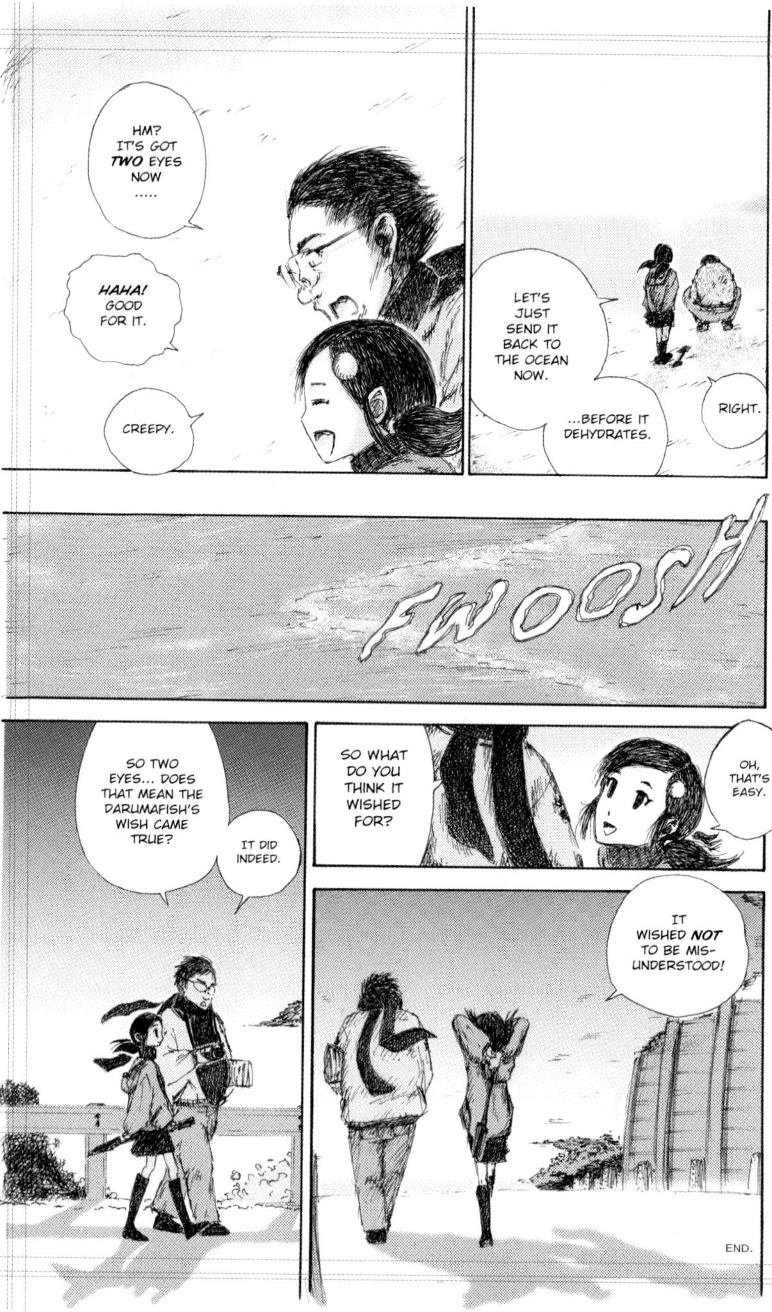
HM? IT'S GOT **TWO** EYES NOW .....
HAHA! GOOD FOR IT.
CREEPY.
LET'S JUST SEND IT BACK TO THE OCEAN NOW.
...BEFORE IT DEHYDRATES.
RIGHT.
FWOOSH
SO TWO EYES... DOES THAT MEAN THE DARUMAFISH'S WISH CAME TRUE?
IT DID INDEED.
SO WHAT DO YOU THINK IT WISHED FOR?
OH, THAT'S EASY.
IT WISHED **NOT** TO BE MIS-UNDERSTOOD!
END.

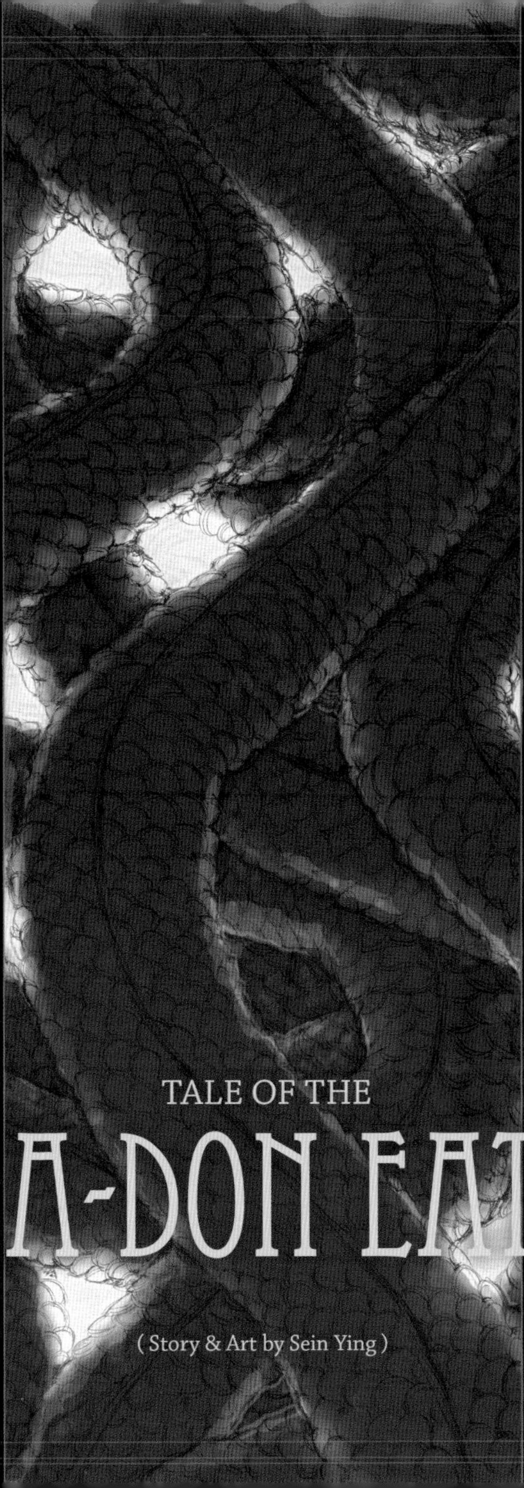

TALE OF THE

UNA-DON EATER

(Story & Art by Sein Ying)

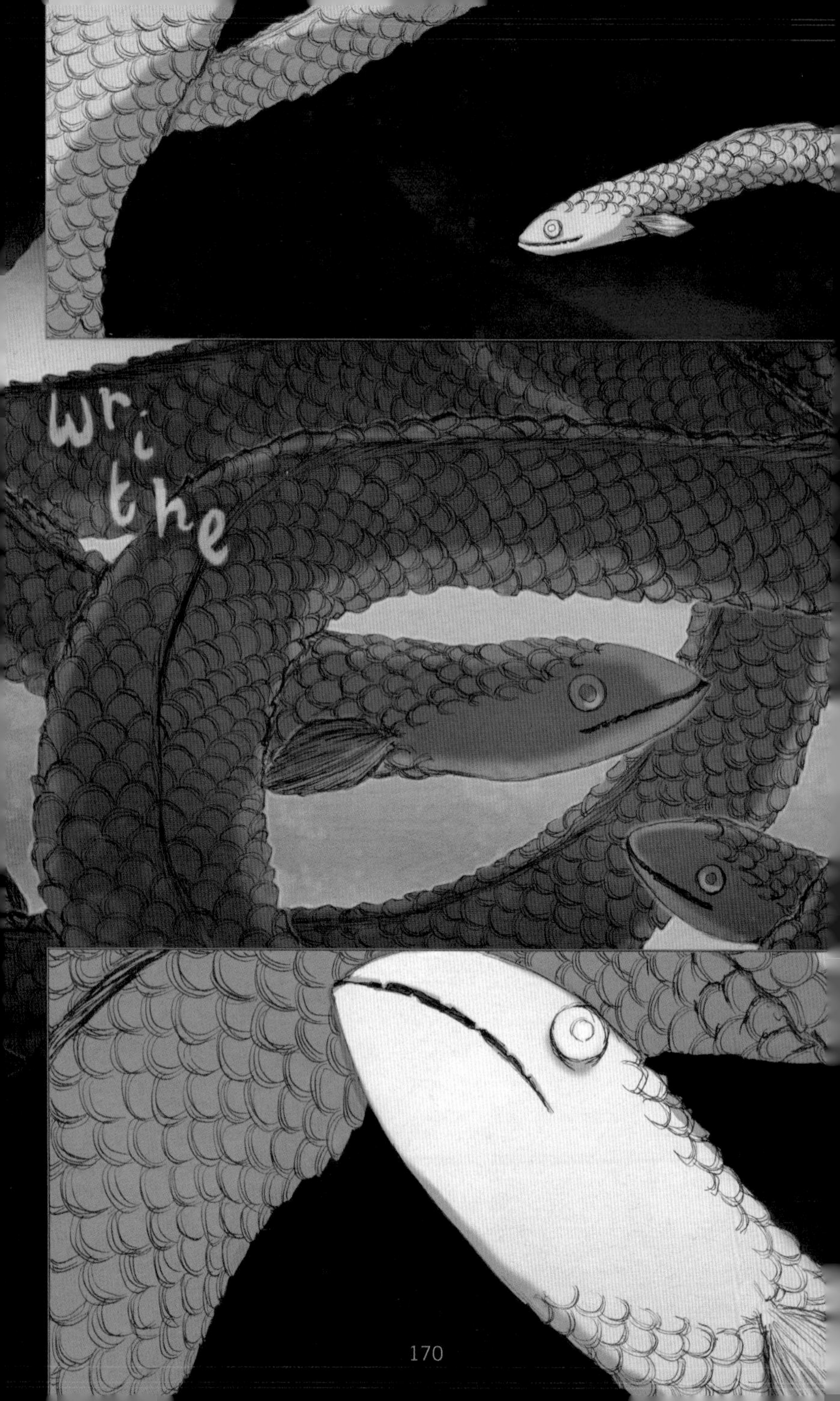
writhe

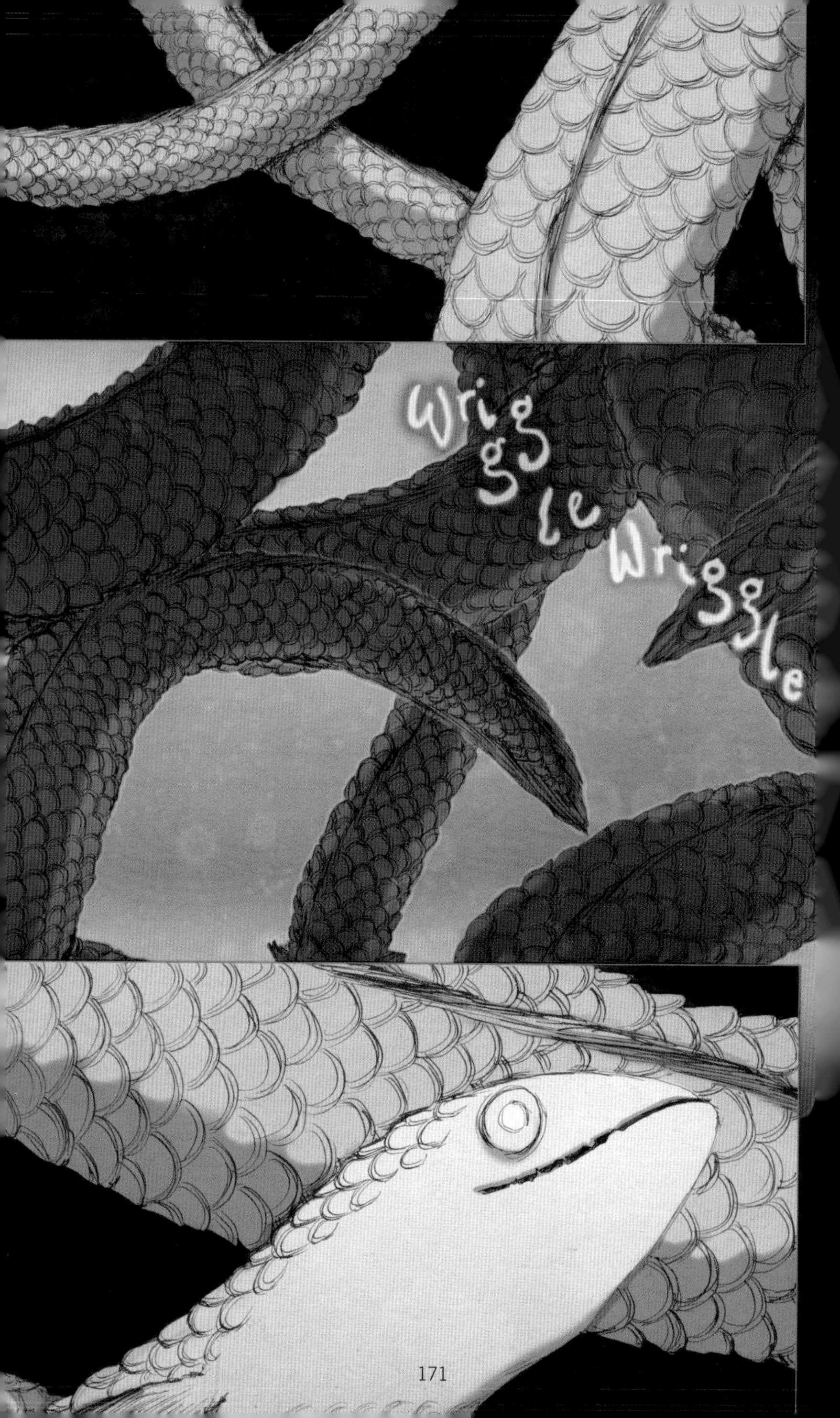
Wriggle
Wriggle

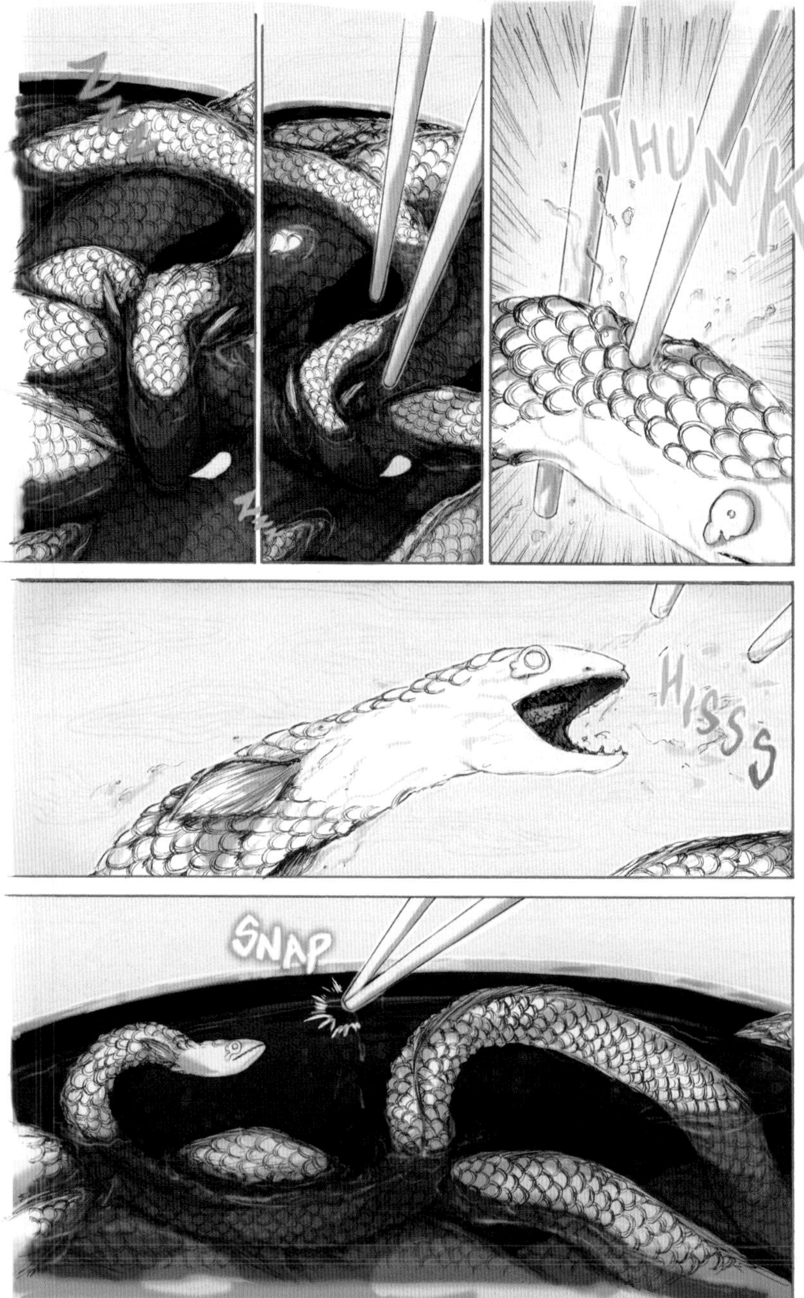
Z Z Z
Z Z Z
THUNK
HISSS
SNAP

GRIP

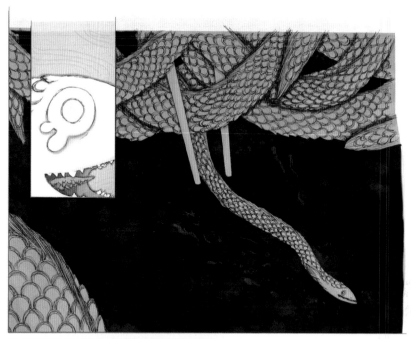

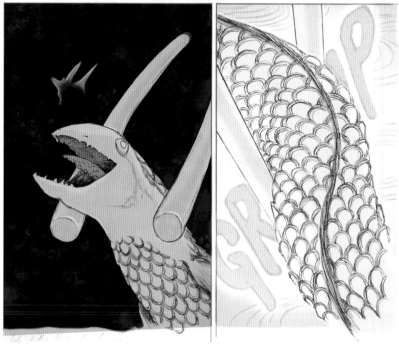

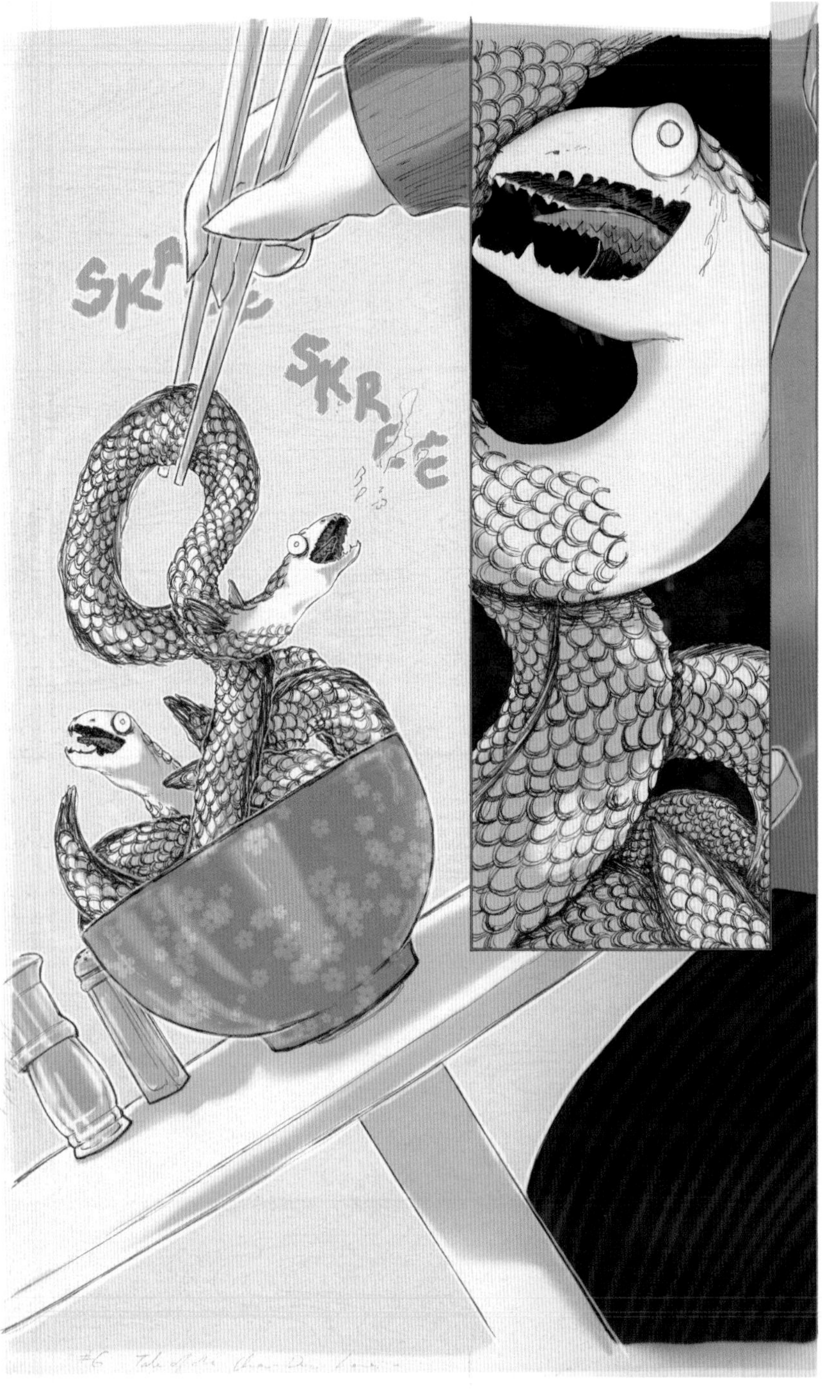
SKREE
SKREE

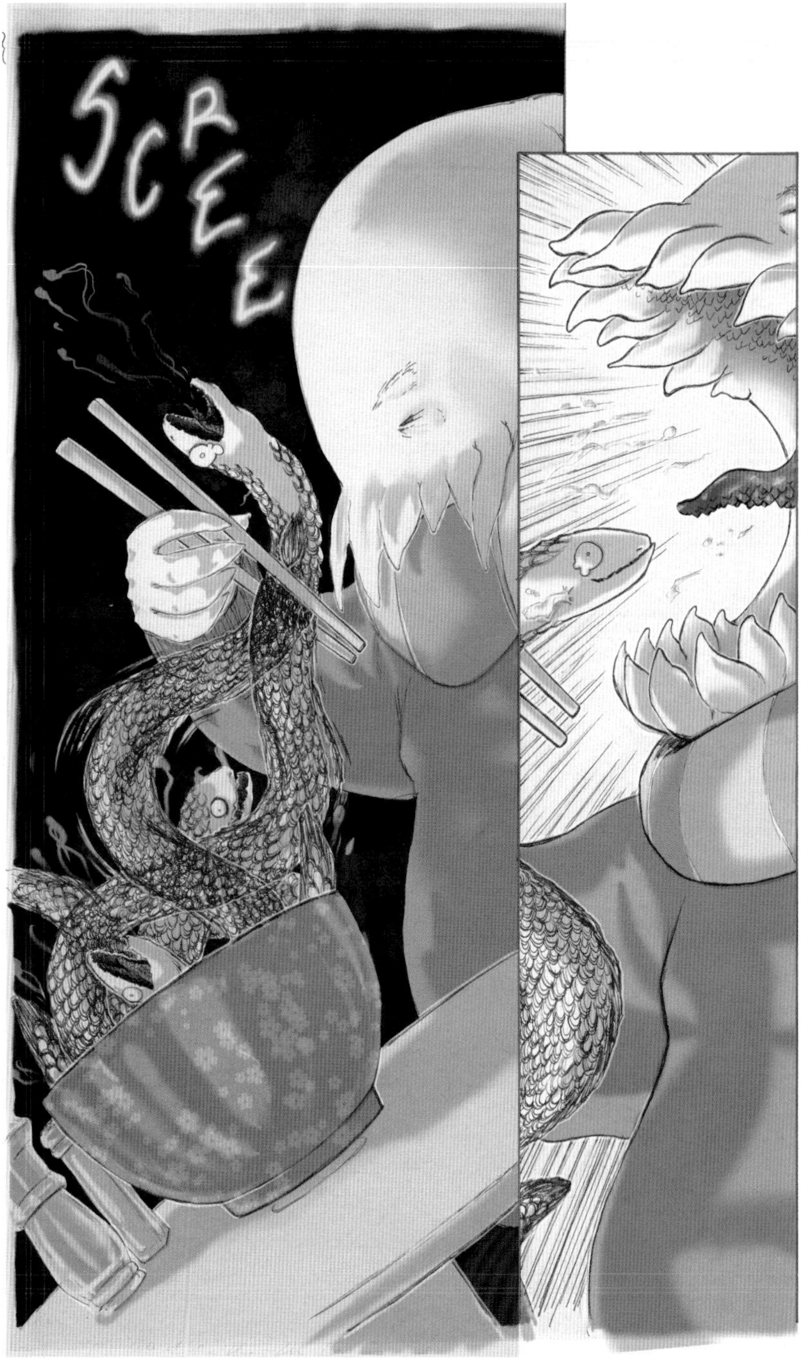
SCREEE

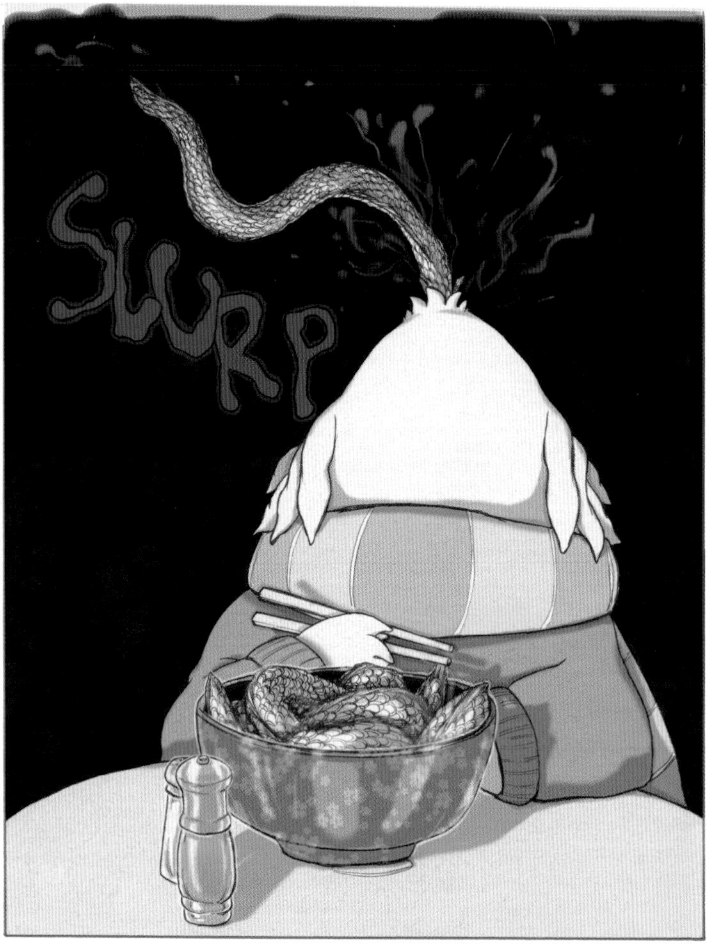
SLURP

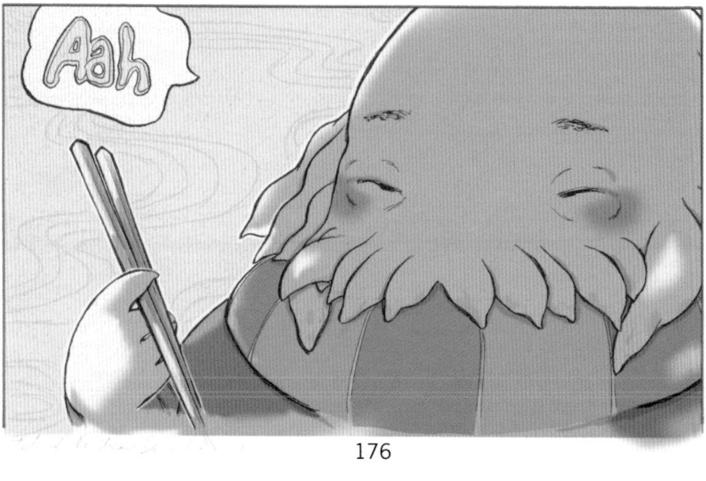
Aah

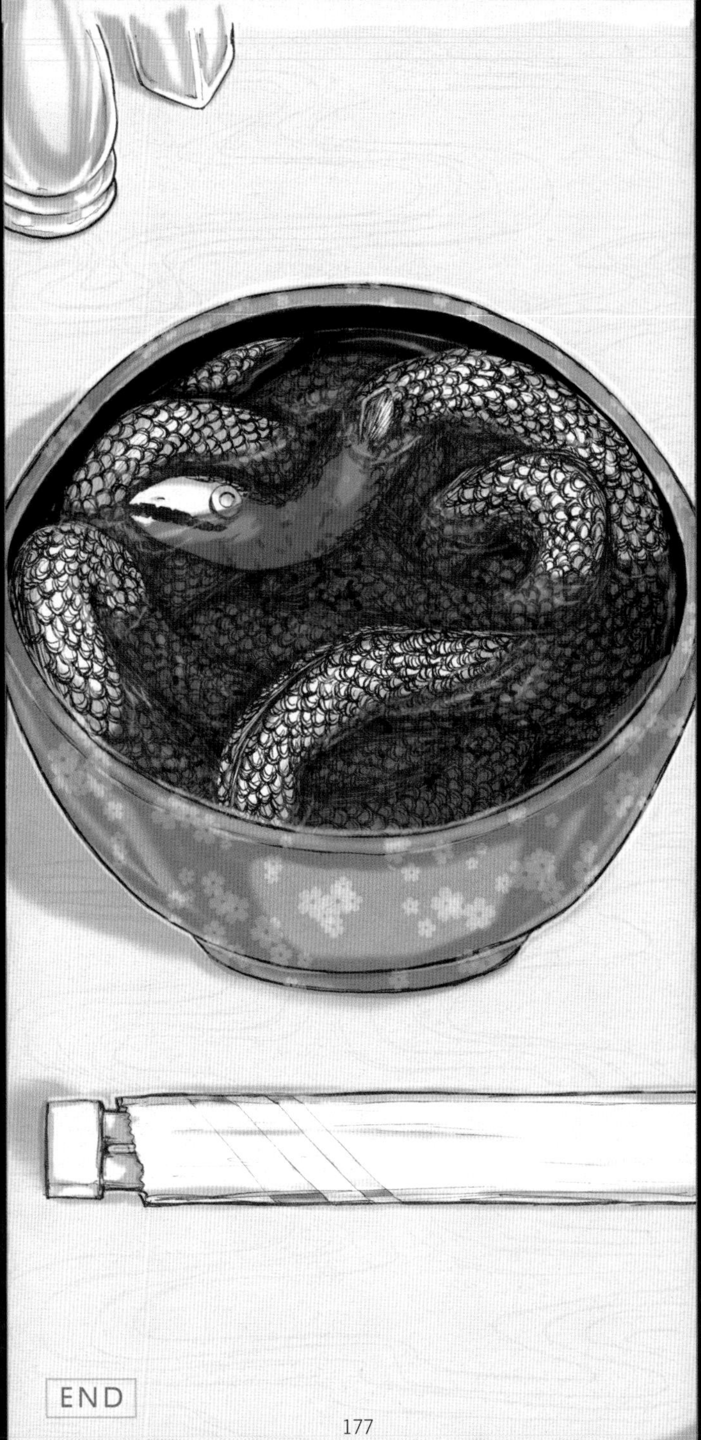
END

Manga Jiman, an interview with Gillian Sein Ying Ha,
first prizewinner of flights to Japan

Where are you from?

Both my parents are originally from Hong Kong, so that makes me Chinese. I was born in London.

How old were you when you drew your first manga?

Probably eleven. I'd been drawing and writing my own comics and children's illustrated stories before this time, but the influence of manga itself didn't properly hit until then.

Who has influenced you most?

From an early age Yoshitaka Amano, in more recent years Takashi Murakami ("pop" fine artist) and Akira Kurosawa (film director). Favourite manga include the intrinsic honesty of *Berserk* (Kentaro Miura), and the laidback spice-of-life application in Kio Shimoku's *Genshiken*. I feel I must also mention Guy Delisle's *Pyongyang*, and Aya Takano. I would love to see *Spaceship EE* translated into English.

What do you do when not creating manga?

I try to practise [drawing] anatomy on a day-to-day basis and watch a lot of documentaries. I read manga but also a variety of magazines and books. Other interests include world cinema and computer games. Thankfully the hardcore gaming only occurs once in a while.

What are you looking forward to when you go to Japan?

Quite simply everything. I'm quite engrossed with the longevity of Japanese culture, how the traditional has continued to complement the contemporary; so I hope to experience as much as I can from Senso-ji Temple to Harajuku and Akihabara

And where did you get the idea?

Having discovered *Daruma* I became very fond of them. Something I had previously overlooked was the custom of painting in the eyes. I felt a bit rattled for how I could miss such a relevant detail. So, in creating the story for Jiman, I wanted to incorporate this somehow as a reminder "never to forget". The idea of the fish came from a design on a Karatsu ware pot. I kept the fish from looking too much like a Daruma because I wanted to present the idea as if it could be mistaken for a real folktale, and I thought that by throwing kimono-inspired patterns onto its body instead, this could retain a special look, yet also remain unusually natural. I watched footage I could find online of particular Japanese beaches; the setting is actually a cross between my memories of a beach I went to with my dad when we visited Hong Kong, and a beach in Weston-Super-Mare, Somerset.

Ed & Ecchi
Me and My Food

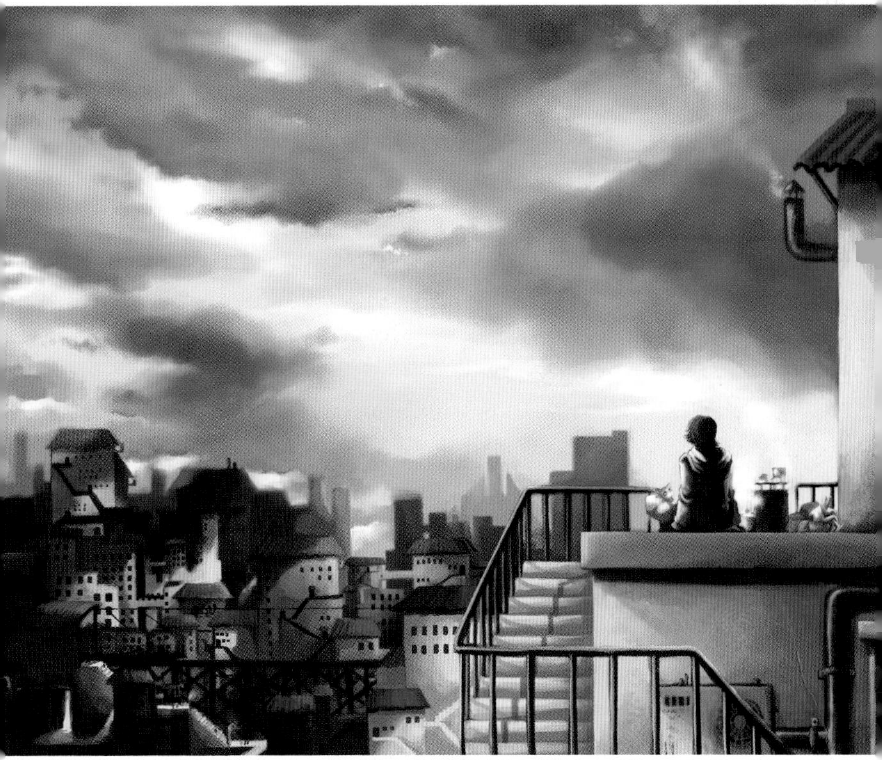

Shari Chankhamma

ED & ECCHI / ME AND MY FOOD
Shari Chankhamma

Some stories defy genre classification, and quite possibly here are two of them. Readers may know Shari from her stories in previous volumes of *Best New Manga*. Done in collaboration with Sweatdrop's Fehed Said, they were gory horrors. So it perhaps comes as something of a surprise for Shari, solo, to produce stories filled with so much light and humour – even when dealing with relative dystopias for her settings.

In the delightful short second story *Me and My Food* we perform a slight return to the island of San Sabian (a sequel of sorts to *The Forgotten Incident of San Sabian* from Volume Two). It isn't what you'd expect!

Shari Chankhamma lives in Thailand. Why she hasn't got publishers queuing up to fling money at her remains a complete mystery.

http://machinegolem.com
www.sharii.com

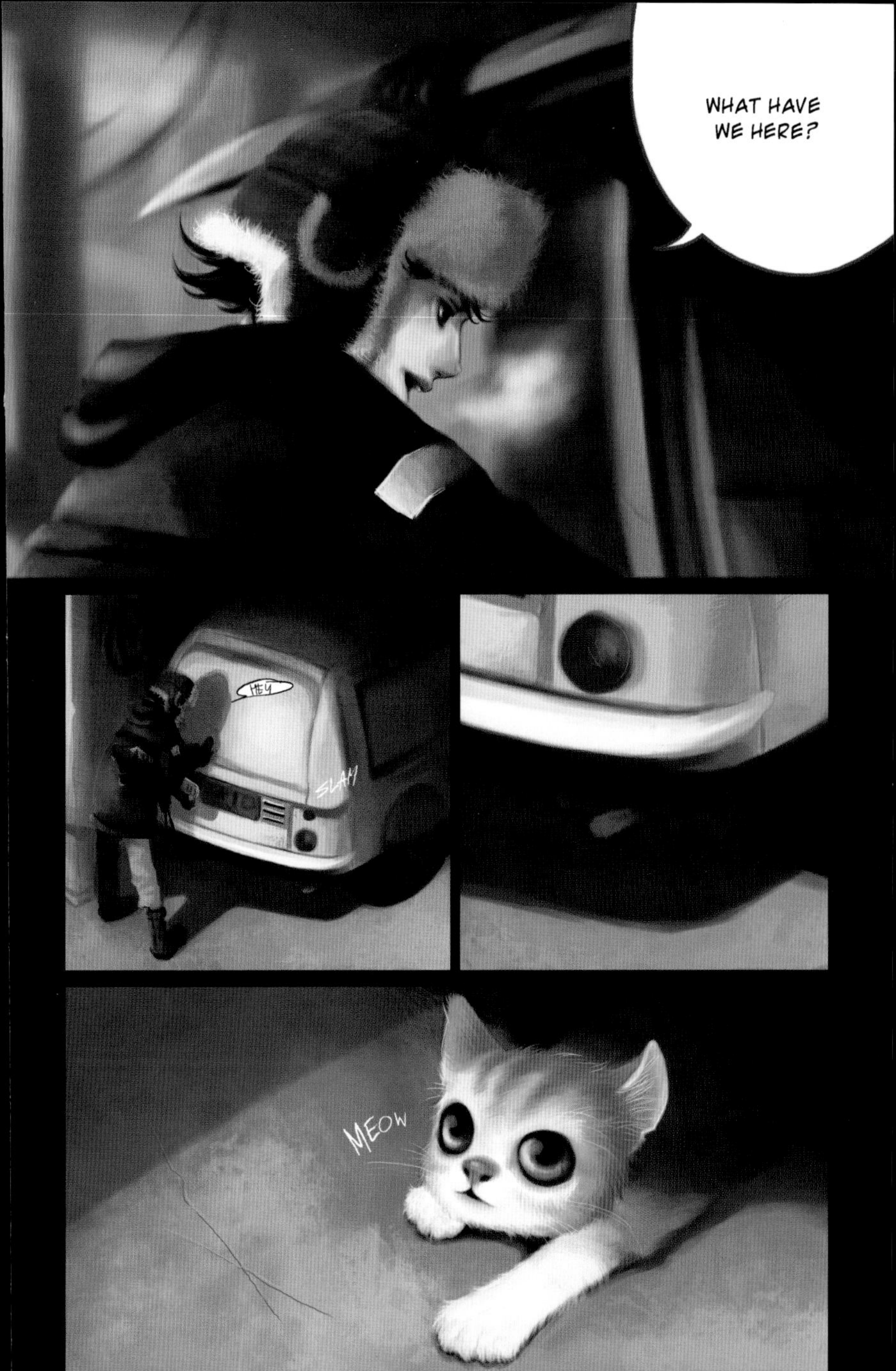
WHAT HAVE WE HERE?
HEY
SLAM
MEOW

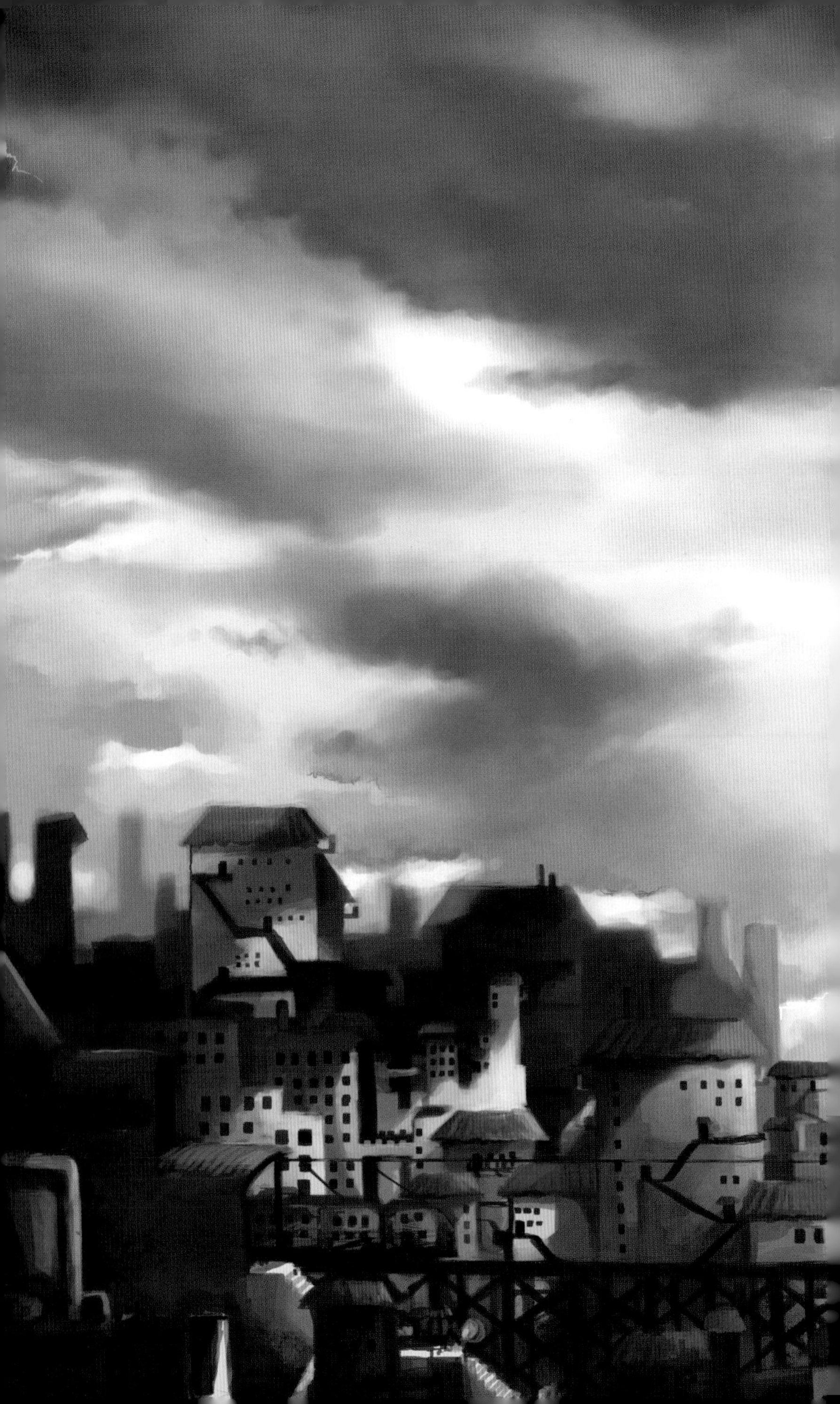

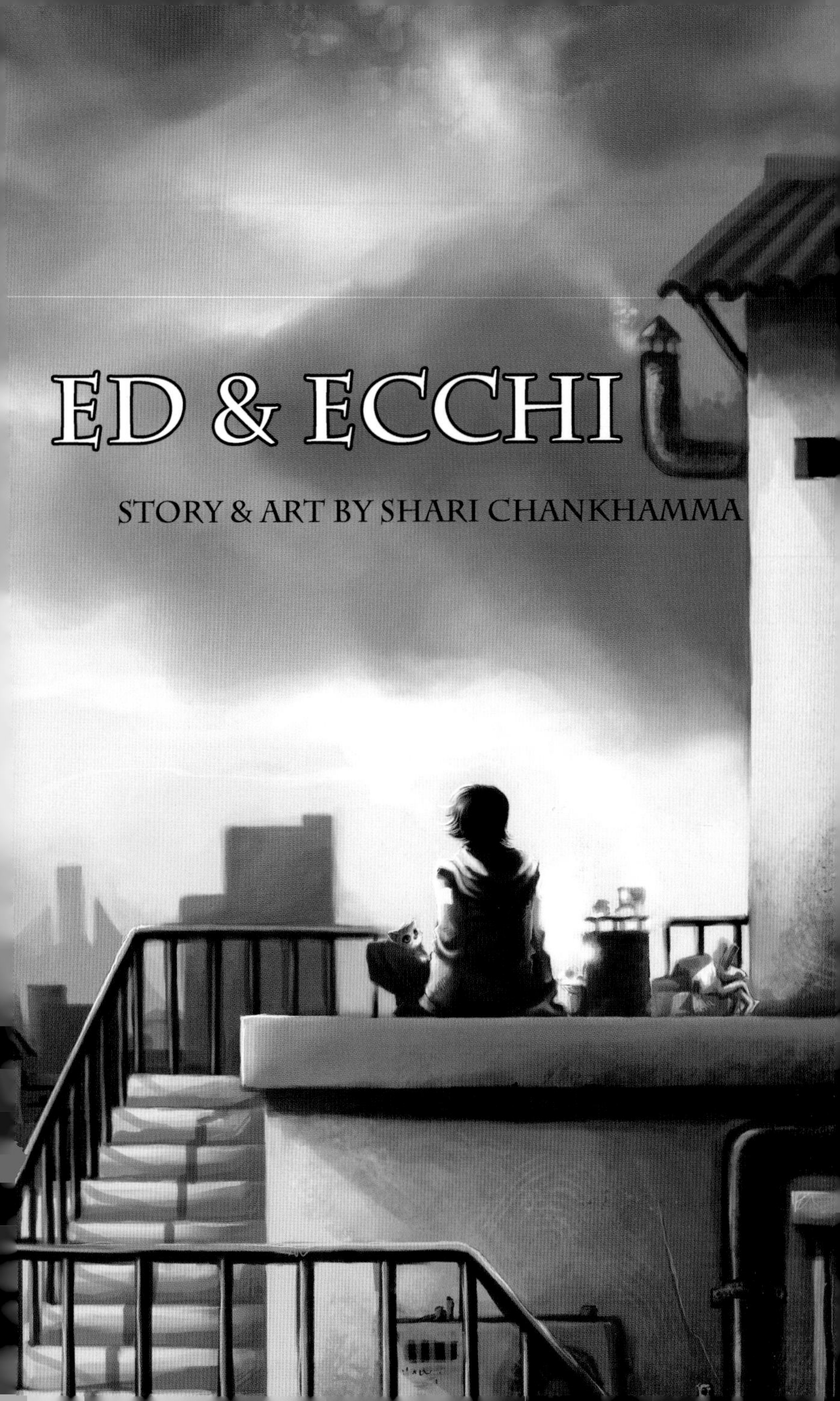
ED & ECCHI
STORY & ART BY SHARI CHANKHAMMA

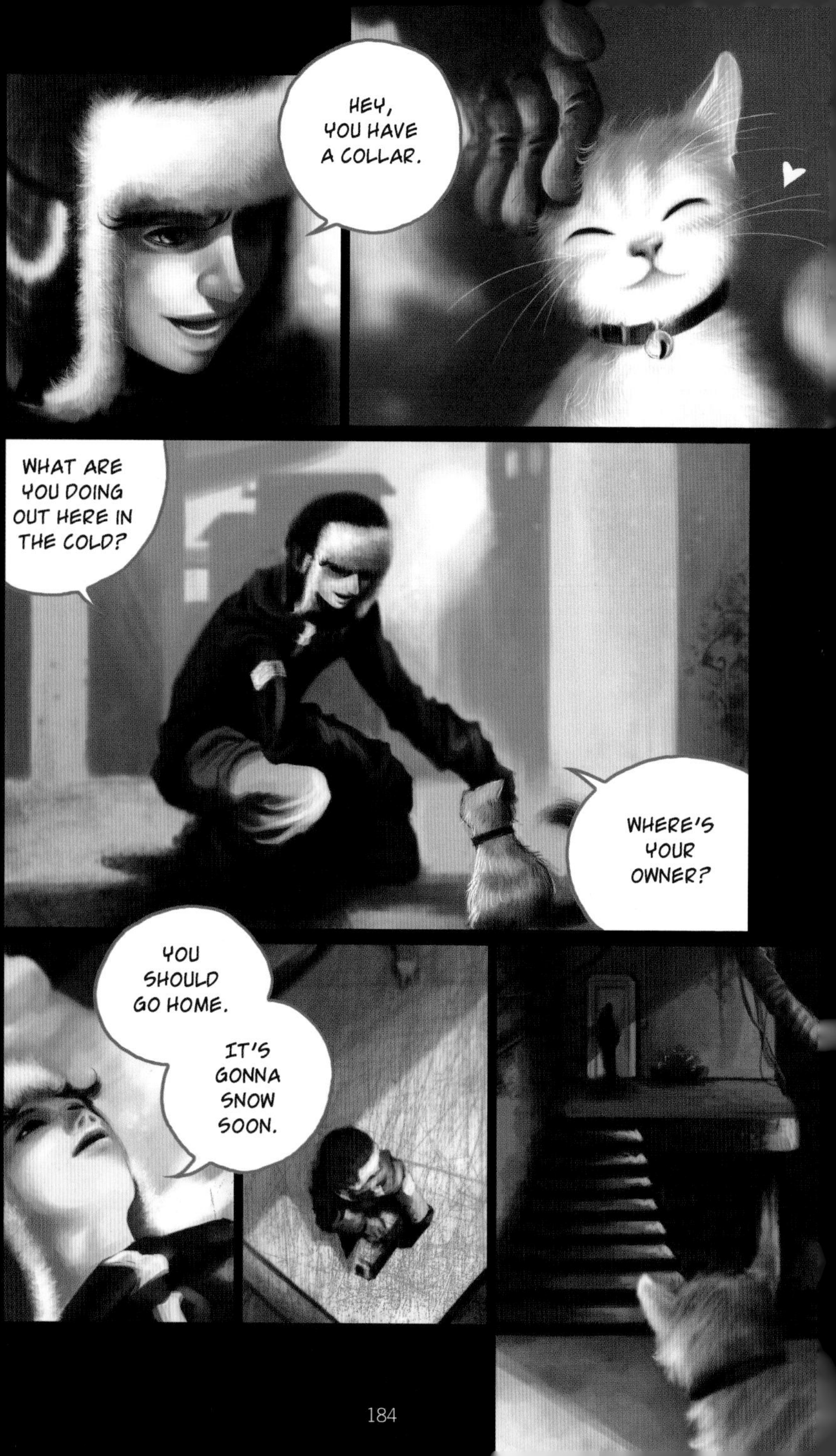
HEY, YOU HAVE A COLLAR.
WHAT ARE YOU DOING OUT HERE IN THE COLD?
WHERE'S YOUR OWNER?
YOU SHOULD GO HOME.
IT'S GONNA SNOW SOON.

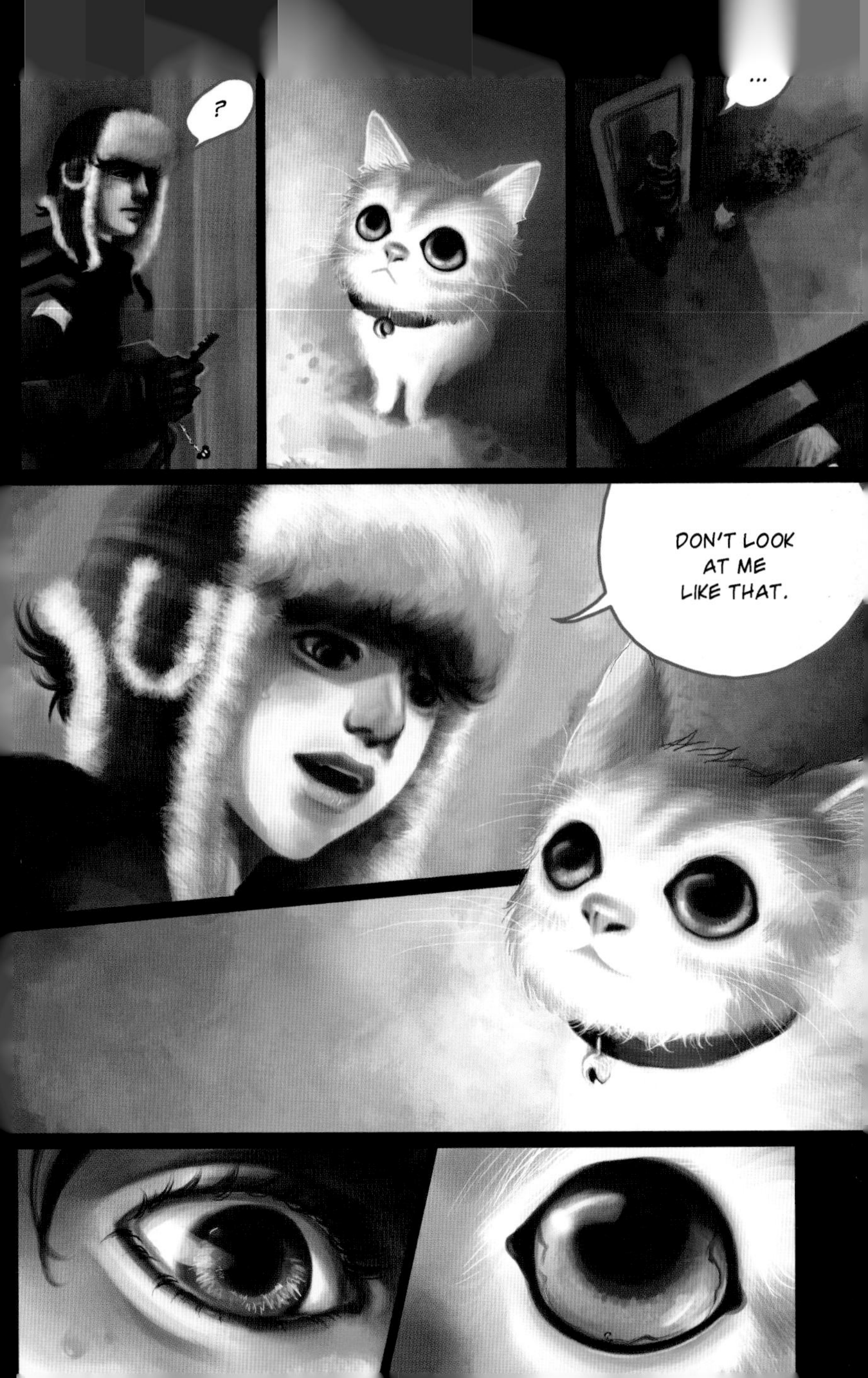
?
...
DON'T LOOK AT ME LIKE THAT.

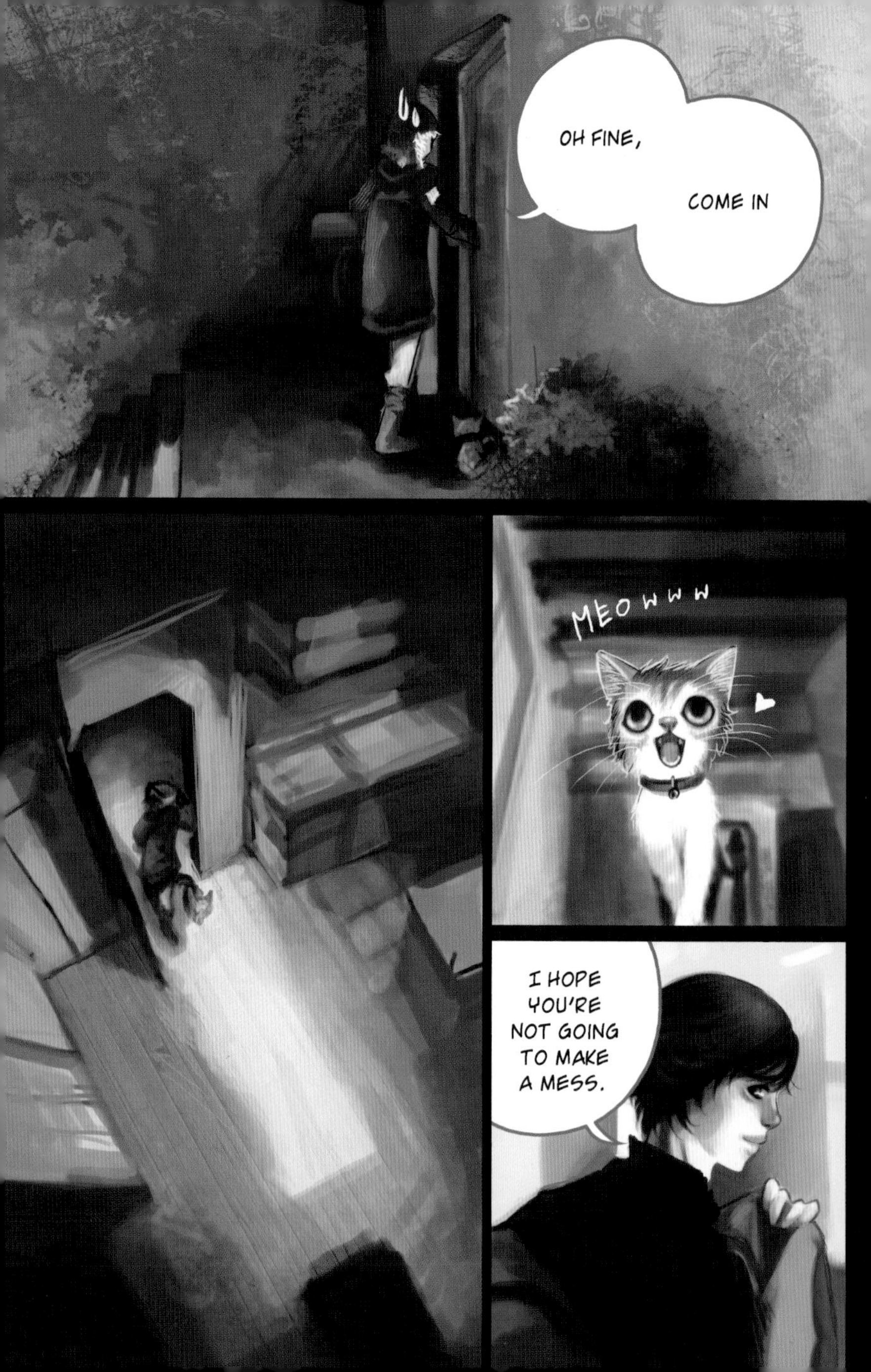
OH FINE, COME IN
MEOWWW
I HOPE YOU'RE NOT GOING TO MAKE A MESS.

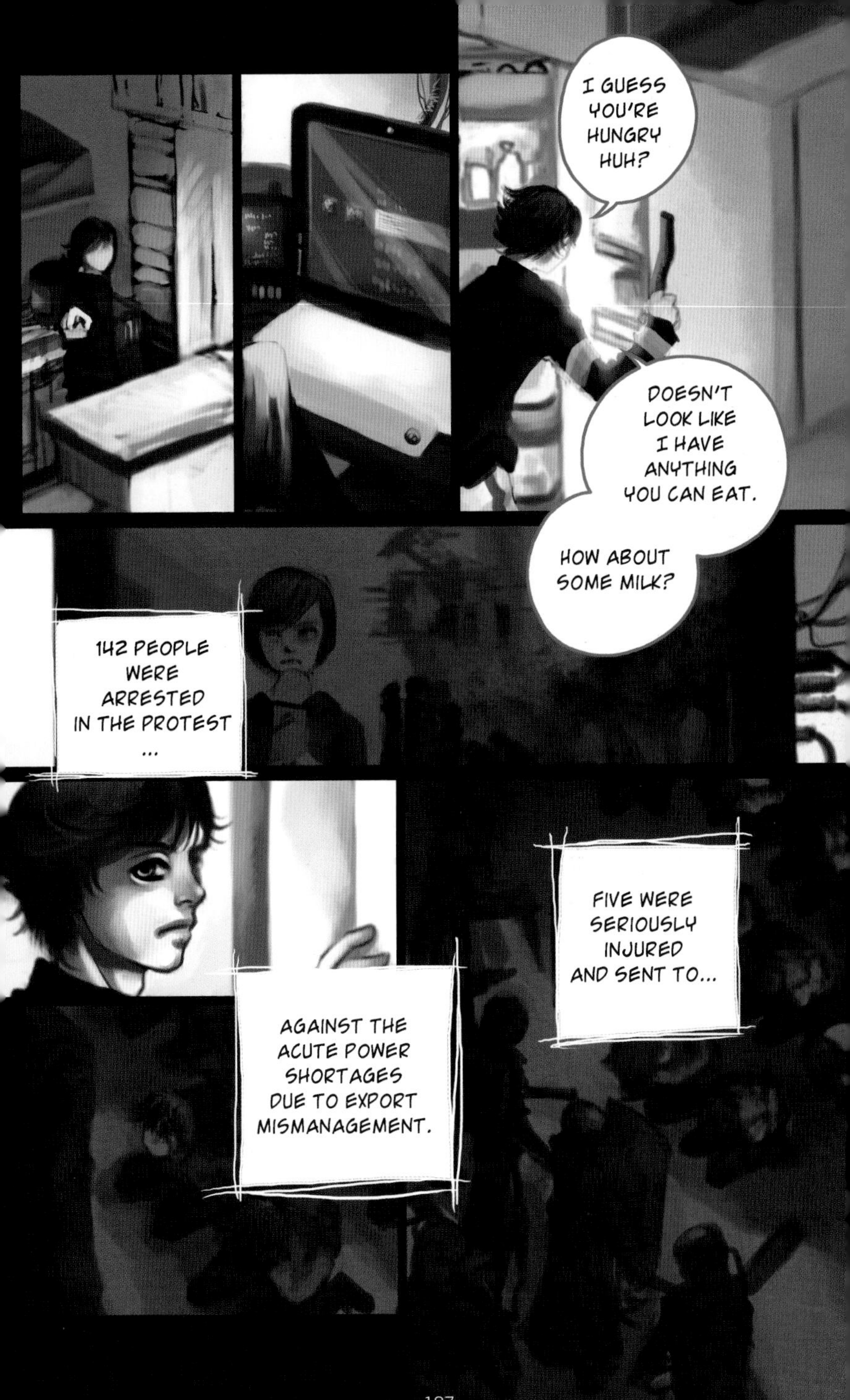
I GUESS YOU'RE HUNGRY HUH?
DOESN'T LOOK LIKE I HAVE ANYTHING YOU CAN EAT.
HOW ABOUT SOME MILK?
142 PEOPLE WERE ARRESTED IN THE PROTEST ...
AGAINST THE ACUTE POWER SHORTAGES DUE TO EXPORT MISMANAGEMENT.
FIVE WERE SERIOUSLY INJURED AND SENT TO...

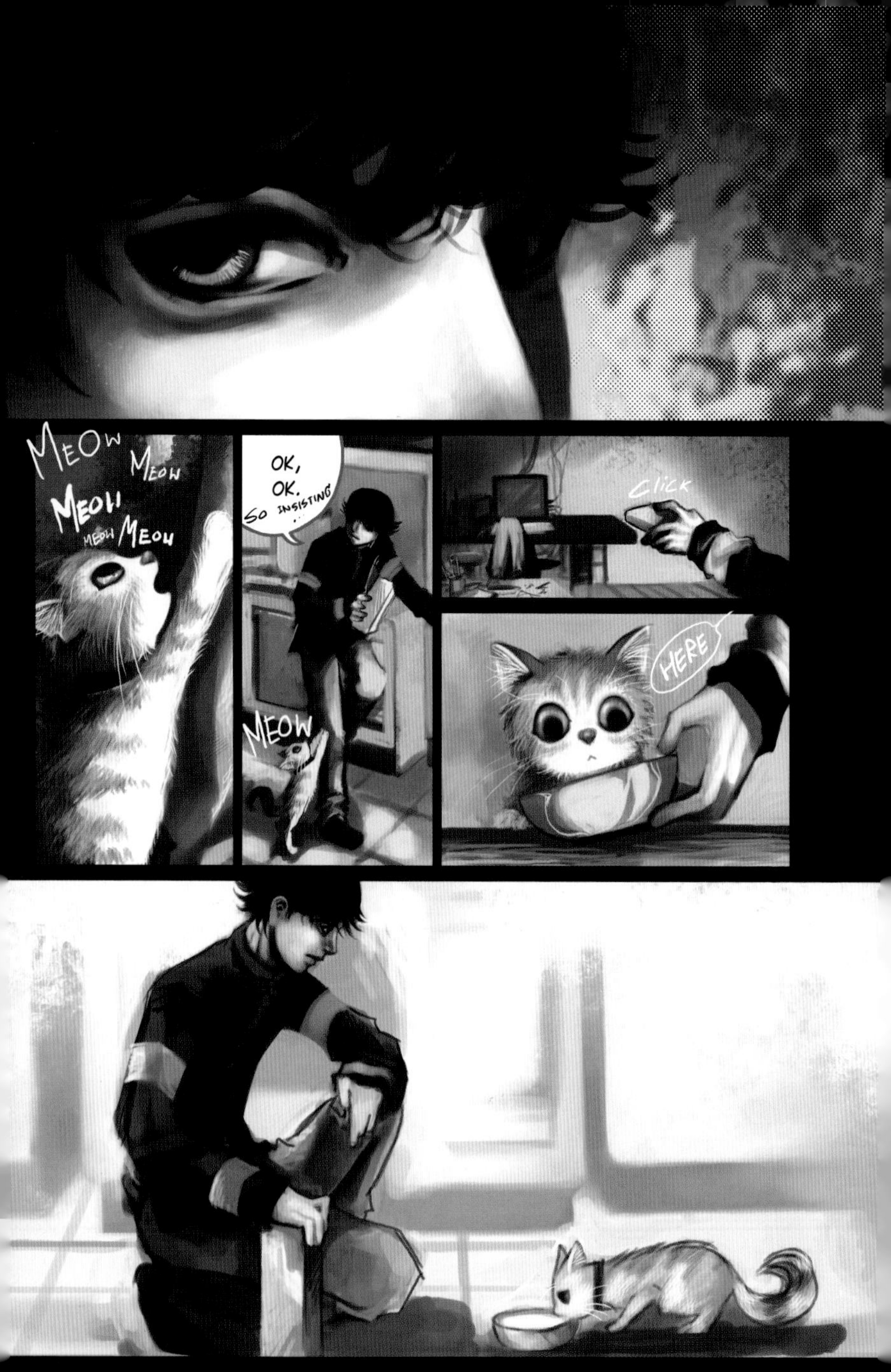
MEOW MEOW
MEOW
MEOW MEOW
OK, OK. SO INSISTING...
MEOW
CLICK
HERE

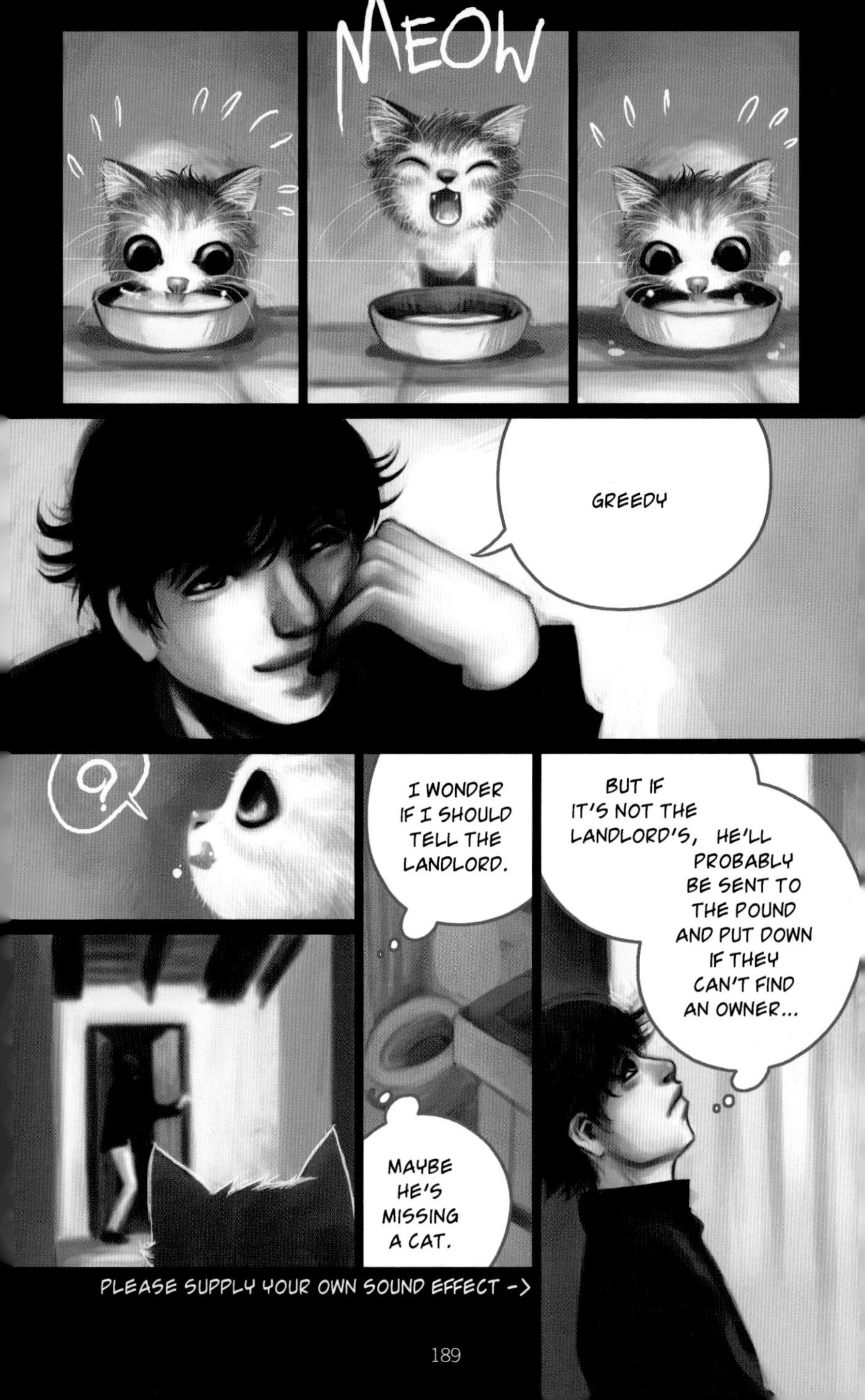
MEOW
GREEDY
?
PLEASE SUPPLY YOUR OWN SOUND EFFECT ->
I WONDER IF I SHOULD TELL THE LANDLORD.
MAYBE HE'S MISSING A CAT.
BUT IF IT'S NOT THE LANDLORD'S, HE'LL PROBABLY BE SENT TO THE POUND AND PUT DOWN IF THEY CAN'T FIND AN OWNER...

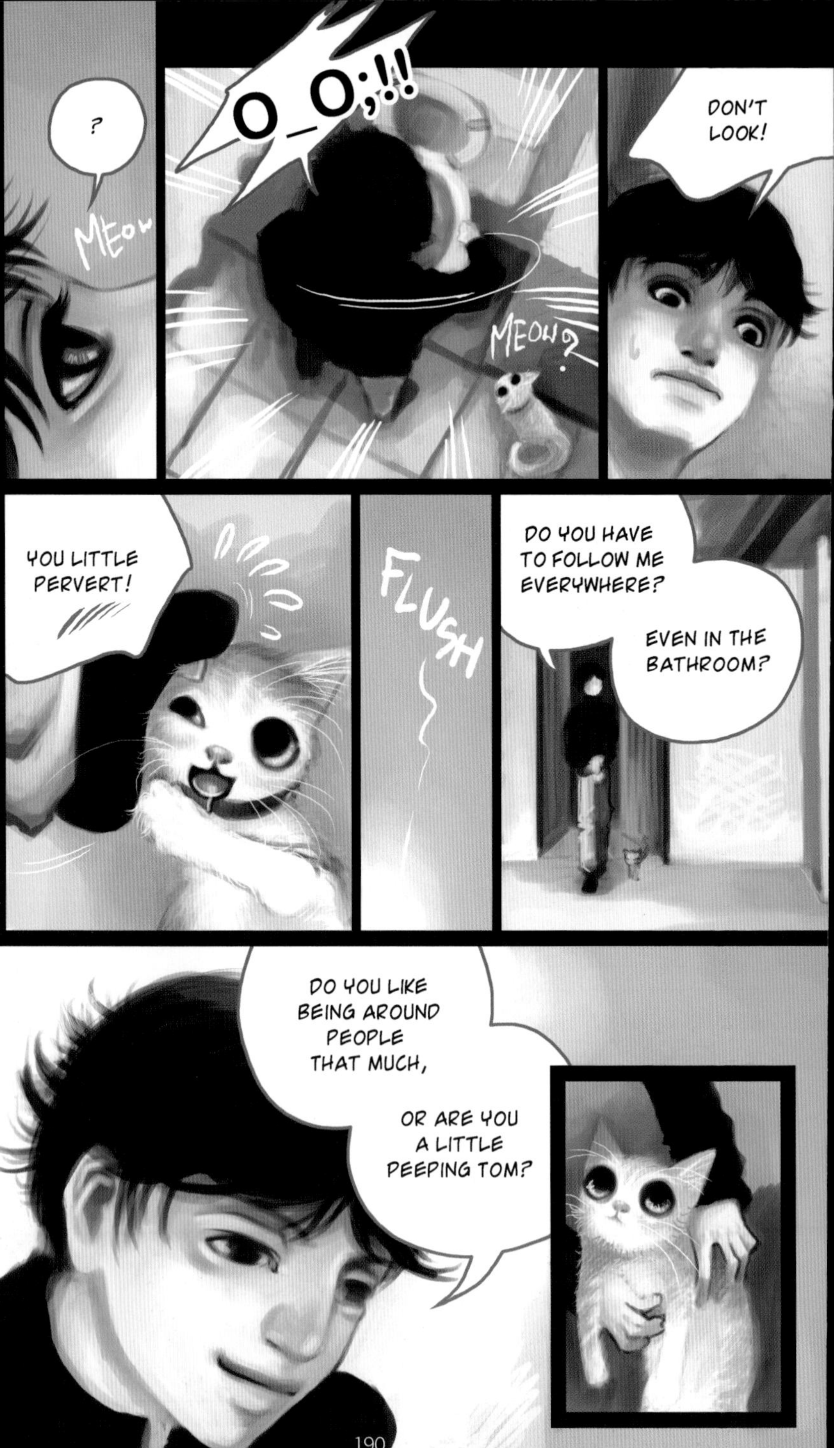
?
MEOW
O_O;!!
MEOW?
DON'T LOOK!
YOU LITTLE PERVERT!
FLUSH
DO YOU HAVE TO FOLLOW ME EVERYWHERE?
EVEN IN THE BATHROOM?
DO YOU LIKE BEING AROUND PEOPLE THAT MUCH,
OR ARE YOU A LITTLE PEEPING TOM?

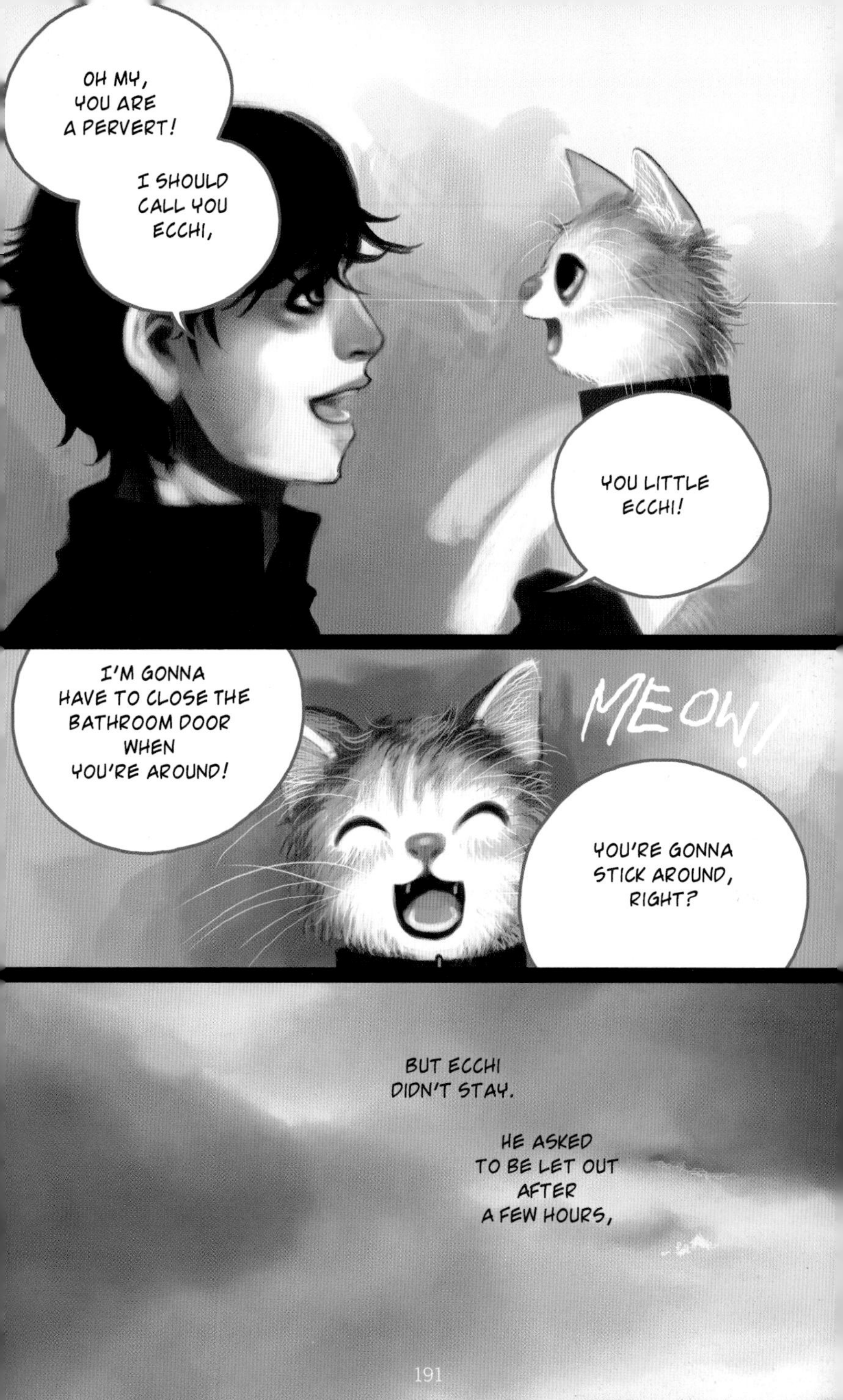
OH MY, YOU ARE A PERVERT!
I SHOULD CALL YOU ECCHI,
YOU LITTLE ECCHI!
I'M GONNA HAVE TO CLOSE THE BATHROOM DOOR WHEN YOU'RE AROUND!
MEOW!
YOU'RE GONNA STICK AROUND, RIGHT?
BUT ECCHI DIDN'T STAY.
HE ASKED TO BE LET OUT AFTER A FEW HOURS,

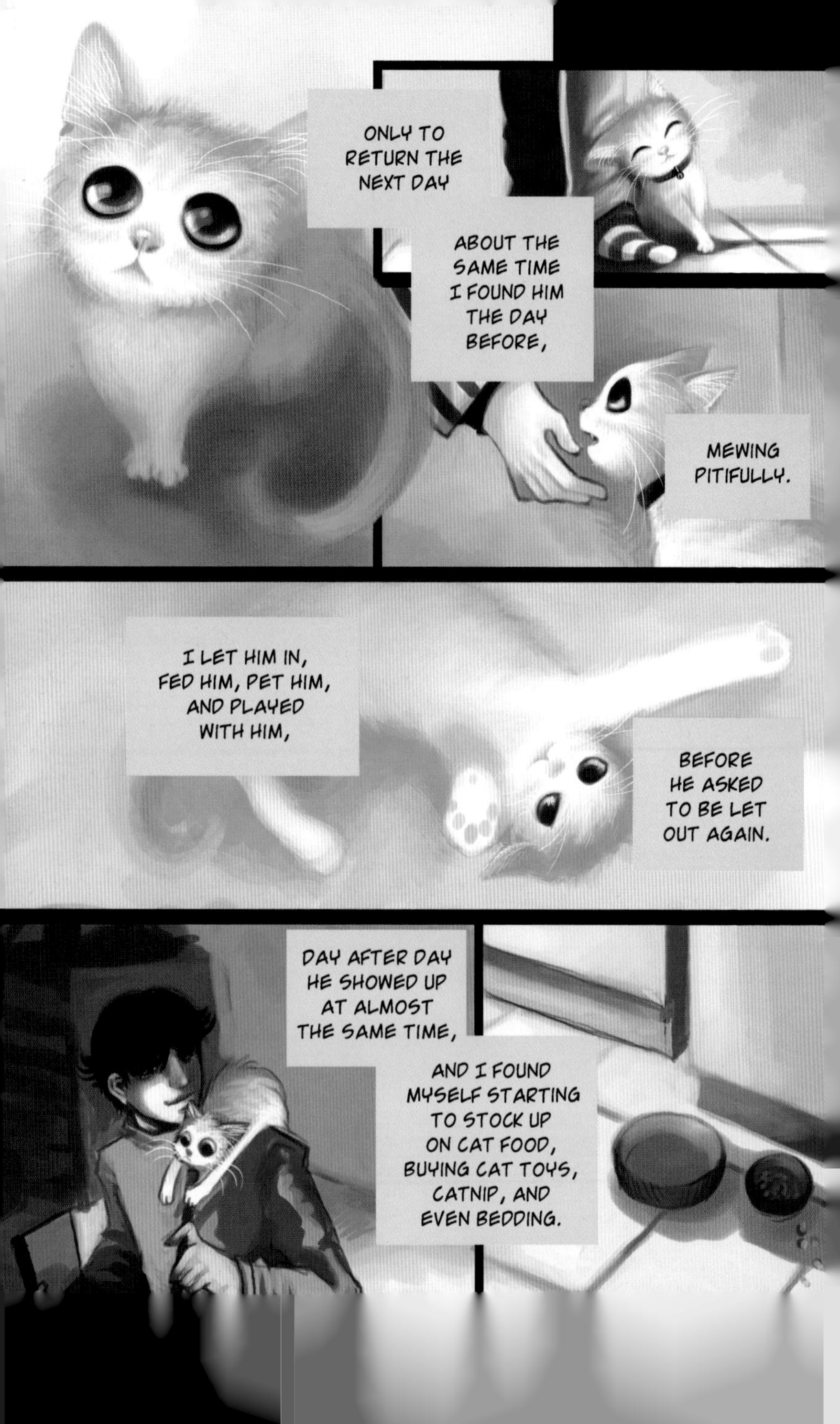
ONLY TO RETURN THE NEXT DAY
ABOUT THE SAME TIME I FOUND HIM THE DAY BEFORE,
MEWING PITIFULLY.
I LET HIM IN, FED HIM, PET HIM, AND PLAYED WITH HIM,
BEFORE HE ASKED TO BE LET OUT AGAIN.
DAY AFTER DAY HE SHOWED UP AT ALMOST THE SAME TIME,
AND I FOUND MYSELF STARTING TO STOCK UP ON CAT FOOD, BUYING CAT TOYS, CATNIP, AND EVEN BEDDING.

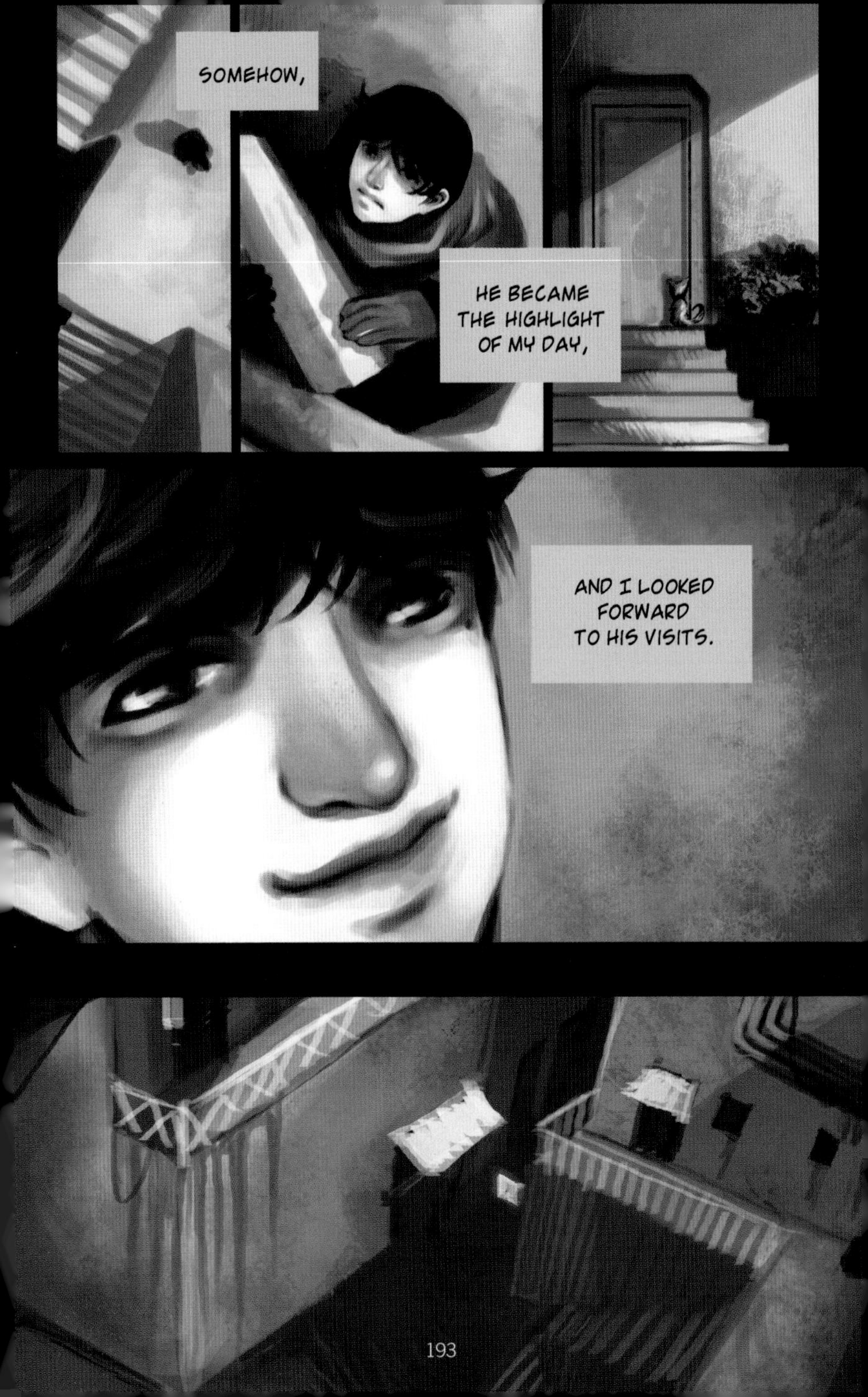
SOMEHOW,
HE BECAME THE HIGHLIGHT OF MY DAY,
AND I LOOKED FORWARD TO HIS VISITS.

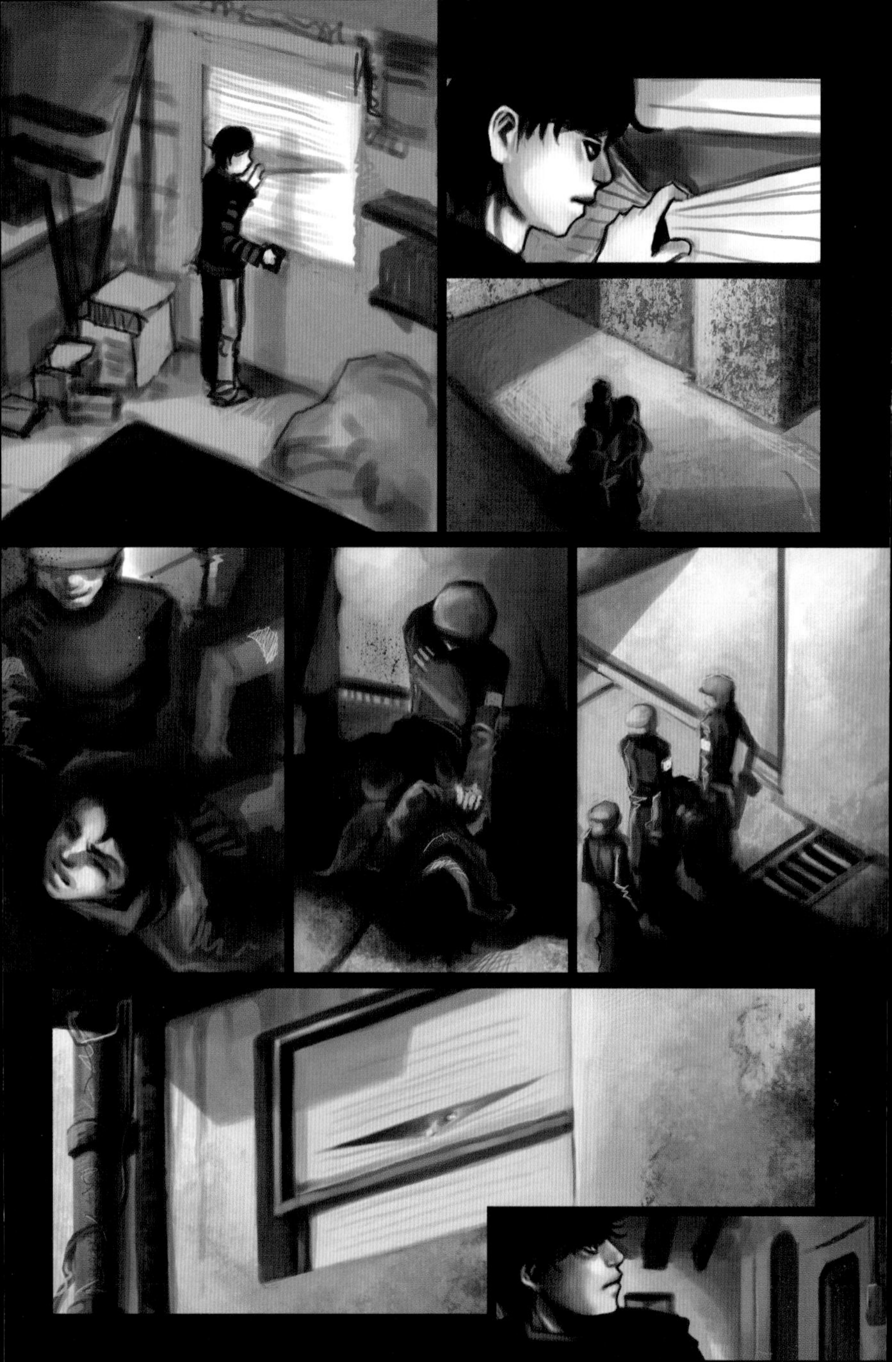

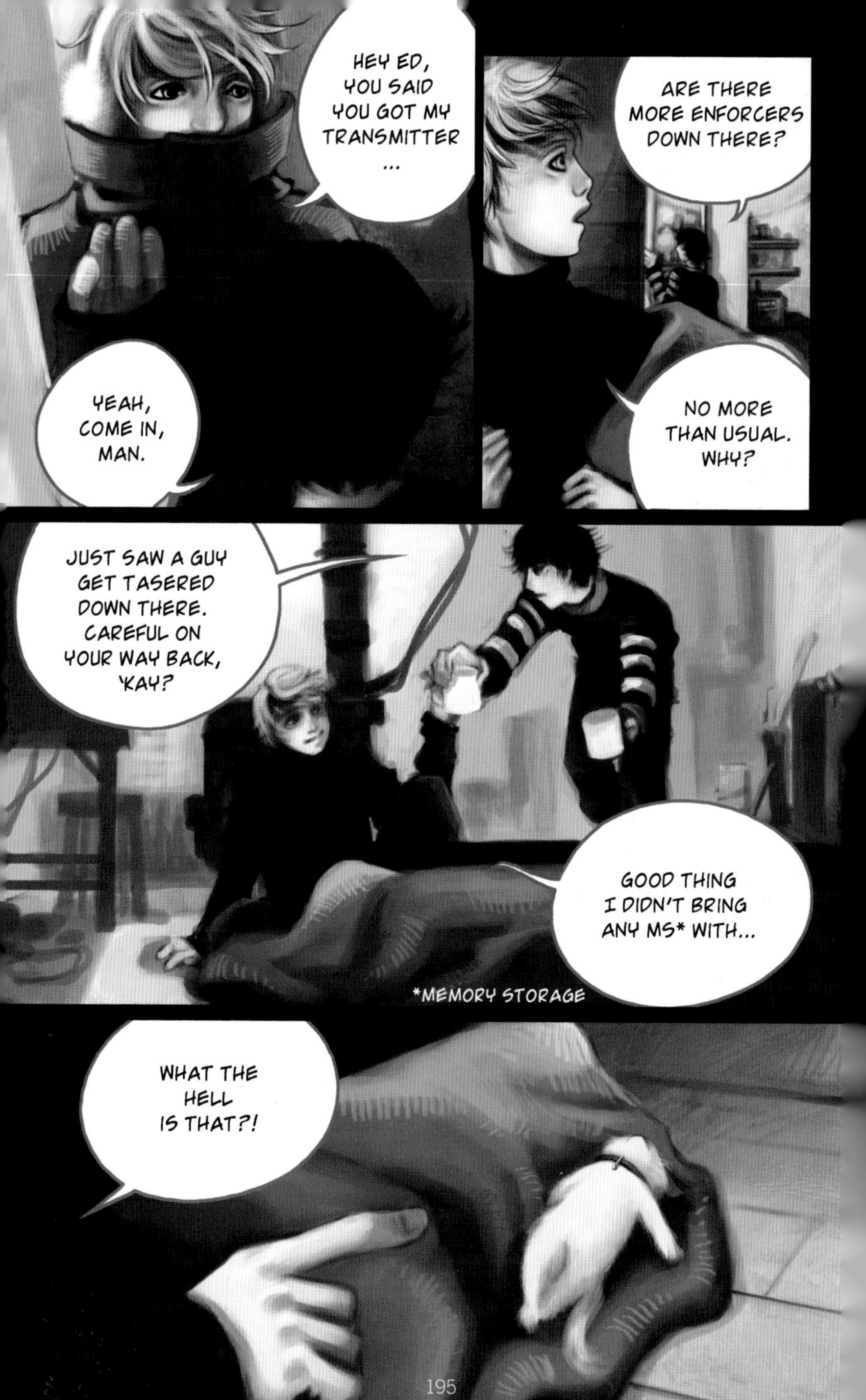
HEY ED, YOU SAID YOU GOT MY TRANSMITTER ...
YEAH, COME IN, MAN.
ARE THERE MORE ENFORCERS DOWN THERE?
NO MORE THAN USUAL. WHY?
JUST SAW A GUY GET TASERED DOWN THERE. CAREFUL ON YOUR WAY BACK, 'KAY?
GOOD THING I DIDN'T BRING ANY MS* WITH...
*MEMORY STORAGE
WHAT THE HELL IS THAT?!

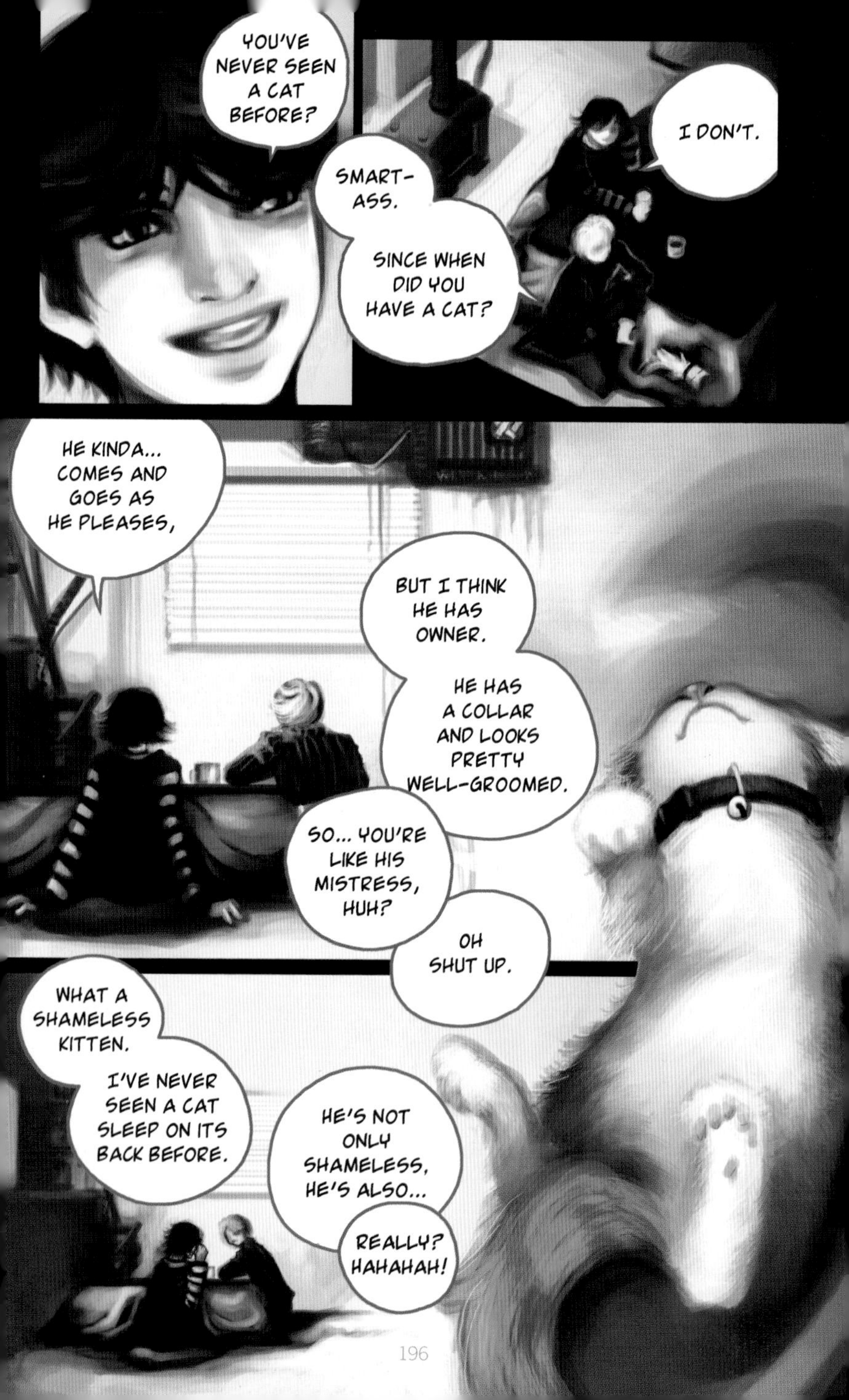
YOU'VE NEVER SEEN A CAT BEFORE?
SMART-ASS.
SINCE WHEN DID YOU HAVE A CAT?
I DON'T.
HE KINDA... COMES AND GOES AS HE PLEASES,
BUT I THINK HE HAS OWNER.
HE HAS A COLLAR AND LOOKS PRETTY WELL-GROOMED.
SO... YOU'RE LIKE HIS MISTRESS, HUH?
OH SHUT UP.
WHAT A SHAMELESS KITTEN.
I'VE NEVER SEEN A CAT SLEEP ON ITS BACK BEFORE.
HE'S NOT ONLY SHAMELESS, HE'S ALSO...
REALLY? HAHAHAH!

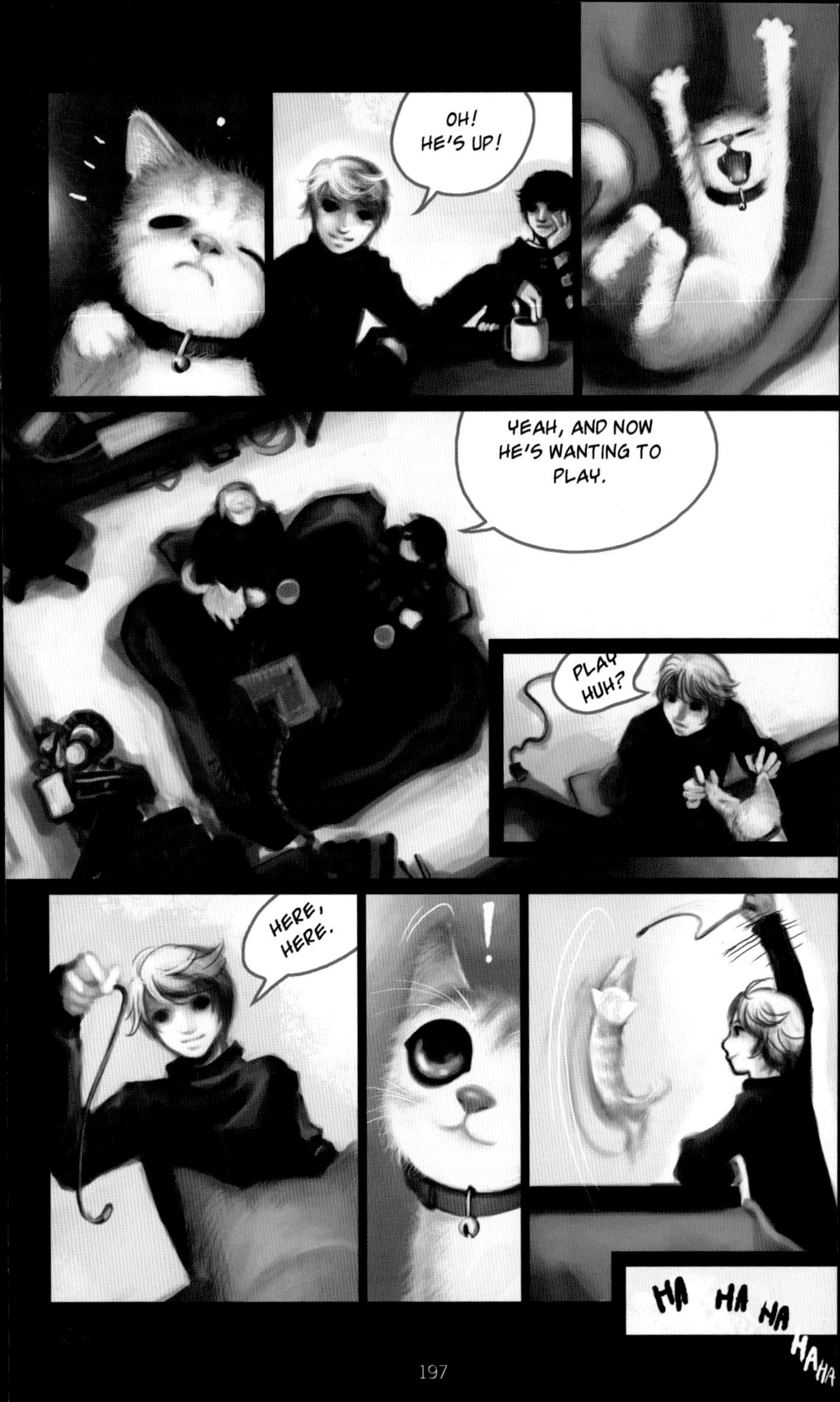
OH! HE'S UP!
YEAH, AND NOW HE'S WANTING TO PLAY.
PLAY HUH?
HERE, HERE.
!
HA HA HA HAHAHA

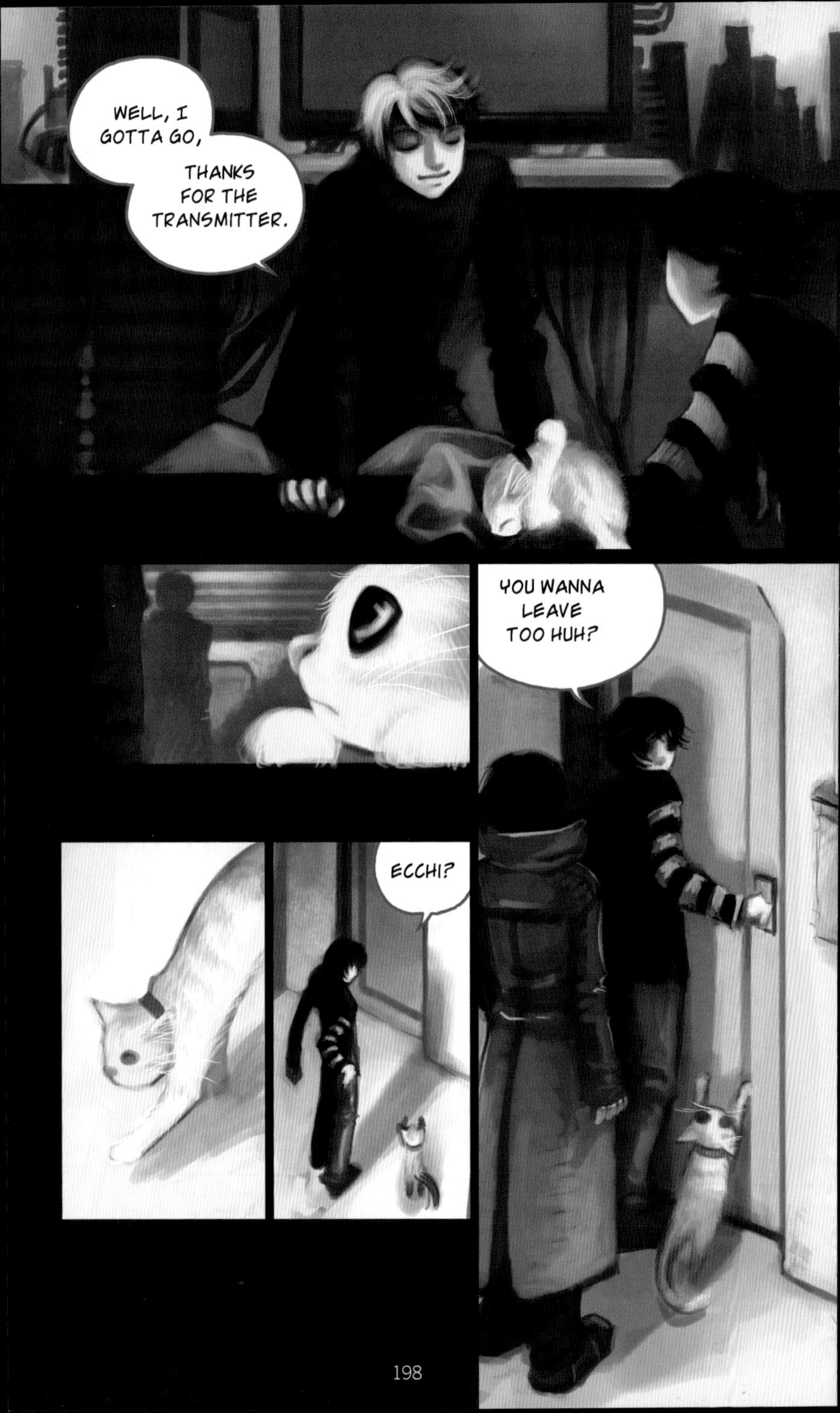
WELL, I GOTTA GO,
THANKS FOR THE TRANSMITTER.
YOU WANNA LEAVE TOO HUH?
ECCHI?

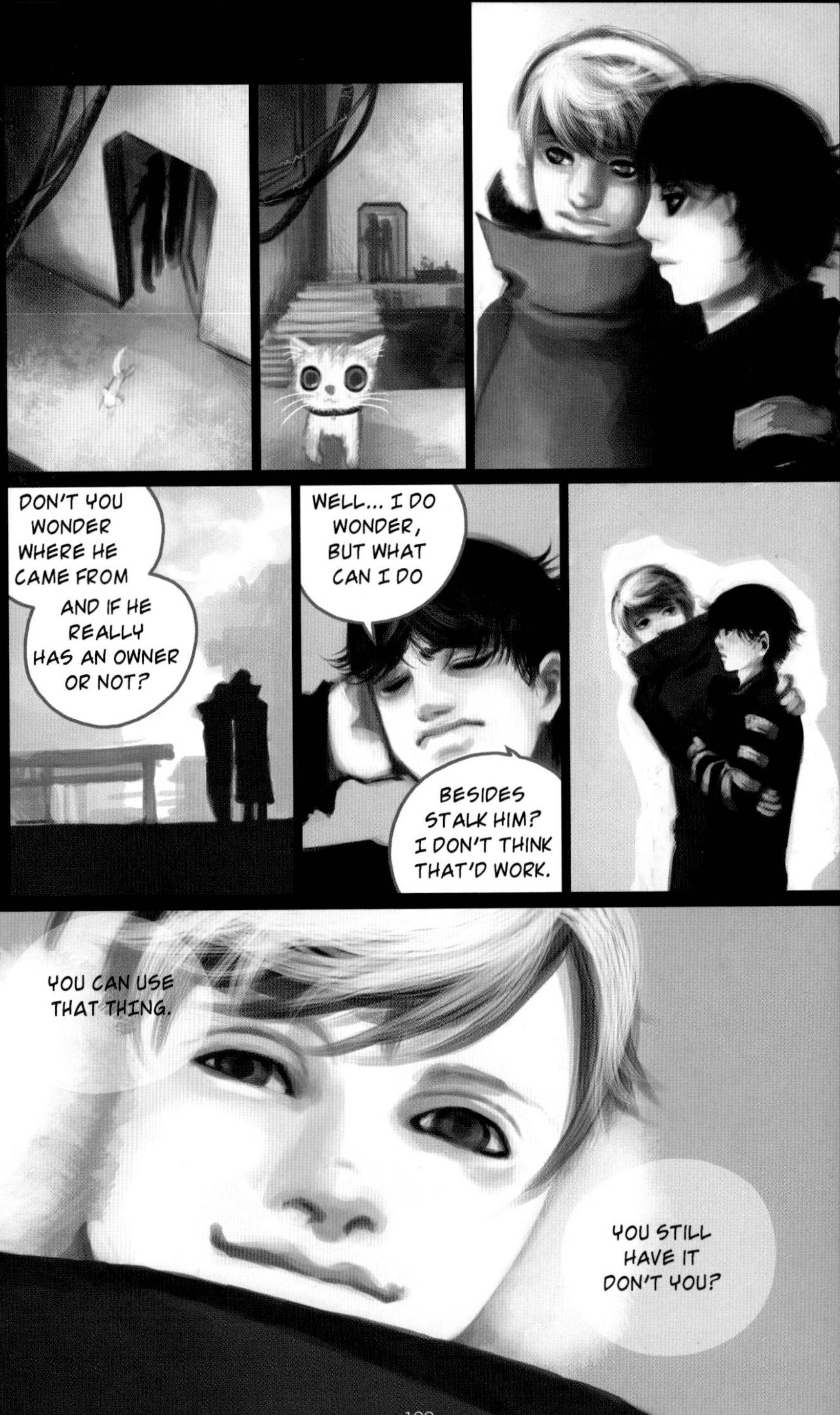
DON'T YOU WONDER WHERE HE CAME FROM
AND IF HE REALLY HAS AN OWNER OR NOT?
WELL... I DO WONDER, BUT WHAT CAN I DO
BESIDES STALK HIM? I DON'T THINK THAT'D WORK.
YOU CAN USE THAT THING.
YOU STILL HAVE IT DON'T YOU?

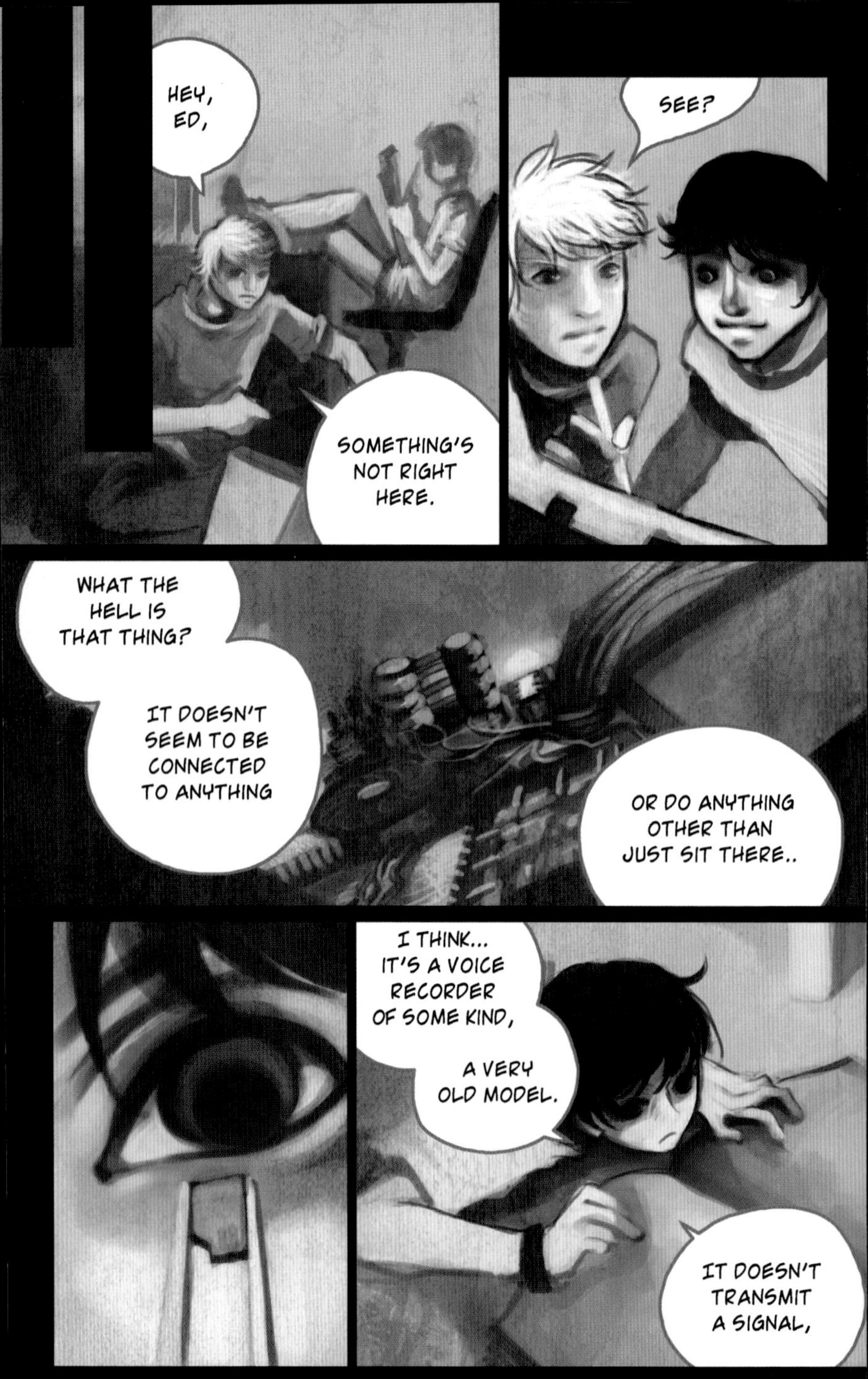
HEY, ED,
SOMETHING'S NOT RIGHT HERE.
SEE?
WHAT THE HELL IS THAT THING?
IT DOESN'T SEEM TO BE CONNECTED TO ANYTHING
OR DO ANYTHING OTHER THAN JUST SIT THERE..
I THINK... IT'S A VOICE RECORDER OF SOME KIND,
A VERY OLD MODEL.
IT DOESN'T TRANSMIT A SIGNAL,

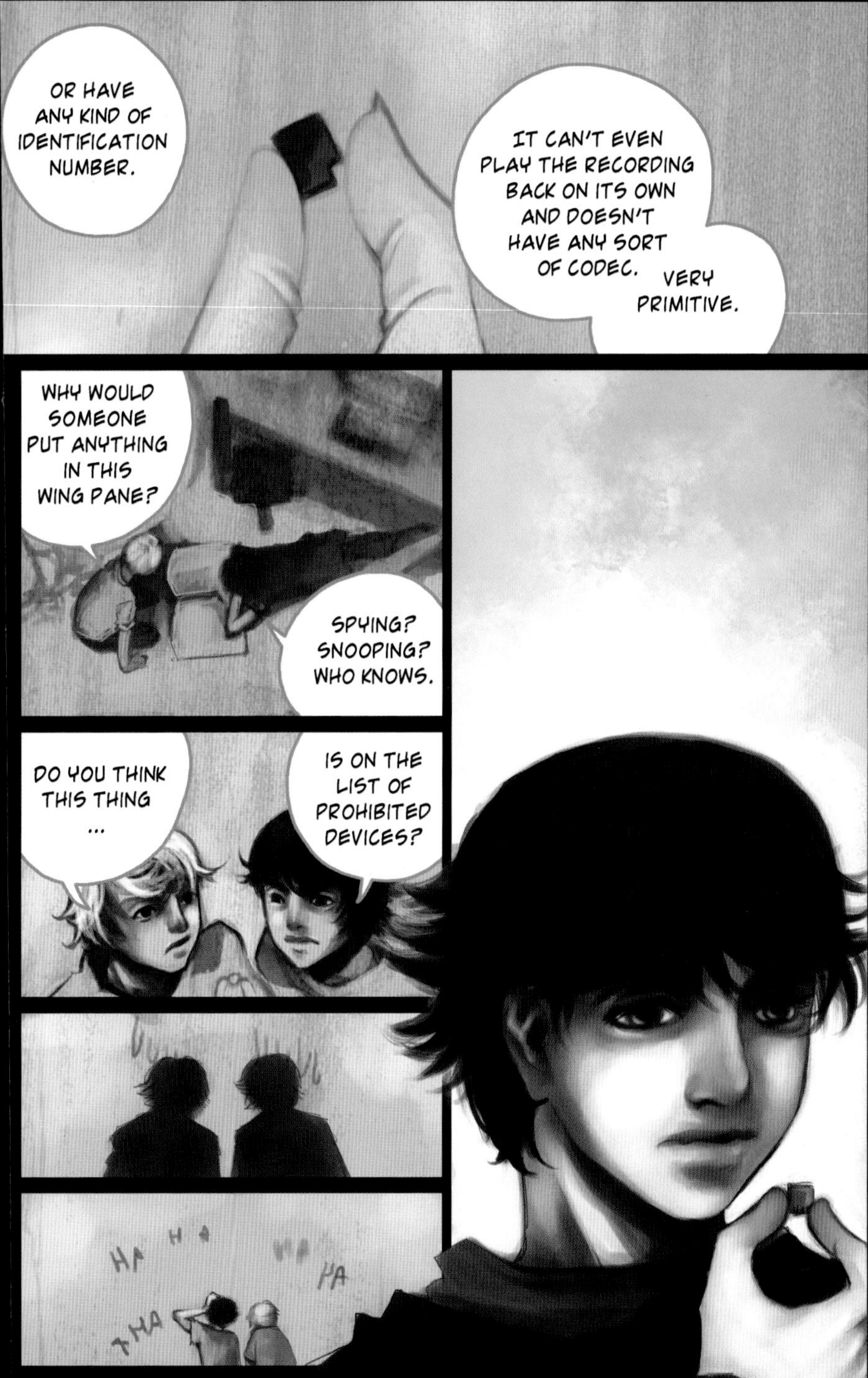
OR HAVE ANY KIND OF IDENTIFICATION NUMBER.
IT CAN'T EVEN PLAY THE RECORDING BACK ON ITS OWN AND DOESN'T HAVE ANY SORT OF CODEC.
VERY PRIMITIVE.
WHY WOULD SOMEONE PUT ANYTHING IN THIS WING PANE?
SPYING? SNOOPING? WHO KNOWS.
DO YOU THINK THIS THING ...
IS ON THE LIST OF PROHIBITED DEVICES?

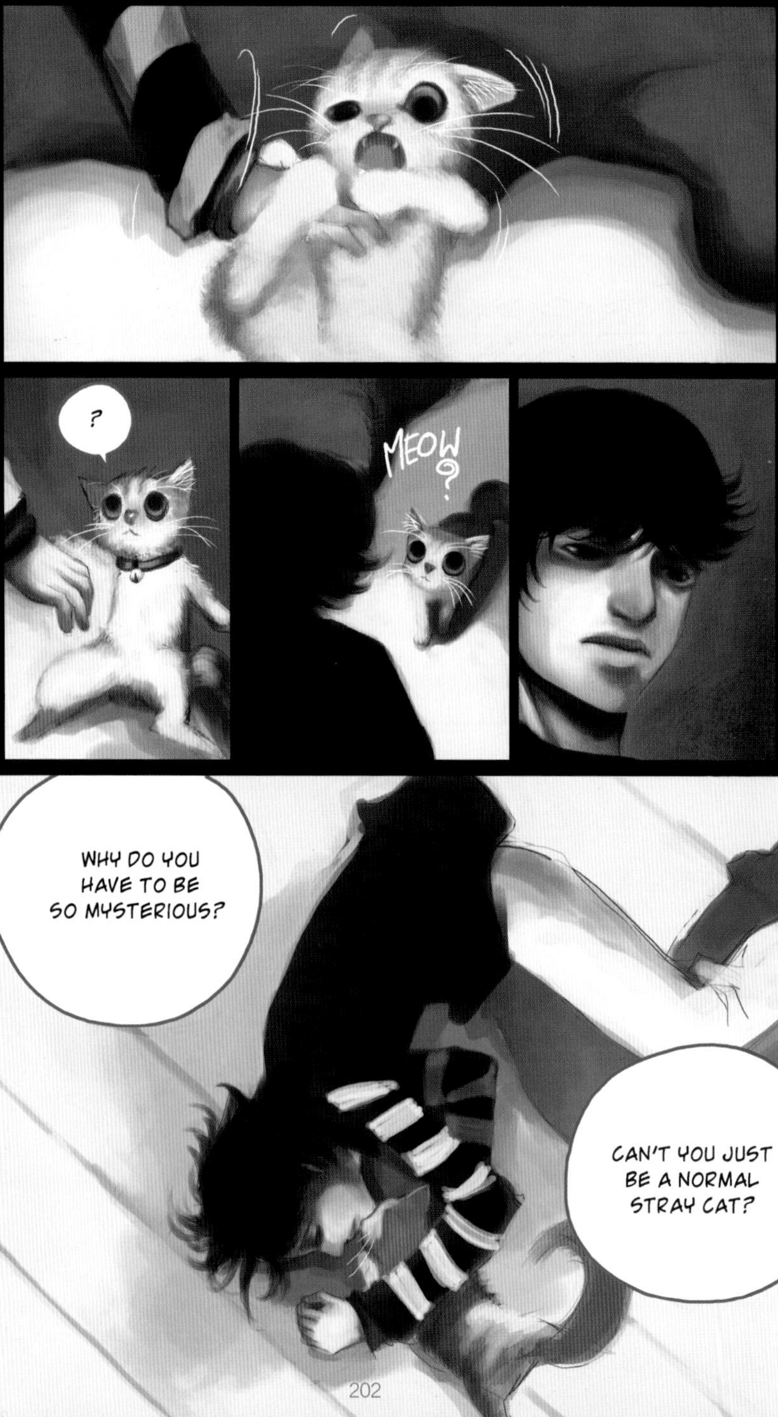
?
MEOW?
WHY DO YOU HAVE TO BE SO MYSTERIOUS?
CAN'T YOU JUST BE A NORMAL STRAY CAT?

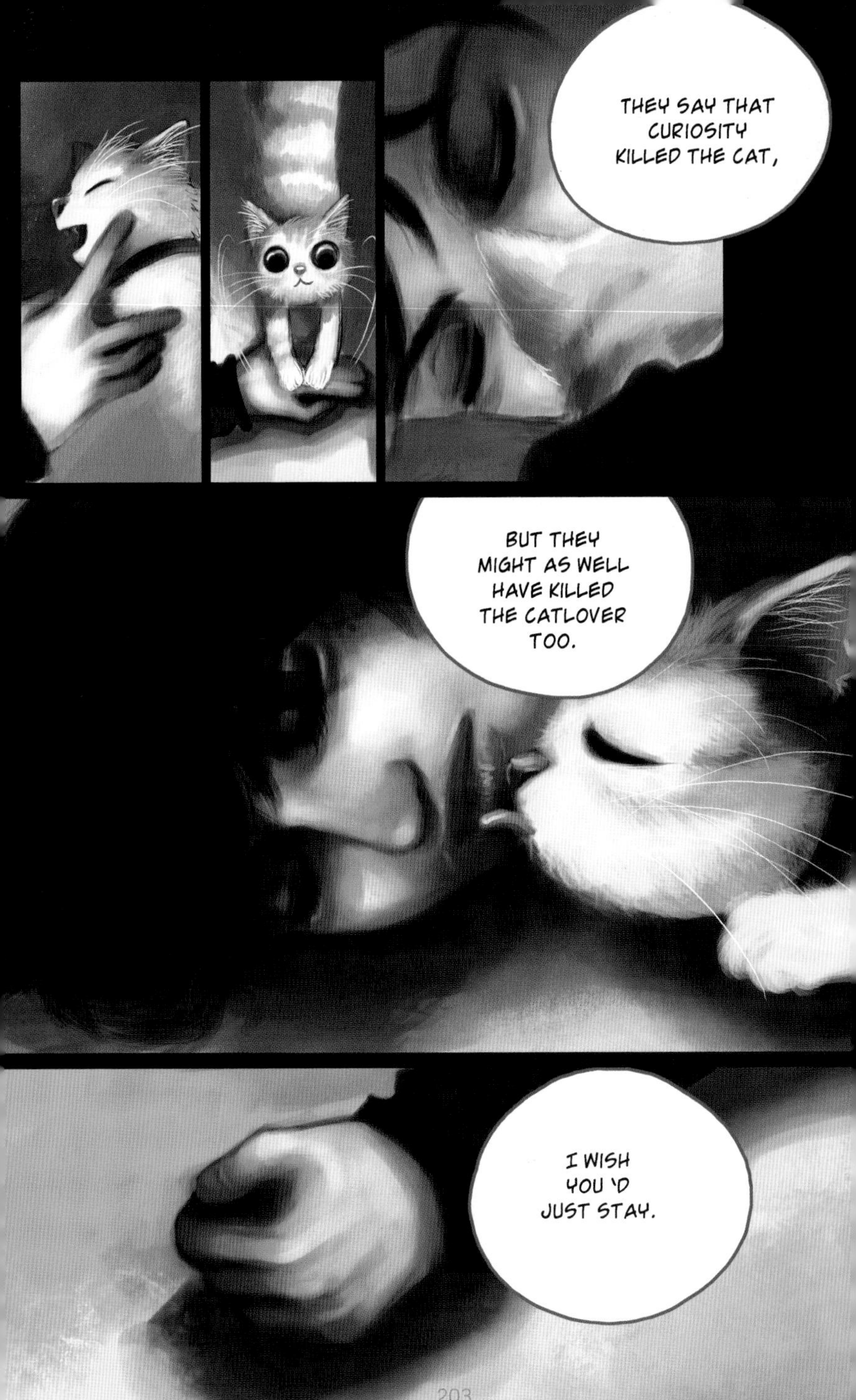
THEY SAY THAT CURIOSITY KILLED THE CAT,
BUT THEY MIGHT AS WELL HAVE KILLED THE CATLOVER TOO.
I WISH YOU 'D JUST STAY.

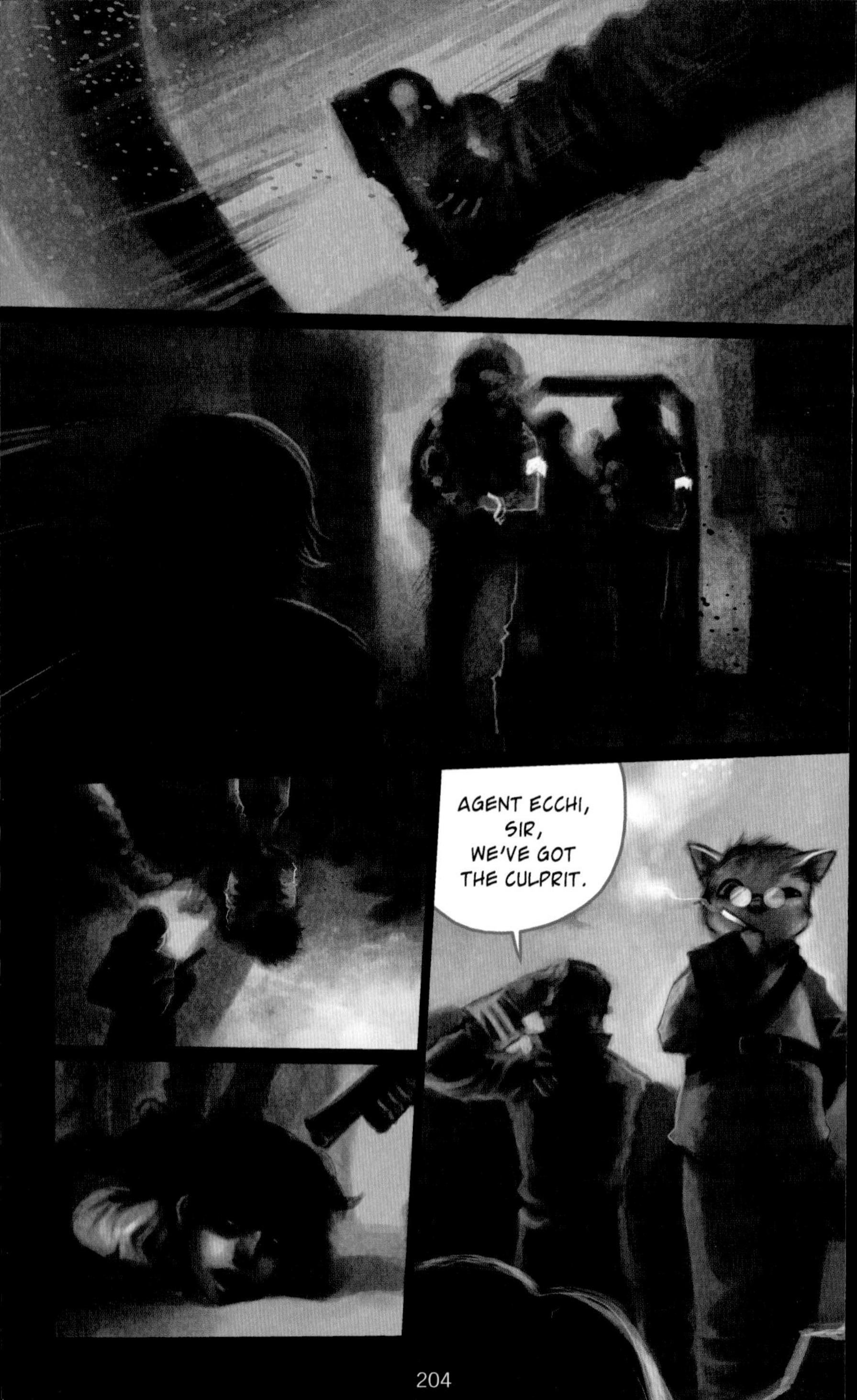
AGENT ECCHI, SIR, WE'VE GOT THE CULPRIT.

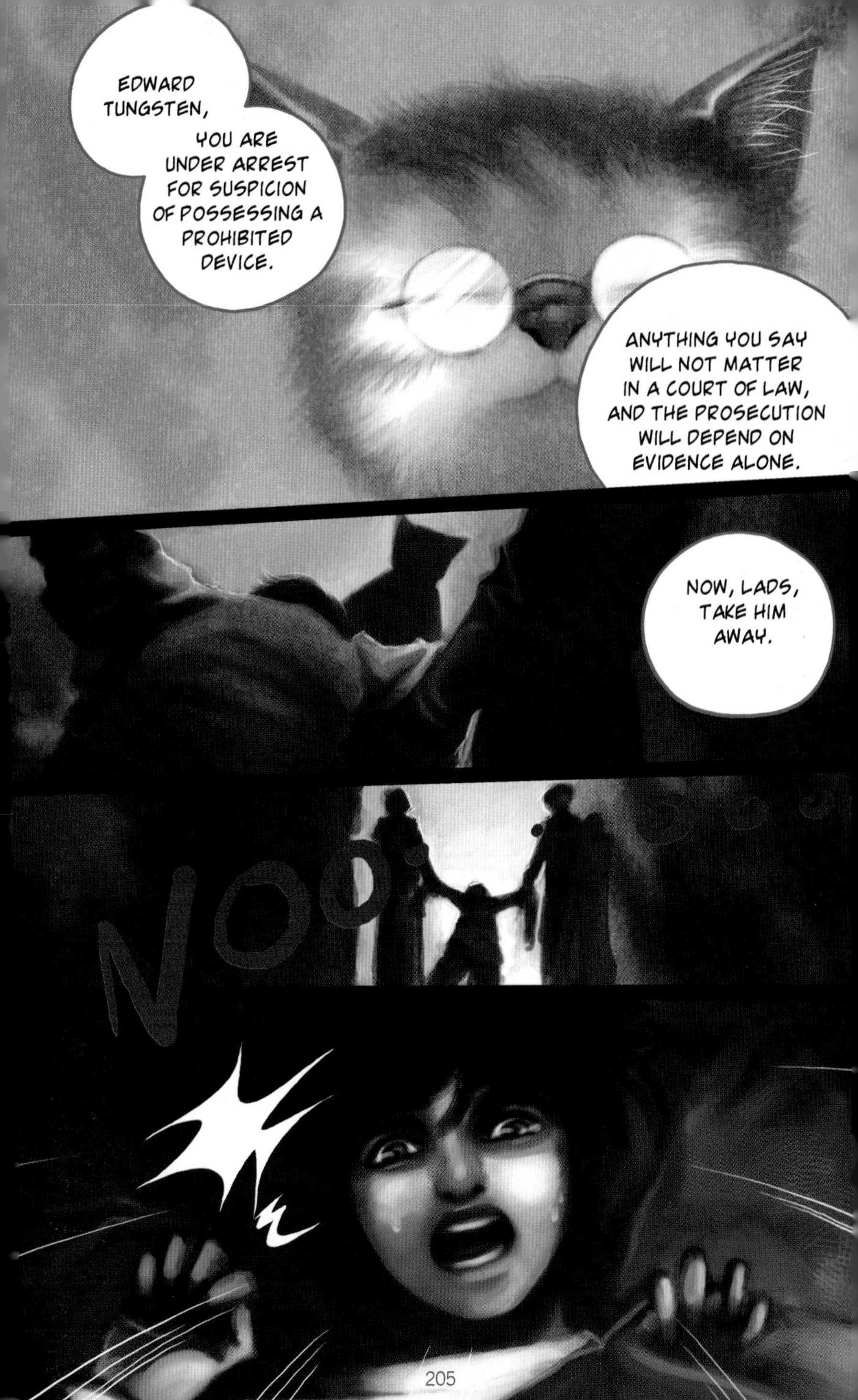
EDWARD TUNGSTEN,
YOU ARE UNDER ARREST FOR SUSPICION OF POSSESSING A PROHIBITED DEVICE.
ANYTHING YOU SAY WILL NOT MATTER IN A COURT OF LAW, AND THE PROSECUTION WILL DEPEND ON EVIDENCE ALONE.
NOW, LADS, TAKE HIM AWAY.
NOOOO...

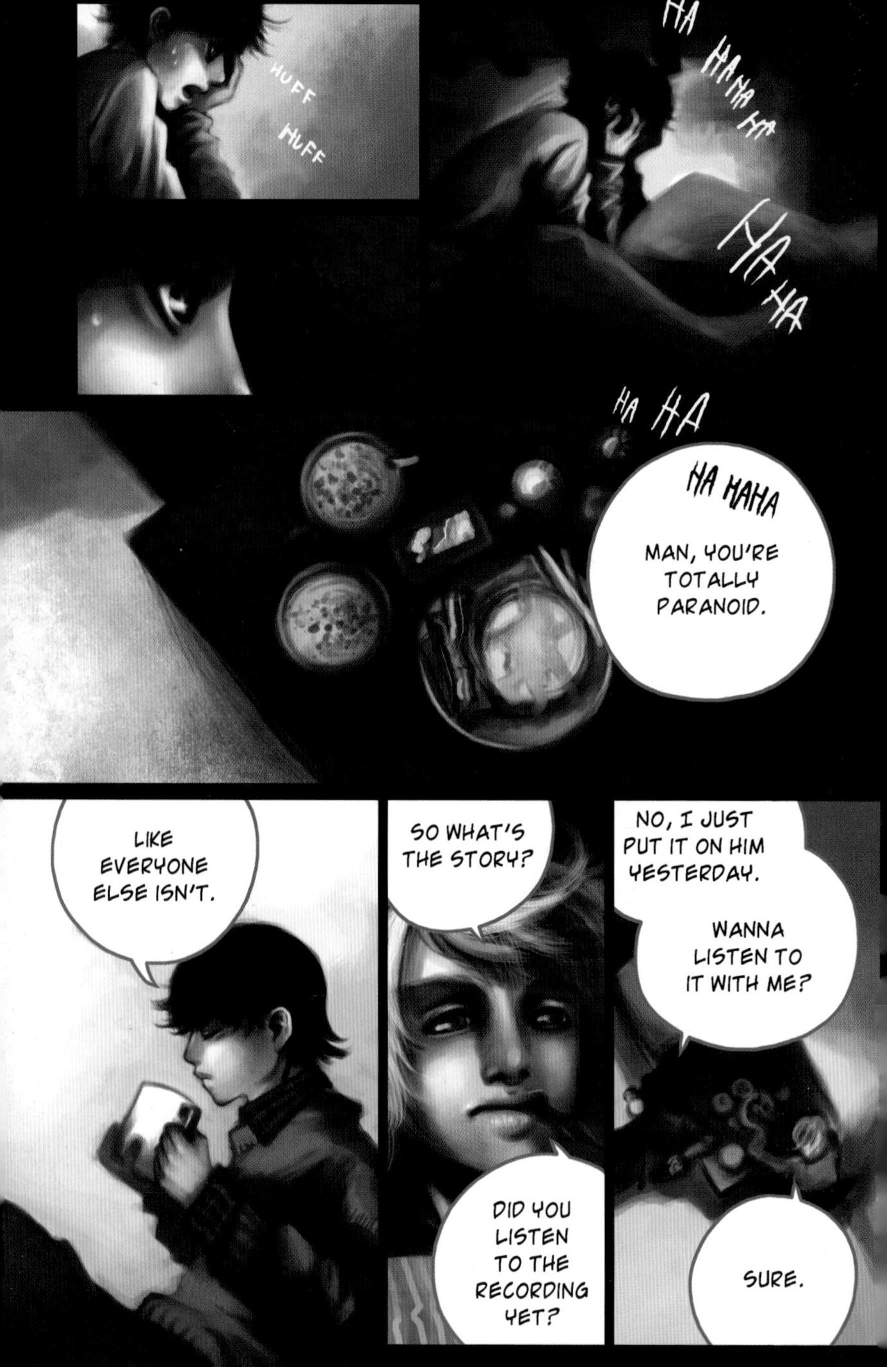
HUFF HUFF
HA HAHAHA HA
HA HA
HA HA
HA HAHA
MAN, YOU'RE TOTALLY PARANOID.
LIKE EVERYONE ELSE ISN'T.
SO WHAT'S THE STORY?
DID YOU LISTEN TO THE RECORDING YET?
NO, I JUST PUT IT ON HIM YESTERDAY.
WANNA LISTEN TO IT WITH ME?
SURE.

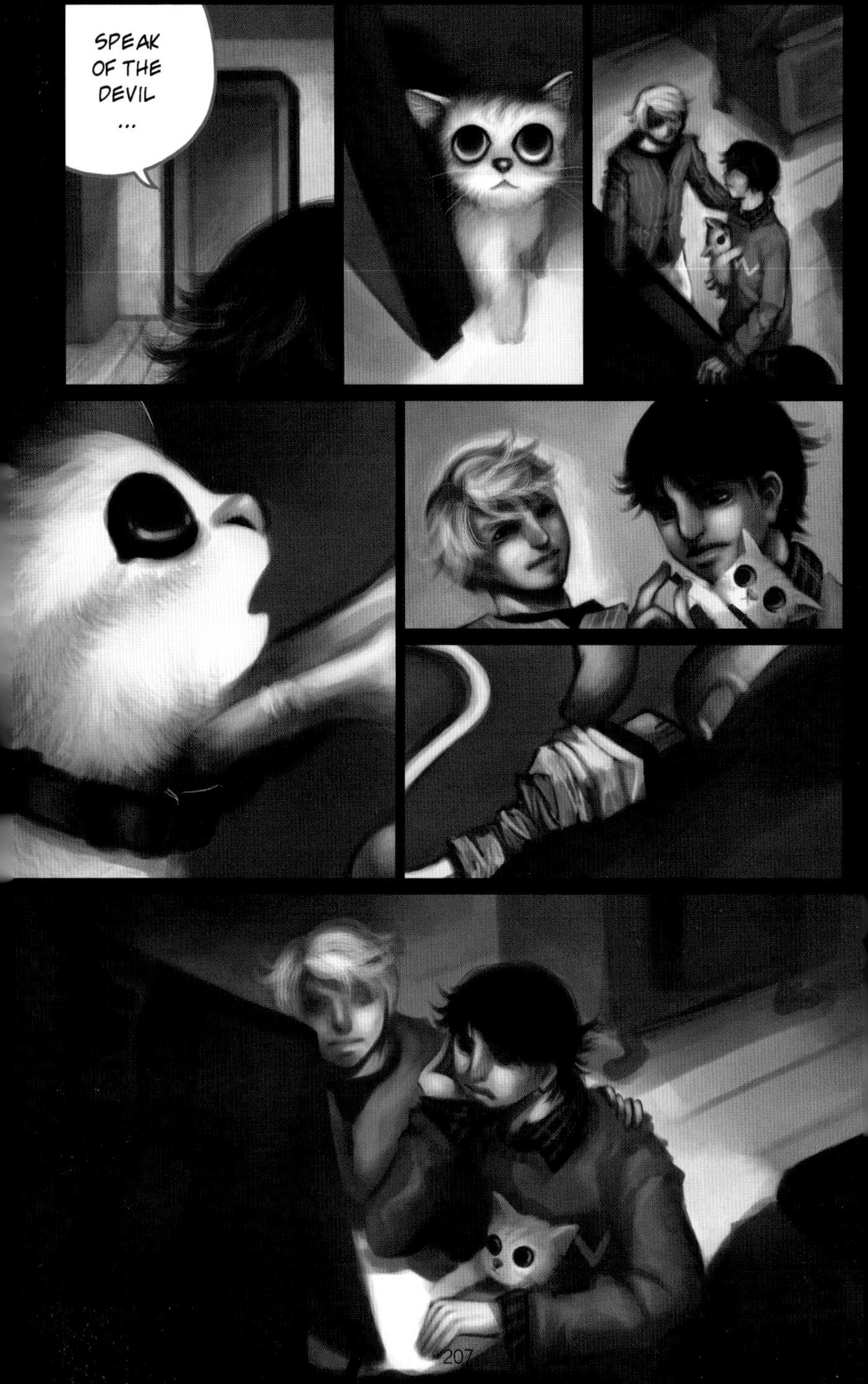
SPEAK OF THE DEVIL ...

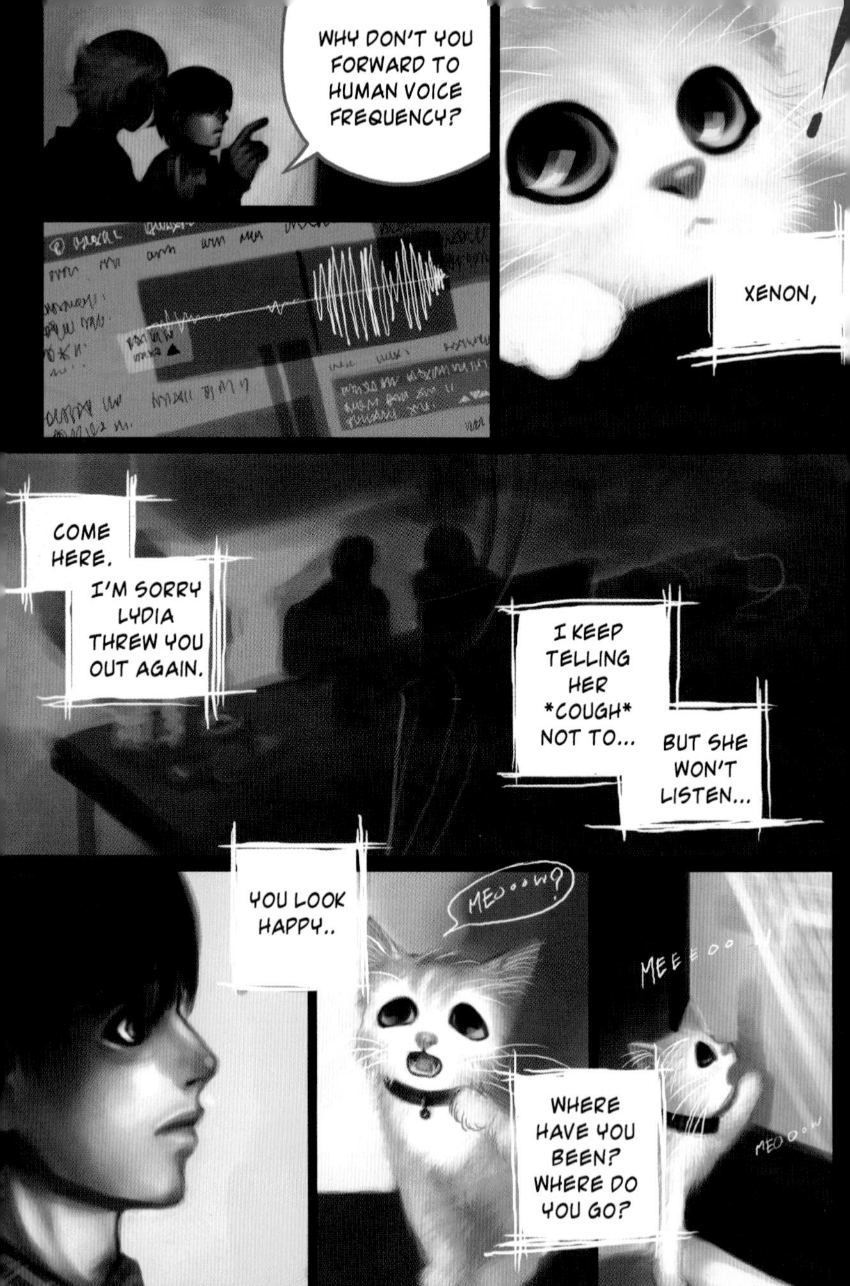
WHY DON'T YOU FORWARD TO HUMAN VOICE FREQUENCY?
XENON,
COME HERE.
I'M SORRY LYDIA THREW YOU OUT AGAIN.
I KEEP TELLING HER *COUGH* NOT TO...
BUT SHE WON'T LISTEN...
YOU LOOK HAPPY..
MEOOW?
MEEEOO
WHERE HAVE YOU BEEN? WHERE DO YOU GO?
MEOOOW

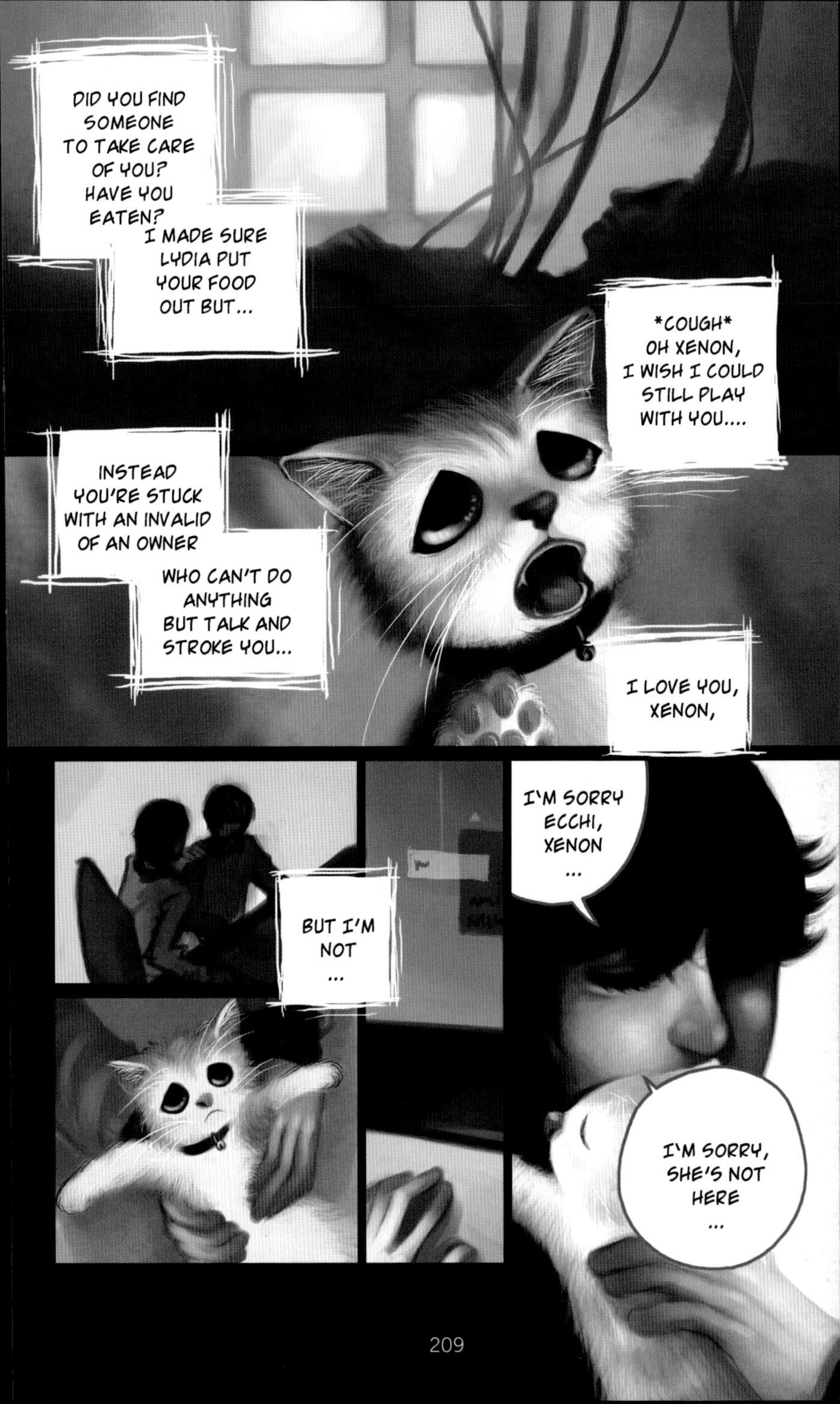
DID YOU FIND SOMEONE TO TAKE CARE OF YOU? HAVE YOU EATEN?
I MADE SURE LYDIA PUT YOUR FOOD OUT BUT...
COUGH OH XENON, I WISH I COULD STILL PLAY WITH YOU....
INSTEAD YOU'RE STUCK WITH AN INVALID OF AN OWNER
WHO CAN'T DO ANYTHING BUT TALK AND STROKE YOU...
I LOVE YOU, XENON,
BUT I'M NOT ...
I'M SORRY ECCHI, XENON ...
I'M SORRY, SHE'S NOT HERE ...

ECCHI IS STILL COMING AND GOING,

BUT I NO LONGER WONDER WHERE HE GOES.

I KNOW NOW IT'S WHERE HE'S NEEDED THE MOST.

AND WHEN HE RETURNS TO ME,

I PAMPER HIM AS BEST AS I CAN

BECAUSE, SOMEHOW, I THINK HE DESERVES A REWARD FOR BEING SO LOYAL

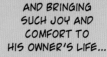

AND BRINGING SUCH JOY AND COMFORT TO HIS OWNER'S LIFE...

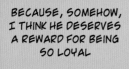

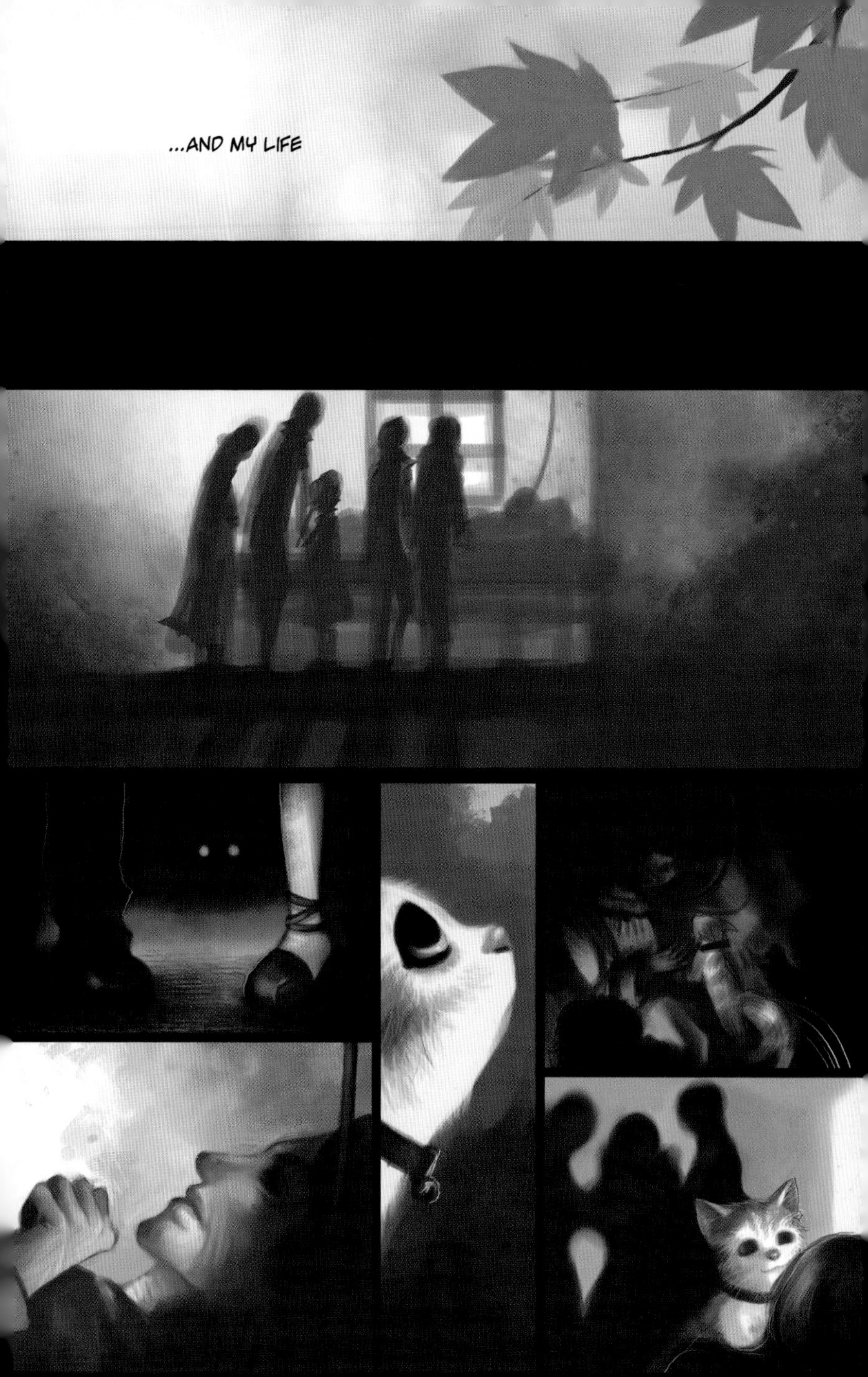
...AND MY LIFE

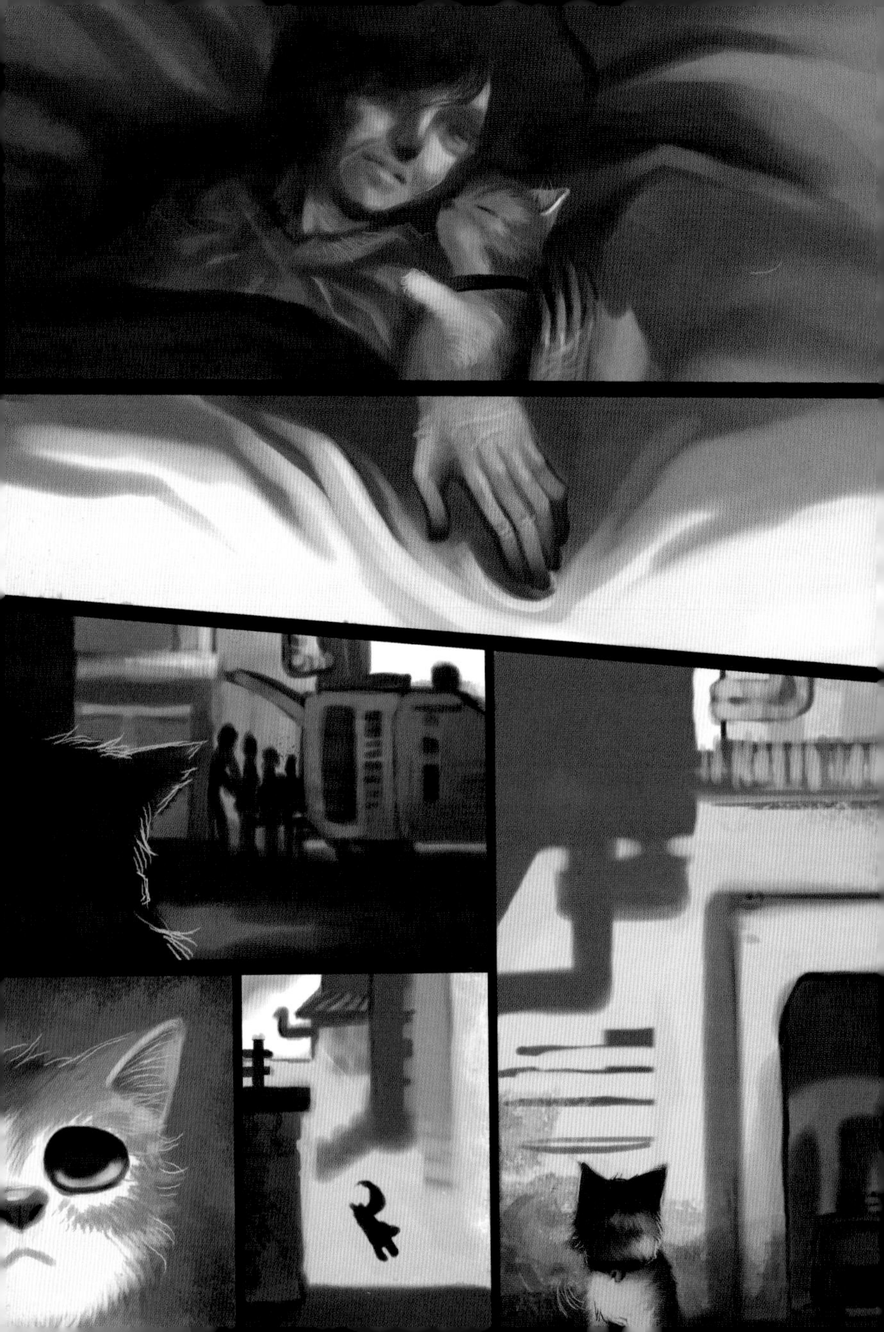

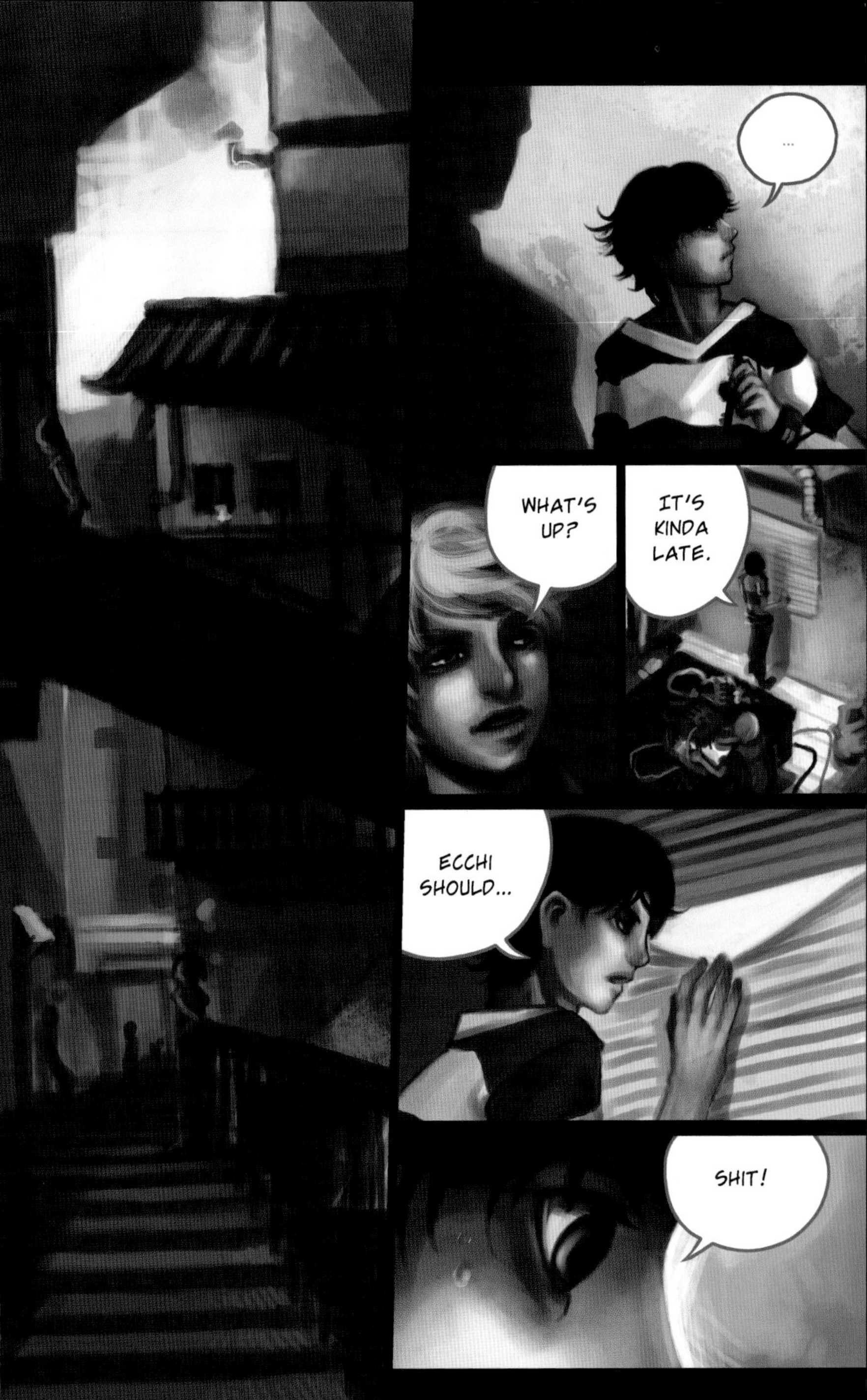
...
WHAT'S UP?
IT'S KINDA LATE.
ECCHI SHOULD...
SHIT!

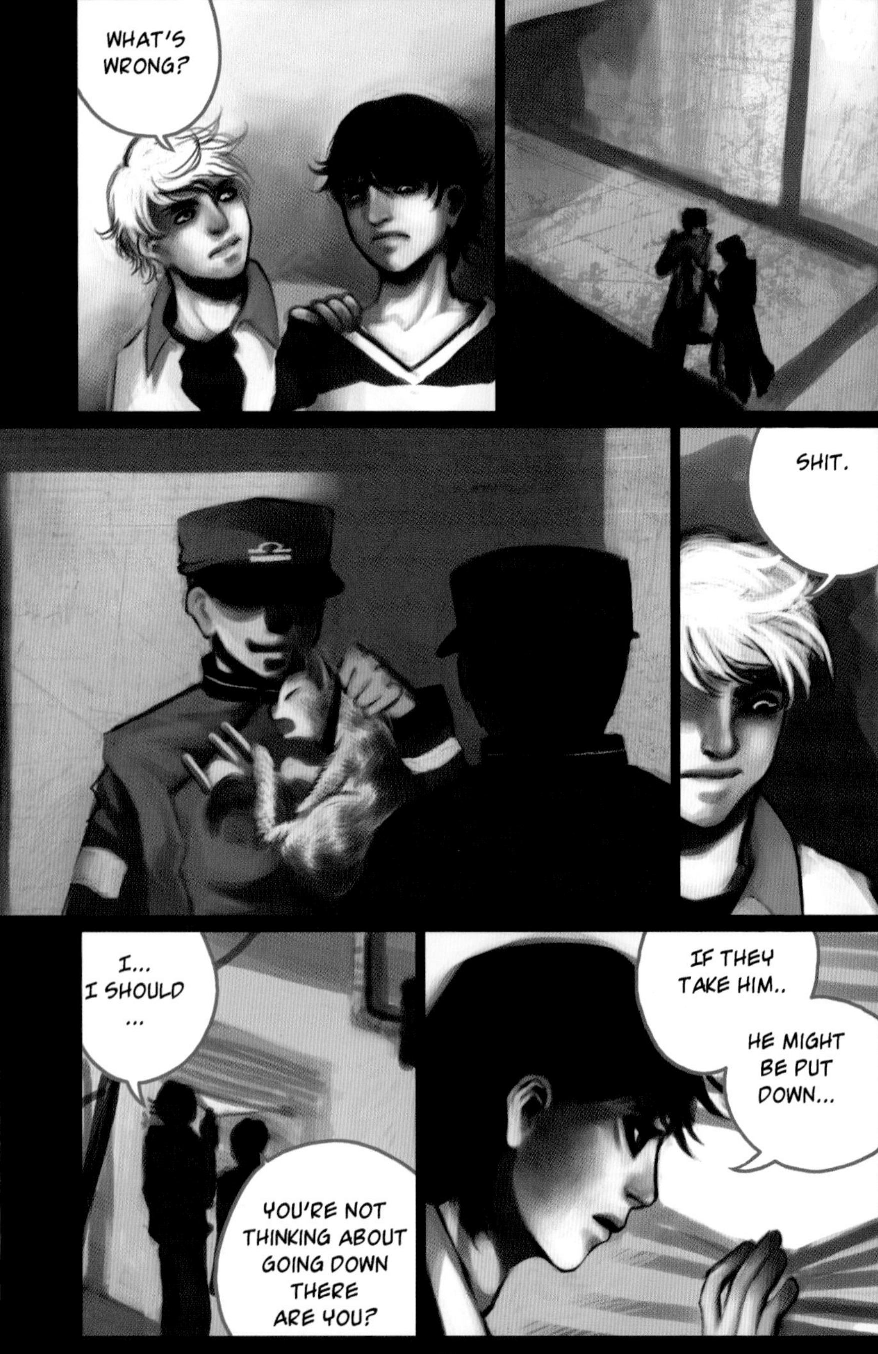
WHAT'S WRONG?
SHIT.
I... I SHOULD ...
YOU'RE NOT THINKING ABOUT GOING DOWN THERE ARE YOU?
IF THEY TAKE HIM..
HE MIGHT BE PUT DOWN...

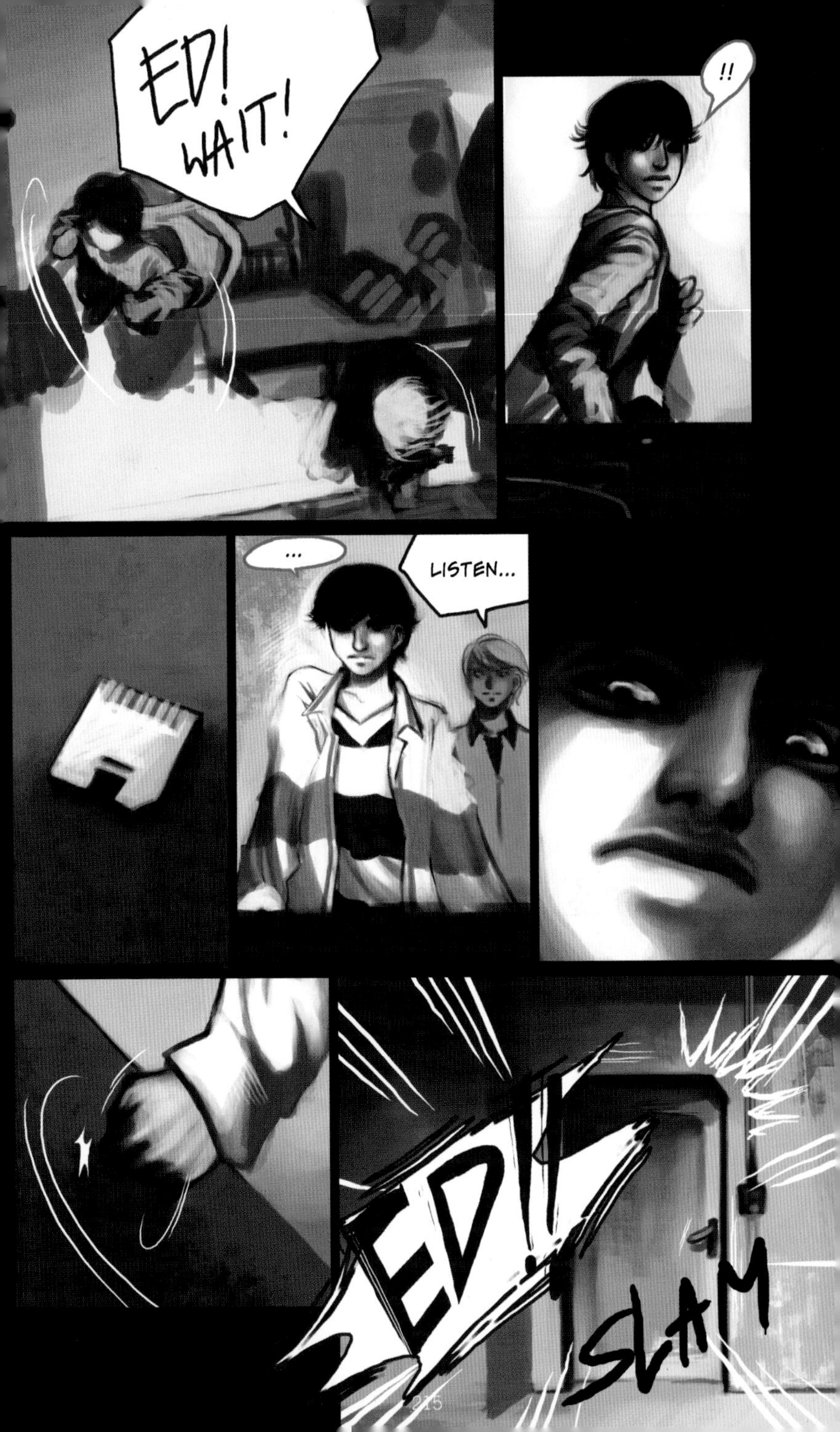
ED! WAIT!
!!
...
LISTEN...
ED!!
SLAM

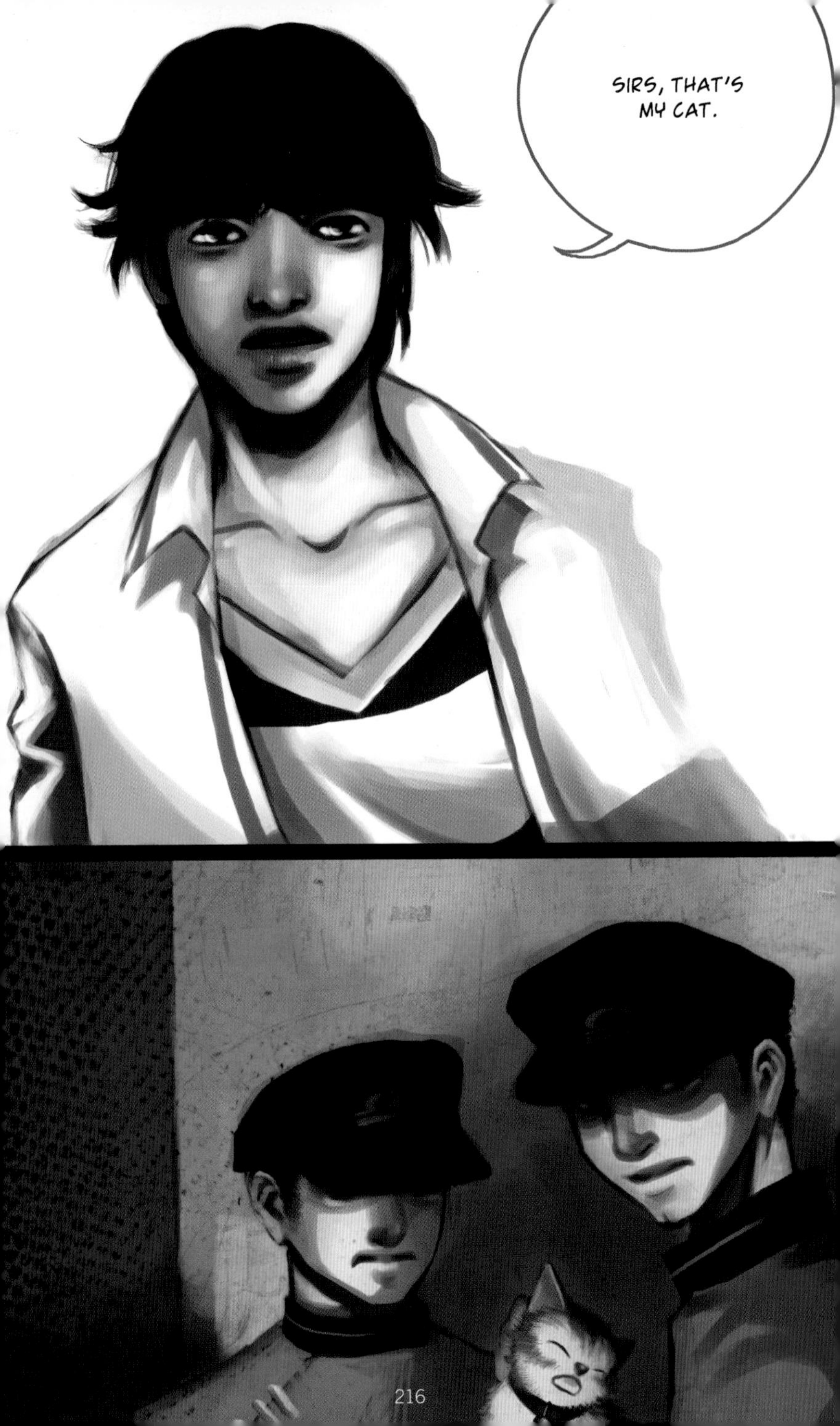
SIRS, THAT'S MY CAT.

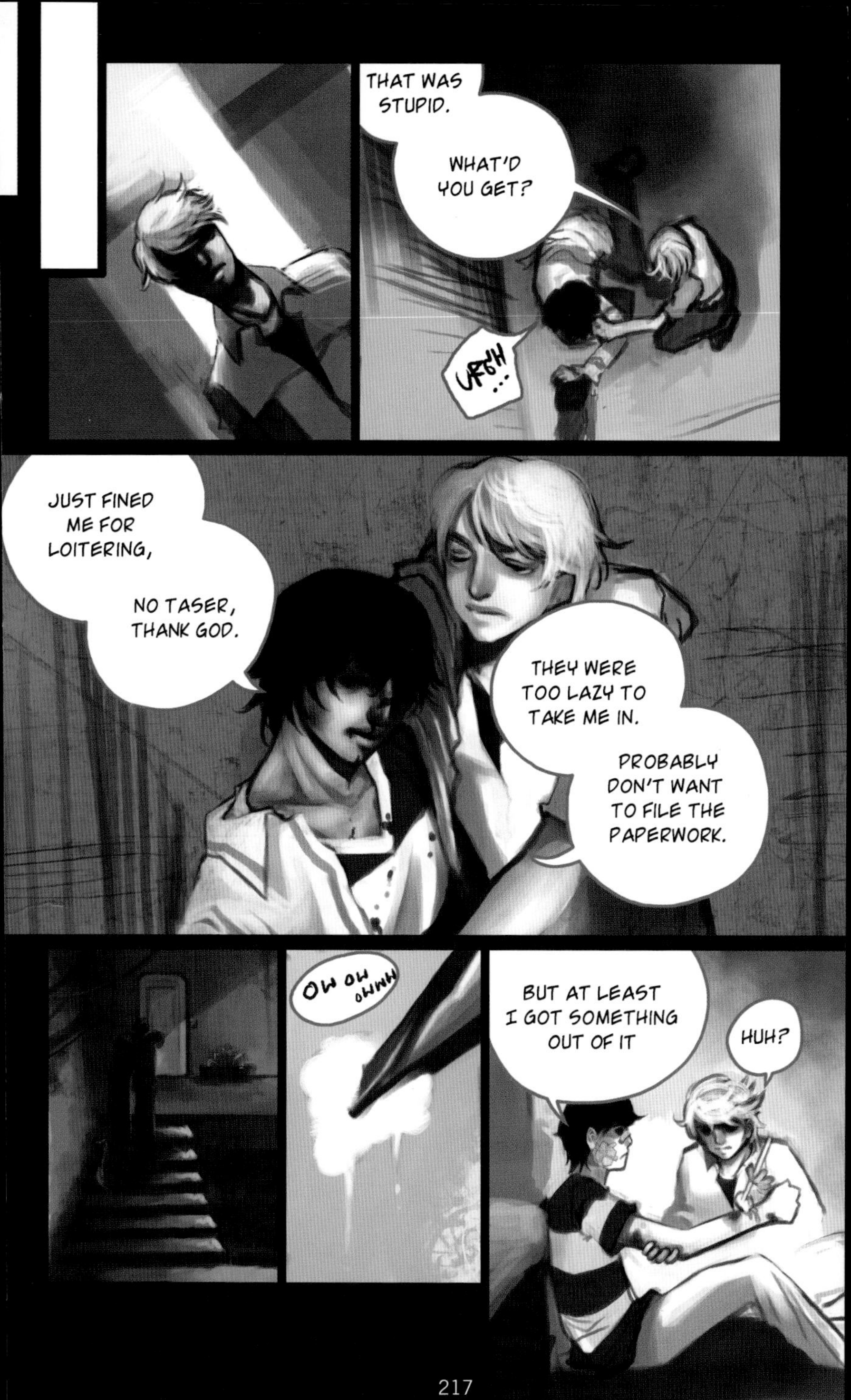
THAT WAS STUPID.
WHAT'D YOU GET?
URGH...
JUST FINED ME FOR LOITERING,
NO TASER, THANK GOD.
THEY WERE TOO LAZY TO TAKE ME IN.
PROBABLY DON'T WANT TO FILE THE PAPERWORK.
OW OW OWWW
BUT AT LEAST I GOT SOMETHING OUT OF IT
HUH?

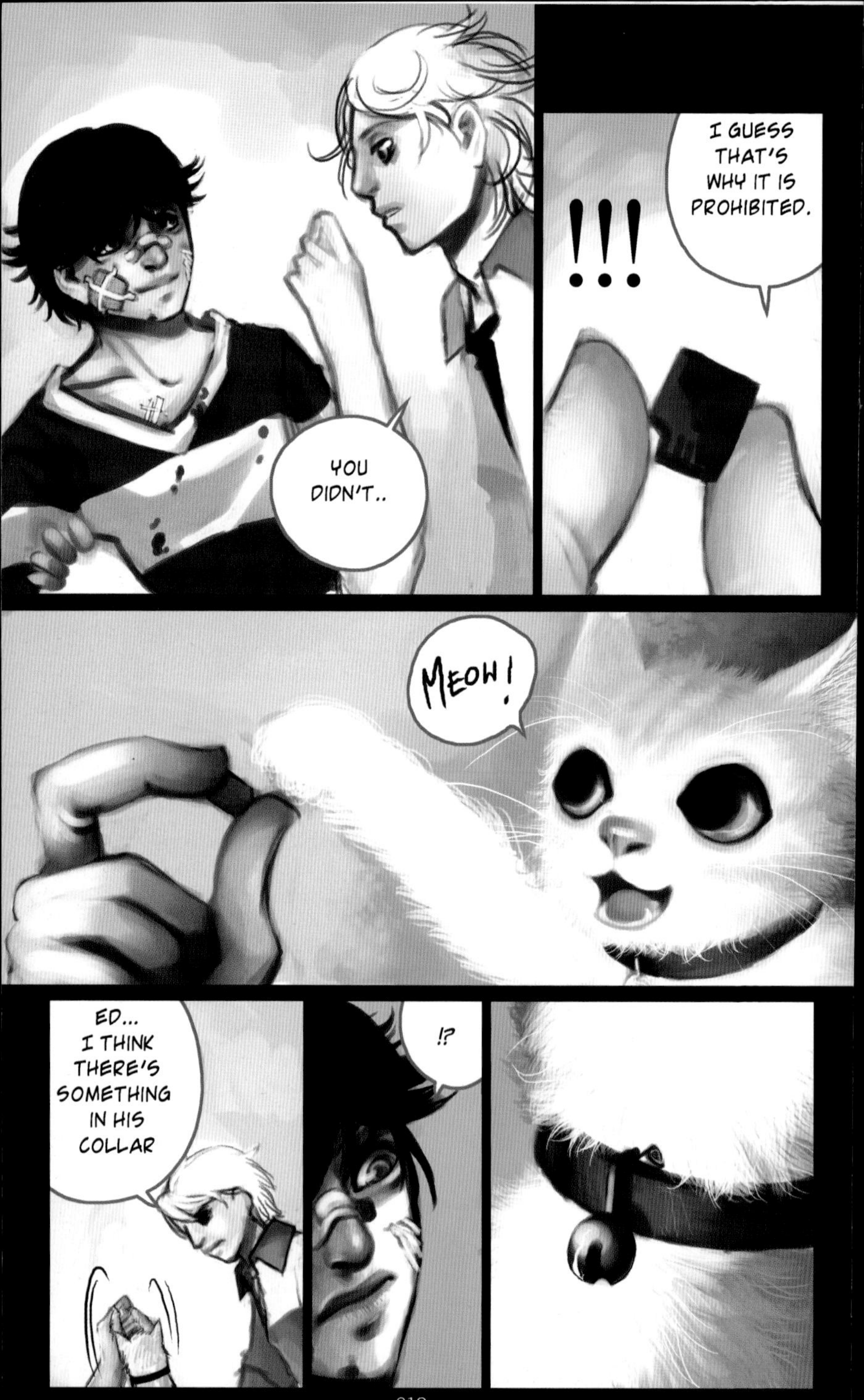
YOU DIDN'T..
!!!
I GUESS THAT'S WHY IT IS PROHIBITED.
MEOW!
ED... I THINK THERE'S SOMETHING IN HIS COLLAR
!?

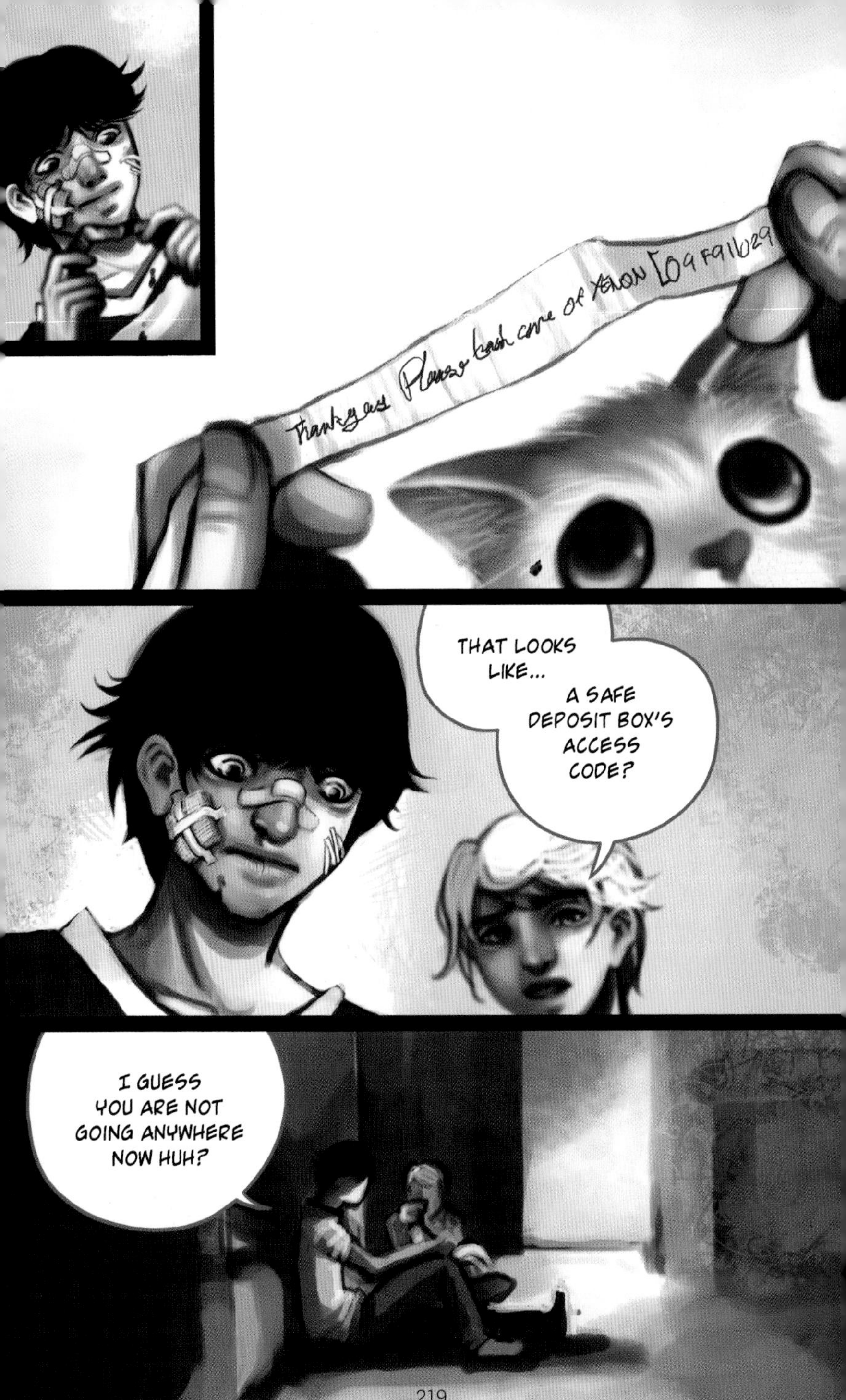
thankyou Please take care of Xenon 09 F911029
THAT LOOKS LIKE... A SAFE DEPOSIT BOX'S ACCESS CODE?
I GUESS YOU ARE NOT GOING ANYWHERE NOW HUH?

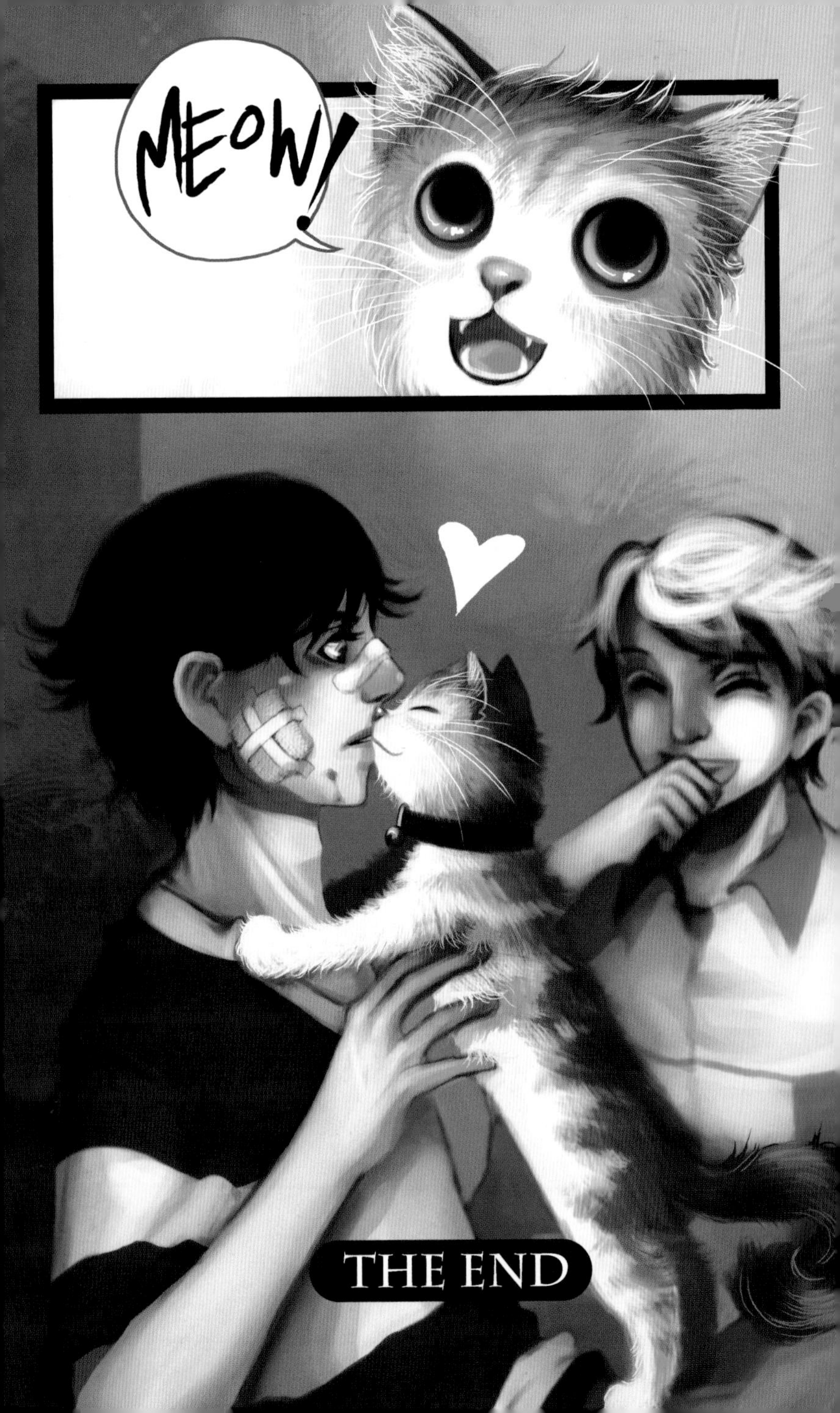
MEOW!
THE END

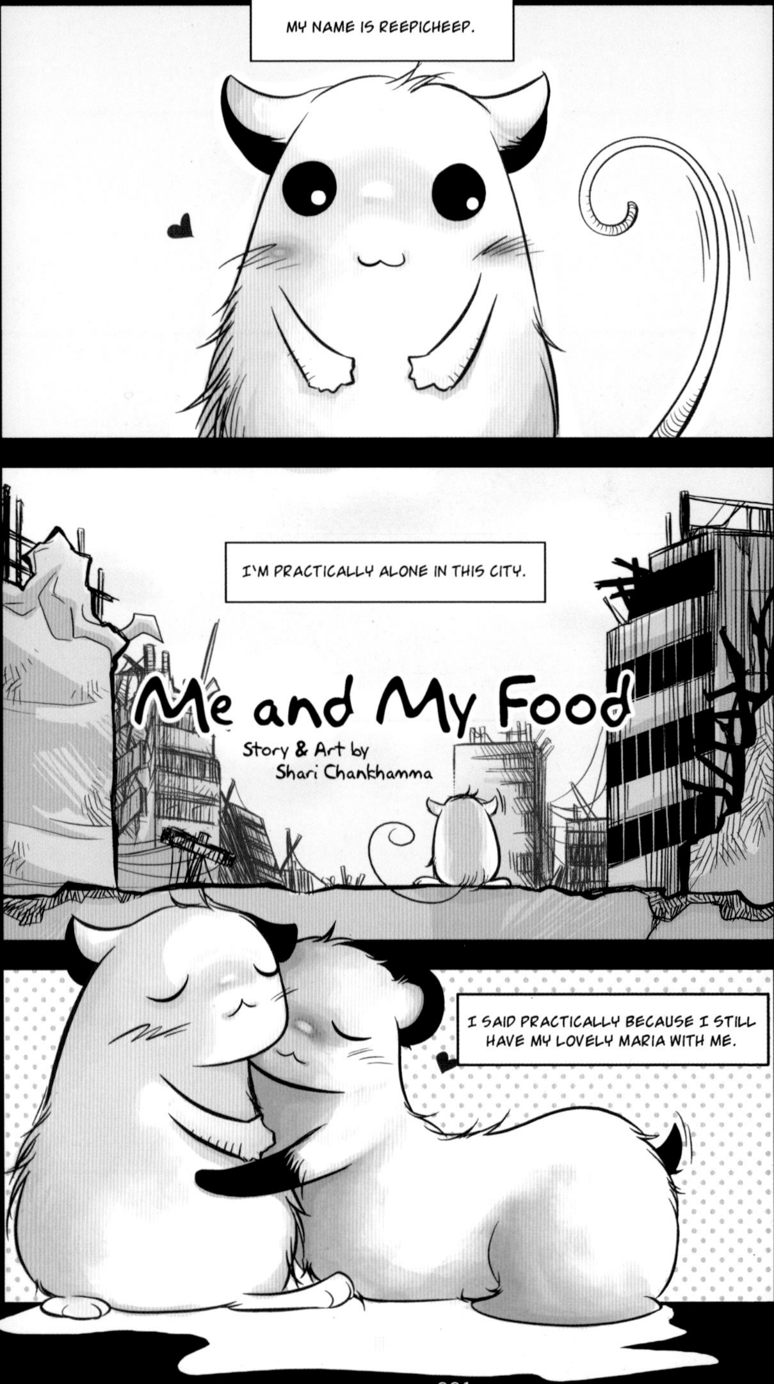
MY NAME IS REEPICHEEP.
I'M PRACTICALLY ALONE IN THIS CITY.
Me and My Food
Story & Art by
Shari Chankhamma
I SAID PRACTICALLY BECAUSE I STILL HAVE MY LOVELY MARIA WITH ME.

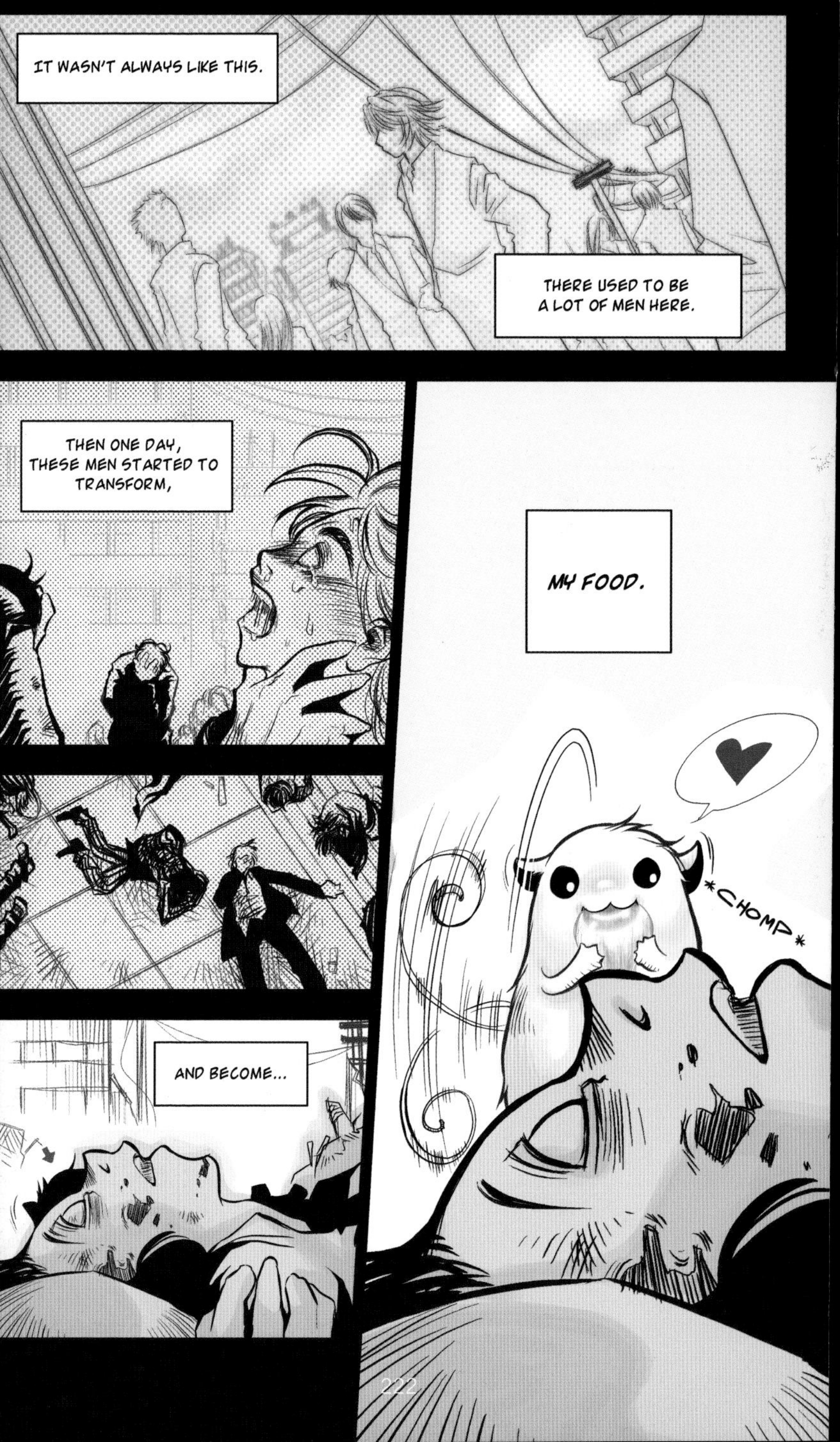
IT WASN'T ALWAYS LIKE THIS.
THERE USED TO BE A LOT OF MEN HERE.
THEN ONE DAY, THESE MEN STARTED TO TRANSFORM,
AND BECOME...
MY FOOD.
CHOMP

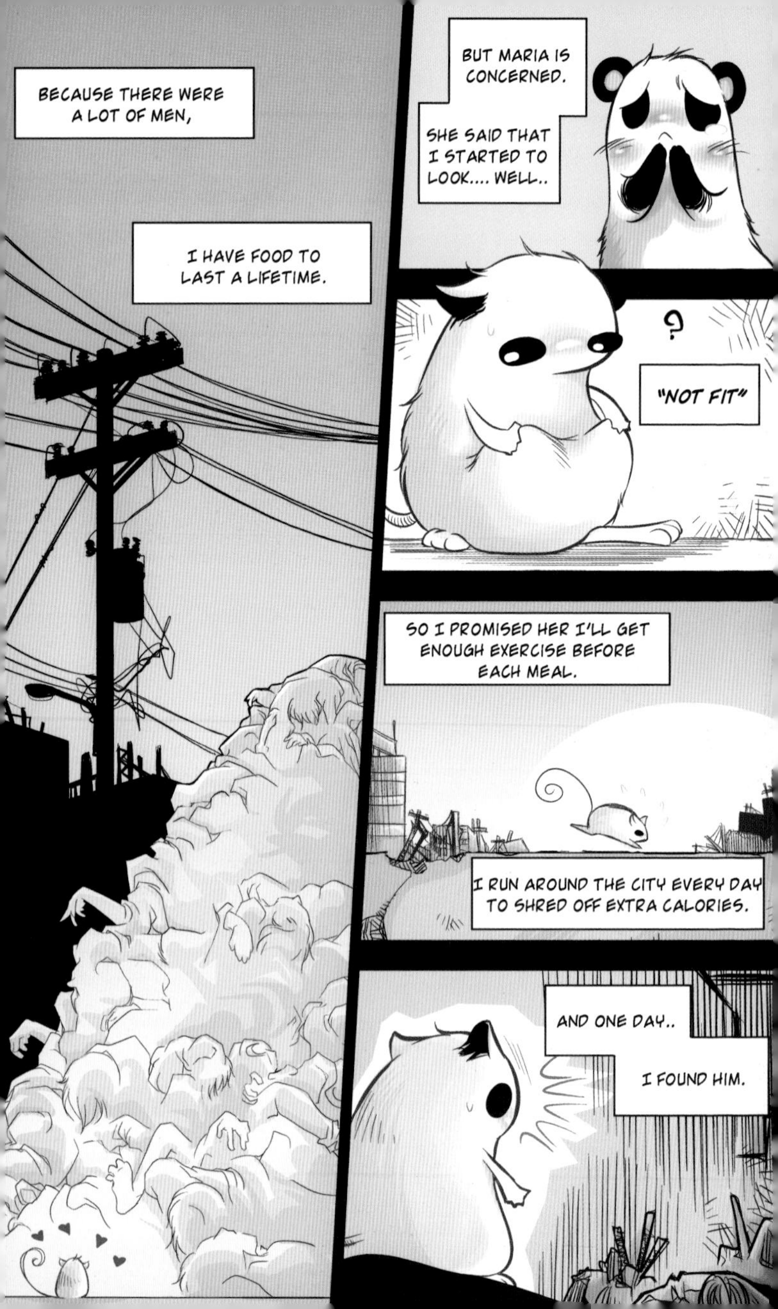

BECAUSE THERE WERE A LOT OF MEN,
I HAVE FOOD TO LAST A LIFETIME.
BUT MARIA IS CONCERNED.
SHE SAID THAT I STARTED TO LOOK.... WELL..
?
"NOT FIT"
SO I PROMISED HER I'LL GET ENOUGH EXERCISE BEFORE EACH MEAL.
I RUN AROUND THE CITY EVERY DAY TO SHRED OFF EXTRA CALORIES.
AND ONE DAY..
I FOUND HIM.

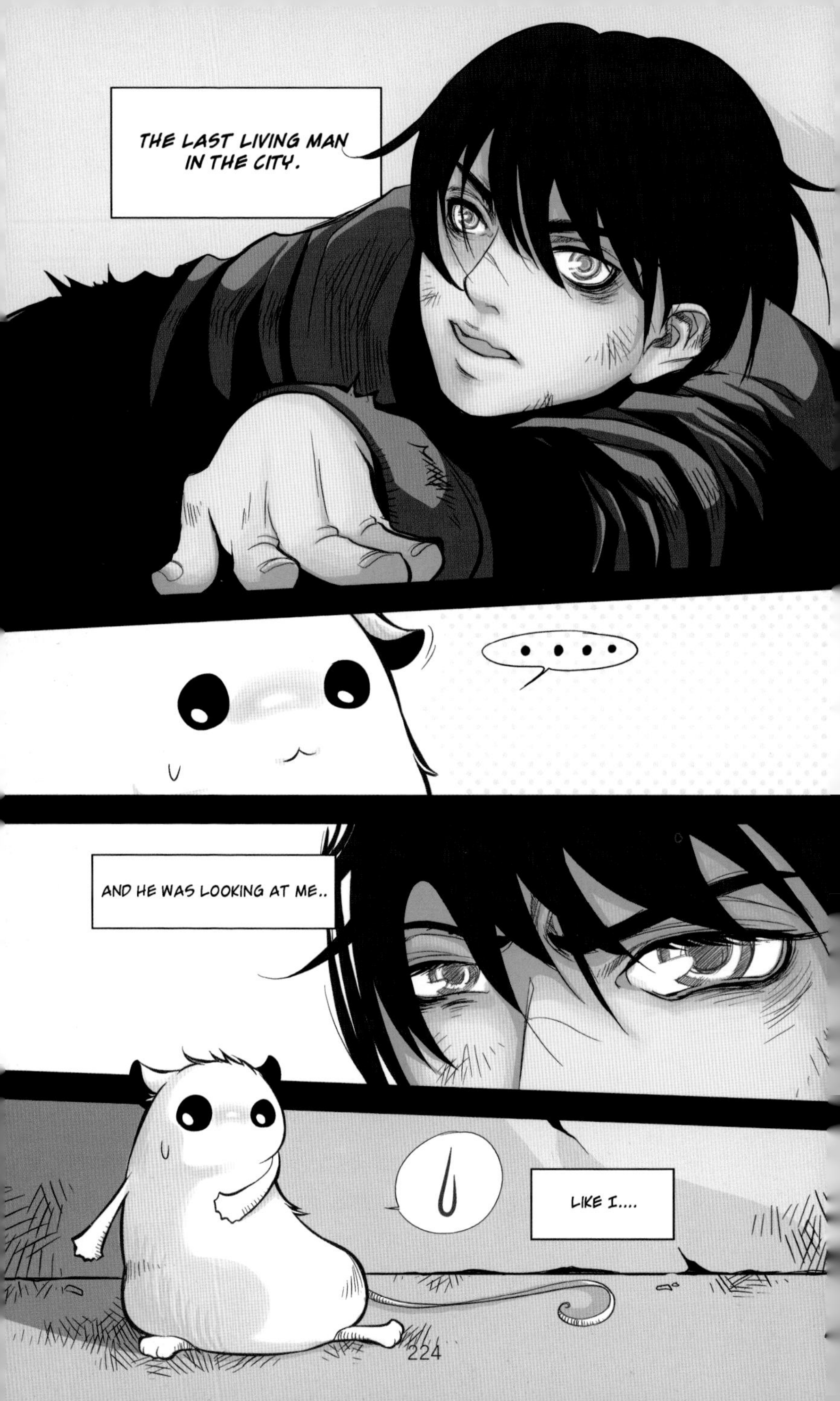
THE LAST LIVING MAN IN THE CITY.
....
AND HE WAS LOOKING AT ME..
LIKE I....

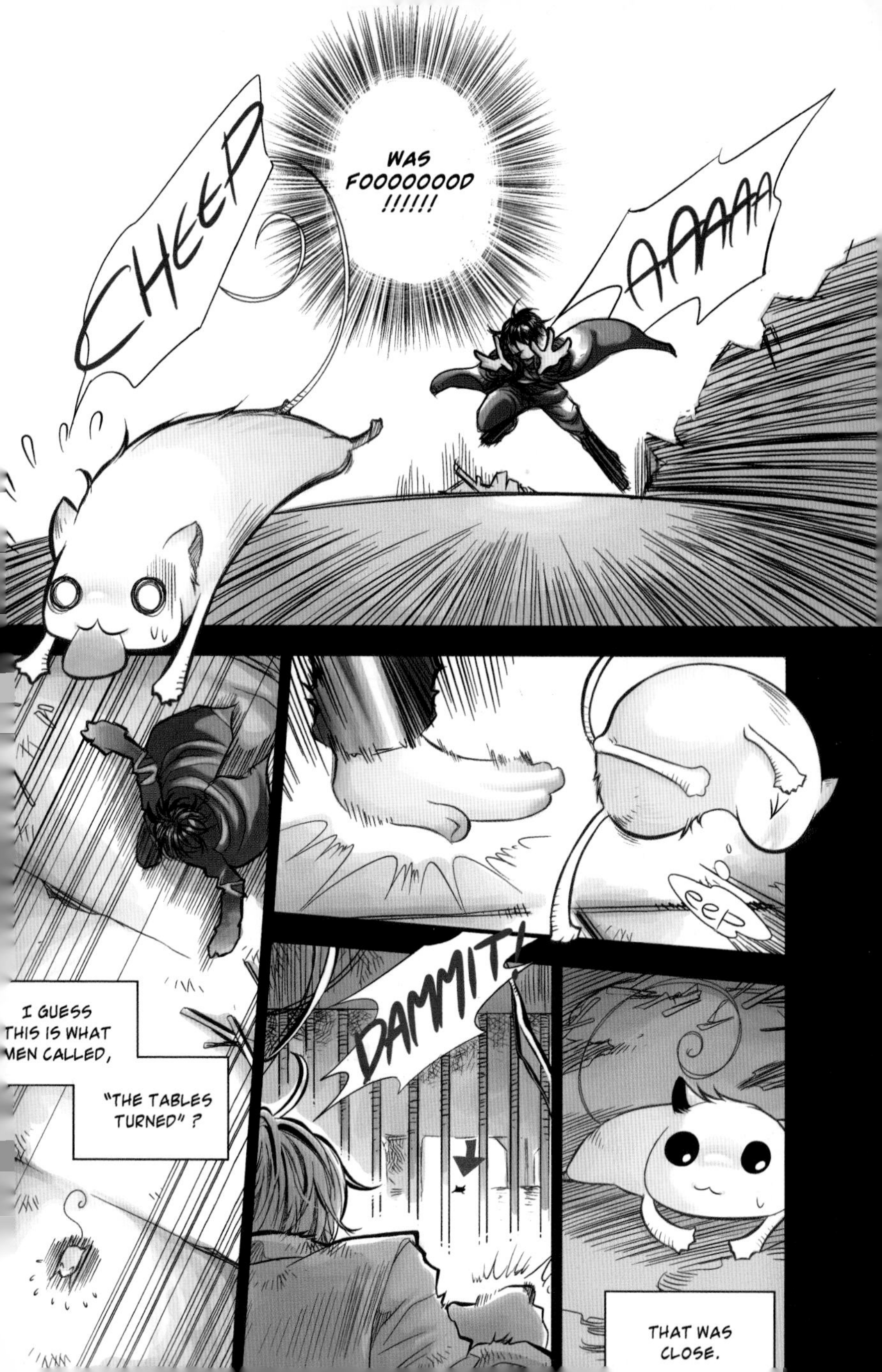
CHEEP
WAS FOOOOOOOD !!!!!!
AAAAA
I GUESS THIS IS WHAT MEN CALLED,
"THE TABLES TURNED" ?
eep
DAMMIT!
THAT WAS CLOSE.

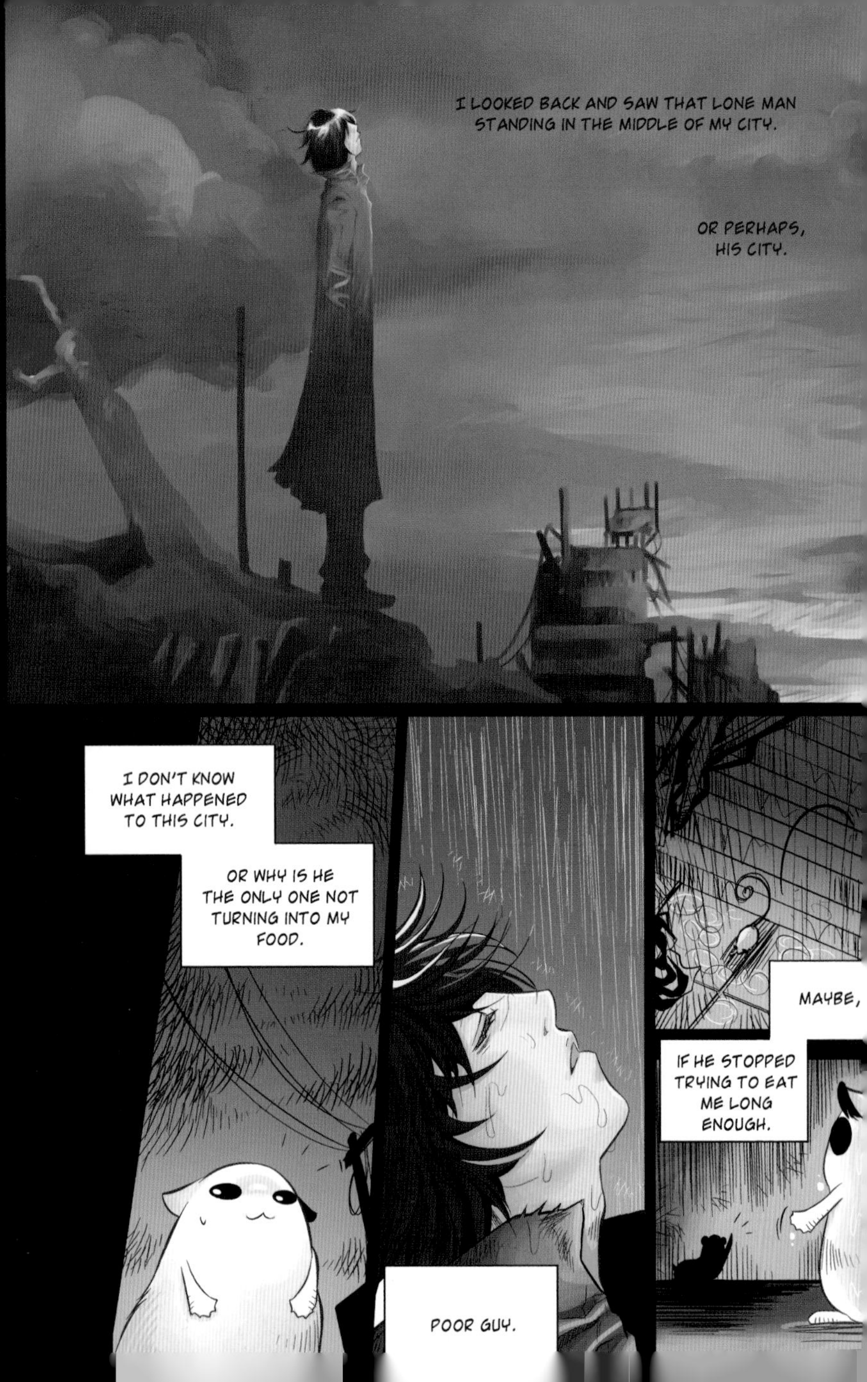
I LOOKED BACK AND SAW THAT LONE MAN STANDING IN THE MIDDLE OF MY CITY.
OR PERHAPS, HIS CITY.
I DON'T KNOW WHAT HAPPENED TO THIS CITY.
OR WHY IS HE THE ONLY ONE NOT TURNING INTO MY FOOD.
POOR GUY.
MAYBE,
IF HE STOPPED TRYING TO EAT ME LONG ENOUGH.

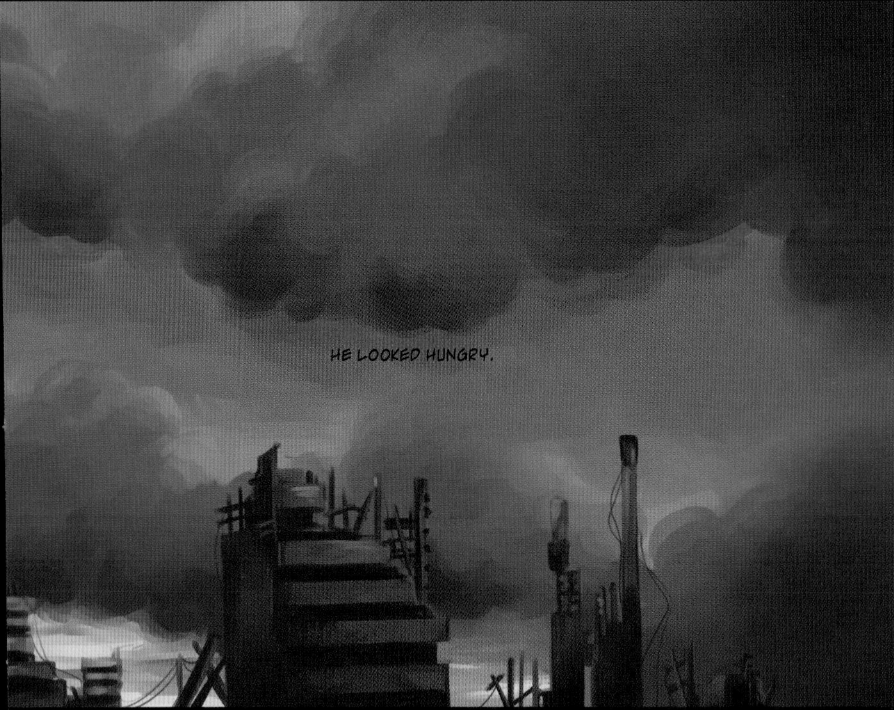
HE LOOKED HUNGRY.

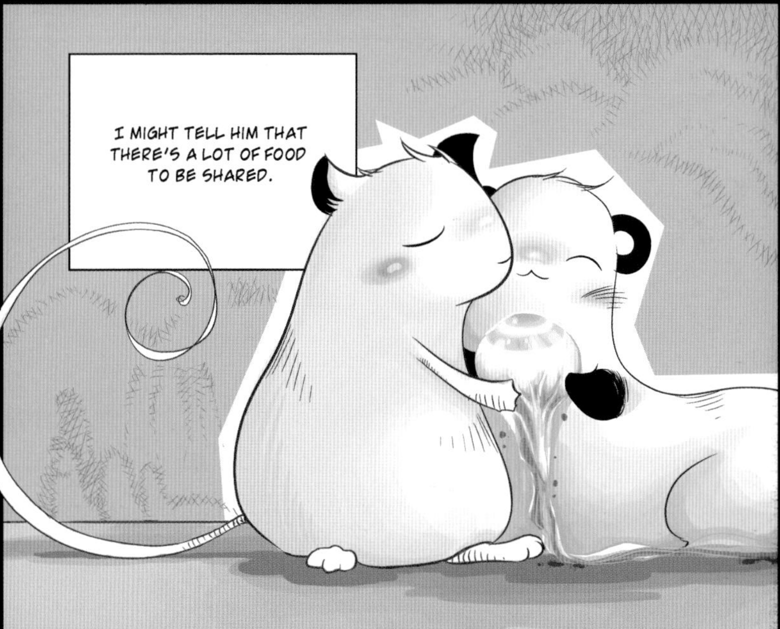
I MIGHT TELL HIM THAT THERE'S A LOT OF FOOD TO BE SHARED.

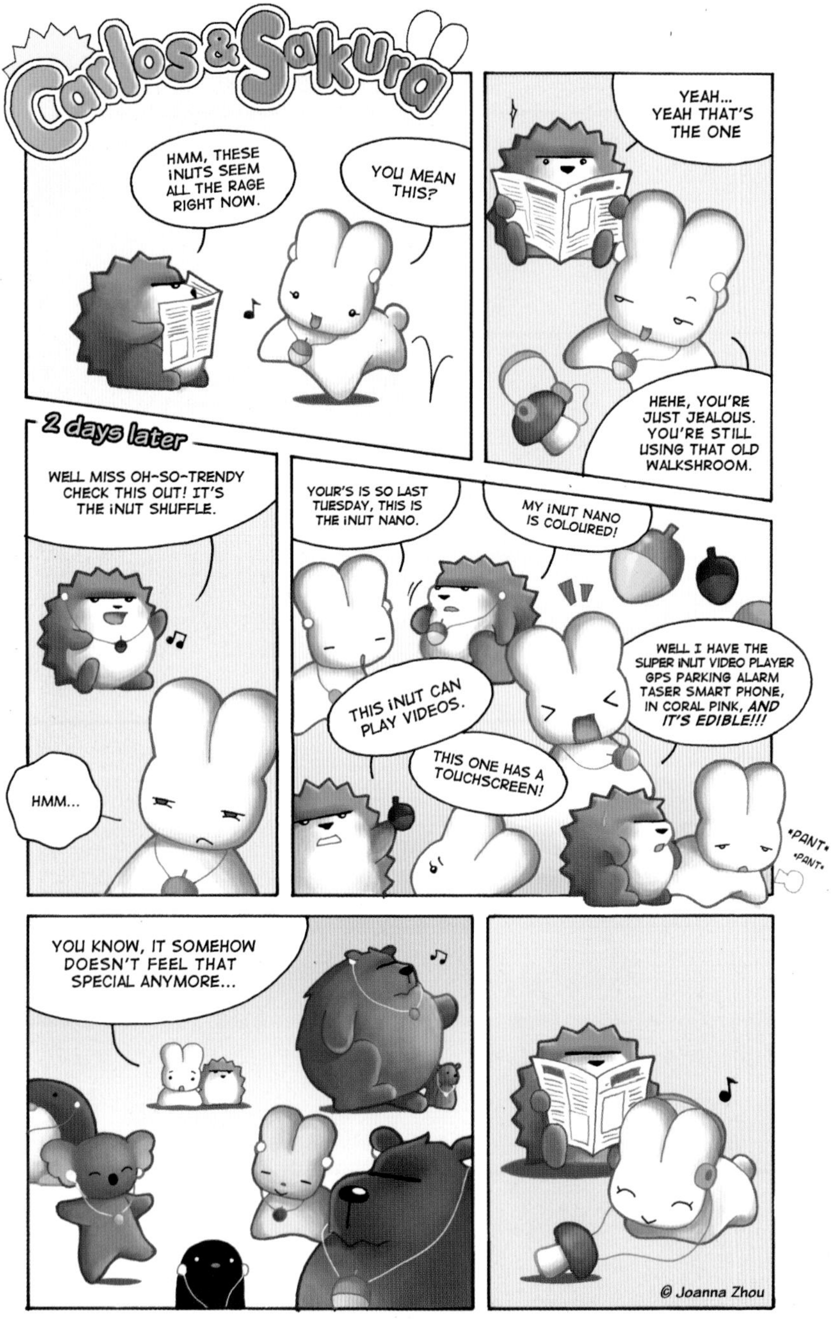
Carlos & Sakura
HMM, THESE iNUTS SEEM ALL THE RAGE RIGHT NOW.
YOU MEAN THIS?
YEAH... YEAH THAT'S THE ONE
HEHE, YOU'RE JUST JEALOUS. YOU'RE STILL USING THAT OLD WALKSHROOM.
2 days later
WELL MISS OH-SO-TRENDY CHECK THIS OUT! IT'S THE iNUT SHUFFLE.
HMM...
YOUR'S IS SO LAST TUESDAY, THIS IS THE iNUT NANO.
MY iNUT NANO IS COLOURED!
THIS iNUT CAN PLAY VIDEOS.
THIS ONE HAS A TOUCHSCREEN!
WELL I HAVE THE SUPER iNUT VIDEO PLAYER GPS PARKING ALARM TASER SMART PHONE, IN CORAL PINK, AND IT'S EDIBLE!!!
PANT *PANT*
YOU KNOW, IT SOMEHOW DOESN'T FEEL THAT SPECIAL ANYMORE...
© Joanna Zhou

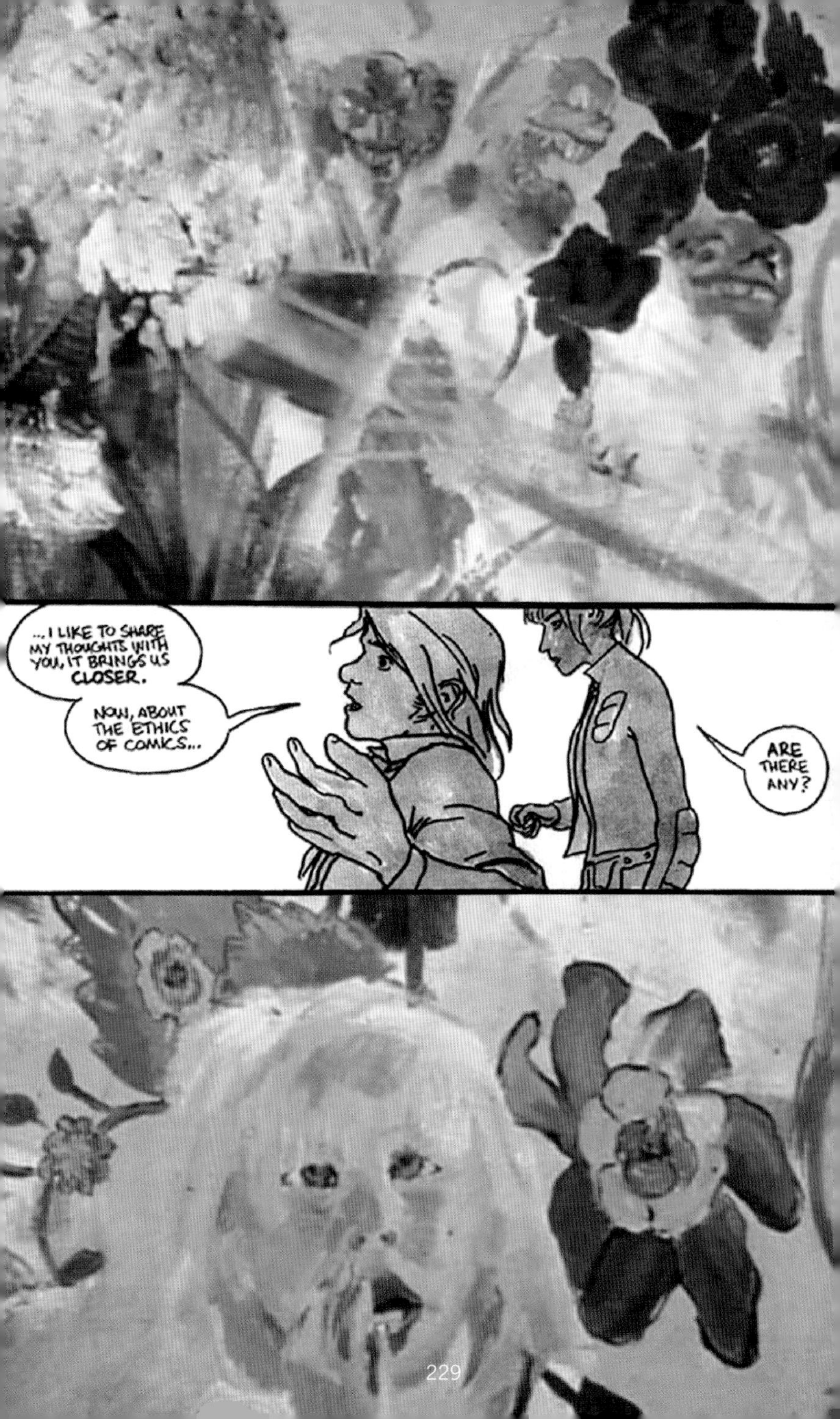
...I LIKE TO SHARE MY THOUGHTS WITH YOU, IT BRINGS US CLOSER.
NOW, ABOUT THE ETHICS OF COMICS...
ARE THERE ANY?

GROUND ZERO – THE WOGE
James Romberger & Marguerite Van Cook

Biography is another popular manga genre (Tezuka himself tackled subjects as varied as Buddha and Adolf Hitler). One of the best single comics published in the 1990s was *Seven Miles A Second*, a collaboration between two New York artists, **James Romberger** and David Wojnariwicz. It told the latter man's life story through the filter of his own writings, with particular haze and focus due to his heavy-duty drug treatments for AIDS, the condition from which David eventually died.

The Woge represents an untold chapter from that superlative exercise in comics narrative, one hopefully to be included within any new edition of the work. Meanwhile, we are proud as all get-out to take this opportunity and include it here, in print for the first time. Written by James' partner **Marguerite Van Cook**, *The Woge* evokes a little of the man by recounting an afternoon's conversation, the layout as free-flowing as their talk.

Look for these upcoming comics titles from James and Marguerite: *The Bronx Kill* with Peter Milligan (DC), *Tales from the Crypt* (Papercutz) and a *Ground Zero* collection.

www.thearteriesgroup.com

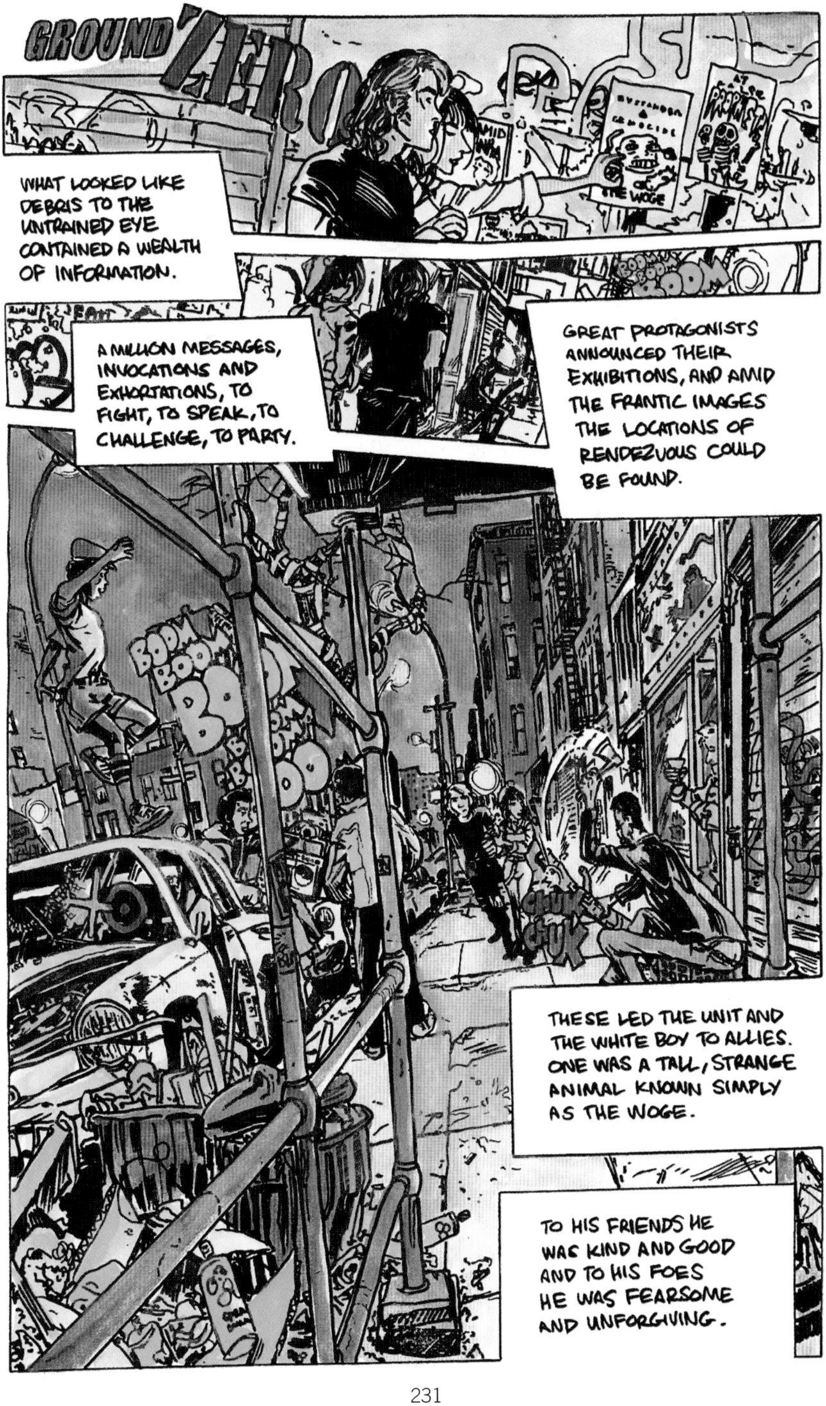
GROUND ZERO
WHAT LOOKED LIKE DEBRIS TO THE UNTRAINED EYE CONTAINED A WEALTH OF INFORMATION.
A MILLION MESSAGES, INVOCATIONS AND EXHORTATIONS, TO FIGHT, TO SPEAK, TO CHALLENGE, TO PARTY.
GREAT PROTAGONISTS ANNOUNCED THEIR EXHIBITIONS, AND AMID THE FRANTIC IMAGES THE LOCATIONS OF RENDEZVOUS COULD BE FOUND.
BOOM BOOM BOOM
CHUK CHUK
THESE LED THE UNIT AND THE WHITE BOY TO ALLIES. ONE WAS A TALL, STRANGE ANIMAL KNOWN SIMPLY AS THE WOGE.
TO HIS FRIENDS HE WAS KIND AND GOOD AND TO HIS FOES HE WAS FEARSOME AND UNFORGIVING.

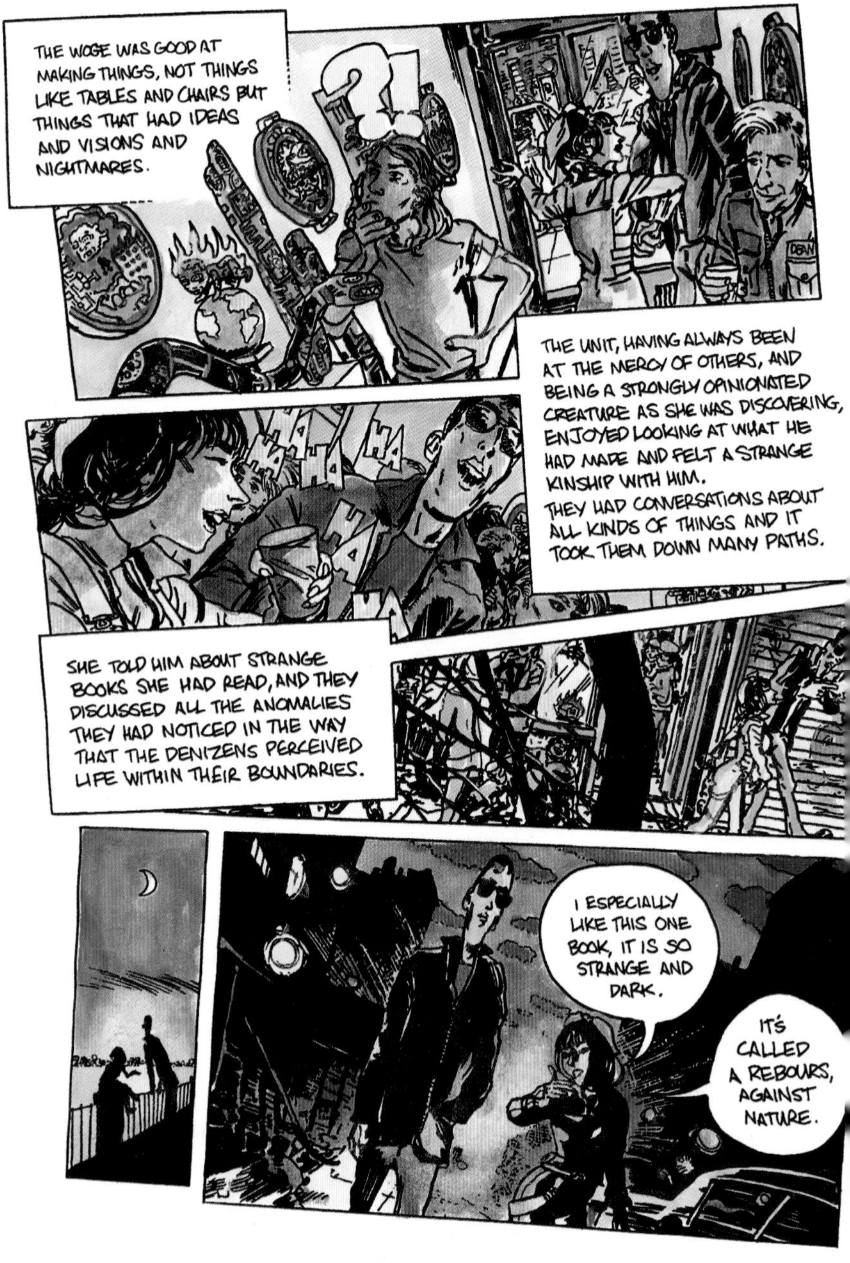
THE WOGE WAS GOOD AT MAKING THINGS, NOT THINGS LIKE TABLES AND CHAIRS BUT THINGS THAT HAD IDEAS AND VISIONS AND NIGHTMARES.
?!
DEAN
THE UNIT, HAVING ALWAYS BEEN AT THE MERCY OF OTHERS, AND BEING A STRONGLY OPINIONATED CREATURE AS SHE WAS DISCOVERING, ENJOYED LOOKING AT WHAT HE HAD MADE AND FELT A STRANGE KINSHIP WITH HIM. THEY HAD CONVERSATIONS ABOUT ALL KINDS OF THINGS AND IT TOOK THEM DOWN MANY PATHS.
HA HA HA HA HA HA HA
SHE TOLD HIM ABOUT STRANGE BOOKS SHE HAD READ, AND THEY DISCUSSED ALL THE ANOMALIES THEY HAD NOTICED IN THE WAY THAT THE DENIZENS PERCEIVED LIFE WITHIN THEIR BOUNDARIES.
I ESPECIALLY LIKE THIS ONE BOOK, IT IS SO STRANGE AND DARK.
IT'S CALLED A REBOURS, AGAINST NATURE.

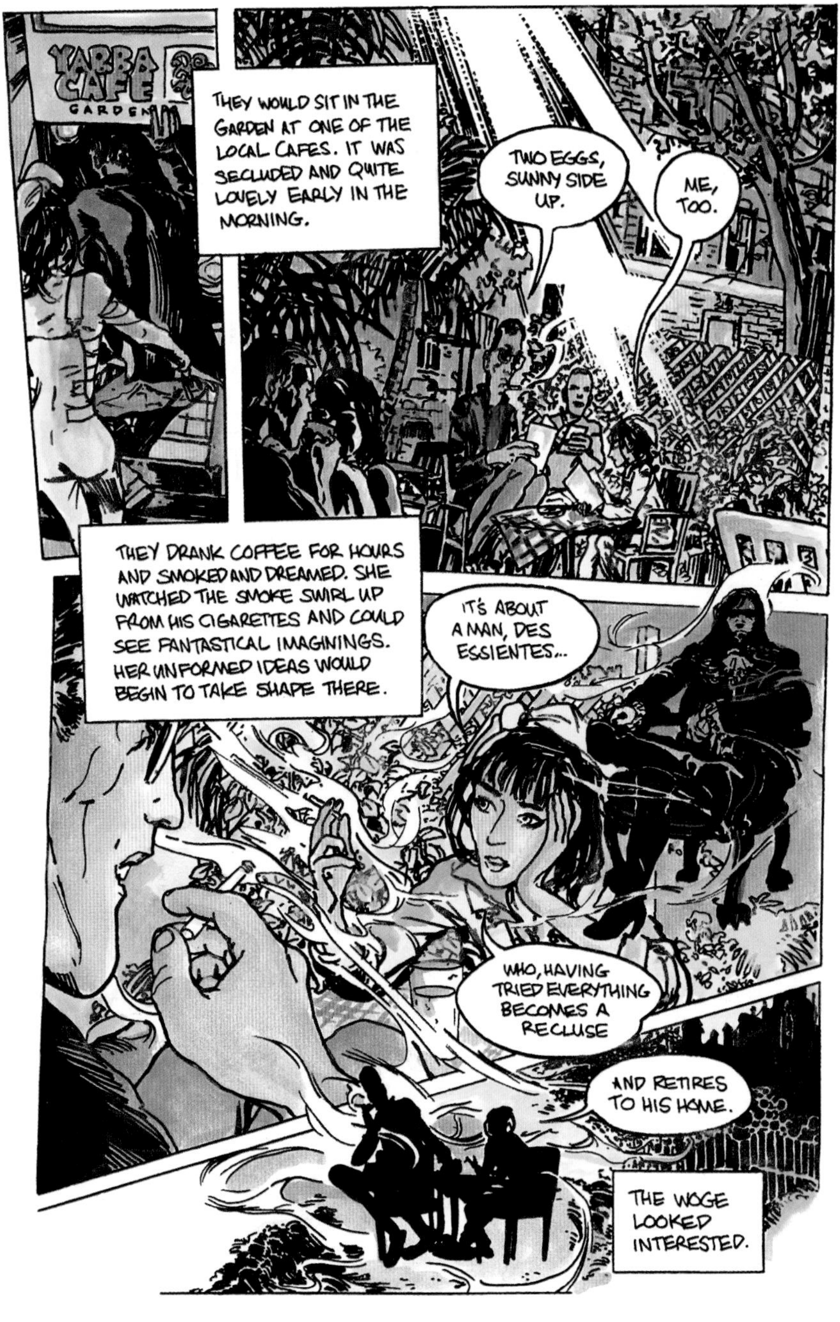
YARBA CAFE GARDEN
THEY WOULD SIT IN THE GARDEN AT ONE OF THE LOCAL CAFES. IT WAS SECLUDED AND QUITE LOVELY EARLY IN THE MORNING.
TWO EGGS, SUNNY SIDE UP.
ME, TOO.
THEY DRANK COFFEE FOR HOURS AND SMOKED AND DREAMED. SHE WATCHED THE SMOKE SWIRL UP FROM HIS CIGARETTES AND COULD SEE FANTASTICAL IMAGININGS. HER UNFORMED IDEAS WOULD BEGIN TO TAKE SHAPE THERE.
IT'S ABOUT A MAN, DES ESSIENTES...
WHO, HAVING TRIED EVERYTHING BECOMES A RECLUSE
AND RETIRES TO HIS HOME.
THE WOGE LOOKED INTERESTED.

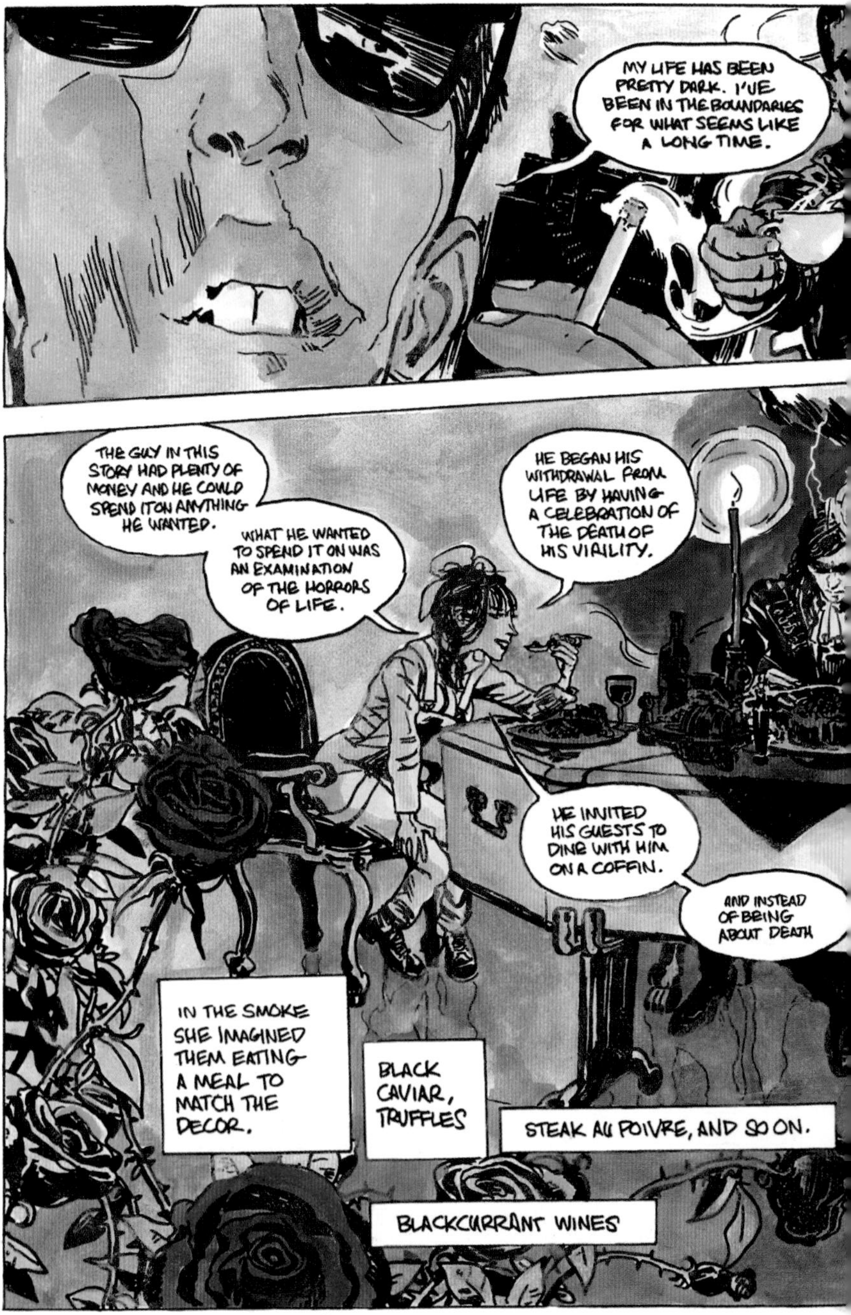
MY LIFE HAS BEEN PRETTY DARK. I'VE BEEN IN THE BOUNDARIES FOR WHAT SEEMS LIKE A LONG TIME.
THE GUY IN THIS STORY HAD PLENTY OF MONEY AND HE COULD SPEND IT ON ANYTHING HE WANTED.
WHAT HE WANTED TO SPEND IT ON WAS AN EXAMINATION OF THE HORRORS OF LIFE.
HE BEGAN HIS WITHDRAWAL FROM LIFE BY HAVING A CELEBRATION OF THE DEATH OF HIS VIRILITY.
HE INVITED HIS GUESTS TO DINE WITH HIM ON A COFFIN.
AND INSTEAD OF BEING ABOUT DEATH
IN THE SMOKE SHE IMAGINED THEM EATING A MEAL TO MATCH THE DECOR.
BLACK CAVIAR, TRUFFLES
STEAK AU POIVRE, AND SO ON.
BLACKCURRANT WINES

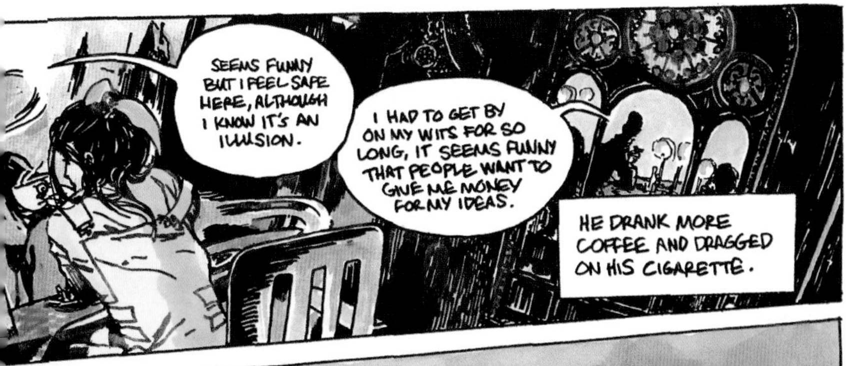
SEEMS FUNNY BUT I FEEL SAFE HERE, ALTHOUGH I KNOW IT'S AN ILLUSION.
I HAD TO GET BY ON MY WITS FOR SO LONG, IT SEEMS FUNNY THAT PEOPLE WANT TO GIVE ME MONEY FOR MY IDEAS.
HE DRANK MORE COFFEE AND DRAGGED ON HIS CIGARETTE.

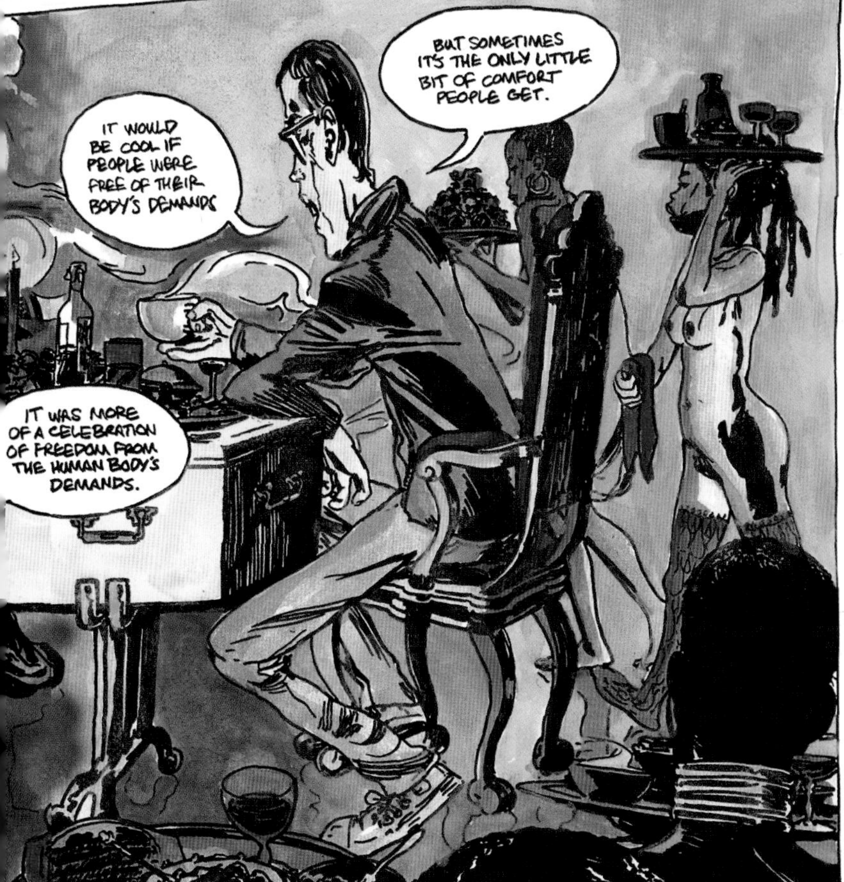
IT WOULD BE COOL IF PEOPLE WERE FREE OF THEIR BODY'S DEMANDS
BUT SOMETIMES IT'S THE ONLY LITTLE BIT OF COMFORT PEOPLE GET.
IT WAS MORE OF A CELEBRATION OF FREEDOM FROM THE HUMAN BODY'S DEMANDS.

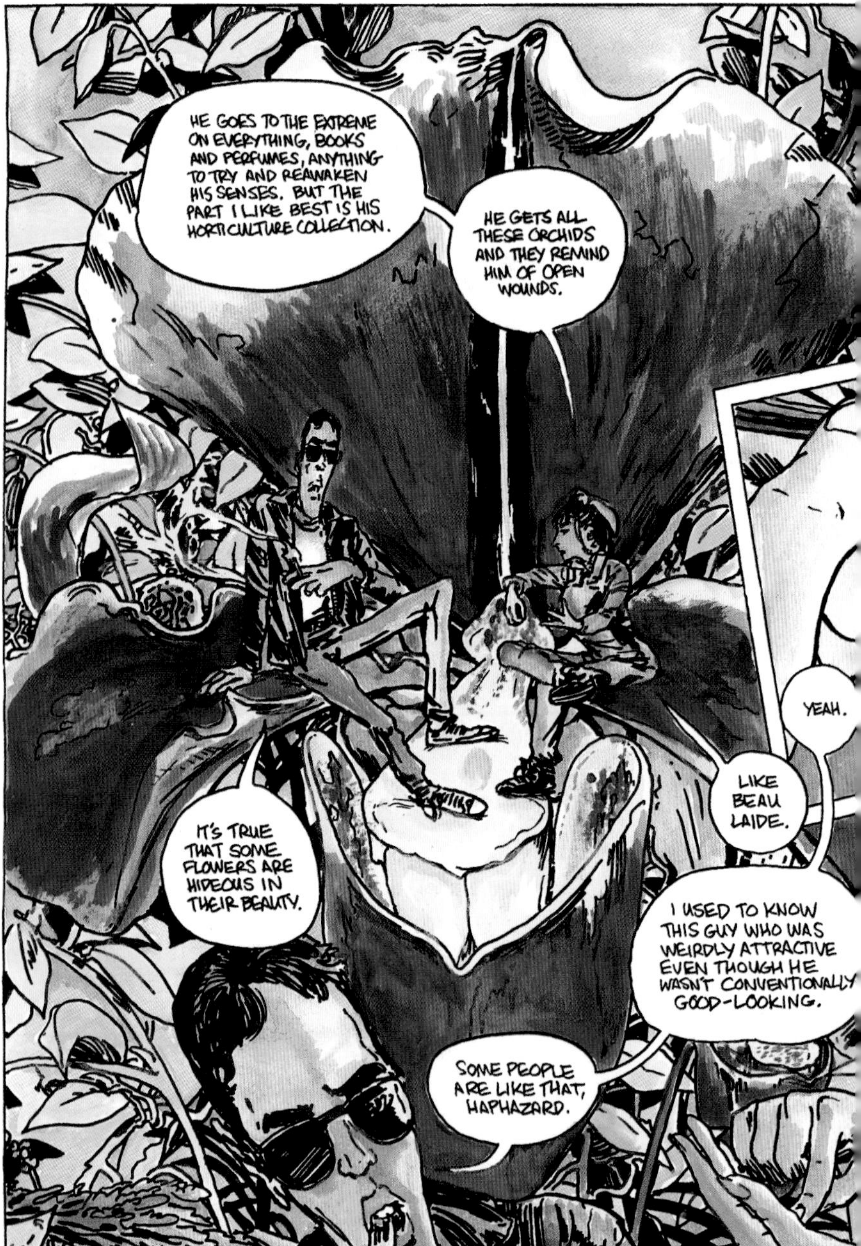
HE GOES TO THE EXTREME ON EVERYTHING, BOOKS AND PERFUMES, ANYTHING TO TRY AND REAWAKEN HIS SENSES. BUT THE PART I LIKE BEST IS HIS HORTICULTURE COLLECTION.
HE GETS ALL THESE ORCHIDS AND THEY REMIND HIM OF OPEN WOUNDS.
YEAH.
LIKE BEAU LAIDE.
IT'S TRUE THAT SOME FLOWERS ARE HIDEOUS IN THEIR BEAUTY.
I USED TO KNOW THIS GUY WHO WAS WEIRDLY ATTRACTIVE EVEN THOUGH HE WASN'T CONVENTIONALLY GOOD-LOOKING.
SOME PEOPLE ARE LIKE THAT, HAPHAZARD.

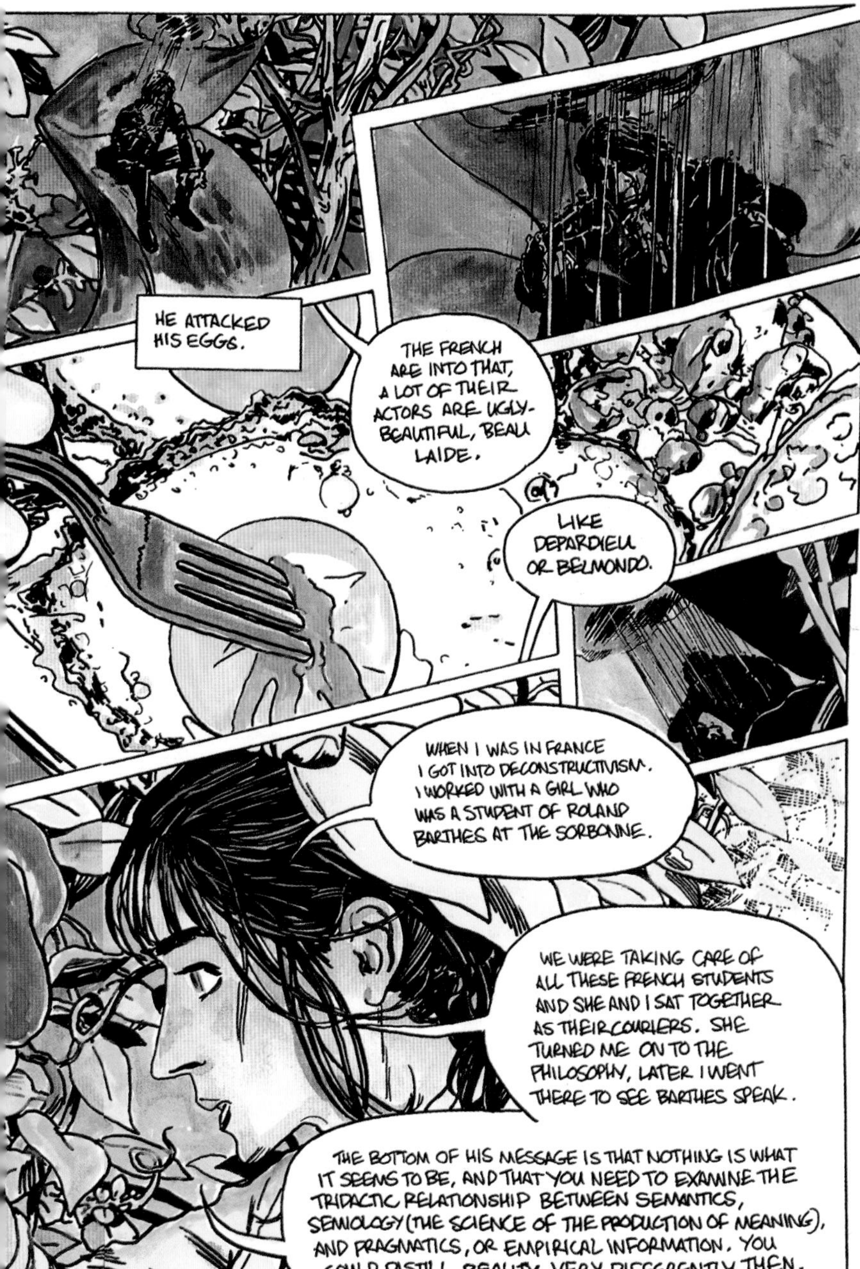
HE ATTACKED HIS EGGS.
THE FRENCH ARE INTO THAT, A LOT OF THEIR ACTORS ARE UGLY-BEAUTIFUL, BEAU LAIDE.
LIKE DEPARDIEU OR BELMONDO.
WHEN I WAS IN FRANCE I GOT INTO DECONSTRUCTIVISM. I WORKED WITH A GIRL WHO WAS A STUDENT OF ROLAND BARTHES AT THE SORBONNE.
WE WERE TAKING CARE OF ALL THESE FRENCH STUDENTS AND SHE AND I SAT TOGETHER AS THEIR COURIERS. SHE TURNED ME ON TO THE PHILOSOPHY, LATER I WENT THERE TO SEE BARTHES SPEAK.
THE BOTTOM OF HIS MESSAGE IS THAT NOTHING IS WHAT IT SEEMS TO BE, AND THAT YOU NEED TO EXAMINE THE TRIDACTIC RELATIONSHIP BETWEEN SEMANTICS, SEMIOLOGY (THE SCIENCE OF THE PRODUCTION OF MEANING), AND PRAGMATICS, OR EMPIRICAL INFORMATION. YOU COULD DISTILL REALITY VERY DIFFERENTLY THEN.

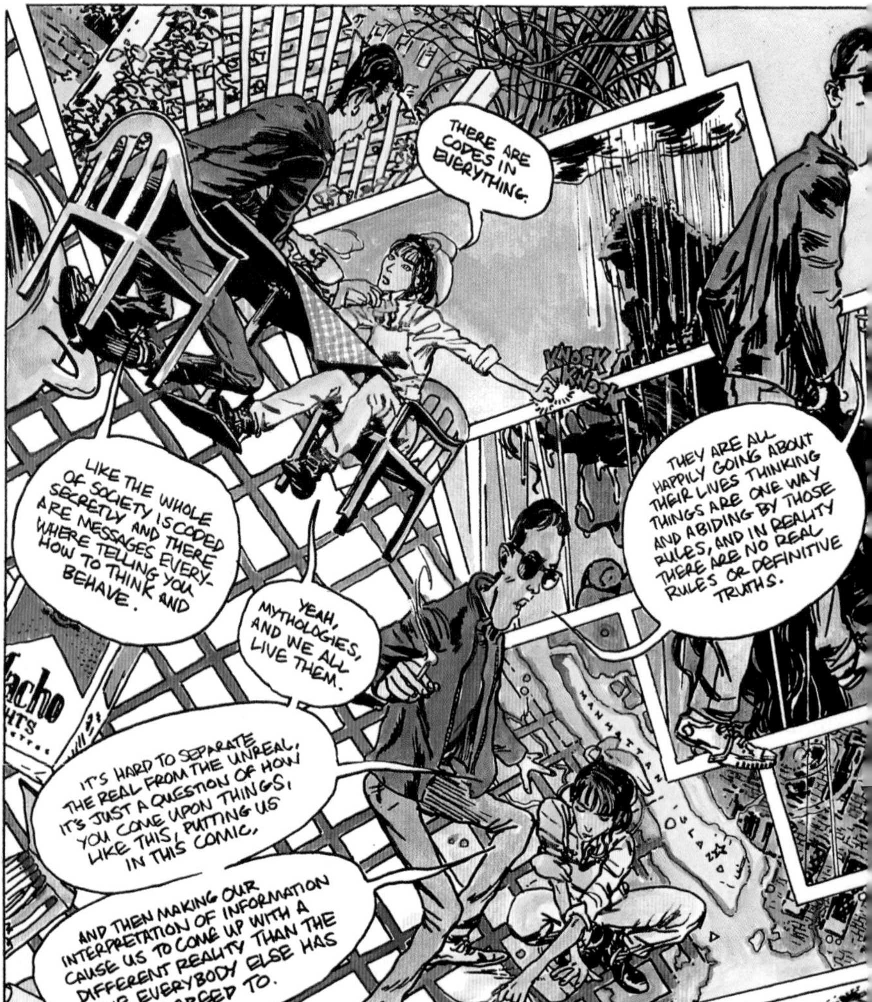
THERE ARE CODES IN EVERYTHING.
LIKE THE WHOLE OF SOCIETY IS CODED SECRETLY AND THERE ARE MESSAGES EVERYWHERE TELLING YOU HOW TO THINK AND BEHAVE.
KNOCK KNOCK
YEAH, MYTHOLOGIES, AND WE ALL LIVE THEM.
THEY ARE ALL HAPPILY GOING ABOUT THEIR LIVES THINKING THINGS ARE ONE WAY AND ABIDING BY THOSE RULES, AND IN REALITY THERE ARE NO REAL RULES OR DEFINITIVE TRUTHS.
IT'S HARD TO SEPARATE THE REAL FROM THE UNREAL, IT'S JUST A QUESTION OF HOW YOU COME UPON THINGS, LIKE THIS, PUTTING US IN THIS COMIC,
AND THEN MAKING OUR INTERPRETATION OF INFORMATION CAUSE US TO COME UP WITH A DIFFERENT REALITY THAN THE ONE EVERYBODY ELSE HAS AGREED TO.

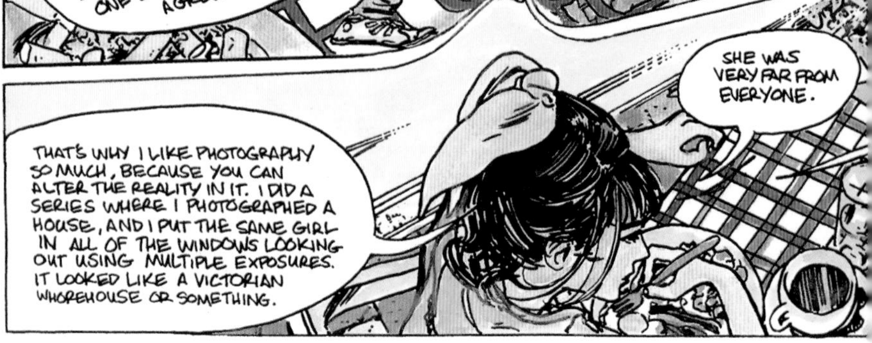
THAT'S WHY I LIKE PHOTOGRAPHY SO MUCH, BECAUSE YOU CAN ALTER THE REALITY IN IT. I DID A SERIES WHERE I PHOTOGRAPHED A HOUSE, AND I PUT THE SAME GIRL IN ALL OF THE WINDOWS LOOKING OUT USING MULTIPLE EXPOSURES. IT LOOKED LIKE A VICTORIAN WHOREHOUSE OR SOMETHING.
SHE WAS VERY FAR FROM EVERYONE.

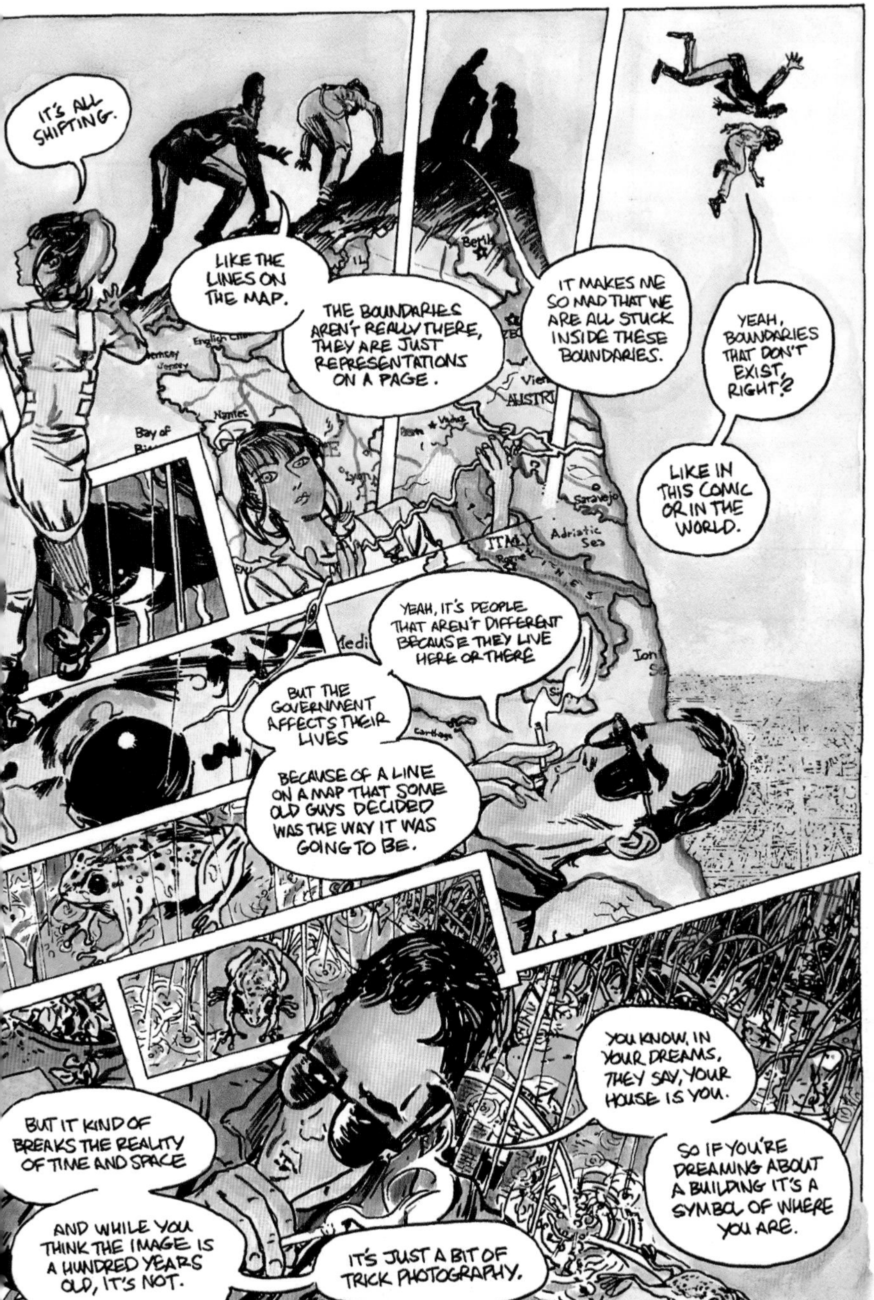
IT'S ALL SHIFTING.
LIKE THE LINES ON THE MAP.
THE BOUNDARIES AREN'T REALLY THERE, THEY ARE JUST REPRESENTATIONS ON A PAGE.
IT MAKES ME SO MAD THAT WE ARE ALL STUCK INSIDE THESE BOUNDARIES.
YEAH, BOUNDARIES THAT DON'T EXIST, RIGHT?
LIKE IN THIS COMIC OR IN THE WORLD.
YEAH, IT'S PEOPLE THAT AREN'T DIFFERENT BECAUSE THEY LIVE HERE OR THERE
BUT THE GOVERNMENT AFFECTS THEIR LIVES
BECAUSE OF A LINE ON A MAP THAT SOME OLD GUYS DECIDED WAS THE WAY IT WAS GOING TO BE.
BUT IT KIND OF BREAKS THE REALITY OF TIME AND SPACE
AND WHILE YOU THINK THE IMAGE IS A HUNDRED YEARS OLD, IT'S NOT.
IT'S JUST A BIT OF TRICK PHOTOGRAPHY.
YOU KNOW, IN YOUR DREAMS, THEY SAY, YOUR HOUSE IS YOU.
SO IF YOU'RE DREAMING ABOUT A BUILDING IT'S A SYMBOL OF WHERE YOU ARE.

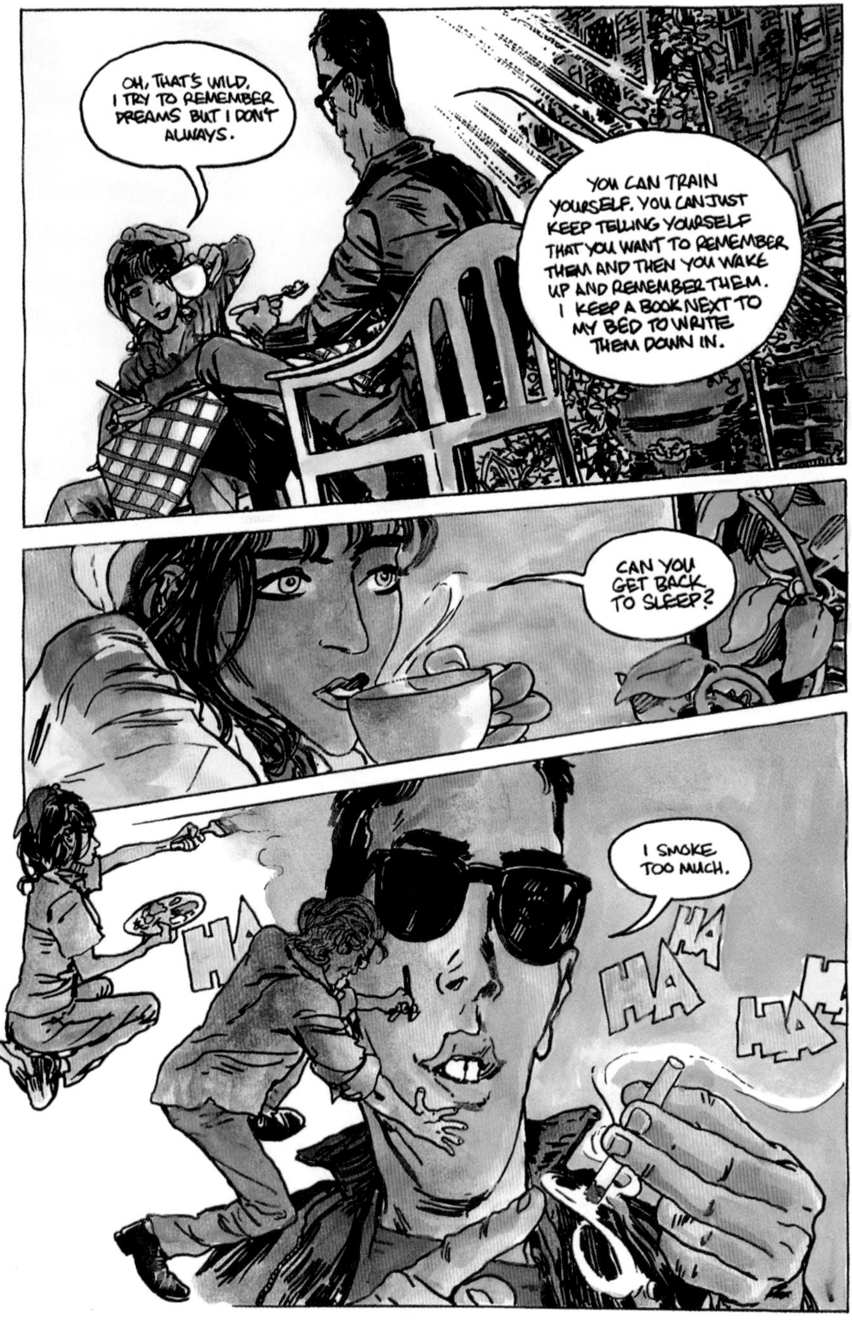
OH, THAT'S WILD, I TRY TO REMEMBER DREAMS BUT I DON'T ALWAYS.
YOU CAN TRAIN YOURSELF. YOU CAN JUST KEEP TELLING YOURSELF THAT YOU WANT TO REMEMBER THEM AND THEN YOU WAKE UP AND REMEMBER THEM. I KEEP A BOOK NEXT TO MY BED TO WRITE THEM DOWN IN.
CAN YOU GET BACK TO SLEEP?
I SMOKE TOO MUCH.
HA
HA
HA
HA

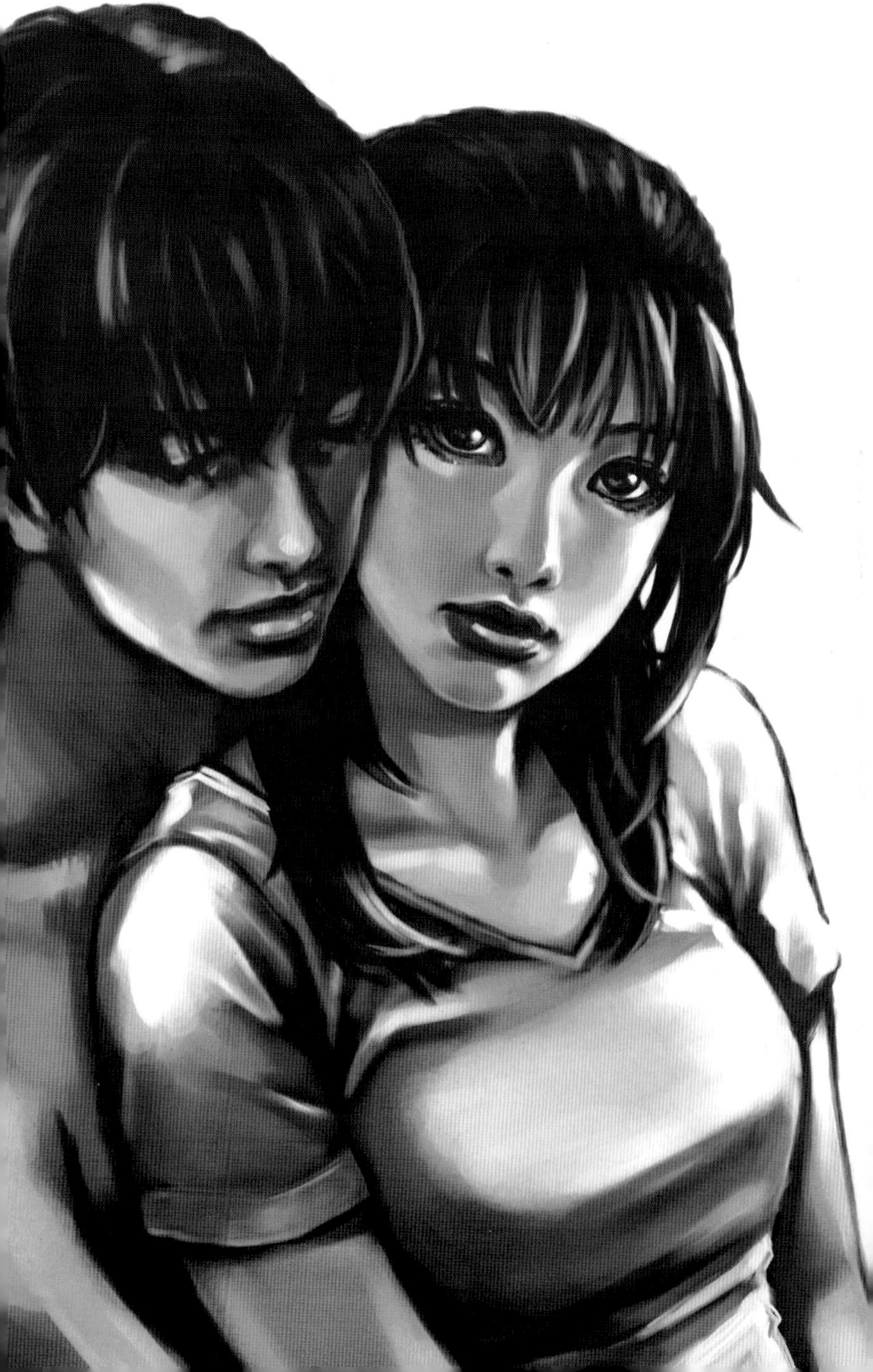

JULY TENTH

Eve Yap

To say more about the genre style of this story might give the game away before you've read it, but roughly speaking it is a *josei*, or everyday drama portrayed in a realistic style. These are most commonly found in Japan among the *redikomi*, or women's titles.

This story was entered in competition for IMAF 2006, where ILYA, Ye Editor, took part in the judging panel. **Eve Yap** lives in Malaysia, where they read comics in either direction – left to right, or right to left. *July Tenth*, at that time, ran right to left (the same reading order as Japanese manga), and has been especially converted by the artist to make its English comics debut here. It was, in fact, Eve's very first coloured comic, planned for her university animation project but turned into a short comic when the animation ended up with a different story. "I enjoyed the process of it," says Eve, "and I hope you guys like it too."

eveyap00@gmail.com
pinkyee.deviantart.com

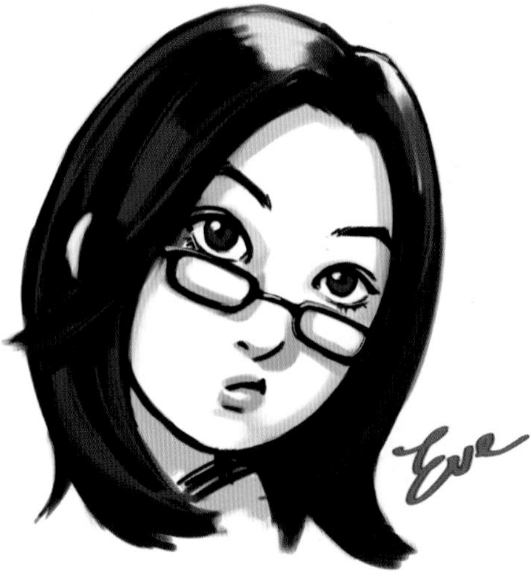
Eve

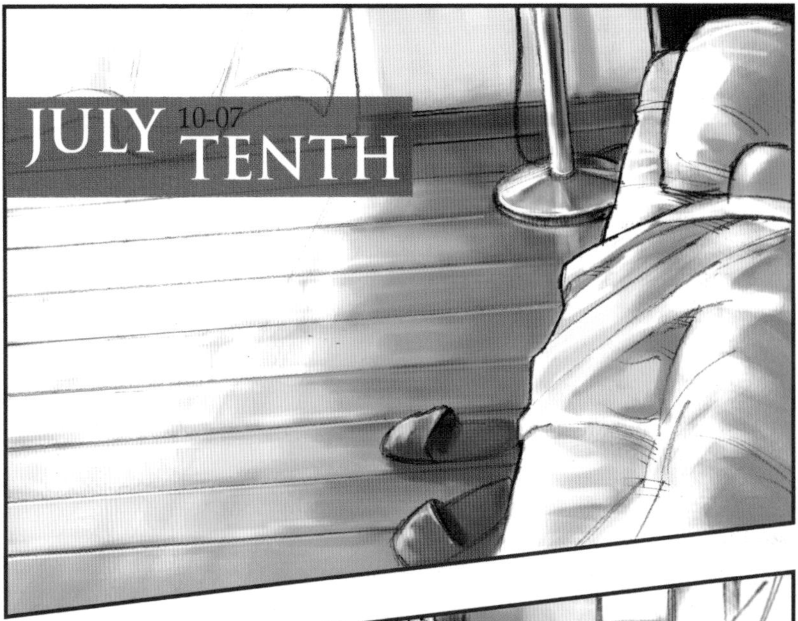
JULY 10-07 TENTH
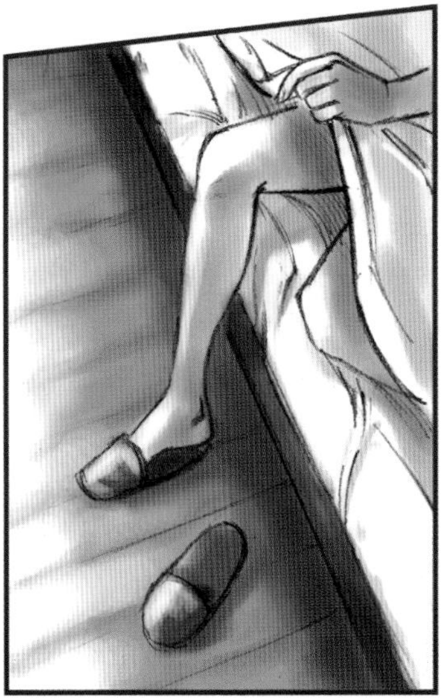
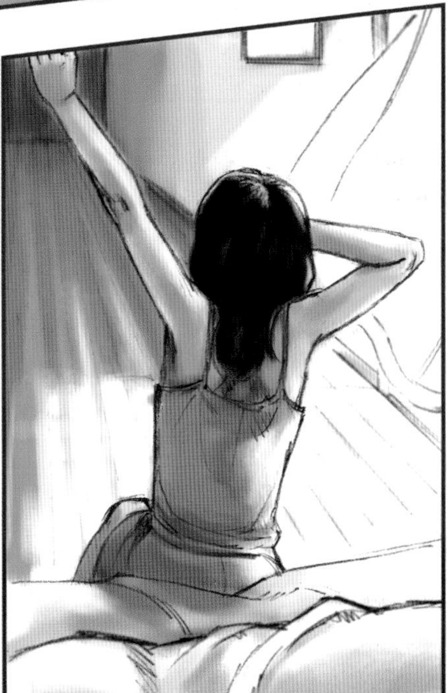

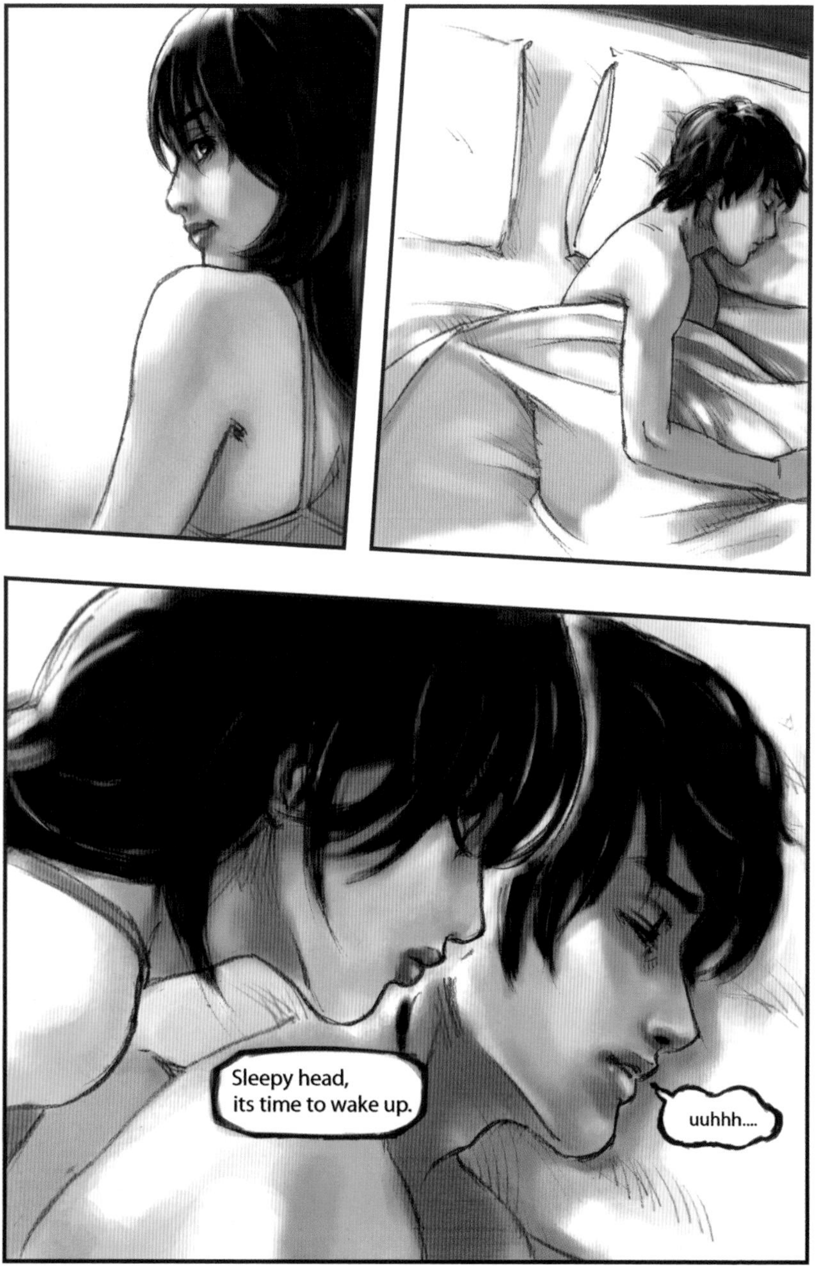
Sleepy head,
its time to wake up.
uuhhh....

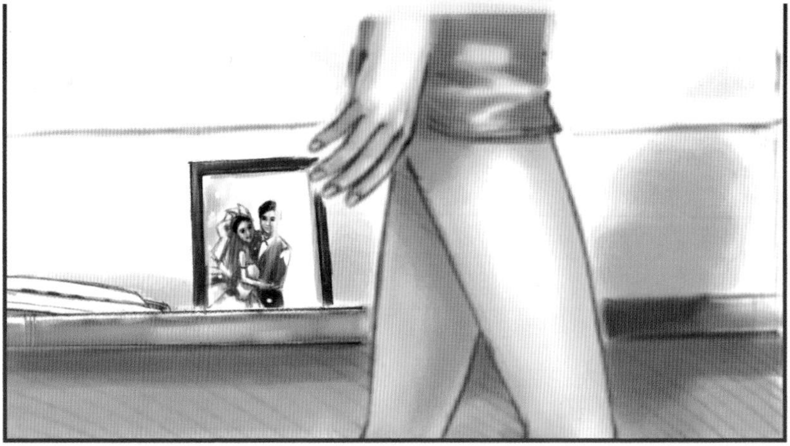

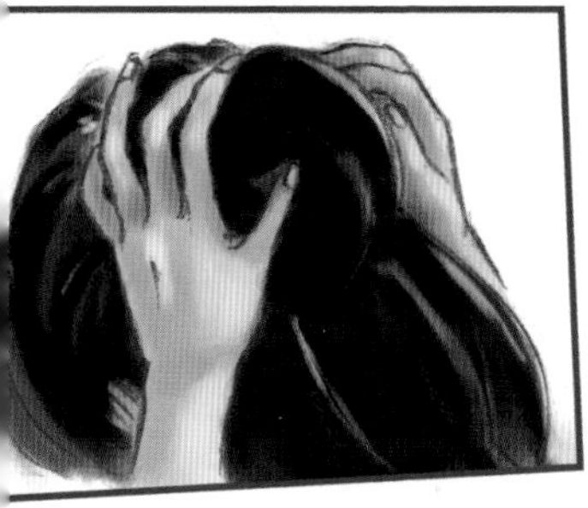

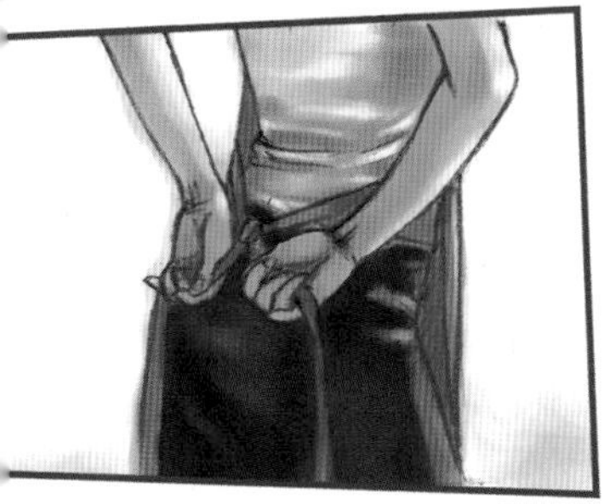

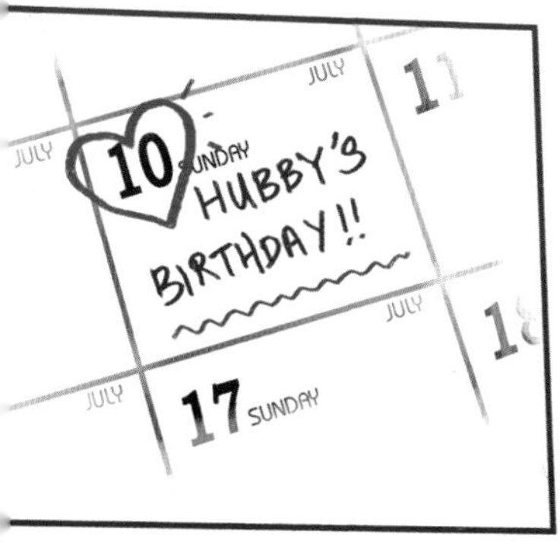
JULY
10 SUNDAY
HUBBY'S BIRTHDAY!!
JULY
JULY
JULY
17 SUNDAY

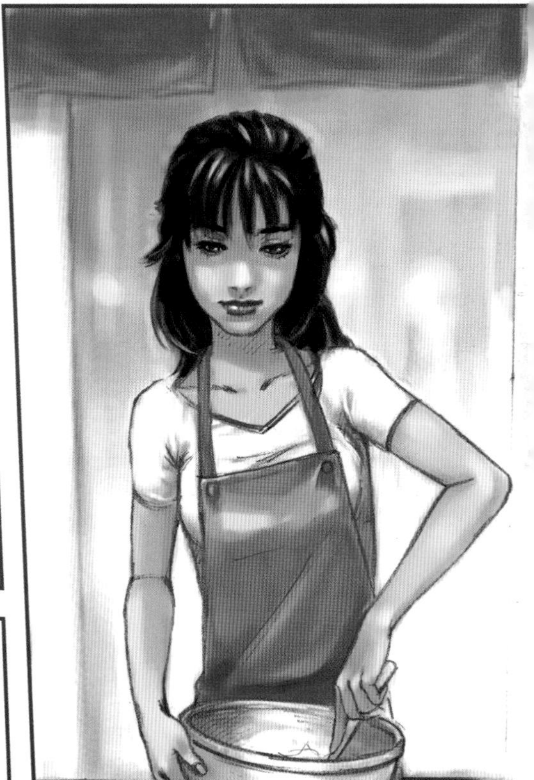

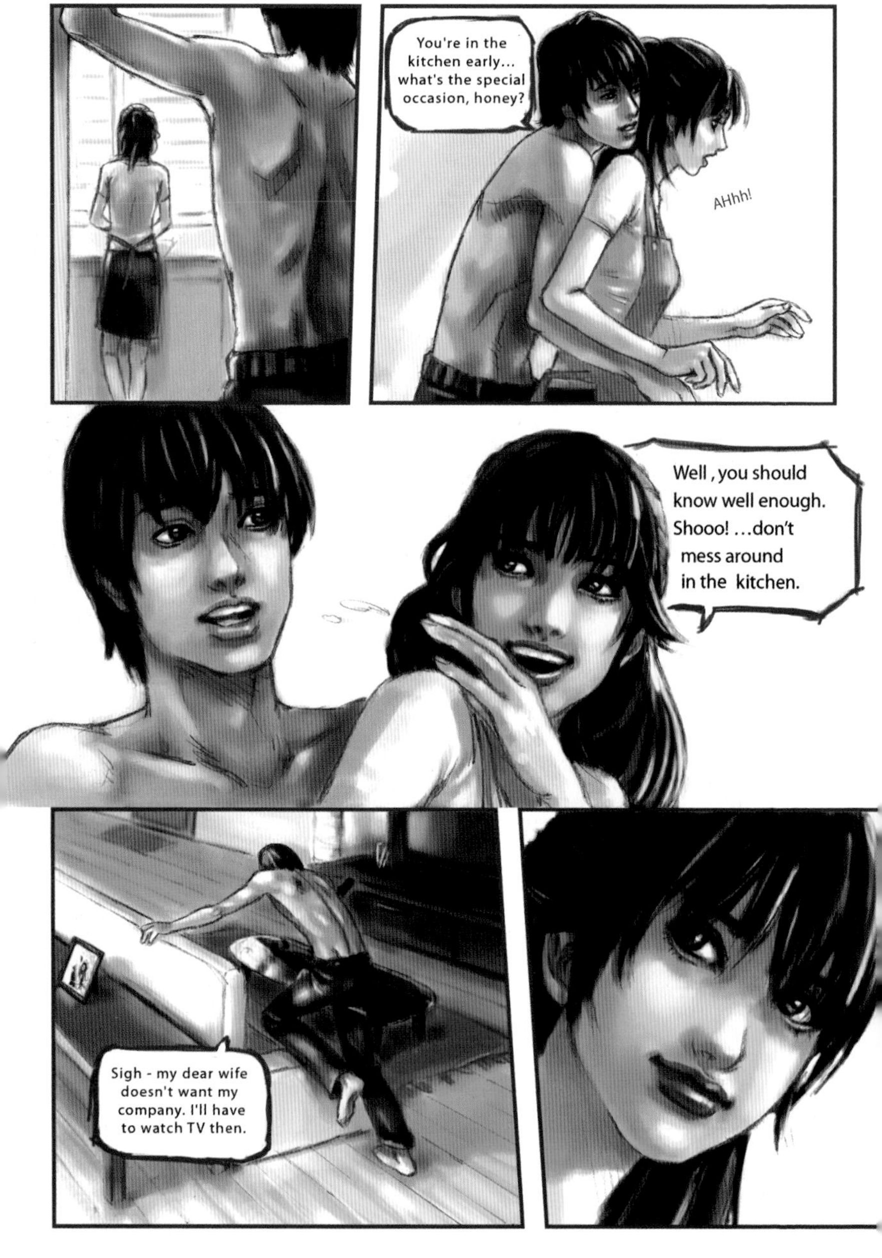

You're in the kitchen early... what's the special occasion, honey?
AHhh!
Well , you should know well enough. Shooo! ...don't mess around in the kitchen.
Sigh - my dear wife doesn't want my company. I'll have to watch TV then.

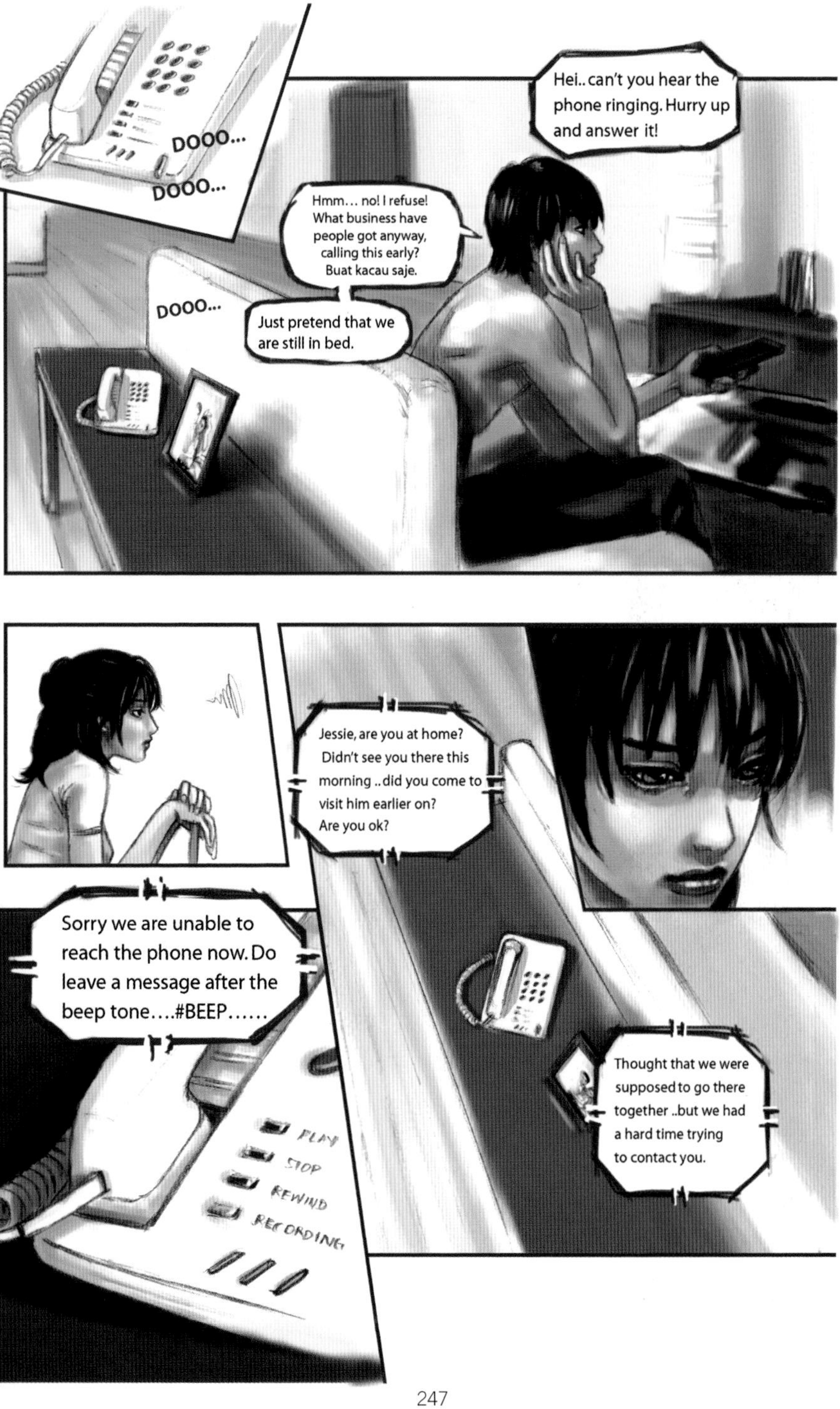
DOOO...
DOOO...
Hei.. can't you hear the phone ringing. Hurry up and answer it!
Hmm… no! I refuse! What business have people got anyway, calling this early? Buat kacau saje.
DOOO...
Just pretend that we are still in bed.
Jessie, are you at home? Didn't see you there this morning ..did you come to visit him earlier on? Are you ok?
Sorry we are unable to reach the phone now. Do leave a message after the beep tone….#BEEP……
PLAY
STOP
REWIND
RECORDING
Thought that we were supposed to go there together ..but we had a hard time trying to contact you.

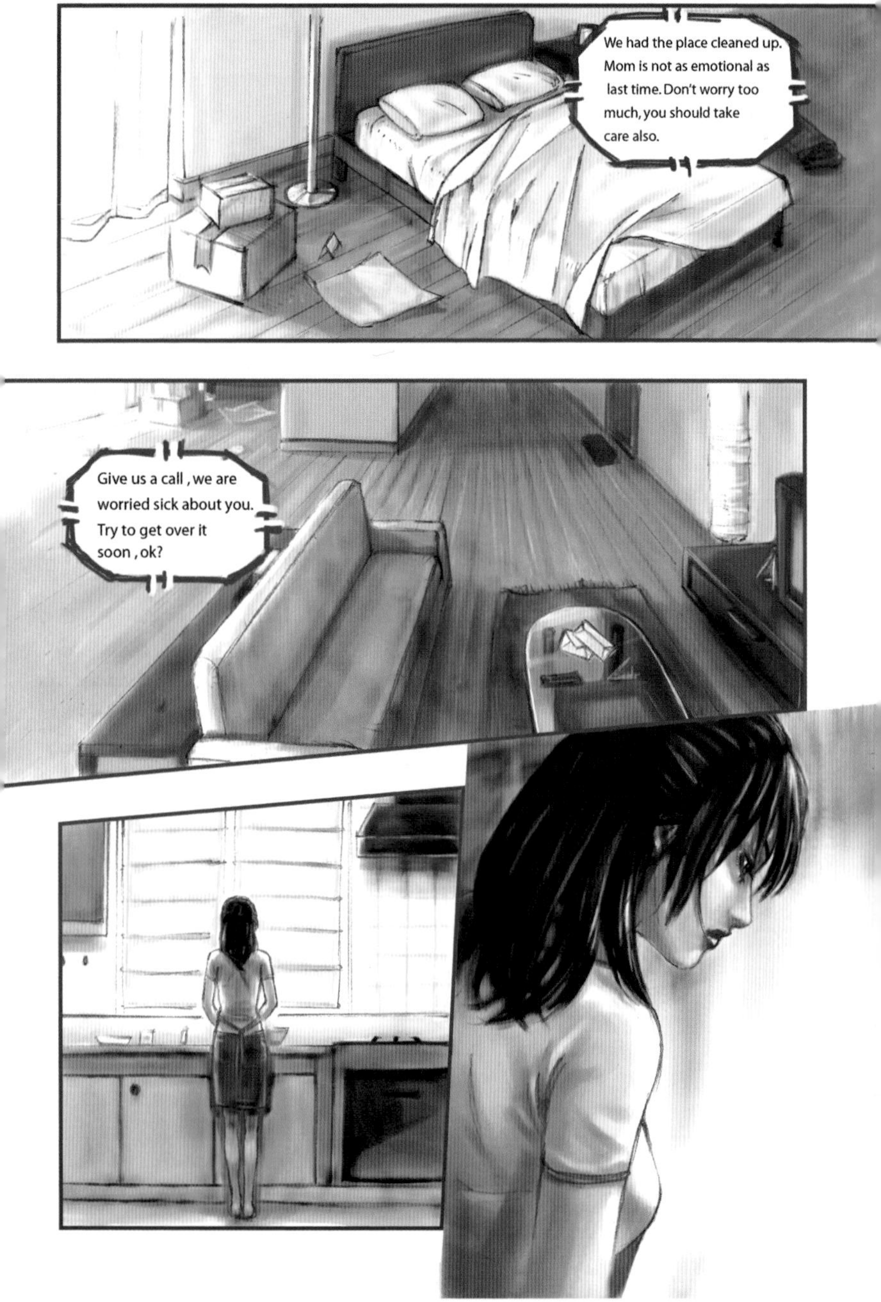
We had the place cleaned up. Mom is not as emotional as last time. Don't worry too much, you should take care also.
Give us a call , we are worried sick about you. Try to get over it soon , ok?

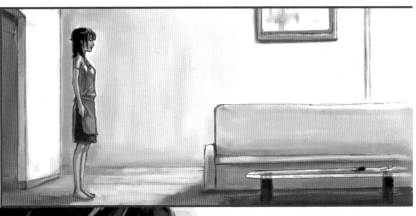
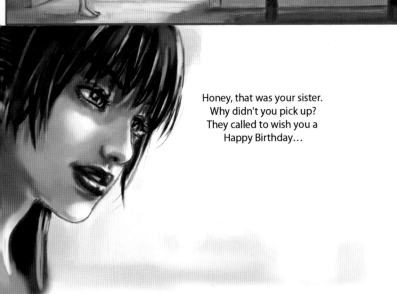

Honey, that was your sister.
Why didn't you pick up?
They called to wish you a
Happy Birthday…

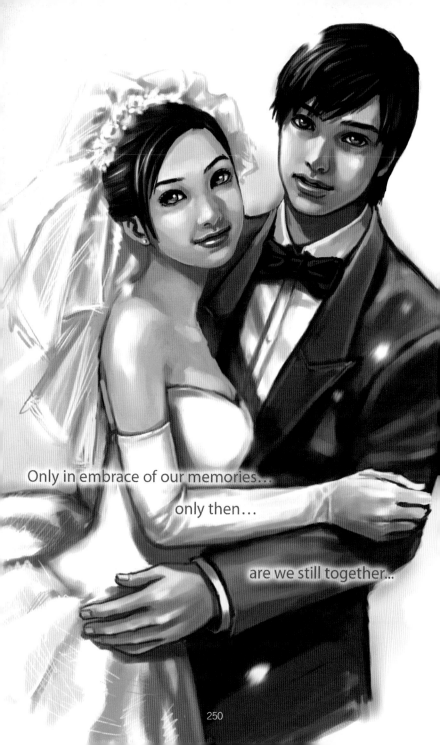

Only in embrace of our memories…

only then…

are we still together…

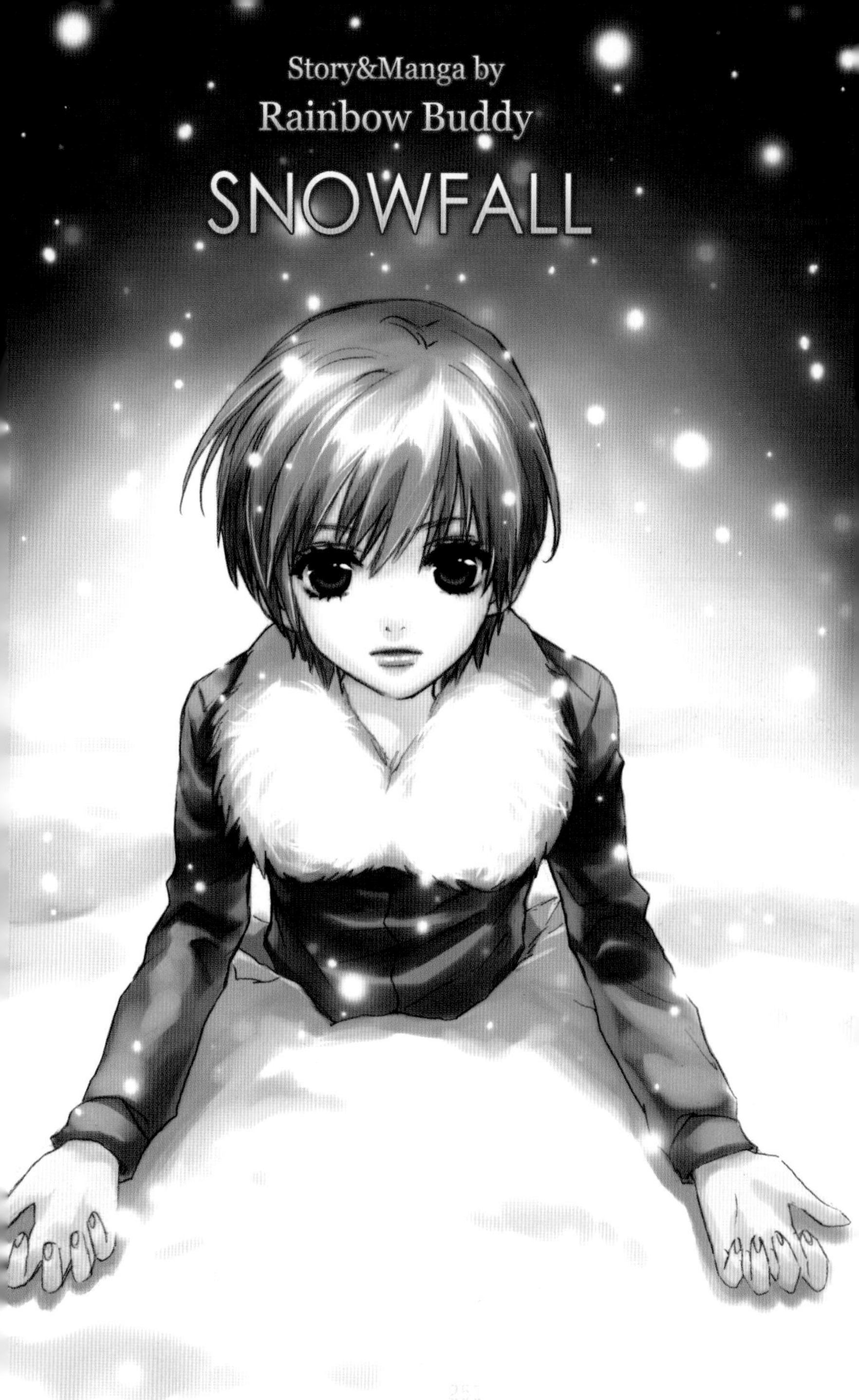
Story&Manga by
Rainbow Buddy
SNOWFALL

SNOWFALL

Rainbow Buddy

This is a *yaoi* or Boys Love story, although it surmounts gender to work as a tale of any first or lost love. As Buddy says, "The story is about some unforgettable memories." *Yaoi* is fast becoming a very popular form of manga – comics principally by and for girls that feature boys falling in love (with each other). Check out our interview with Chie Kutsuwada in *Volume Two* for more background.

Buddy (Yifan or "Ivy" Ling), born in Beijing in 1983, has been widely published as an illustrator for magazines and novels. Her manga *Delicious Seasons* is serialized every month in *comicfans* (a manhua – Chinese manga – anthology), also published as a book in the USA. "In China," she reports, "original manga is growing really fast. I hope that more Chinese manga artists can be introduced to the global market. My newest artwork is *Spy Goddess*, co-published by Tokyopop and Harper Collins."

Readers might also recall *Eve3000*, Buddy's collaboration with American songstress Anna Mercedes (*Volume Two*): exciting things are happening, with a pilot for an animated feature already in production. For more original Chinese manga, see our special Summer Studio China section.

www.buddy-net.net
www.tokyopop.com/buddy

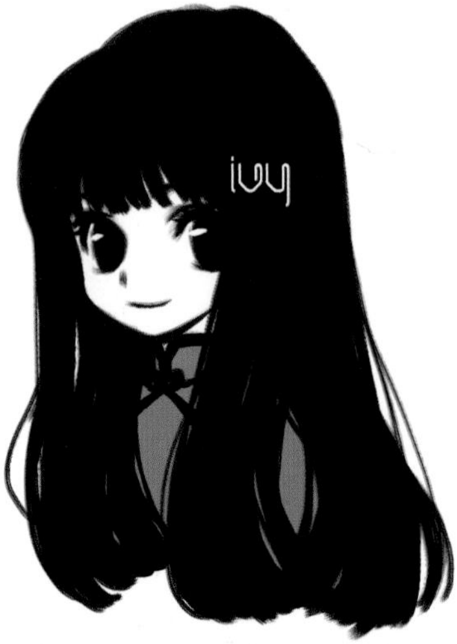
ivy

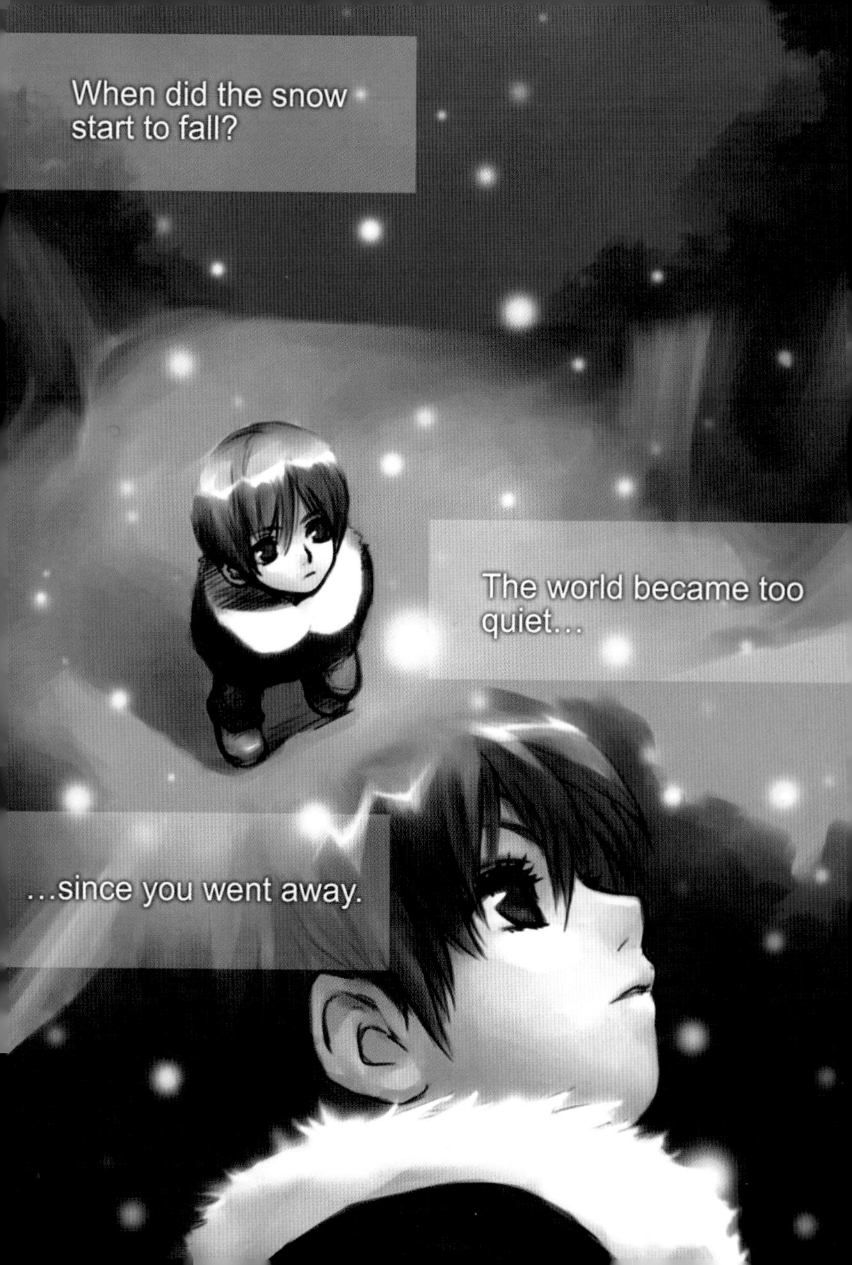
When did the snow start to fall?
The world became too quiet…
…since you went away.

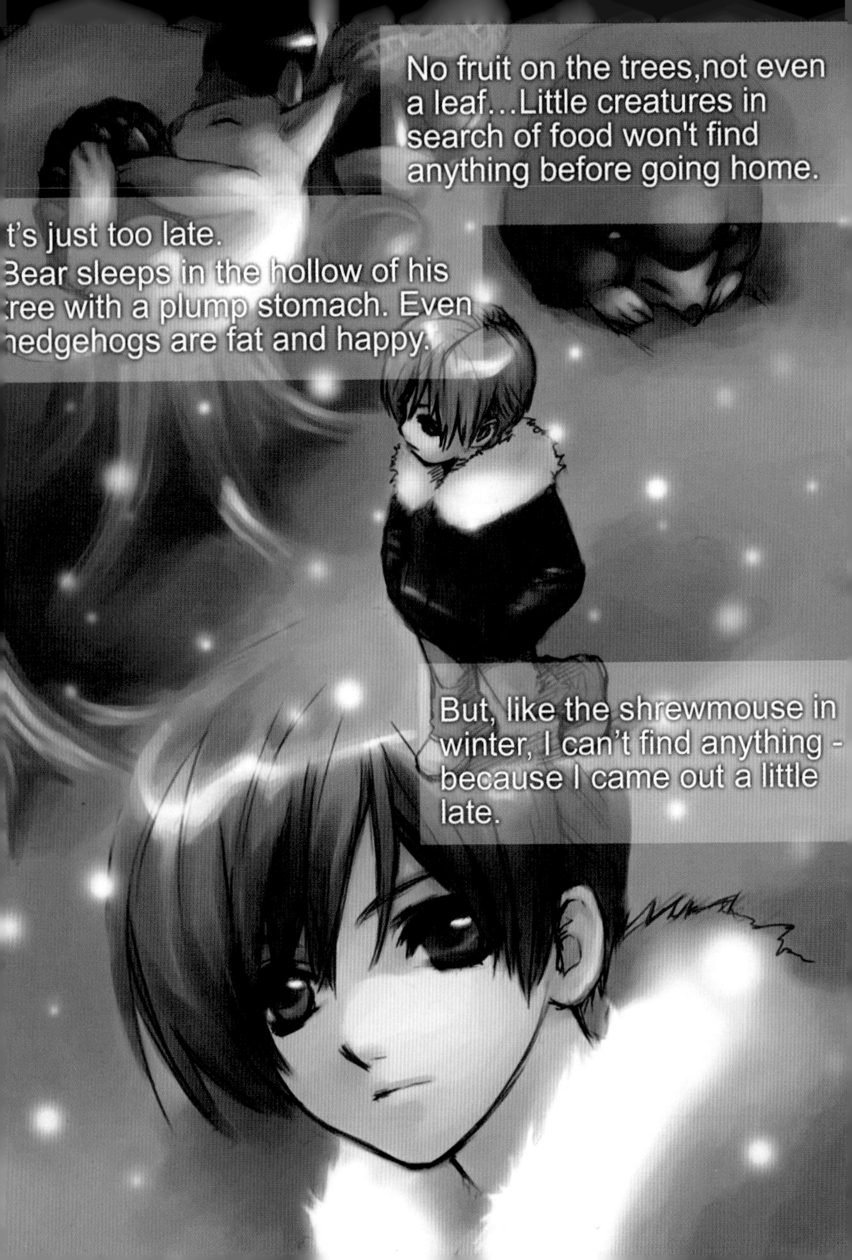
No fruit on the trees,not even a leaf…Little creatures in search of food won't find anything before going home.
t’s just too late. ear sleeps in the hollow of his ree with a plump stomach. Even edgehogs are fat and happy.
But, like the shrewmouse in winter, I can’t find anything - because I came out a little late.

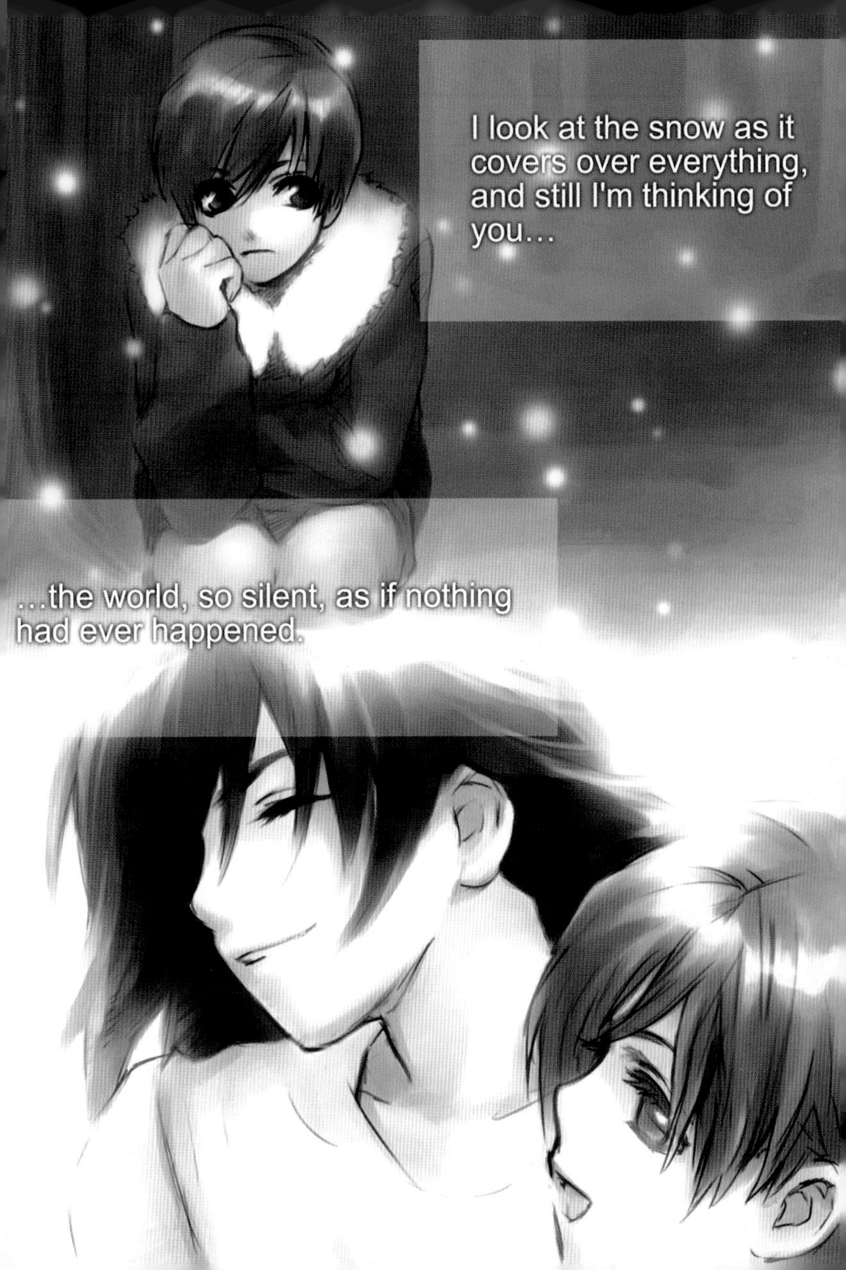
I look at the snow as it covers over everything, and still I'm thinking of you…
…the world, so silent, as if nothing had ever happened.

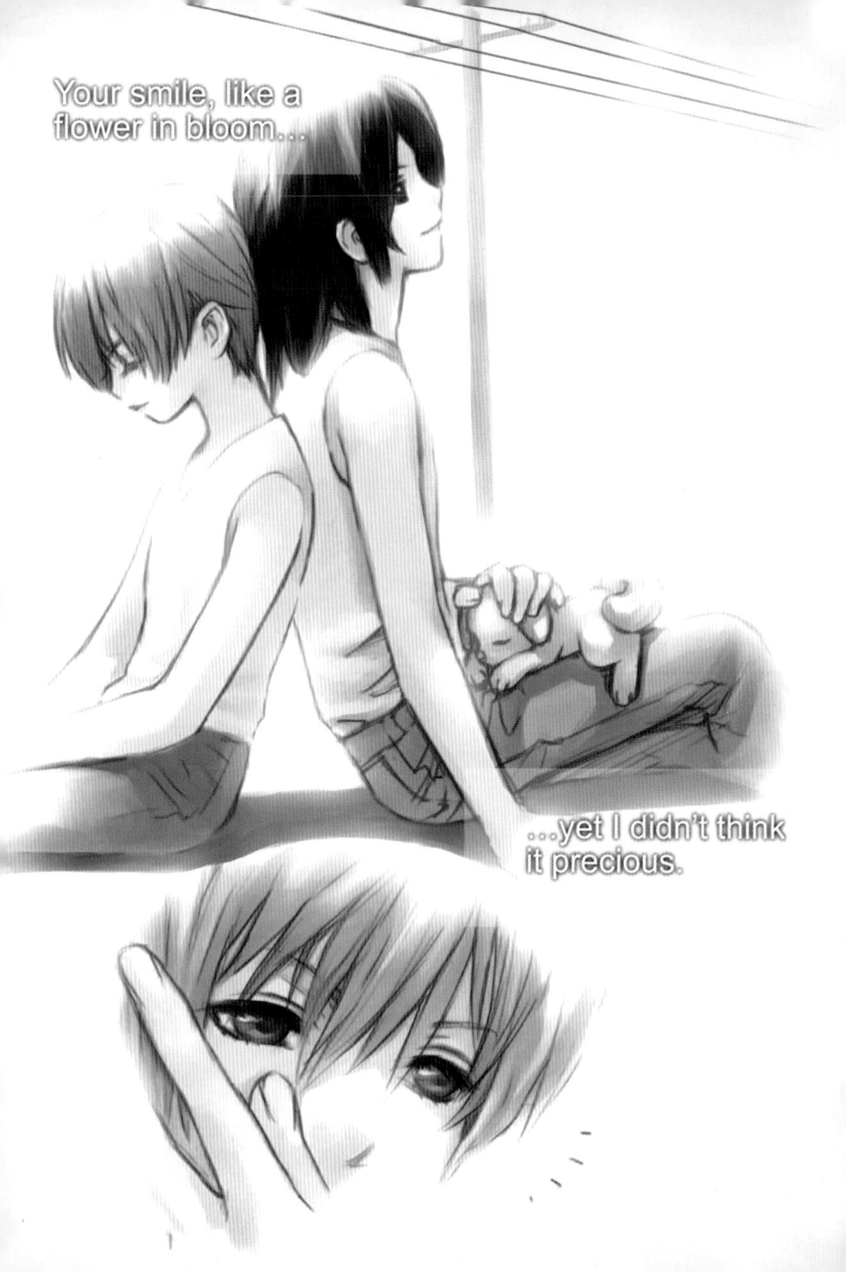
Your smile, like a flower in bloom...
...yet I didn't think it precious.

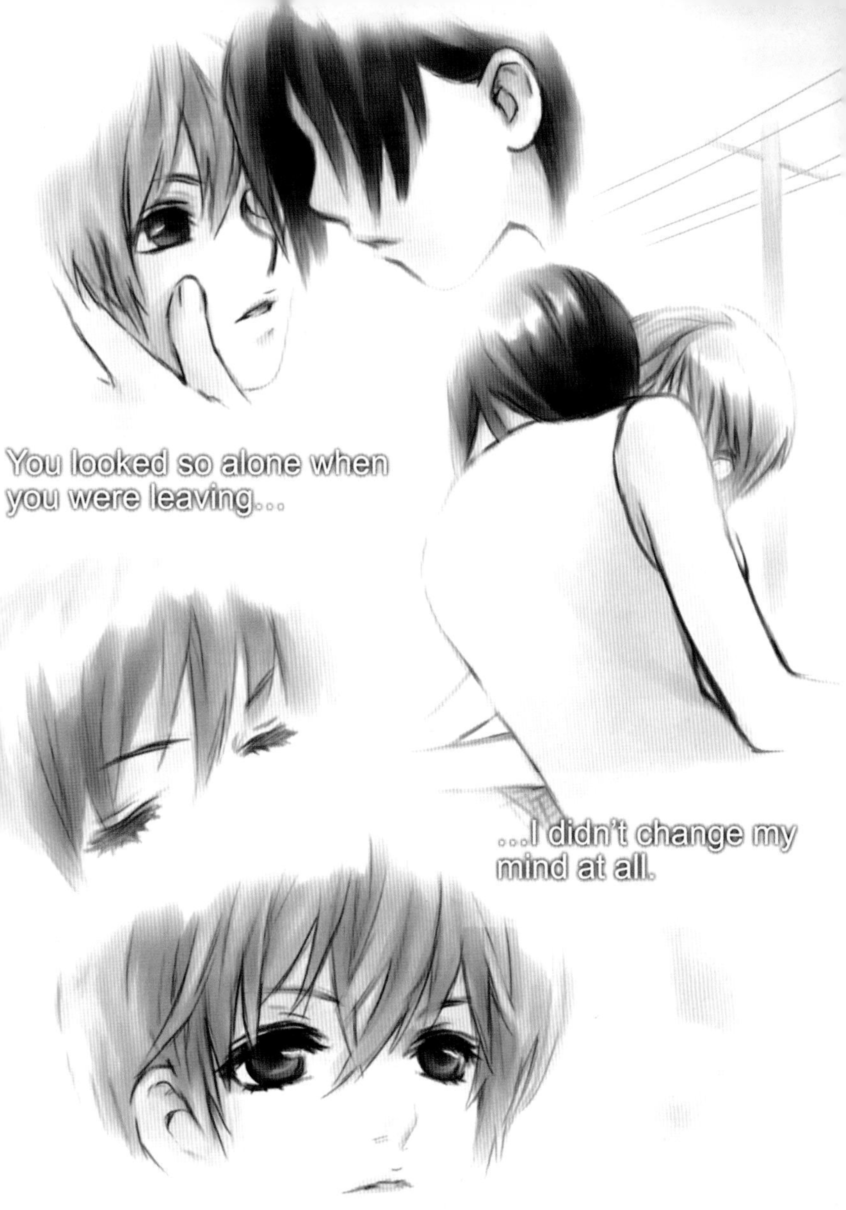
You looked so alone when you were leaving...
...I didn't change my mind at all.

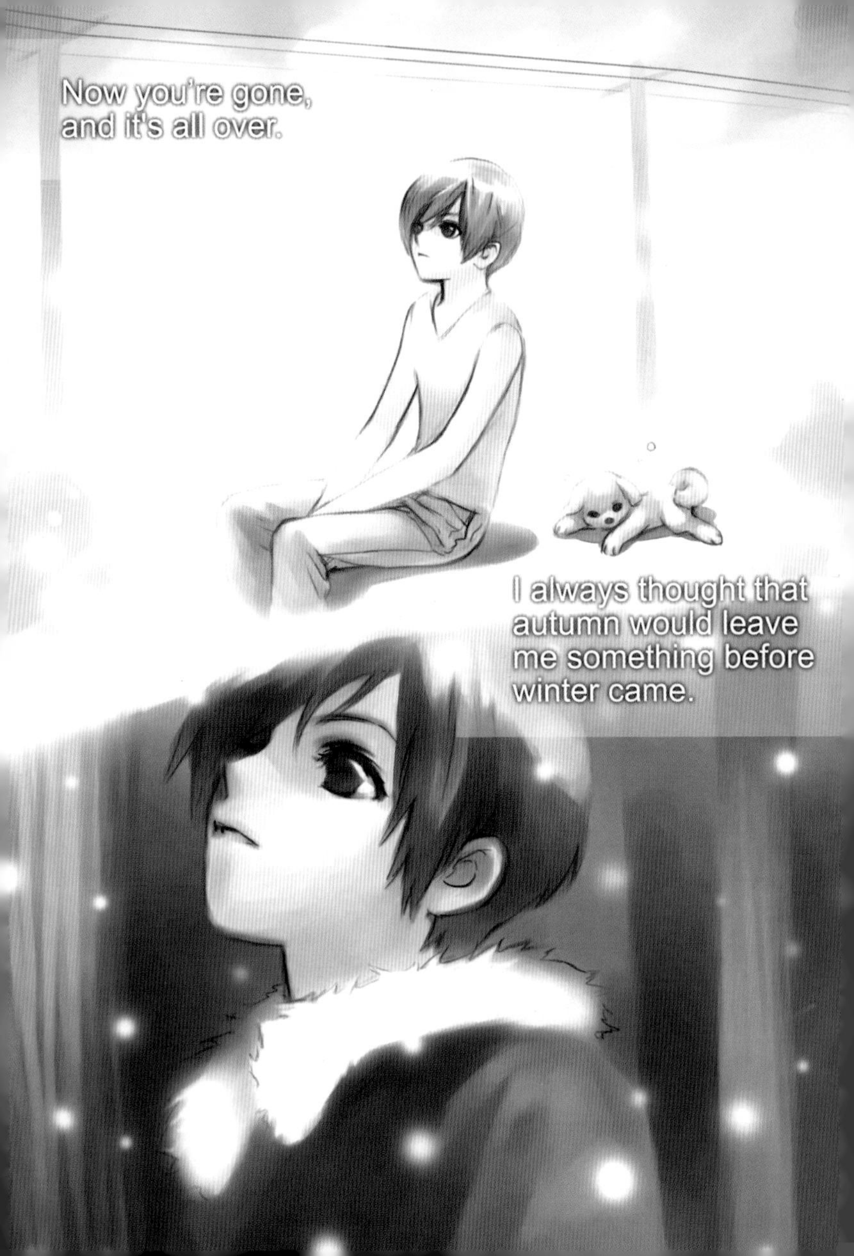
Now you're gone, and it's all over.
I always thought that autumn would leave me something before winter came.

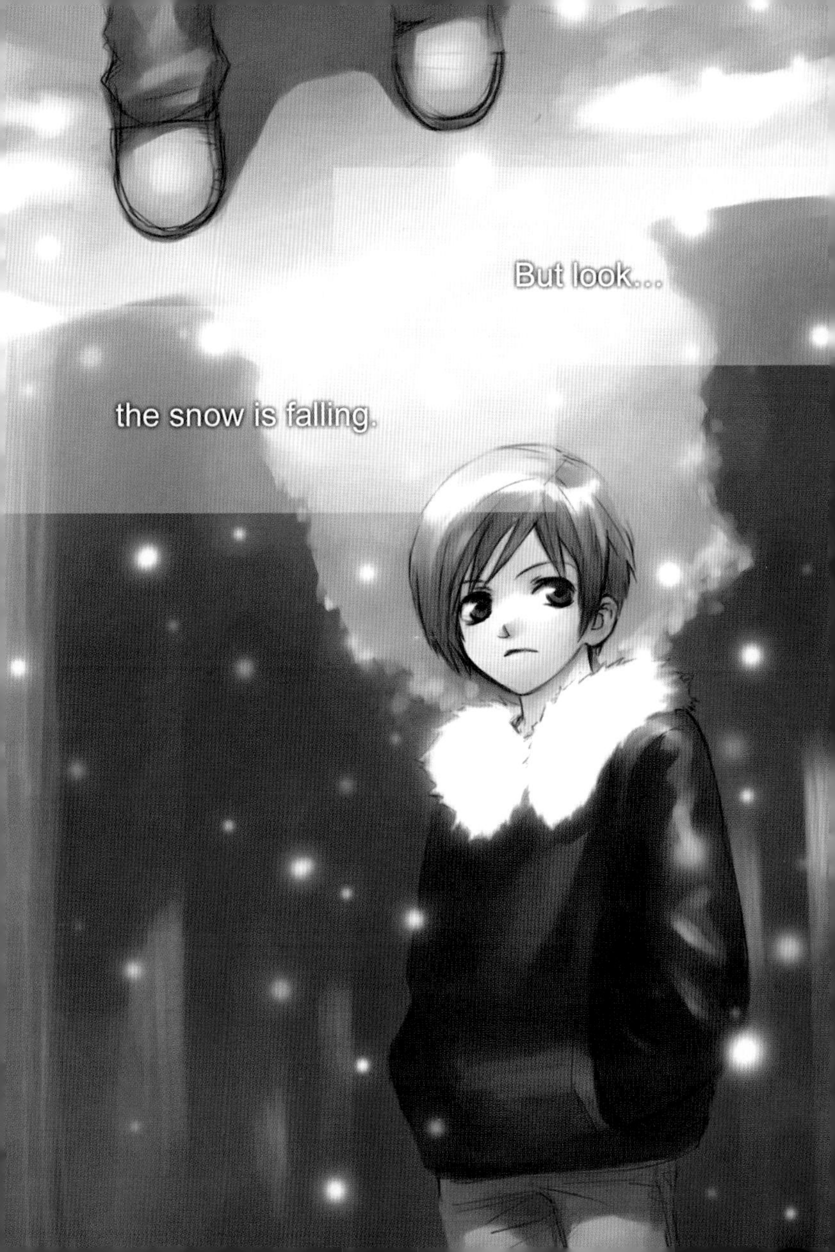
But look...
the snow is falling.

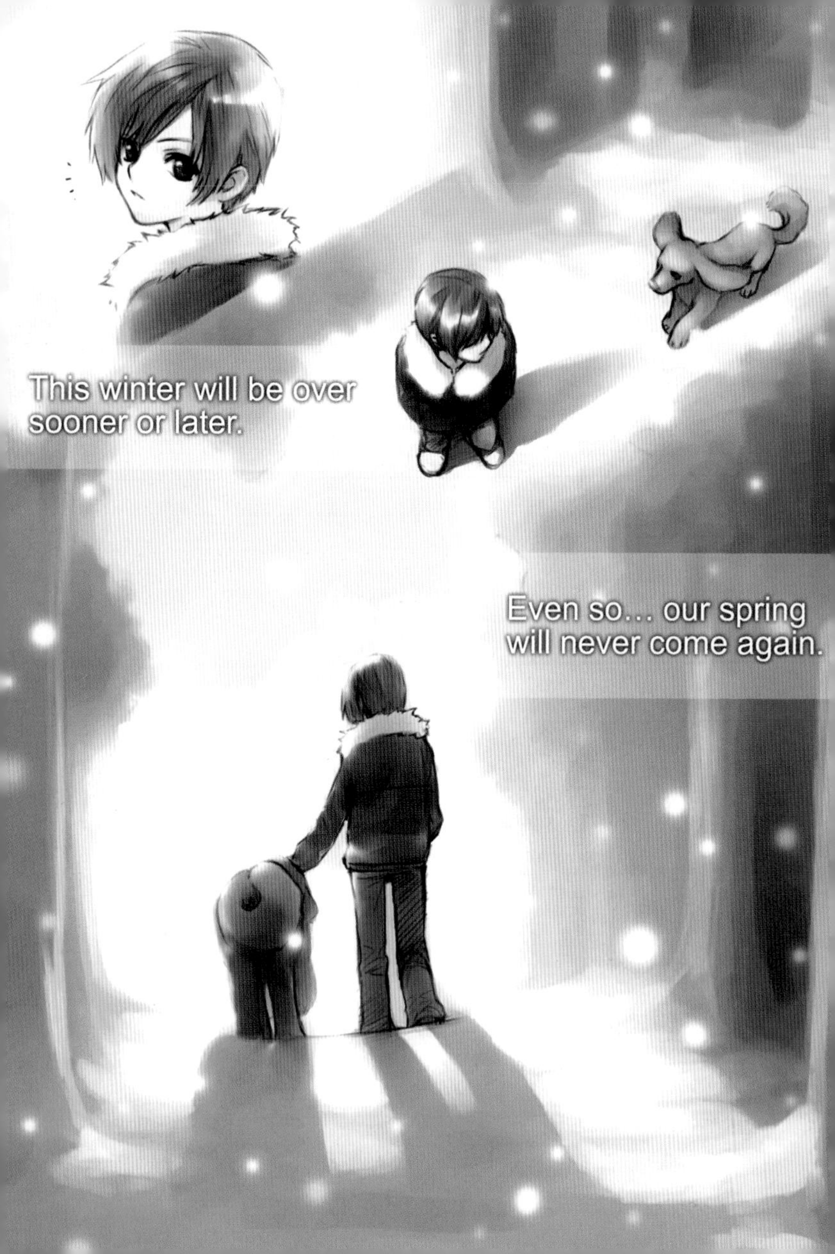
This winter will be over sooner or later.
Even so... our spring will never come again.

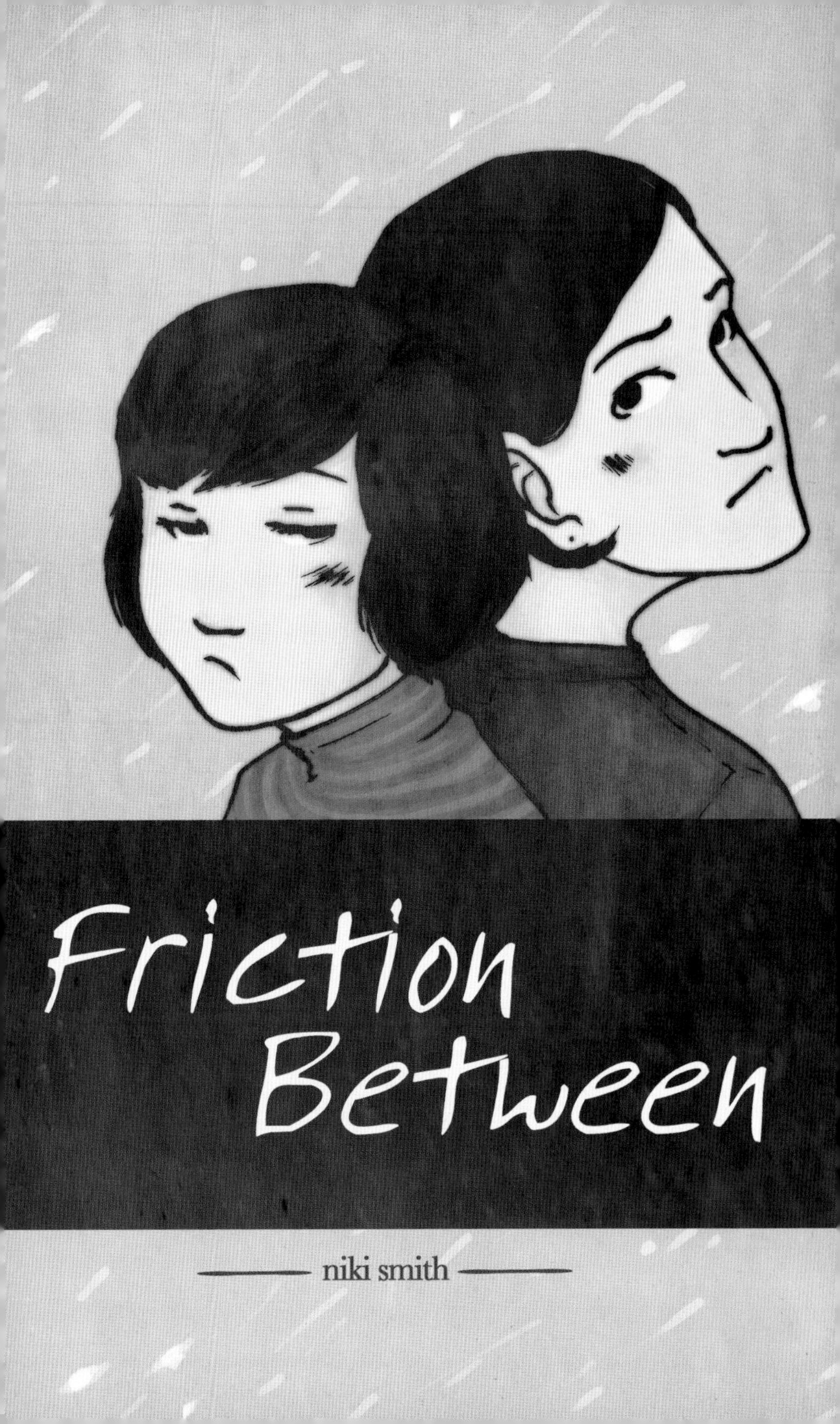
Friction Between
niki smith

FRICTION BETWEEN
Niki Smith

From *yaoi* to a *yuri*, or Girls Love story, although in style it most resembles a *josei*. "A lot less idealized, and more realistic," as the artist herself describes it. "Not as much fluff and sparkles! *Josei* is typically aimed at women in their twenties."

Niki Smith is in her fourth year at the Cleveland Institute of Art, Ohio. Once graduated, she hopes to take a crack at a full-length graphic novel. We await with interest, reckoning Niki one of the most interesting and accomplished writers to come along in a while – at the same time being no slouch as an artist. Niki tells us that she enjoys spending her vacation time in Europe (most especially Germany), and likes to create stories about subtly-foreign climes that still resonate for her (mostly!) American audience.

At *Best New Manga* towers we get many submissions from hopeful contributors. Very few make the grade, but that's just how Niki Smith came to be included.

www.niki-smith.com

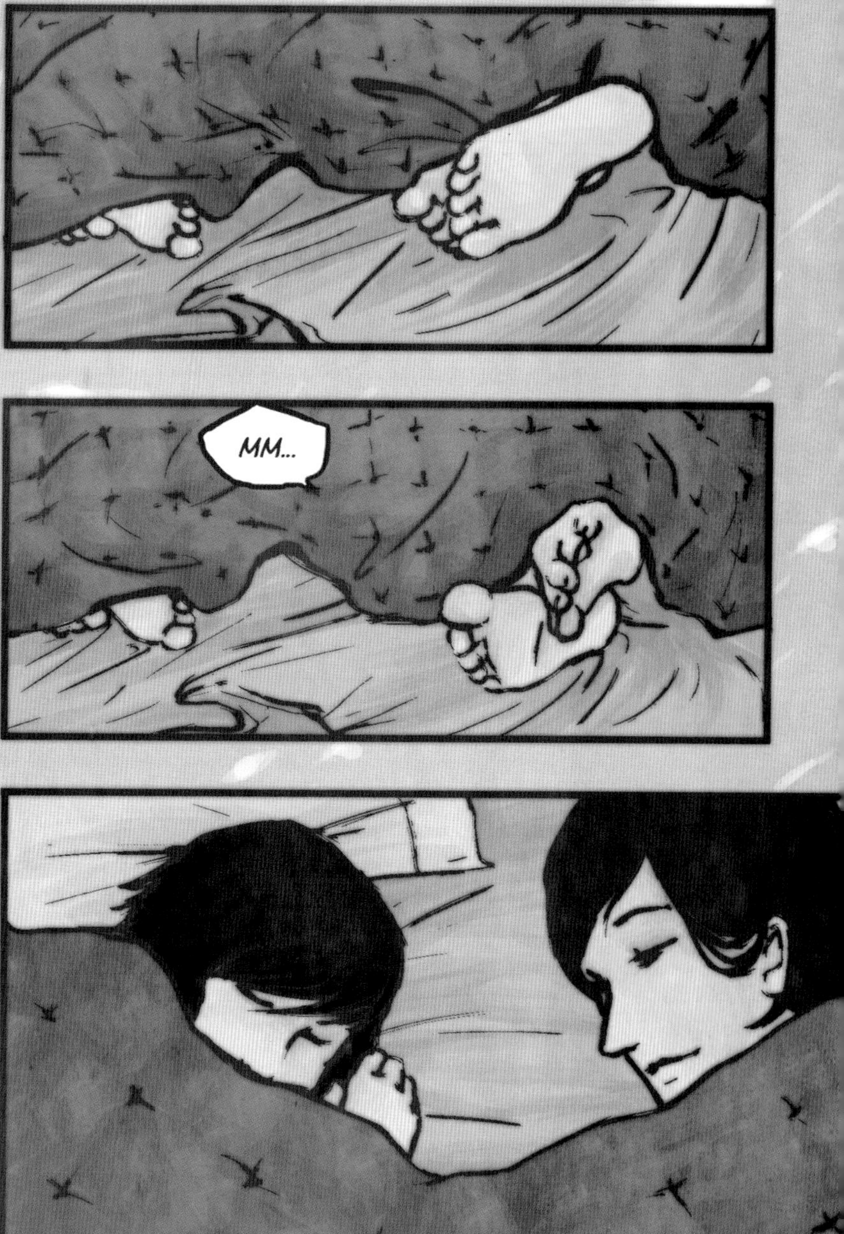
MM...

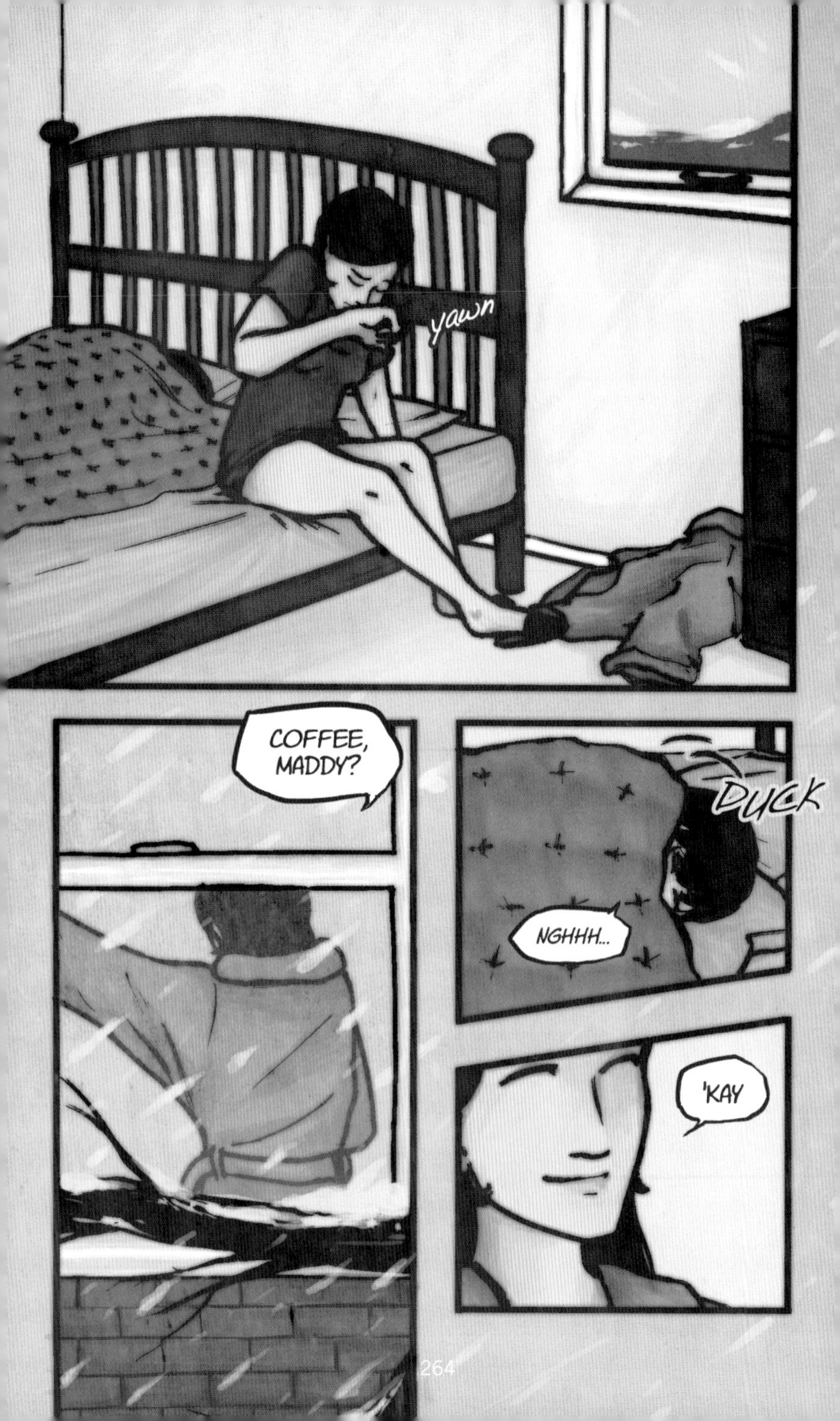
yawn
COFFEE, MADDY?
DUCK
NGHHH...
'KAY

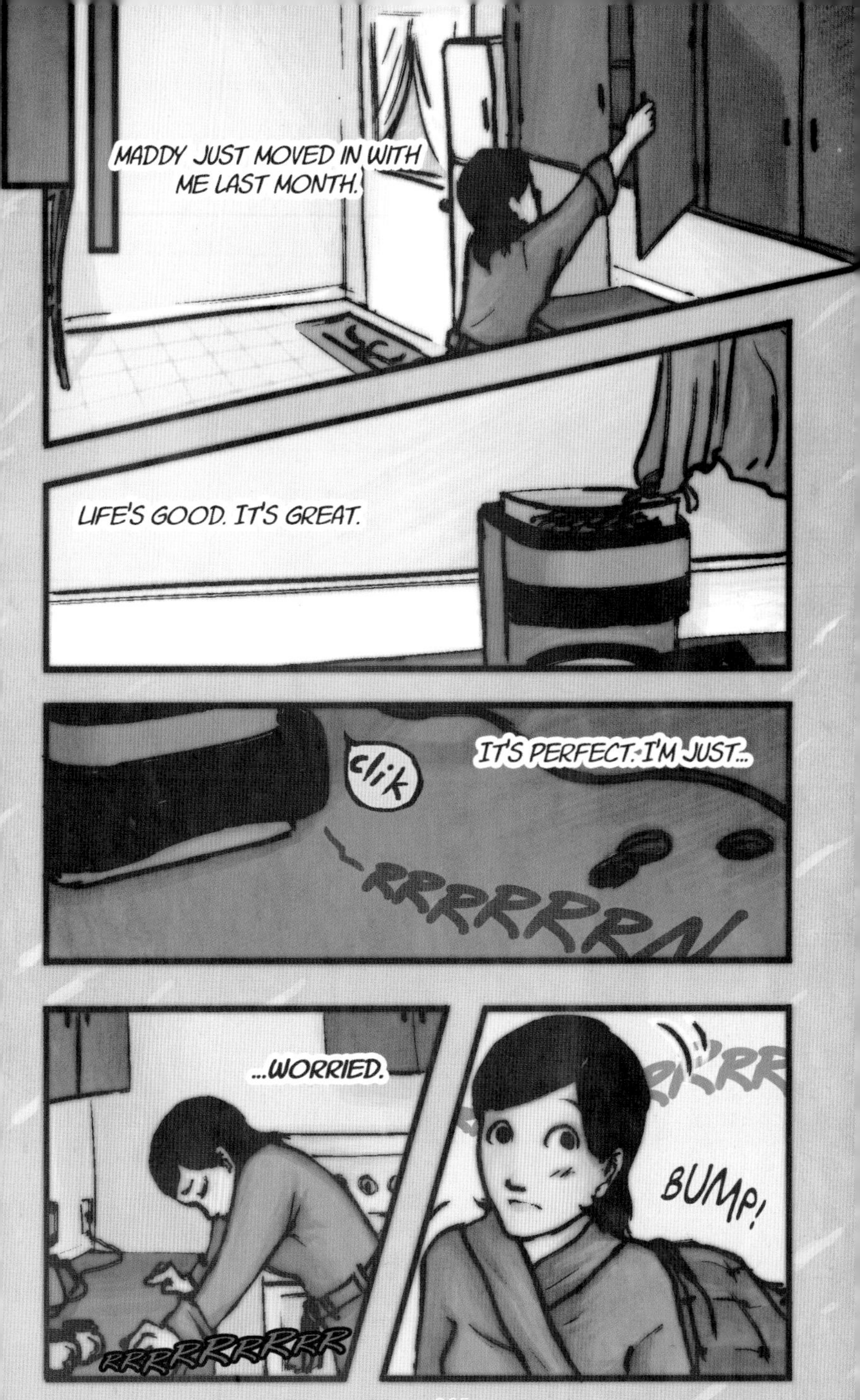
MADDY JUST MOVED IN WITH ME LAST MONTH.
LIFE'S GOOD. IT'S GREAT.
clik
IT'S PERFECT. I'M JUST...
RRRRRRN
...WORRIED.
RRRRRRRRRR
RRRR
BUMP!

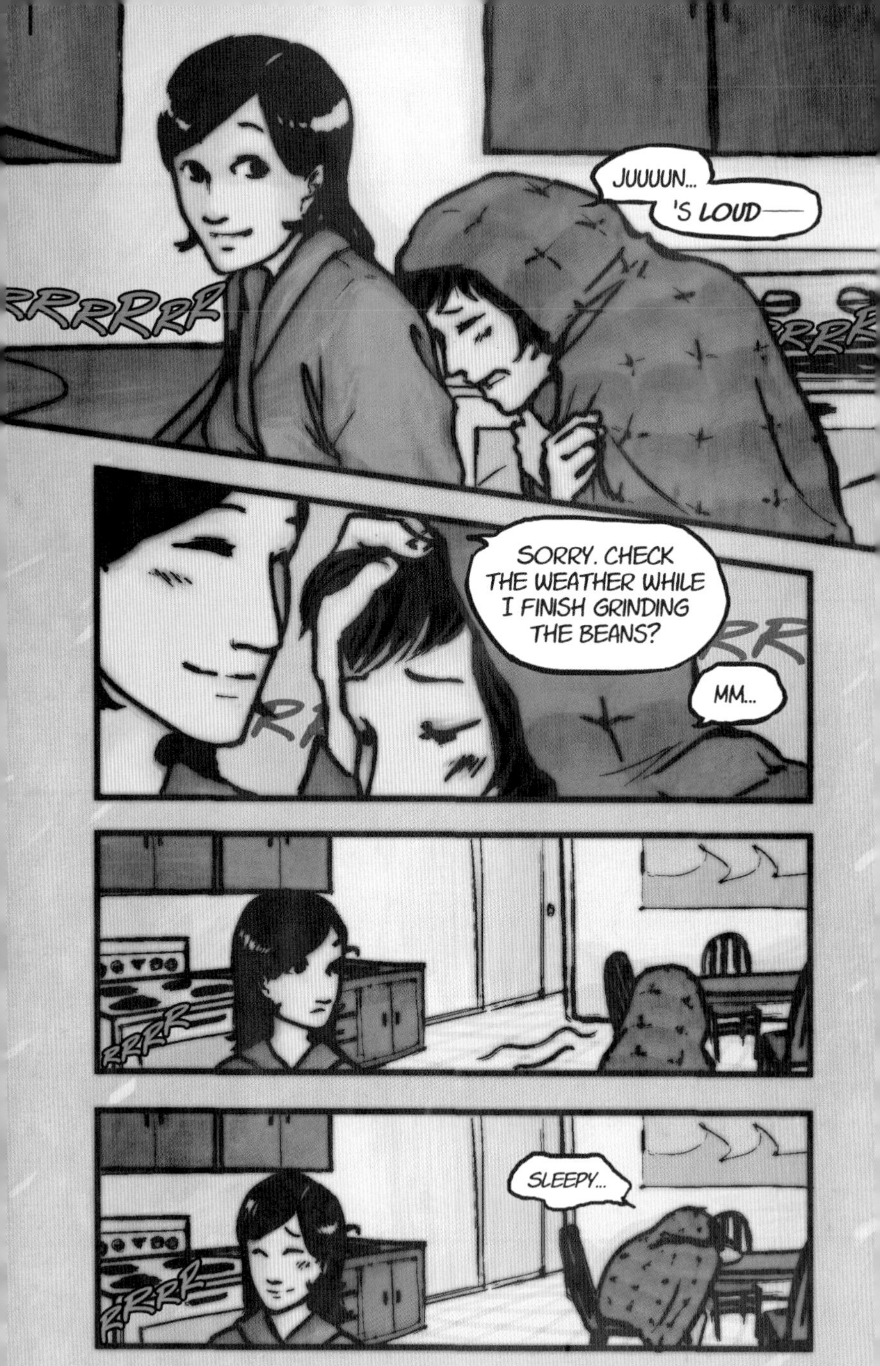
JUUUUN...
'S LOUD
RRRRRR
SORRY. CHECK THE WEATHER WHILE I FINISH GRINDING THE BEANS?
MM...
RRRR
SLEEPY...
RRRR

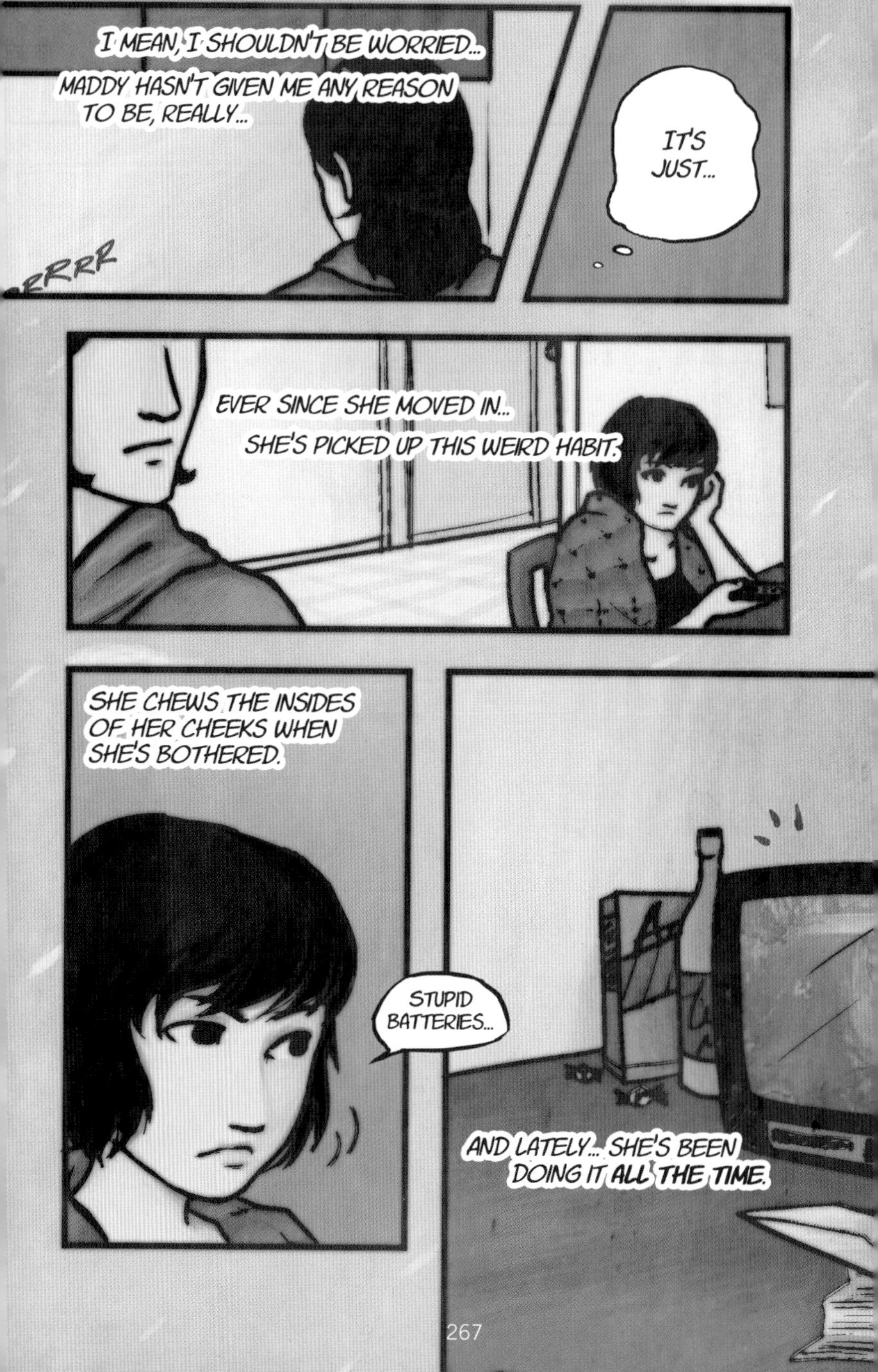
I MEAN, I SHOULDN'T BE WORRIED...
MADDY HASN'T GIVEN ME ANY REASON TO BE, REALLY...
RRRRR
IT'S JUST...
EVER SINCE SHE MOVED IN...
SHE'S PICKED UP THIS WEIRD HABIT.
SHE CHEWS THE INSIDES OF HER CHEEKS WHEN SHE'S BOTHERED.
STUPID BATTERIES...
AND LATELY... SHE'S BEEN DOING IT **ALL THE TIME.**

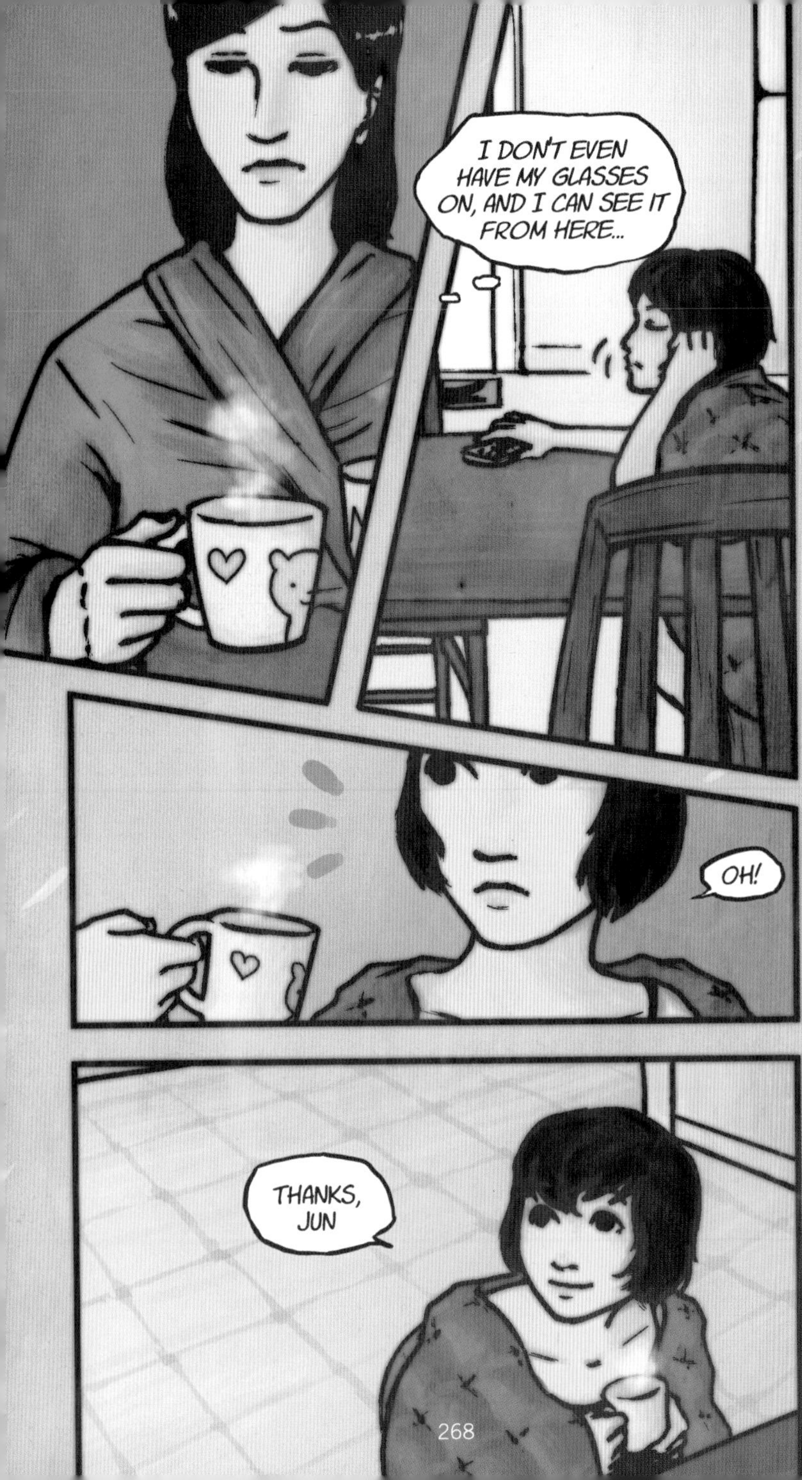
I DON'T EVEN HAVE MY GLASSES ON, AND I CAN SEE IT FROM HERE...
OH!
THANKS, JUN

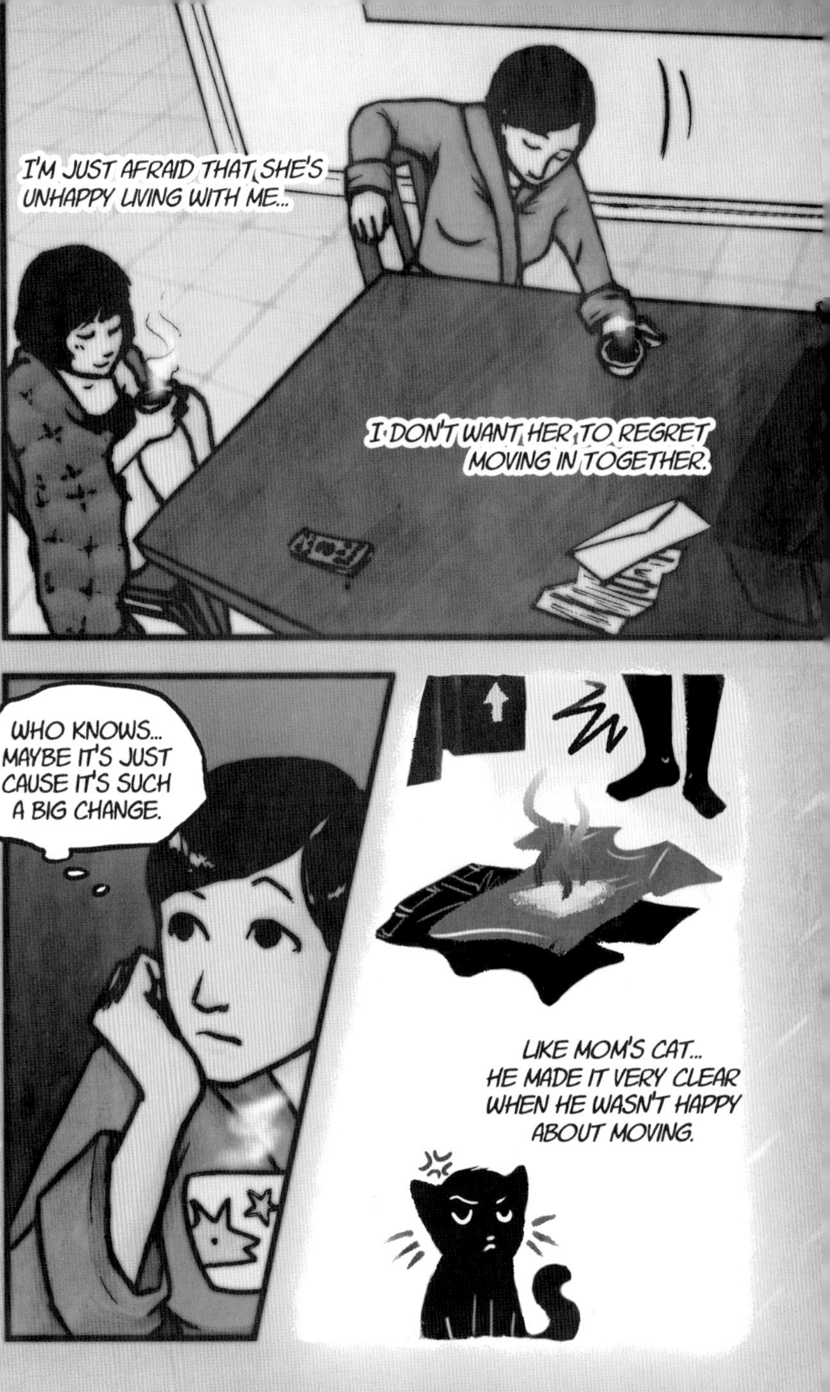
I'M JUST AFRAID THAT SHE'S UNHAPPY LIVING WITH ME...
I DON'T WANT HER TO REGRET MOVING IN TOGETHER.
WHO KNOWS... MAYBE IT'S JUST CAUSE IT'S SUCH A BIG CHANGE.
LIKE MOM'S CAT... HE MADE IT VERY CLEAR WHEN HE WASN'T HAPPY ABOUT MOVING.

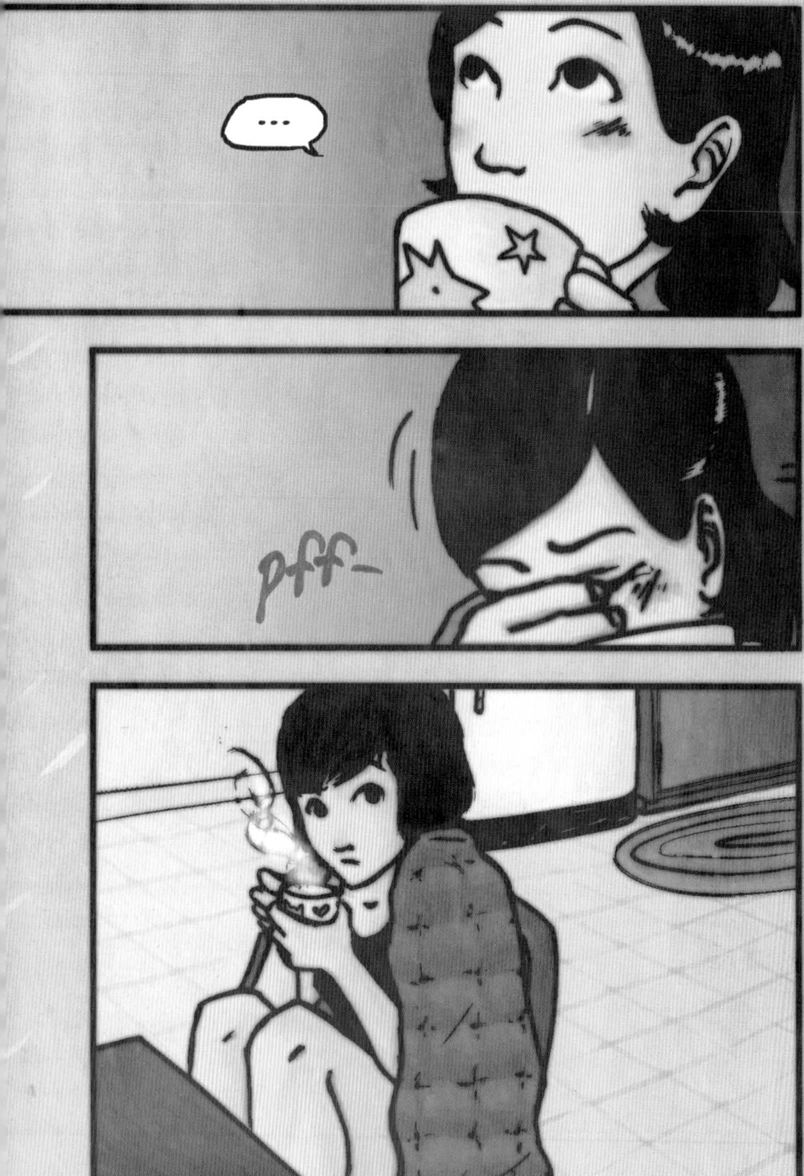
...
pff_

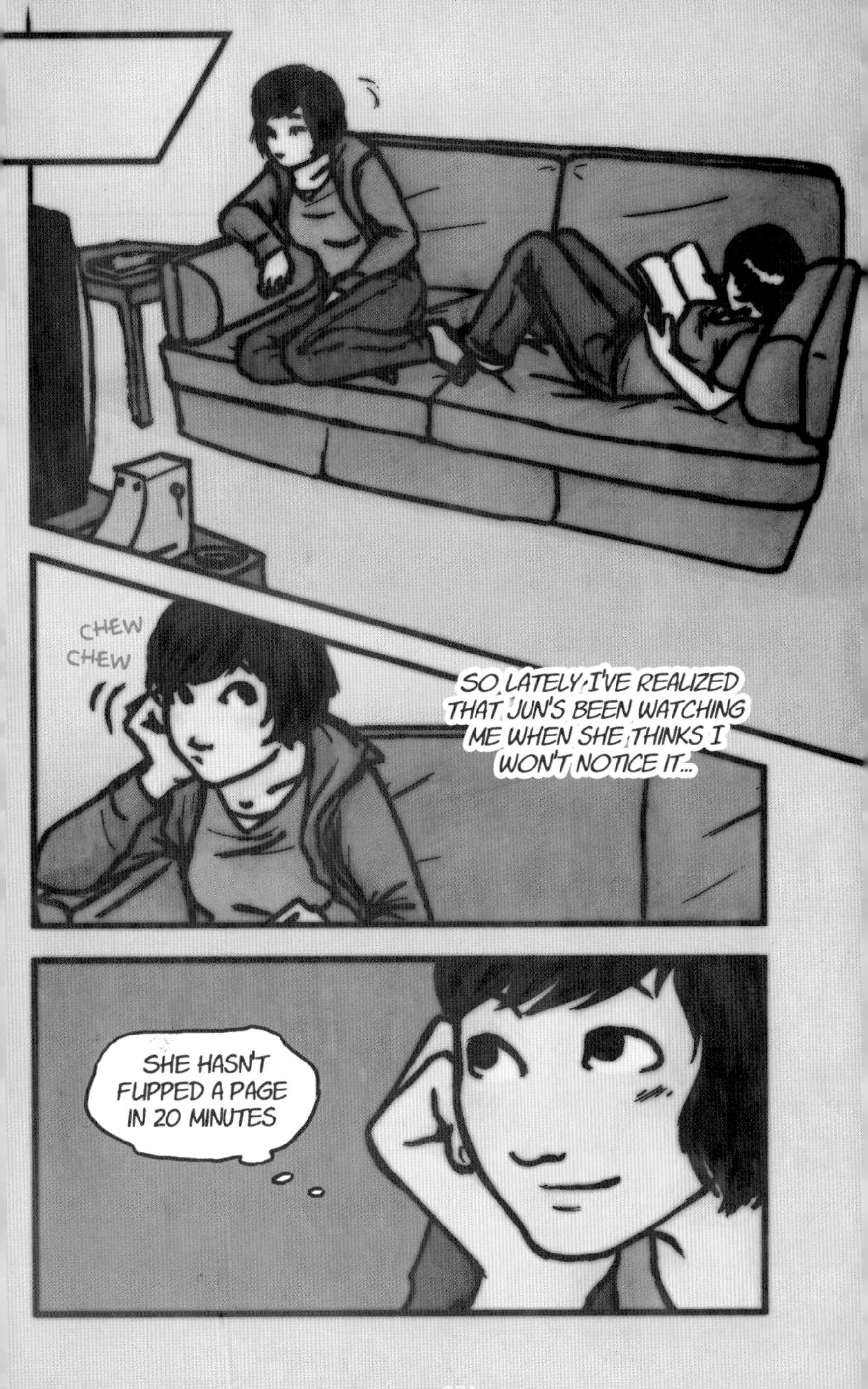
CHEW
CHEW
SO LATELY I'VE REALIZED THAT JUN'S BEEN WATCHING ME WHEN SHE THINKS I WON'T NOTICE IT...
SHE HASN'T FLIPPED A PAGE IN 20 MINUTES

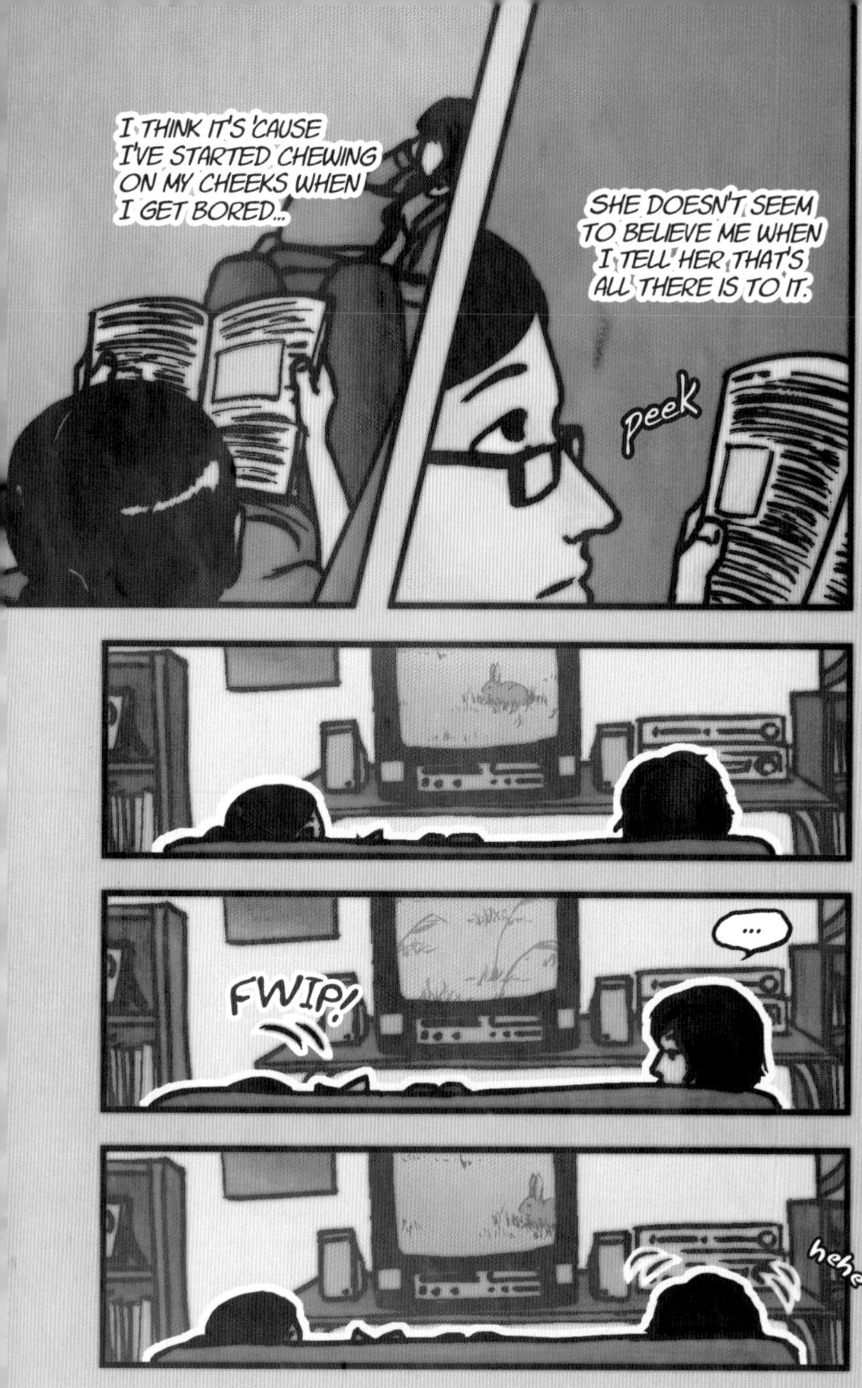

I THINK IT'S 'CAUSE I'VE STARTED CHEWING ON MY CHEEKS WHEN I GET BORED...
SHE DOESN'T SEEM TO BELIEVE ME WHEN I TELL HER THAT'S ALL THERE IS TO IT.
peek
FWIP!
...
hehe

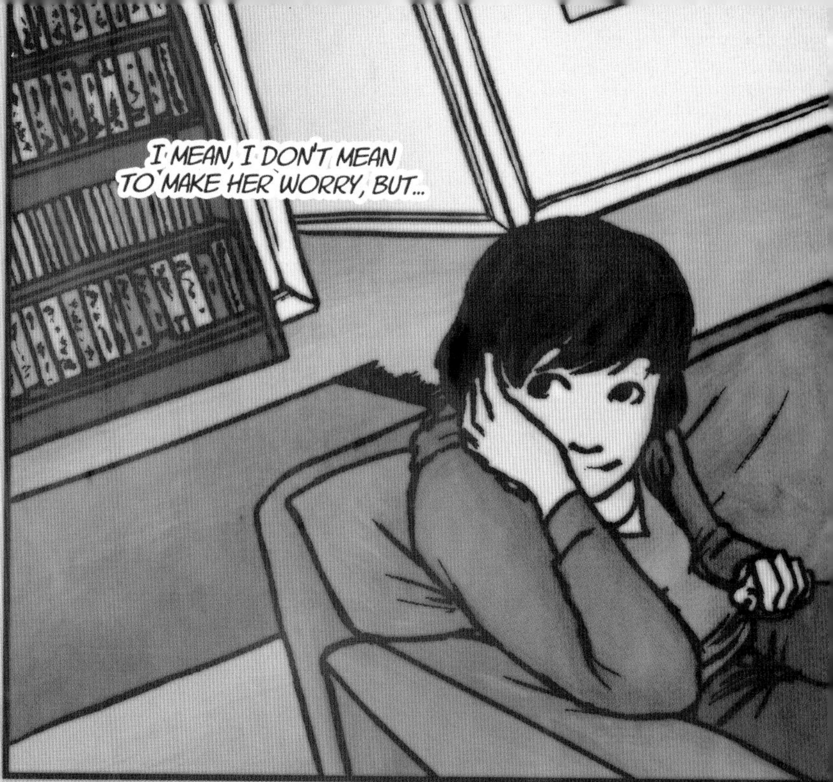
I MEAN, I DON'T MEAN TO MAKE HER WORRY, BUT...
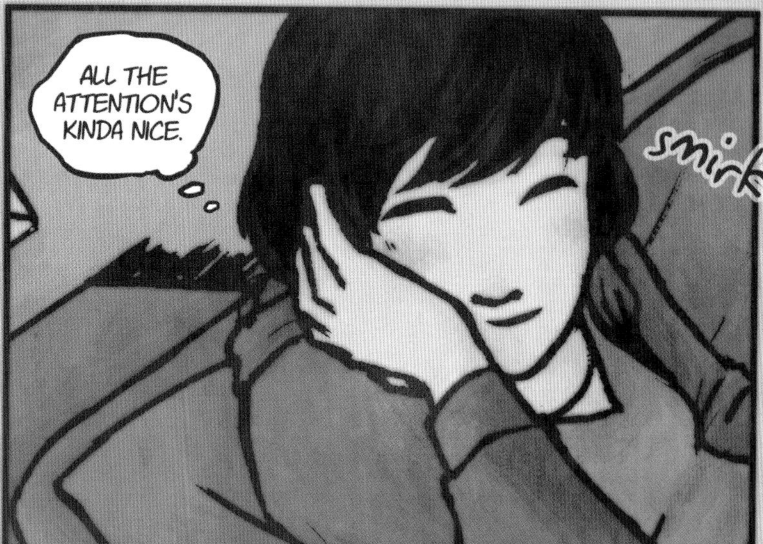
ALL THE ATTENTION'S KINDA NICE.
smirk

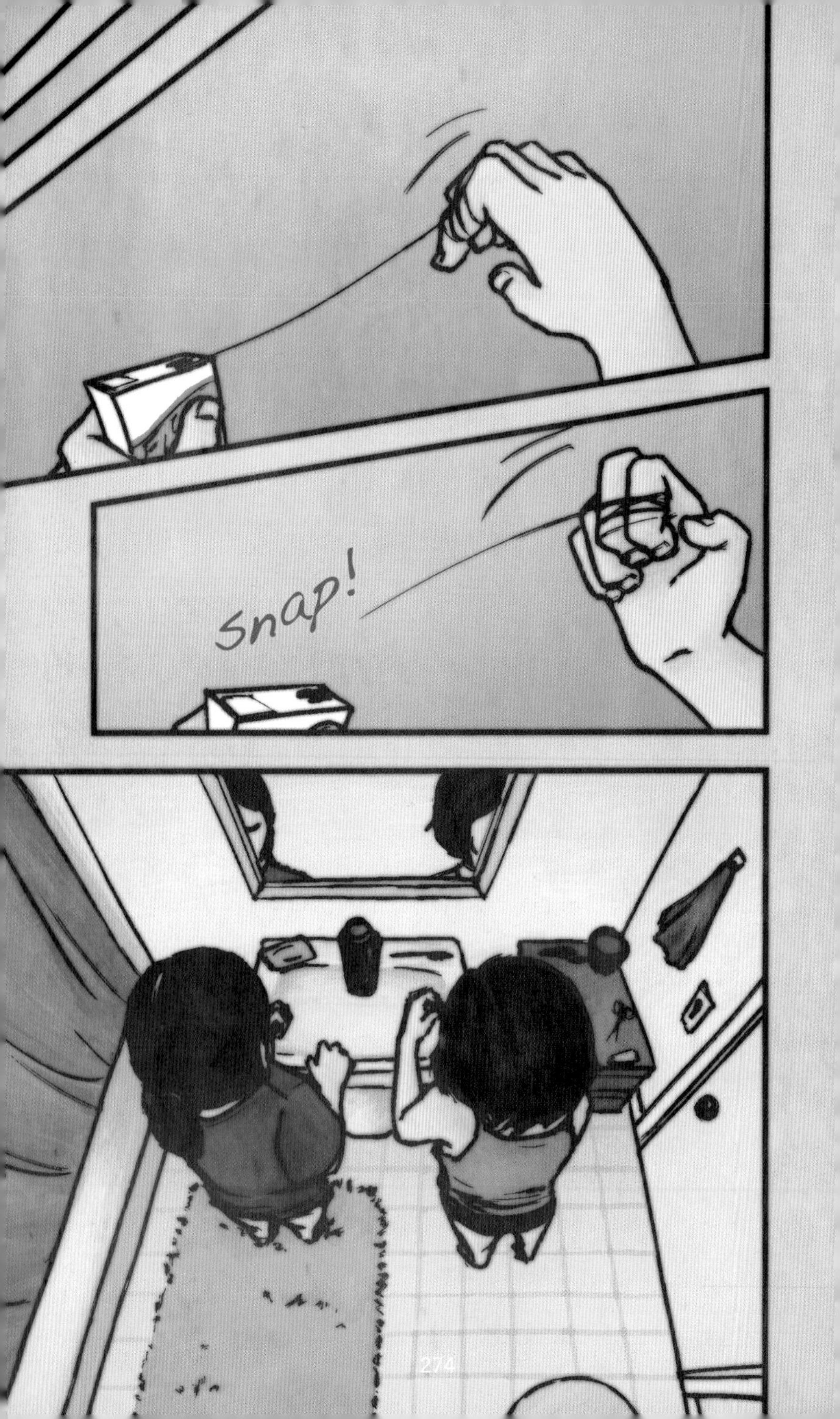
Snap!

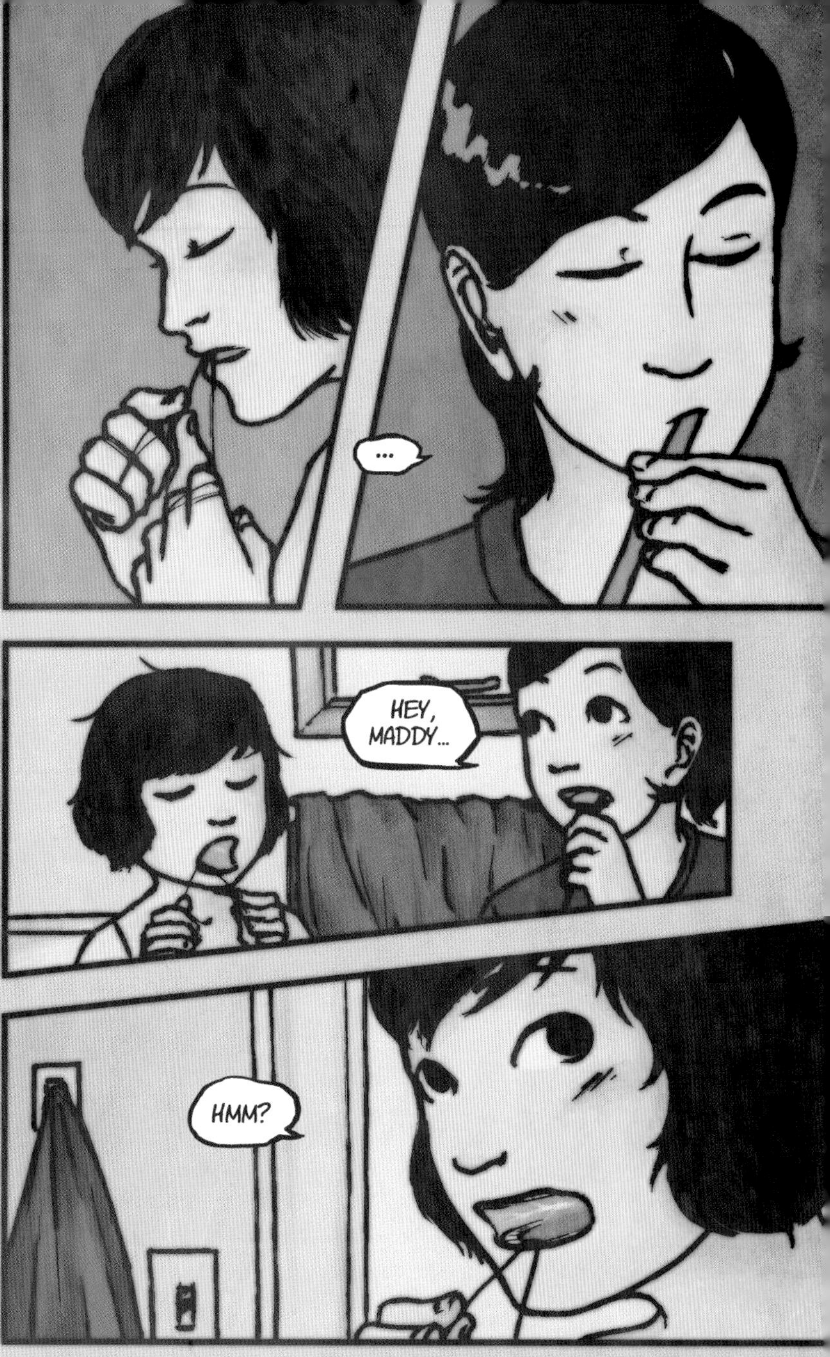
...
HEY, MADDY...
HMM?

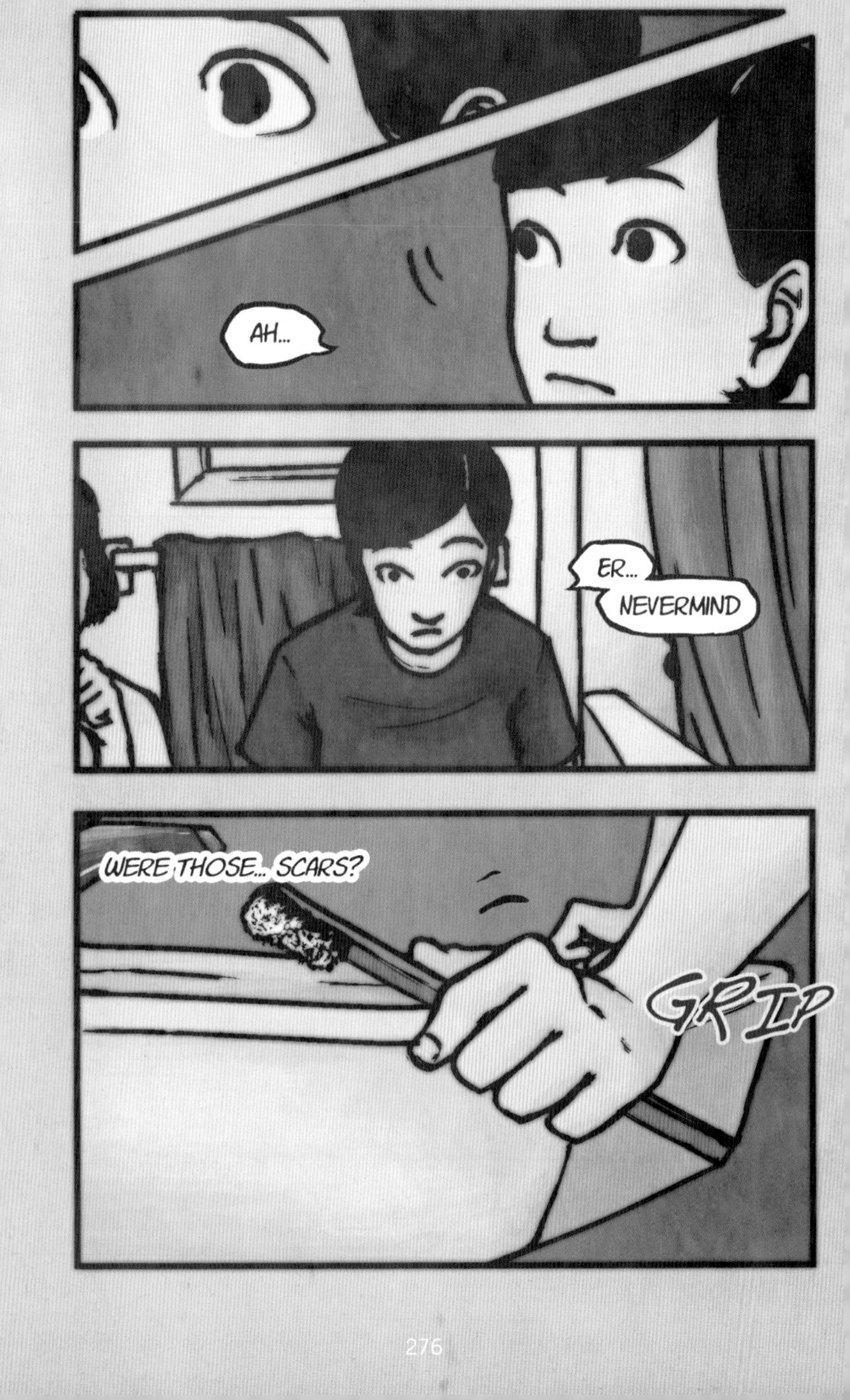
AH...
ER...
NEVERMIND
WERE THOSE... SCARS?
GRIP

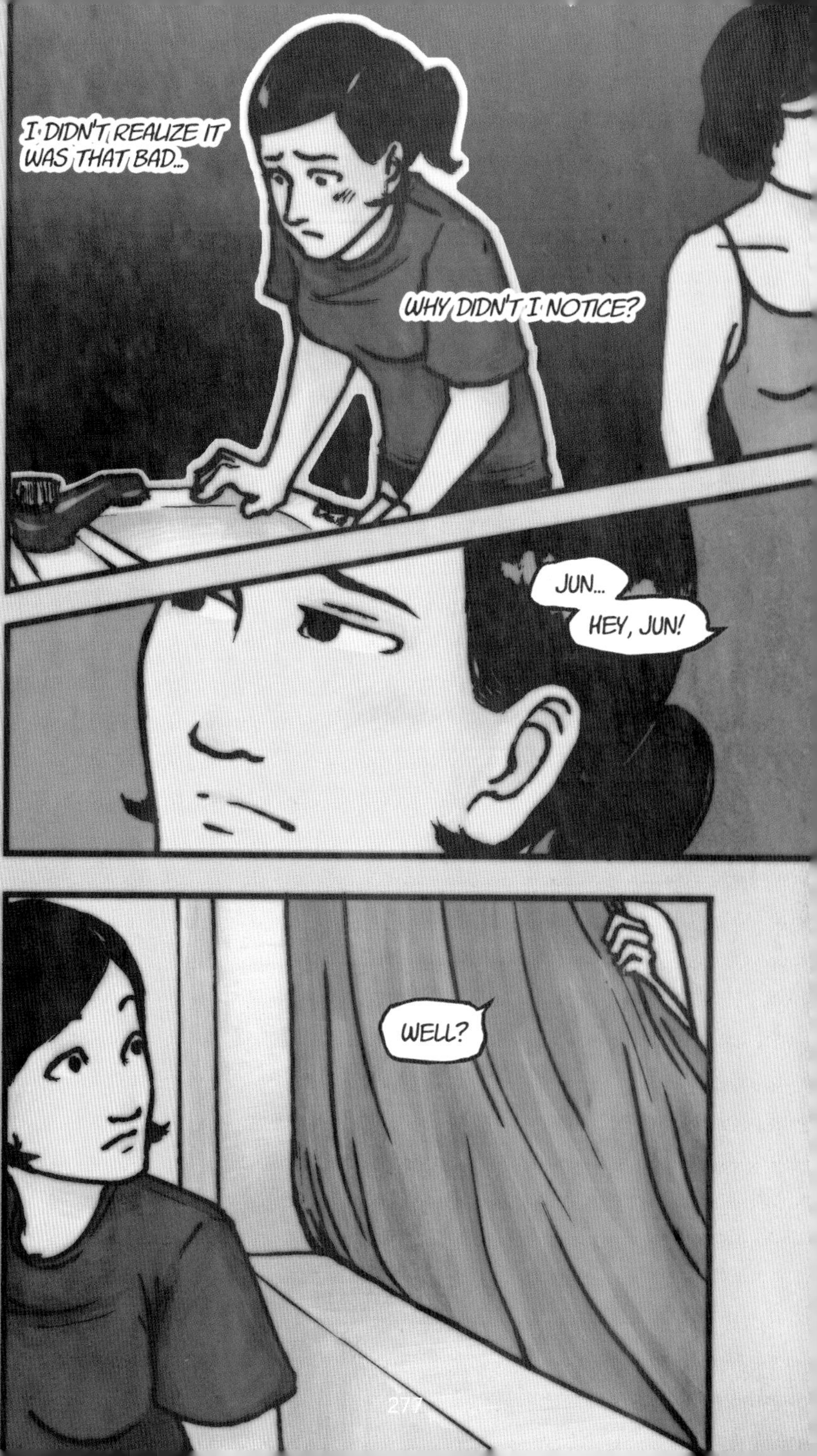
I DIDN'T REALIZE IT WAS THAT BAD...
WHY DIDN'T I NOTICE?
JUN...
HEY, JUN!
WELL?

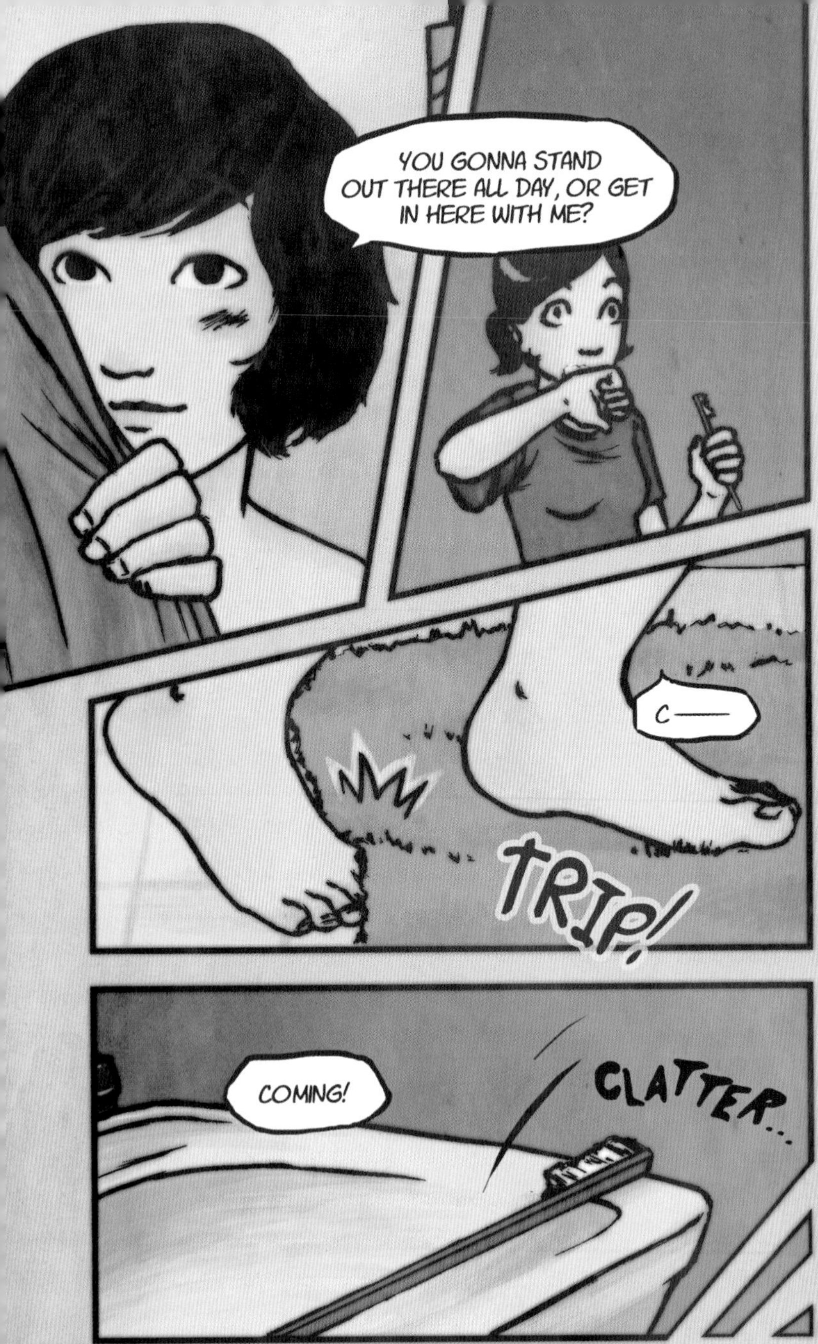
YOU GONNA STAND OUT THERE ALL DAY, OR GET IN HERE WITH ME?
C——
TRIP!
COMING!
CLATTER...

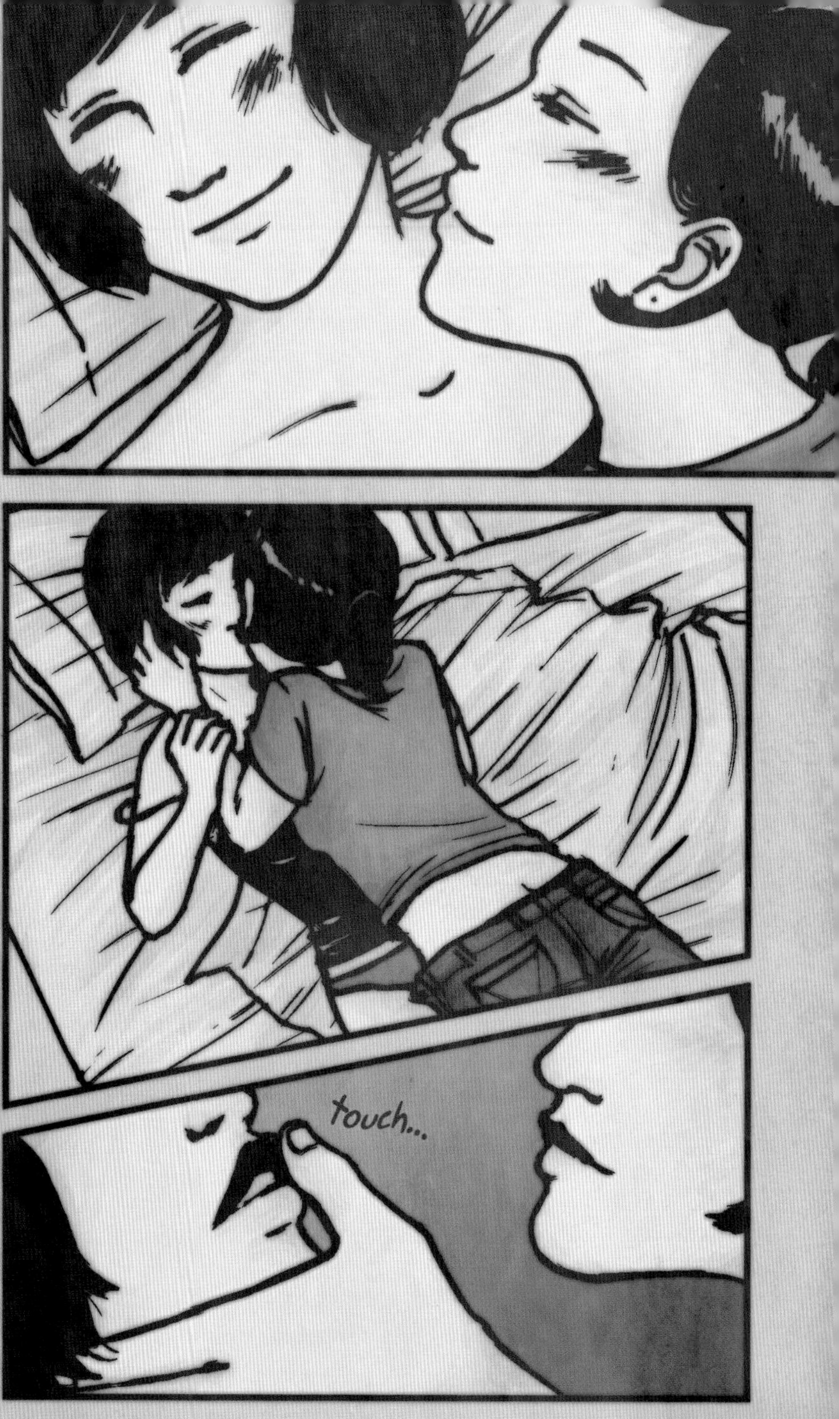
touch...

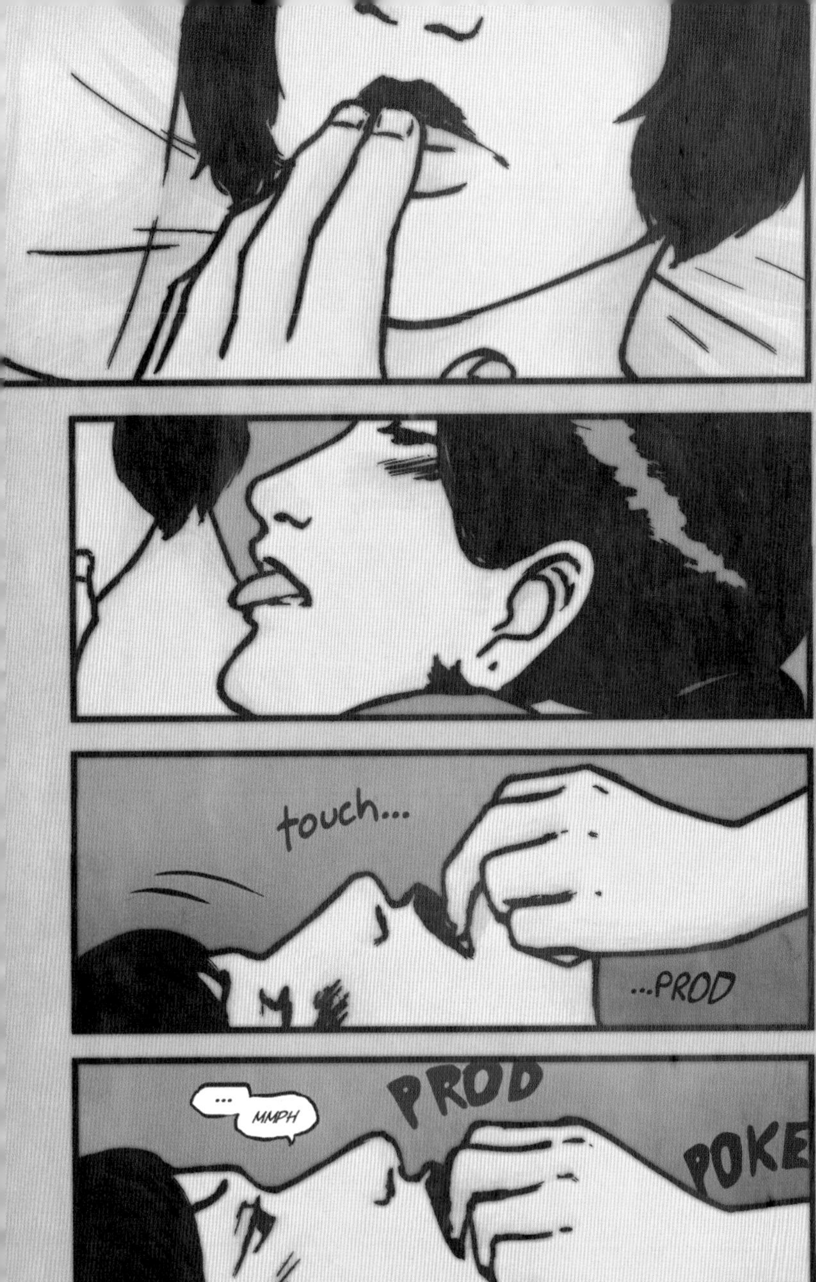
touch...
...PROD
...
MMPH
PROD
POKE

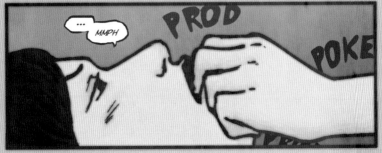

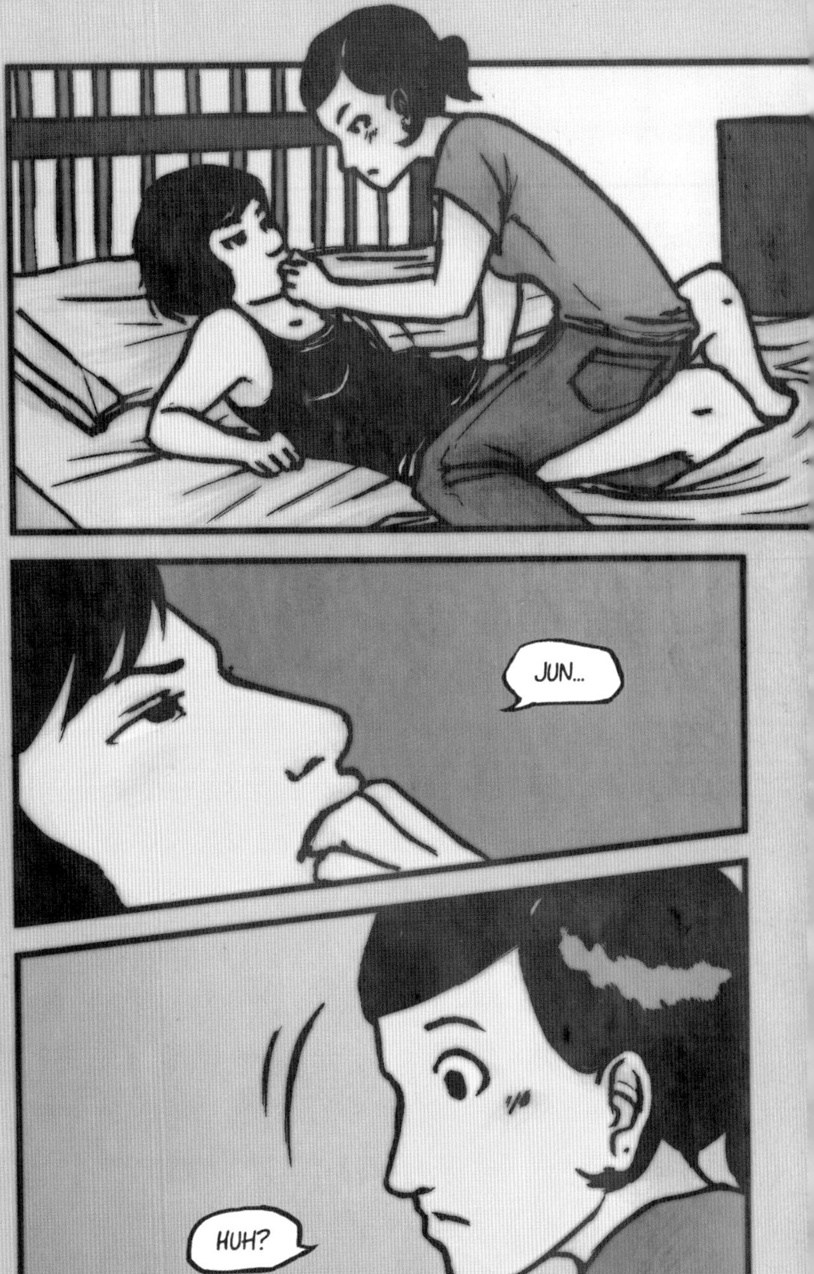
JUN...
HUH?

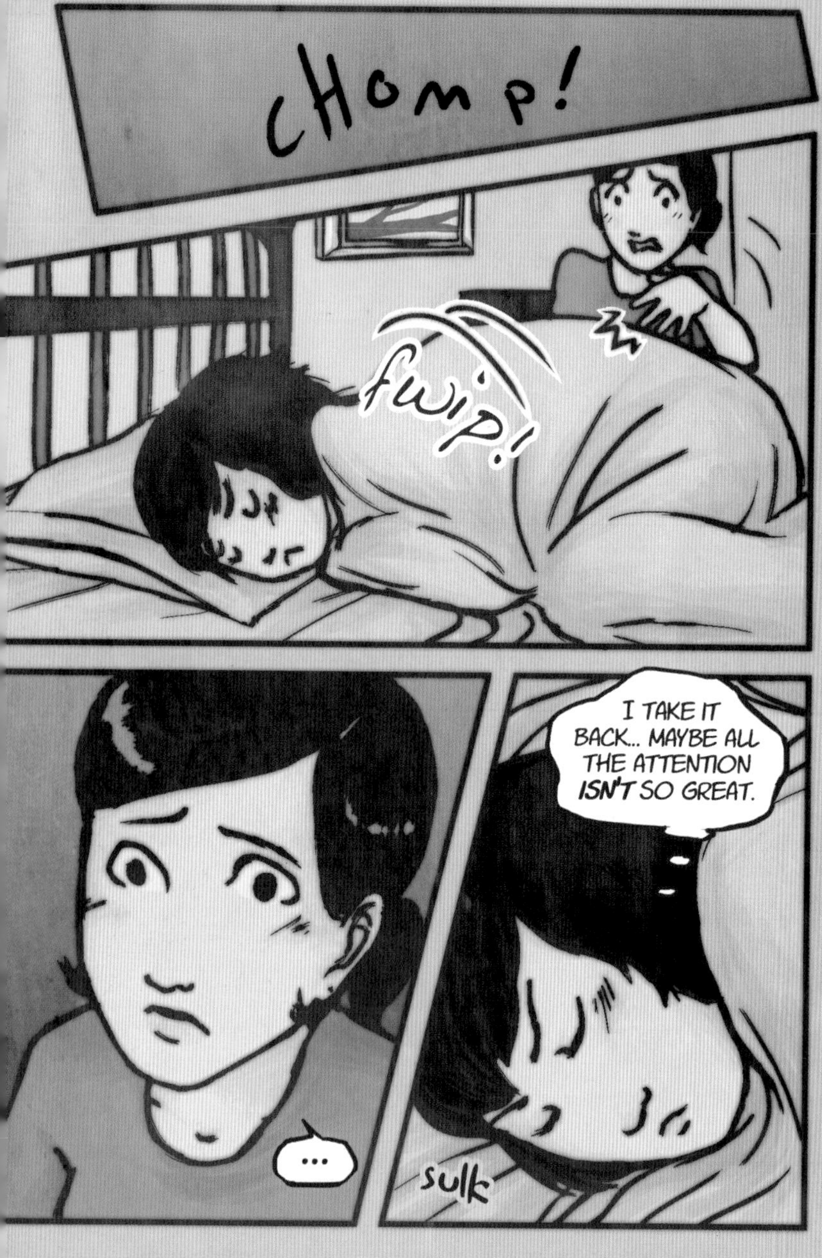
cHOmp!
fwip!
I TAKE IT BACK... MAYBE ALL THE ATTENTION **ISN'T** SO GREAT.
...
sulk

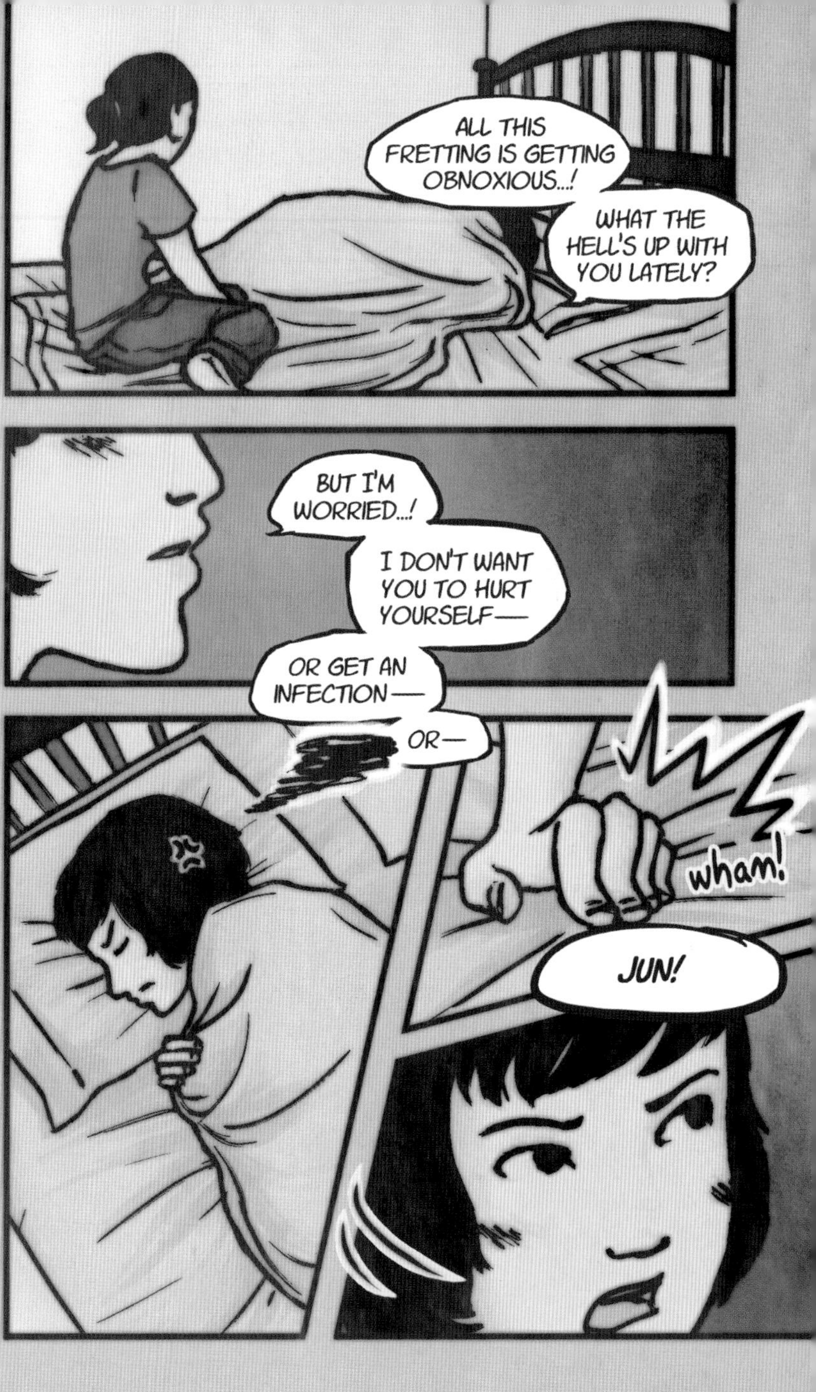
ALL THIS FRETTING IS GETTING OBNOXIOUS...!
WHAT THE HELL'S UP WITH YOU LATELY?
BUT I'M WORRIED...!
I DON'T WANT YOU TO HURT YOURSELF—
OR GET AN INFECTION—
OR—
whan!
JUN!

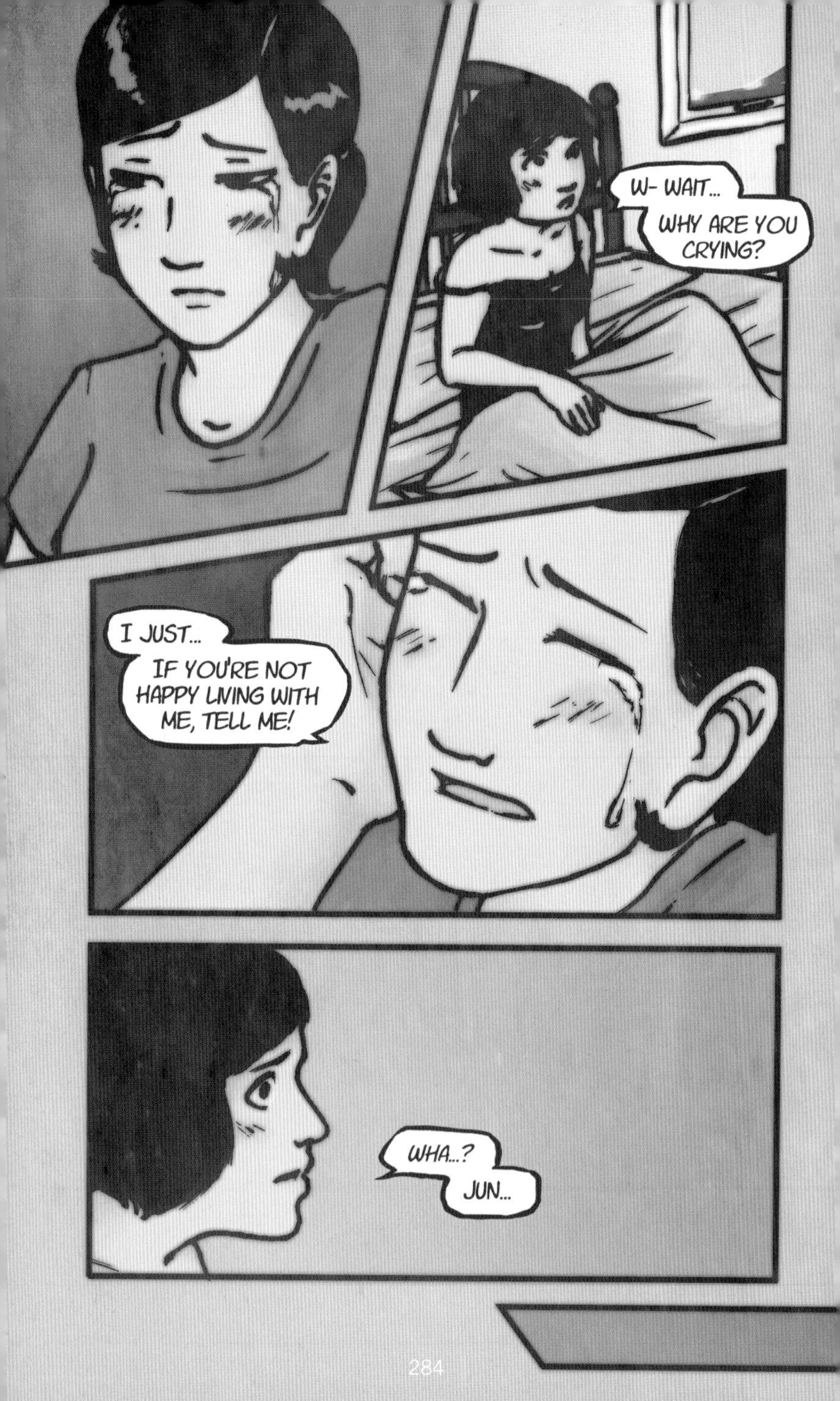
W- WAIT...
WHY ARE YOU CRYING?
I JUST...
IF YOU'RE NOT HAPPY LIVING WITH ME, TELL ME!
WHA...?
JUN...

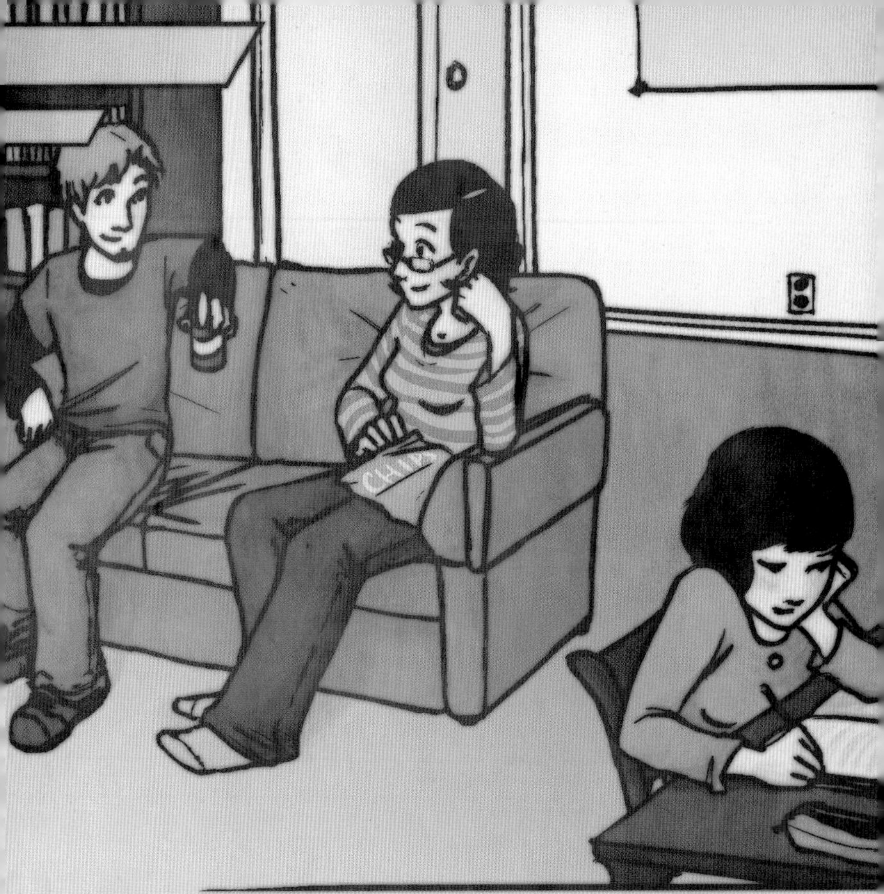

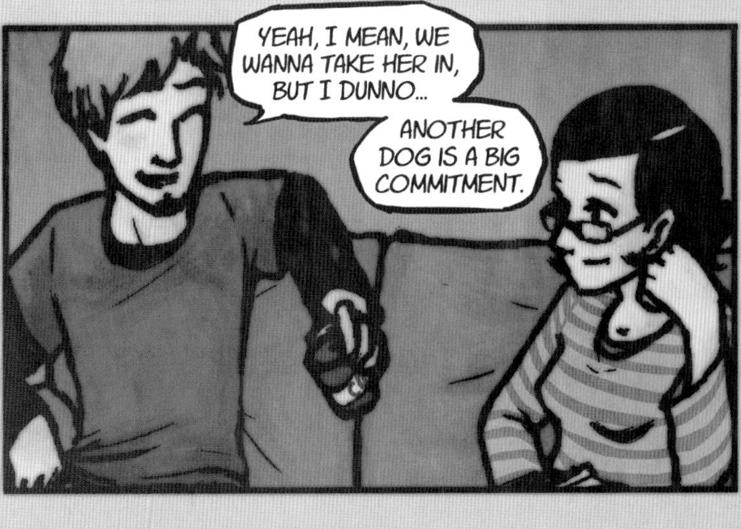
YEAH, I MEAN, WE WANNA TAKE HER IN, BUT I DUNNO...
ANOTHER DOG IS A BIG COMMITMENT.

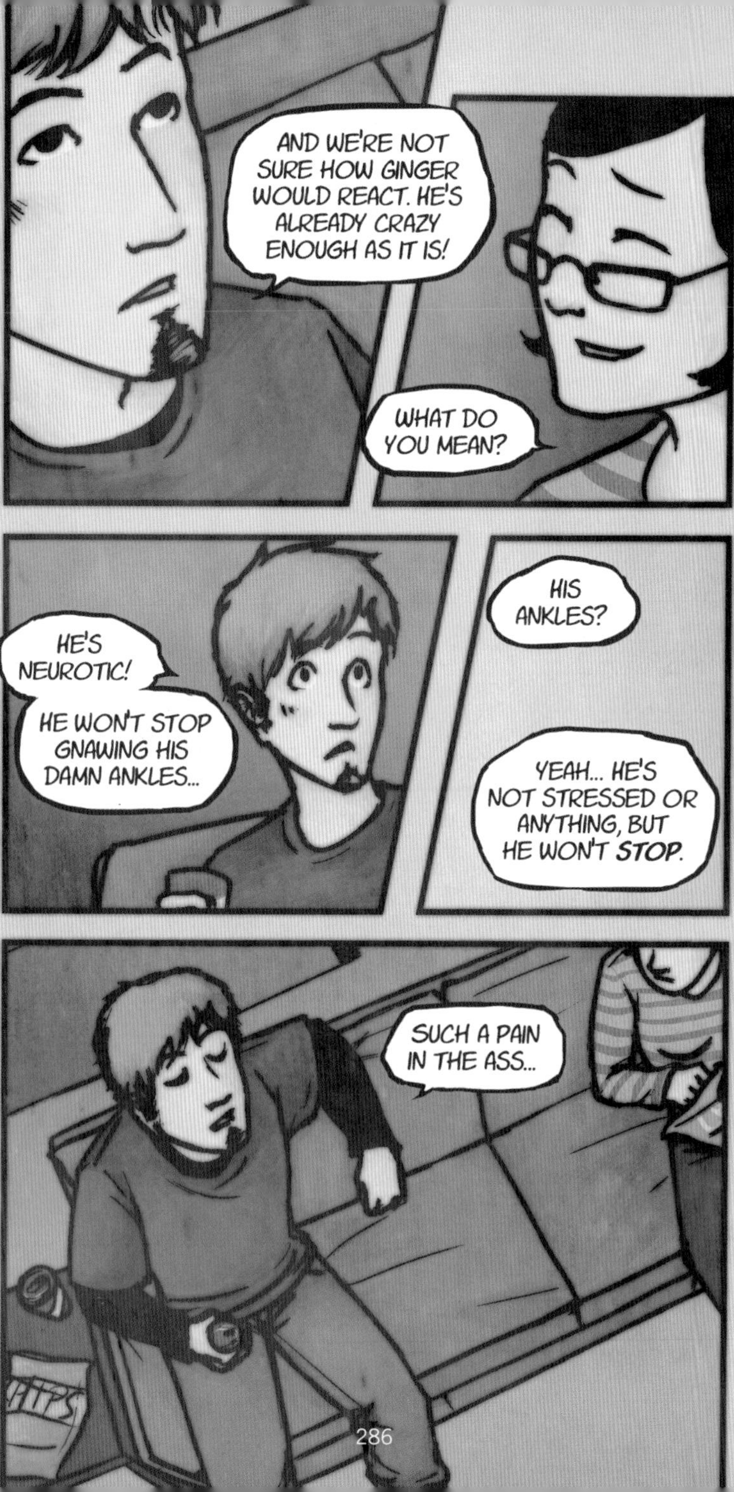
AND WE'RE NOT SURE HOW GINGER WOULD REACT. HE'S ALREADY CRAZY ENOUGH AS IT IS!
WHAT DO YOU MEAN?
HE'S NEUROTIC!
HE WON'T STOP GNAWING HIS DAMN ANKLES...
HIS ANKLES?
YEAH... HE'S NOT STRESSED OR ANYTHING, BUT HE WON'T **STOP**.
SUCH A PAIN IN THE ASS...
CHIPS

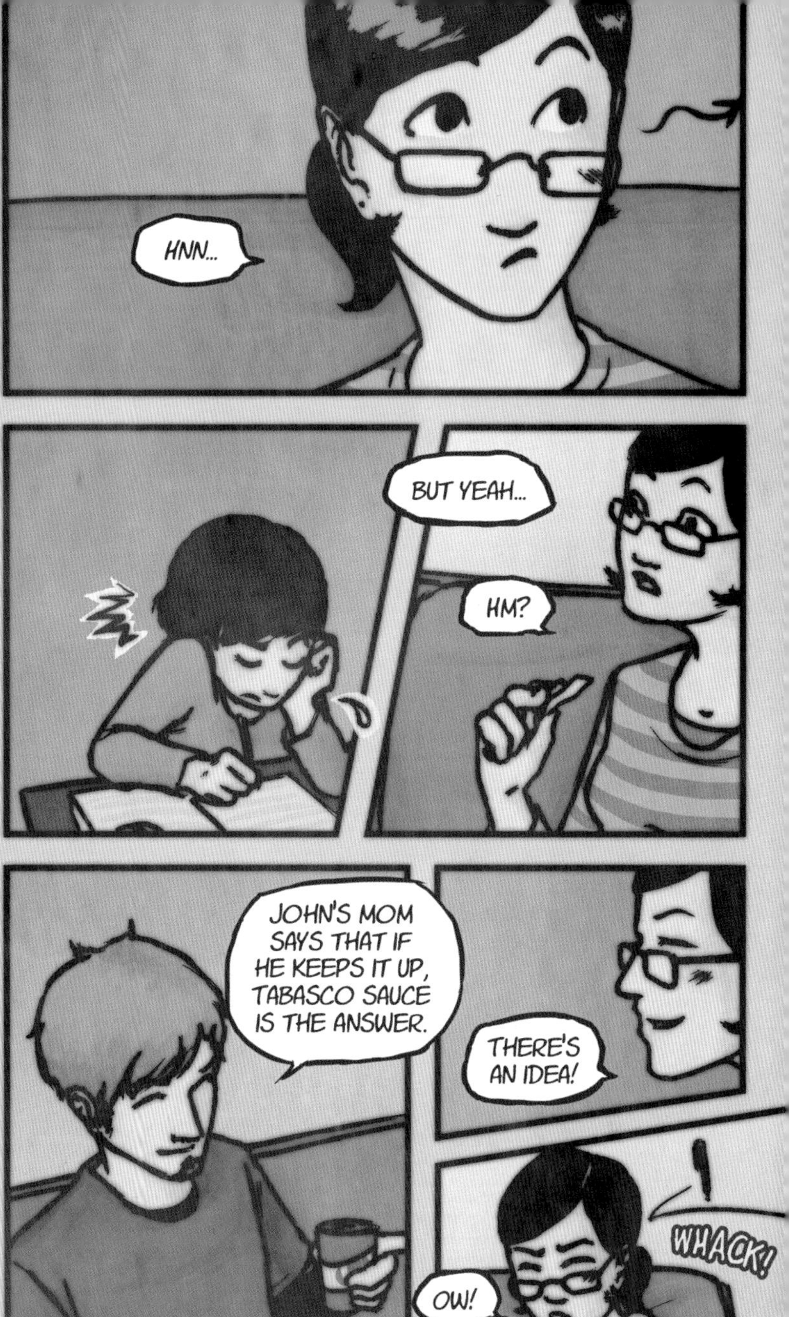
HNN...
BUT YEAH...
HM?
JOHN'S MOM SAYS THAT IF HE KEEPS IT UP, TABASCO SAUCE IS THE ANSWER.
THERE'S AN IDEA!
WHACK!
OW!

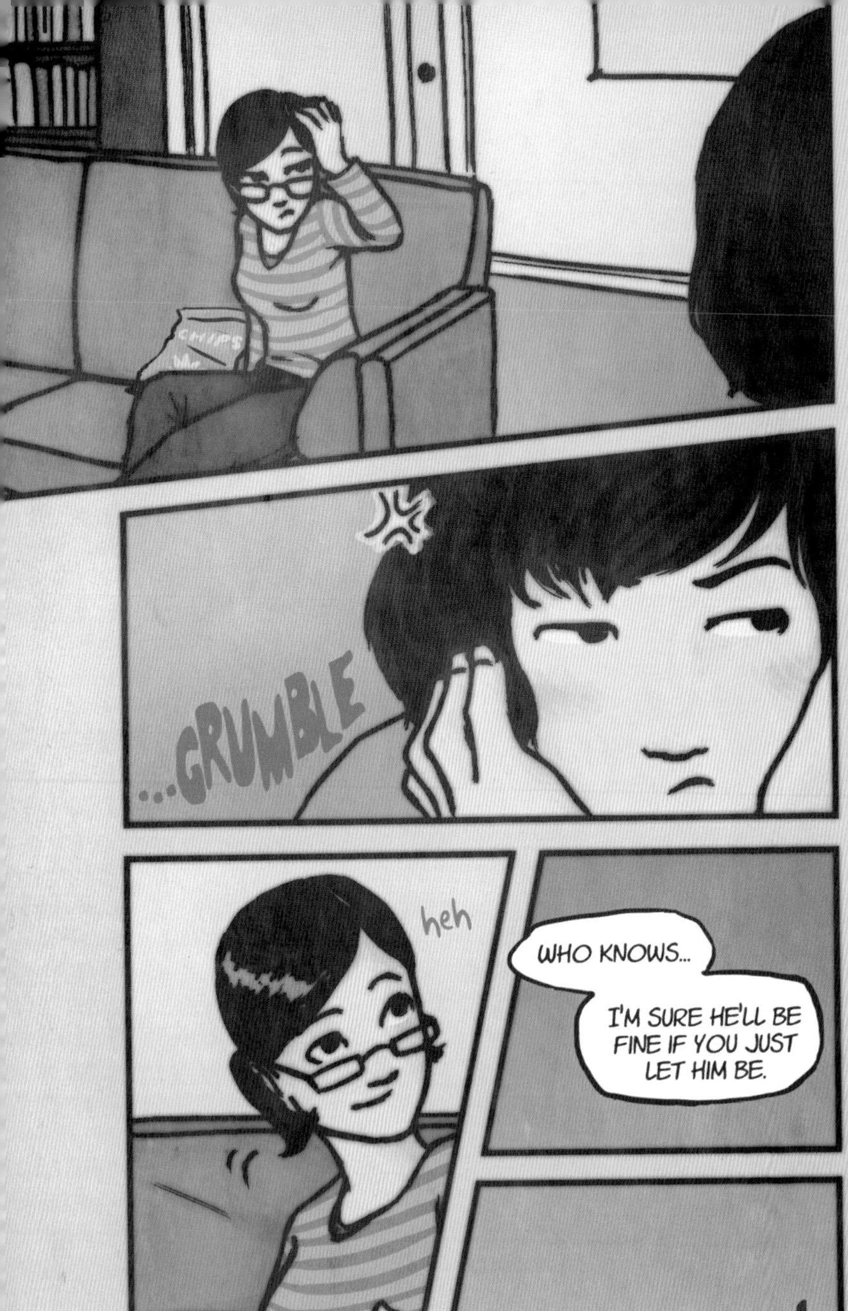
CHIPS
...GRUMBLE
heh
WHO KNOWS...
I'M SURE HE'LL BE FINE IF YOU JUST LET HIM BE.
-end-

ATTACK OF THE PEACH BLOSSOMS

Yao Feila (FLY)

In a movie somebody once said, "Life is full of surprises", which impressed me a lot.

When I was a little boy, first I dreamed of being Superman. Later I dreamed of being a comic artist, though I thought it was impossible at that time. I just wool-gathered without any misgivings.

Years later, I woke up one morning and was surprised to find that I really became a cartoonist. I started to think perhaps I could realize more dreams? Rescue the world, for example... ok, it's not for me to do that yet. Then at least I can create comic books that may save the world! To a cartoonist, anything is possible!'

www.summerzoo.com
email: manga@126.com
email: summerzoo@yahoo.cn

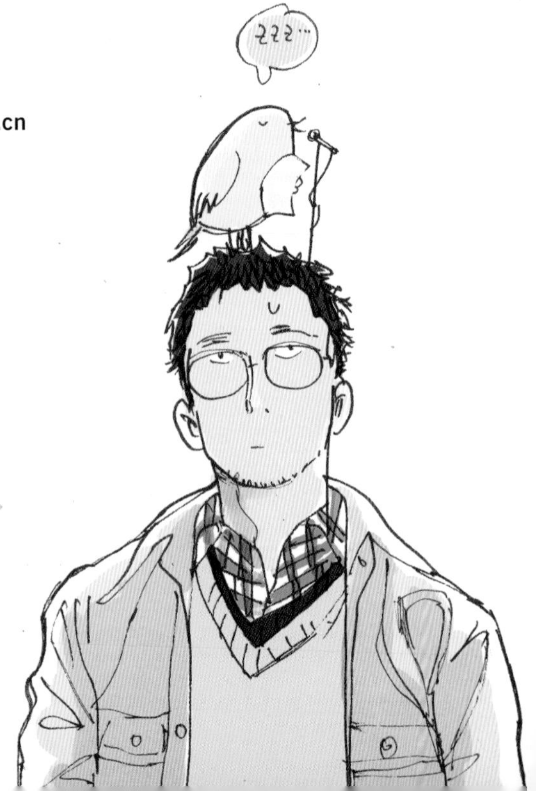

SUMMER
www.summerzoo.com

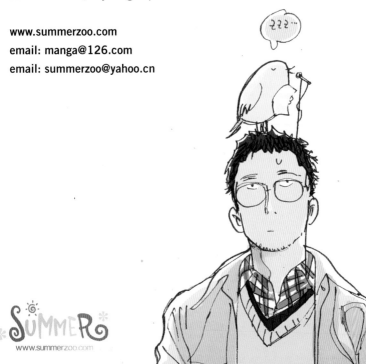

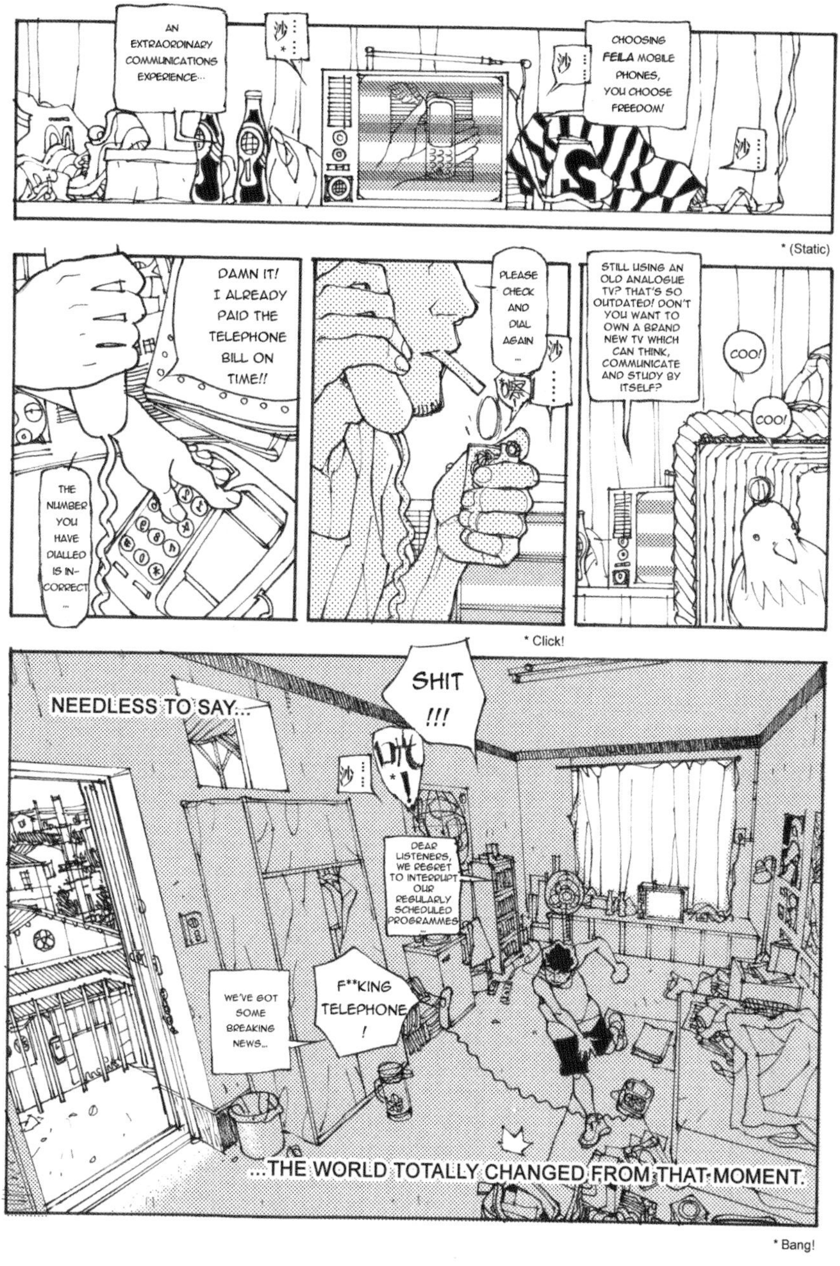
AN EXTRAORDINARY COMMUNICATIONS EXPERIENCE...
沙 ... * ...
CHOOSING FEILA MOBILE PHONES, YOU CHOOSE FREEDOM!
DAMN IT! I ALREADY PAID THE TELEPHONE BILL ON TIME!!
THE NUMBER YOU HAVE DIALLED IS INCORRECT ...
PLEASE CHECK AND DIAL AGAIN ...
STILL USING AN OLD ANALOGUE TV? THAT'S SO OUTDATED! DON'T YOU WANT TO OWN A BRAND NEW TV WHICH CAN THINK, COMMUNICATE AND STUDY BY ITSELF?
COO!
COO!
NEEDLESS TO SAY...
SHIT !!!
DEAR LISTENERS, WE REGRET TO INTERRUPT OUR REGULARLY SCHEDULED PROGRAMMES ...
WE'VE GOT SOME BREAKING NEWS...
F**KING TELEPHONE !
...THE WORLD TOTALLY CHANGED FROM THAT MOMENT.

* (Static)

* Click!

* Bang!

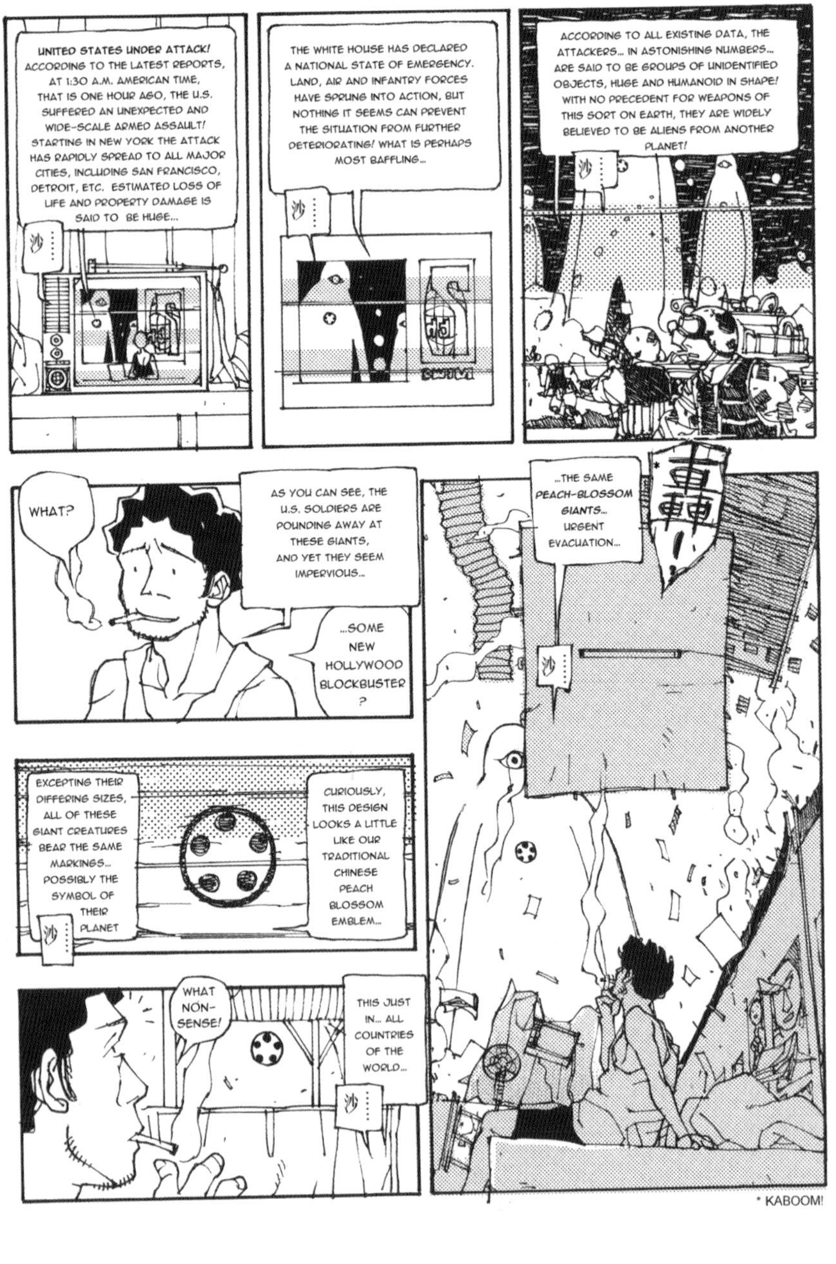
UNITED STATES UNDER ATTACK! ACCORDING TO THE LATEST REPORTS, AT 1:30 A.M. AMERICAN TIME, THAT IS ONE HOUR AGO, THE U.S. SUFFERED AN UNEXPECTED AND WIDE-SCALE ARMED ASSAULT! STARTING IN NEW YORK THE ATTACK HAS RAPIDLY SPREAD TO ALL MAJOR CITIES, INCLUDING SAN FRANCISCO, DETROIT, ETC. ESTIMATED LOSS OF LIFE AND PROPERTY DAMAGE IS SAID TO BE HUGE...
沙 ......
THE WHITE HOUSE HAS DECLARED A NATIONAL STATE OF EMERGENCY. LAND, AIR AND INFANTRY FORCES HAVE SPRUNG INTO ACTION, BUT NOTHING IT SEEMS CAN PREVENT THE SITUATION FROM FURTHER DETERIORATING! WHAT IS PERHAPS MOST BAFFLING...
沙 ......
ACCORDING TO ALL EXISTING DATA, THE ATTACKERS... IN ASTONISHING NUMBERS... ARE SAID TO BE GROUPS OF UNIDENTIFIED OBJECTS, HUGE AND HUMANOID IN SHAPE! WITH NO PRECEDENT FOR WEAPONS OF THIS SORT ON EARTH, THEY ARE WIDELY BELIEVED TO BE ALIENS FROM ANOTHER PLANET!
沙 ......
WHAT?
AS YOU CAN SEE, THE U.S. SOLDIERS ARE POUNDING AWAY AT THESE GIANTS, AND YET THEY SEEM IMPERVIOUS...
...SOME NEW HOLLYWOOD BLOCKBUSTER ?
...THE SAME PEACH-BLOSSOM GIANTS... URGENT EVACUATION...
沙 ......
EXCEPTING THEIR DIFFERING SIZES, ALL OF THESE GIANT CREATURES BEAR THE SAME MARKINGS... POSSIBLY THE SYMBOL OF THEIR PLANET
沙 ......
CURIOUSLY, THIS DESIGN LOOKS A LITTLE LIKE OUR TRADITIONAL CHINESE PEACH BLOSSOM EMBLEM...
WHAT NON-SENSE!
THIS JUST IN... ALL COUNTRIES OF THE WORLD...
沙 ......

* KABOOM!

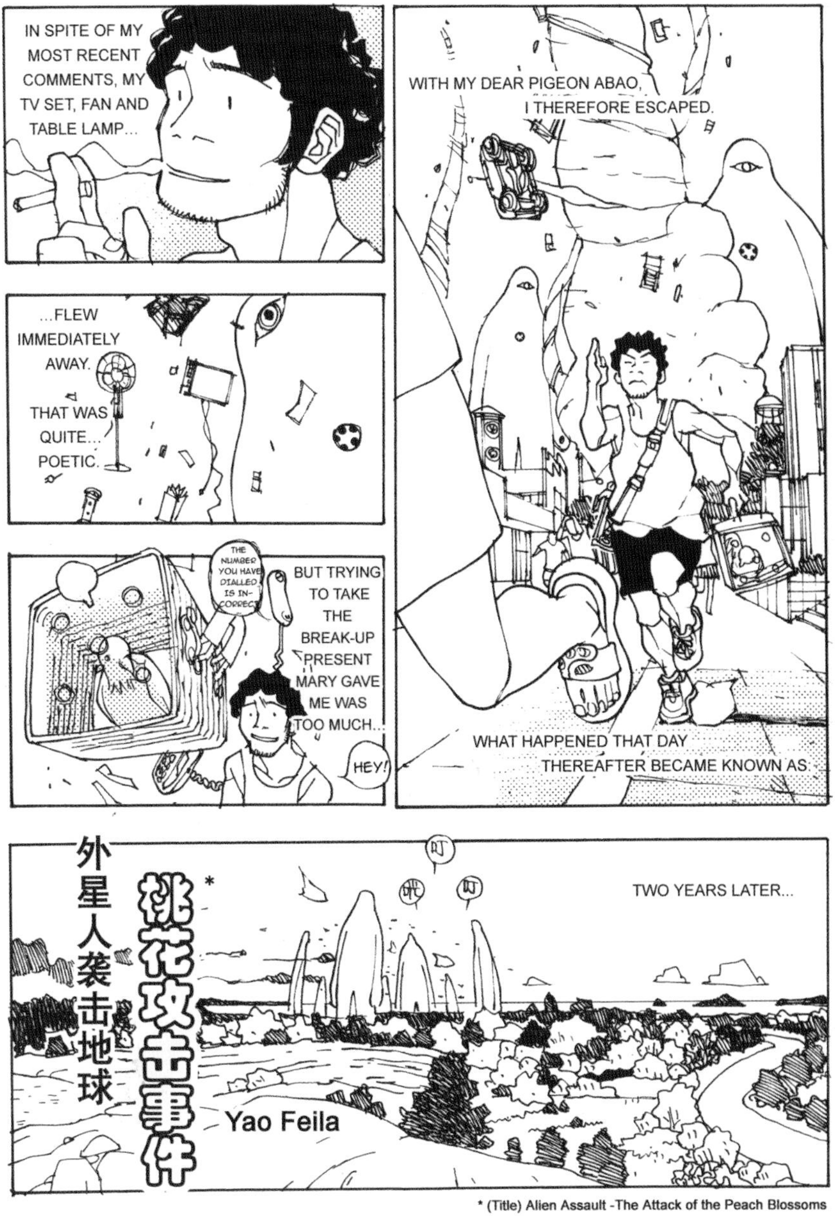
IN SPITE OF MY MOST RECENT COMMENTS, MY TV SET, FAN AND TABLE LAMP...
...FLEW IMMEDIATELY AWAY.
THAT WAS QUITE... POETIC.
THE NUMBER YOU HAVE DIALLED IS IN-CORRECT
BUT TRYING TO TAKE THE BREAK-UP PRESENT MARY GAVE ME WAS TOO MUCH...
HEY!
WITH MY DEAR PIGEON ABAO, I THEREFORE ESCAPED.
WHAT HAPPENED THAT DAY THEREAFTER BECAME KNOWN AS:
叮
叮
TWO YEARS LATER...
桃花攻击事件*
外星人袭击地球
Yao Feila

* (Title) Alien Assault -The Attack of the Peach Blossoms

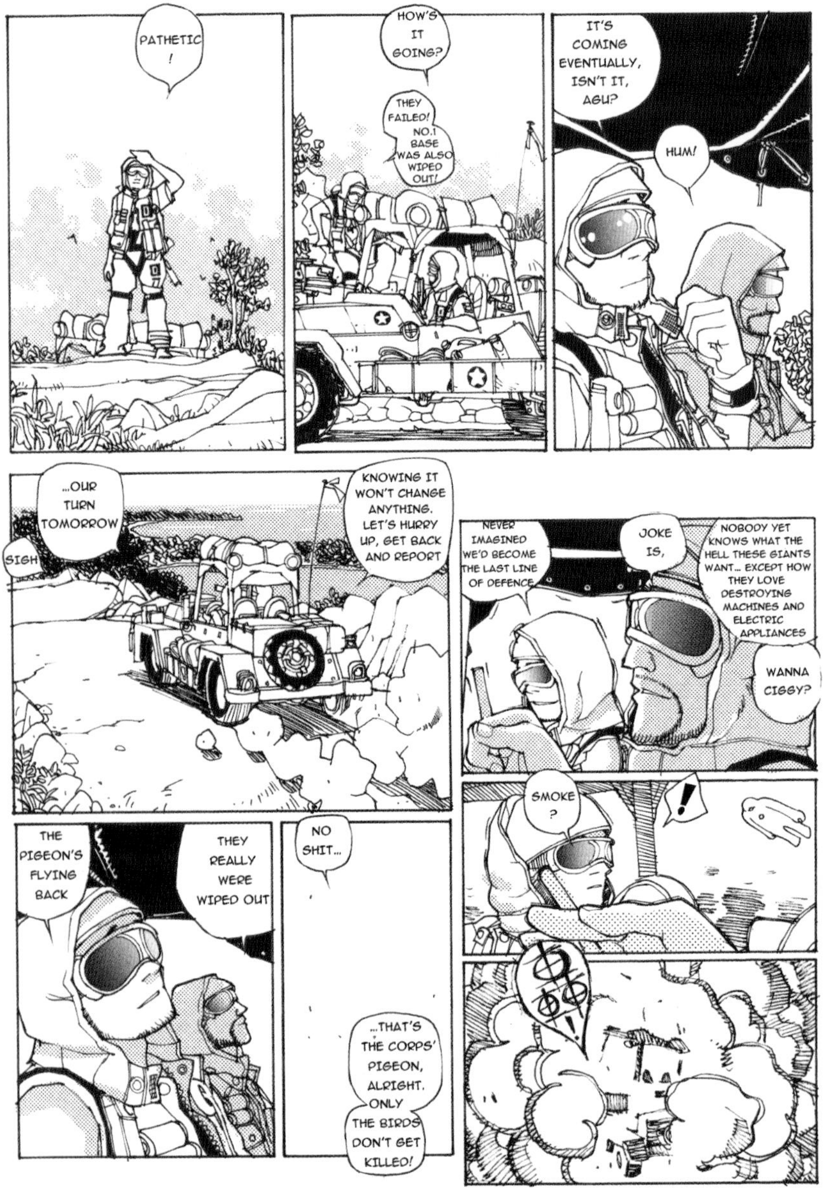
PATHETIC!
HOW'S IT GOING?
THEY FAILED! NO.1 BASE WAS ALSO WIPED OUT!
IT'S COMING EVENTUALLY, ISN'T IT, AGU?
HUM!
...OUR TURN TOMORROW
SIGH
KNOWING IT WON'T CHANGE ANYTHING. LET'S HURRY UP, GET BACK AND REPORT
NEVER IMAGINED WE'D BECOME THE LAST LINE OF DEFENCE
JOKE IS,
NOBODY YET KNOWS WHAT THE HELL THESE GIANTS WANT... EXCEPT HOW THEY LOVE DESTROYING MACHINES AND ELECTRIC APPLIANCES
WANNA CIGGY?
SMOKE?
!
THE PIGEON'S FLYING BACK
THEY REALLY WERE WIPED OUT
NO SHIT...
...THAT'S THE CORPS' PIGEON, ALRIGHT. ONLY THE BIRDS DON'T GET KILLED!

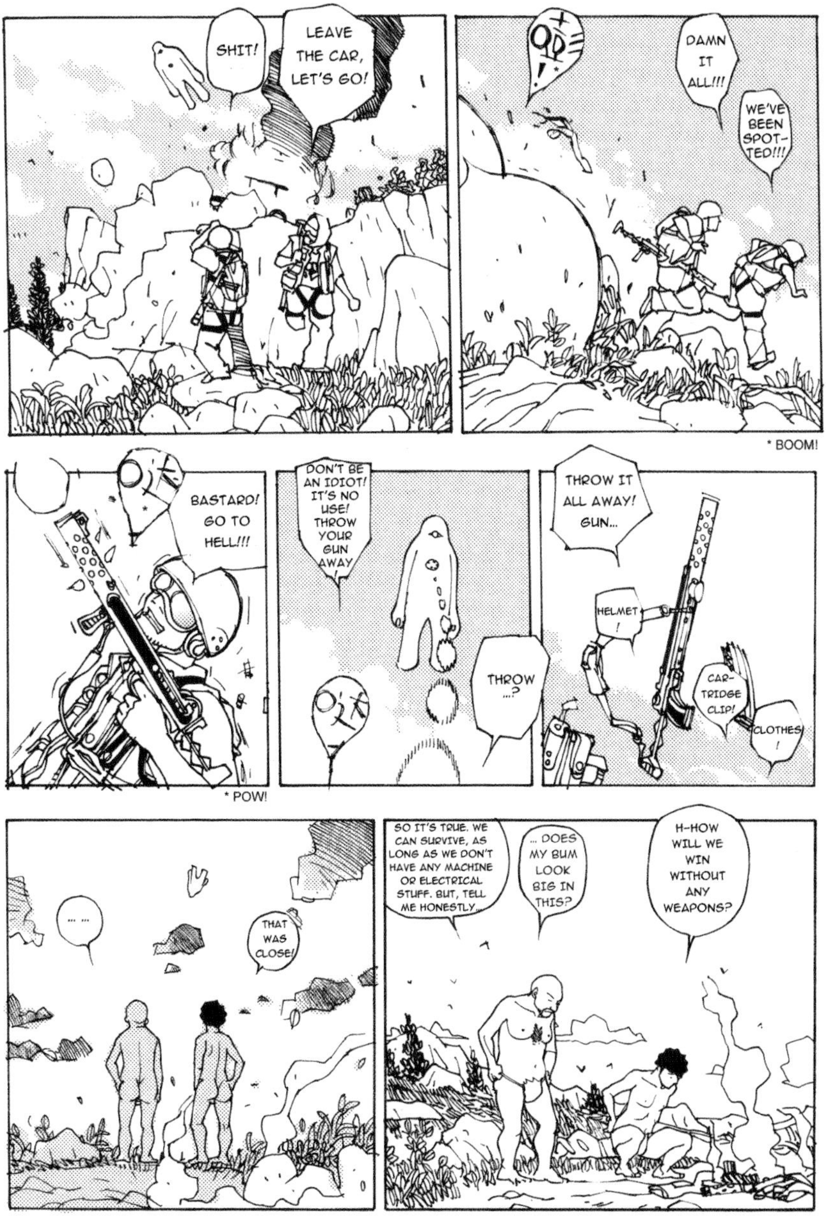
SHIT!
LEAVE THE CAR, LET'S GO!
DAMN IT ALL!!!
WE'VE BEEN SPOT-TED!!!
* BOOM!
BASTARD! GO TO HELL!!!
* POW!
DON'T BE AN IDIOT! IT'S NO USE! THROW YOUR GUN AWAY!
THROW ...?
THROW IT ALL AWAY! GUN...
HELMET!
CAR-TRIDGE CLIP!
CLOTHES!
... ...
THAT WAS CLOSE!
SO IT'S TRUE. WE CAN SURVIVE, AS LONG AS WE DON'T HAVE ANY MACHINE OR ELECTRICAL STUFF. BUT, TELL ME HONESTLY...
... DOES MY BUM LOOK BIG IN THIS?
H-HOW WILL WE WIN WITHOUT ANY WEAPONS?

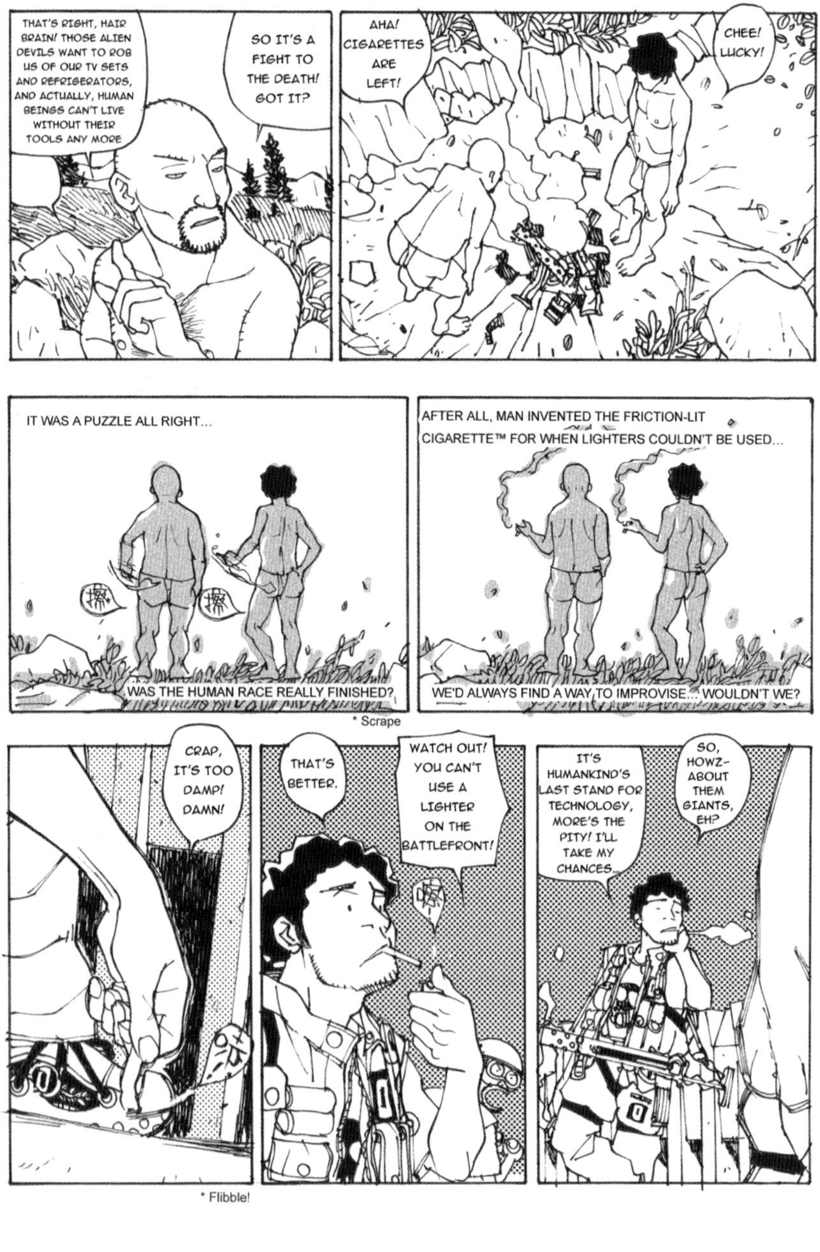

THAT'S RIGHT, HAIR BRAIN! THOSE ALIEN DEVILS WANT TO ROB US OF OUR TV SETS AND REFRIGERATORS, AND ACTUALLY, HUMAN BEINGS CAN'T LIVE WITHOUT THEIR TOOLS ANY MORE
SO IT'S A FIGHT TO THE DEATH! GOT IT?
AHA! CIGARETTES ARE LEFT!
CHEE! LUCKY!
IT WAS A PUZZLE ALL RIGHT...
擦
擦
WAS THE HUMAN RACE REALLY FINISHED?
AFTER ALL, MAN INVENTED THE FRICTION-LIT CIGARETTE™ FOR WHEN LIGHTERS COULDN'T BE USED...
WE'D ALWAYS FIND A WAY TO IMPROVISE... WOULDN'T WE?
* Scrape
CRAP, IT'S TOO DAMP! DAMN!
THAT'S BETTER.
WATCH OUT! YOU CAN'T USE A LIGHTER ON THE BATTLEFRONT!
IT'S HUMANKIND'S LAST STAND FOR TECHNOLOGY, MORE'S THE PITY! I'LL TAKE MY CHANCES...
SO, HOWZ-ABOUT THEM GIANTS, EH?

* Flibble!

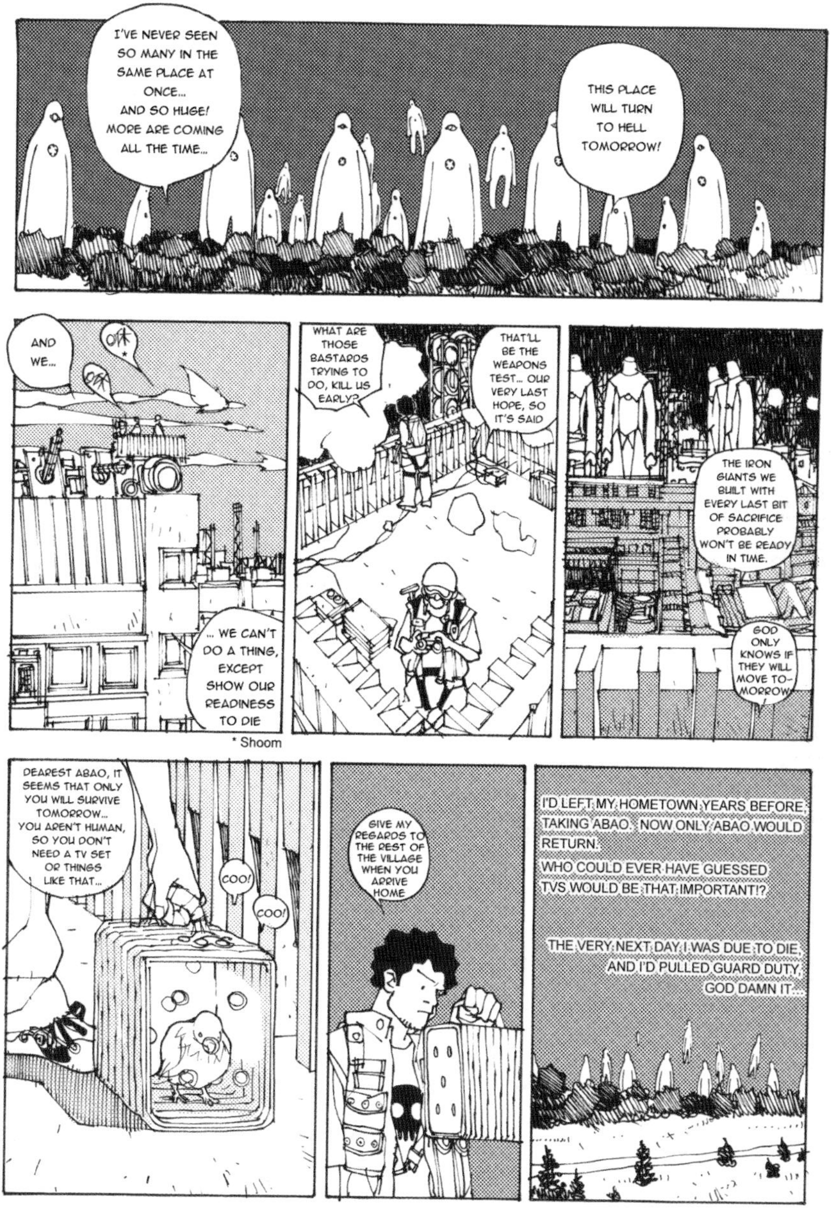

I'VE NEVER SEEN SO MANY IN THE SAME PLACE AT ONCE... AND SO HUGE! MORE ARE COMING ALL THE TIME...
THIS PLACE WILL TURN TO HELL TOMORROW!
AND WE...
... WE CAN'T DO A THING, EXCEPT SHOW OUR READINESS TO DIE
* Shoom
WHAT ARE THOSE BASTARDS TRYING TO DO, KILL US EARLY?
THAT'LL BE THE WEAPONS TEST... OUR VERY LAST HOPE, SO IT'S SAID
THE IRON GIANTS WE BUILT WITH EVERY LAST BIT OF SACRIFICE PROBABLY WON'T BE READY IN TIME.
GOD ONLY KNOWS IF THEY WILL MOVE TO-MORROW!
DEAREST ABAO, IT SEEMS THAT ONLY YOU WILL SURVIVE TOMORROW... YOU AREN'T HUMAN, SO YOU DON'T NEED A TV SET OR THINGS LIKE THAT...
COO!
COO!
GIVE MY REGARDS TO THE REST OF THE VILLAGE WHEN YOU ARRIVE HOME
I'D LEFT MY HOMETOWN YEARS BEFORE, TAKING ABAO. NOW ONLY ABAO WOULD RETURN.
WHO COULD EVER HAVE GUESSED TVS WOULD BE THAT IMPORTANT!?
THE VERY NEXT DAY I WAS DUE TO DIE, AND I'D PULLED GUARD DUTY, GOD DAMN IT...

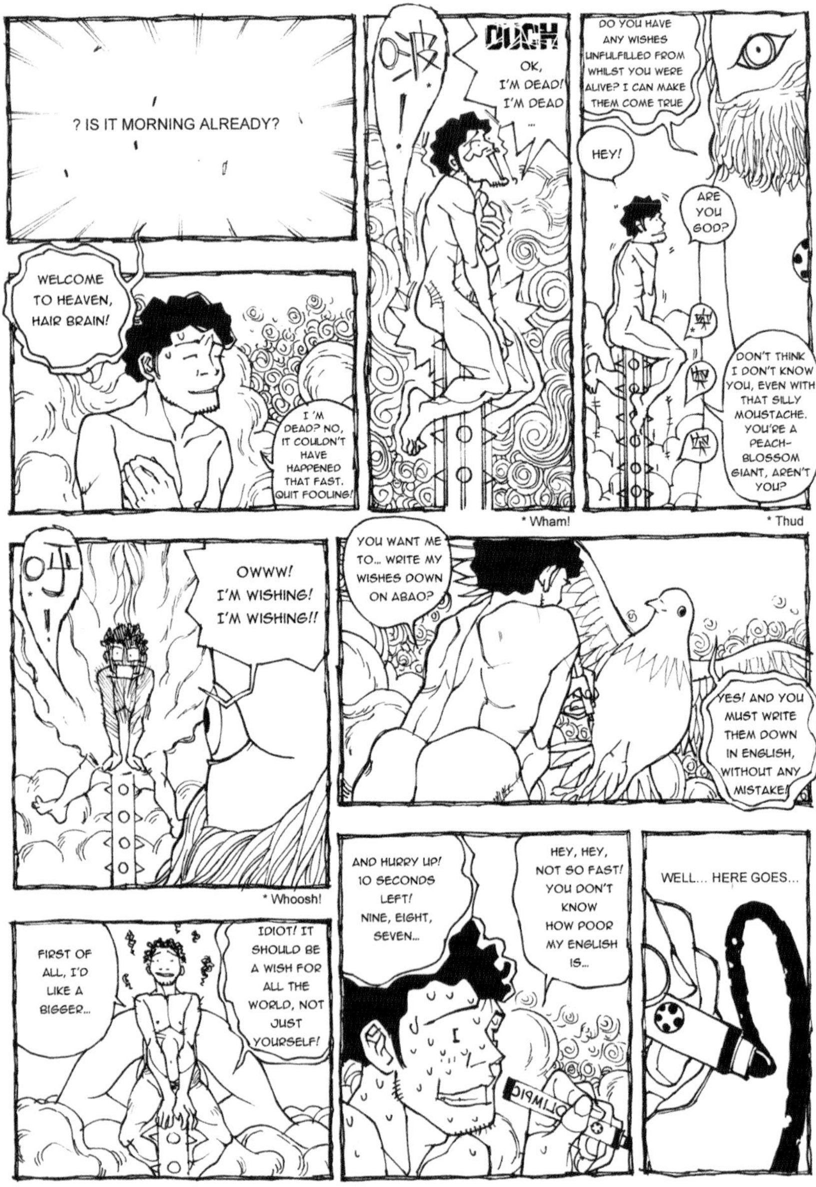

? IS IT MORNING ALREADY?
WELCOME TO HEAVEN, HAIR BRAIN!
I'M DEAD? NO, IT COULDN'T HAVE HAPPENED THAT FAST. QUIT FOOLING!
OUCH
OK, I'M DEAD! I'M DEAD ...
* Wham!
DO YOU HAVE ANY WISHES UNFULFILLED FROM WHILST YOU WERE ALIVE? I CAN MAKE THEM COME TRUE
HEY!
ARE YOU GOD?
DON'T THINK I DON'T KNOW YOU, EVEN WITH THAT SILLY MOUSTACHE. YOU'RE A PEACH-BLOSSOM GIANT, AREN'T YOU?
* Thud
OWWW! I'M WISHING! I'M WISHING!!
* Whoosh!
YOU WANT ME TO... WRITE MY WISHES DOWN ON ABAO?
YES! AND YOU MUST WRITE THEM DOWN IN ENGLISH, WITHOUT ANY MISTAKE!
FIRST OF ALL, I'D LIKE A BIGGER...
IDIOT! IT SHOULD BE A WISH FOR ALL THE WORLD, NOT JUST YOURSELF!
AND HURRY UP! 10 SECONDS LEFT! NINE, EIGHT, SEVEN...
HEY, HEY, NOT SO FAST! YOU DON'T KNOW HOW POOR MY ENGLISH IS...
OLIMPIC
WELL... HERE GOES...

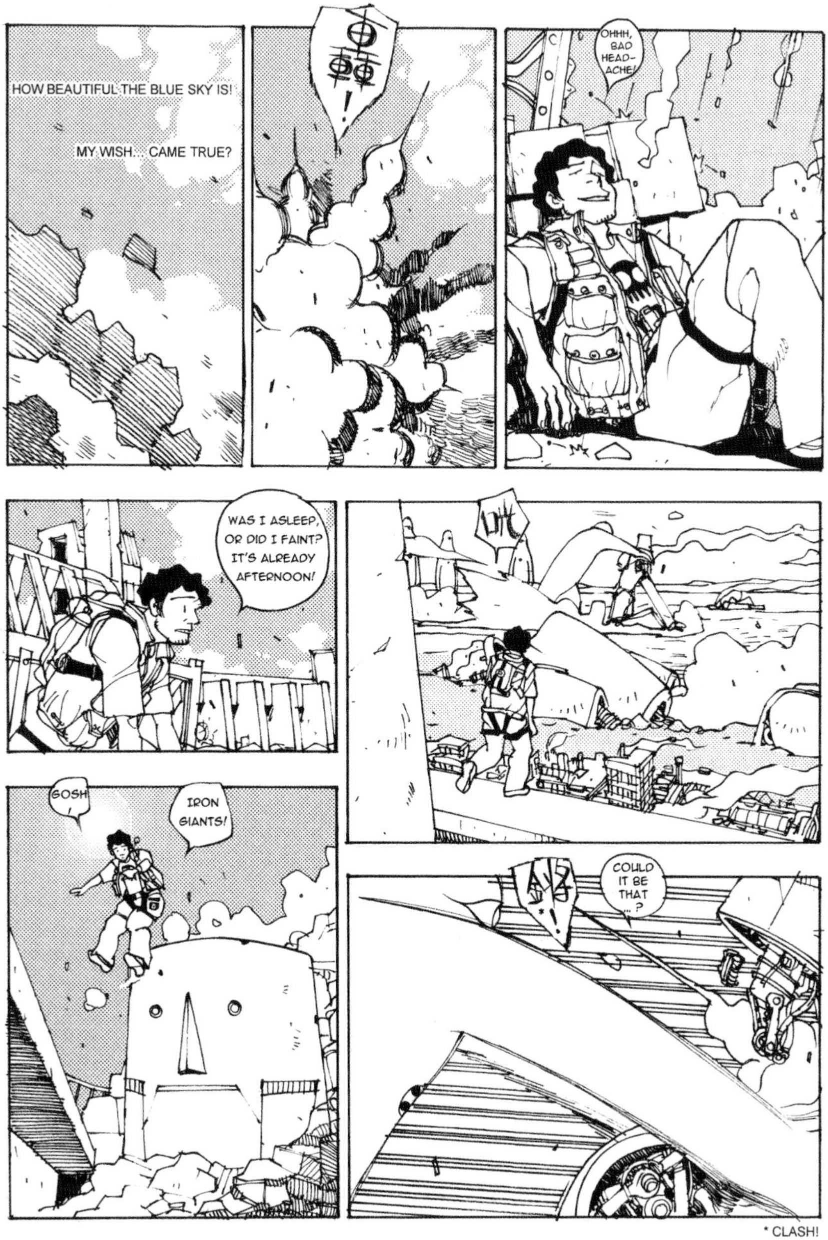
HOW BEAUTIFUL THE BLUE SKY IS!
MY WISH... CAME TRUE?
OHHH, BAD HEAD-ACHE!
WAS I ASLEEP, OR DID I FAINT? IT'S ALREADY AFTERNOON!
GOSH
IRON GIANTS!
COULD IT BE THAT ...?
* CLASH!

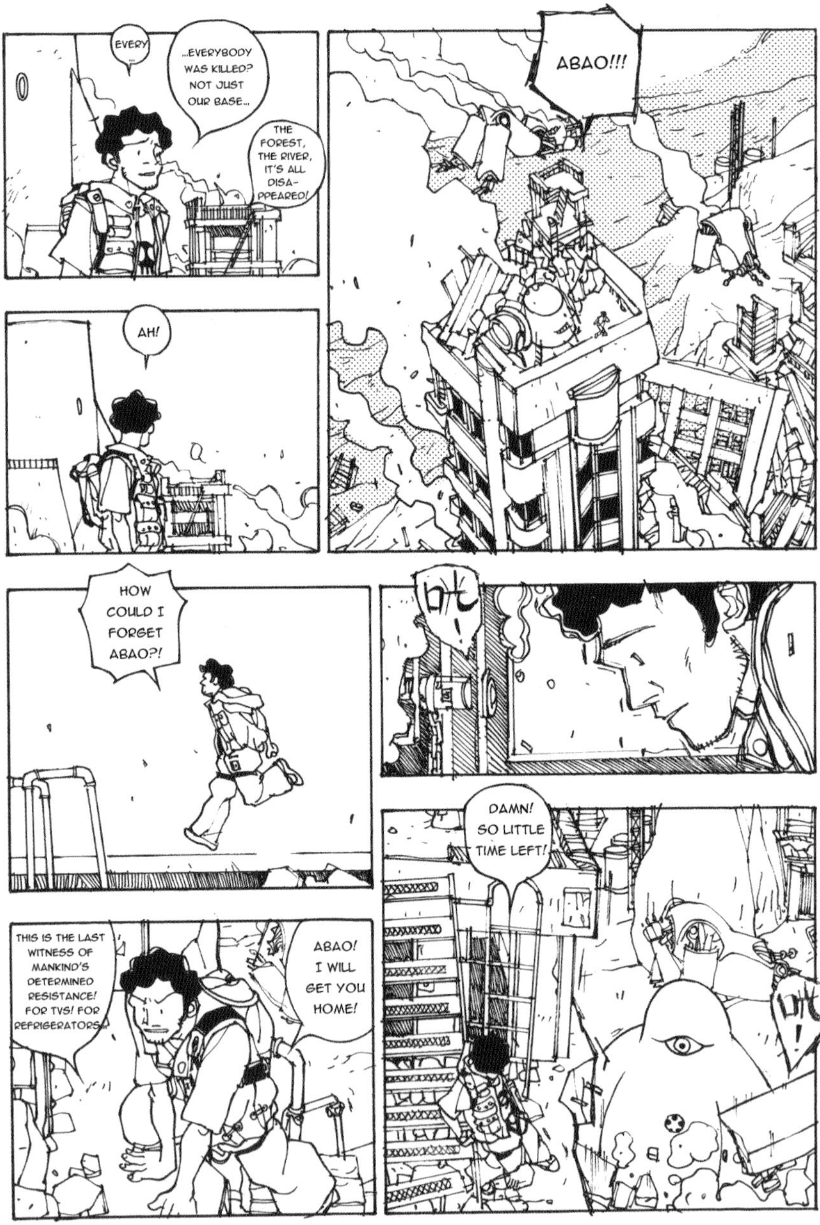
EVERY...
...EVERYBODY WAS KILLED? NOT JUST OUR BASE...
THE FOREST, THE RIVER, IT'S ALL DISA-PPEARED!
AH!
ABAO!!!
HOW COULD I FORGET ABAO?!
THIS IS THE LAST WITNESS OF MANKIND'S DETERMINED RESISTANCE! FOR TVS! FOR REFRIGERATORS...
ABAO! I WILL GET YOU HOME!
DAMN! SO LITTLE TIME LEFT!

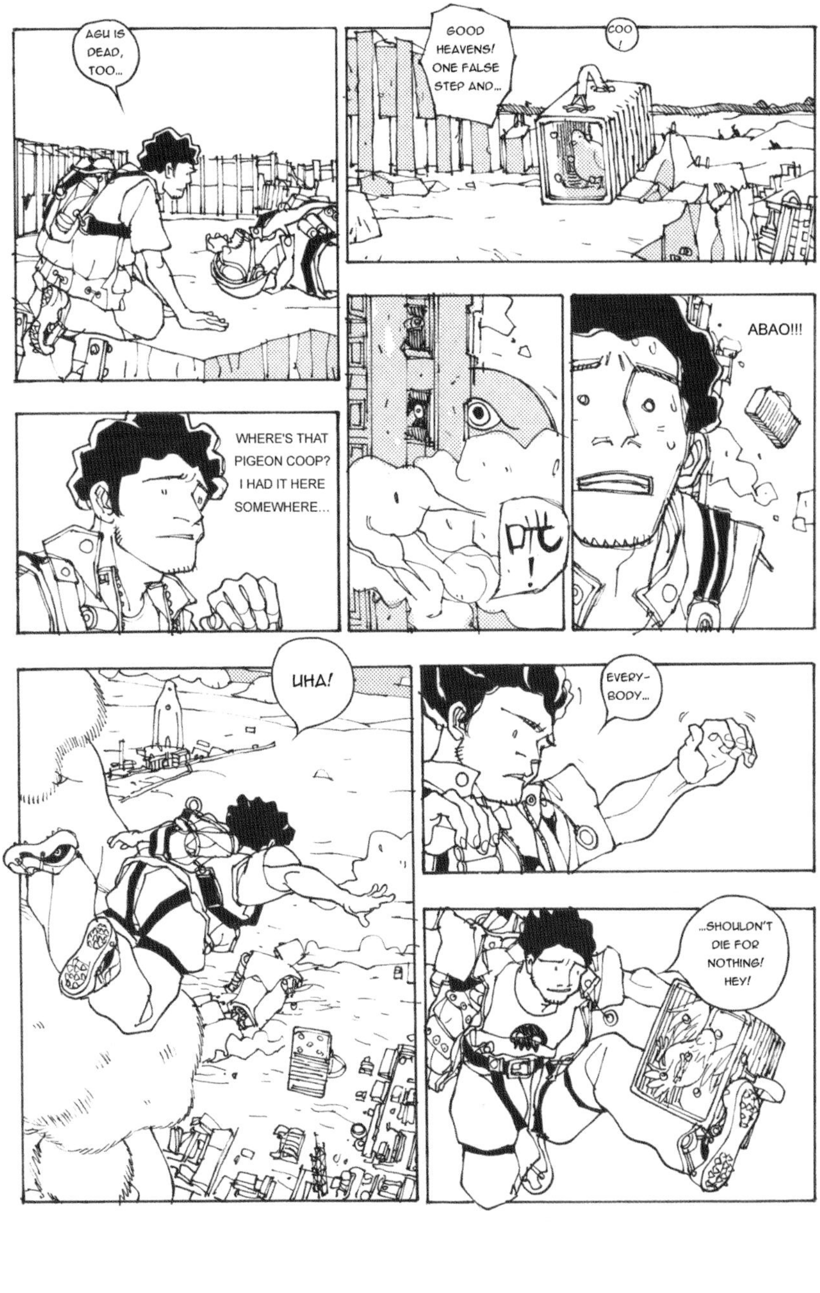
AGU IS DEAD, TOO...
GOOD HEAVENS! ONE FALSE STEP AND...
COO!
WHERE'S THAT PIGEON COOP? I HAD IT HERE SOMEWHERE...
PIT!
ABAO!!!
UHA!
EVERY-BODY...
...SHOULDN'T DIE FOR NOTHING! HEY!

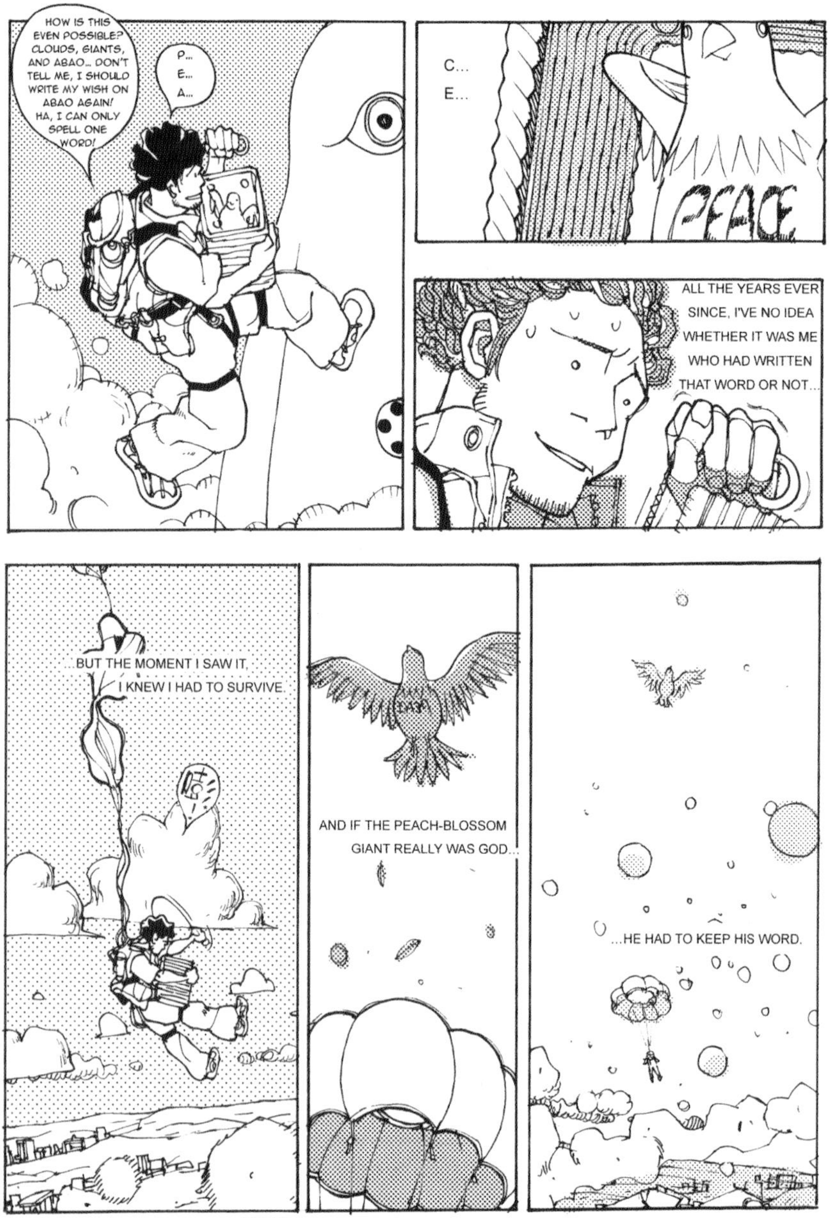
HOW IS THIS EVEN POSSIBLE? CLOUDS, GIANTS, AND ABAO... DON'T TELL ME, I SHOULD WRITE MY WISH ON ABAO AGAIN! HA, I CAN ONLY SPELL ONE WORD!
P... E... A...
C... E...
PEACE
ALL THE YEARS EVER SINCE, I'VE NO IDEA WHETHER IT WAS ME WHO HAD WRITTEN THAT WORD OR NOT...
...BUT THE MOMENT I SAW IT, I KNEW I HAD TO SURVIVE.
AND IF THE PEACH-BLOSSOM GIANT REALLY WAS GOD...
...HE HAD TO KEEP HIS WORD.

* Bloomph!

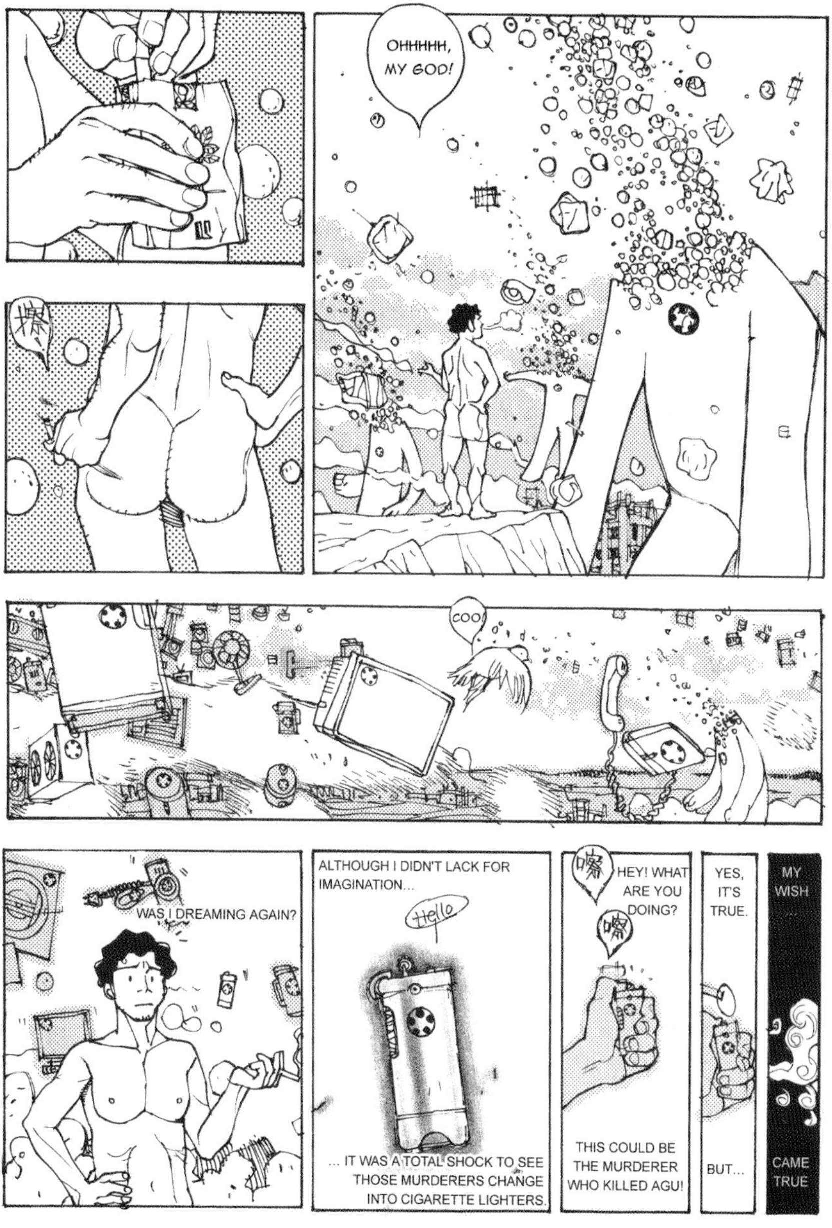
OHHHHH, MY GOD!
COO!
WAS I DREAMING AGAIN?
ALTHOUGH I DIDN'T LACK FOR IMAGINATION…
Hello
… IT WAS A TOTAL SHOCK TO SEE THOSE MURDERERS CHANGE INTO CIGARETTE LIGHTERS.
HEY! WHAT ARE YOU DOING?
THIS COULD BE THE MURDERER WHO KILLED AGU!
YES, IT'S TRUE.
BUT…
MY WISH …
CAME TRUE

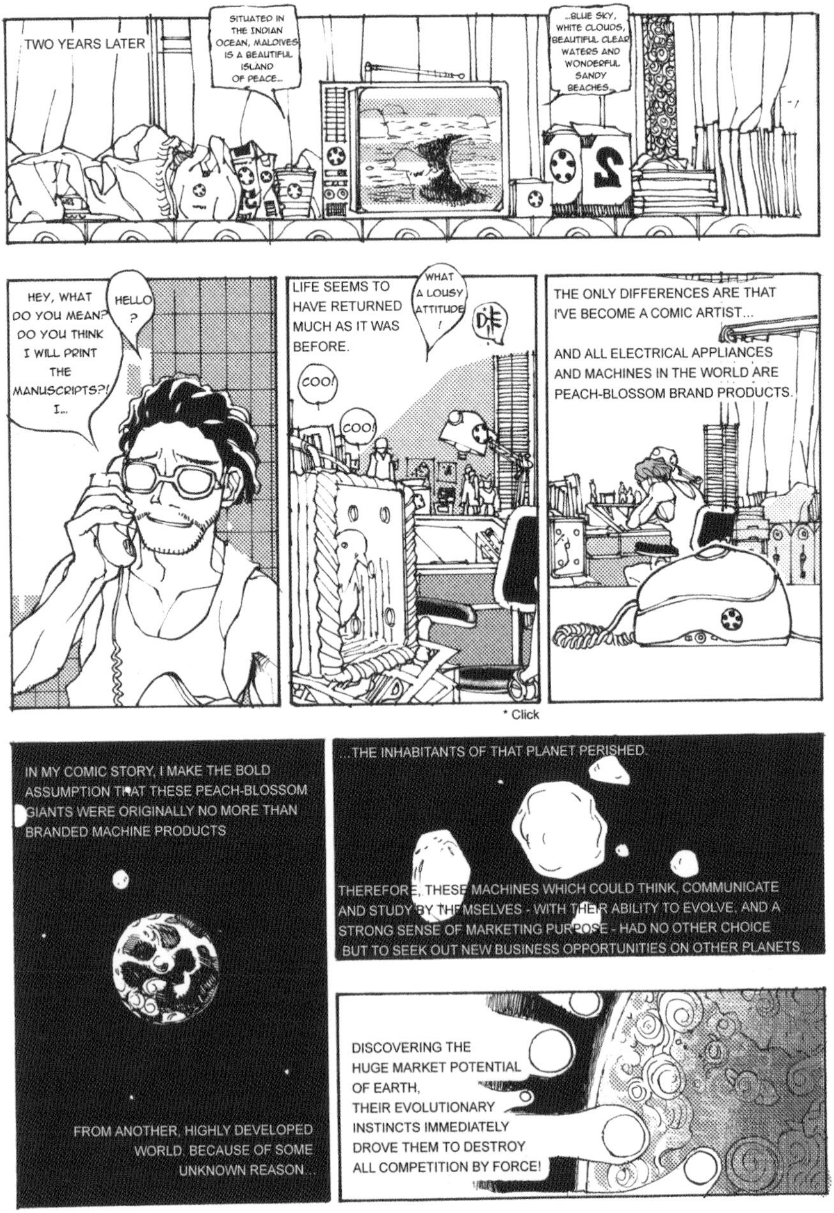

TWO YEARS LATER
SITUATED IN THE INDIAN OCEAN, MALDIVES IS A BEAUTIFUL ISLAND OF PEACE...
...BLUE SKY, WHITE CLOUDS, BEAUTIFUL CLEAR WATERS AND WONDERFUL SANDY BEACHES.
HEY, WHAT DO YOU MEAN? DO YOU THINK I WILL PRINT THE MANUSCRIPTS?! I...
HELLO ?
LIFE SEEMS TO HAVE RETURNED MUCH AS IT WAS BEFORE.
WHAT A LOUSY ATTITUDE !
DIE
COO!
COO!
THE ONLY DIFFERENCES ARE THAT I'VE BECOME A COMIC ARTIST...
AND ALL ELECTRICAL APPLIANCES AND MACHINES IN THE WORLD ARE PEACH-BLOSSOM BRAND PRODUCTS.
* Click
IN MY COMIC STORY, I MAKE THE BOLD ASSUMPTION THAT THESE PEACH-BLOSSOM GIANTS WERE ORIGINALLY NO MORE THAN BRANDED MACHINE PRODUCTS
FROM ANOTHER, HIGHLY DEVELOPED WORLD. BECAUSE OF SOME UNKNOWN REASON...
...THE INHABITANTS OF THAT PLANET PERISHED.
THEREFORE, THESE MACHINES WHICH COULD THINK, COMMUNICATE AND STUDY BY THEMSELVES - WITH THEIR ABILITY TO EVOLVE, AND A STRONG SENSE OF MARKETING PURPOSE - HAD NO OTHER CHOICE BUT TO SEEK OUT NEW BUSINESS OPPORTUNITIES ON OTHER PLANETS.
DISCOVERING THE HUGE MARKET POTENTIAL OF EARTH, THEIR EVOLUTIONARY INSTINCTS IMMEDIATELY DROVE THEM TO DESTROY ALL COMPETITION BY FORCE!

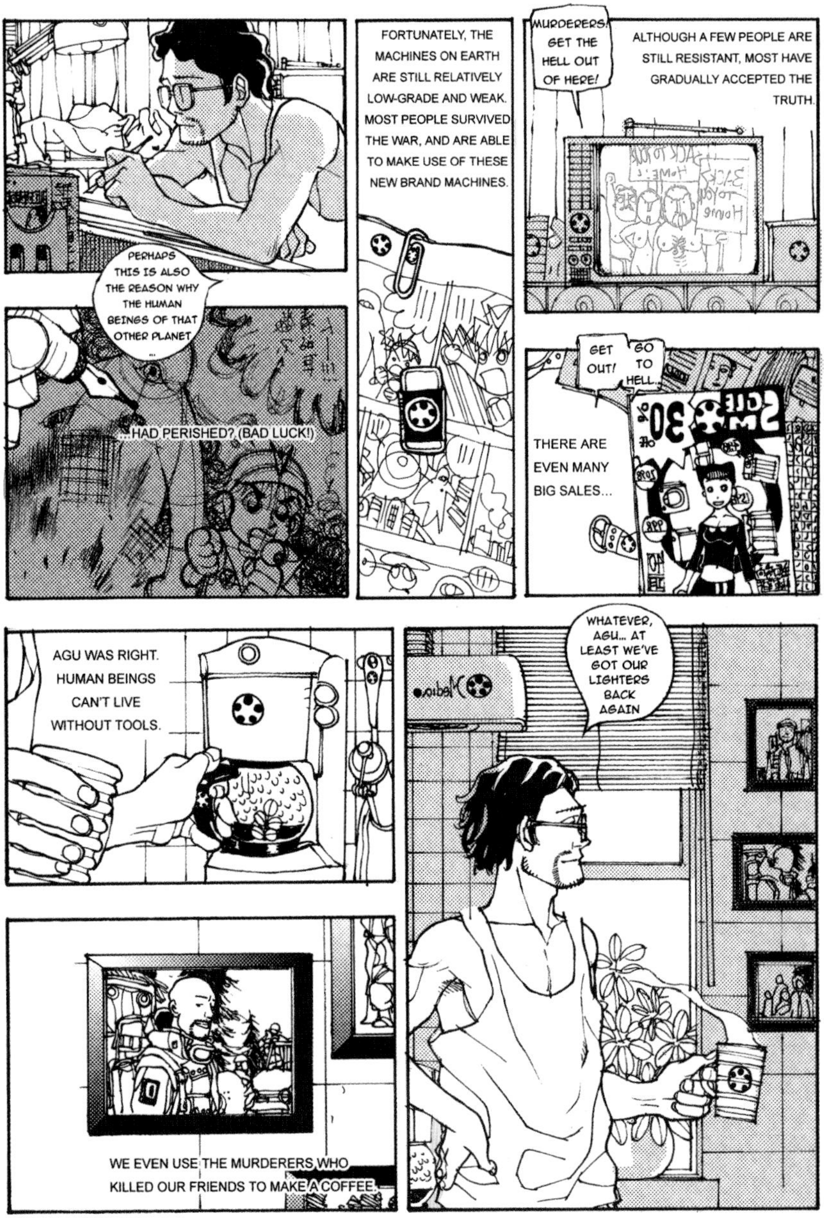
PERHAPS THIS IS ALSO THE REASON WHY THE HUMAN BEINGS OF THAT OTHER PLANET ...
...HAD PERISHED? (BAD LUCK!)
FORTUNATELY, THE MACHINES ON EARTH ARE STILL RELATIVELY LOW-GRADE AND WEAK. MOST PEOPLE SURVIVED THE WAR, AND ARE ABLE TO MAKE USE OF THESE NEW BRAND MACHINES.
MURDERERS! GET THE HELL OUT OF HERE!
ALTHOUGH A FEW PEOPLE ARE STILL RESISTANT, MOST HAVE GRADUALLY ACCEPTED THE TRUTH.
GET OUT!
GO TO HELL.
THERE ARE EVEN MANY BIG SALES...
30
AGU WAS RIGHT. HUMAN BEINGS CAN'T LIVE WITHOUT TOOLS.
WE EVEN USE THE MURDERERS WHO KILLED OUR FRIENDS TO MAKE A COFFEE.
WHATEVER, AGU... AT LEAST WE'VE GOT OUR LIGHTERS BACK AGAIN

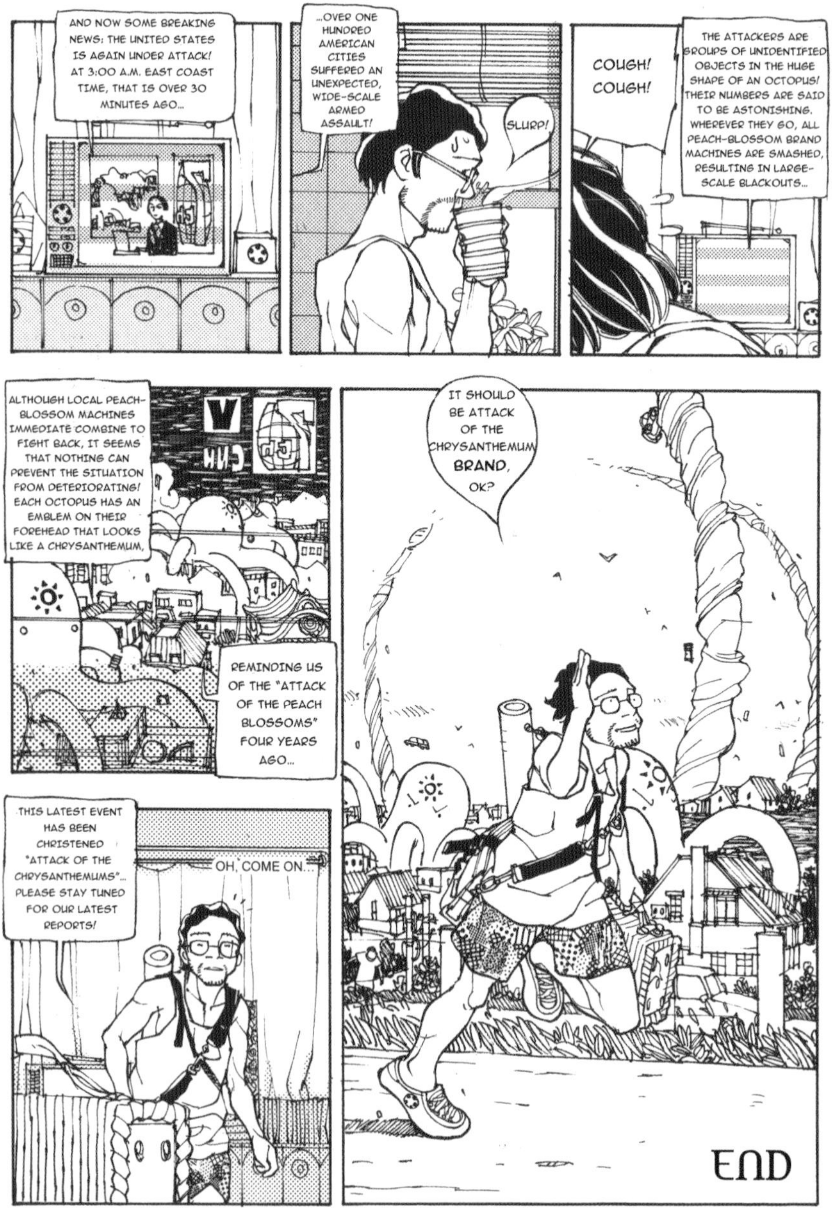
AND NOW SOME BREAKING NEWS: THE UNITED STATES IS AGAIN UNDER ATTACK! AT 3:00 A.M. EAST COAST TIME, THAT IS OVER 30 MINUTES AGO...
...OVER ONE HUNDRED AMERICAN CITIES SUFFERED AN UNEXPECTED, WIDE-SCALE ARMED ASSAULT!
SLURP!
COUGH! COUGH!
THE ATTACKERS ARE GROUPS OF UNIDENTIFIED OBJECTS IN THE HUGE SHAPE OF AN OCTOPUS! THEIR NUMBERS ARE SAID TO BE ASTONISHING. WHEREVER THEY GO, ALL PEACH-BLOSSOM BRAND MACHINES ARE SMASHED, RESULTING IN LARGE-SCALE BLACKOUTS...
ALTHOUGH LOCAL PEACH-BLOSSOM MACHINES IMMEDIATE COMBINE TO FIGHT BACK, IT SEEMS THAT NOTHING CAN PREVENT THE SITUATION FROM DETERIORATING! EACH OCTOPUS HAS AN EMBLEM ON THEIR FOREHEAD THAT LOOKS LIKE A CHRYSANTHEMUM,
REMINDING US OF THE "ATTACK OF THE PEACH BLOSSOMS" FOUR YEARS AGO...
THIS LATEST EVENT HAS BEEN CHRISTENED "ATTACK OF THE CHRYSANTHEMUMS"... PLEASE STAY TUNED FOR OUR LATEST REPORTS!
OH, COME ON...
IT SHOULD BE ATTACK OF THE CHRYSANTHEMUM BRAND, OK?
END

as a king

AS A KING
Yu Yanshu

"The little boy who used to love doodling on his textbooks now becomes a professional comic artist. It's weird because I always thought I would be a machinist, fond of car racing, when I grew up. I wish for a peaceful world, I wish for less greenhouse effects and more alternative energy, and I wish I didn't have to pay tax. Besides, I have created a cartoon story called *Grim Reapersz.z.*"

www.summerzoo.com
email: manga@126.com
email: summerzoo@yahoo.cn

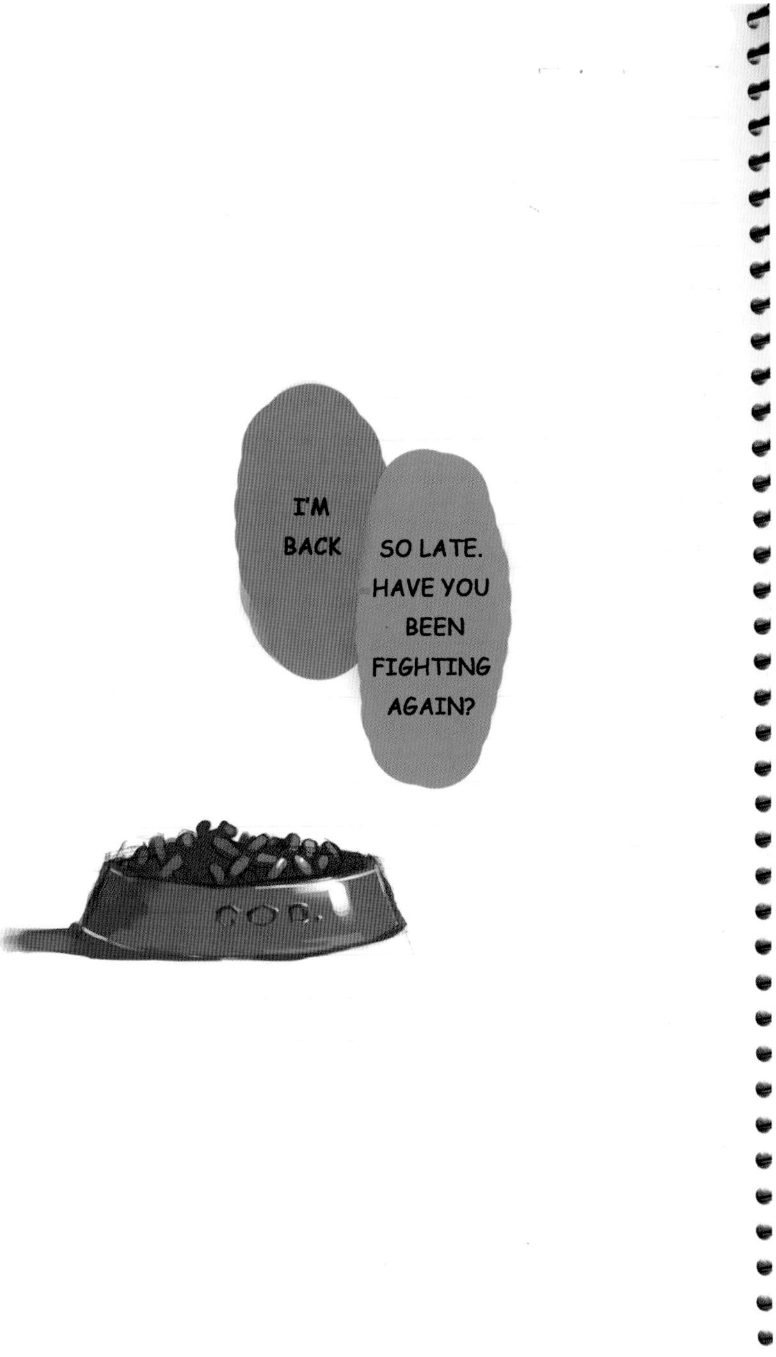
I'M BACK
SO LATE. HAVE YOU BEEN FIGHTING AGAIN?

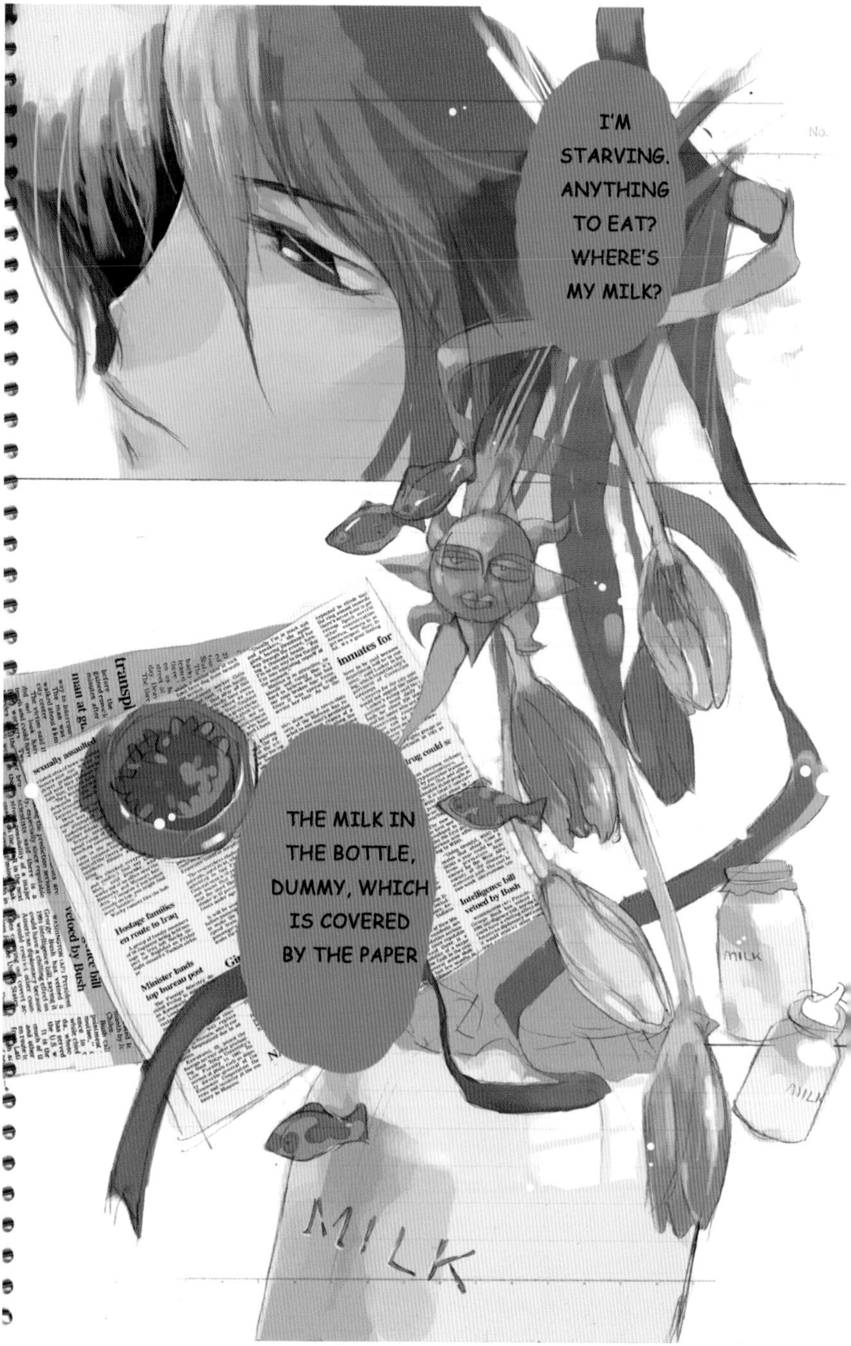
I'M STARVING. ANYTHING TO EAT? WHERE'S MY MILK?
THE MILK IN THE BOTTLE, DUMMY, WHICH IS COVERED BY THE PAPER
MILK
MILK
MILK

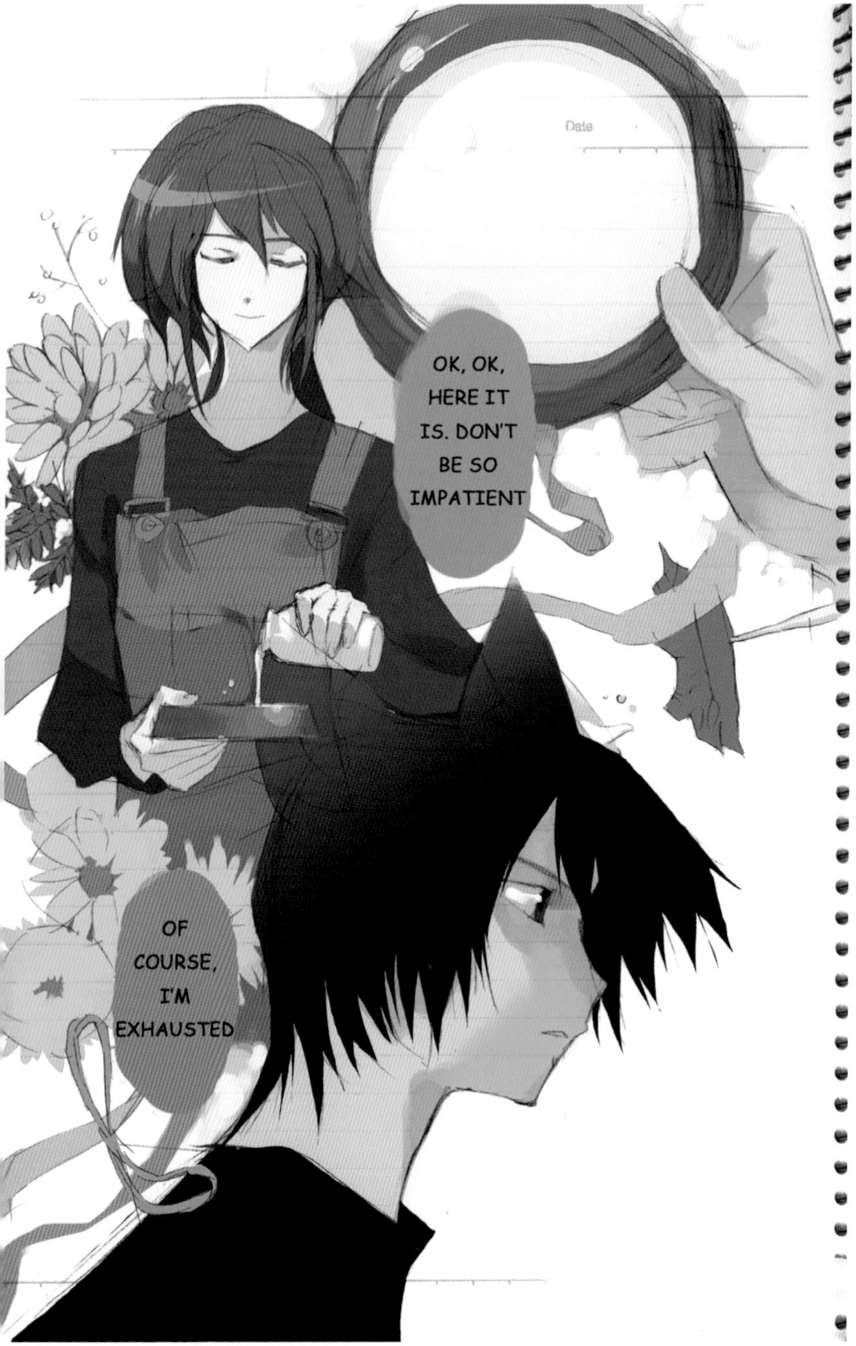
Date
OK, OK, HERE IT IS. DON'T BE SO IMPATIENT
OF COURSE, I'M EXHAUSTED

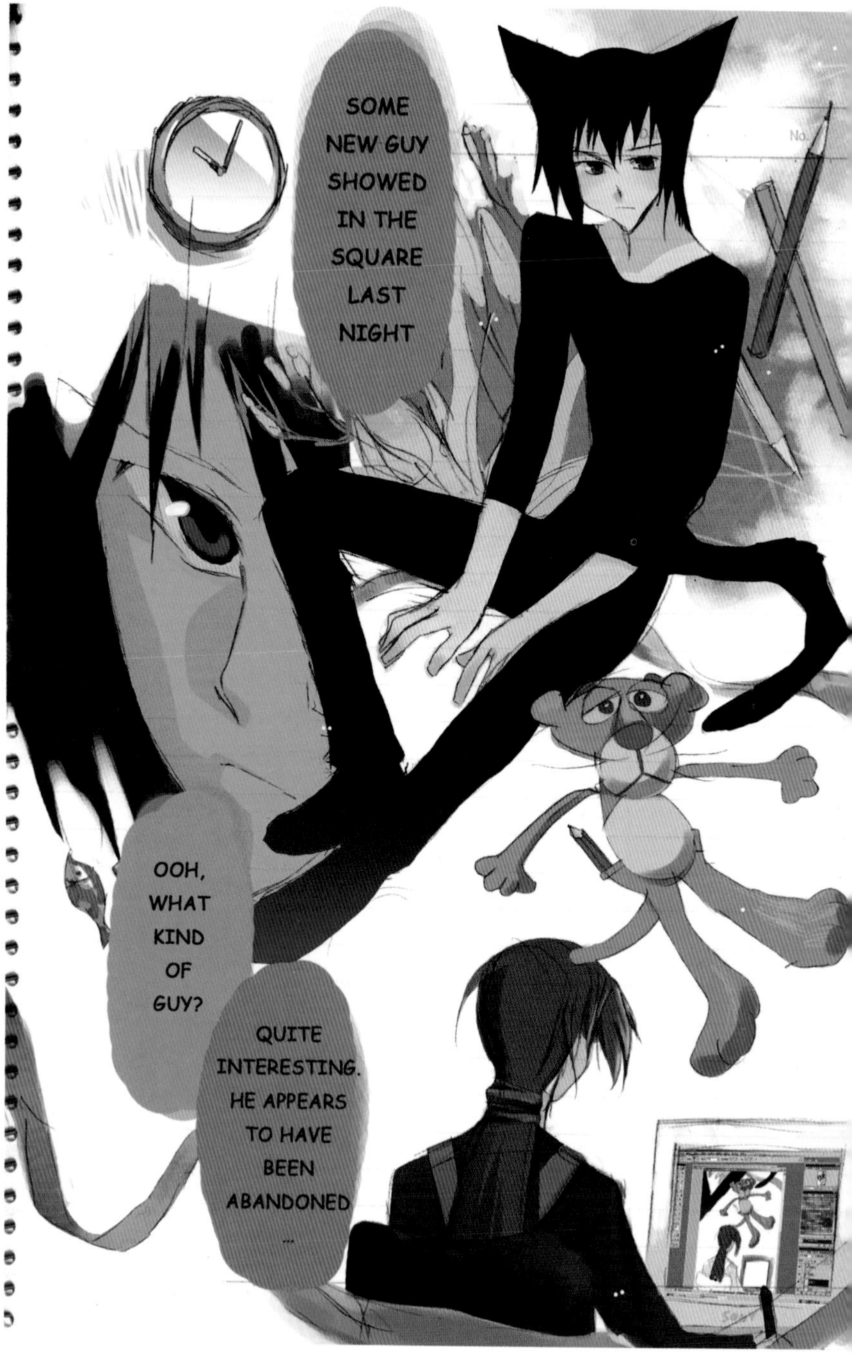
SOME NEW GUY SHOWED IN THE SQUARE LAST NIGHT
OOH, WHAT KIND OF GUY?
QUITE INTERESTING. HE APPEARS TO HAVE BEEN ABANDONED ...

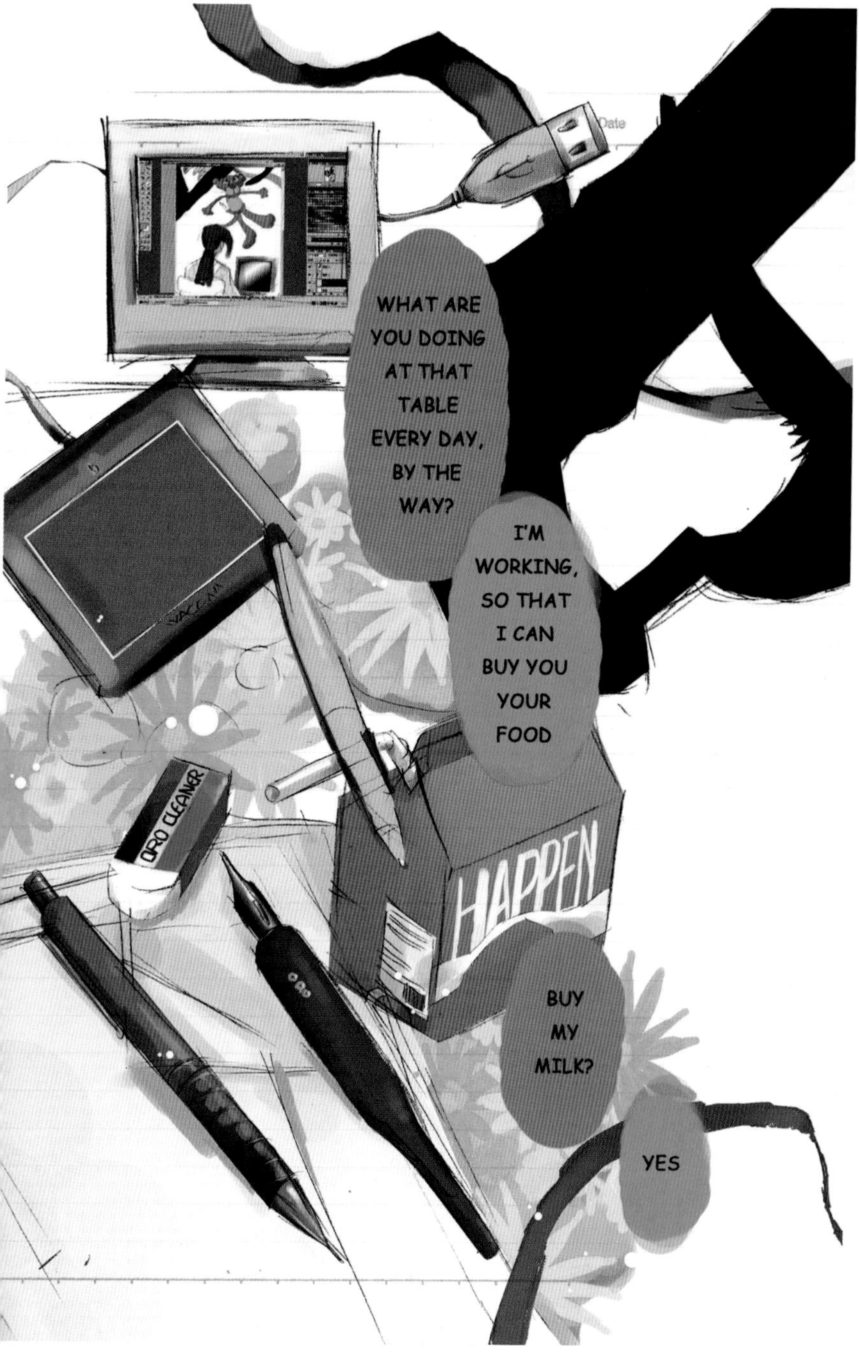
WHAT ARE YOU DOING AT THAT TABLE EVERY DAY, BY THE WAY?
I'M WORKING, SO THAT I CAN BUY YOU YOUR FOOD
QRO CLEANER
HAPPEN
BUY MY MILK?
YES

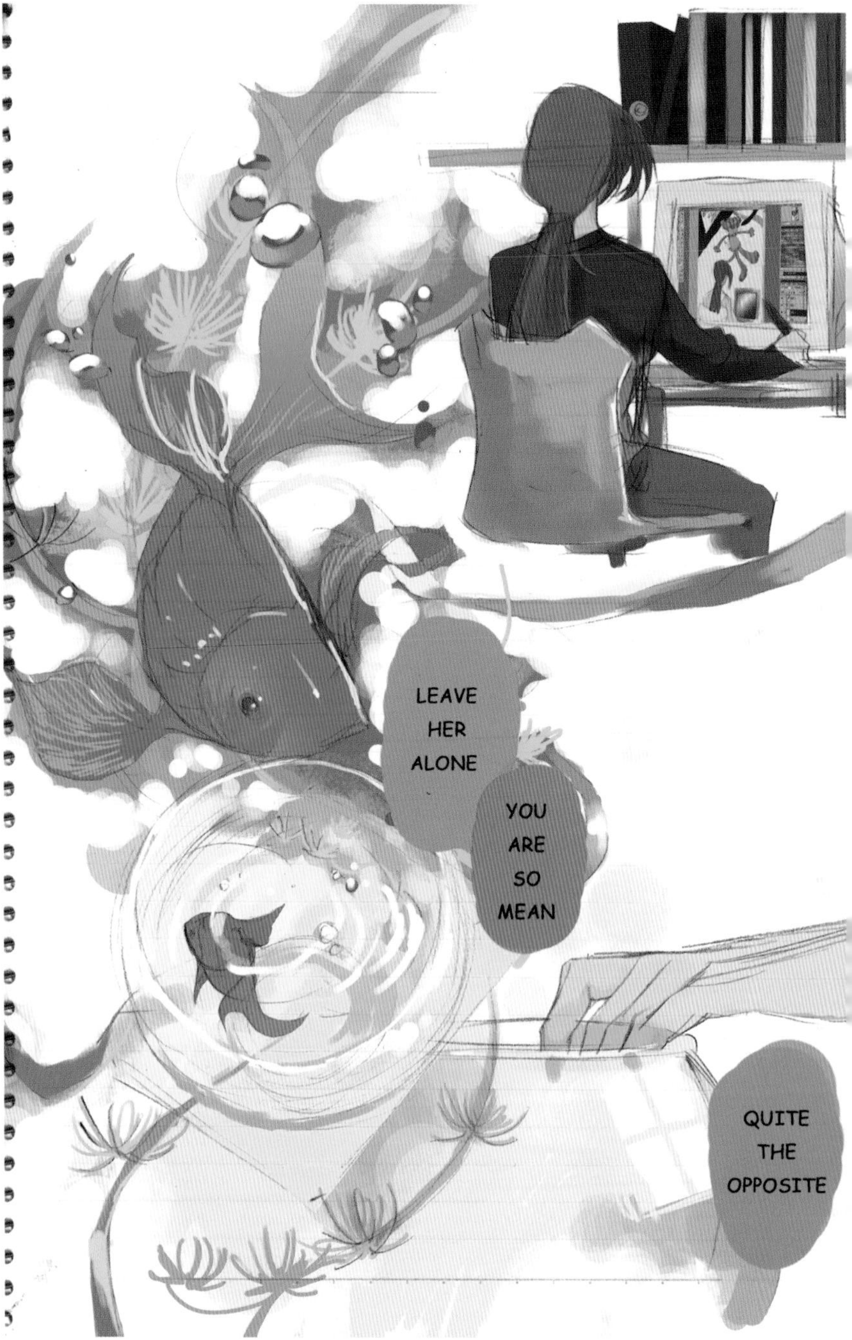
LEAVE HER ALONE
YOU ARE SO MEAN
QUITE THE OPPOSITE

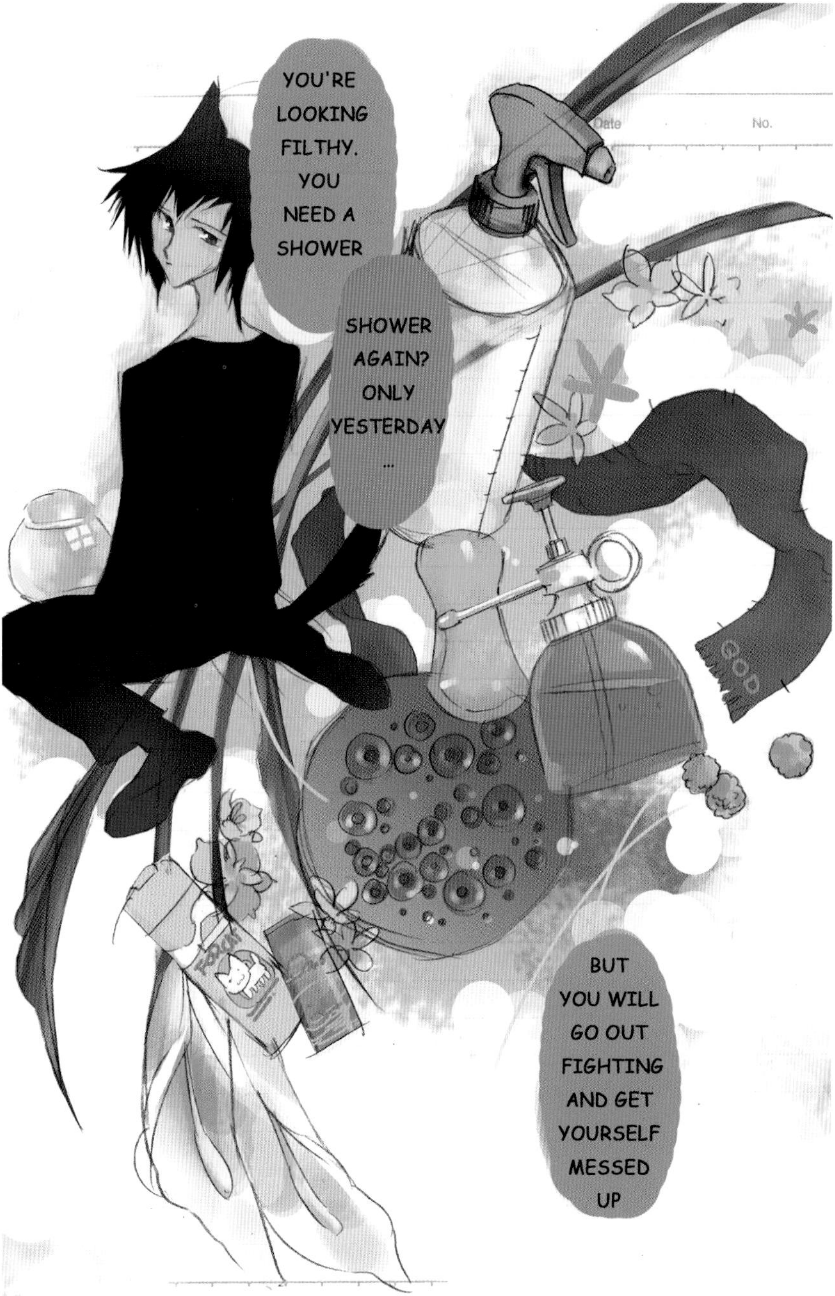
YOU'RE LOOKING FILTHY. YOU NEED A SHOWER
SHOWER AGAIN? ONLY YESTERDAY ...
BUT YOU WILL GO OUT FIGHTING AND GET YOURSELF MESSED UP
Date
No.
GOD

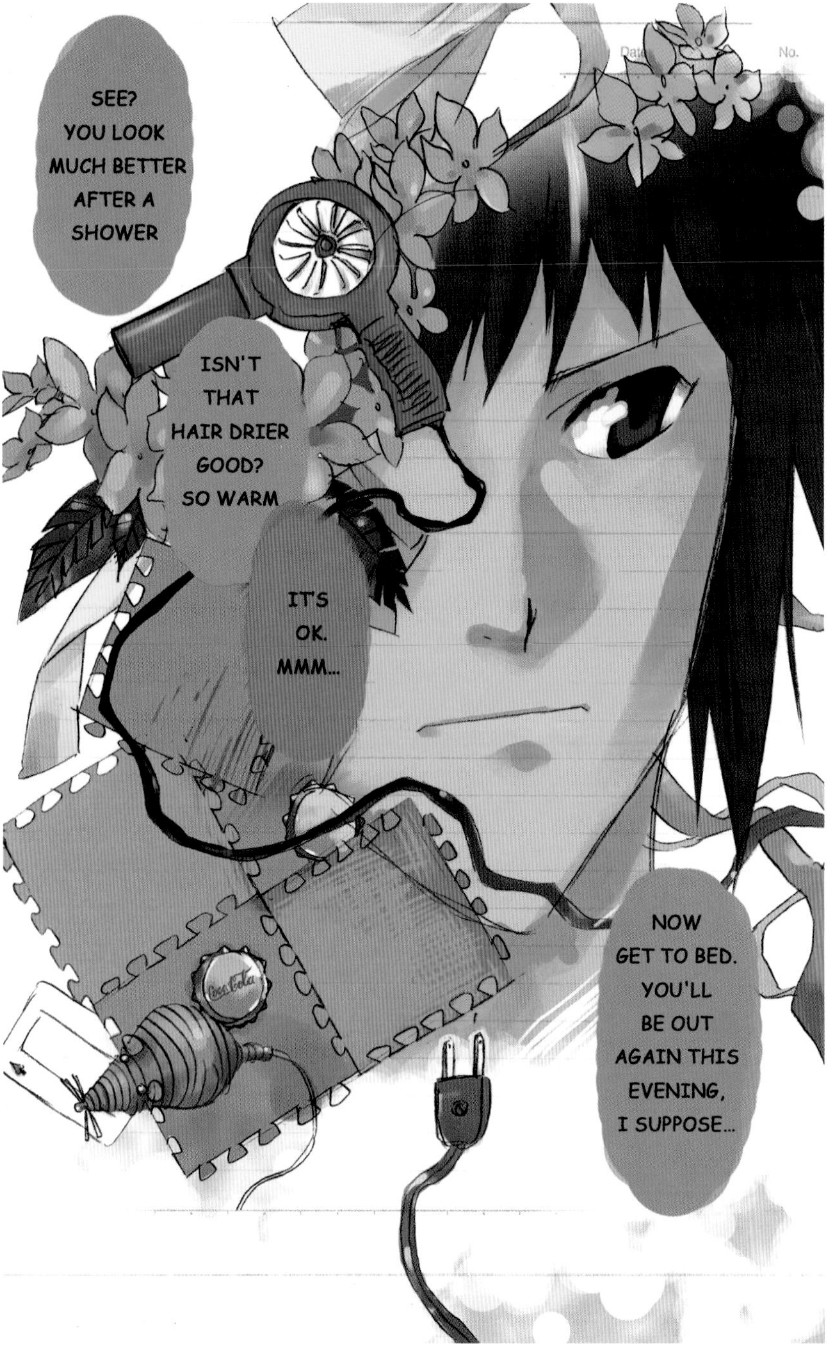
SEE? YOU LOOK MUCH BETTER AFTER A SHOWER
Date
No.
ISN'T THAT HAIR DRIER GOOD? SO WARM
IT'S OK. MMM...
NOW GET TO BED. YOU'LL BE OUT AGAIN THIS EVENING, I SUPPOSE...

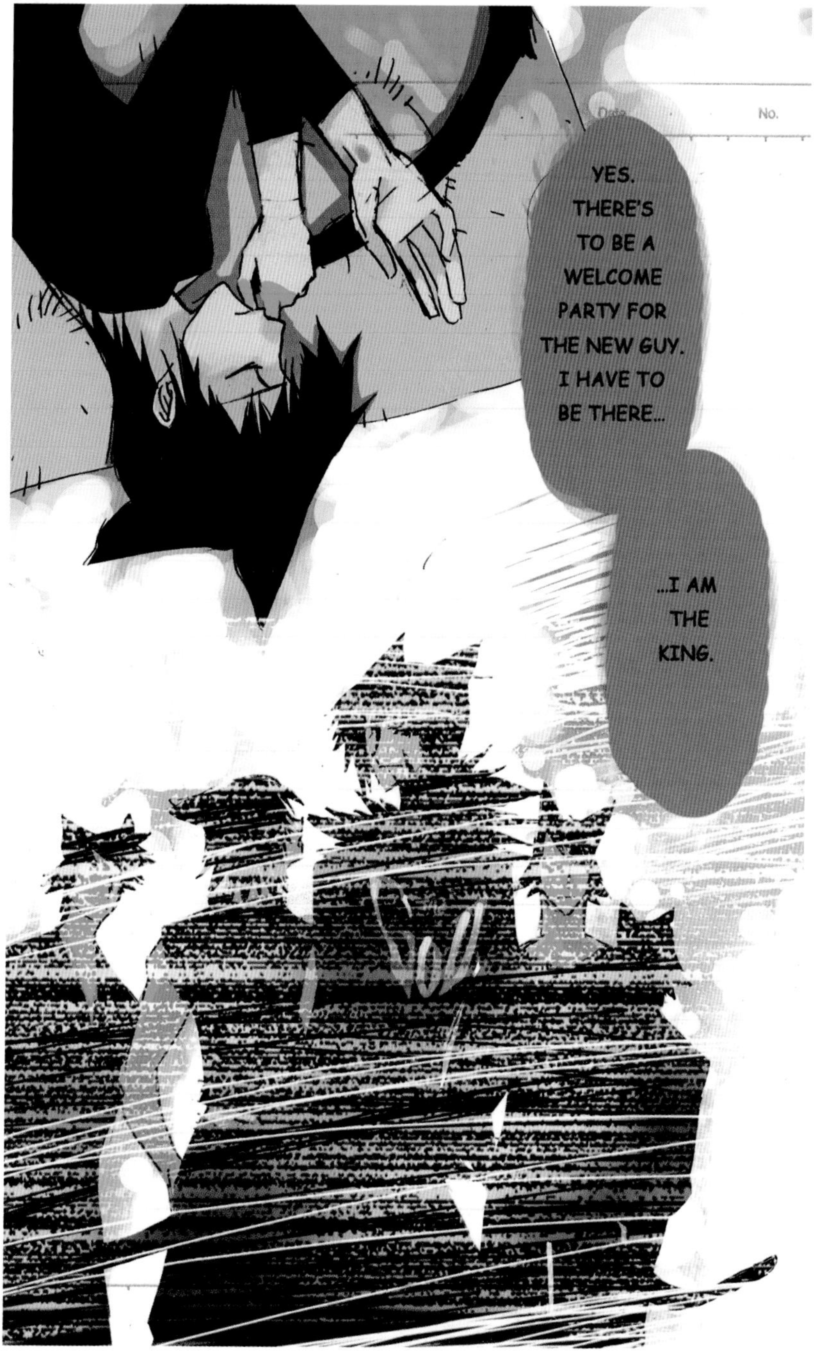
Date
No.
YES. THERE'S TO BE A WELCOME PARTY FOR THE NEW GUY. I HAVE TO BE THERE...
...I AM THE KING.

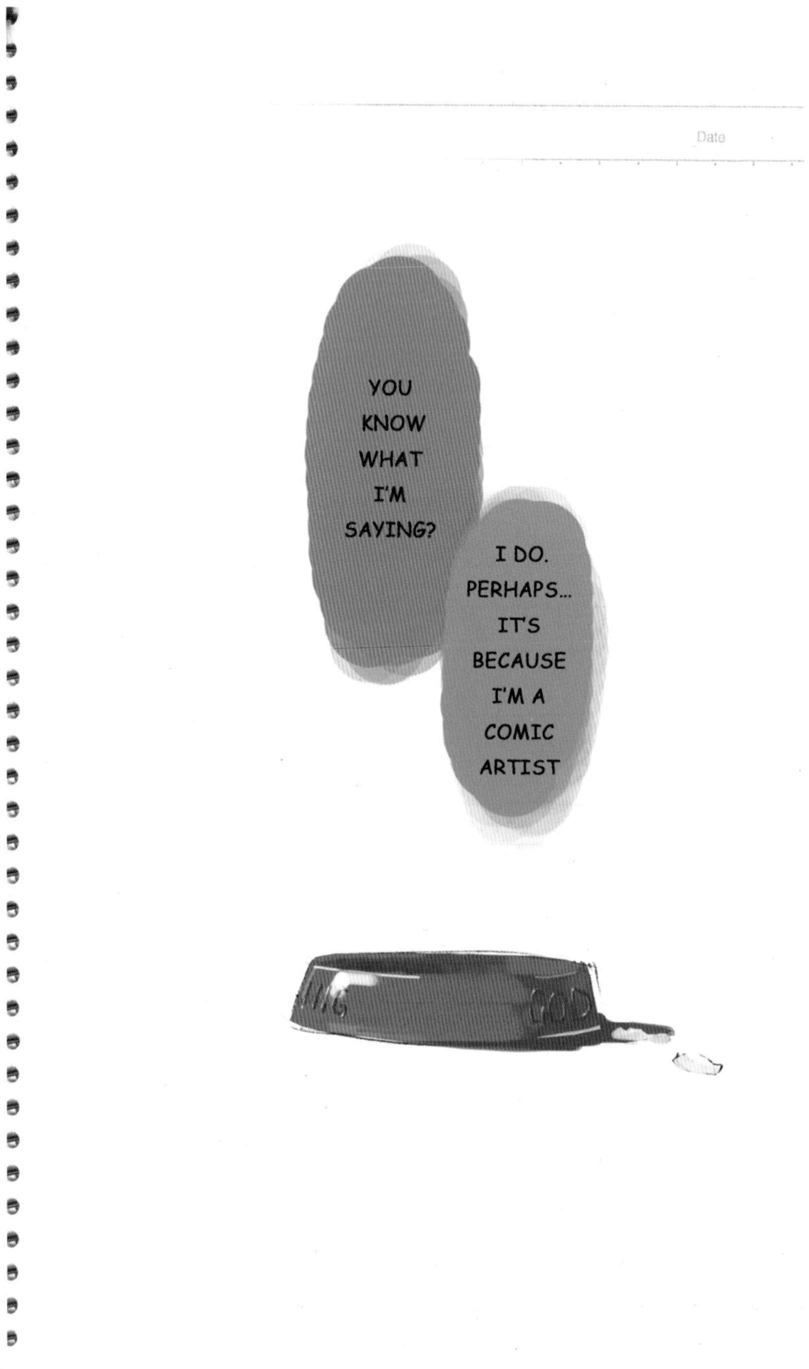
Date
YOU KNOW WHAT I'M SAYING?
I DO. PERHAPS... IT'S BECAUSE I'M A COMIC ARTIST

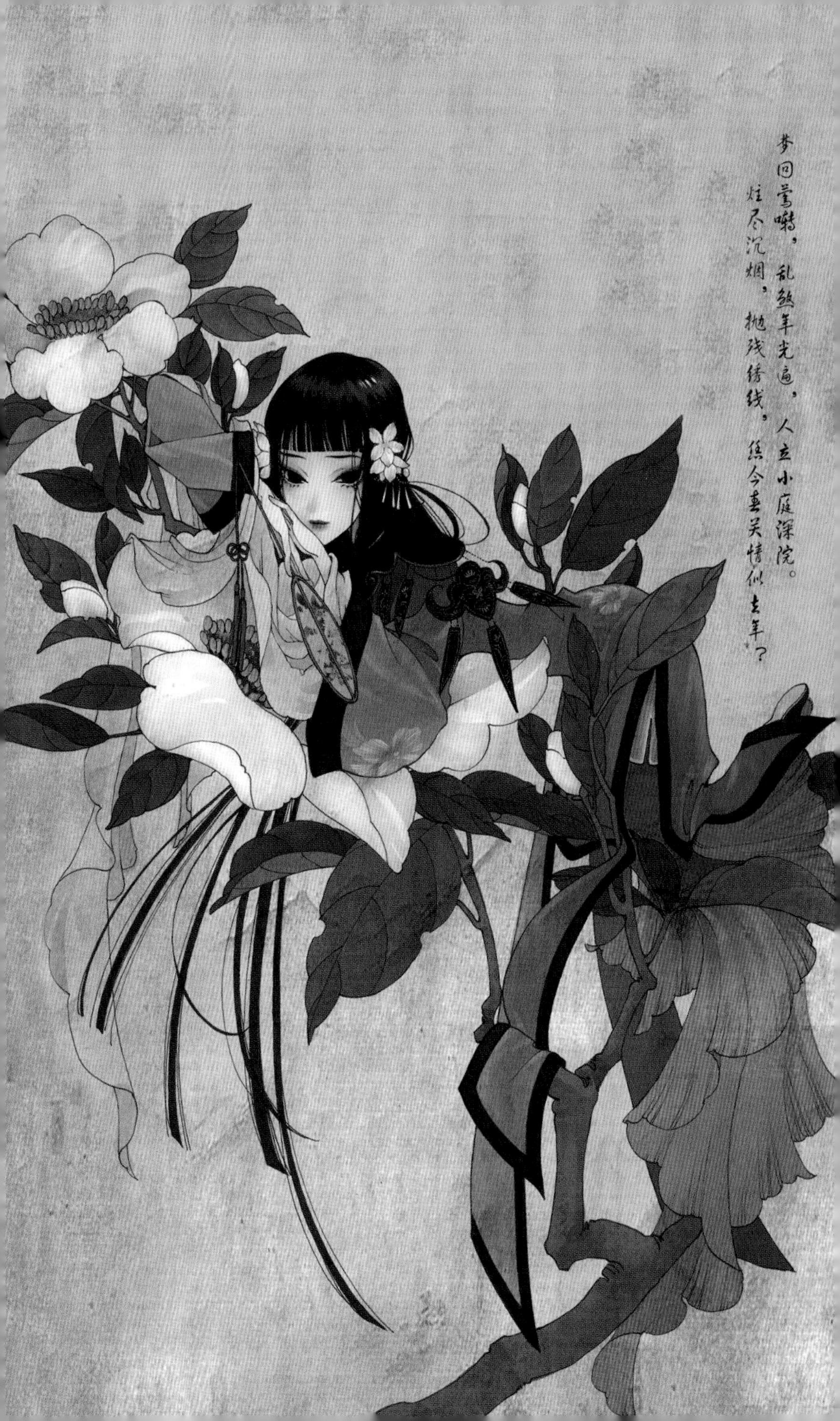
梦回莺啭，乱煞年光遍，人立小庭深院。
炷尽沉烟，抛残绣线，恁今春关情似去年？

A DREAM IN GARDEN
Xia Da

A long time ago, there was a philosopher in China called Zhuangzi. One night he dreamed that he changed to a butterfly. When he woke up, he sighed:

> "Did I change to the butterfly or did the butterfly change to me? Perhaps my present being is no more than a dream of the butterfly?"

However, I'm too young to understand a question like that. The story following began in a sunny afternoon. A butterfly passed my eyes when I was daydreaming, and when the naughty wind was turning the pages of *The Peony Pavilion*...

www.summerzoo.com
email: manga@126.com
email: summerzoo@yahoo.cn

Translation: courtesy and
copyright © Lindy Li Mark

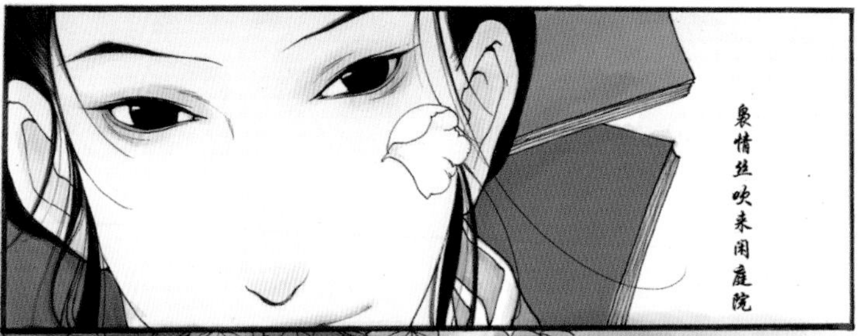

袅情丝吹来闲庭院

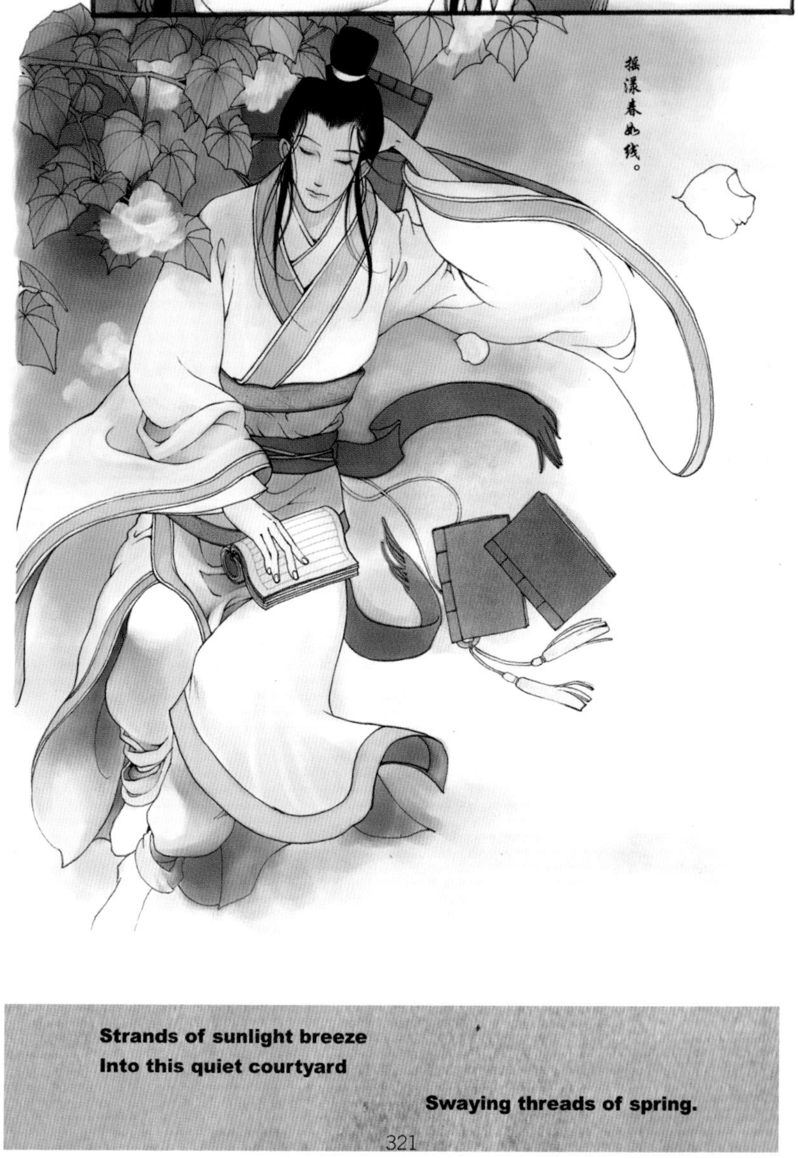

摇漾春如线。

Strands of sunlight breeze
Into this quiet courtyard

Swaying threads of spring.

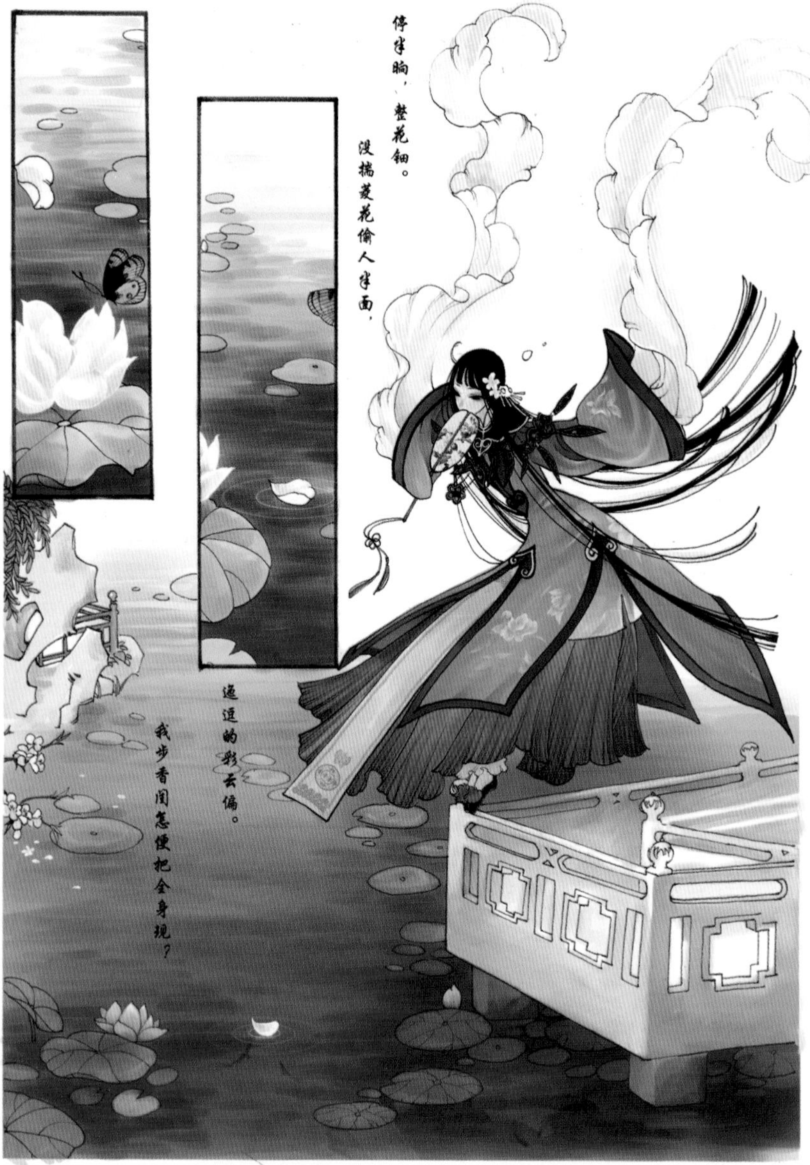
停半晌，整花钿。
没揣菱花偷人半面，
迤逗的彩云偏。
我步香闺怎便把全身现？

Pausing awhile, I fix my hairpin

Contemplating the mirror, that stole my silhouette.

Cloud like tresses trailing to one side.

Pacing my chamber dare I step outside.

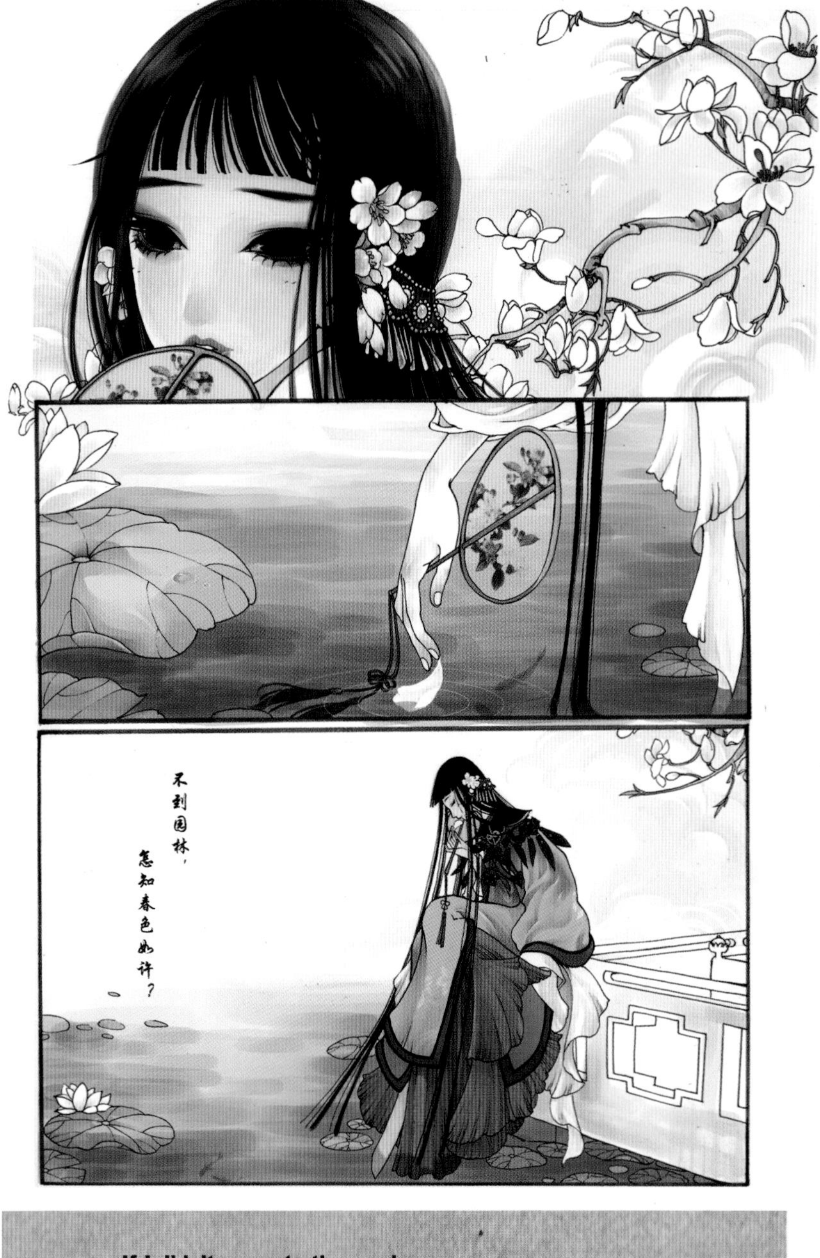
不到园林，
怎知春色如许？

If I didn't come to the garden,
How should I know that springtime is like this.

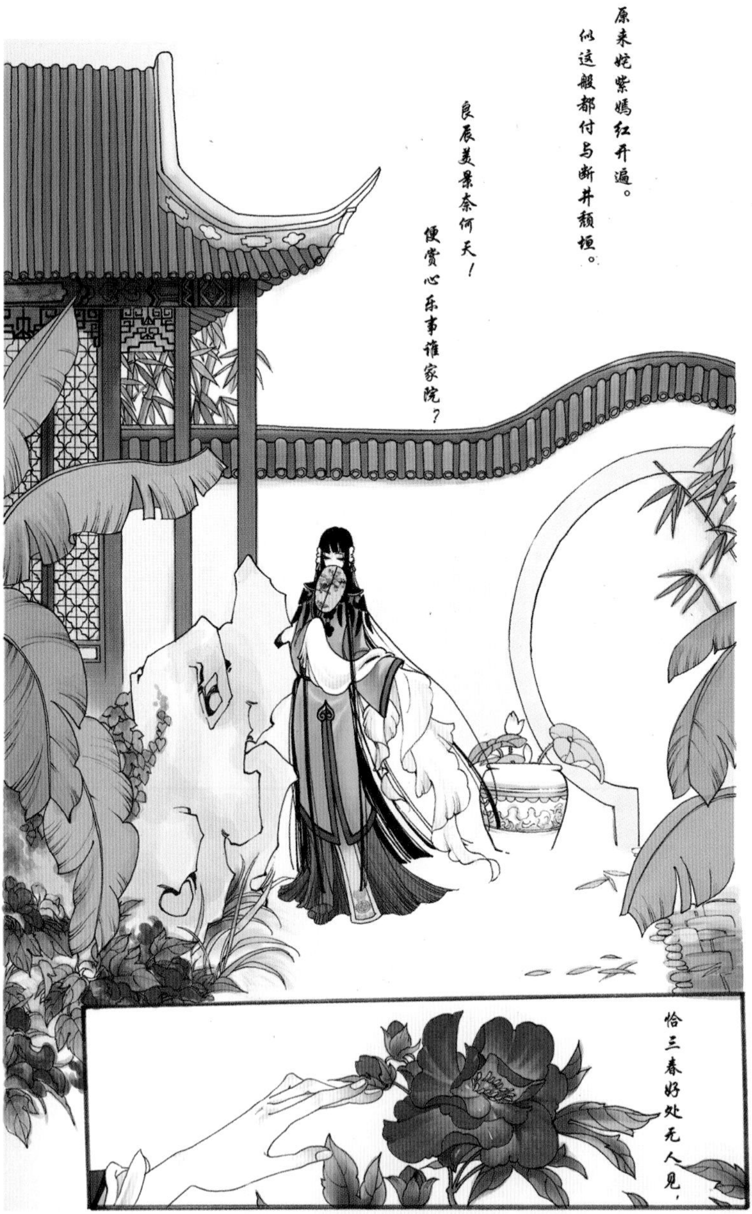
原来姹紫嫣红开遍。
似这般都付与断井颓垣。
良辰美景奈何天！
便赏心乐事谁家院？
恰三春好处无人见，

Already, bright purple and
passion pink bloom in profusion.

Yet to crumbling well, faded walls,
such splendour is abandoned.

But in this glorious season,
Where are sounds of joy in this garden?

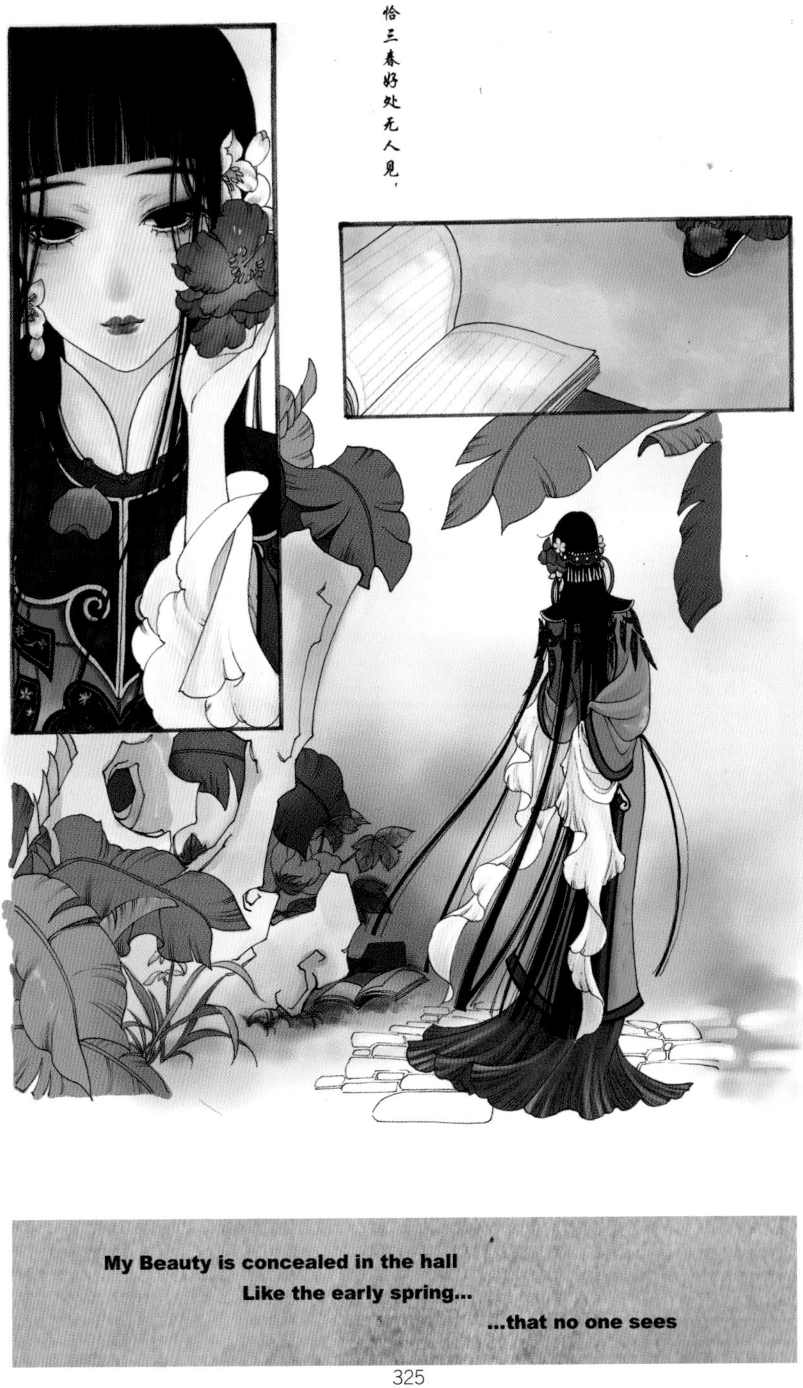
恰三春好处无人见，
My Beauty is concealed in the hall
Like the early spring...
...that no one sees

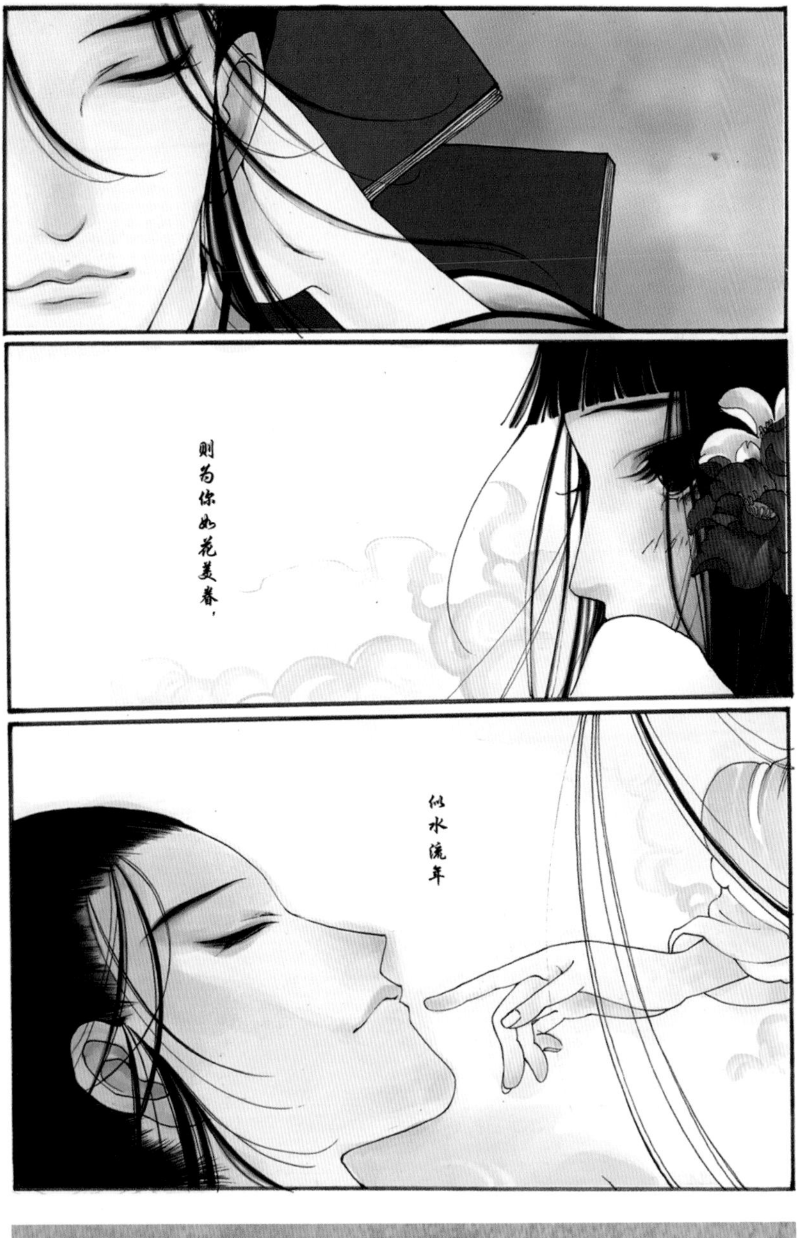
则为你如花美眷，
似水流年

For your beauty
that flowers
with the flowing river of time

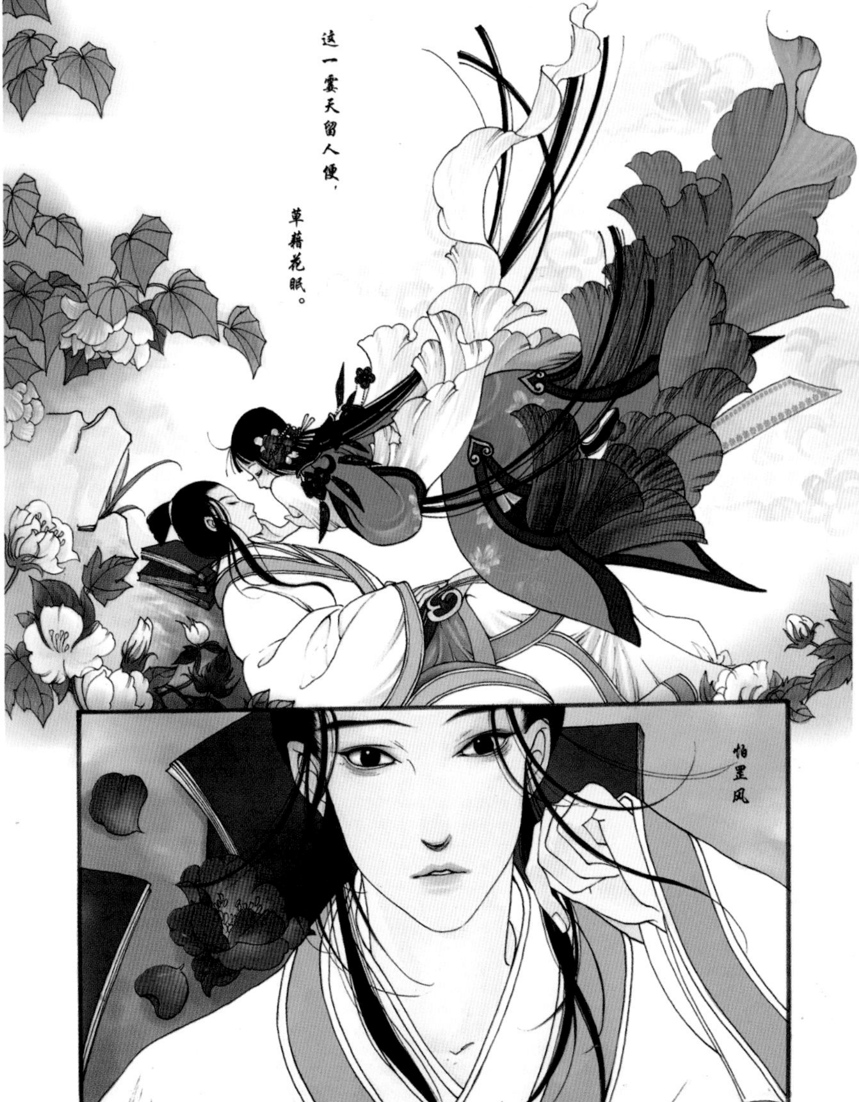
这一霎天留人便，
草藉花眠。
怕罡风

This brief moment
is made in heaven,
Pillowed on grass, bedded among flowers.
The annoying strong wind,

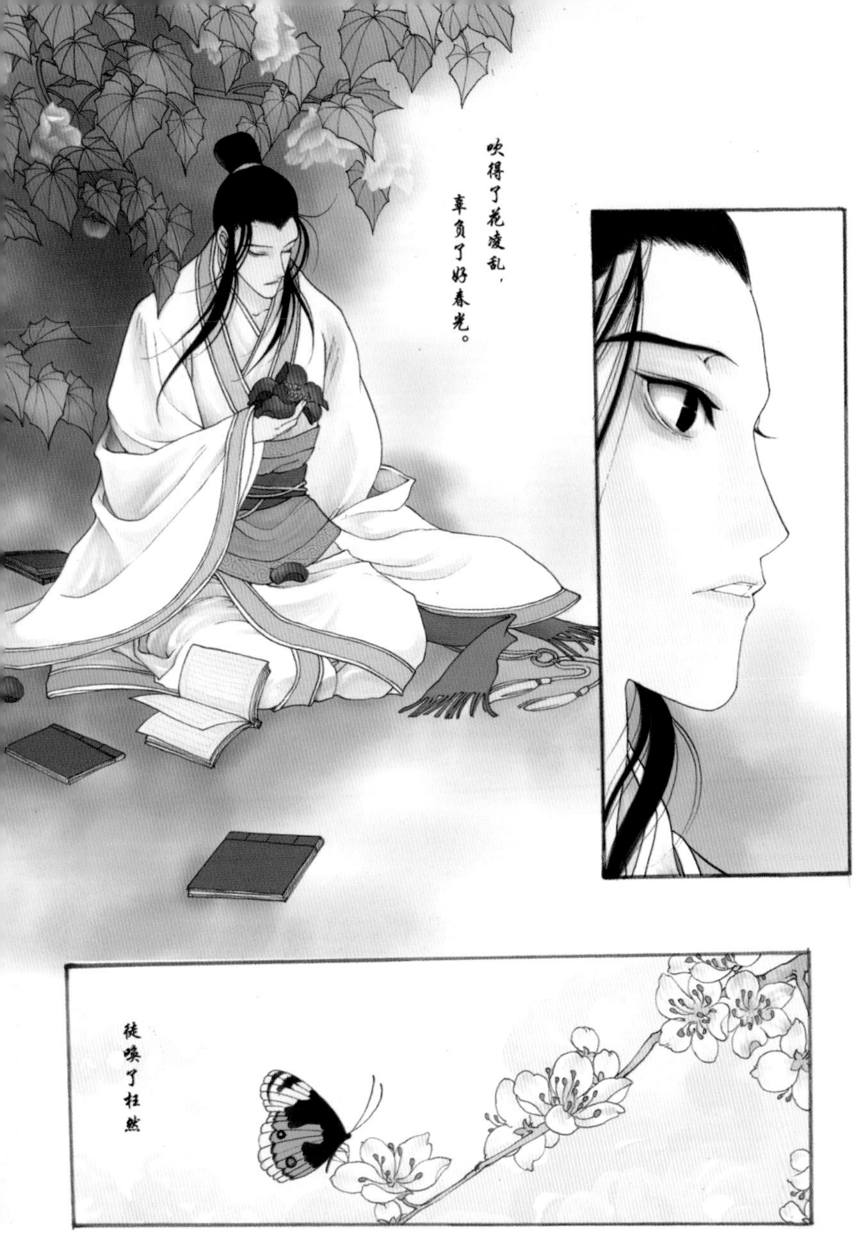
吹得了花凌乱，
辜负了好春光。
徒叹了枉然

Messes flowers,
betrays the beauty of springtime.

As thus, the whole view is wasted.

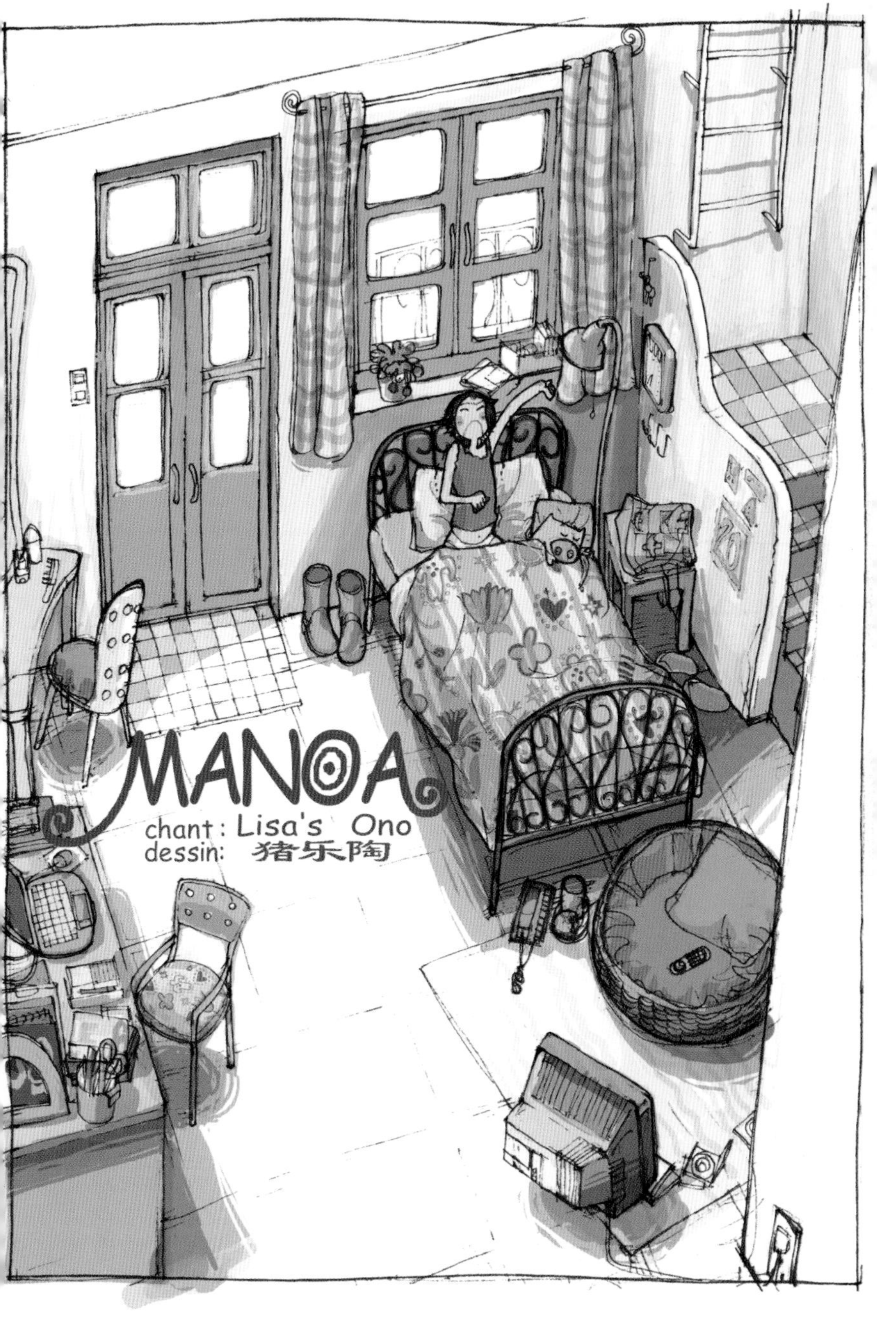
MANOA
chant : Lisa's Ono
dessin: 猪乐陶

IN MANOA

Zhu Letao

Zhu Letao, whose birth name is Qi Xiao, was born in Shanghai and later moved to Yunnan, Yangzhou, Shanghai and Beijing. Now she's living in Hangzhou. Before she officially launched her career in drawing cartoons, Letao has also worked as a clothes shopping-guide, a secretary, a Yoga teacher and so on.

Published artwork: *The Magic Soup of Love*
MATA – The Adventure on Lighthouse Island
MATA – The Adventure in the Golden Country 1–2
Xishuangbanna, My Home

Biggest wish: Happily and healthily drawing cartoons
Smallest wish: Become Superman

www.summerzoo.com
email: manga@126.com
email: summerzoo@yahoo.cn

Original lyrics © Lisa Ono

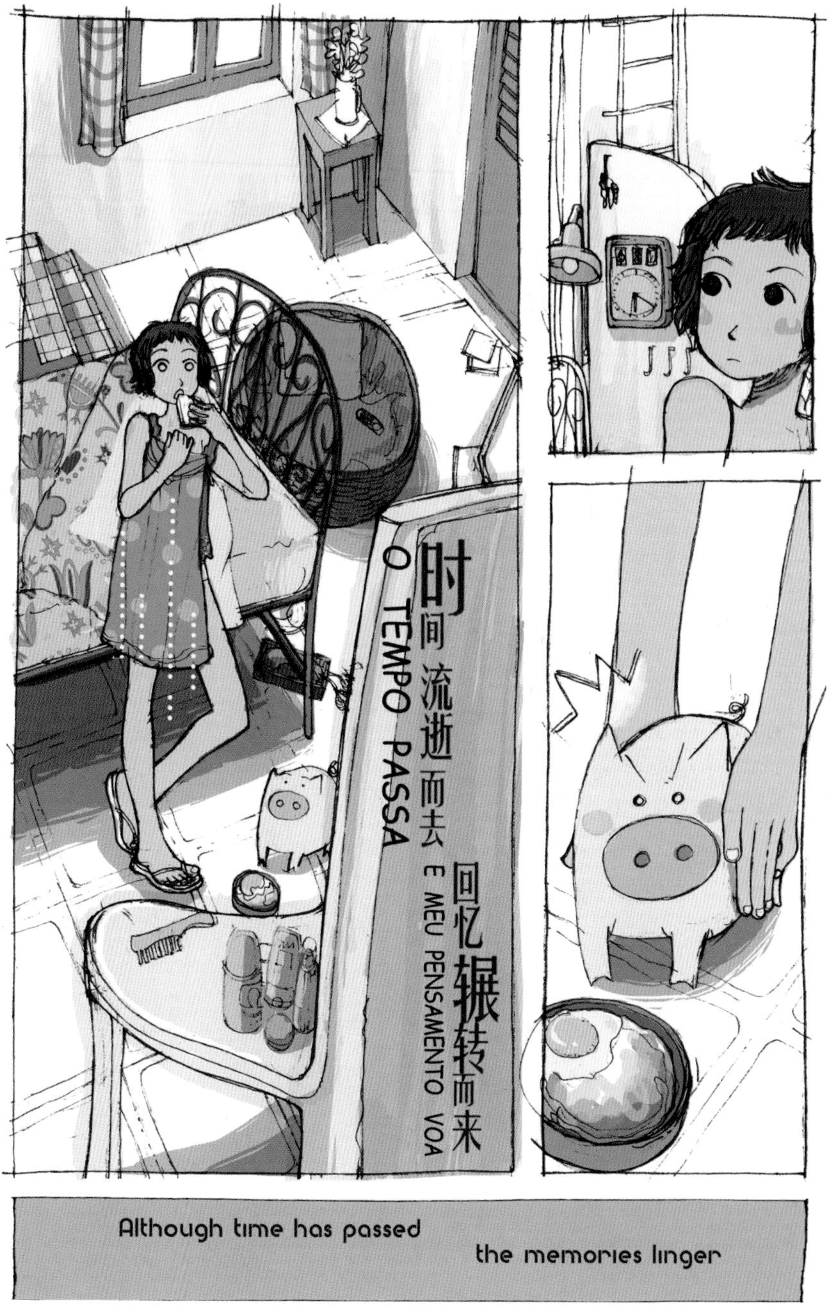
时间流逝而去
回忆辗转而来
O TEMPO PASSA
E MEU PENSAMENTO VOA
Although time has passed
the memories linger

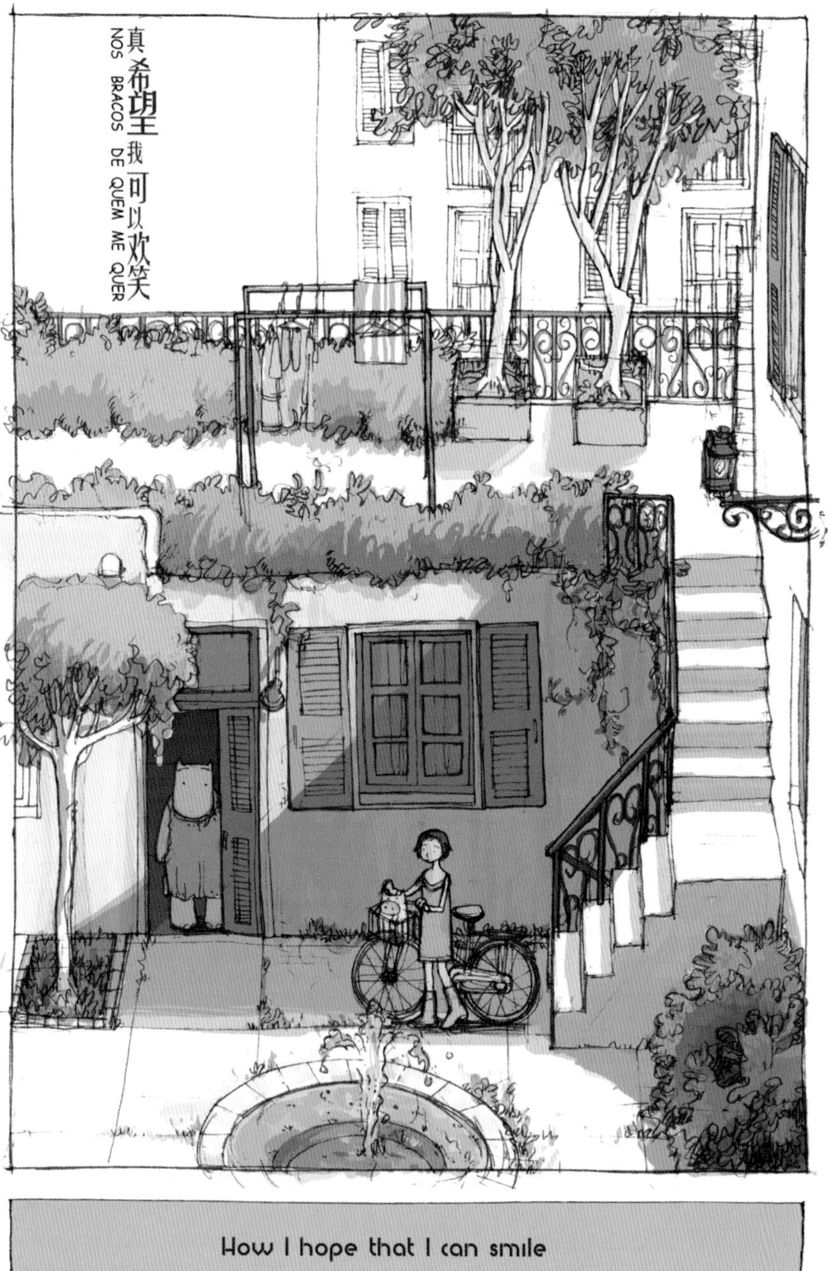
真希望我可以欢笑
NOS BRACOS DE QUEM ME QUER

How I hope that I can smile

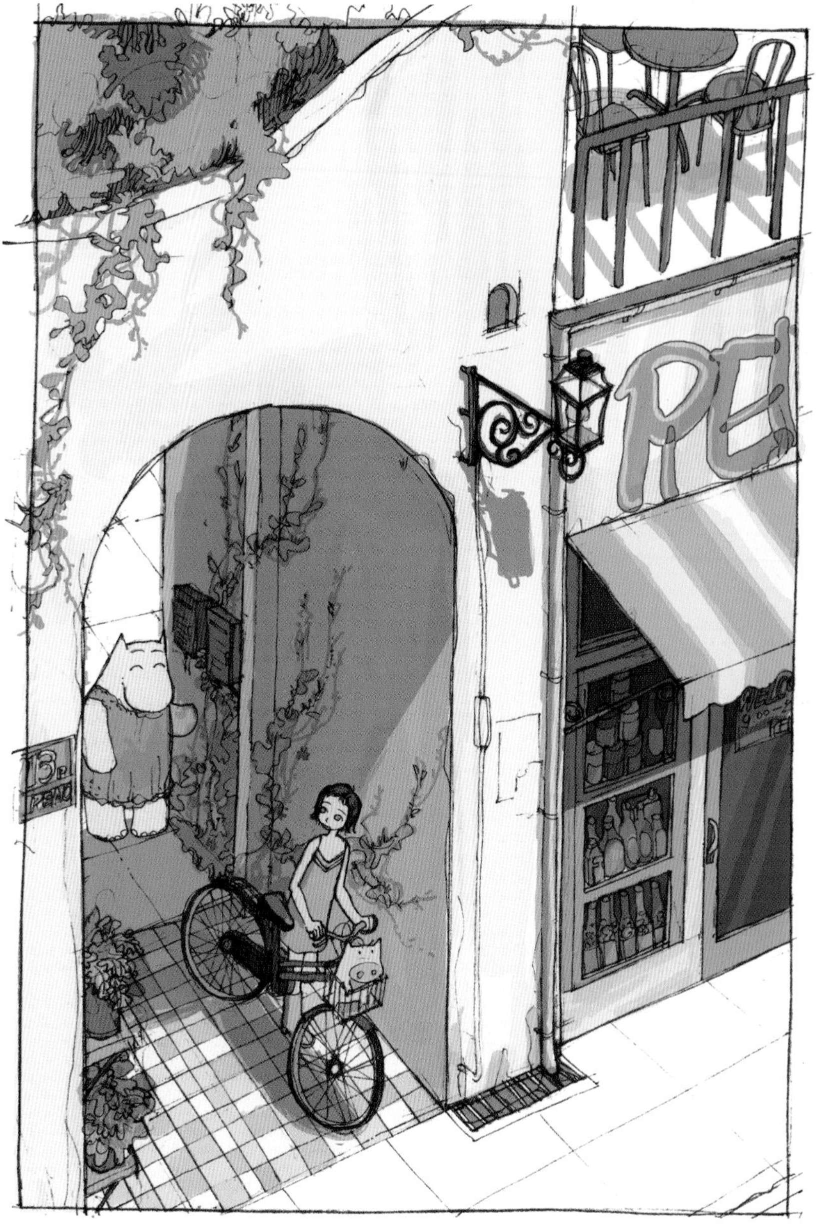
PE

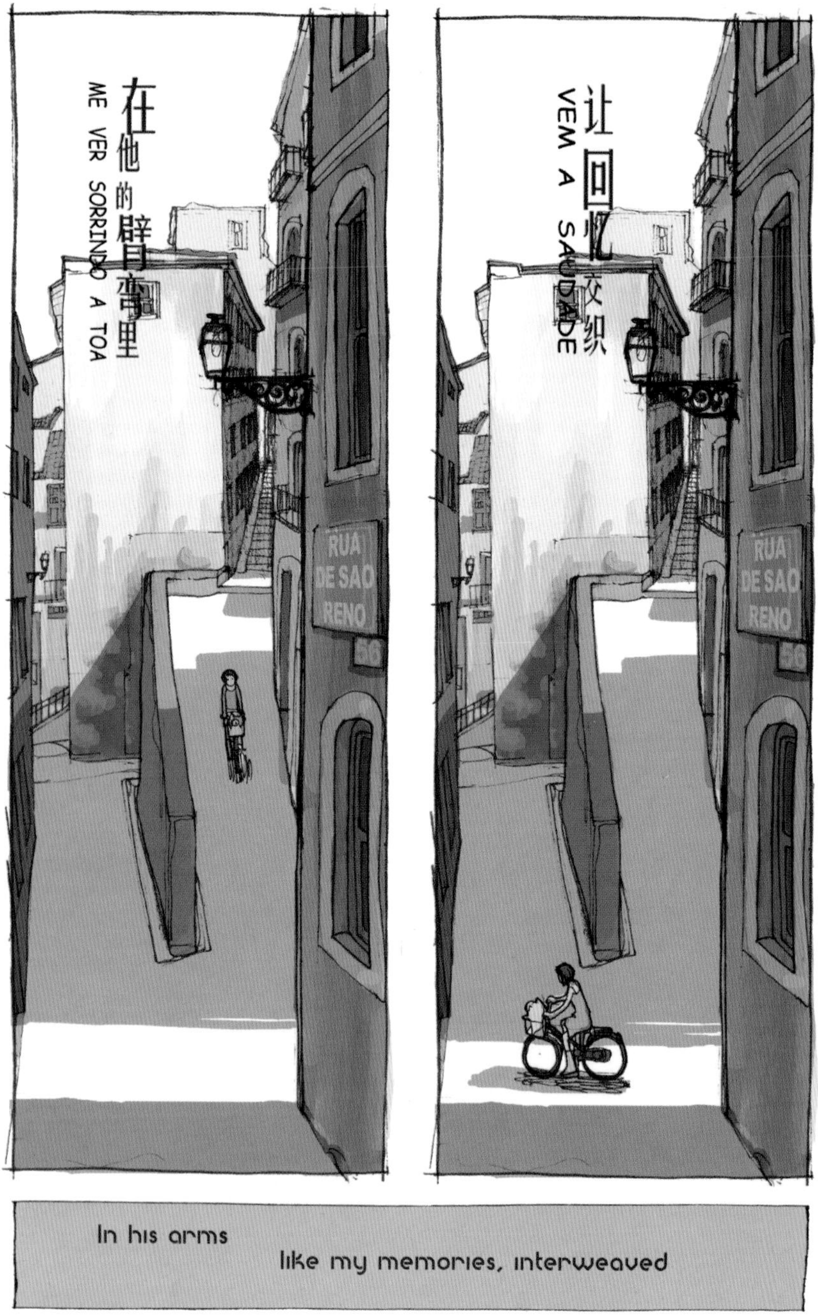
在他的臂弯里
ME VER SORRINDO A TOA
让回忆交织
VEM A SAUDADE
RUA DE SAO RENO
56
RUA DE SAO RENO
56
In his arms
like my memories, interweaved

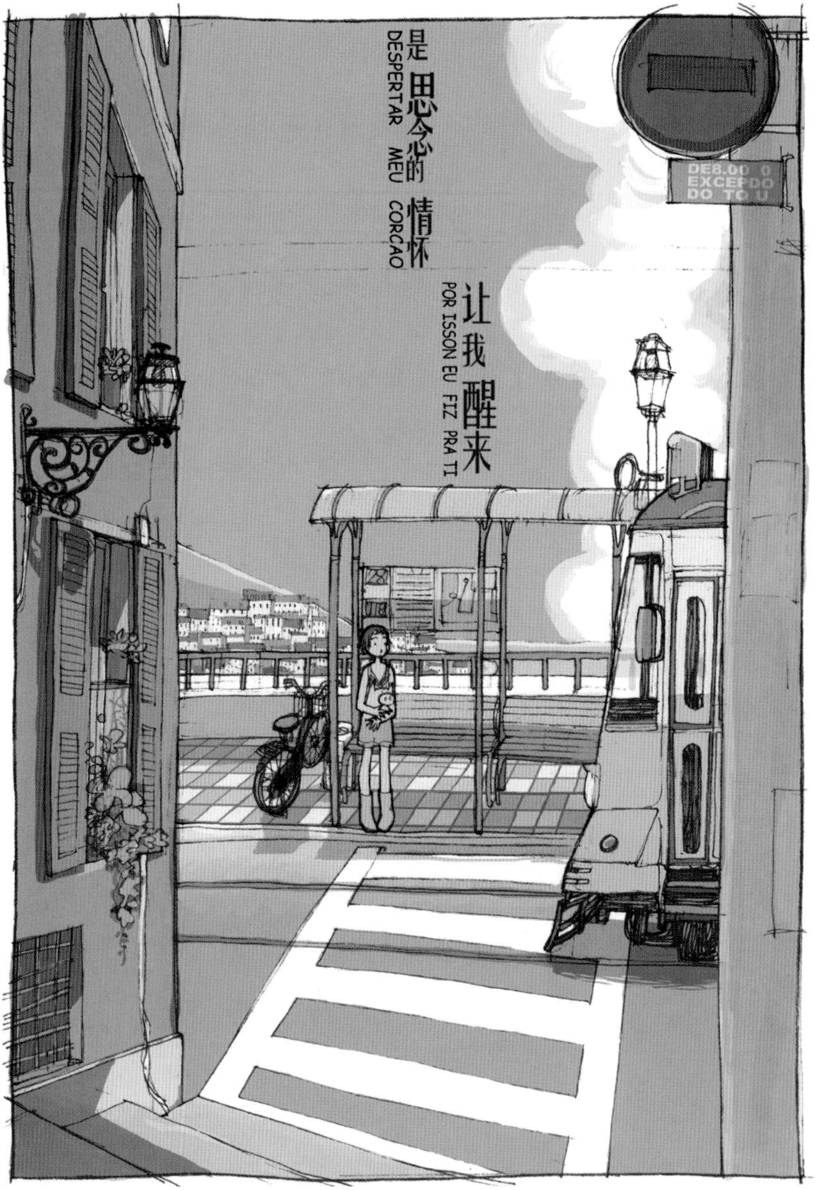
是思念的情怀
DESPERTAR MEU CORCAO
让我醒来
POR ISSON EU FIZ PRA TI

It is this yearning feeling that woke me up

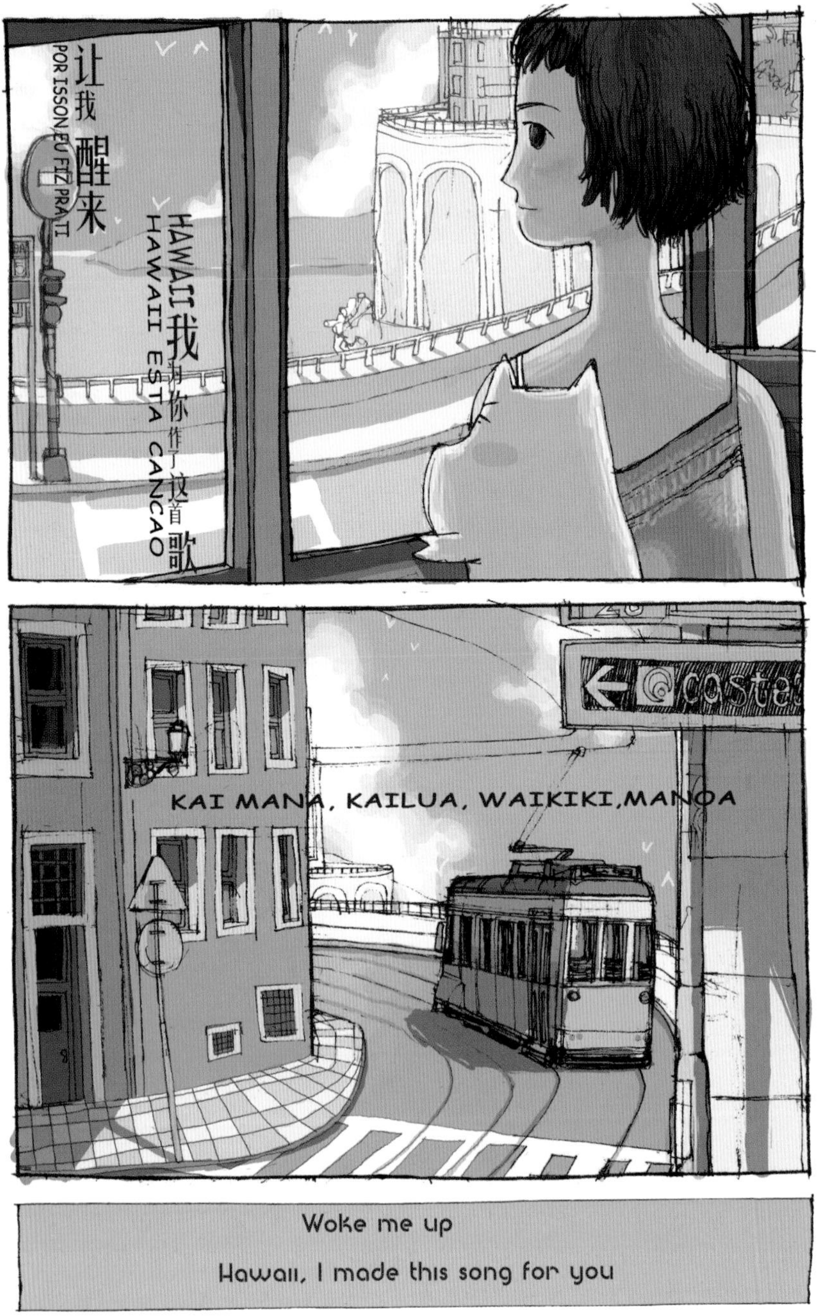
HAWAII我为你作了这首歌
HAWAII ESTA CANCAO
让我醒来
POR ISSON,EU FIZ PRA TI
KAI MANA, KAILUA, WAIKIKI,MANOA
Woke me up
Hawaii, I made this song for you

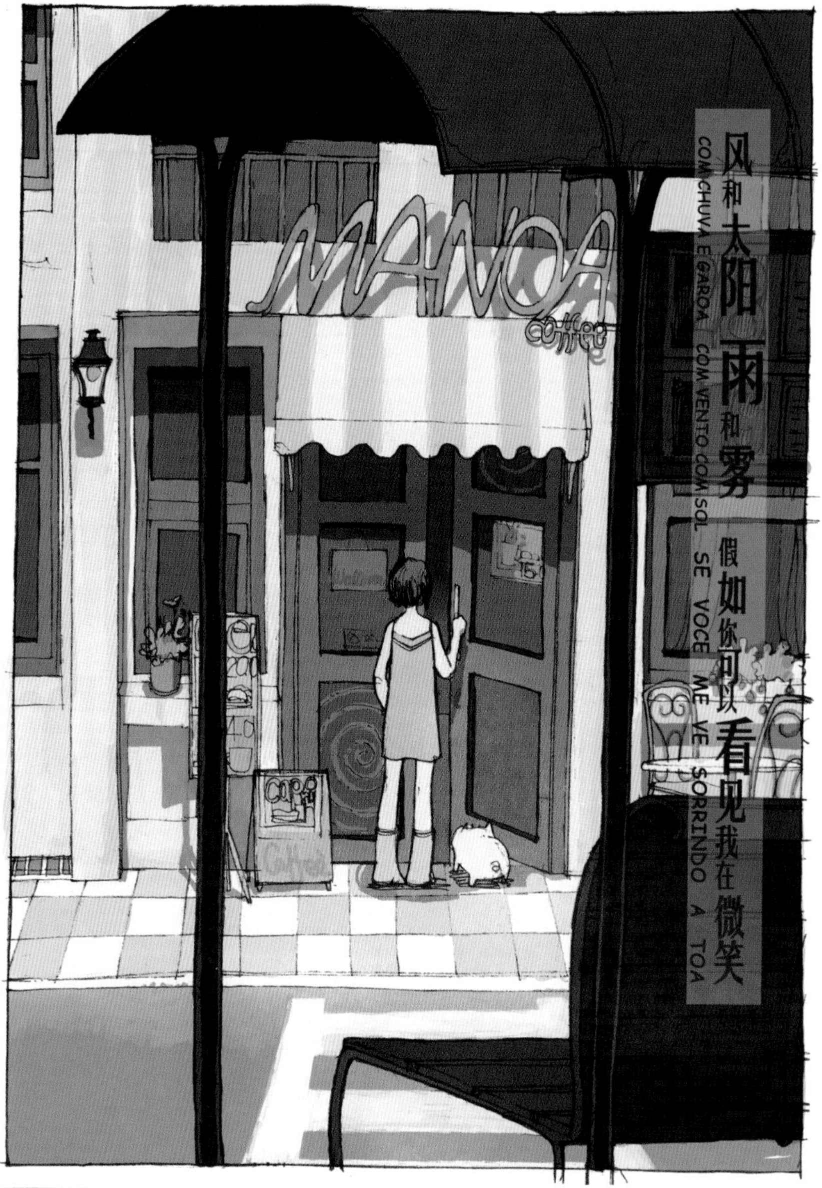
MANOA
coffee
风和太阳雨和雾
假如你可以看见我在微笑
COM CHUVA E GAROA COM VENTO COM SOL SE VOCE ME VE SORRINDO A TOA

The wind and the sun, the rain and the fog
If you can see me smiling...

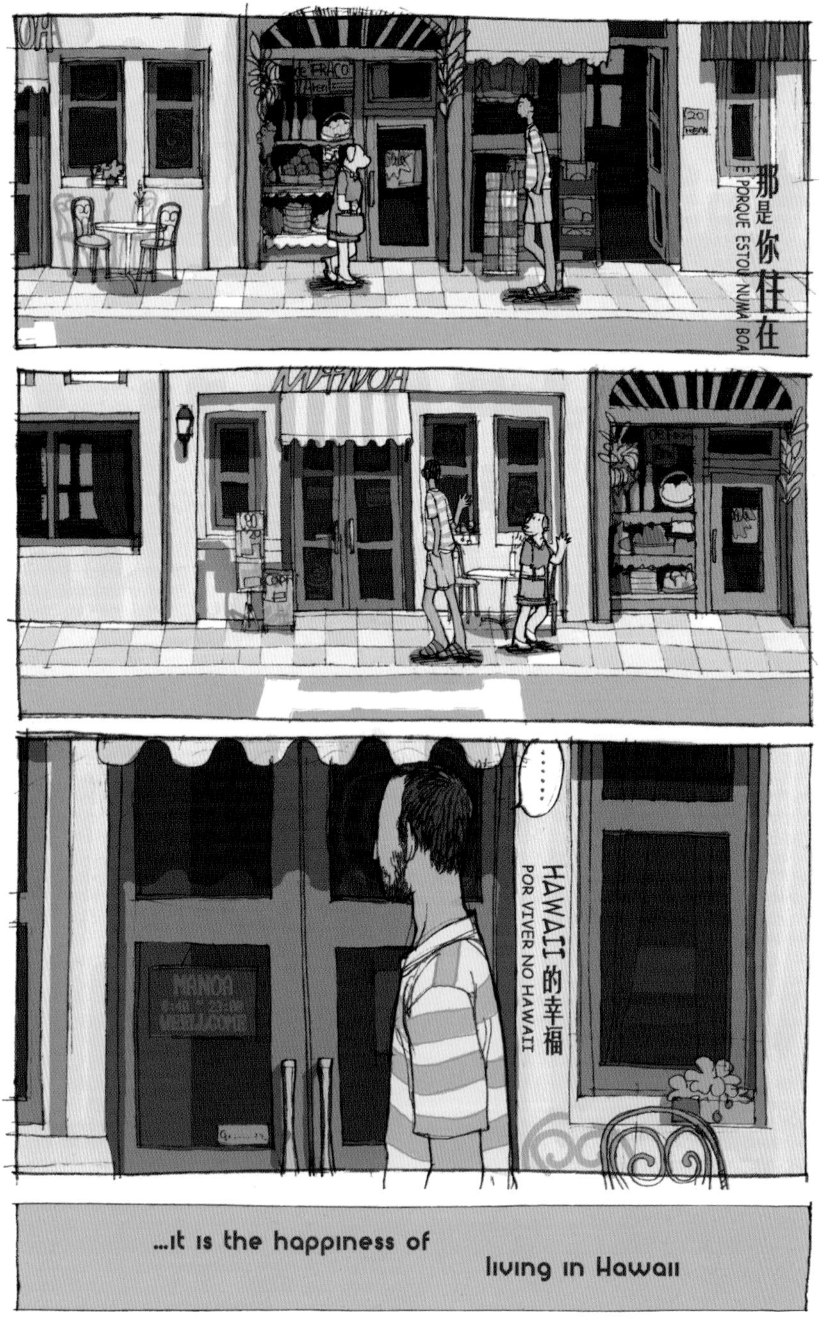
那是你住在
E PORQUE ESTOU NUMA BOA
......
HAWAII的幸福
POR VIVER NO HAWAII
...it is the happiness of
living in Hawaii

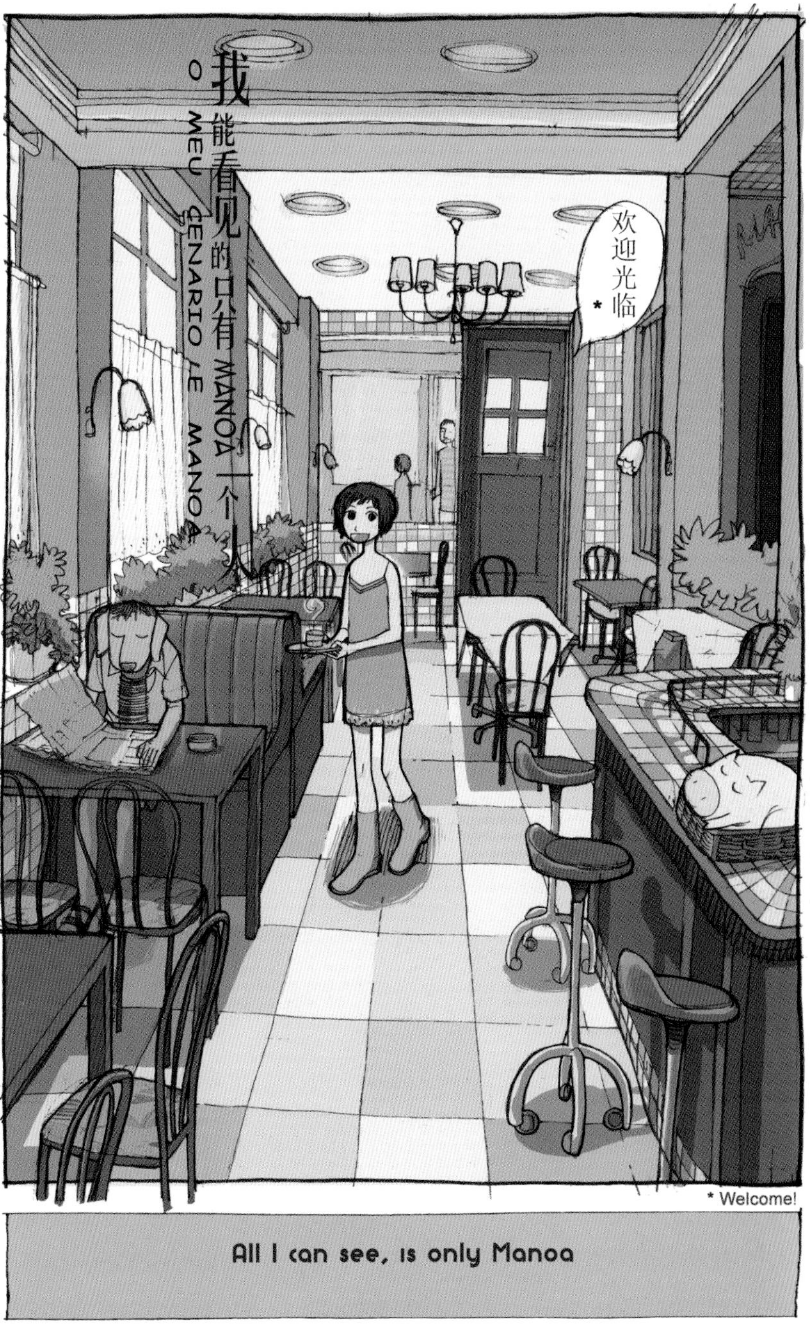
我能看见的只有MANOA一个人
O MEU CENARIO É MANOA
欢迎光临*
* Welcome!
All I can see, is only Manoa

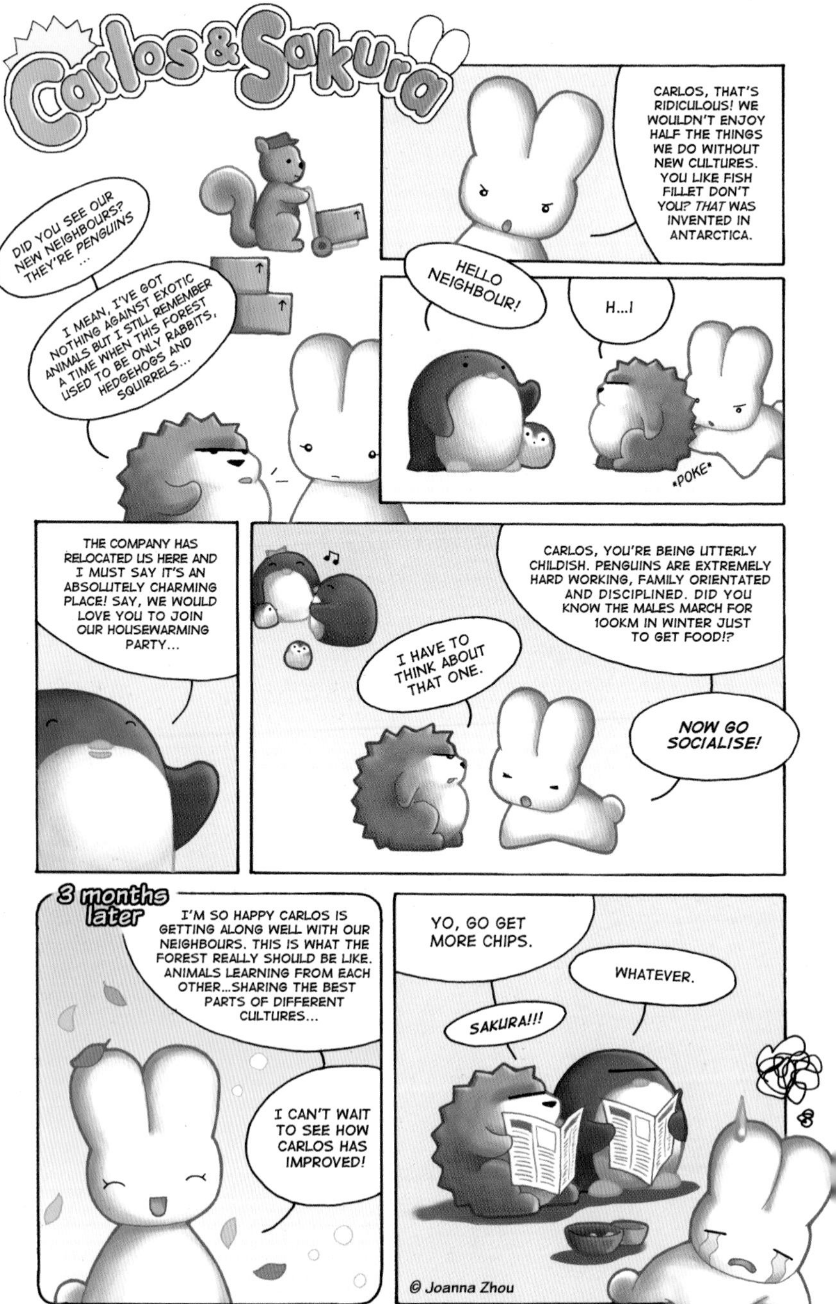
Carlos & Sakura
DID YOU SEE OUR NEW NEIGHBOURS? THEY'RE *PENGUINS* ...
I MEAN, I'VE GOT NOTHING AGAINST EXOTIC ANIMALS BUT I STILL REMEMBER A TIME WHEN THIS FOREST USED TO BE ONLY RABBITS, HEDGEHOGS AND SQUIRRELS...
CARLOS, THAT'S RIDICULOUS! WE WOULDN'T ENJOY HALF THE THINGS WE DO WITHOUT NEW CULTURES. YOU LIKE FISH FILLET DON'T YOU? *THAT* WAS INVENTED IN ANTARCTICA.
HELLO NEIGHBOUR!
H...I
POKE
THE COMPANY HAS RELOCATED US HERE AND I MUST SAY IT'S AN ABSOLUTELY CHARMING PLACE! SAY, WE WOULD LOVE YOU TO JOIN OUR HOUSEWARMING PARTY...
CARLOS, YOU'RE BEING UTTERLY CHILDISH. PENGUINS ARE EXTREMELY HARD WORKING, FAMILY ORIENTATED AND DISCIPLINED. DID YOU KNOW THE MALES MARCH FOR 100KM IN WINTER JUST TO GET FOOD!?
I HAVE TO THINK ABOUT THAT ONE.
NOW GO SOCIALISE!
3 months later
I'M SO HAPPY CARLOS IS GETTING ALONG WELL WITH OUR NEIGHBOURS. THIS IS WHAT THE FOREST REALLY SHOULD BE LIKE. ANIMALS LEARNING FROM EACH OTHER...SHARING THE BEST PARTS OF DIFFERENT CULTURES...
I CAN'T WAIT TO SEE HOW CARLOS HAS IMPROVED!
YO, GO GET MORE CHIPS.
WHATEVER.
SAKURA!!!
© Joanna Zhou

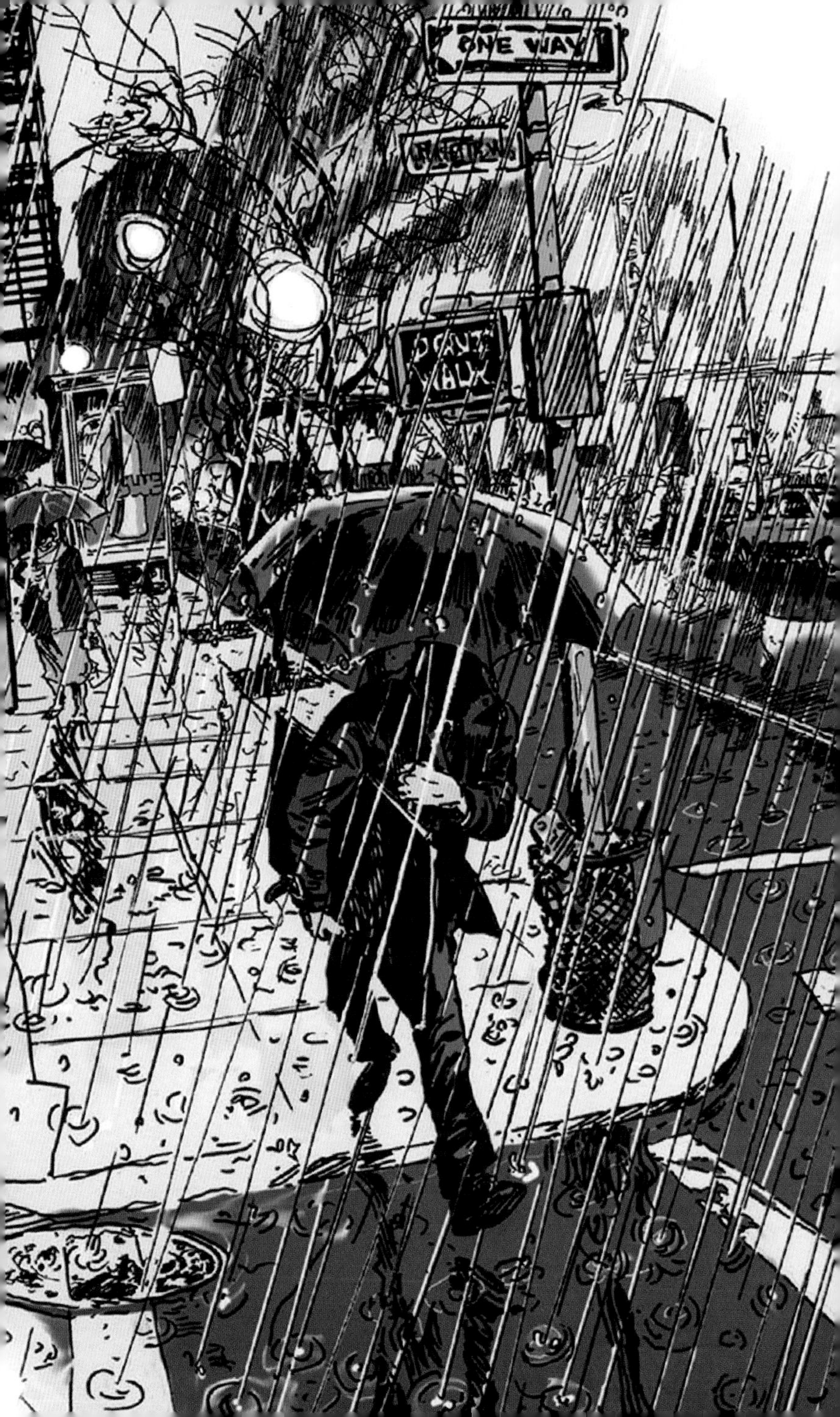
ONE WAY

NEW YORK STORIES
James Romberger & Crosby Romberger

Summer's over, here comes the rain. The Romberger family circus rolls back into *BNM* town with a short cycle of stories redolent of their home, New York City. **James Romberger,** one of the best storytellers in the business, counts classic manga among his many and diverse comics influences, as evinced by his dynamic and yet perfectly poised layouts (**Crosby** is James and Marguerite's son; he helped his father out by writing the words for their tag-tale).

Tensions ride high in any highly concentrated urban area; modern city life is filled with incidents of confrontation, acted out each second of every day. Citizens cope by blanking most everyone they meet, fellow-feeling denied to the point of walking as soon as looking through one another. Is it any accident then, that *chambara*, or "fencing" dramas – samurai swordfighting to you and me – should be such a popular modern manga genre? They also function as living history of braver times, when life was lived by the bushido warrior code, and where such meetings along the path were swiftly resolved with cathartic action and bloody violence. This may be entirely Ye Editor's crackpot opinion, but *St Mark's Jaguar*, in its way, suggests nothing so much as a very American fencing drama.

www.thearteriesgroup.com

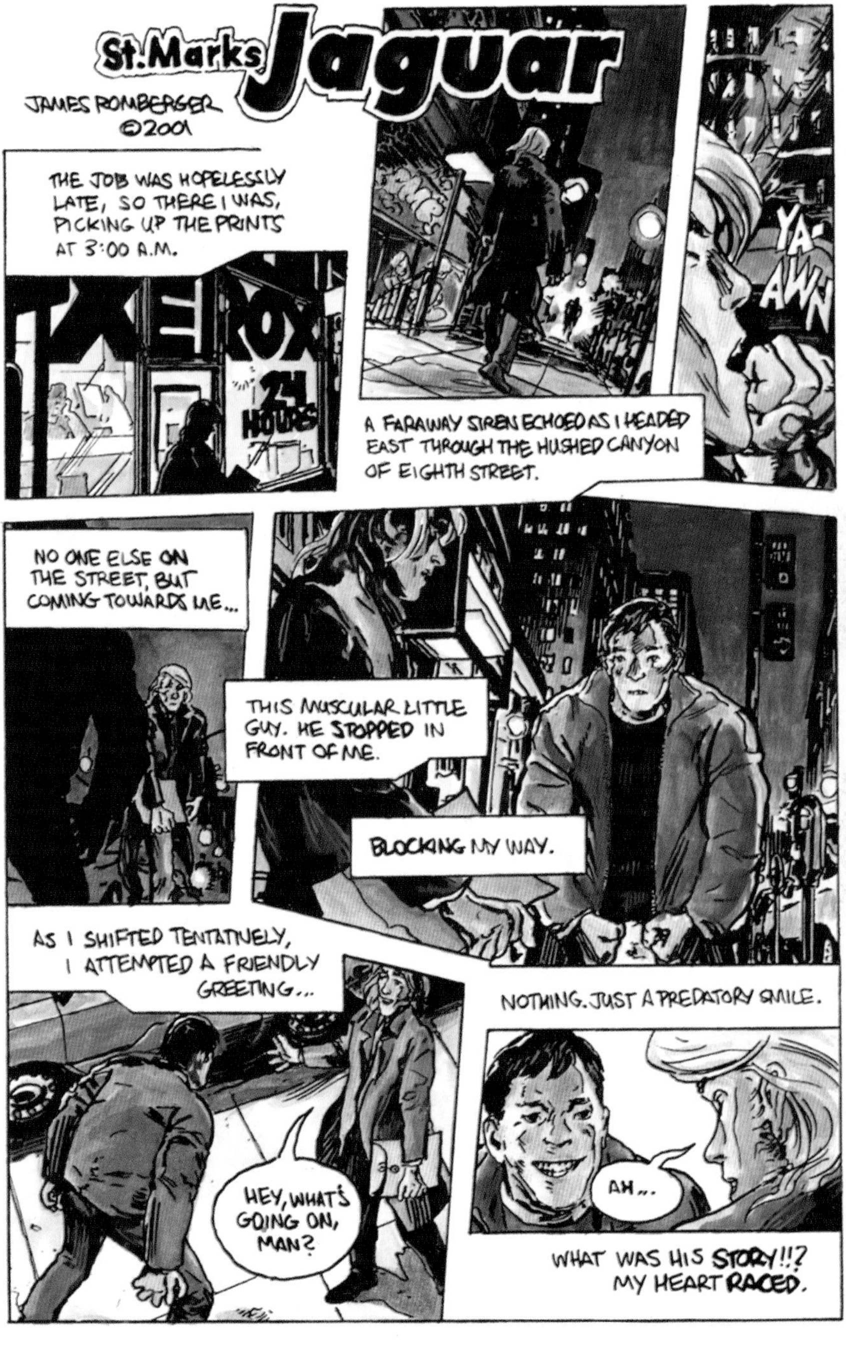

St. Marks Jaguar
JAMES ROMBERGER ©2001
THE JOB WAS HOPELESSLY LATE, SO THERE I WAS, PICKING UP THE PRINTS AT 3:00 A.M.
XEROX
24 HOURS
A FARAWAY SIREN ECHOED AS I HEADED EAST THROUGH THE HUSHED CANYON OF EIGHTH STREET.
YA-AWN
NO ONE ELSE ON THE STREET, BUT COMING TOWARDS ME...
THIS MUSCULAR LITTLE GUY. HE STOPPED IN FRONT OF ME.
BLOCKING MY WAY.
AS I SHIFTED TENTATIVELY, I ATTEMPTED A FRIENDLY GREETING...
HEY, WHAT'S GOING ON, MAN?
NOTHING. JUST A PREDATORY SMILE.
AH...
WHAT WAS HIS STORY!!? MY HEART RACED.

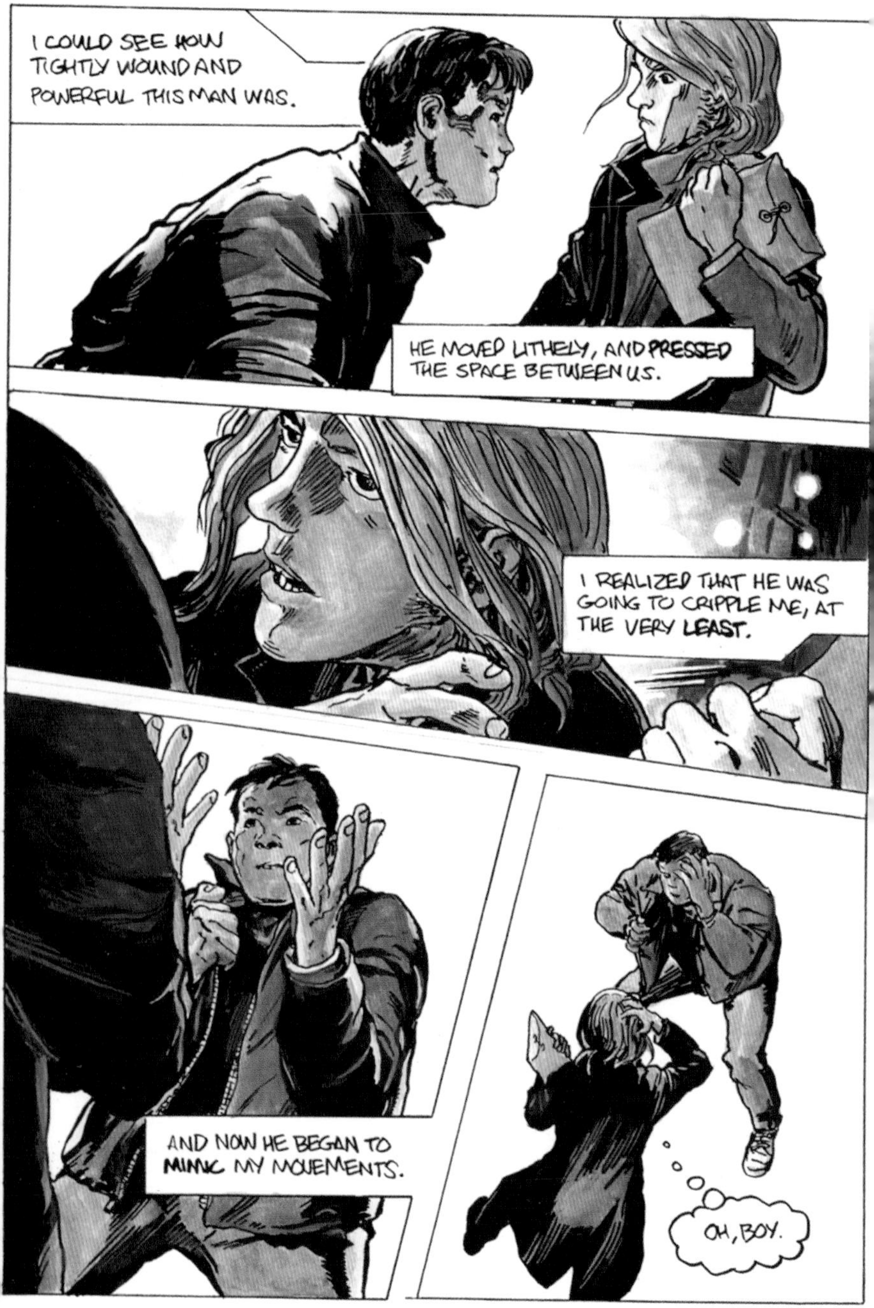
I COULD SEE HOW TIGHTLY WOUND AND POWERFUL THIS MAN WAS.
HE MOVED LITHELY, AND PRESSED THE SPACE BETWEEN US.
I REALIZED THAT HE WAS GOING TO CRIPPLE ME, AT THE VERY LEAST.
AND NOW HE BEGAN TO MIMIC MY MOVEMENTS.
OH, BOY.

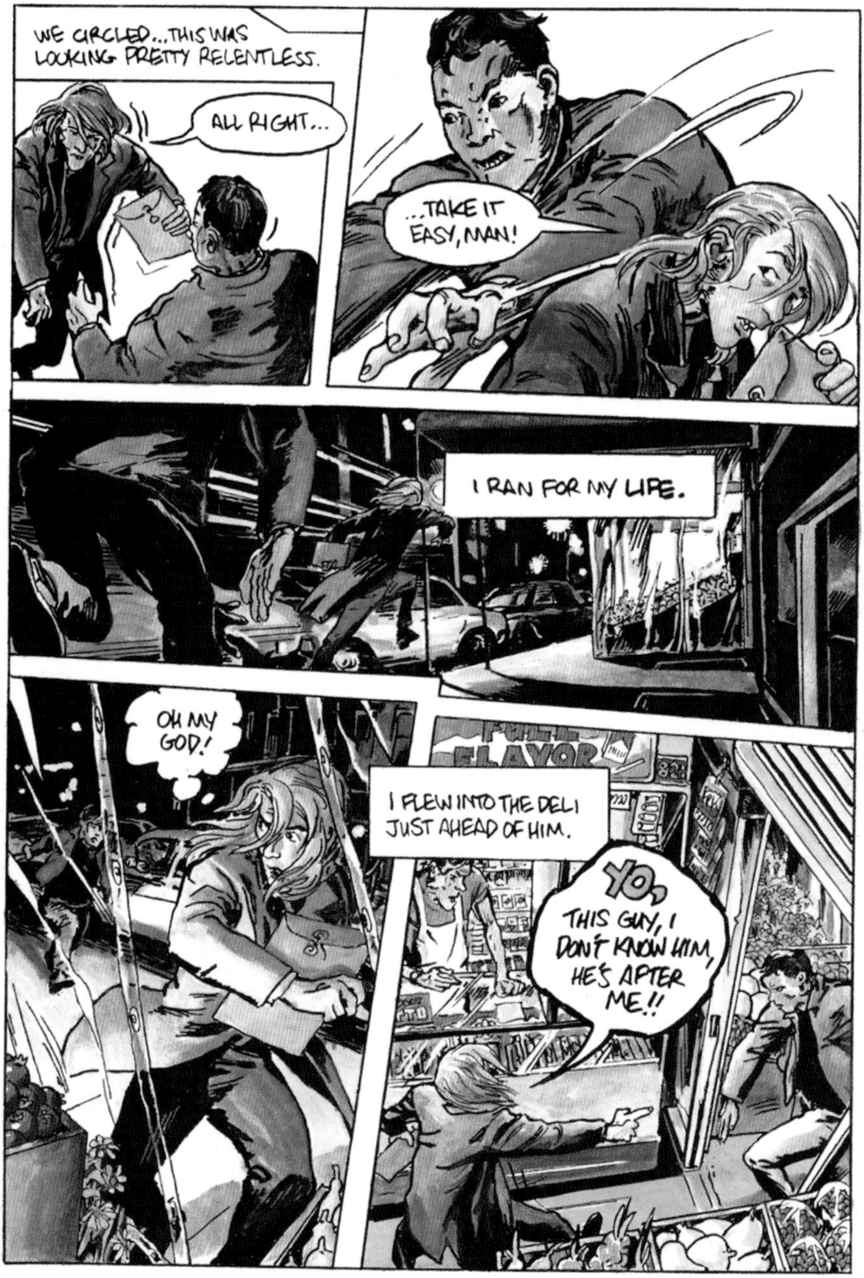
WE CIRCLED... THIS WAS LOOKING PRETTY RELENTLESS.
ALL RIGHT...
...TAKE IT EASY, MAN!
I RAN FOR MY LIFE.
OH MY GOD!
I FLEW INTO THE DELI JUST AHEAD OF HIM.
YO, THIS GUY, I DON'T KNOW HIM, HE'S AFTER ME!!

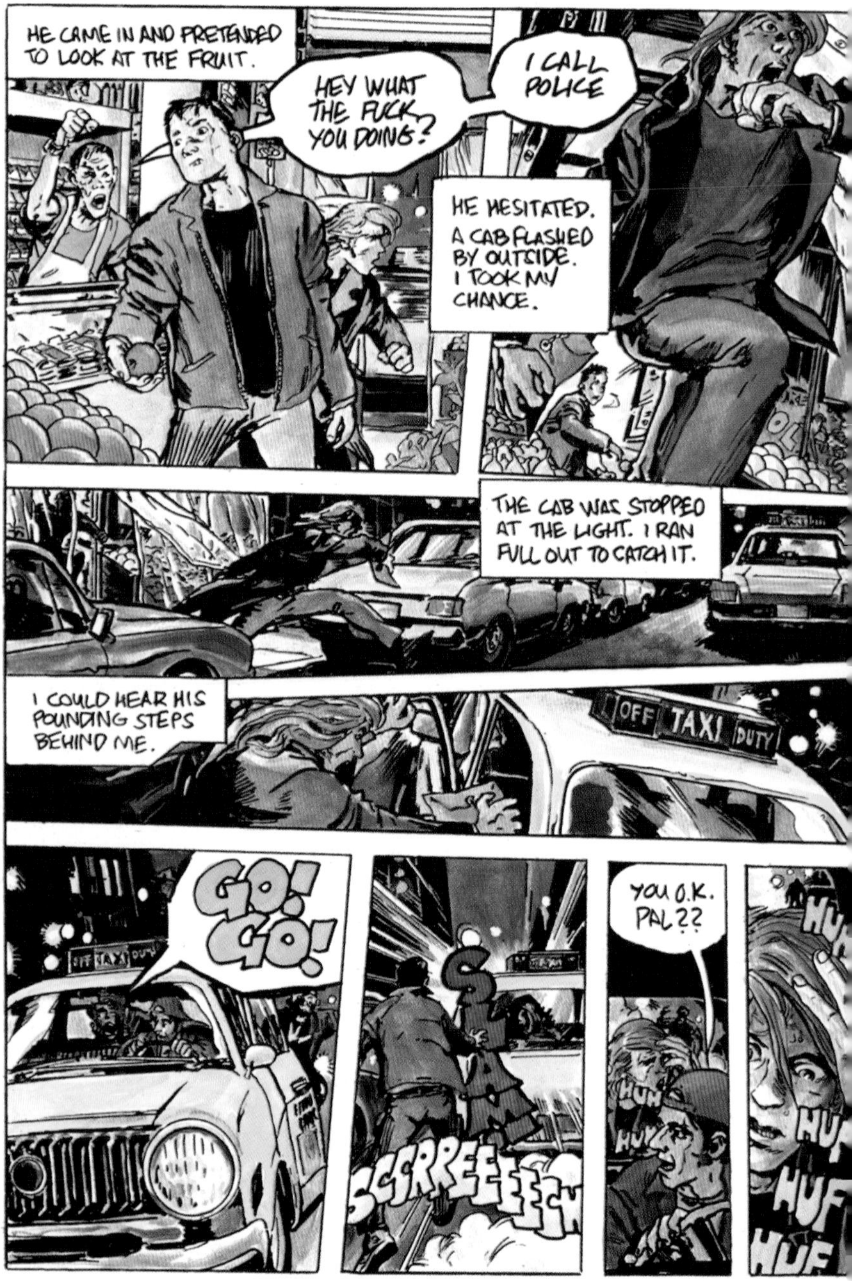
HE CAME IN AND PRETENDED TO LOOK AT THE FRUIT.
HEY WHAT THE FUCK YOU DOING?
I CALL POLICE
HE HESITATED. A CAB FLASHED BY OUTSIDE. I TOOK MY CHANCE.
THE CAB WAS STOPPED AT THE LIGHT. I RAN FULL OUT TO CATCH IT.
I COULD HEAR HIS POUNDING STEPS BEHIND ME.
OFF TAXI DUTY
GO! GO!
SCRREEEECH
YOU O.K. PAL??
HUF HUF HUF HUF

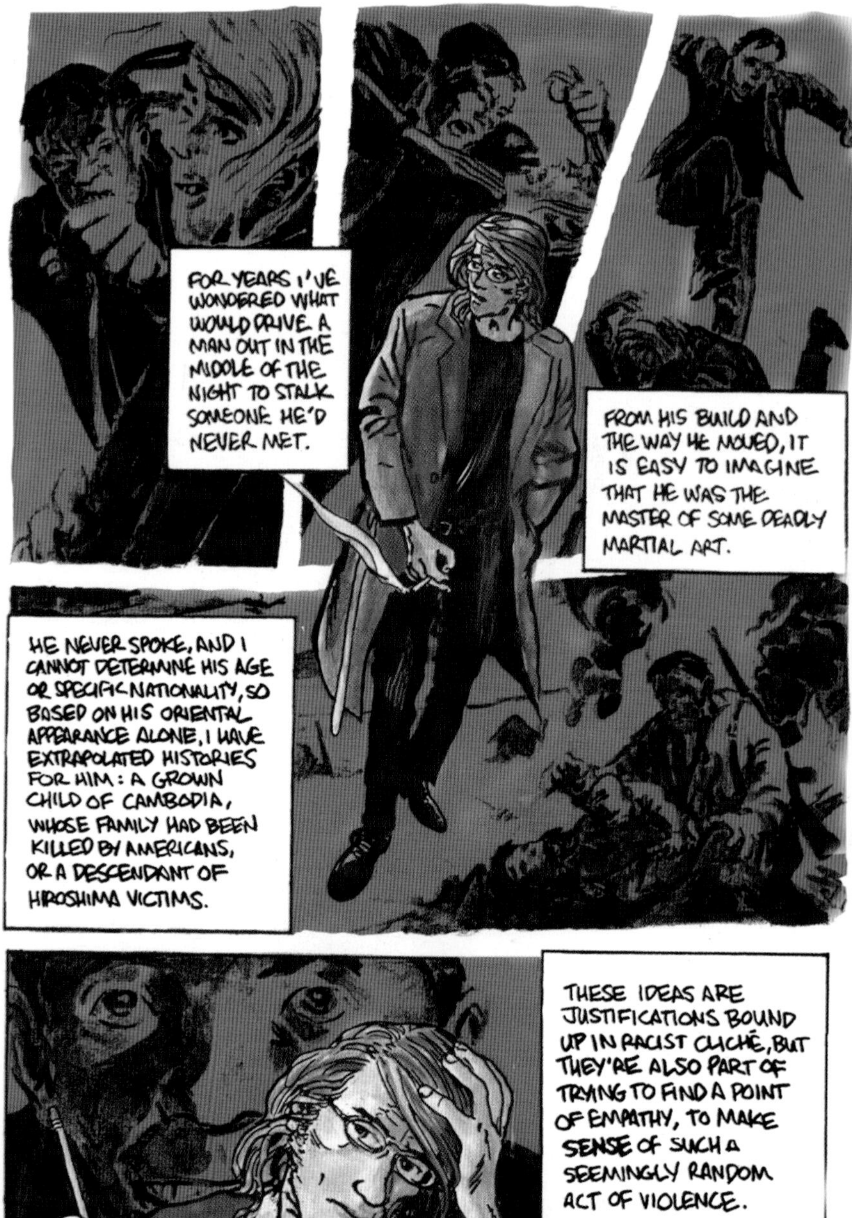
FOR YEARS I'VE WONDERED WHAT WOULD DRIVE A MAN OUT IN THE MIDDLE OF THE NIGHT TO STALK SOMEONE HE'D NEVER MET.
FROM HIS BUILD AND THE WAY HE MOVED, IT IS EASY TO IMAGINE THAT HE WAS THE MASTER OF SOME DEADLY MARTIAL ART.
HE NEVER SPOKE, AND I CANNOT DETERMINE HIS AGE OR SPECIFIC NATIONALITY, SO BASED ON HIS ORIENTAL APPEARANCE ALONE, I HAVE EXTRAPOLATED HISTORIES FOR HIM: A GROWN CHILD OF CAMBODIA, WHOSE FAMILY HAD BEEN KILLED BY AMERICANS, OR A DESCENDANT OF HIROSHIMA VICTIMS.
THESE IDEAS ARE JUSTIFICATIONS BOUND UP IN RACIST CLICHÉ, BUT THEY'RE ALSO PART OF TRYING TO FIND A POINT OF EMPATHY, TO MAKE SENSE OF SUCH A SEEMINGLY RANDOM ACT OF VIOLENCE.
END

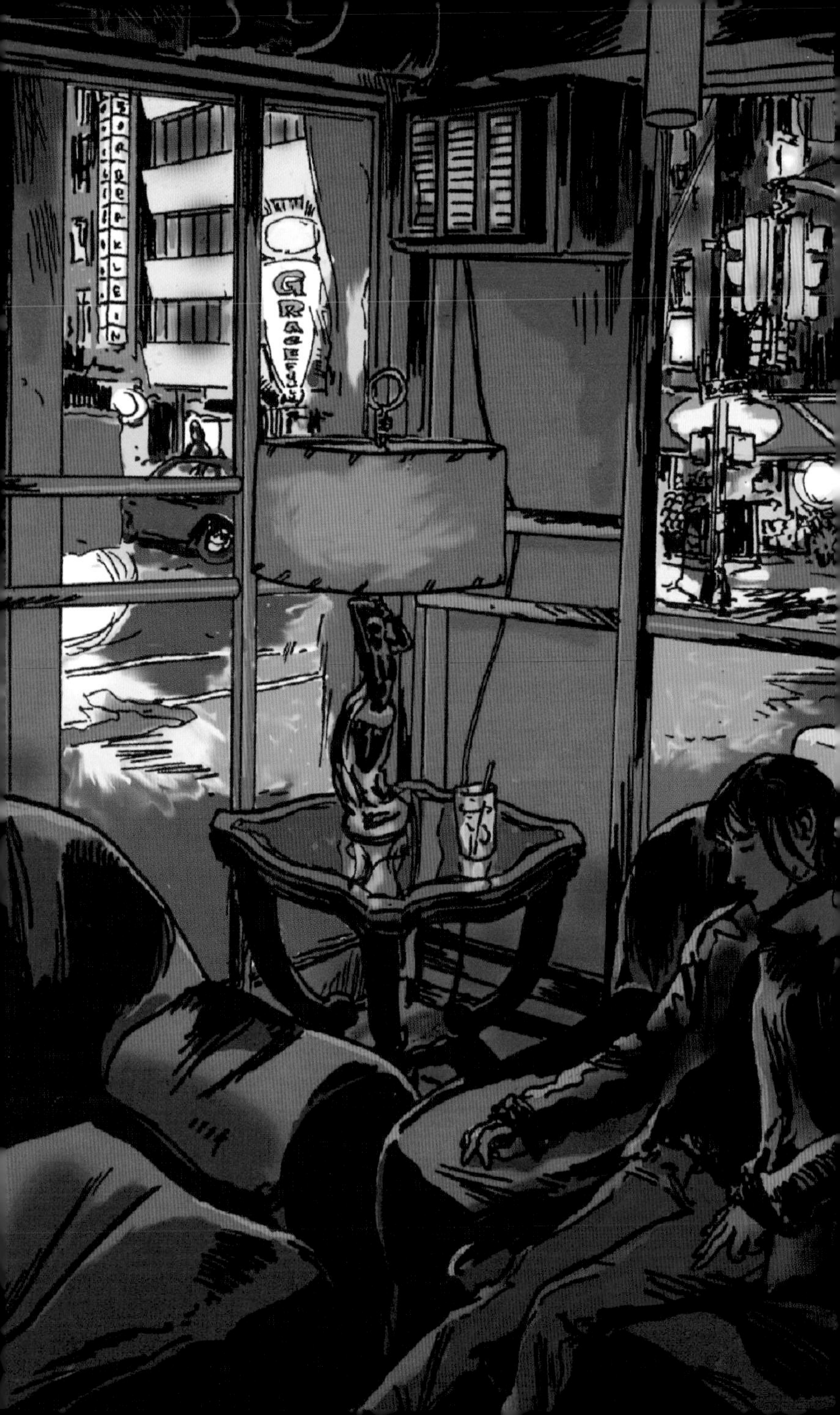

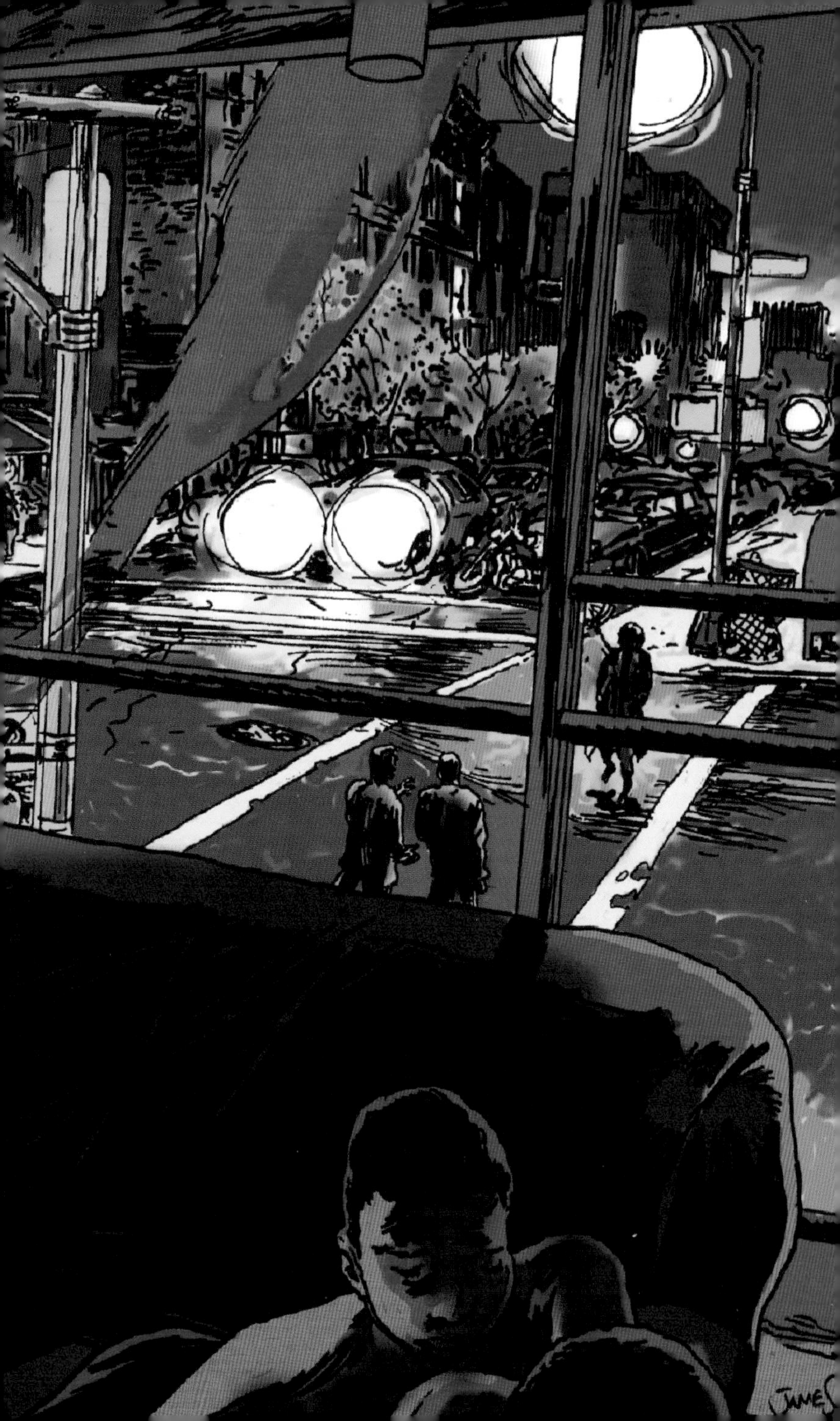
JAMES

IN THE YARD...

THE GREAT LIGHT MOVES FROM SIDE TO SIDE, HUNTING.

CHK-! CHK-! CHK!

THE RATTLE OF SNAKES IS HEARD, LOUDLY.

CH-CHANK!

SSSSS

WHO GOES THERE??

TAX

FLEEING LIKE A RAT...

KLATH RATL

SUN IN A CAN, THE ONLY THING THAT THE LIGHT BEARER DREADS.

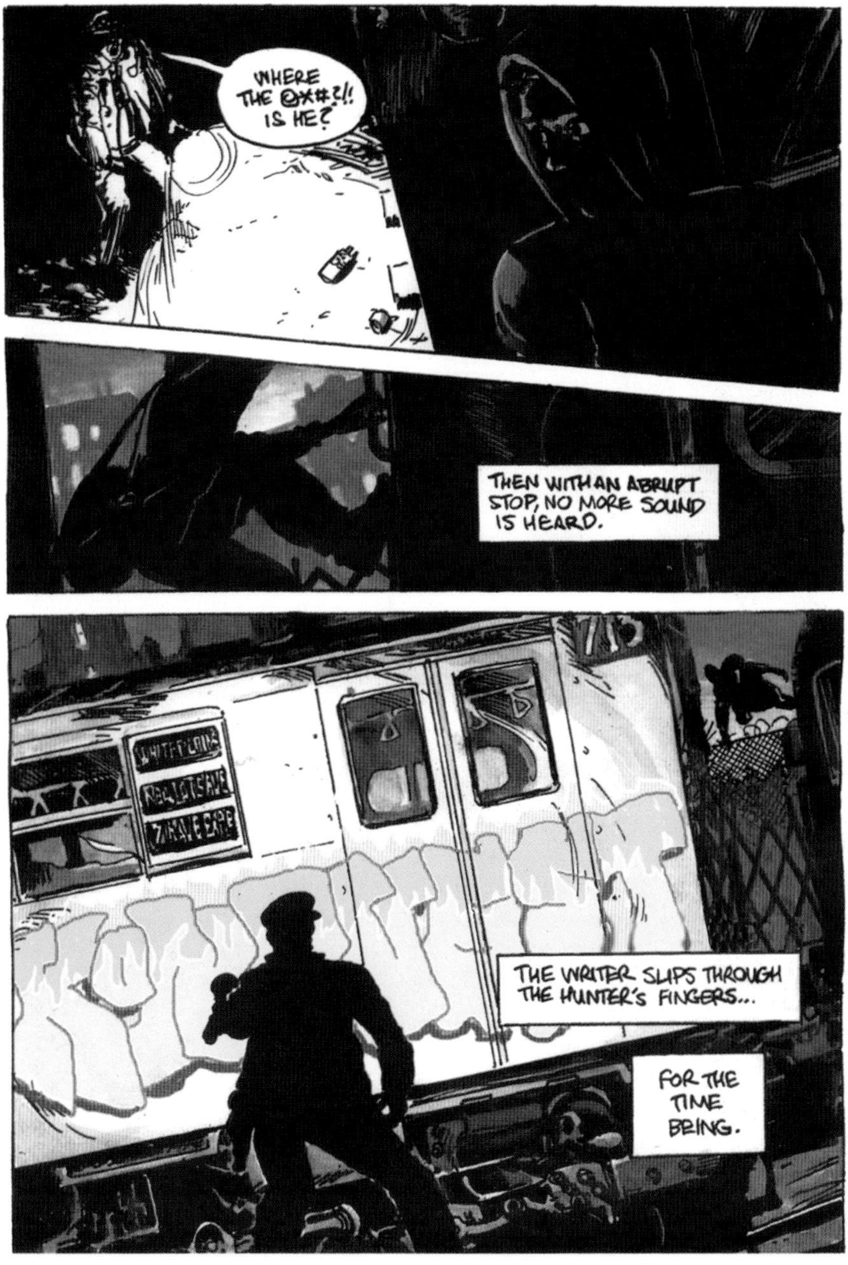
WHERE THE @X#?!! IS HE?
THEN WITH AN ABRUPT STOP, NO MORE SOUND IS HEARD.
THE WRITER SLIPS THROUGH THE HUNTER'S FINGERS...
FOR THE TIME BEING.

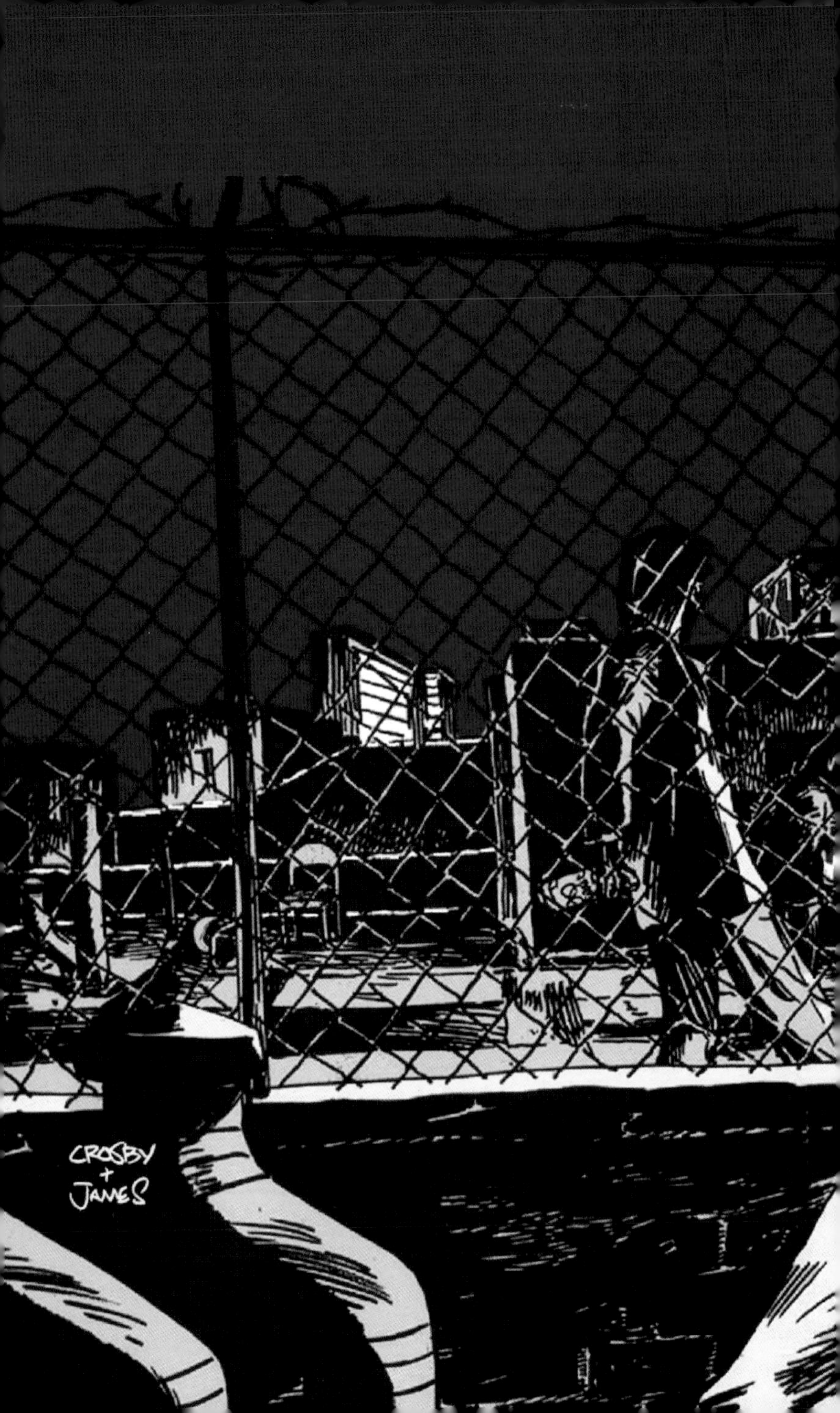
CROSBY
+
JAMES

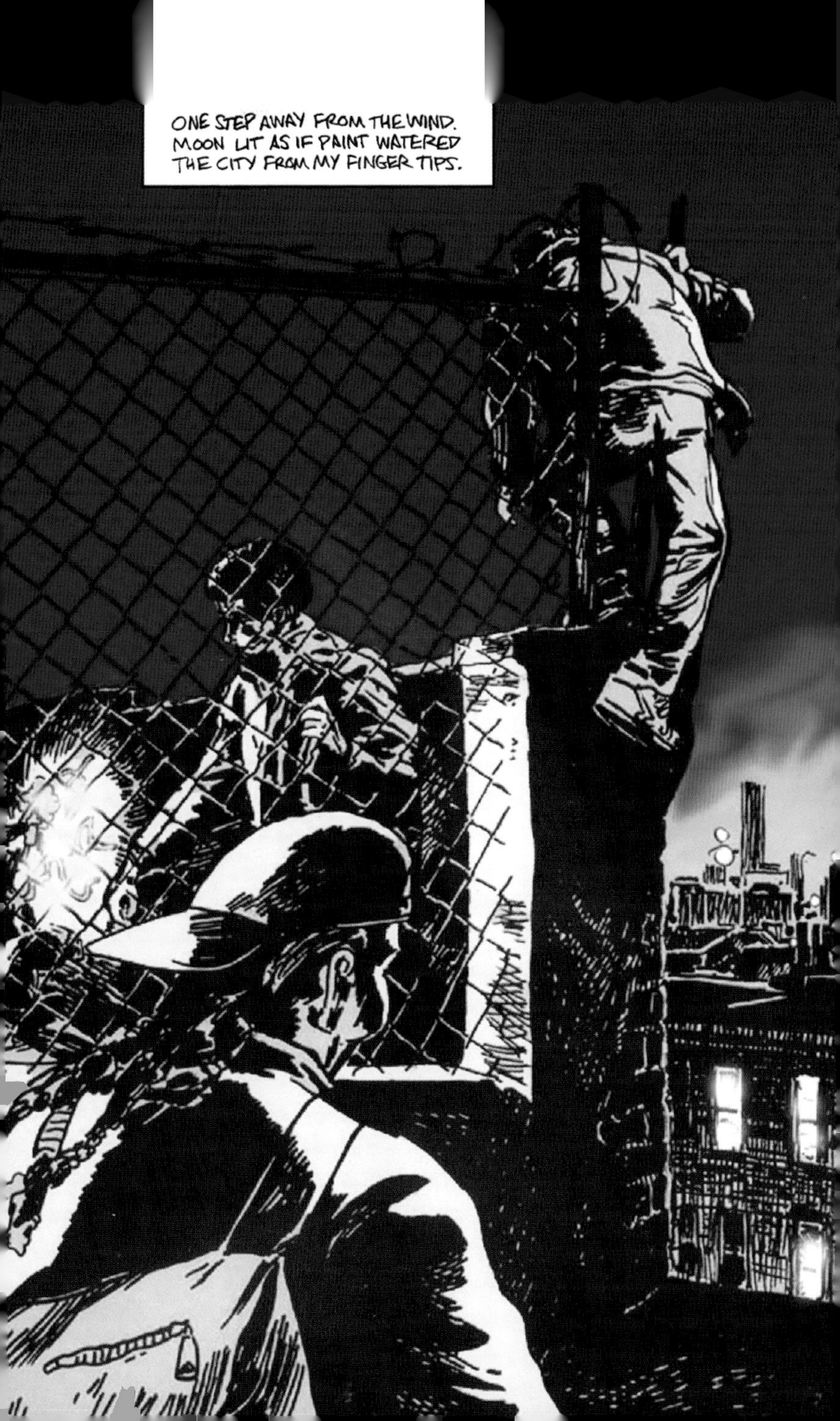
ONE STEP AWAY FROM THE WIND. MOON LIT AS IF PAINT WATERED THE CITY FROM MY FINGER TIPS.

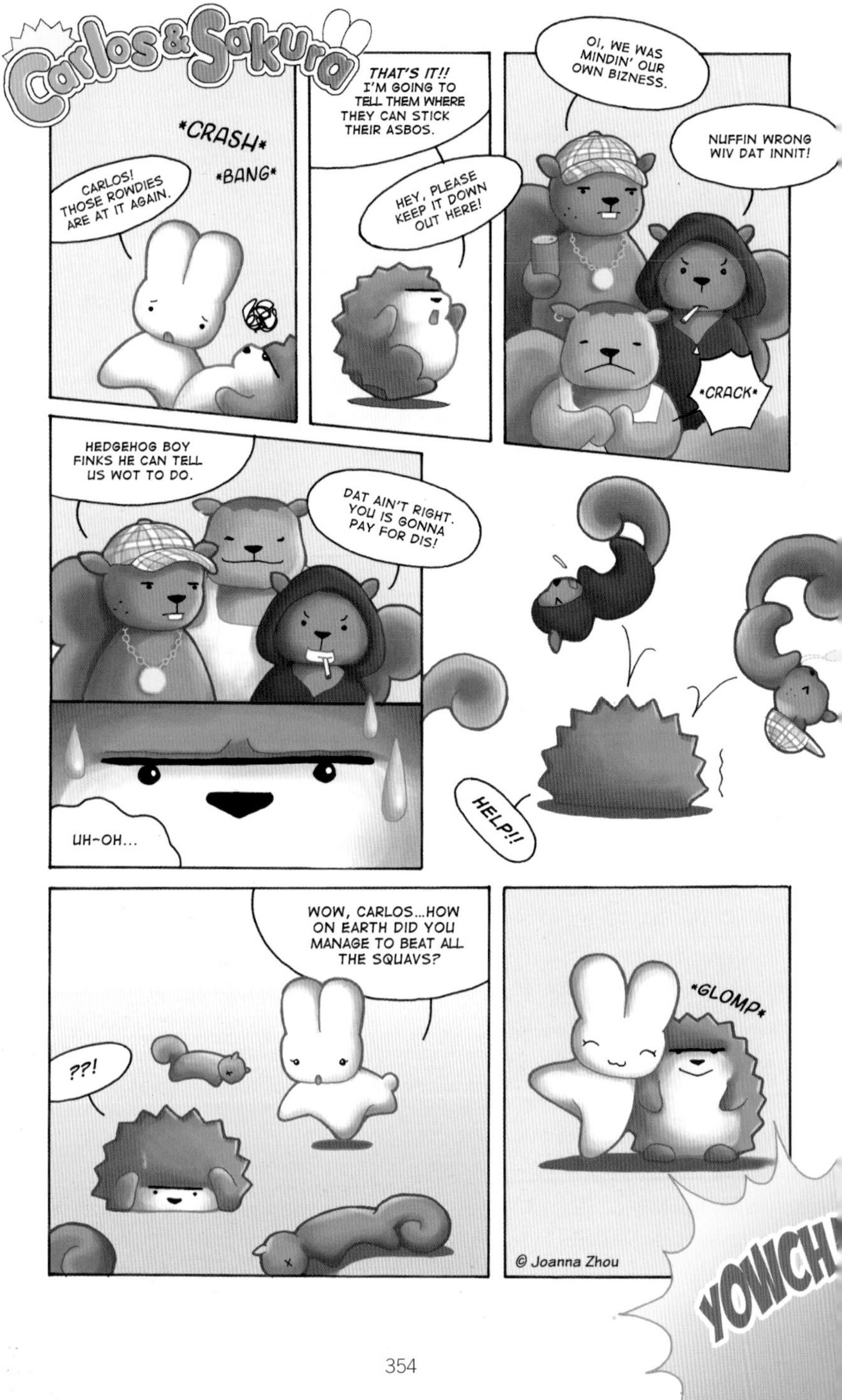

Carlos & Sakura
CRASH
BANG
CARLOS! THOSE ROWDIES ARE AT IT AGAIN.
THAT'S IT!! I'M GOING TO TELL THEM WHERE THEY CAN STICK THEIR ASBOS.
HEY, PLEASE KEEP IT DOWN OUT HERE!
OI, WE WAS MINDIN' OUR OWN BIZNESS.
NUFFIN WRONG WIV DAT INNIT!
CRACK
HEDGEHOG BOY FINKS HE CAN TELL US WOT TO DO.
DAT AIN'T RIGHT. YOU IS GONNA PAY FOR DIS!
UH-OH...
HELP!!
WOW, CARLOS...HOW ON EARTH DID YOU MANAGE TO BEAT ALL THE SQUAVS?
??!
GLOMP
© Joanna Zhou
YOWCH!

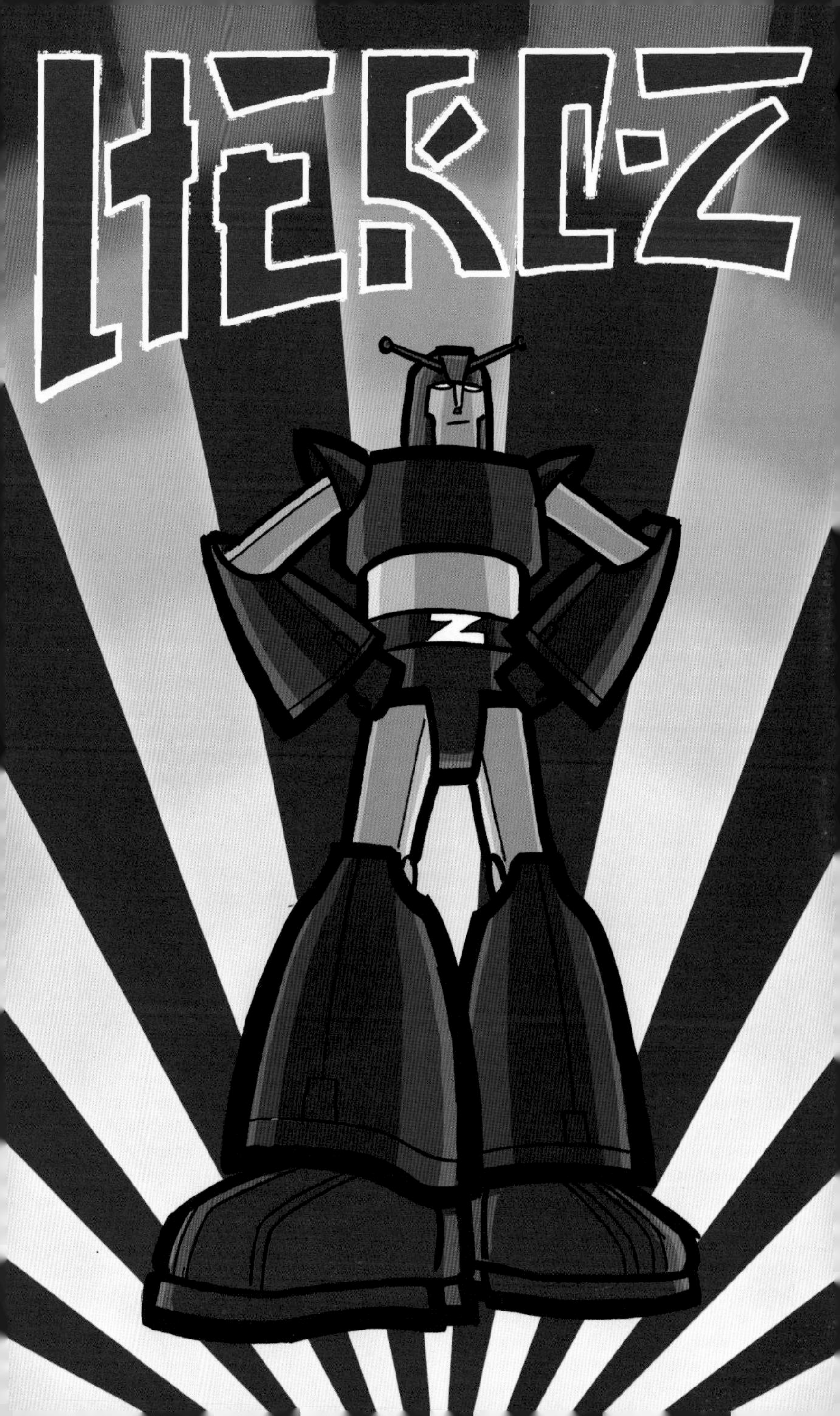
HERO-Z
Z

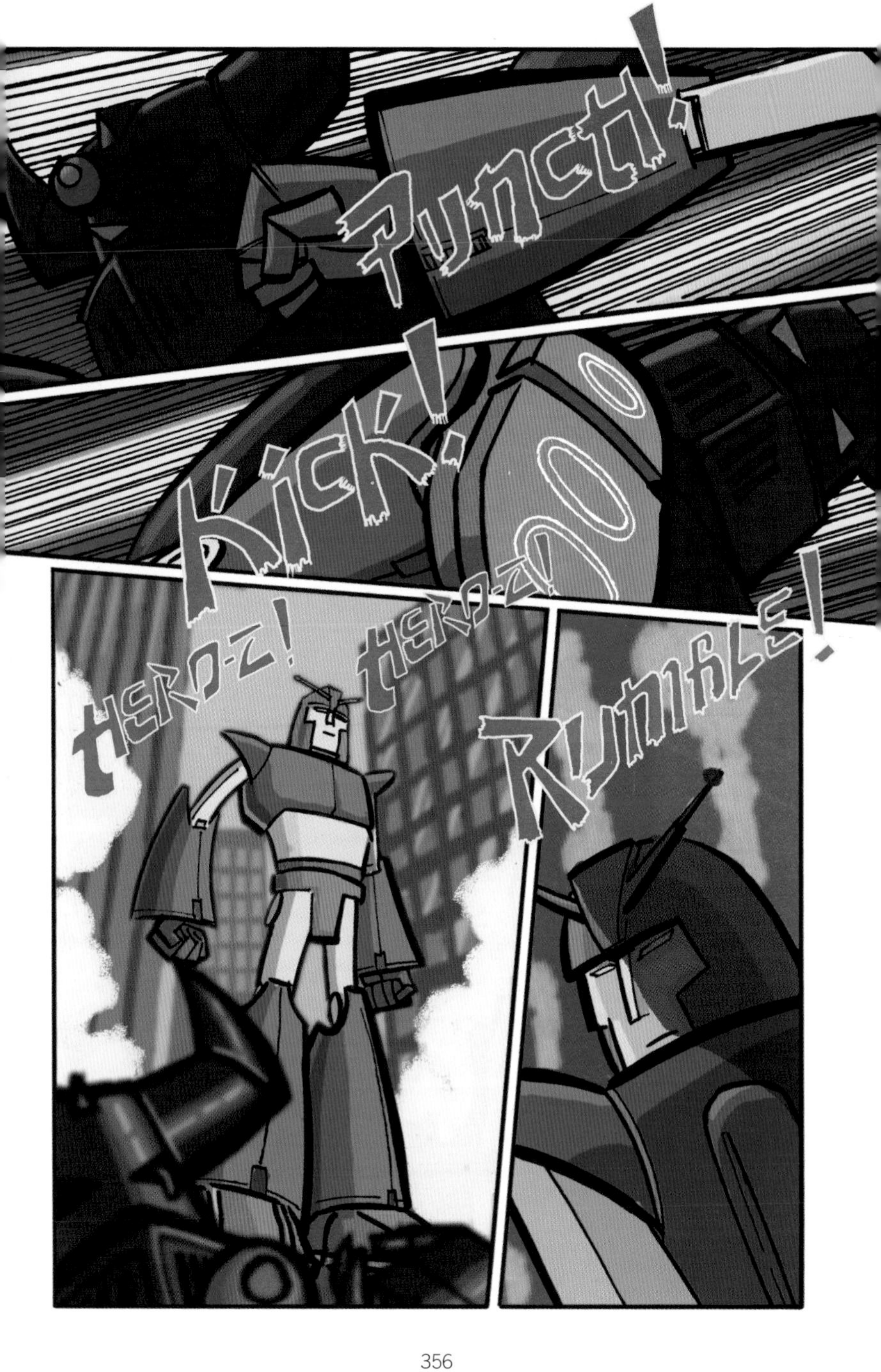
PUNCH!
KICK!
HERO-Z! HERO-Z!
RUMBLE!

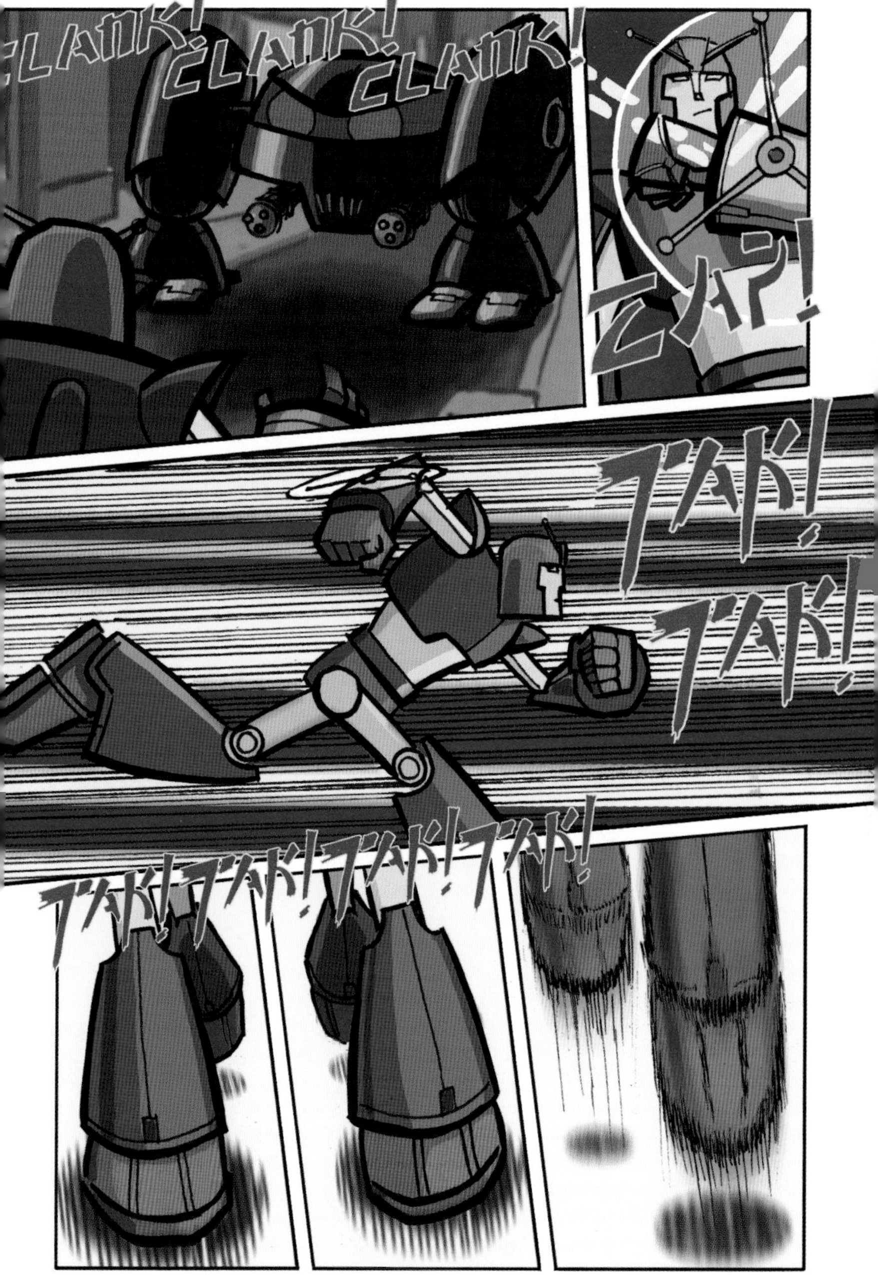
CLANK! CLANK! CLANK!

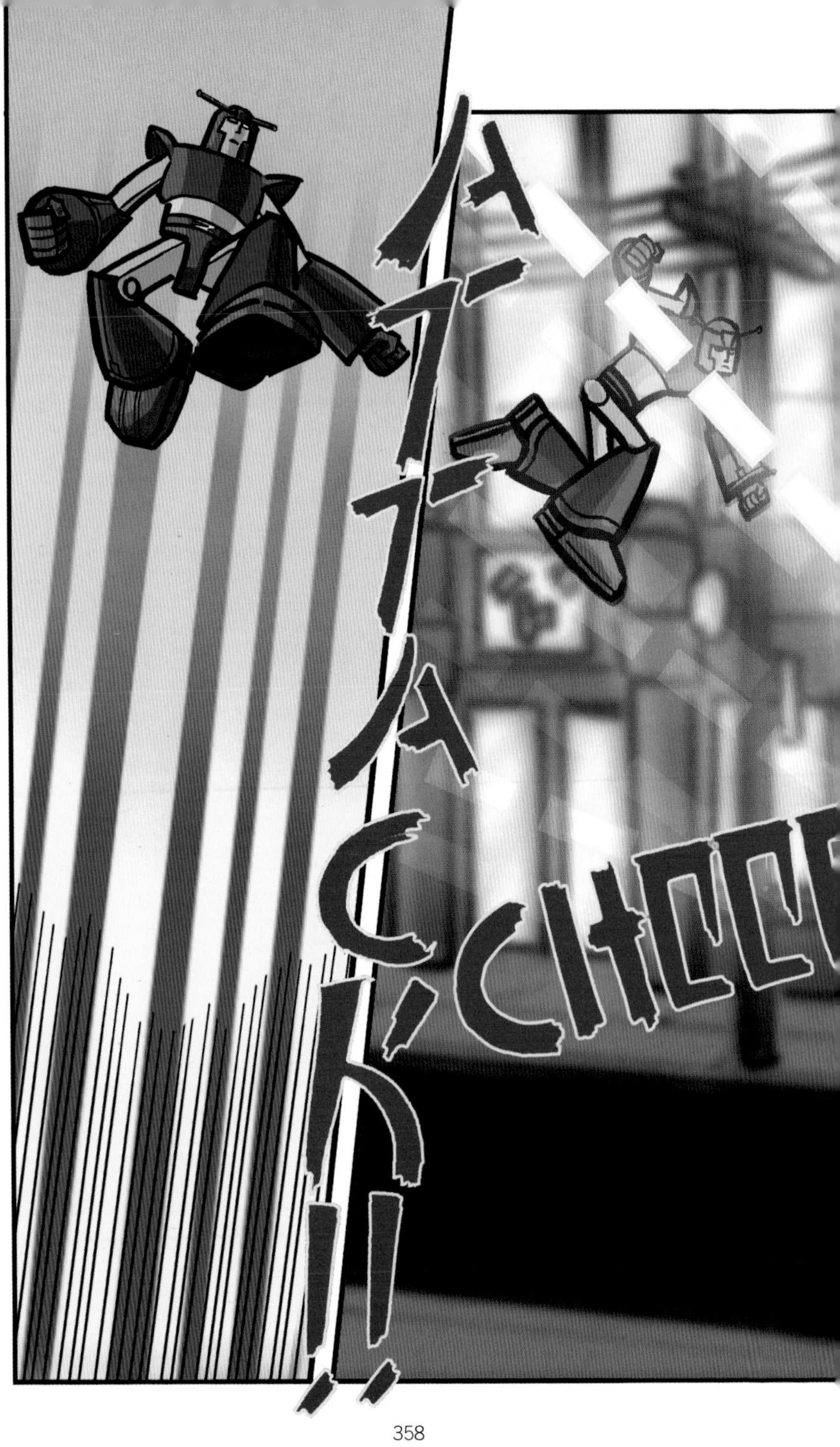

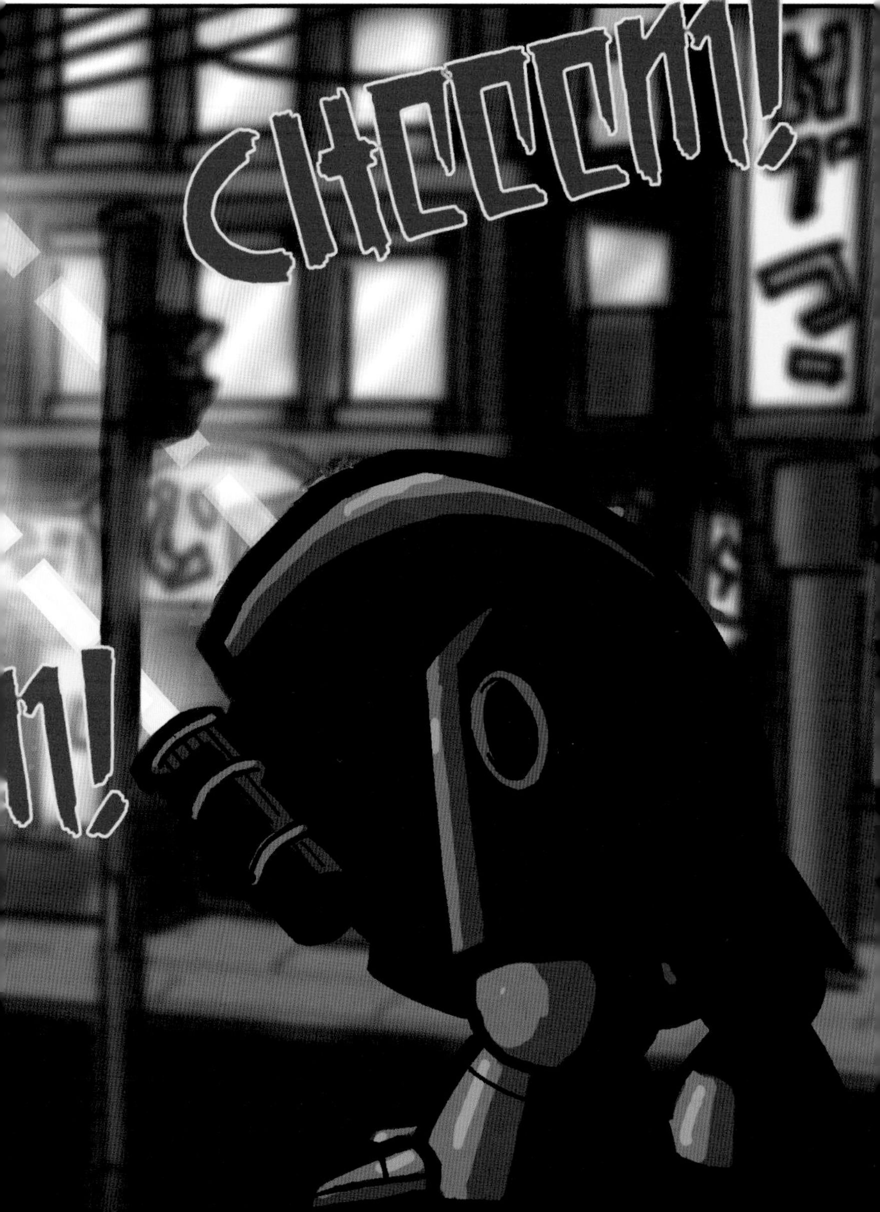
CHOOOM!

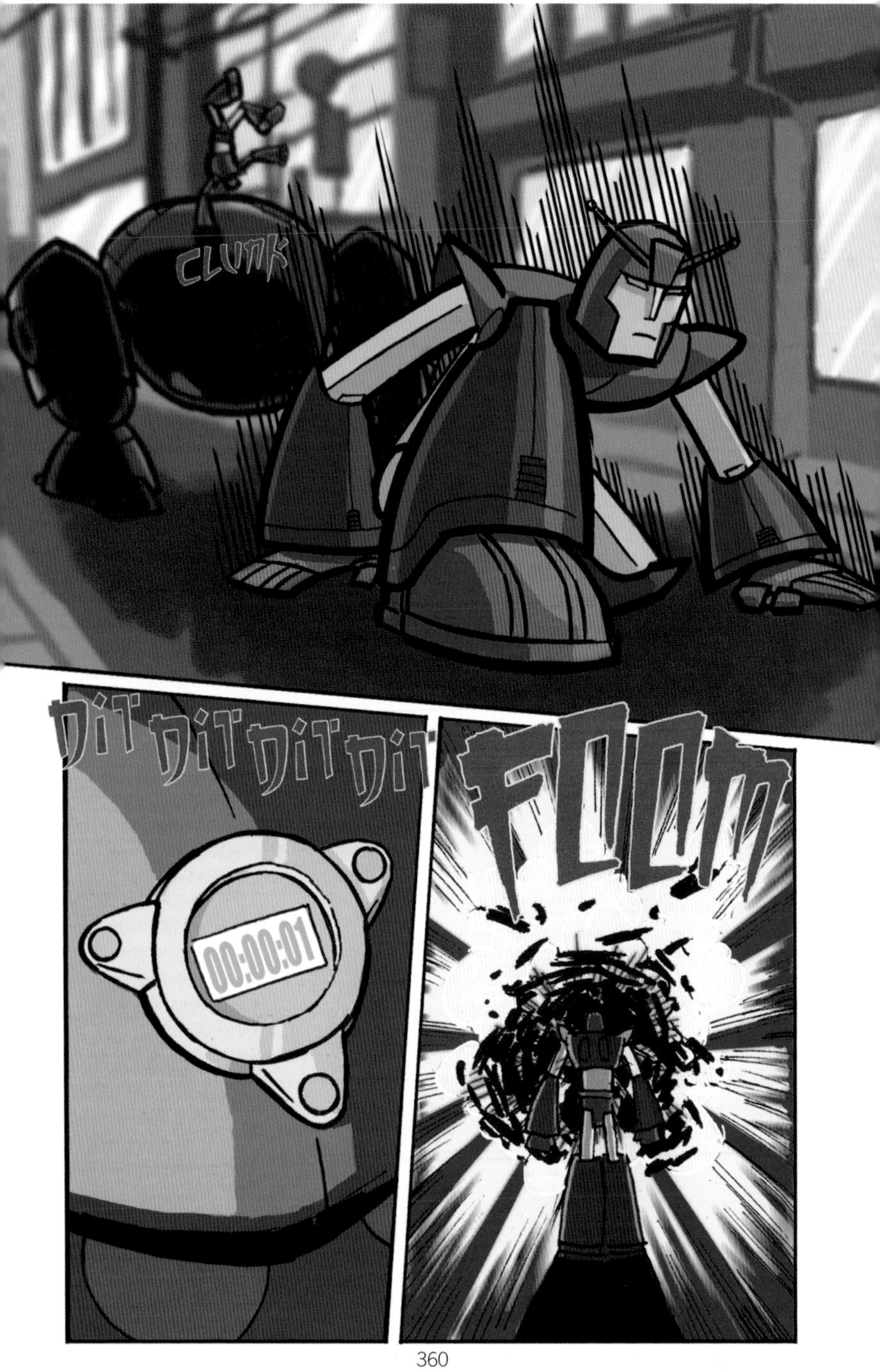
CLUNK
DIT DIT DIT DIT
00:00:01
FOOM

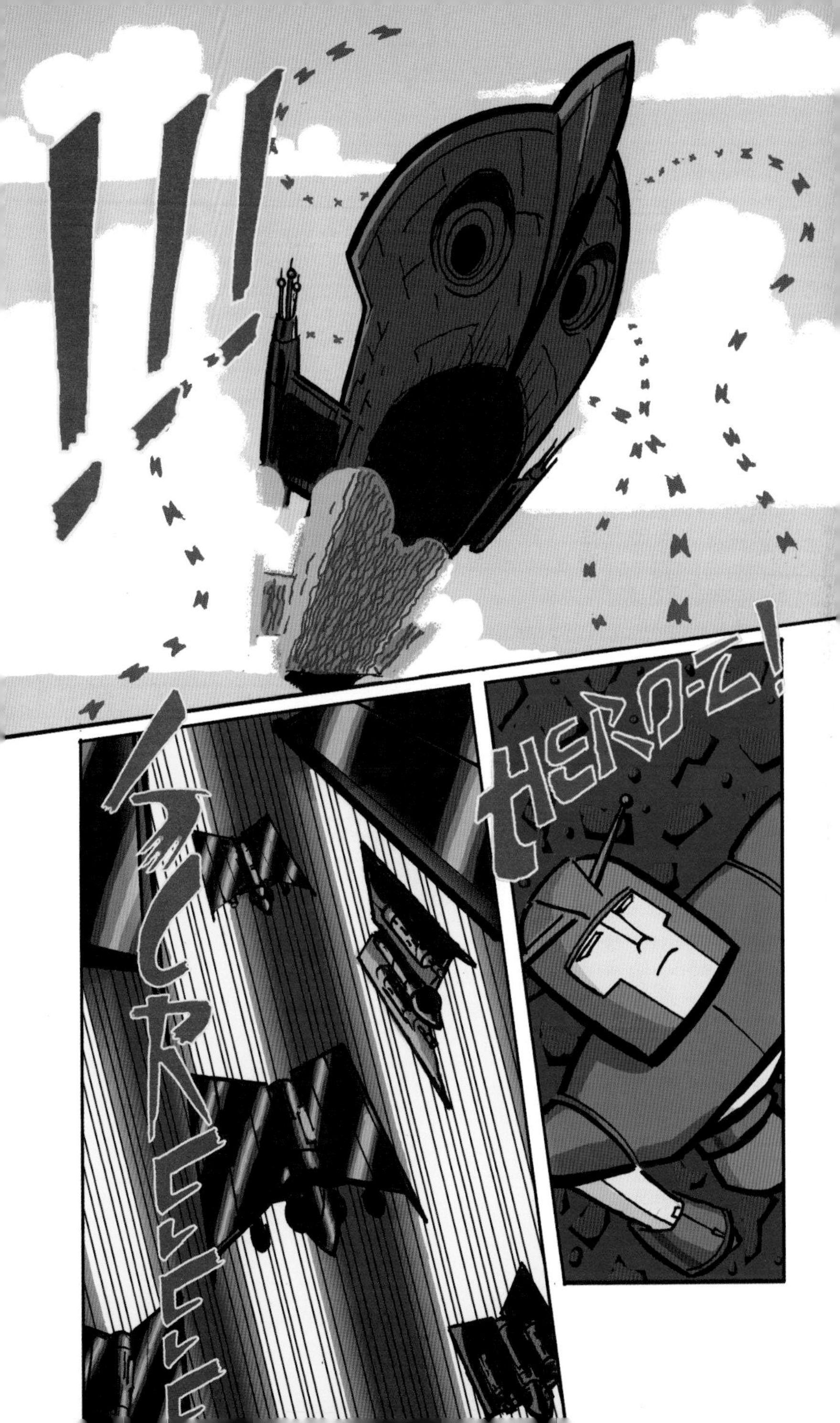
!!!
HERO-Z!

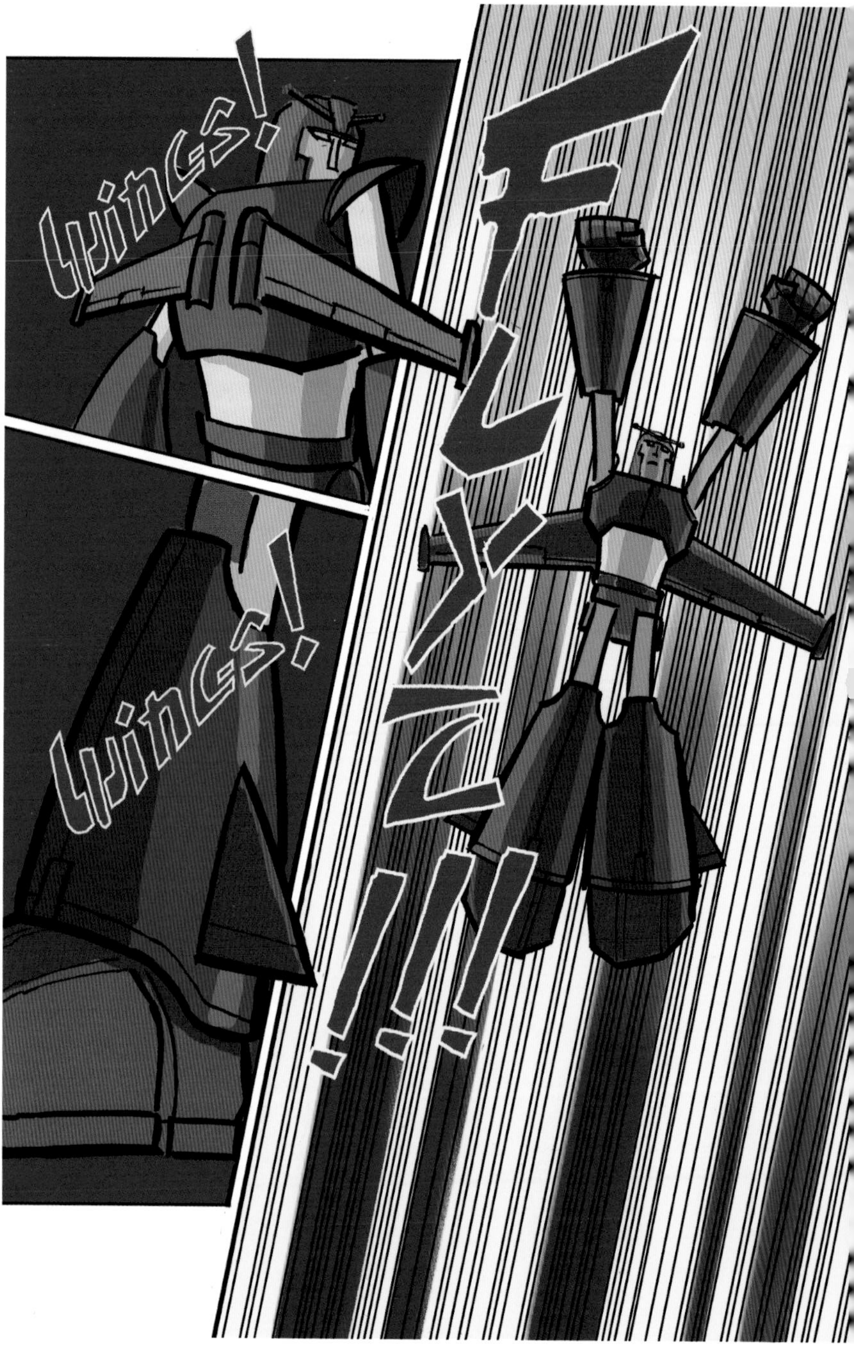
Wings!
Wings!
FLY!!!!

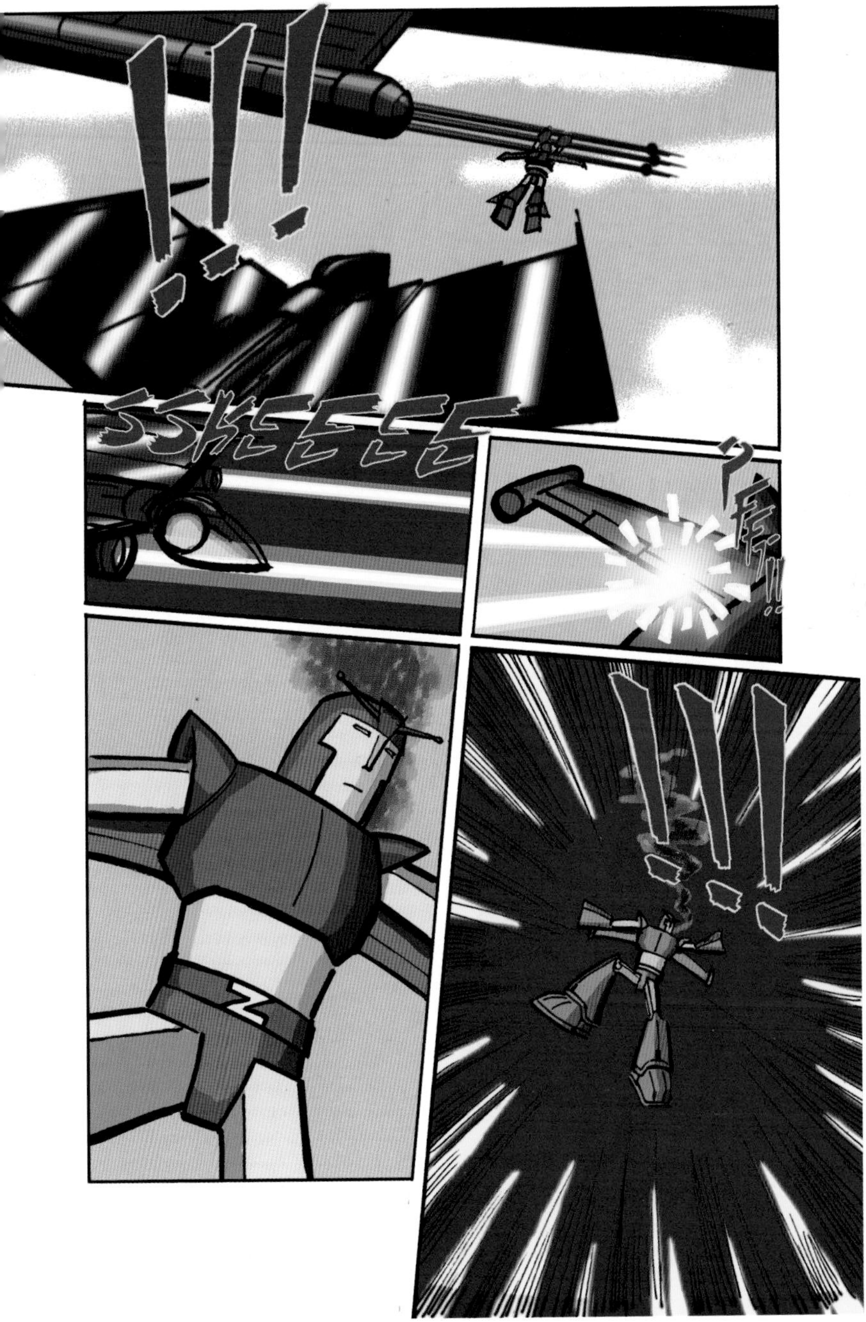
!!!
SSKEEEEE
!!
!!!

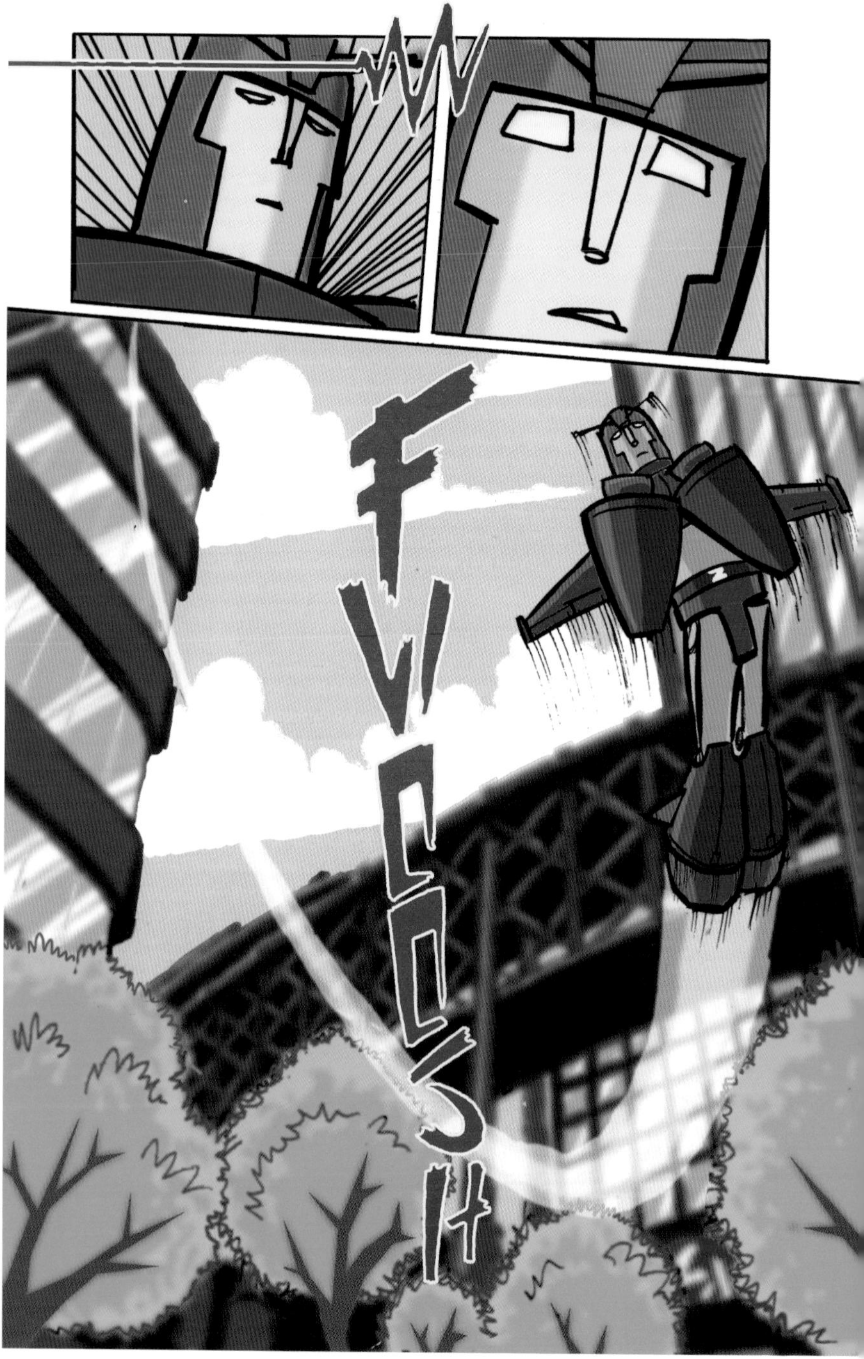
FWOOSH

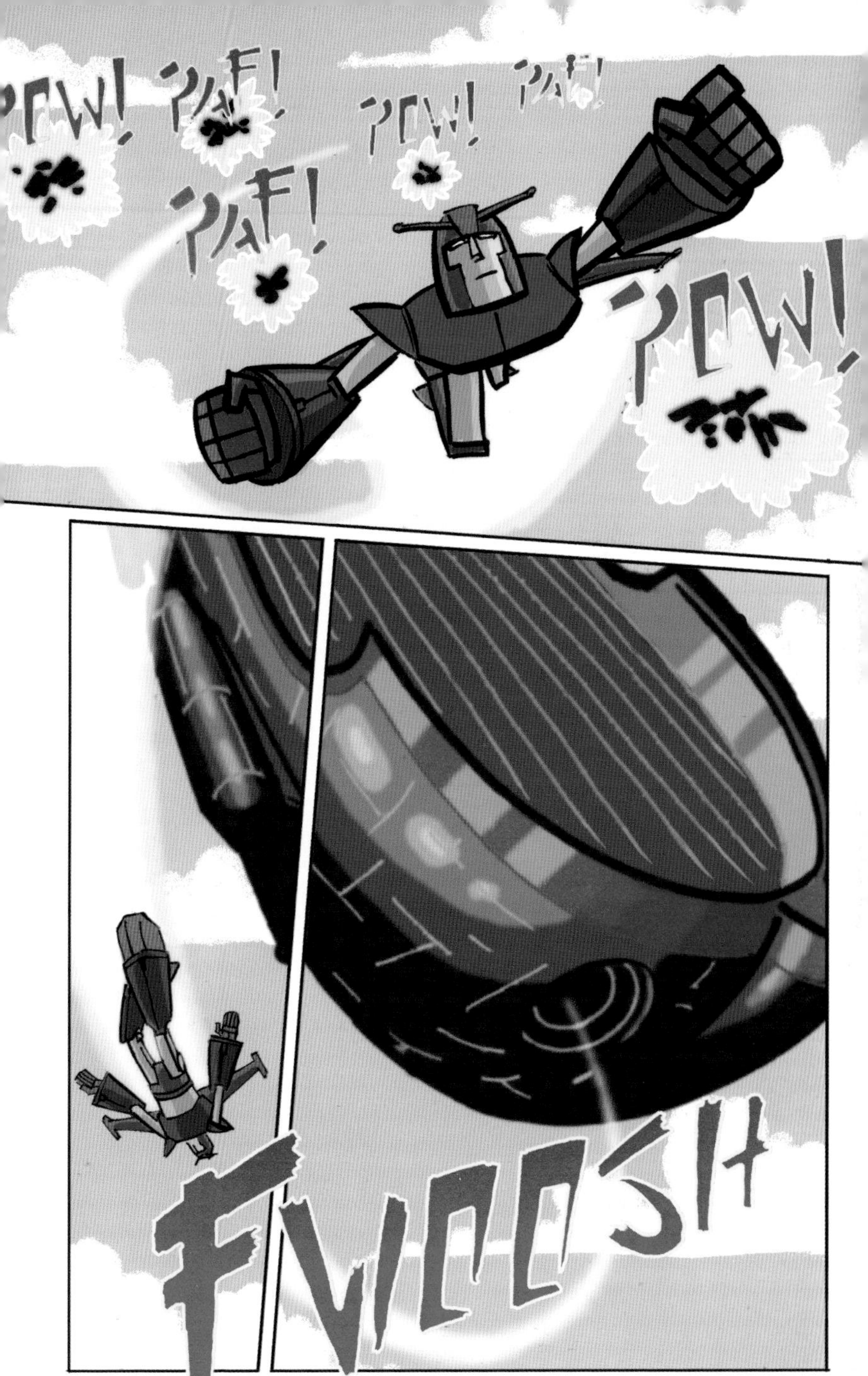
POW!
PAF!
POW!
PAF!
PAF!
POW!
FWOOSH

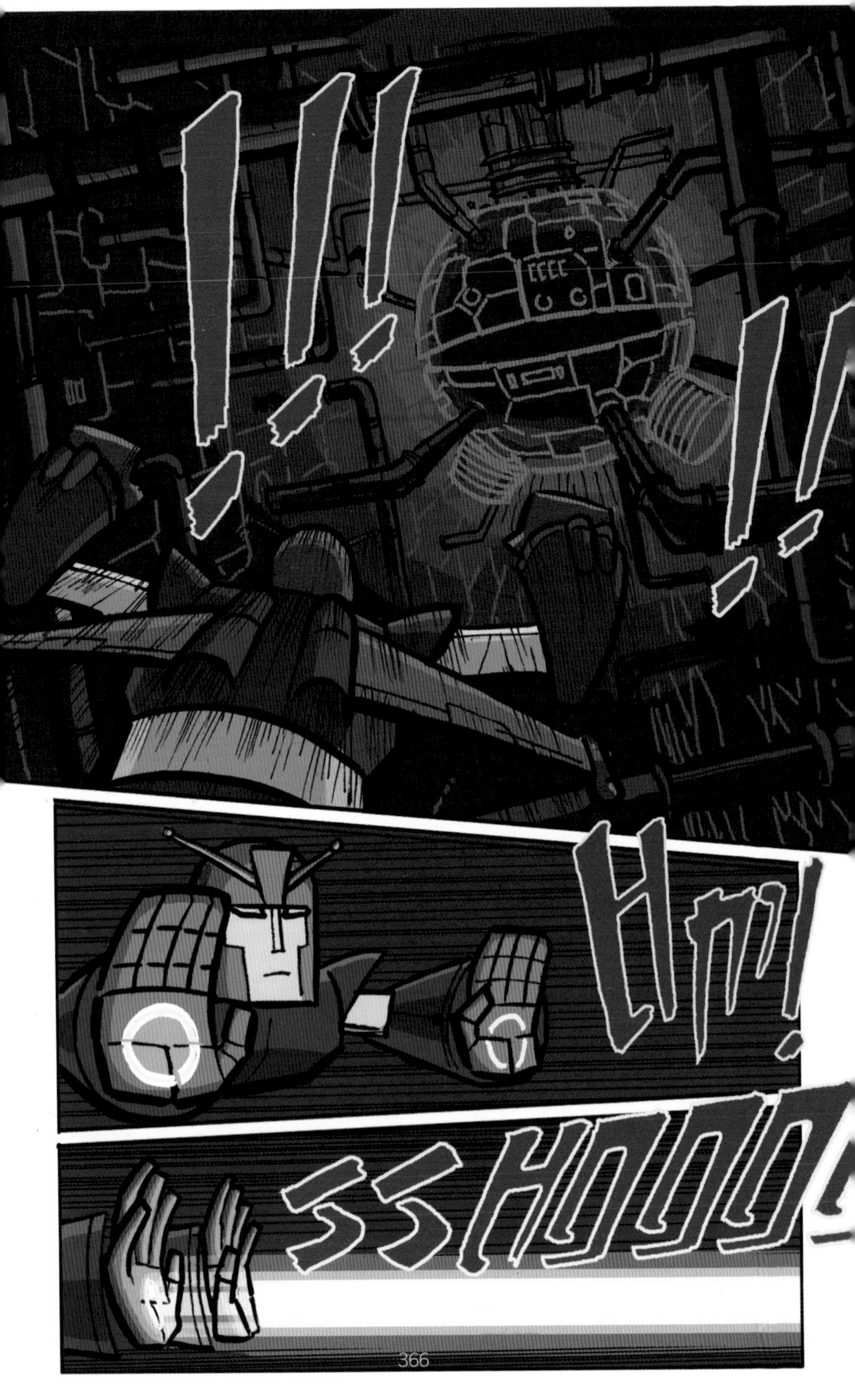
!!!
!!
HM!
SSHOOO

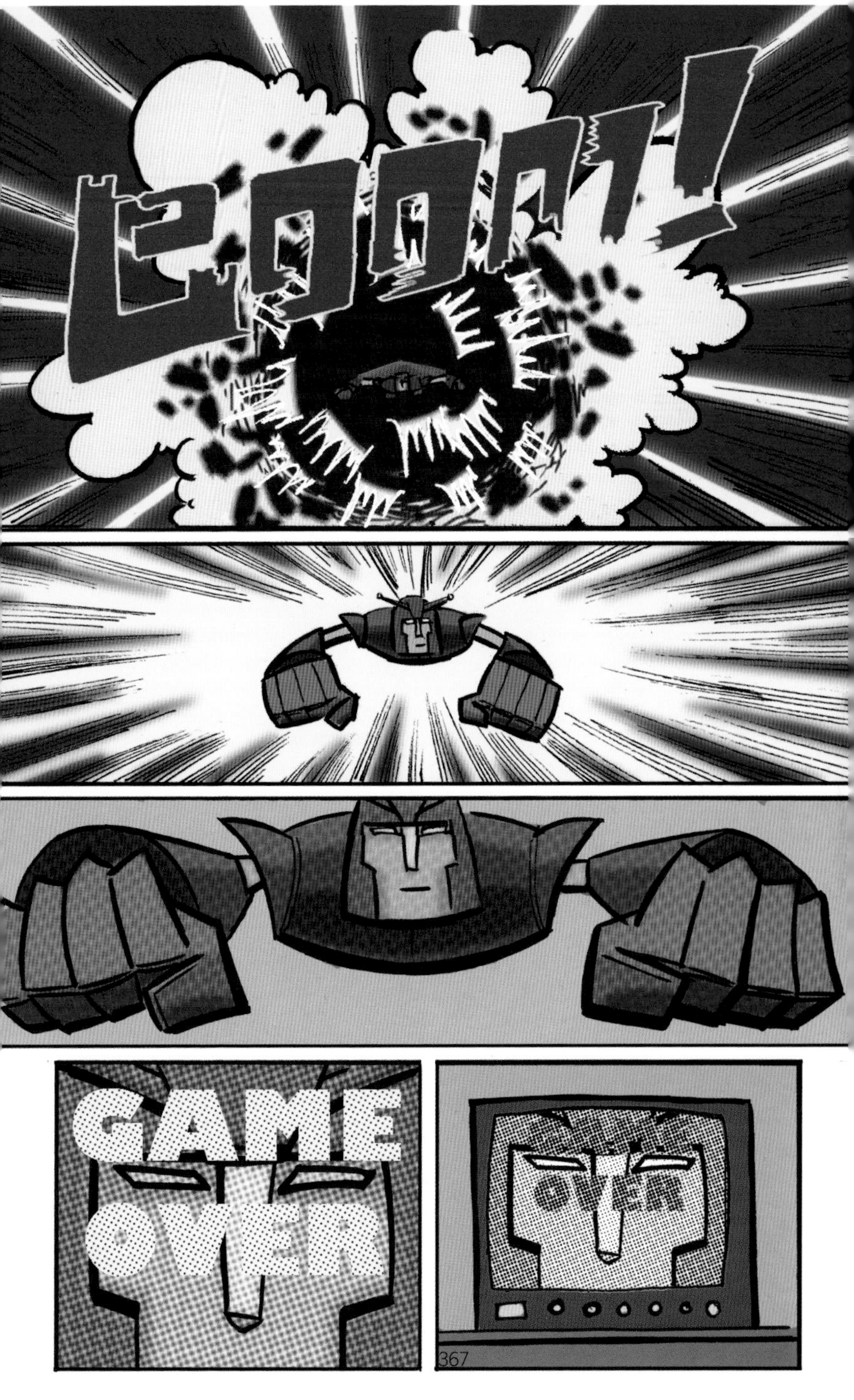
BOOM!
GAME OVER
OVER

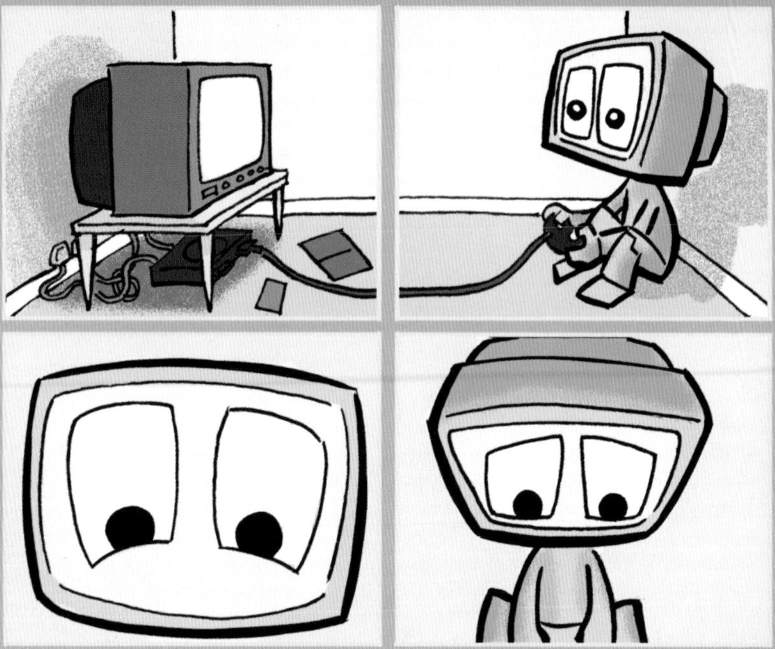

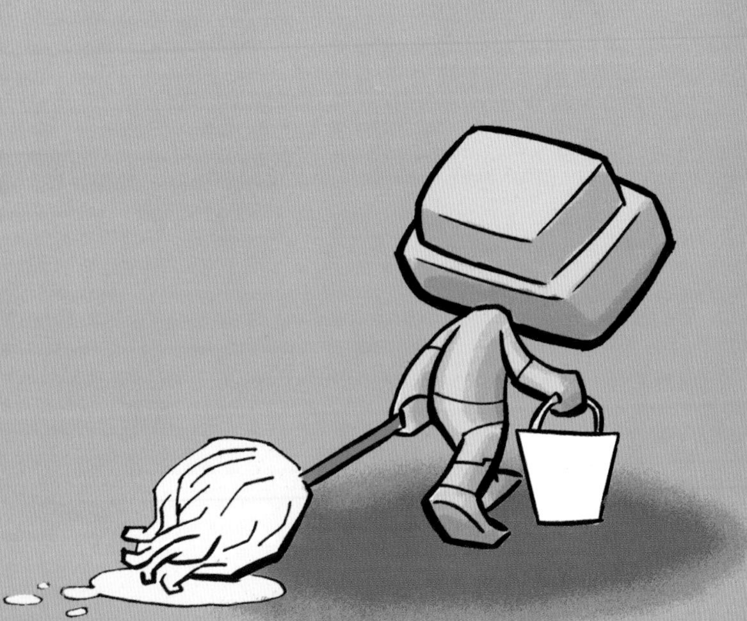

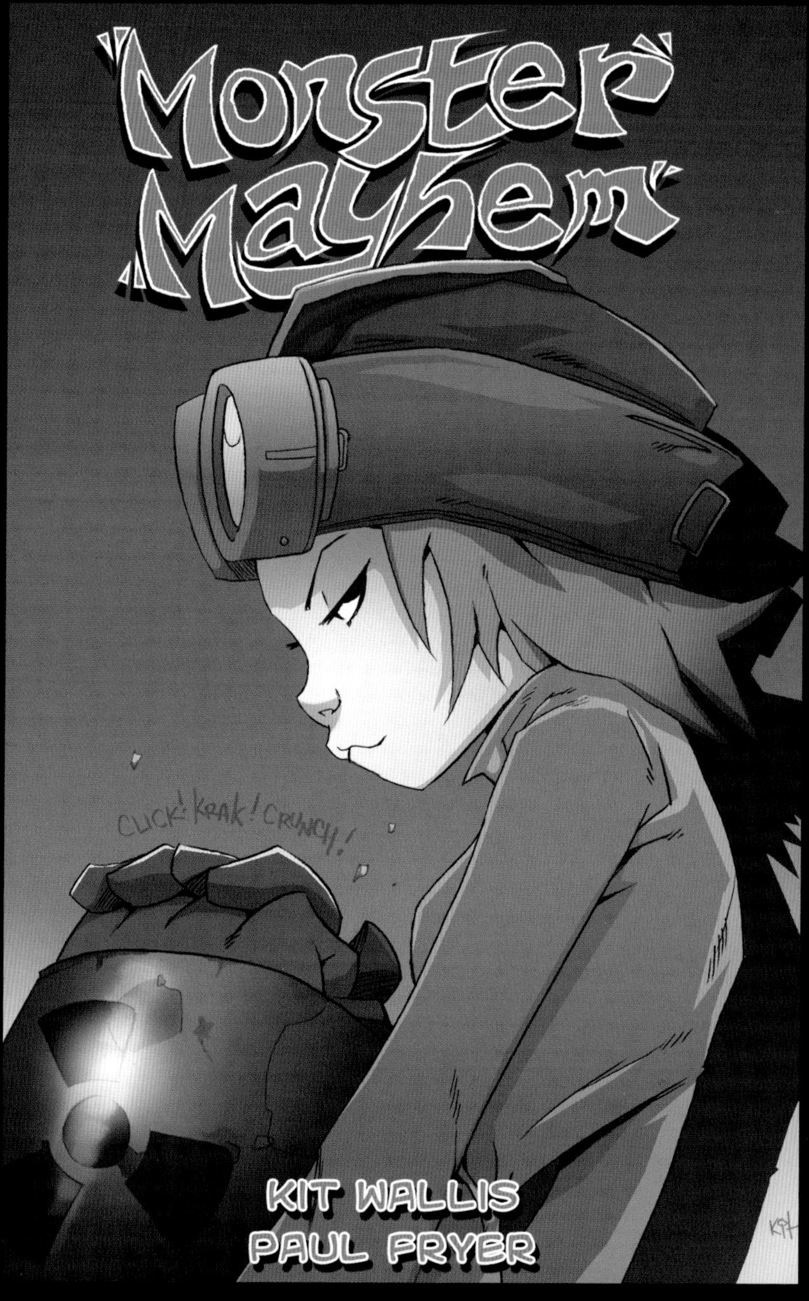
Monster Mayhem
CLICK! KRAK! CRUNCH!
KIT WALLIS
PAUL FRYER

MONSTER MAYHEM

Kit Wallis & Paul Fryer

Kit Wallis started making comics aged ten, photocopying his drawings and handing them out at school. Main influences are Jamie (*Tank Girl/Gorillaz*) Hewlett, Abe Yoshitoshi, Koji Morimoto, Paul Pope and Tatsuyuki Tanaka.

Monster Club, his own creation, was Kit's first professionally published work, followed by *Wonderland* (Image), *Breathe* (Markosia), and many others. His colourful style first caught our attention as an entrant to IMAF 2005. We're delighted to finally be able to show it off here, with a brand new monsterwork.

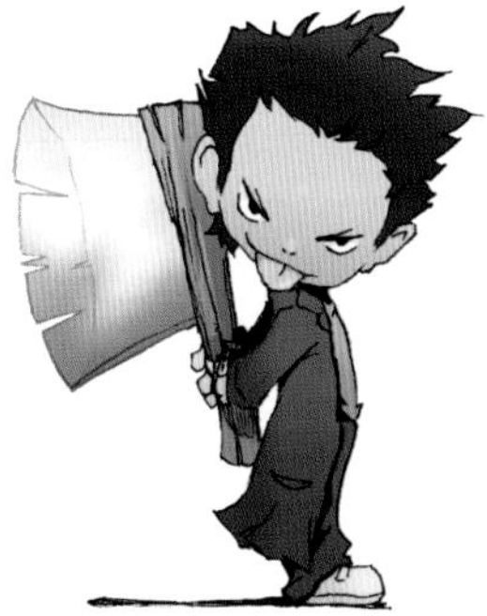

kitwallis@hotmail.com
www.kitwallis.com

"Just wanna say cheers to Paul for the story and colouring help!" says Kit, "Cheers!"

Paul Fryer lists Yukito Kishiro and Erika Sakurazawa among his "thieving elements" (influences), as well as Bill (*Calvin & Hobbes*) Watterson and Mike (*Hellboy*) Mignola. "I firmly believe that comics have the potential to heal the ozone layer and patch up global disagreements," declares Paul. "And that they glow in the dark when you're not looking. 'Cos comics are awesome, right?" :D

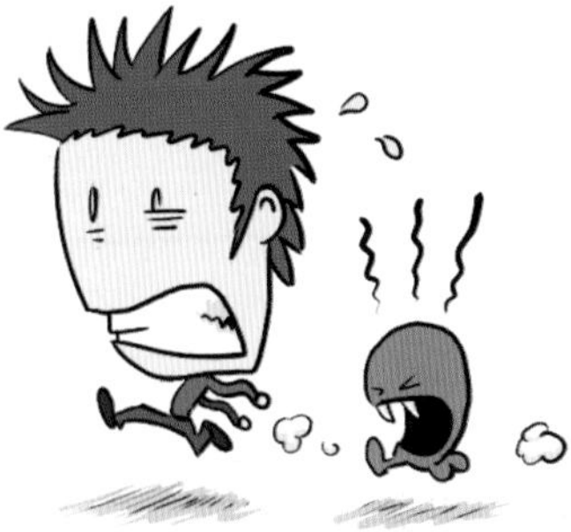

www.greatvagueness.co.uk

Says Paul: "I'd like to dedicate a big jug of beer to Kit for letting me stomp around in his story like some kinda pencil Godzilla! Wuargh! – pf!"

(Either that last bit is Paul signing off, or he just farted.)

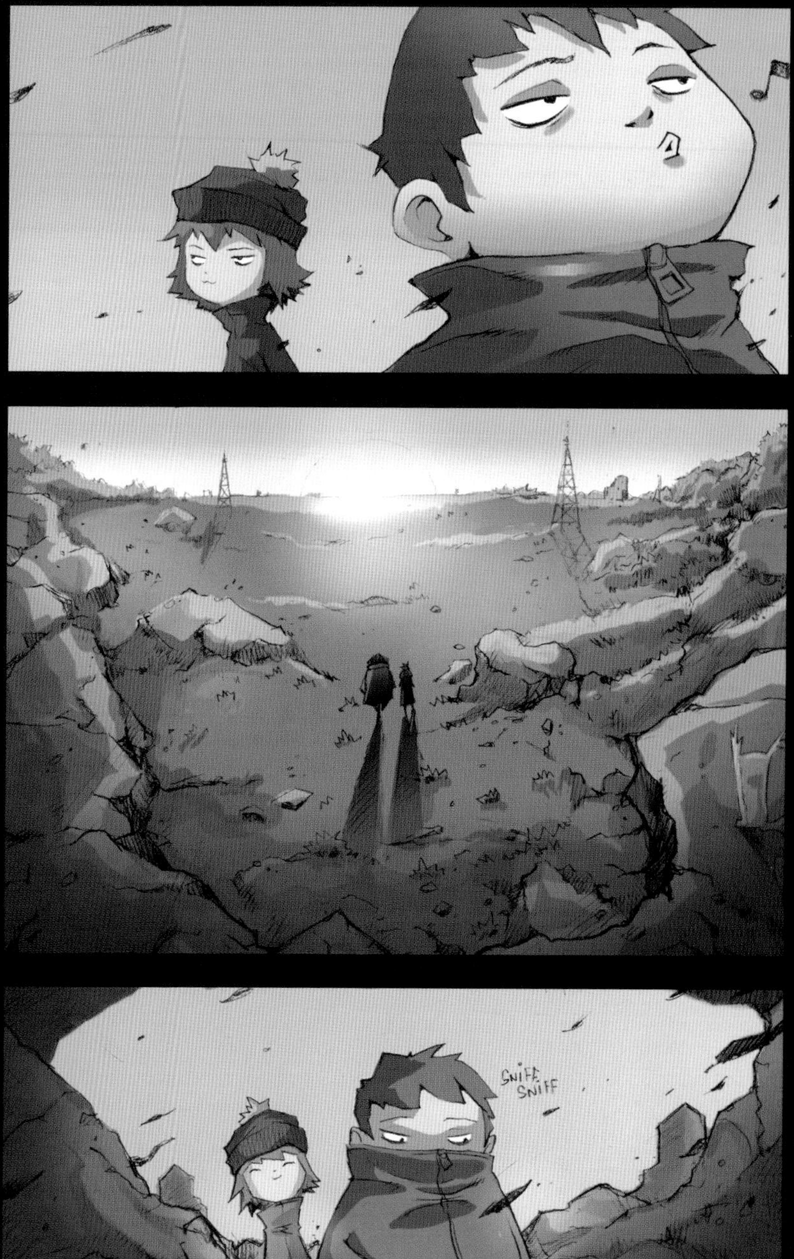
SNIFF SNIFF

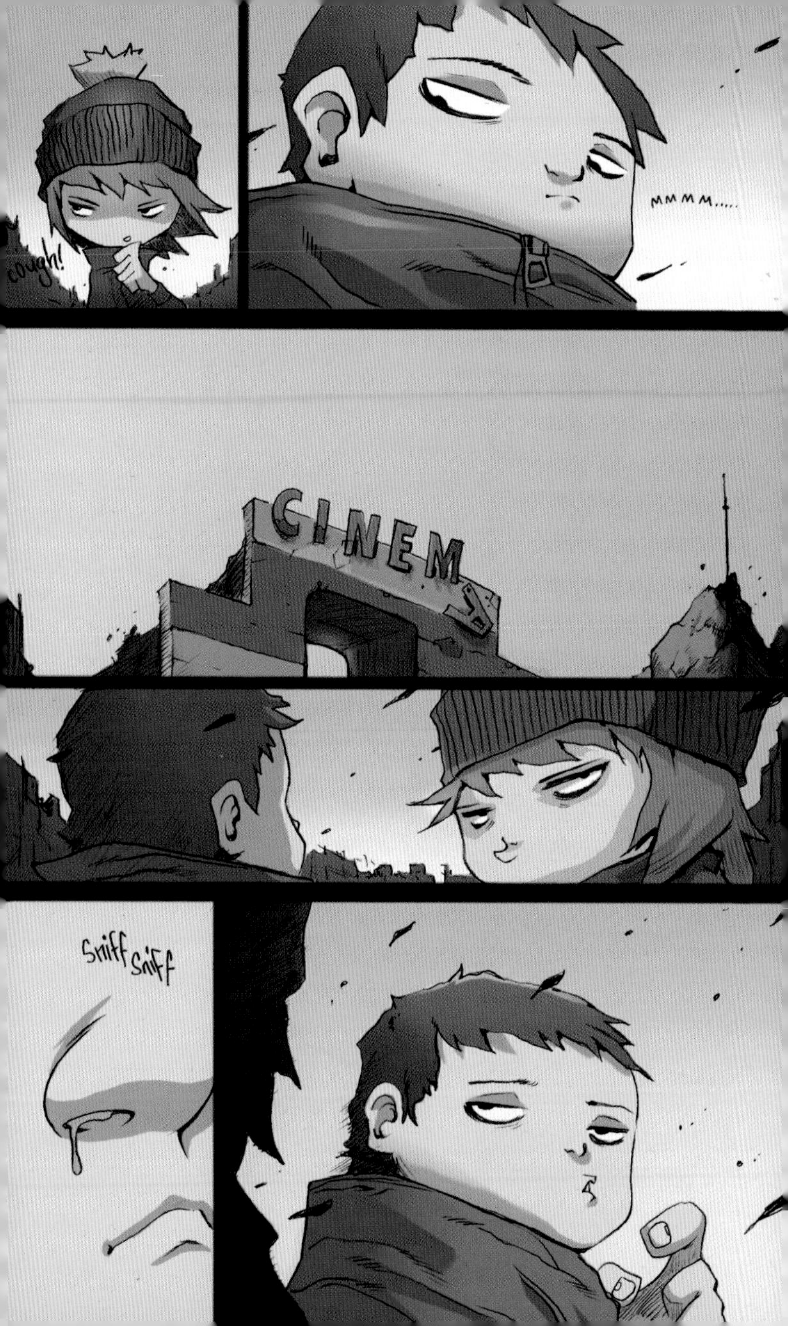
cough!
MMMM.....
CINEM
Sniff Sniff

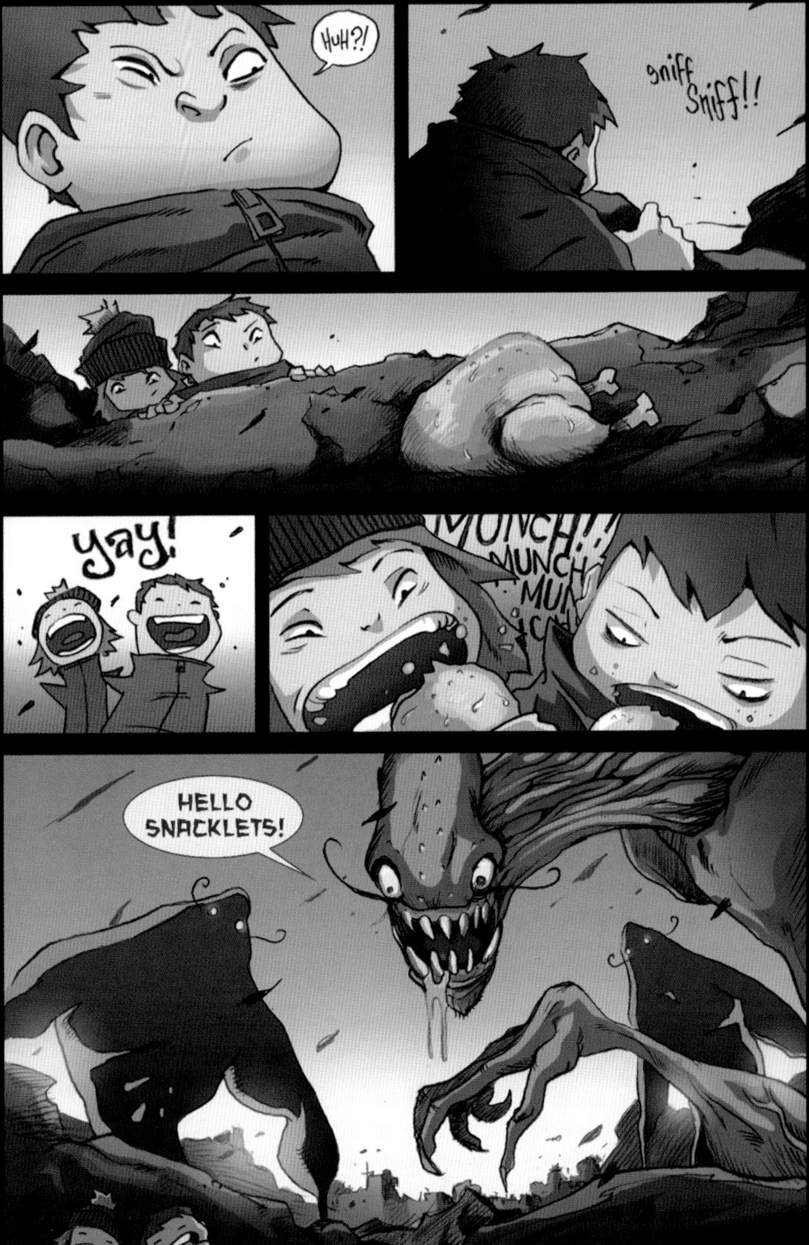
HUH?!
sniff Sniff!!
yay!
MUNCH!! MUNCH MUN
HELLO SNACKLETS!

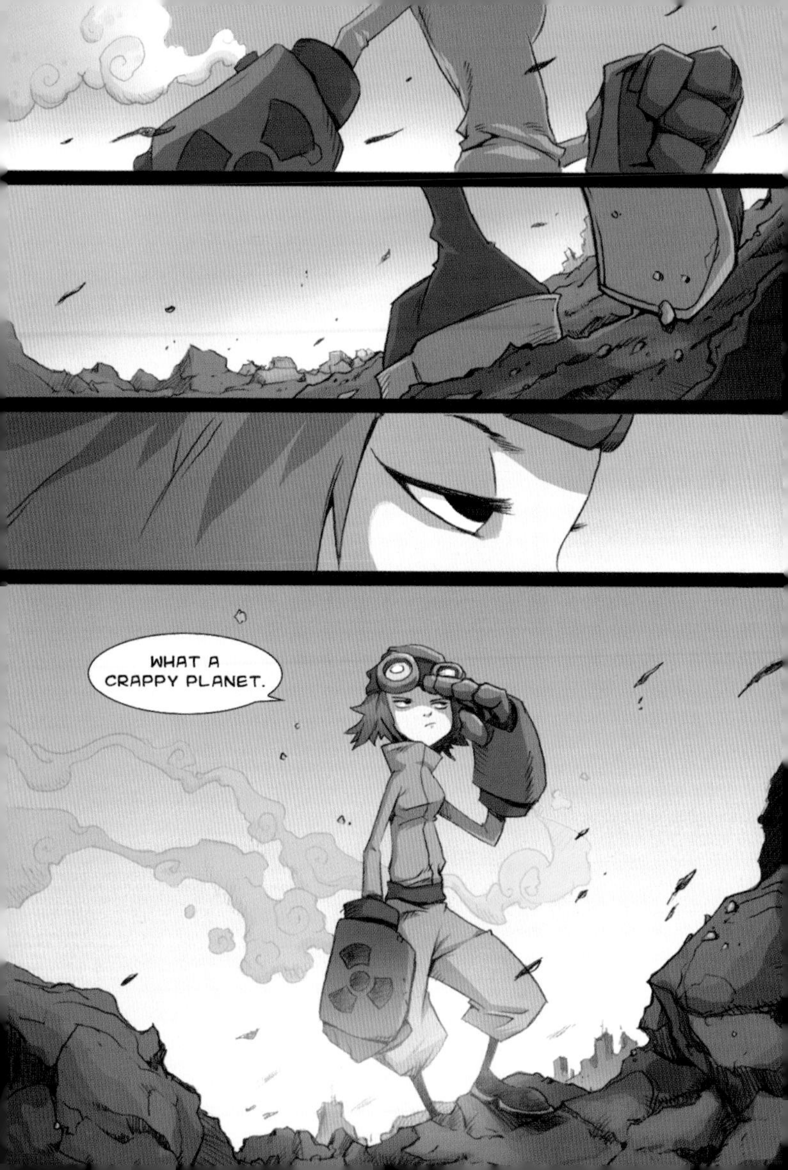
WHAT A CRAPPY PLANET.

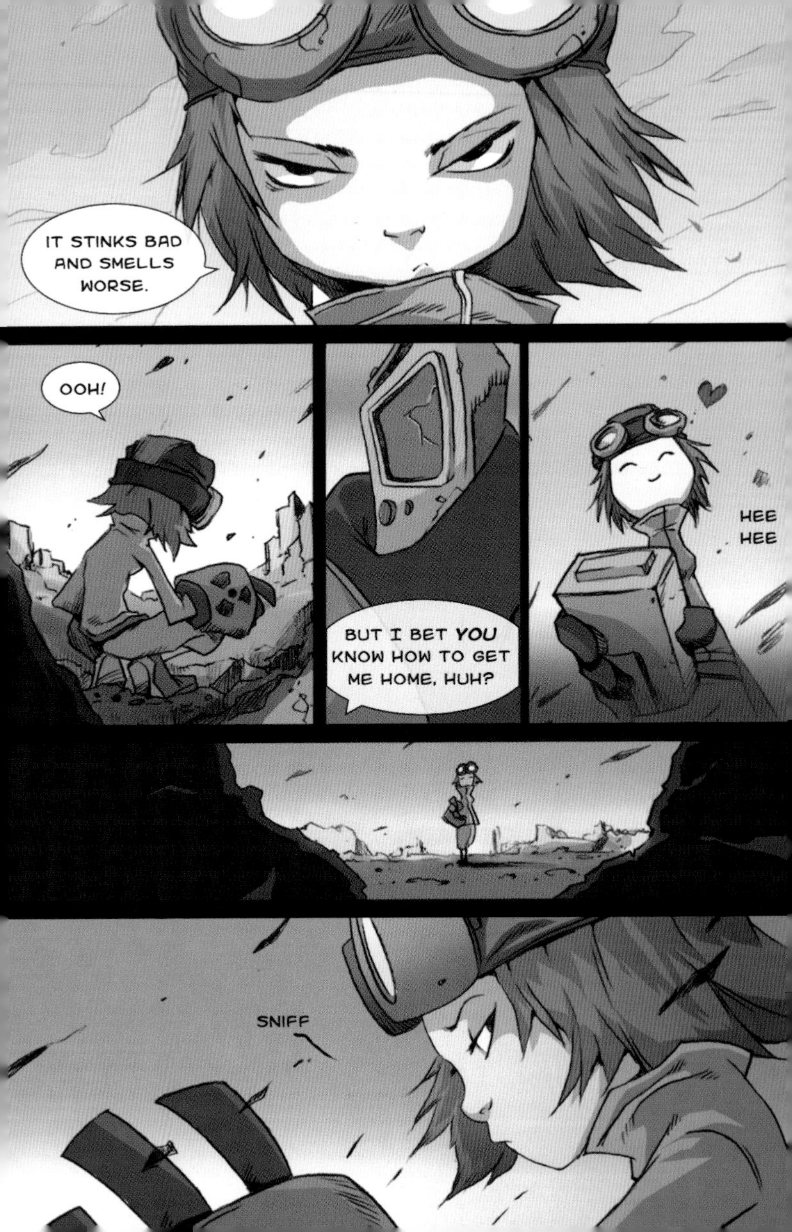

IT STINKS BAD AND SMELLS WORSE.
OOH!
BUT I BET *YOU* KNOW HOW TO GET ME HOME, HUH?
HEE HEE
SNIFF

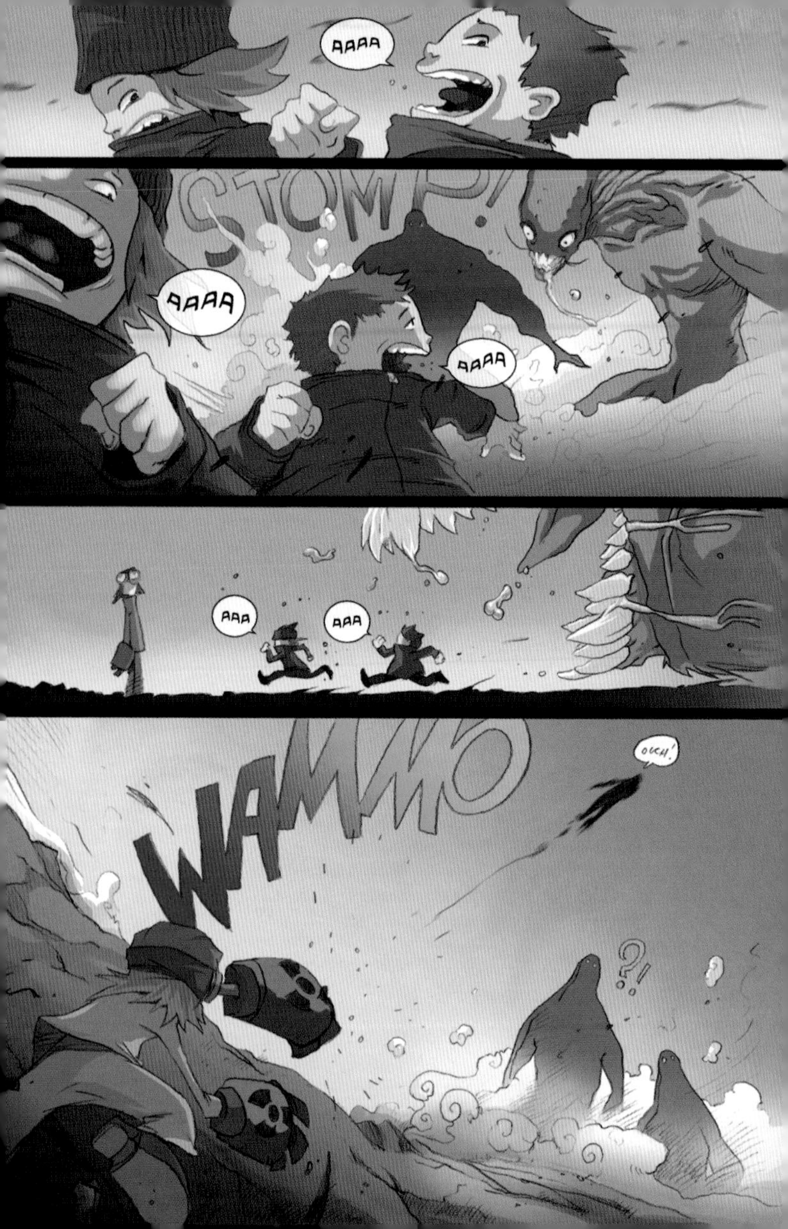
AAAA
STOMP!
AAAA
AAAA
AAA
AAA
WAMMO
OUCH!
?!

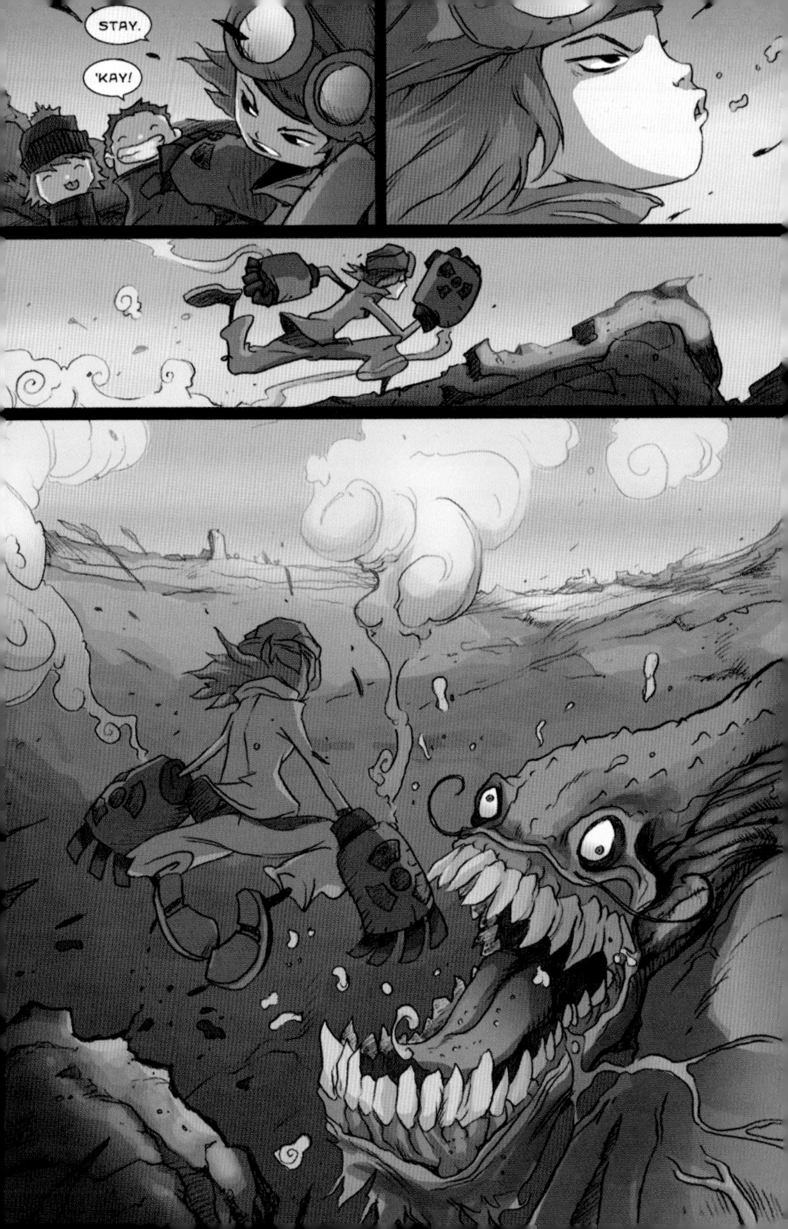
STAY.
'KAY!

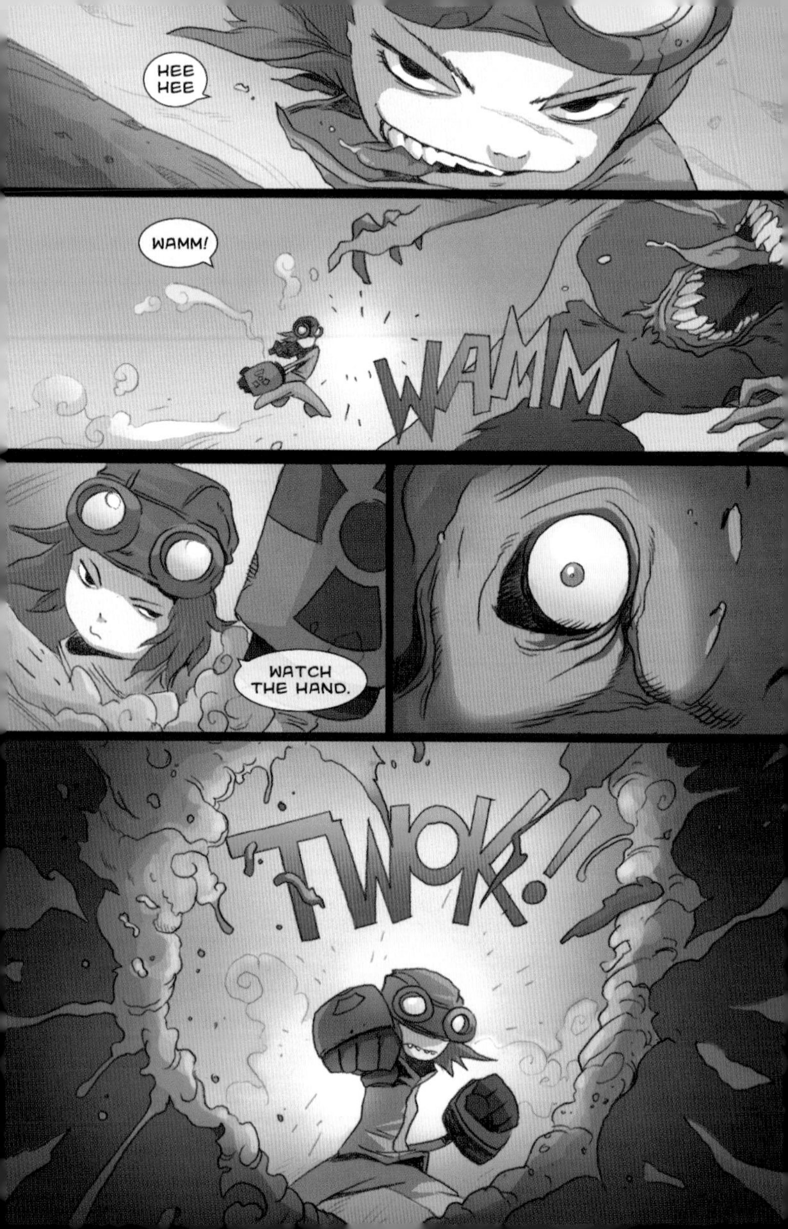
HEE HEE
WAMM!
WAMM
WATCH THE HAND.
TWOK!!

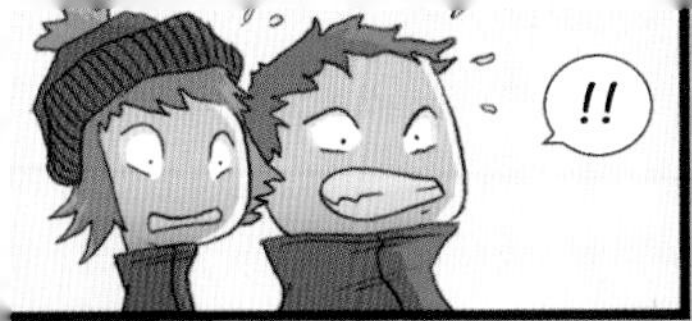
!!
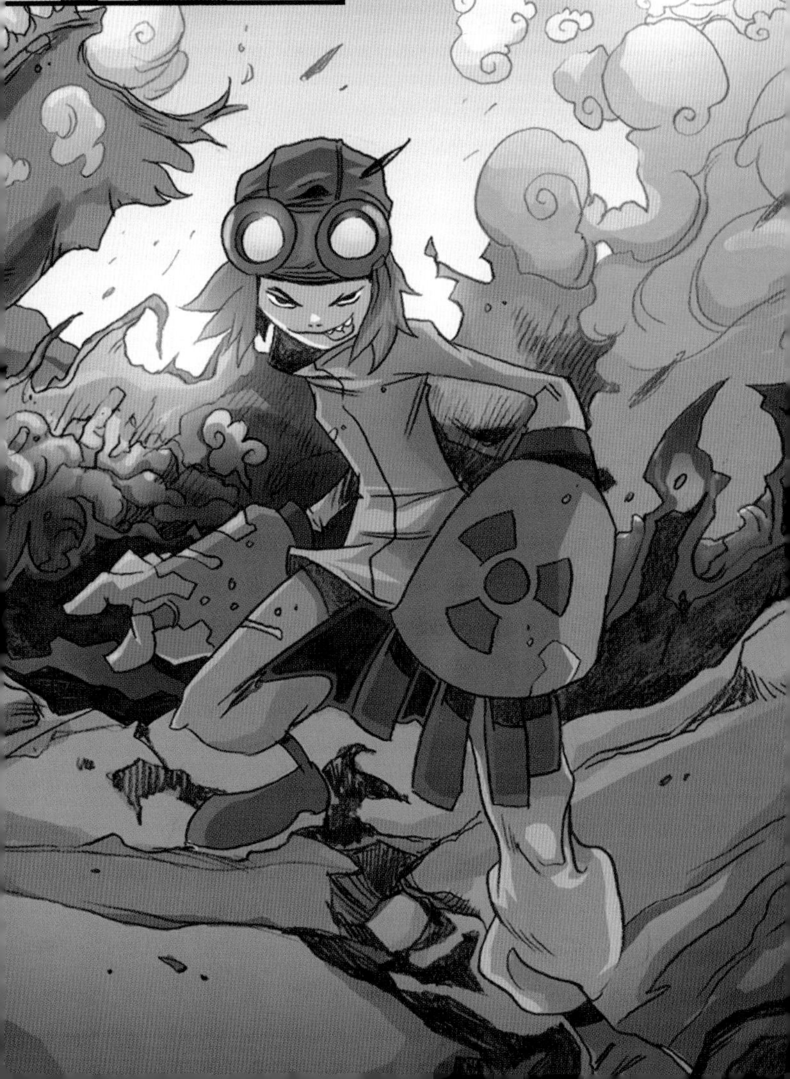

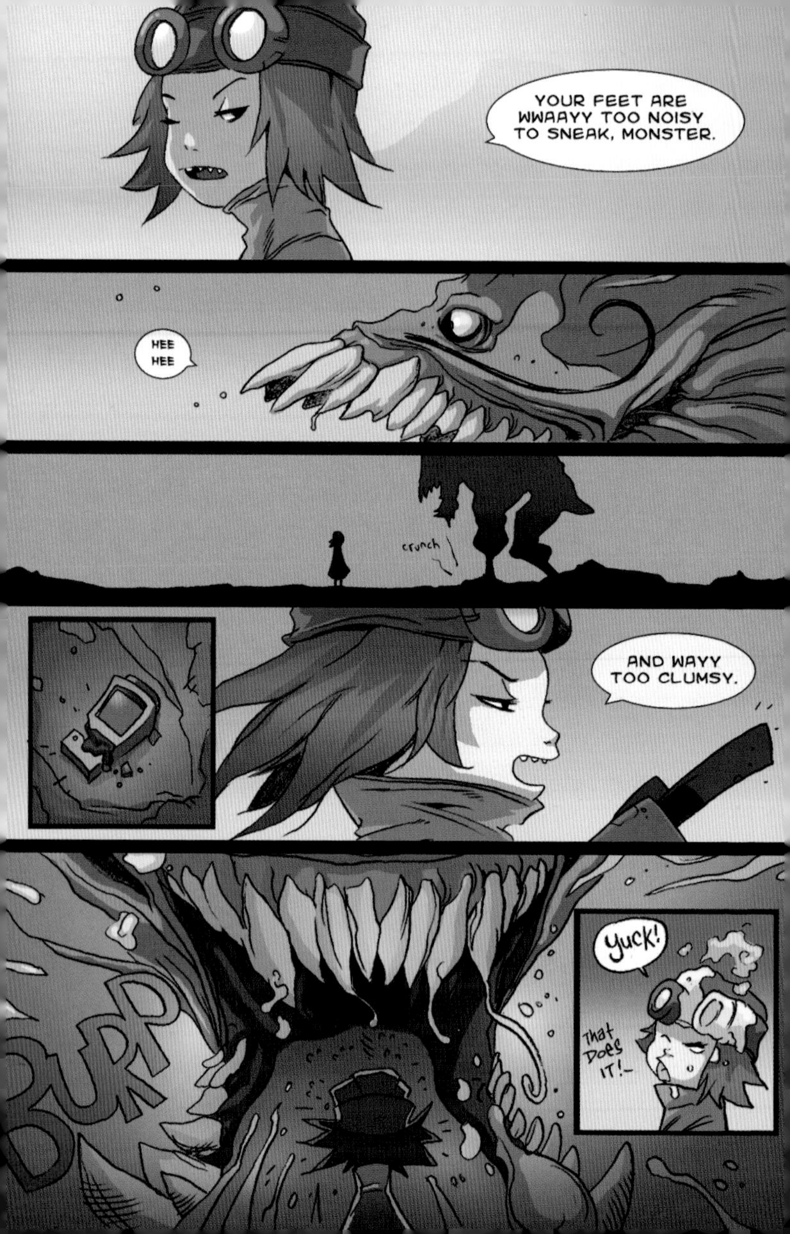
YOUR FEET ARE WWAAYY TOO NOISY TO SNEAK, MONSTER.
HEE HEE
crunch
AND WAYY TOO CLUMSY.
YUCK!
That DOES IT!

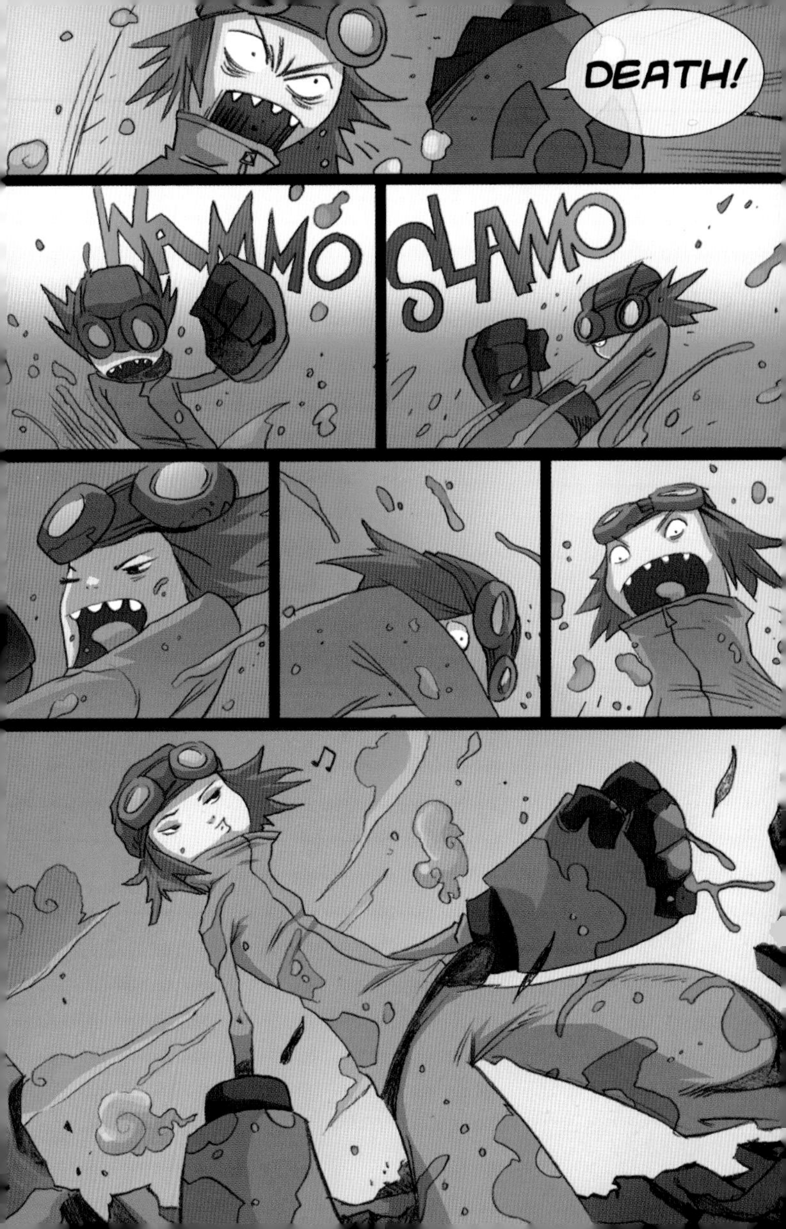
DEATH!
WAMMO
SLAMO

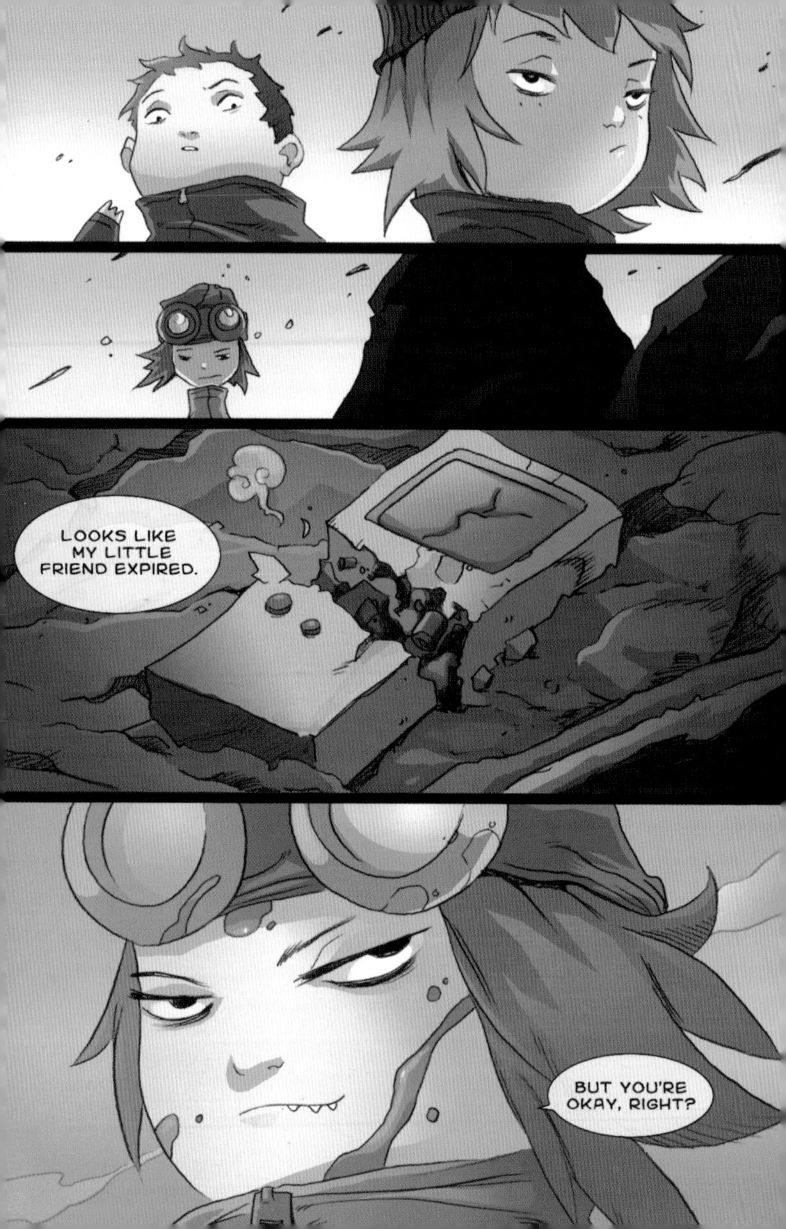
LOOKS LIKE MY LITTLE FRIEND EXPIRED.
BUT YOU'RE OKAY, RIGHT?

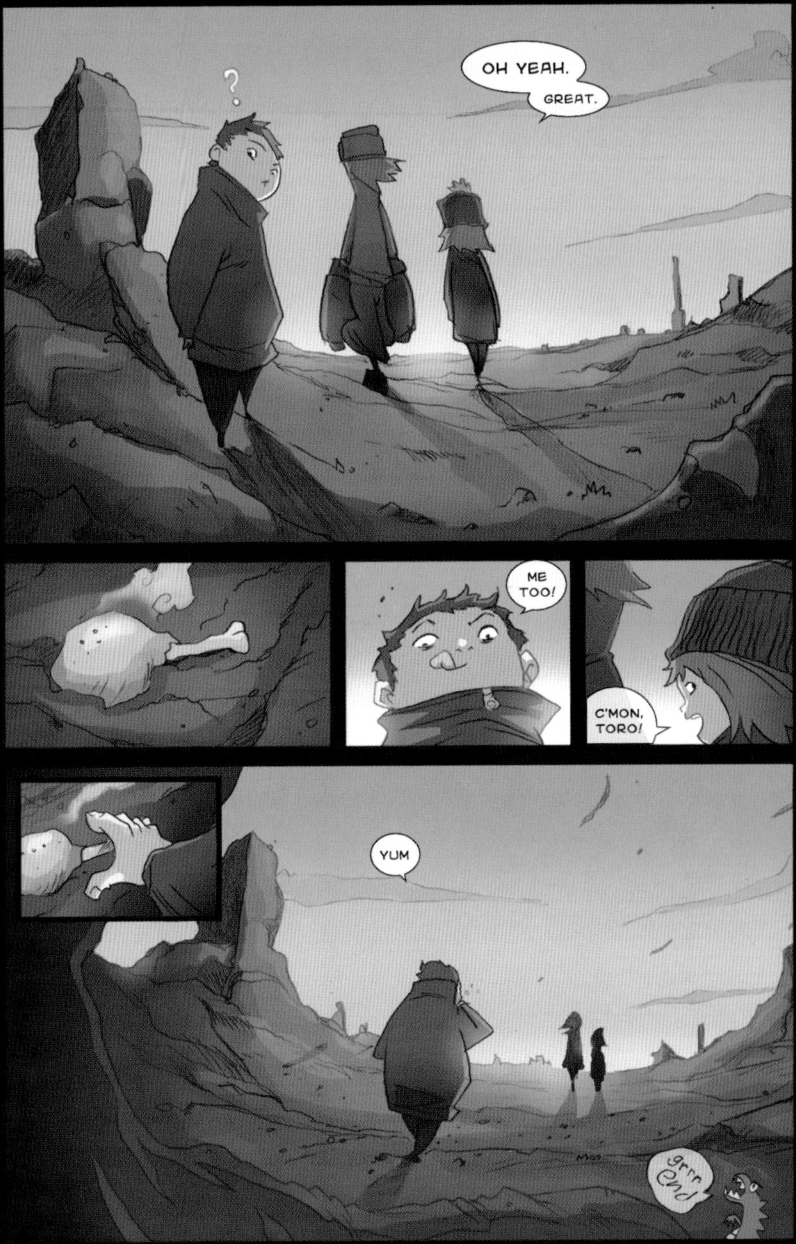
OH YEAH.
GREAT.
ME TOO!
C'MON, TORO!
YUM
grrr

PURIKURA*

Sarah Burgess

Romance, a *shojo* manga staple, receives few portrayals so raw and pure as here. Evocative body language such as the tentative fumbling of hands displays a rare gem of comic narrative. A Manga Jiman entry, this scene alone leapt this story out of the stack for sheer sincerity of intent.

"When I draw," says **Sarah Burgess**, "I want to back away from the obsession with symmetry, accuracy of bodies and form. I prefer to give a natural life, movement and expression to my characters. I always try to make my comics flow rather than look stiff, wishing to put my heart and tears into every stroke! My favourite kinds of stories are gentle and slow paced. My ultimate inspiration is Umino Chika, whose art and storytelling is gentle, unique and focused on the realities of life; if I aspire to be like anyone, it is her. Every story that I write is loosely based on a personal experience I have had. More than anything, I want my readers to feel passionately when they read." Job done, Sarah.

denji-chan.deviantart.com
www.drunkduck.com/Between_kingdoms

WHITE

Sofia Falkenhem

White **is a romance** of an altogether different stripe – entirely more adult and compromised, yet no less reticent; evoked with equal and painful sincerity for all of its relative sophistication. This story got bumped from *Volume Two* at the last gasp due to a shortfall in available pages, but bounces rather neatly off the other romantic mini-dramas included this time around. **Sofia Falkenhem** is from Sweden, a European nation with a lively and popular manga scene. She was originally introduced to *Best New Manga* by comics expert Paul Gravett, following one of his fact-finding trips. Thanks for the tip, PG!

www.sofiafalkenhem.com

*Print Club Machines

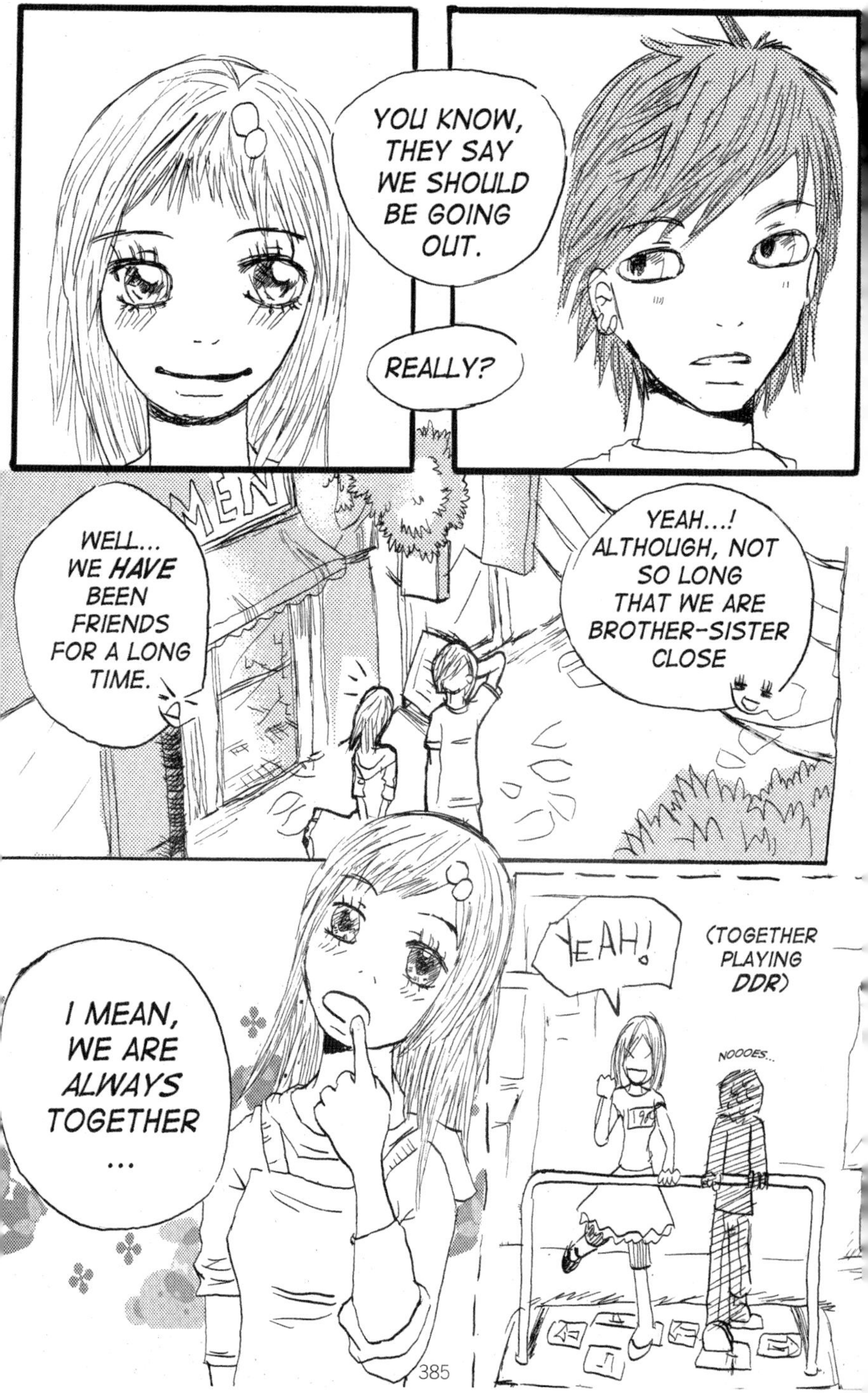
YOU KNOW, THEY SAY WE SHOULD BE GOING OUT.
REALLY?
WELL... WE *HAVE* BEEN FRIENDS FOR A LONG TIME.
MEN
YEAH...! ALTHOUGH, NOT SO LONG THAT WE ARE BROTHER-SISTER CLOSE
I MEAN, WE ARE *ALWAYS* TOGETHER ...
YEAH!
(TOGETHER PLAYING *DDR*)
NOOOES...

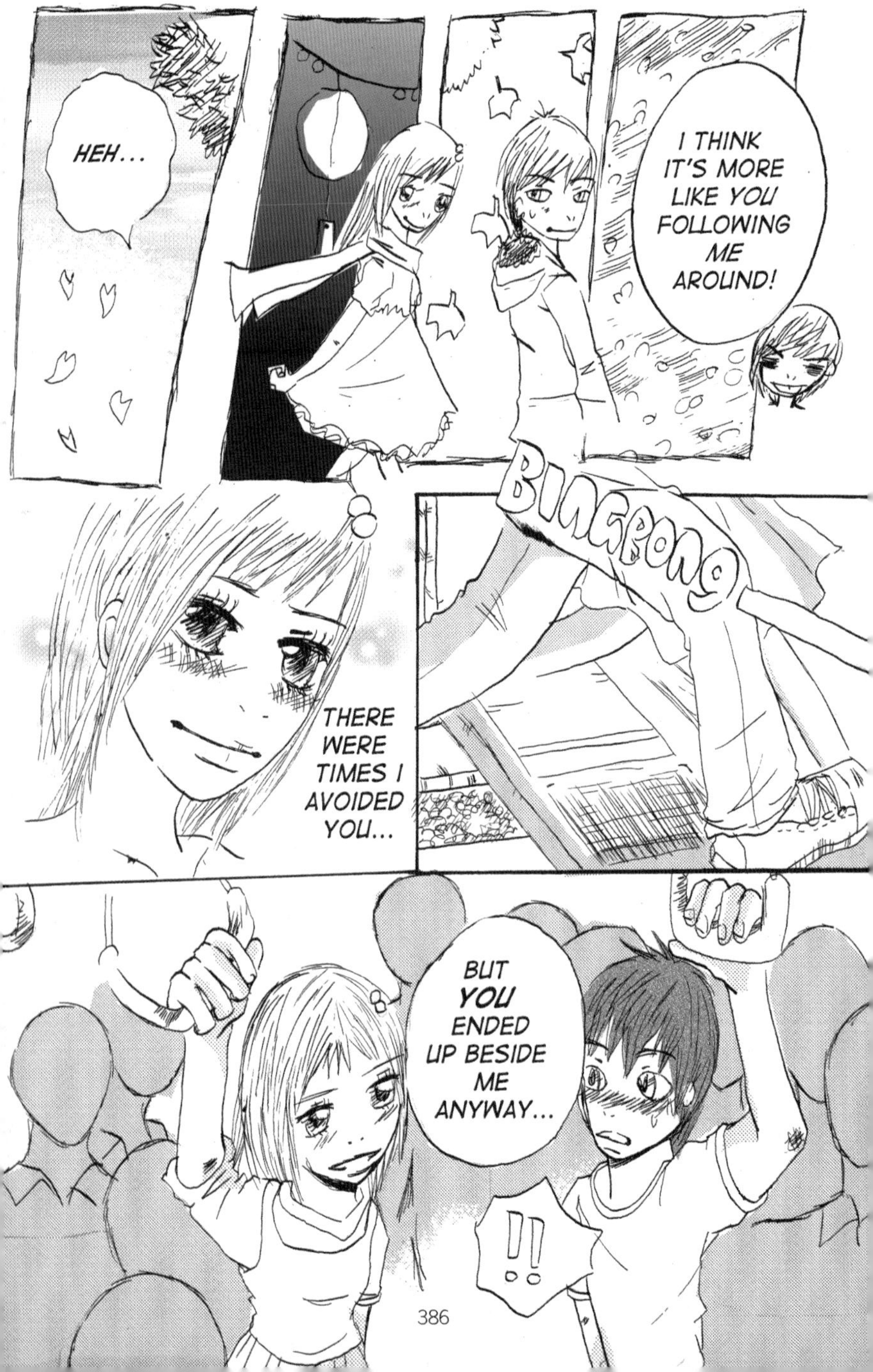
HEH...
I THINK IT'S MORE LIKE YOU FOLLOWING ME AROUND!
BINGPONG
THERE WERE TIMES I AVOIDED YOU...
BUT YOU ENDED UP BESIDE ME ANYWAY...
!!

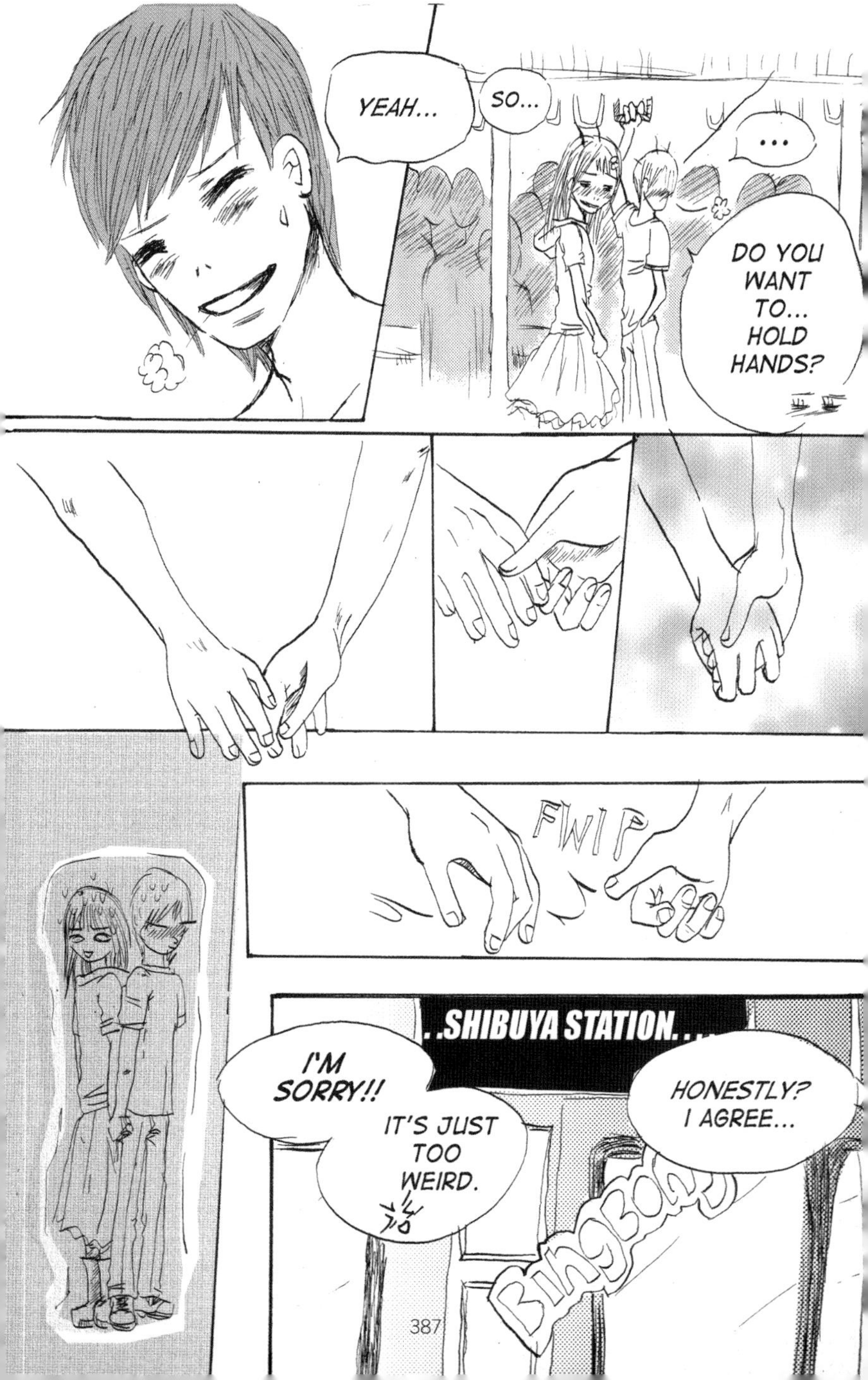
YEAH...
SO...
...
DO YOU WANT TO... HOLD HANDS?
FWIP
. .SHIBUYA STATION. . .
I'M SORRY!!
IT'S JUST TOO WEIRD.
HONESTLY? I AGREE...
BINGBONG

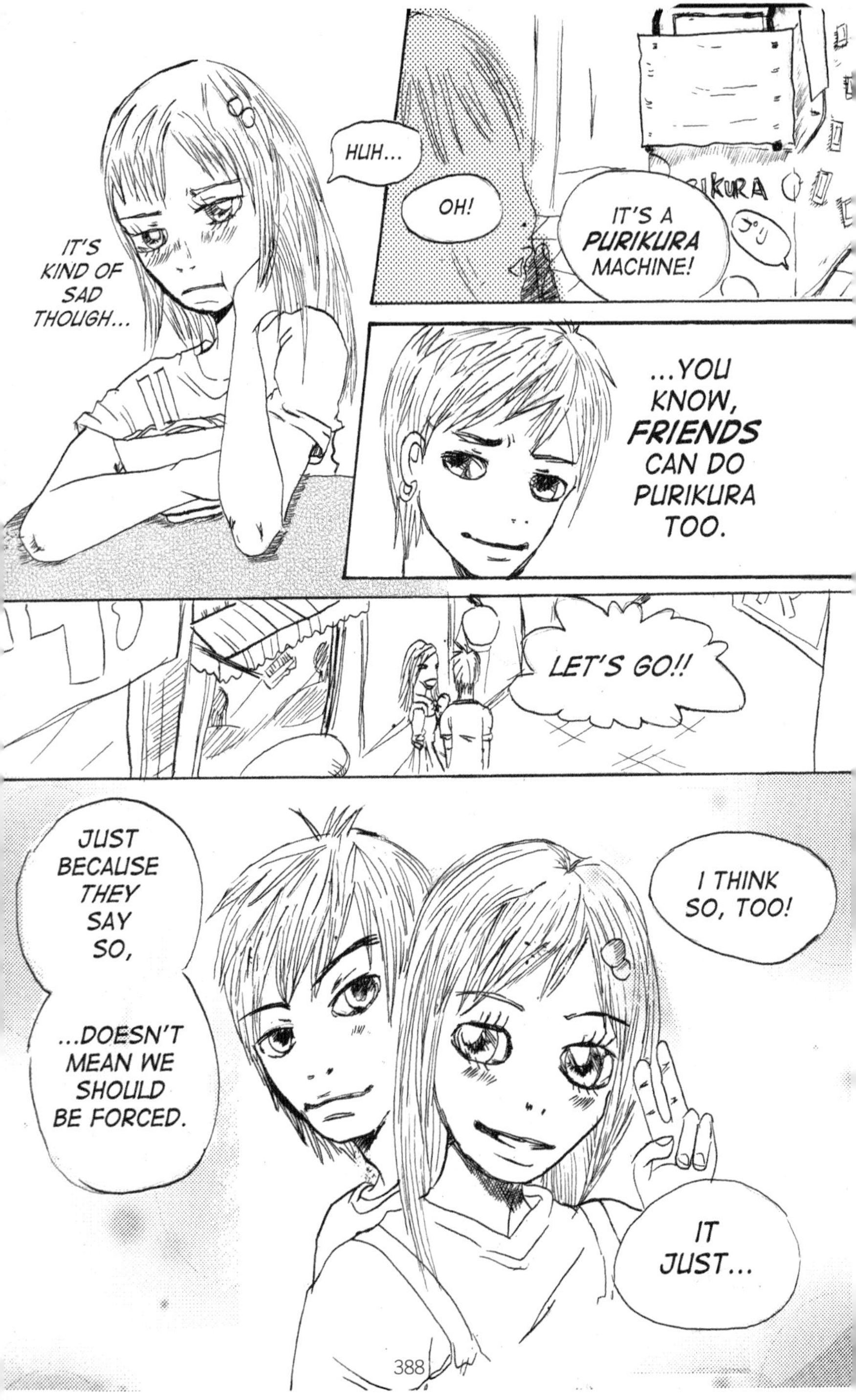

IT'S KIND OF SAD THOUGH...
HUH...
OH!
IT'S A **PURIKURA** MACHINE!
...YOU KNOW, **FRIENDS** CAN DO PURIKURA TOO.
LET'S GO!!
JUST BECAUSE THEY SAY SO,
...DOESN'T MEAN WE SHOULD BE FORCED.
I THINK SO, TOO!
IT JUST...

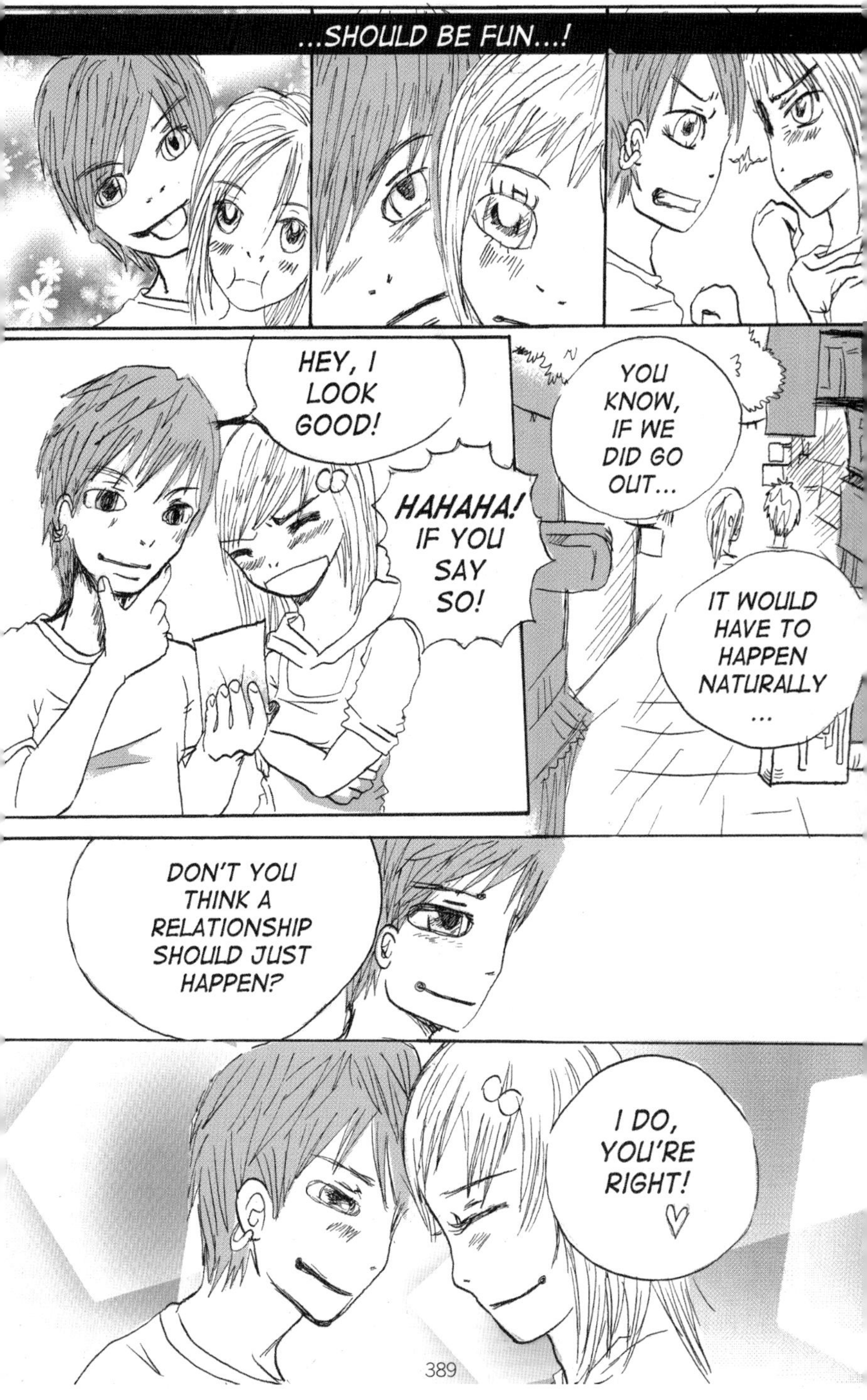
...SHOULD BE FUN...!
HEY, I LOOK GOOD!
HAHAHA! IF YOU SAY SO!
YOU KNOW, IF WE DID GO OUT...
IT WOULD HAVE TO HAPPEN NATURALLY ...
DON'T YOU THINK A RELATIONSHIP SHOULD JUST HAPPEN?
I DO, YOU'RE RIGHT! ♡

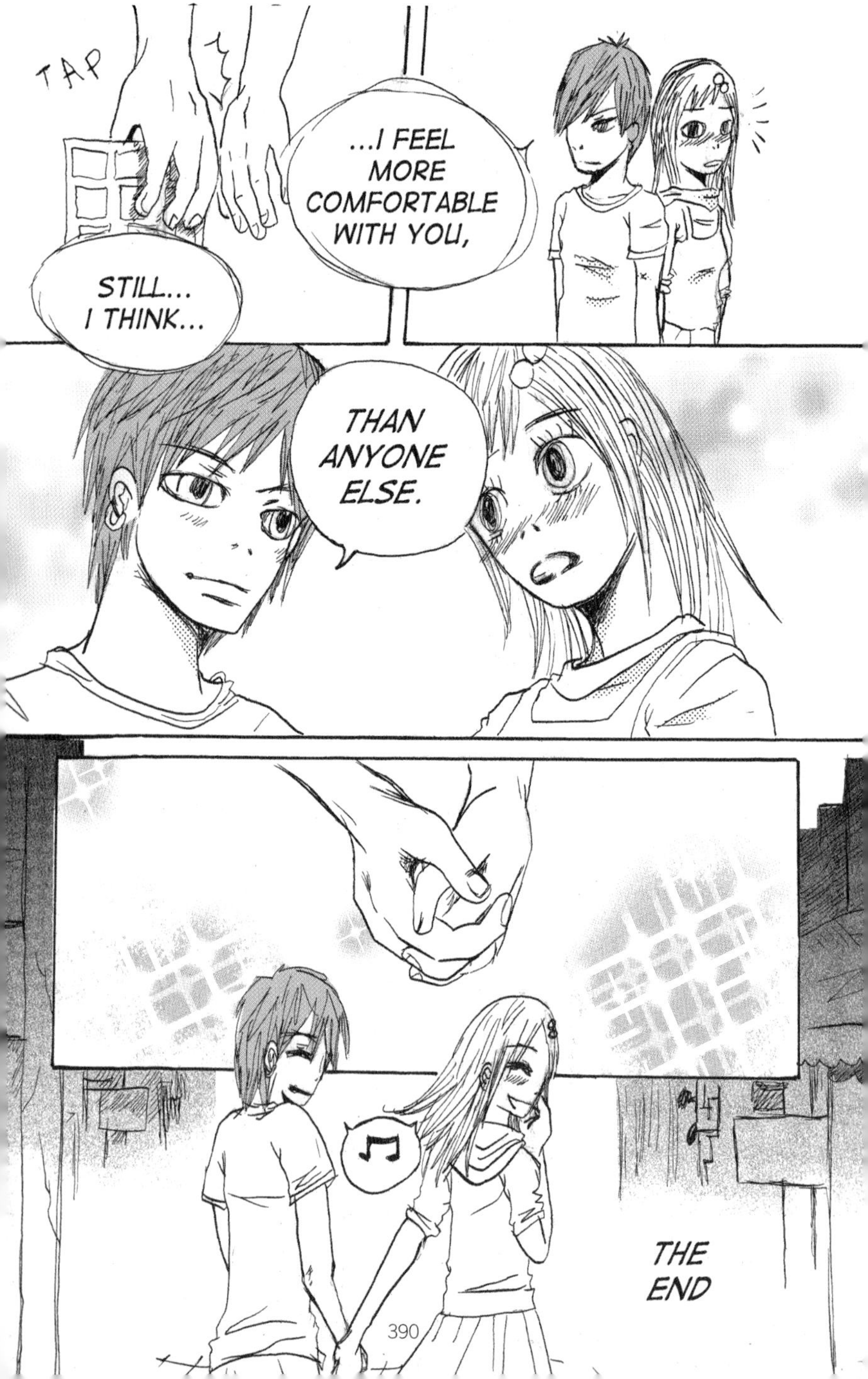
TAP
STILL... I THINK...
...I FEEL MORE COMFORTABLE WITH YOU,
THAN ANYONE ELSE.
THE END

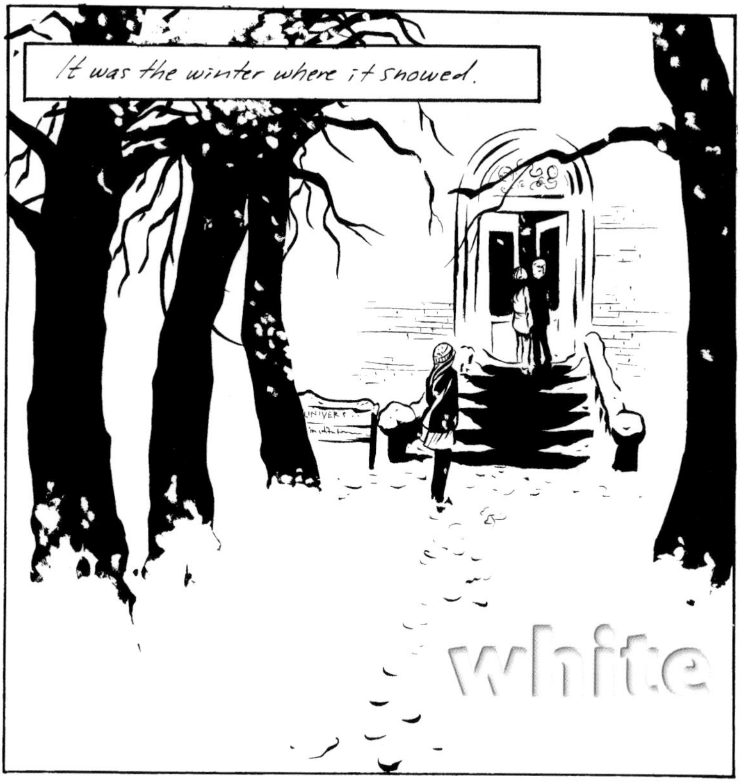
It was the winter where it snowed.
white

There was to be an exam that afternoon, and everyone was really too stressed to enjoy the films under discussion.

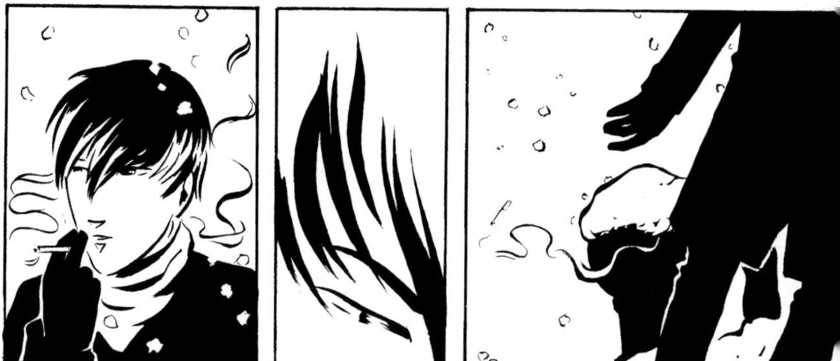

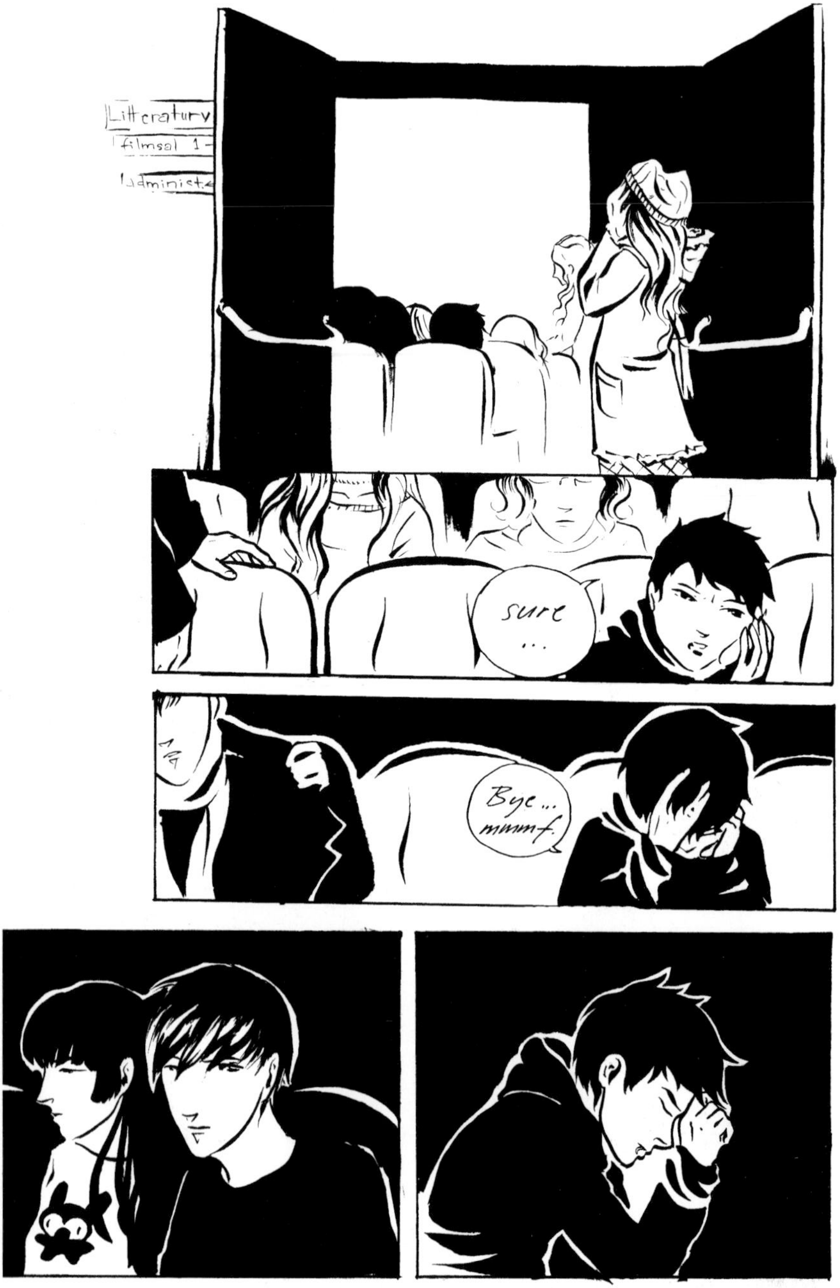
Litteraturv
filmsal 1-
administ
sure ...
Bye... mmmf.

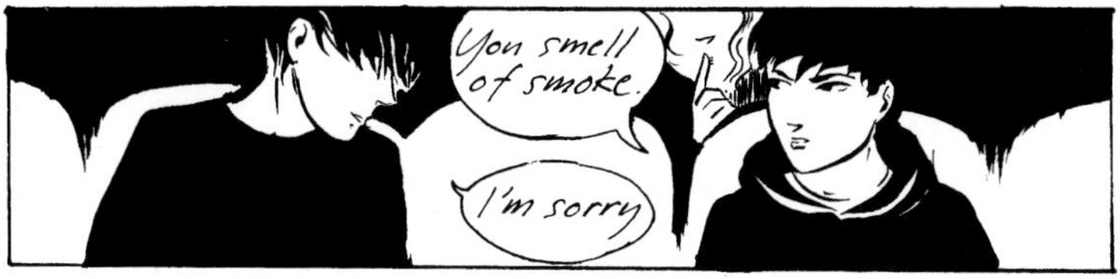
You smell of smoke.
I'm sorry

I think it was the first time you noticed me.

Of course I had been watching you many times, you being so petite kind of drew the attention.

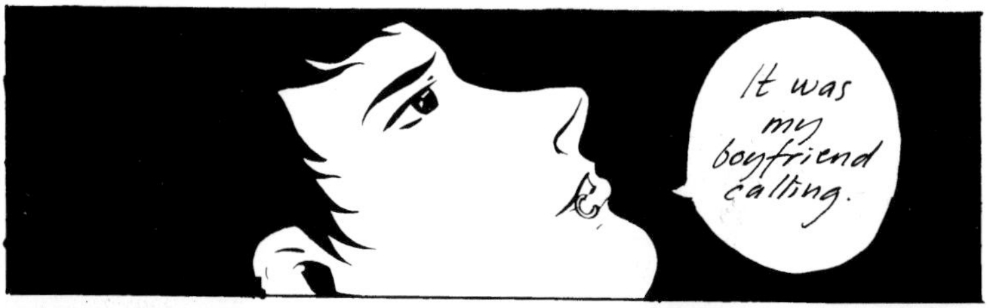
It was my boyfriend calling.

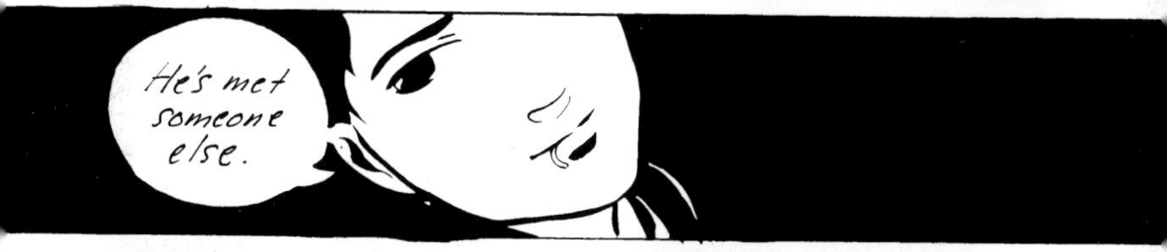
He's met someone else.

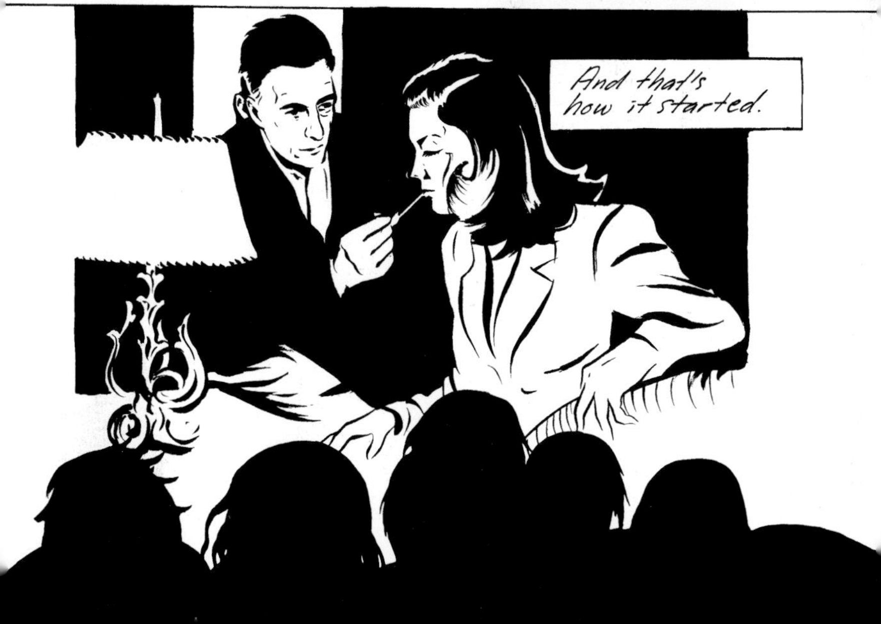
And that's how it started.

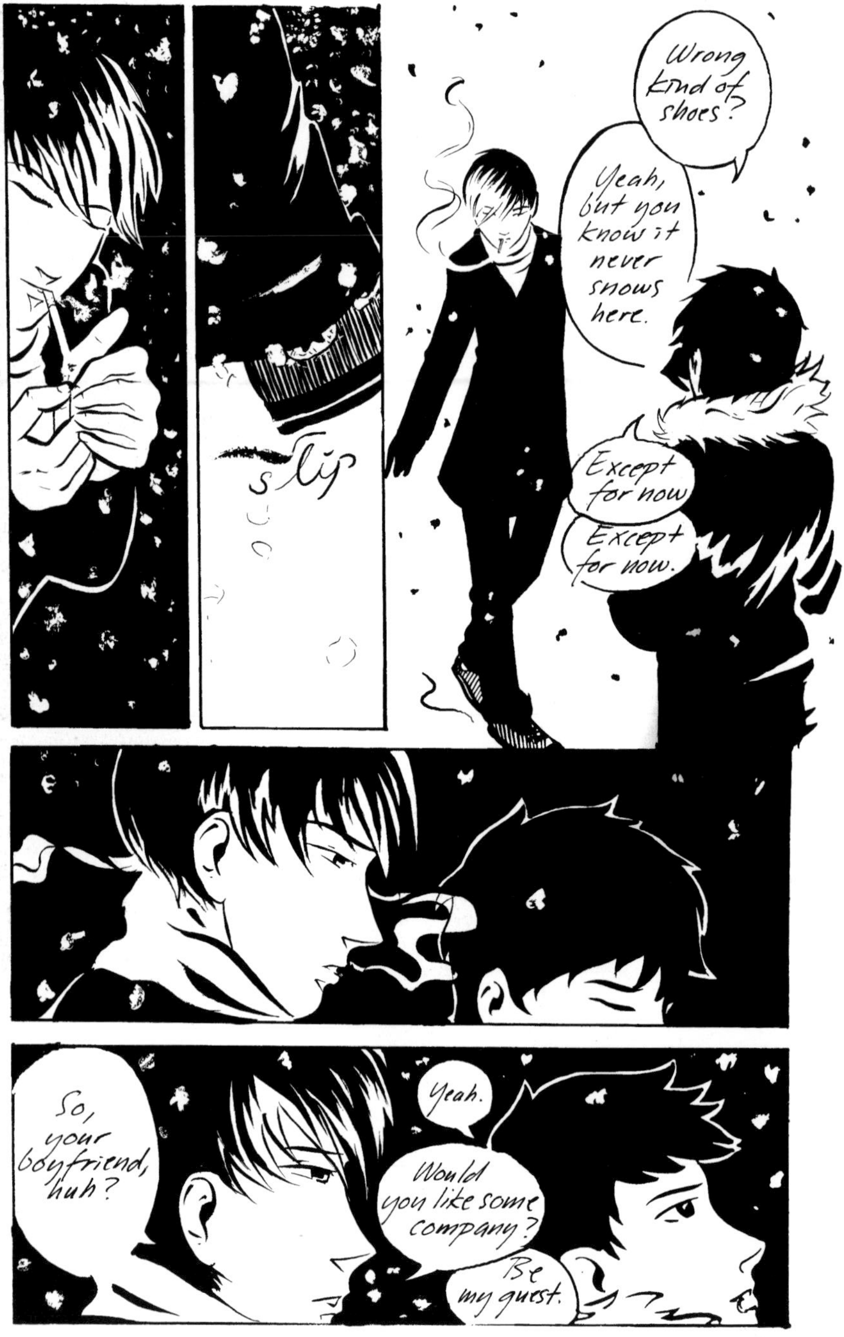
slip
Wrong kind of shoes?
Yeah, but you know it never snows here.
Except for now.
Except for now.
So, your boyfriend, huh?
Yeah.
Would you like some company?
Be my guest.

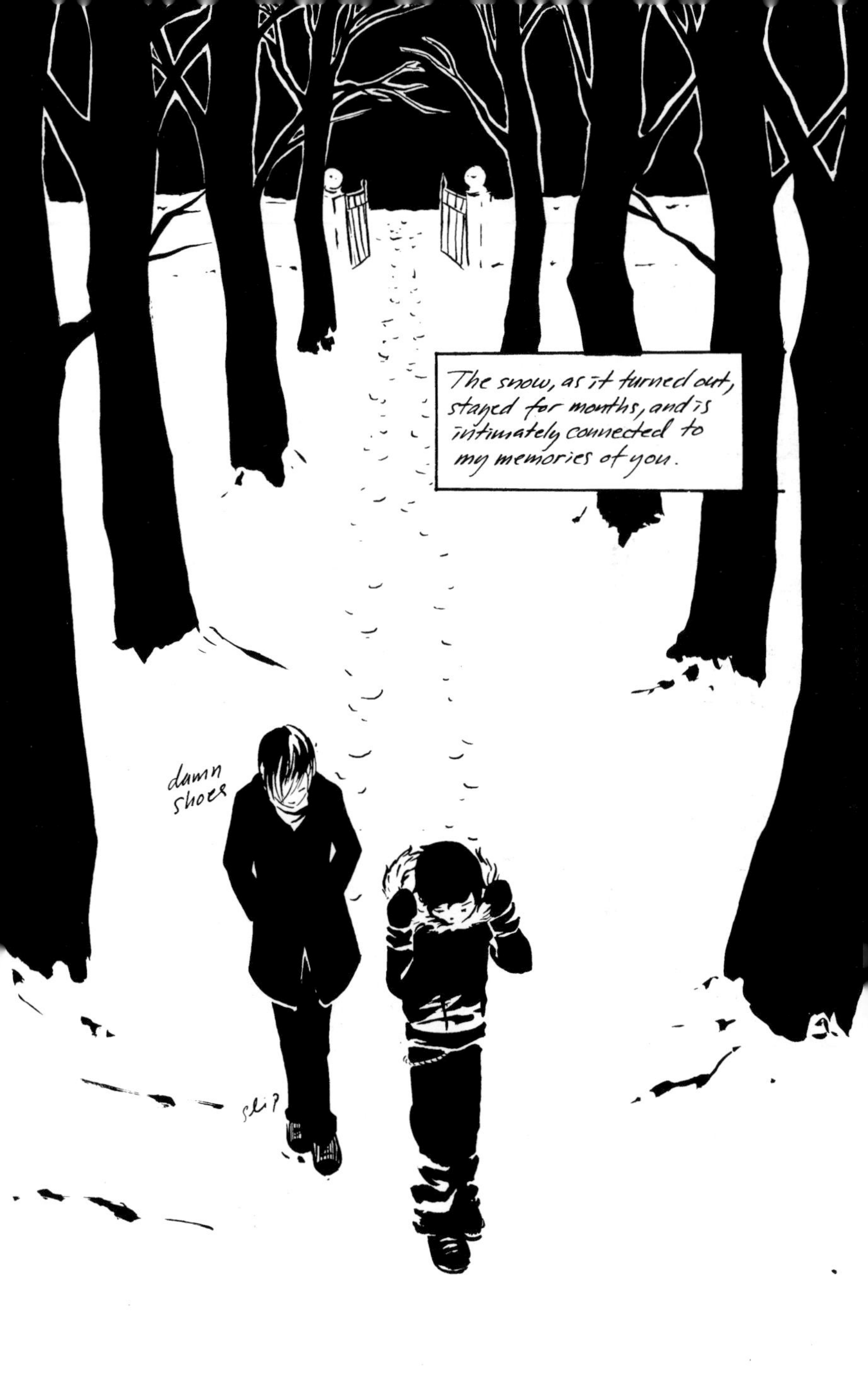
The snow, as it turned out, stayed for months, and is intimately connected to my memories of you.
damn shoes
slip

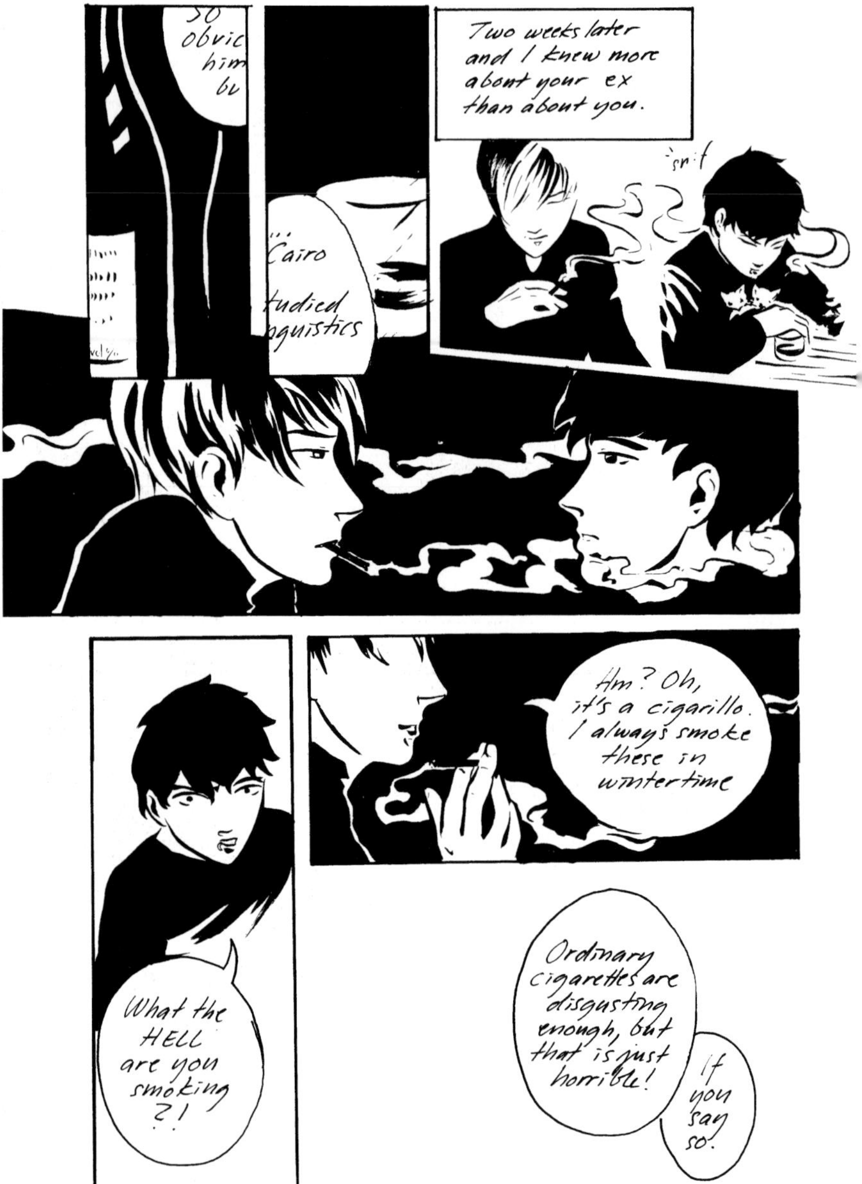
SO obvic him bu
... Cairo tudied guistics
Two weeks later and I knew more about your ex than about you.
snif
What the HELL are you smoking?!
Hm? Oh, it's a cigarillo. I always smoke these in wintertime
Ordinary cigarettes are disgusting enough, but that is just horrible!
If you say so.

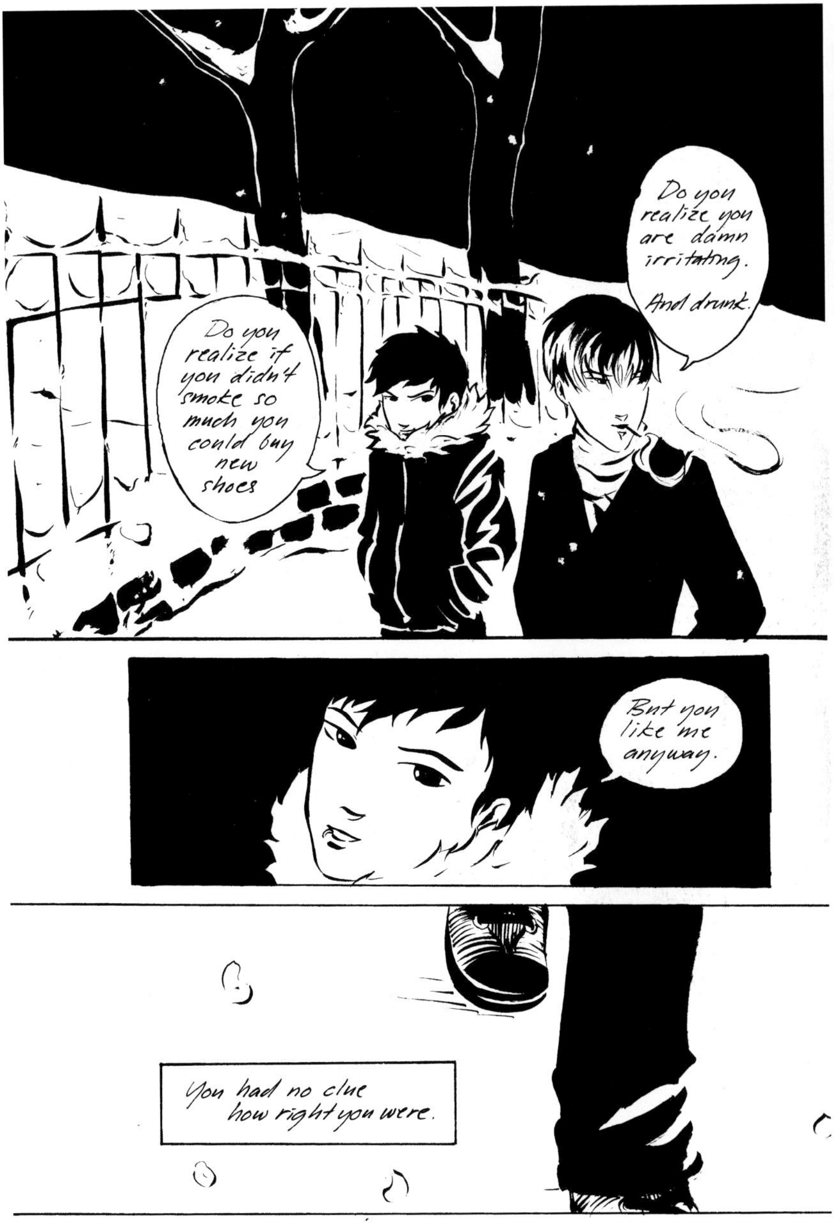
Do you realize if you didn't smoke so much you could buy new shoes
Do you realize you are damn irritating.
And drunk.
But you like me anyway.
You had no clue how right you were.

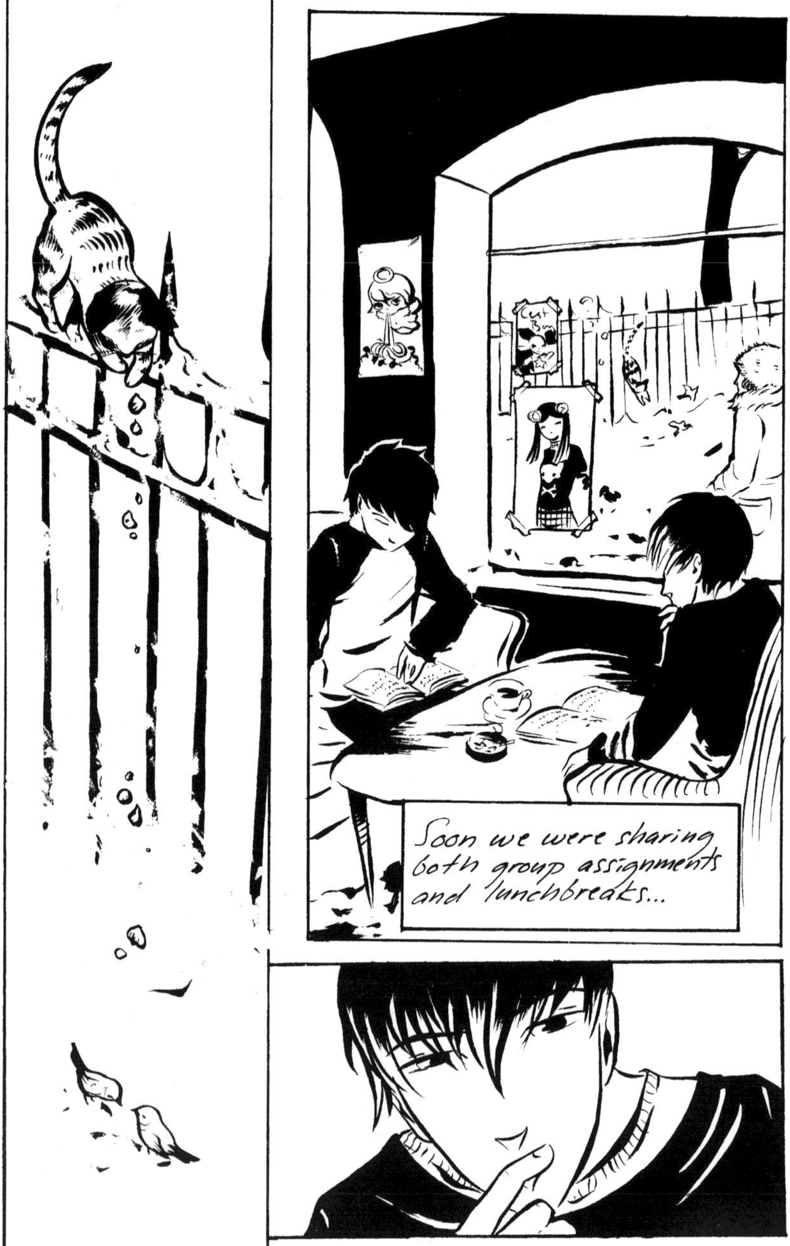
Soon we were sharing both group assignments and lunchbreaks...

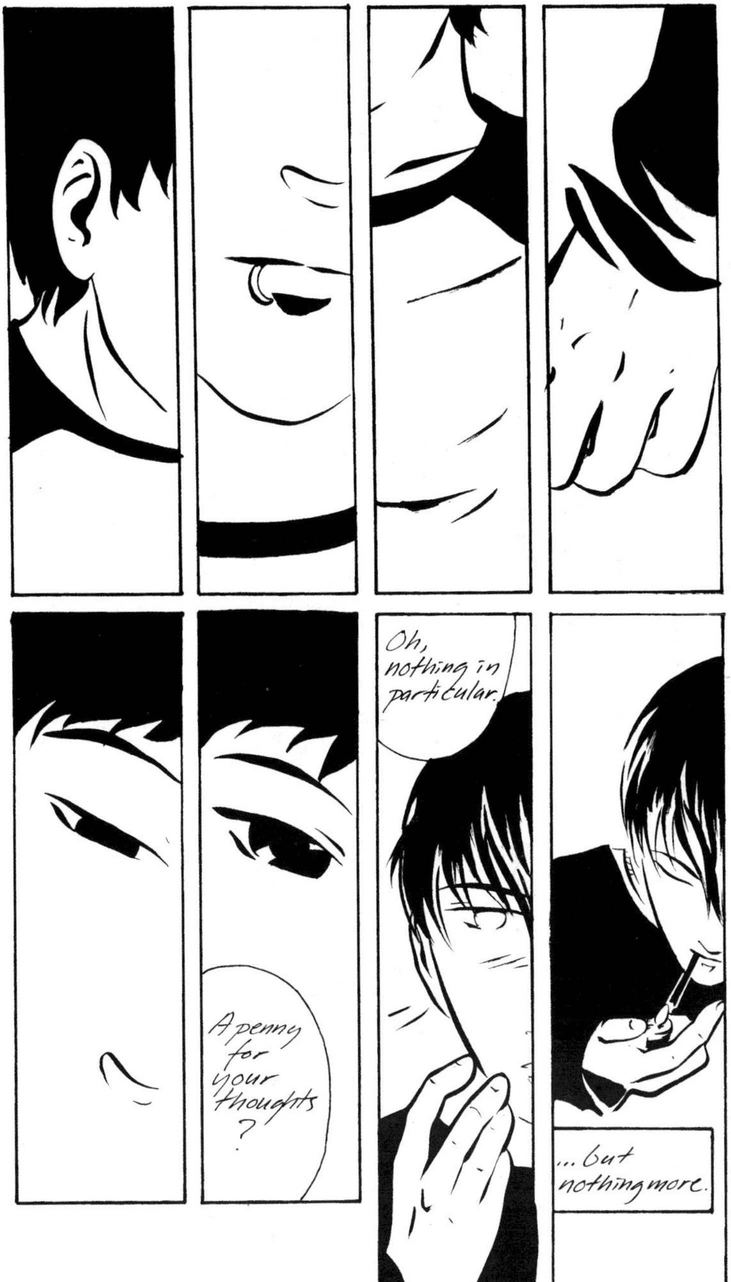
A penny for your thoughts?
Oh, nothing in particular.
...but nothing more.

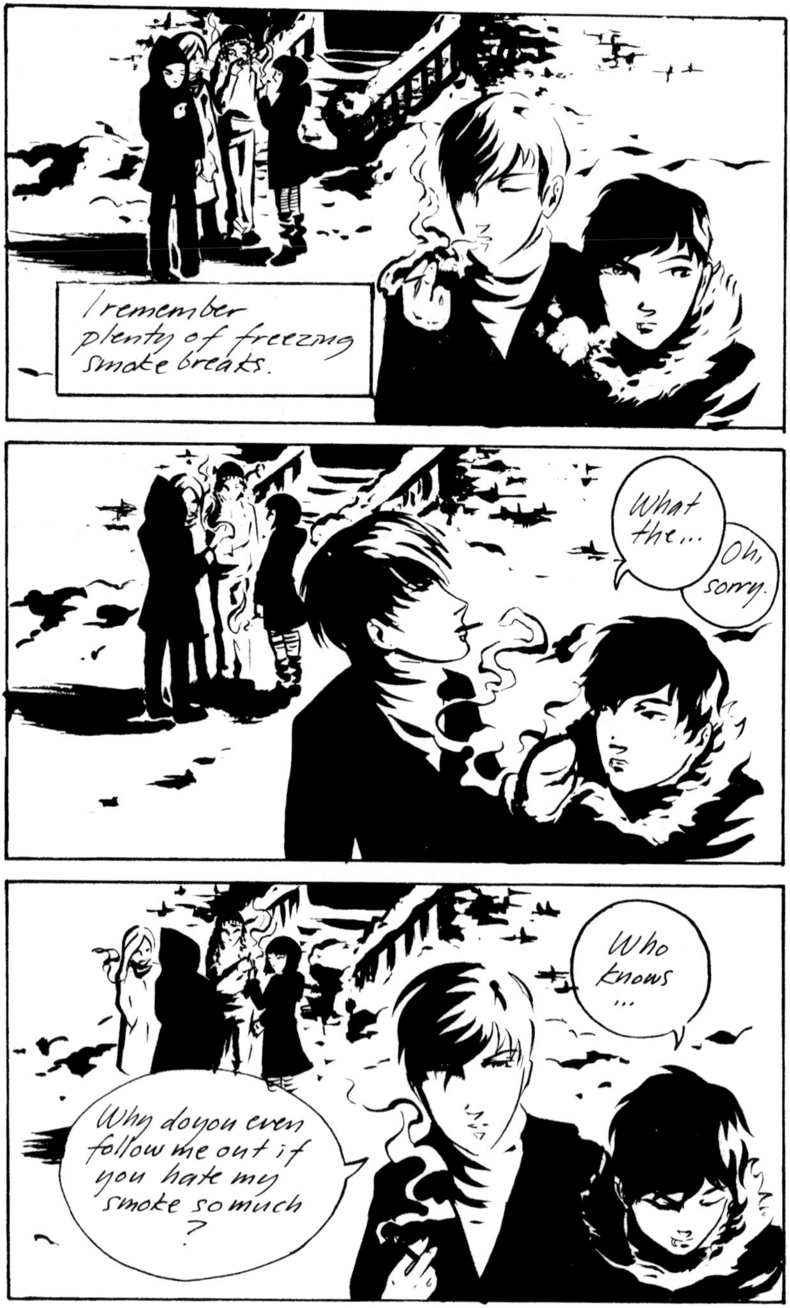

I remember plenty of freezing smoke breaks.
What the...
Oh, sorry.
Who knows ...
Why do you even follow me out if you hate my smoke so much ?

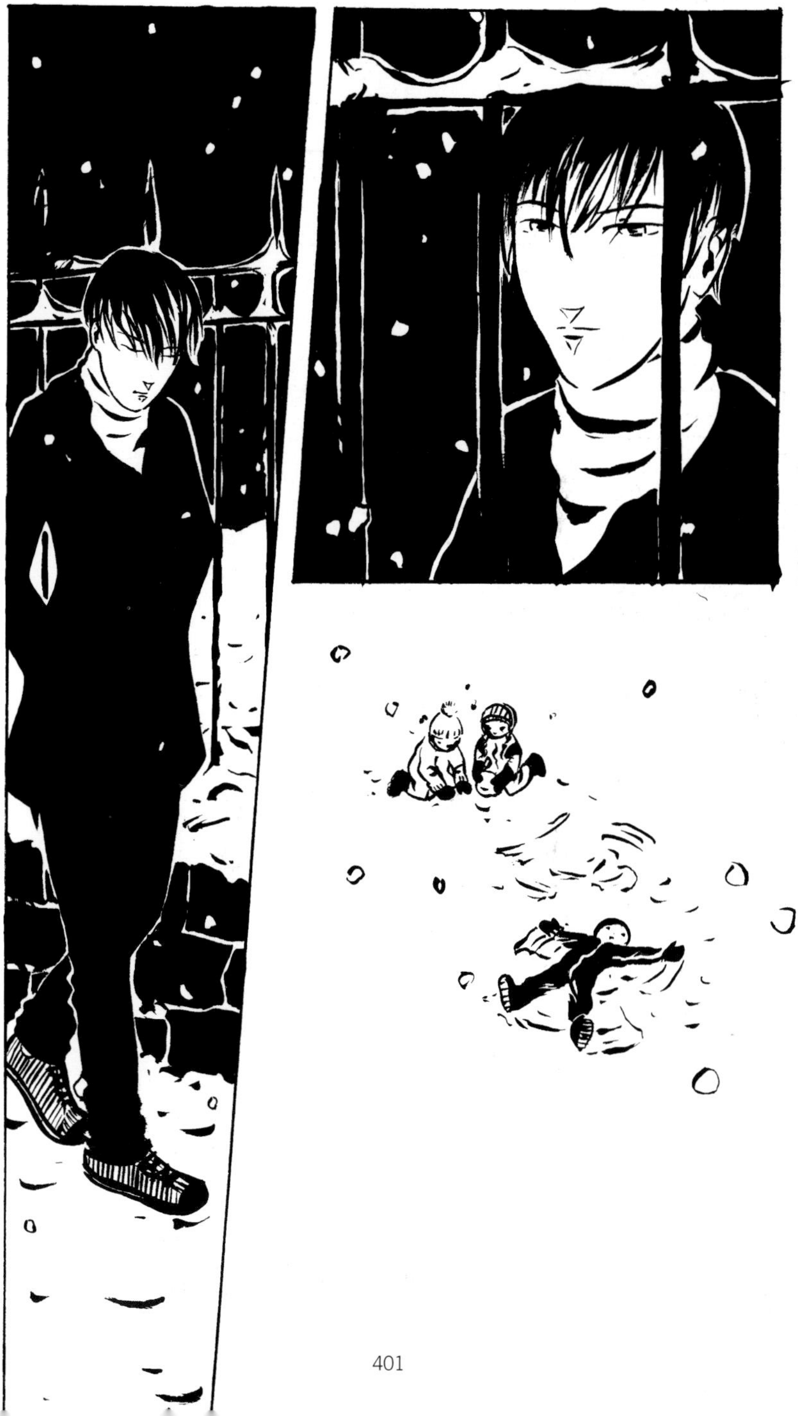

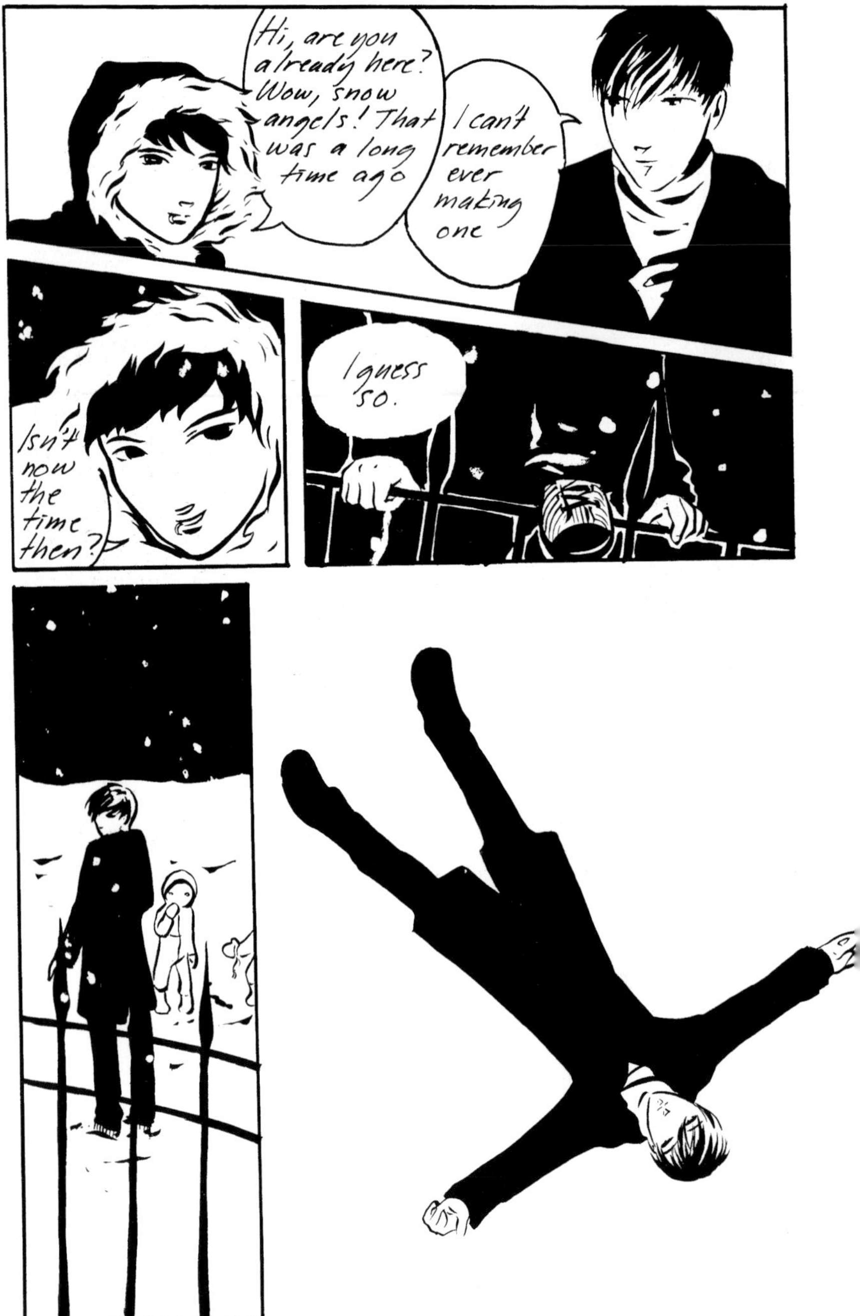
Hi, are you already here? Wow, snow angels! That was a long time ago
I can't remember ever making one
Isn't now the time then?
I guess so.

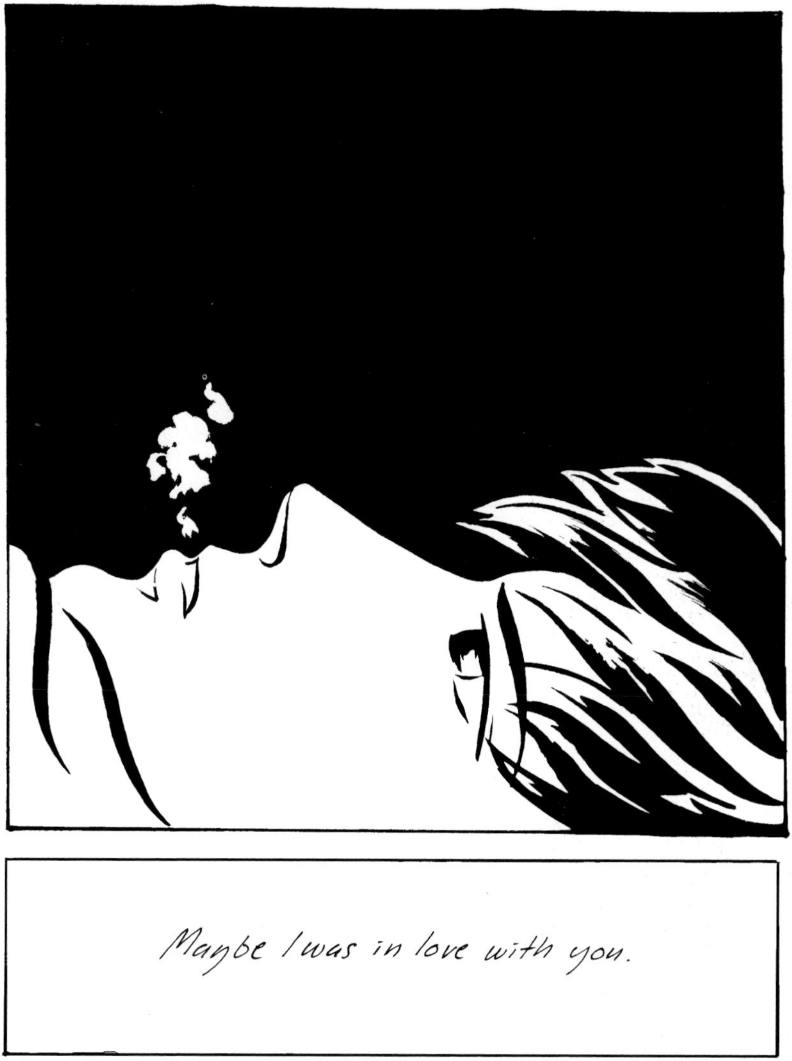
Maybe I was in love with you.

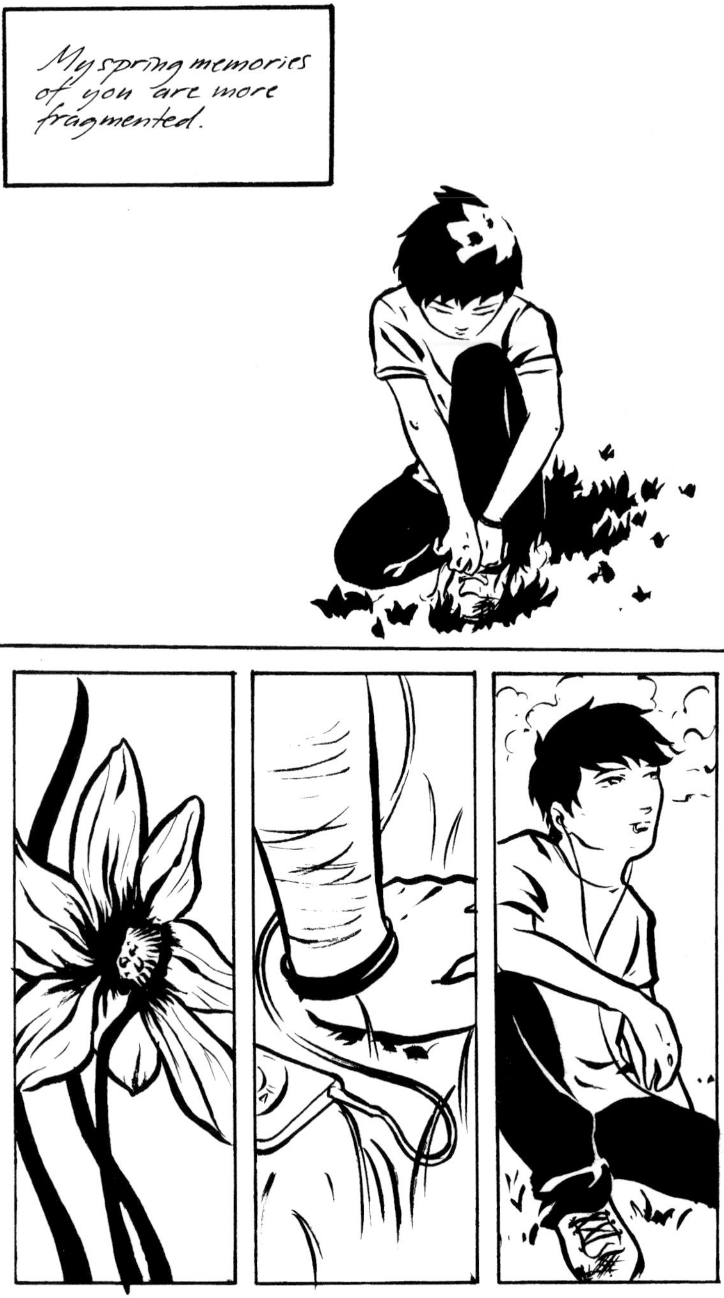
My spring memories of you are more fragmented.

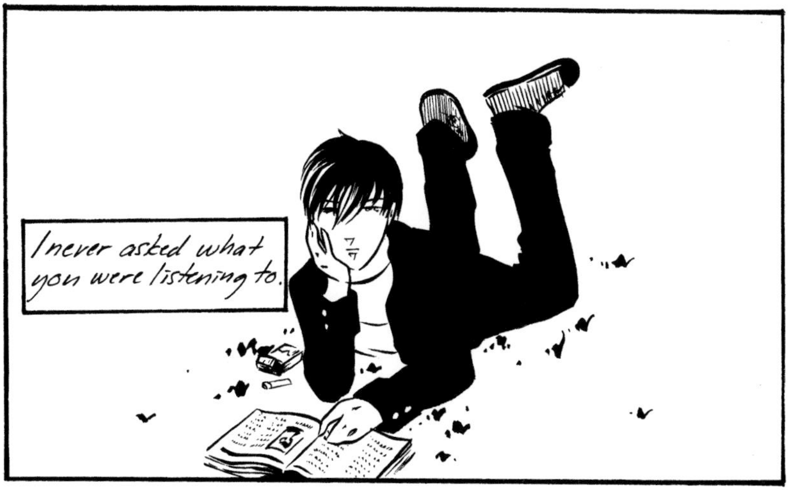
I never asked what you were listening to.

and then it ended.

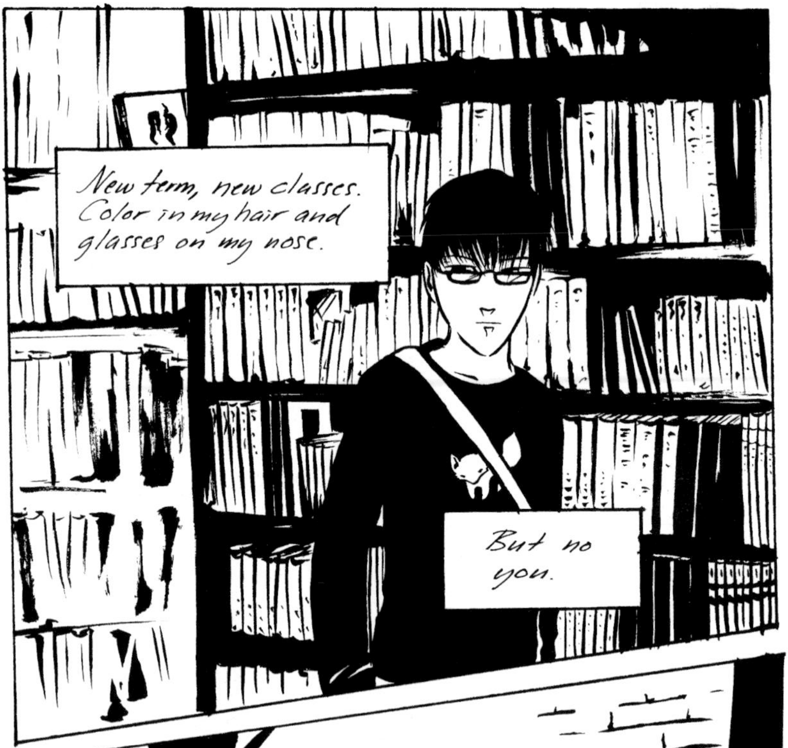
New term, new classes. Color in my hair and glasses on my nose.
But no you.
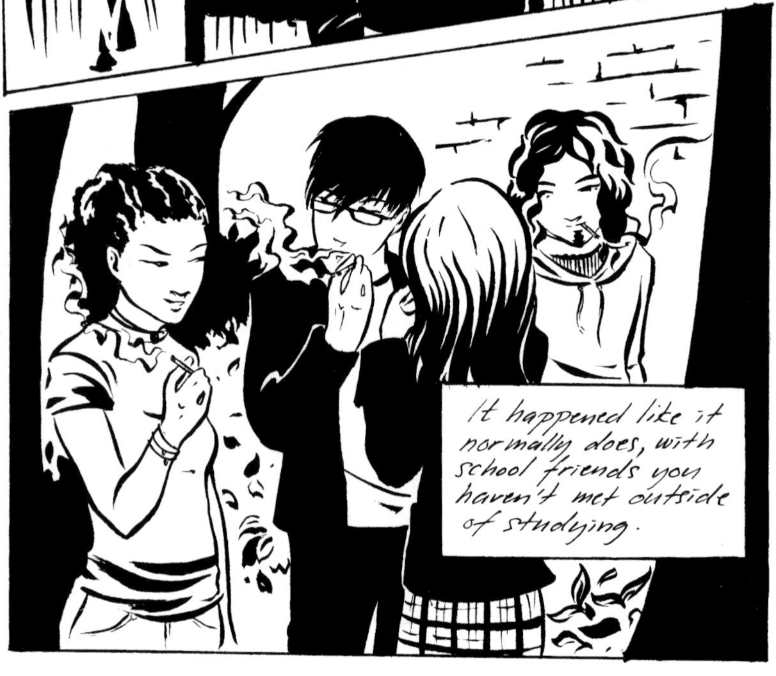
It happened like it normally does, with school friends you haven't met outside of studying.

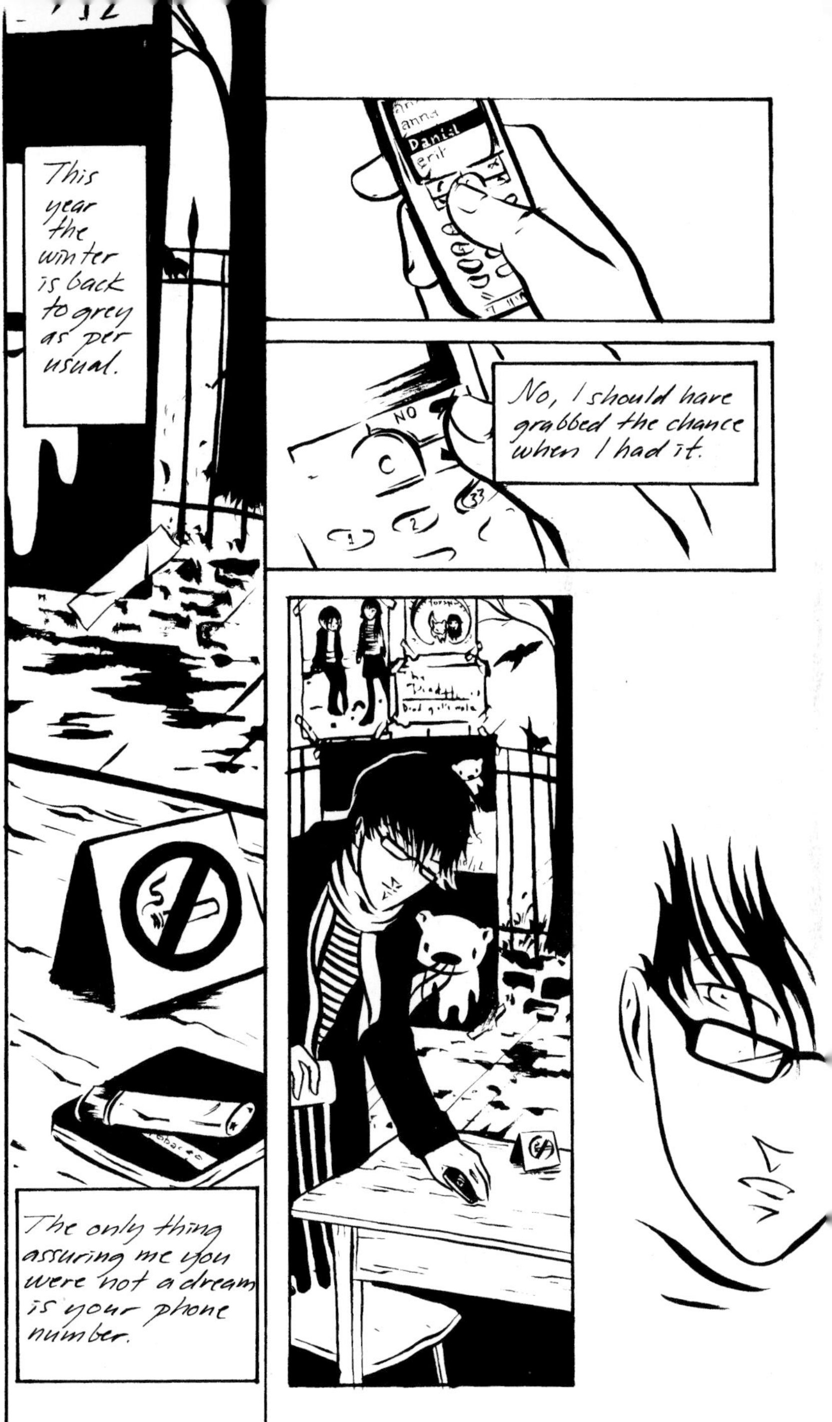
This year the winter is back to grey as per usual.
The only thing assuring me you were not a dream is your phone number.
NO
No, I should have grabbed the chance when I had it.

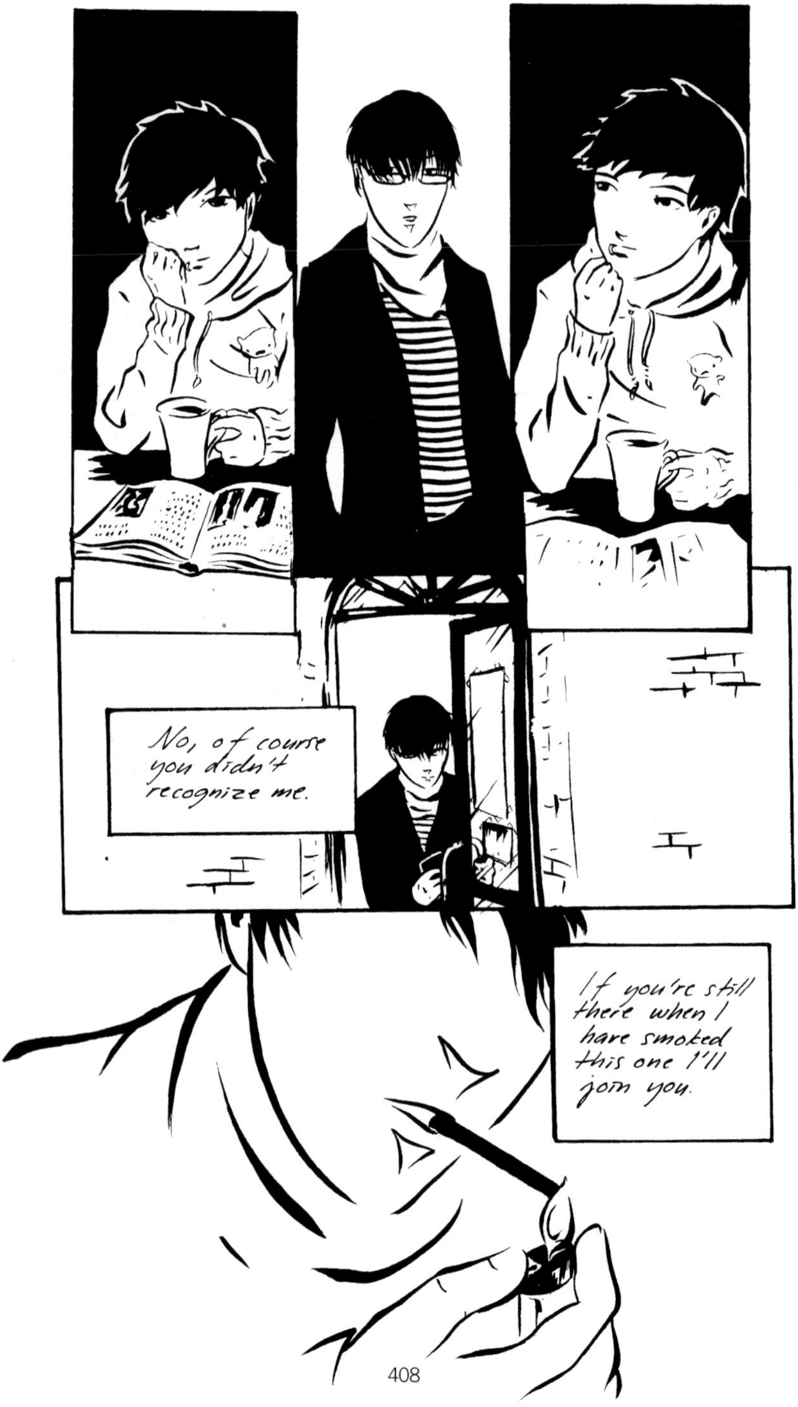
No, of course you didn't recognize me.
If you're still there when I have smoked this one I'll join you.

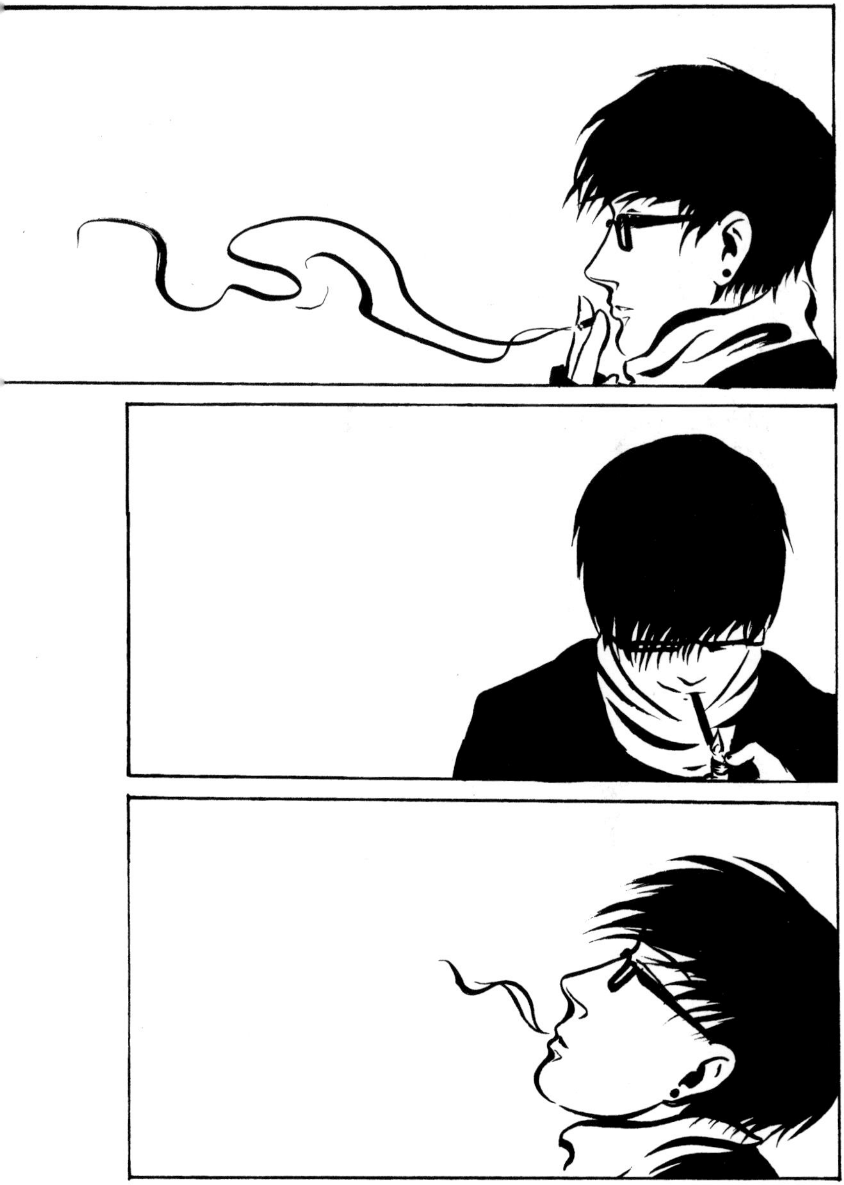

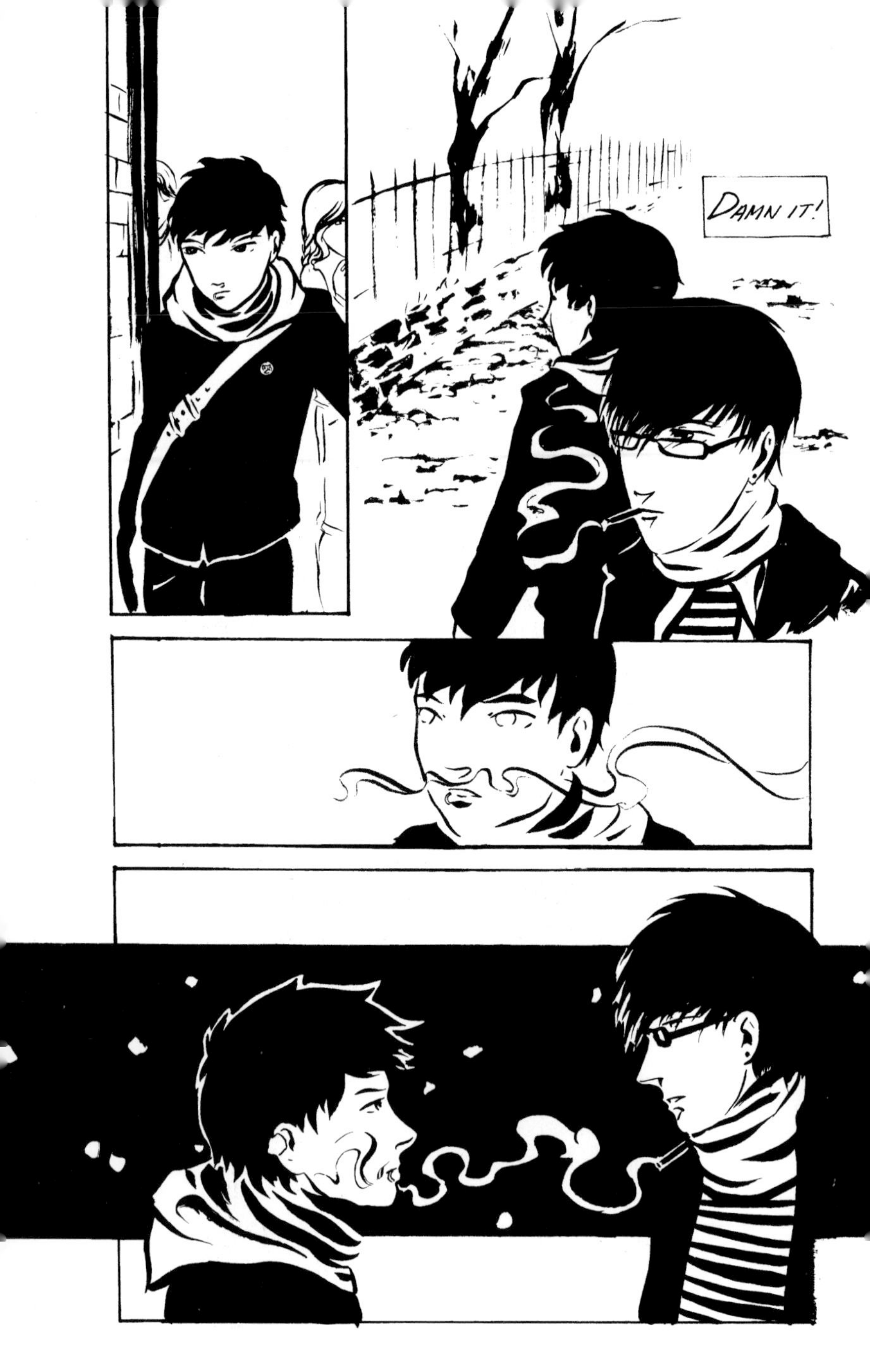
DAMN IT!

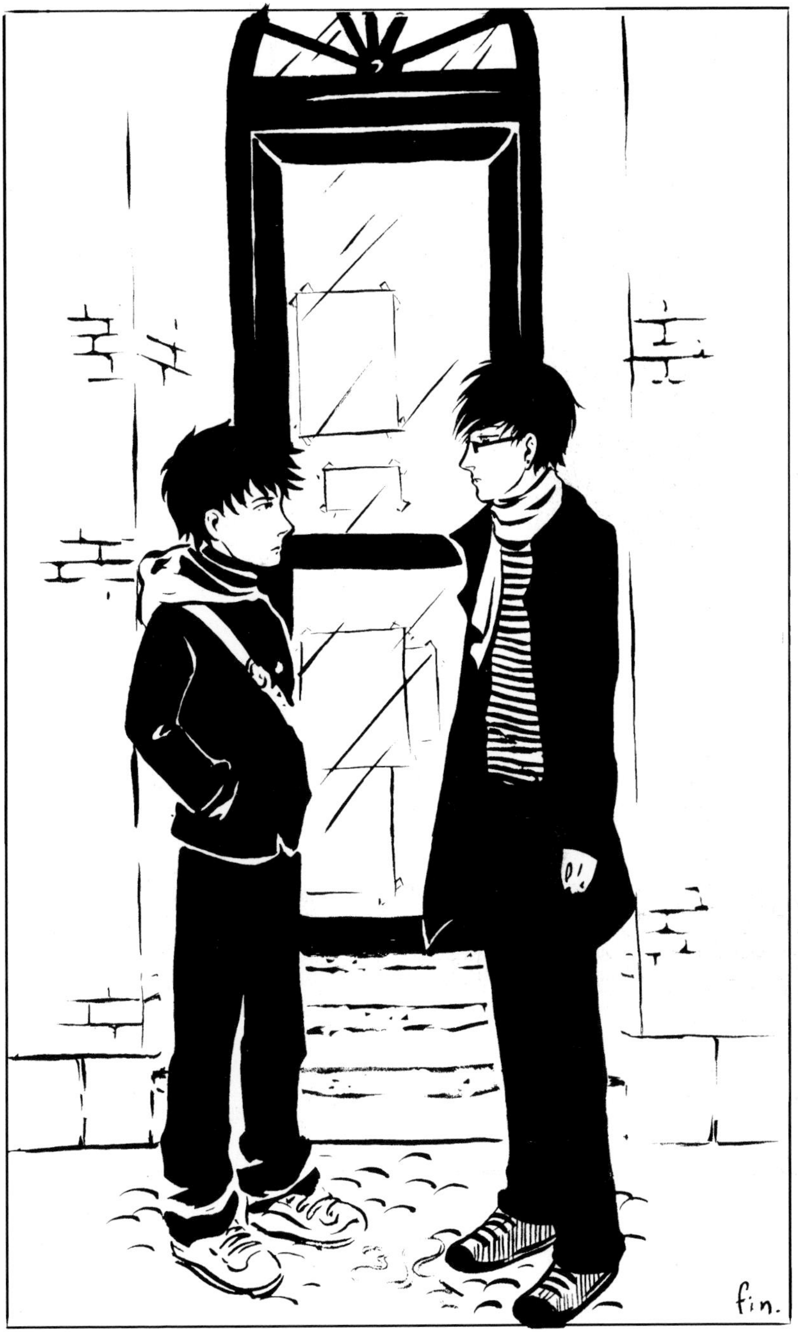
fin.

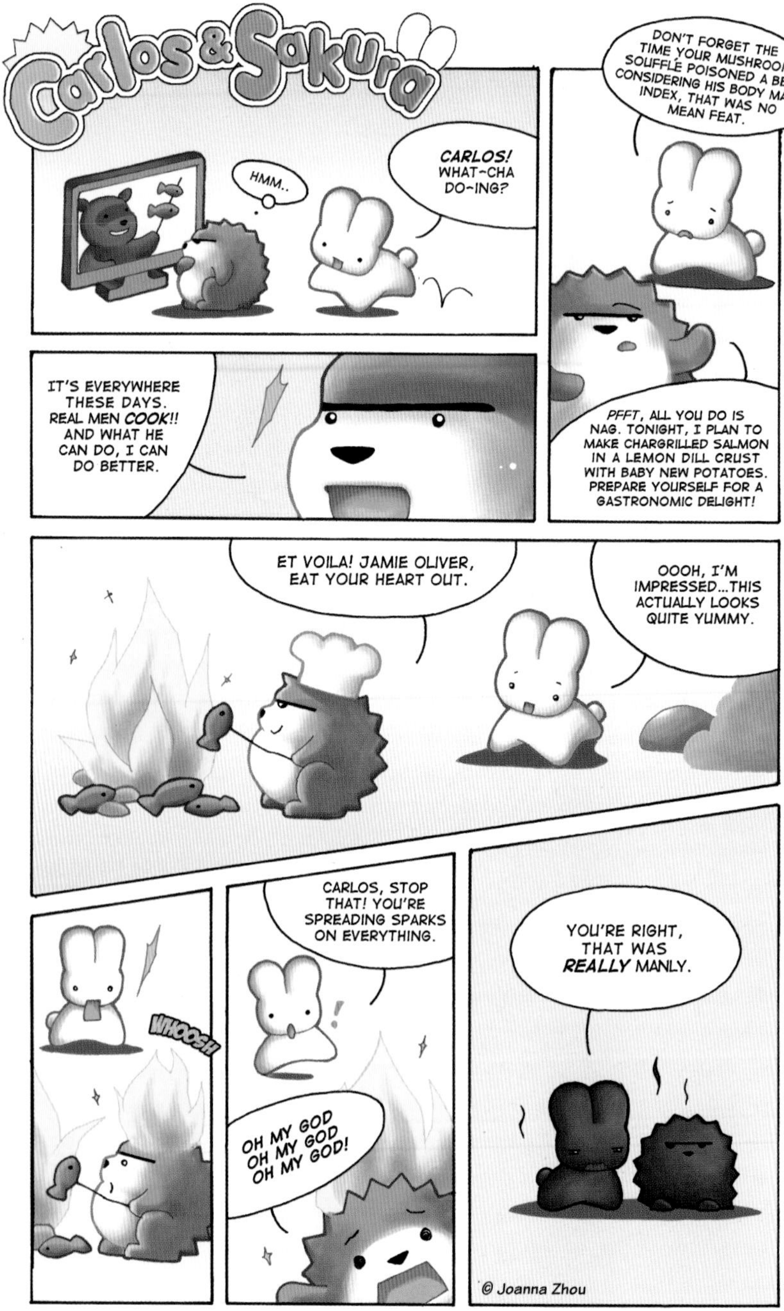
Carlos & Sakura
HMM..
CARLOS! WHAT-CHA DO-ING?
DON'T FORGET THE TIME YOUR MUSHROOM SOUFFLÉ POISONED A BEAR. CONSIDERING HIS BODY MASS INDEX, THAT WAS NO MEAN FEAT.
IT'S EVERYWHERE THESE DAYS. REAL MEN COOK!! AND WHAT HE CAN DO, I CAN DO BETTER.
PFFT, ALL YOU DO IS NAG. TONIGHT, I PLAN TO MAKE CHARGRILLED SALMON IN A LEMON DILL CRUST WITH BABY NEW POTATOES. PREPARE YOURSELF FOR A GASTRONOMIC DELIGHT!
ET VOILA! JAMIE OLIVER, EAT YOUR HEART OUT.
OOOH, I'M IMPRESSED...THIS ACTUALLY LOOKS QUITE YUMMY.
WHOOSH
CARLOS, STOP THAT! YOU'RE SPREADING SPARKS ON EVERYTHING.
!
OH MY GOD OH MY GOD OH MY GOD!
YOU'RE RIGHT, THAT WAS REALLY MANLY.
© Joanna Zhou

IN DRE AMS

CELIA MACHUCA A. • STORY
ELISABET BASANTA • ART

IN DREAMS
Eli Basanta

We don't encourage *shojo* or *shonen* styles because they are so prevalent elsewhere, but there's always a welcome to be found here for the very best *shojo*. Enter **Eli Basanta**, a leading manga practitioner in her home country of Spain (cover artist Ken Niimura also lives there). She originally entered this strip as part of the late, lamented IMAF; we saw it, liked it, and remembered it for that day when we could print it in full colour as it was always meant to be. Like various others around the world – Anike Hage in Germany, Benjamin in China, Adam Warren and many others in the USA – Eli has managed to carve herself a career out of making manga.

www.elibasanta.com
lely.deviantart.com

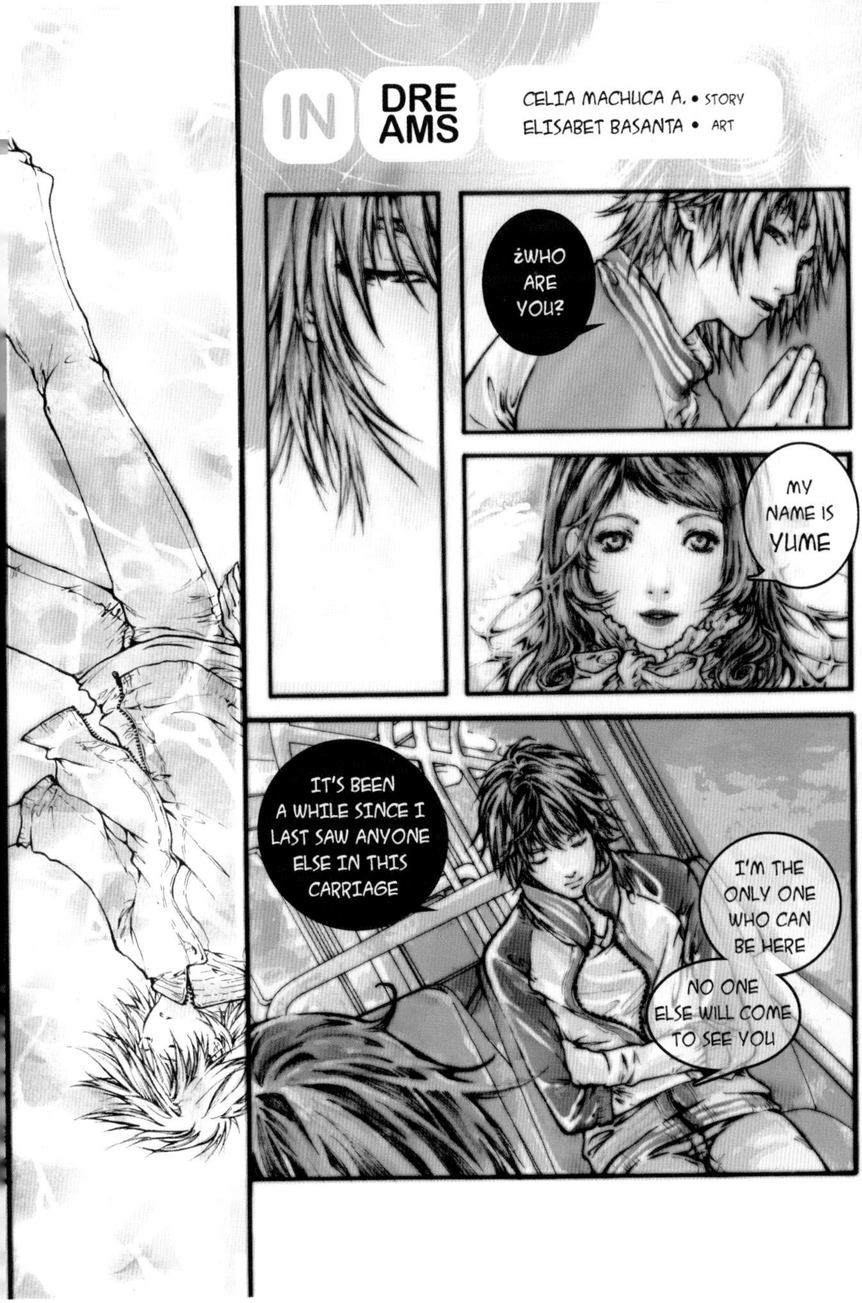
IN DREAMS
CELIA MACHUCA A. • STORY
ELISABET BASANTA • ART
¿WHO ARE YOU?
MY NAME IS YUME
IT'S BEEN A WHILE SINCE I LAST SAW ANYONE ELSE IN THIS CARRIAGE
I'M THE ONLY ONE WHO CAN BE HERE
NO ONE ELSE WILL COME TO SEE YOU

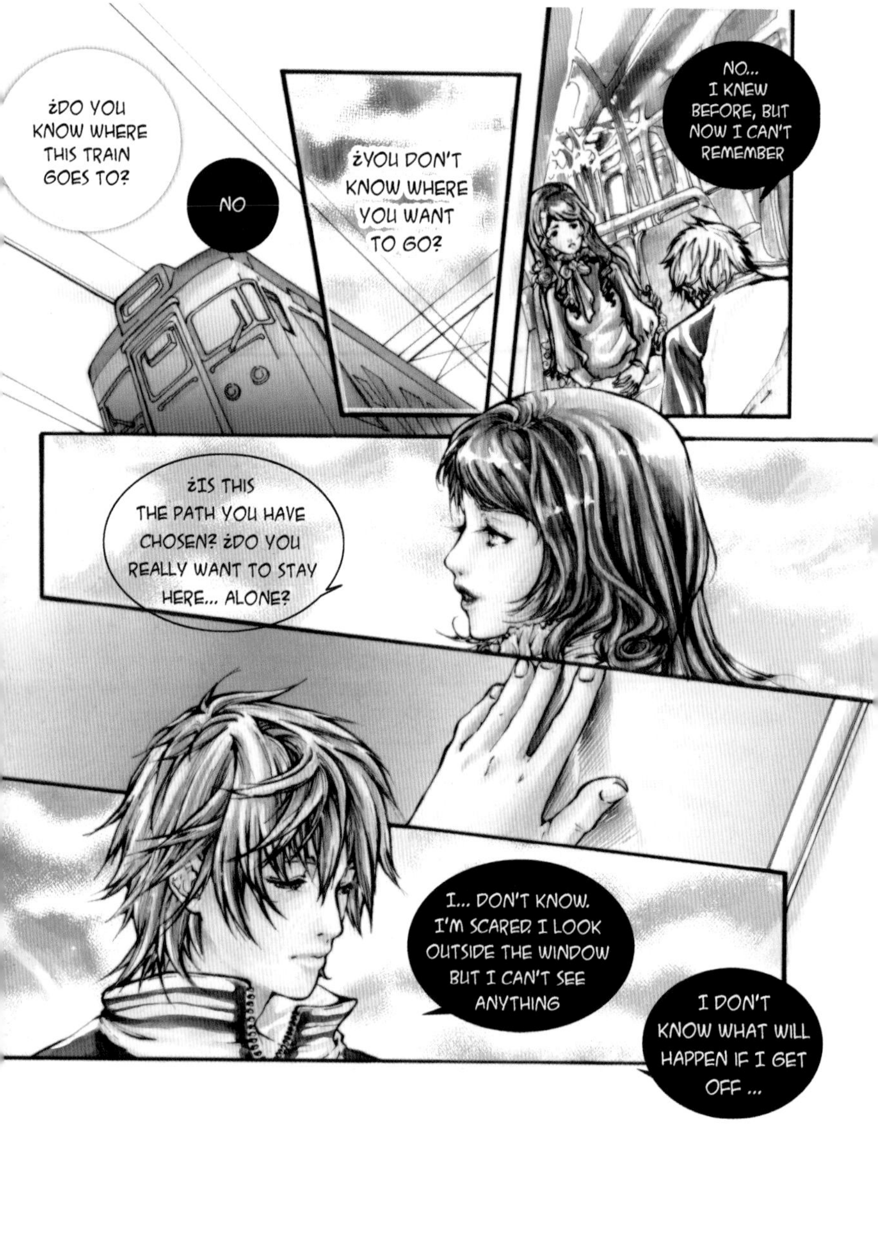
¿DO YOU KNOW WHERE THIS TRAIN GOES TO?
NO
¿YOU DON'T KNOW WHERE YOU WANT TO GO?
NO... I KNEW BEFORE, BUT NOW I CAN'T REMEMBER
¿IS THIS THE PATH YOU HAVE CHOSEN? ¿DO YOU REALLY WANT TO STAY HERE... ALONE?
I... DON'T KNOW. I'M SCARED. I LOOK OUTSIDE THE WINDOW BUT I CAN'T SEE ANYTHING
I DON'T KNOW WHAT WILL HAPPEN IF I GET OFF ...

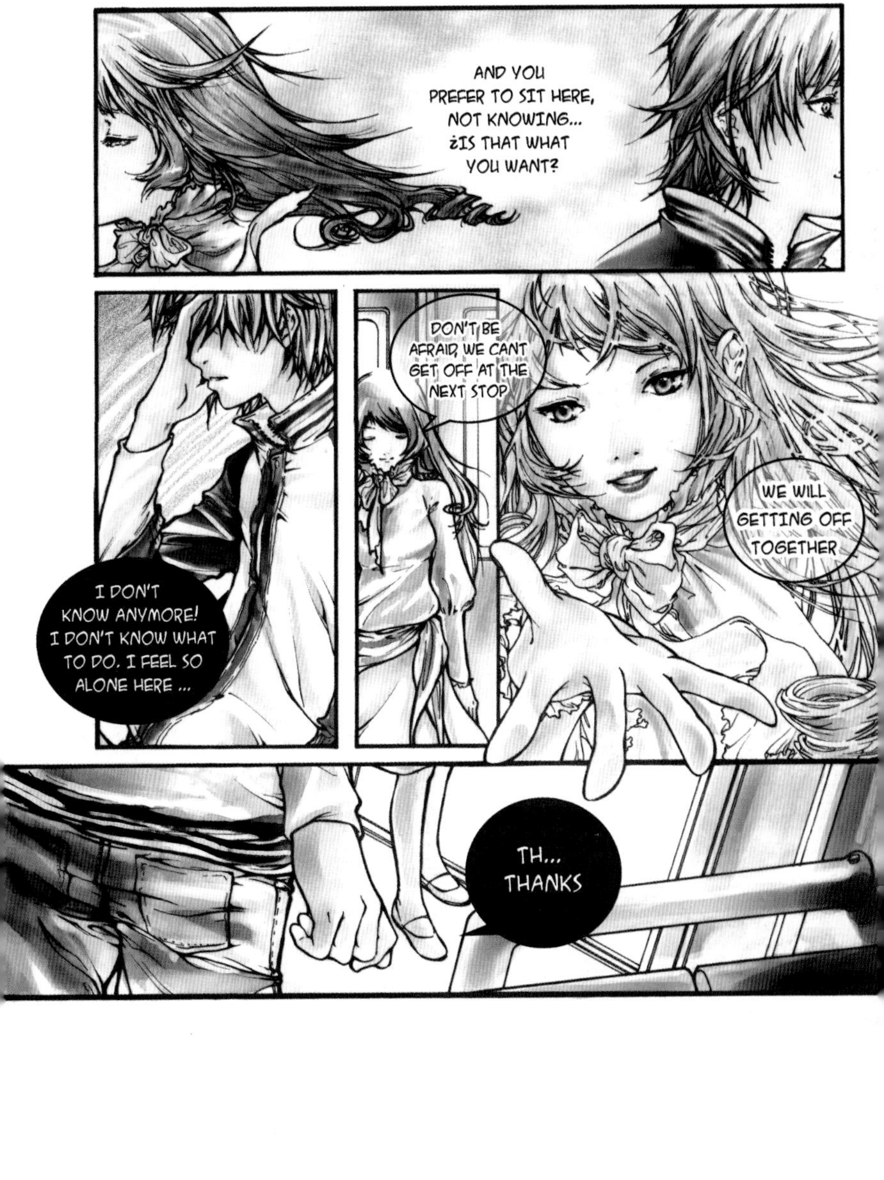

AND YOU PREFER TO SIT HERE, NOT KNOWING... ¿IS THAT WHAT YOU WANT?
I DON'T KNOW ANYMORE! I DON'T KNOW WHAT TO DO. I FEEL SO ALONE HERE ...
DON'T BE AFRAID, WE CANT GET OFF AT THE NEXT STOP
WE WILL GETTING OFF TOGETHER
TH... THANKS

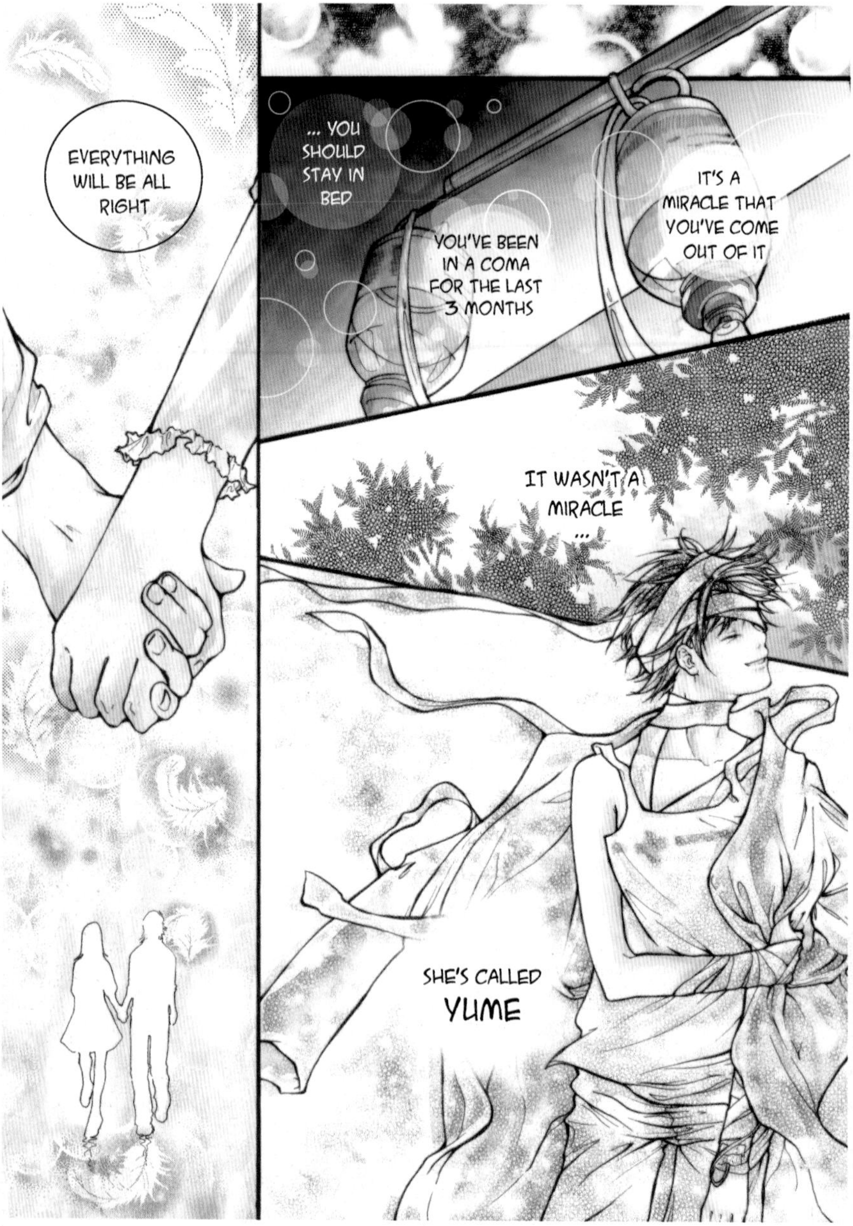
EVERYTHING WILL BE ALL RIGHT
... YOU SHOULD STAY IN BED
YOU'VE BEEN IN A COMA FOR THE LAST 3 MONTHS
IT'S A MIRACLE THAT YOU'VE COME OUT OF IT
IT WASN'T A MIRACLE ...
SHE'S CALLED YUME

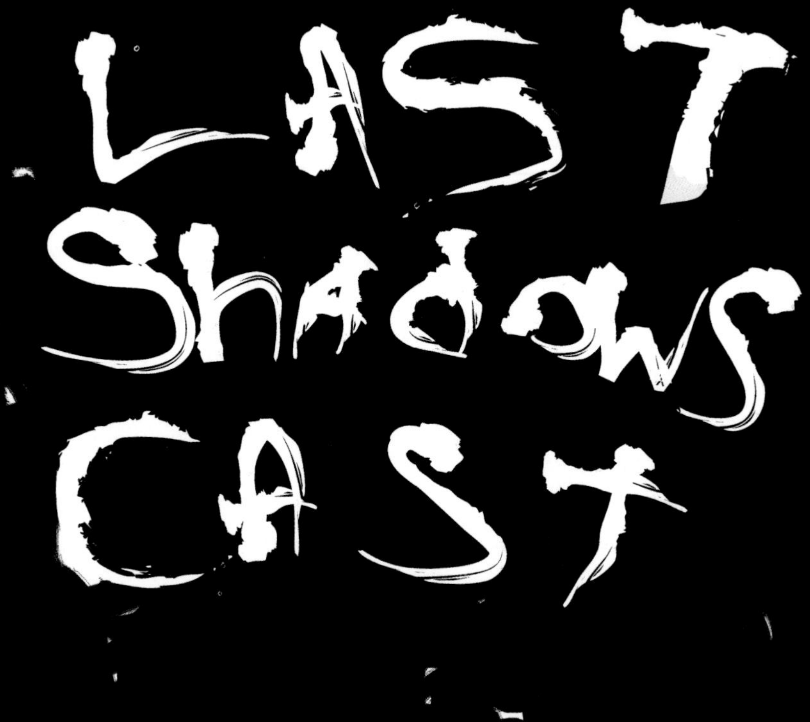
LAST
Shadows
CAST

BY CASPAR WIJNGAARD

LAST SHADOWS CAST

Caspar Wijngaard

In a *Mad World* (as the song goes), the dreams in which you're dying are the best you'll ever have. *Last Shadows Cast* is a neat end-times fable; apocalyptic, revelatory (wait for it...) eschatological, revolving around a final twist so subtle that in its sobriety it might easily be missed. Look to the title. **Caspar Wijngaard** originally drew our attention as part of IMAF 2005, with his scurrilous and goofy full-colour strip, *You, Me & Yesterday.* Caspar tells us, "Drawing since I could pick up a pencil, I was first introduced to manga at about eight years old. My older brother and I started buying manga comics and would sit there copying the panels, creating pictures crammed with a medley of all our favourite characters, cool-looking robots and cute girls...

Nowadays he works full time in an uptown fashion-house boutique, but still managed to wangle enough days off and time out to craft especially for us this intense little futuristic fable. Filled to bursting with tales to tell, we feel it won't be long before he's looking for another line of work entirely: and who knows, it may well involve manga!

"So please," says Casper, "enjoy this tale of the last moments on earth."

caspart8@yahoo.com

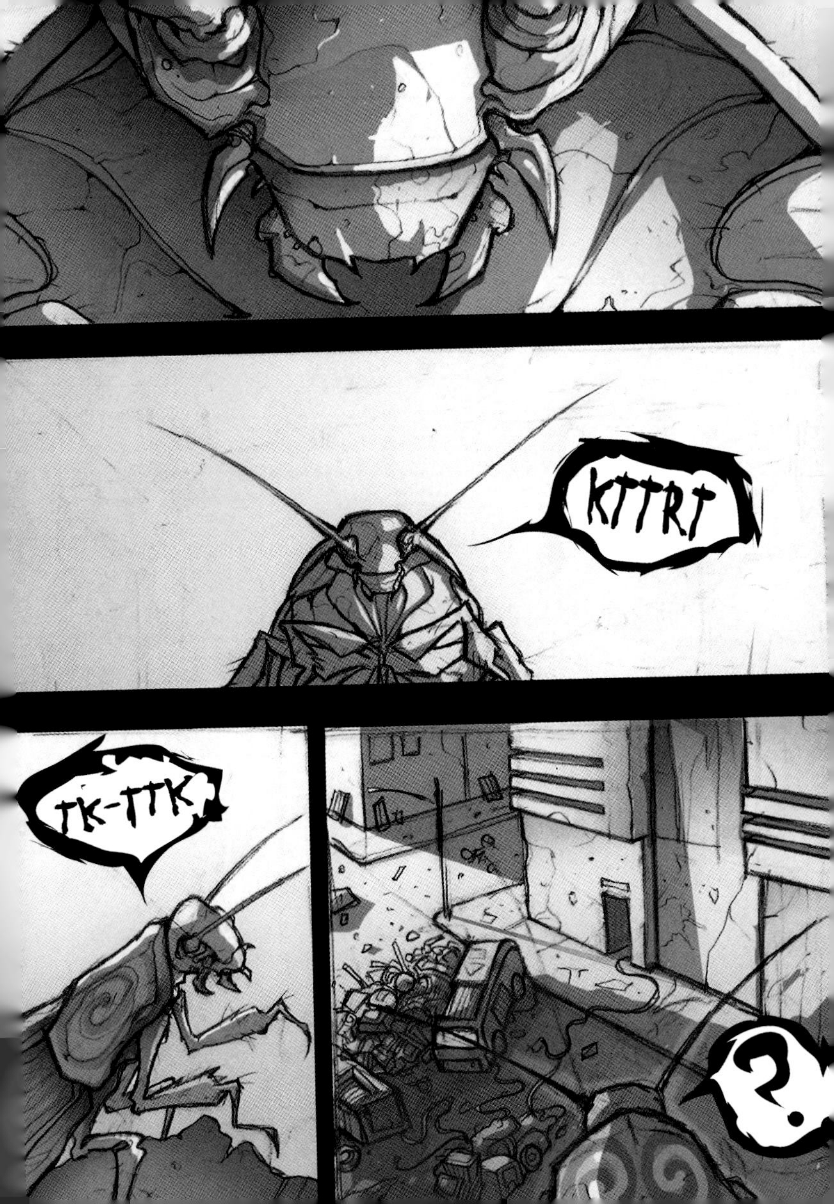
KTTRT
TK-TTK
?

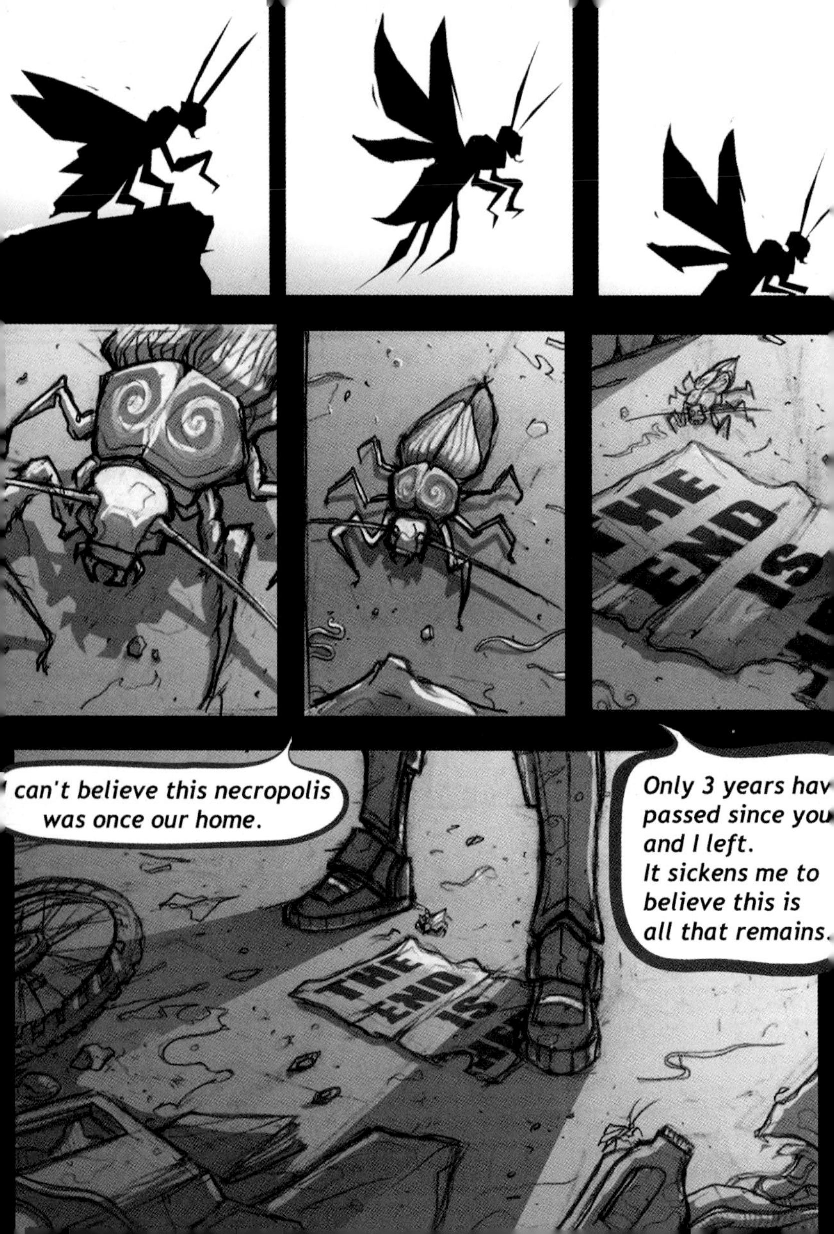
THE END IS
THE END IS
can't believe this necropolis was once our home.
Only 3 years hav passed since you and I left. It sickens me to believe this is all that remains.
THE END IS

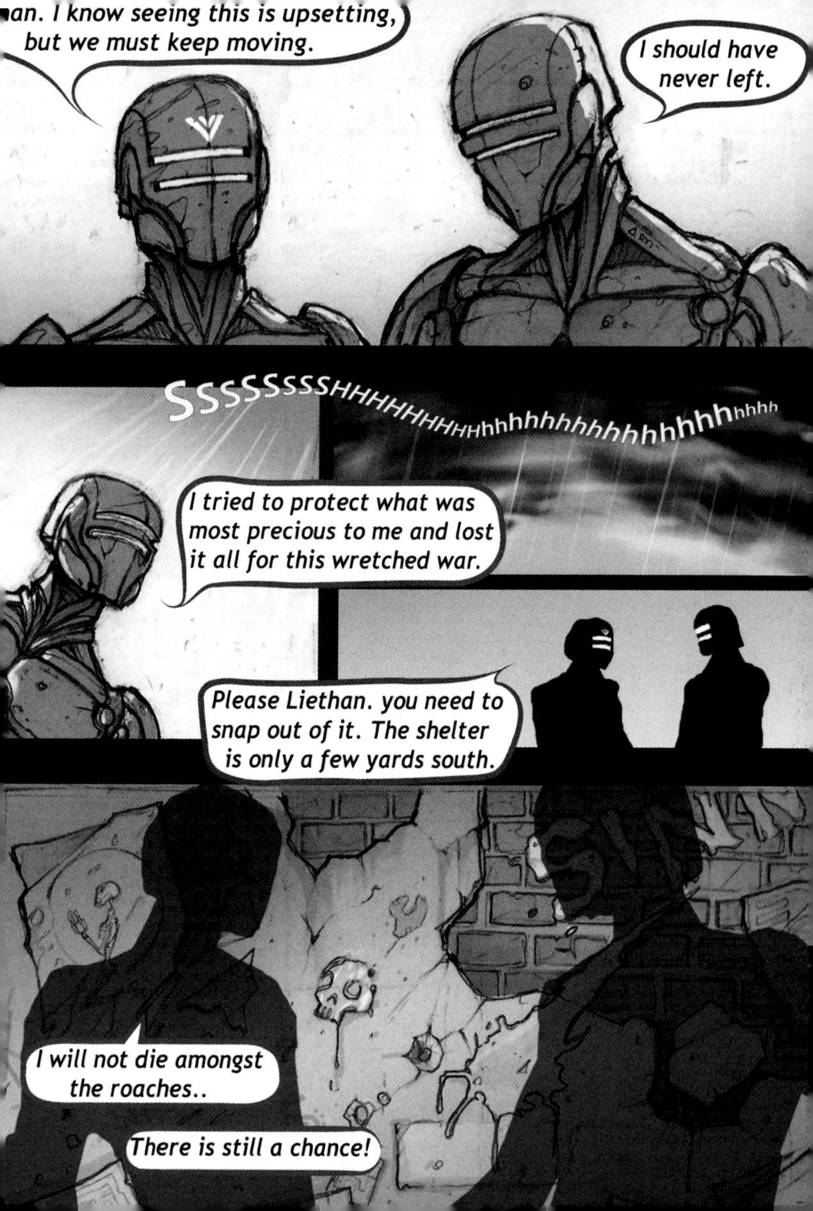
an. I know seeing this is upsetting, but we must keep moving.
I should have never left.
SSSSSSSSHHHHHHHHhhhhhhhhhhhhhhhhhh
I tried to protect what was most precious to me and lost it all for this wretched war.
Please Liethan. you need to snap out of it. The shelter is only a few yards south.
I will not die amongst the roaches..
There is still a chance!

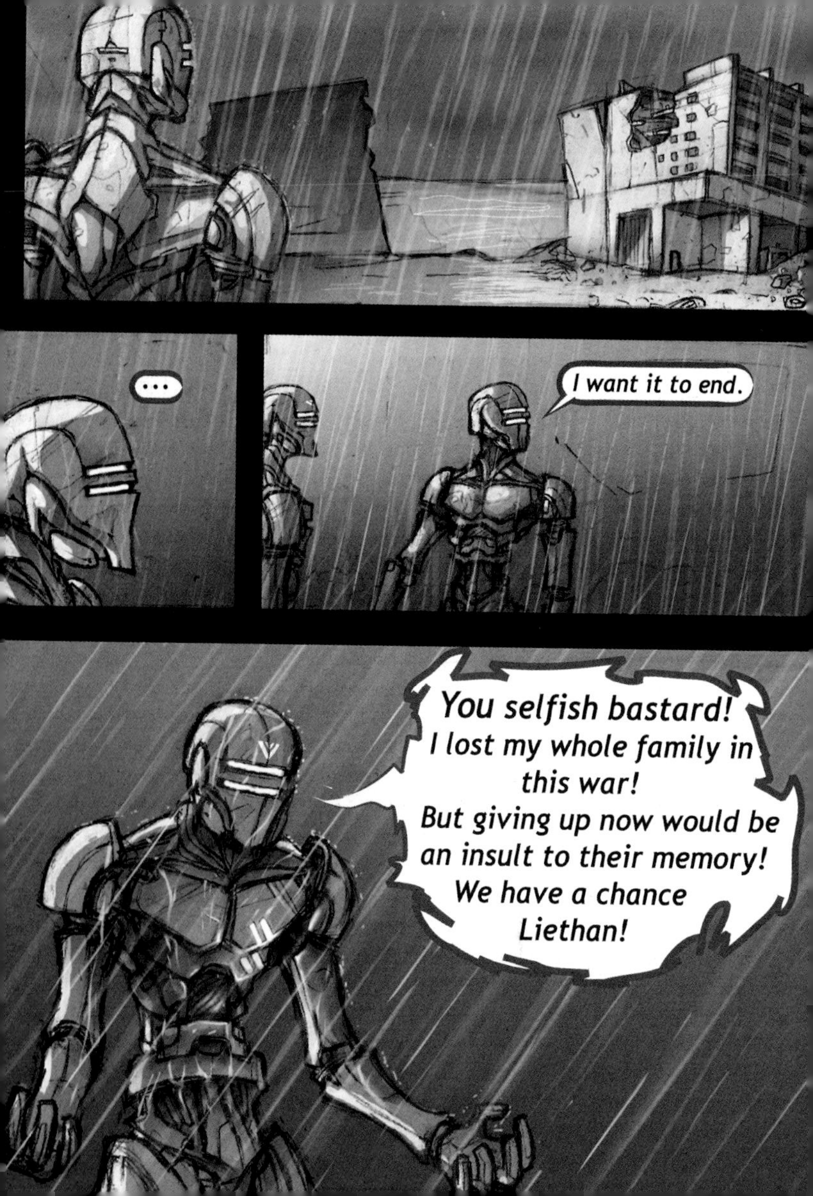
...
I want it to end.
You selfish bastard! I lost my whole family in this war! But giving up now would be an insult to their memory! We have a chance Liethan!

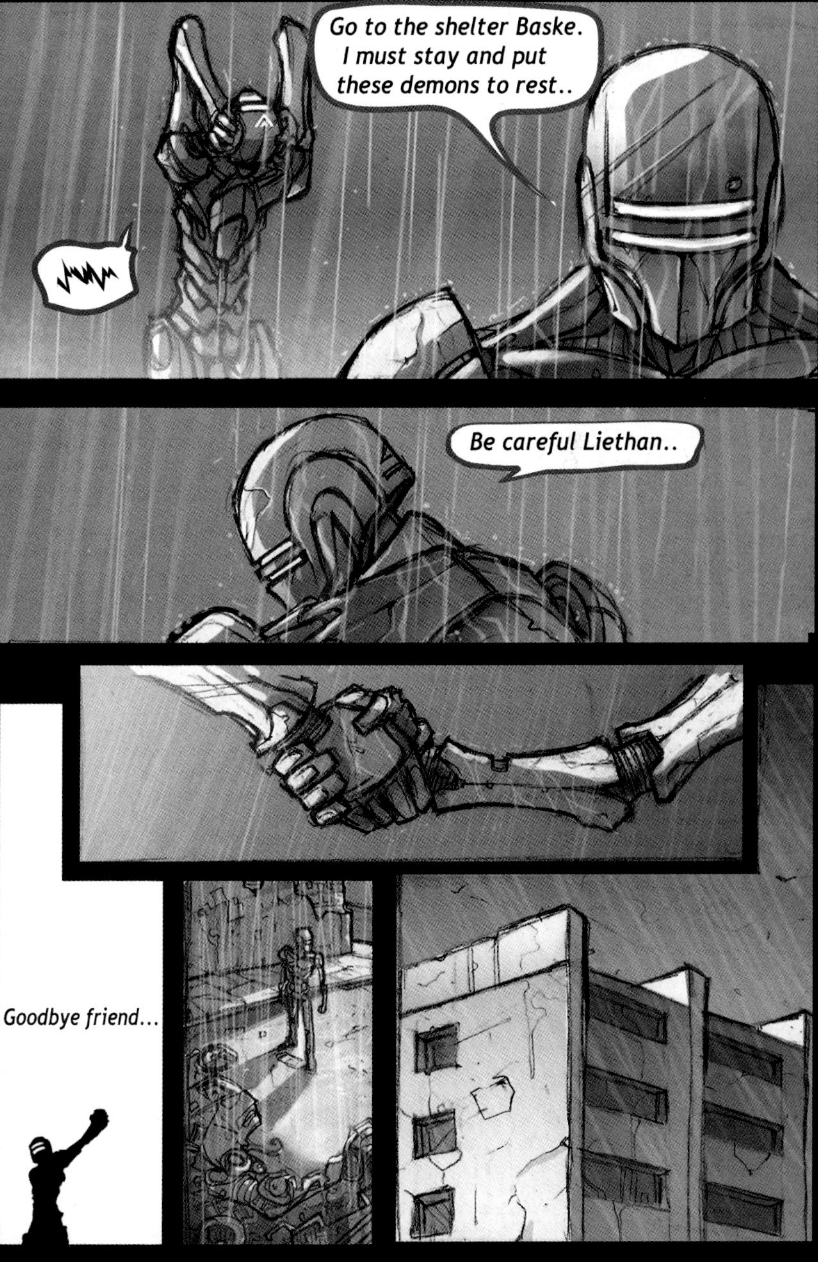
Go to the shelter Baske. I must stay and put these demons to rest..
Be careful Liethan..
Goodbye friend...

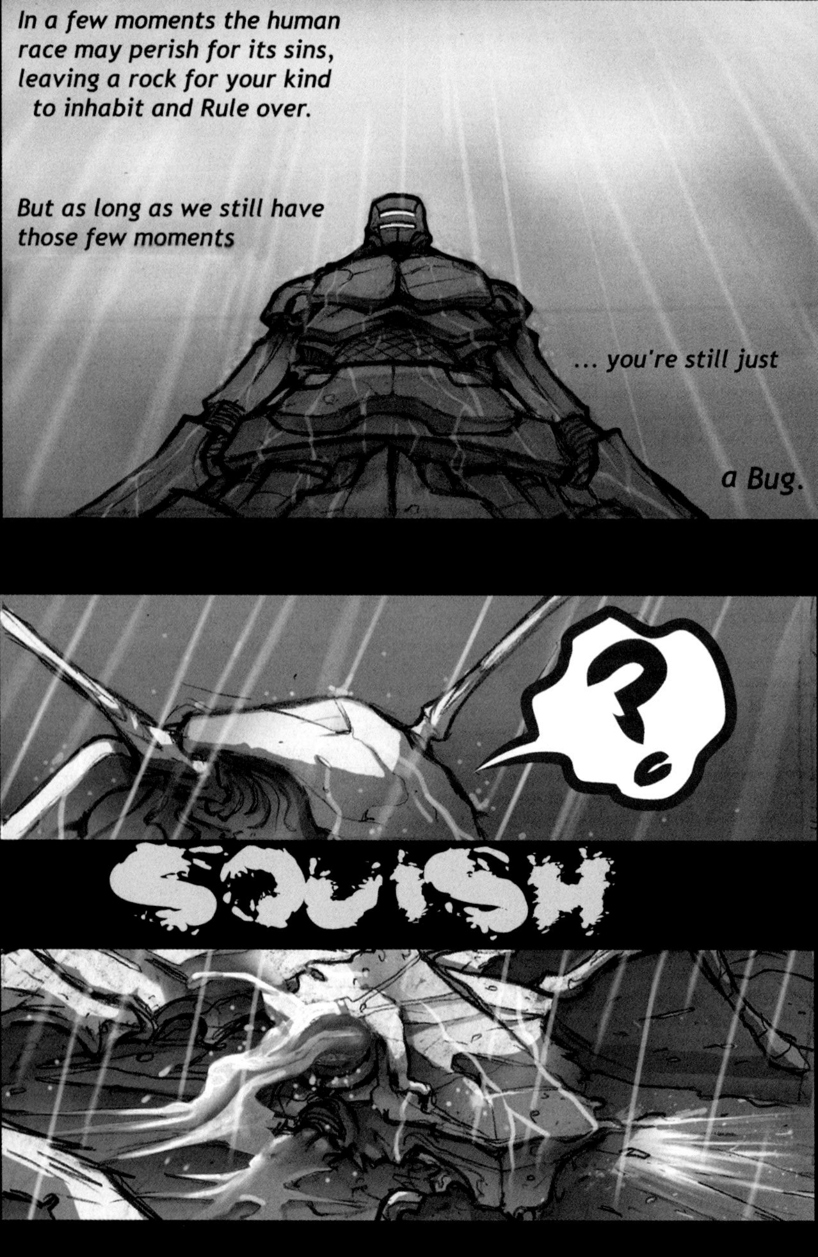
In a few moments the human race may perish for its sins, leaving a rock for your kind to inhabit and Rule over.
But as long as we still have those few moments
... you're still just
a Bug.
?
SQUISH

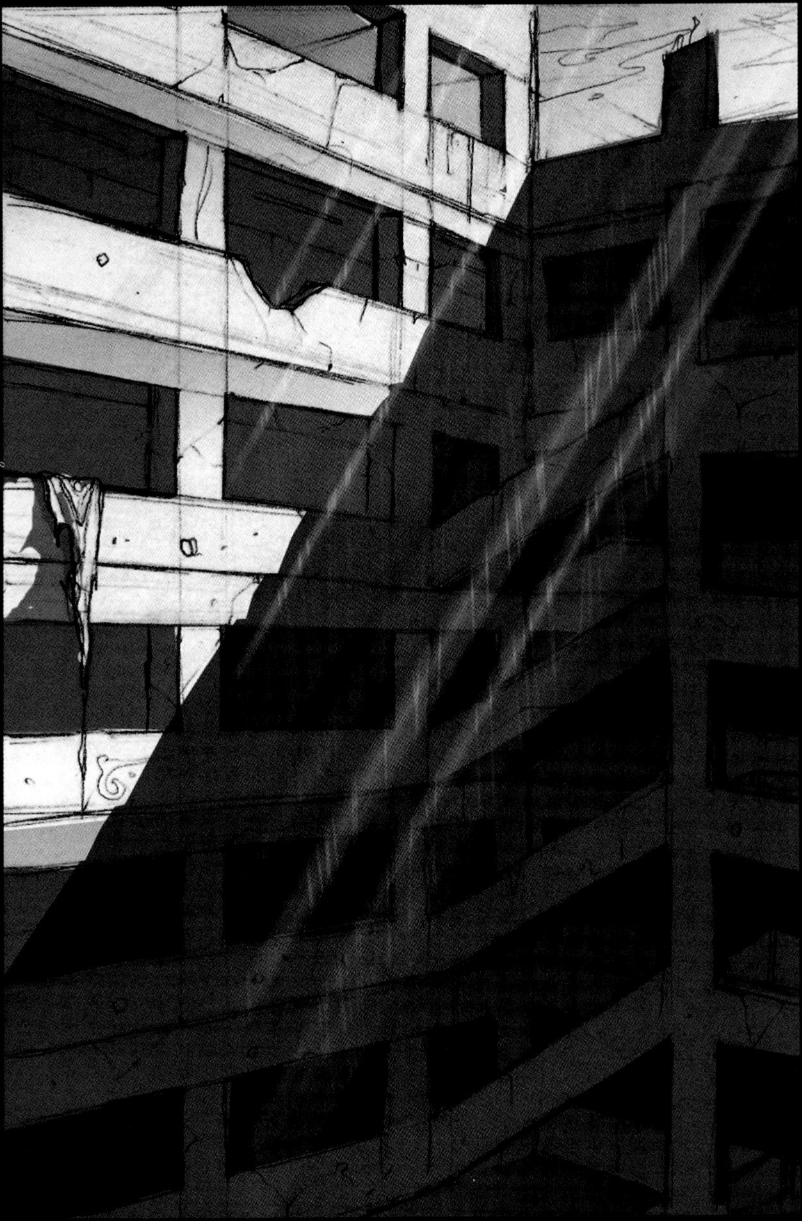

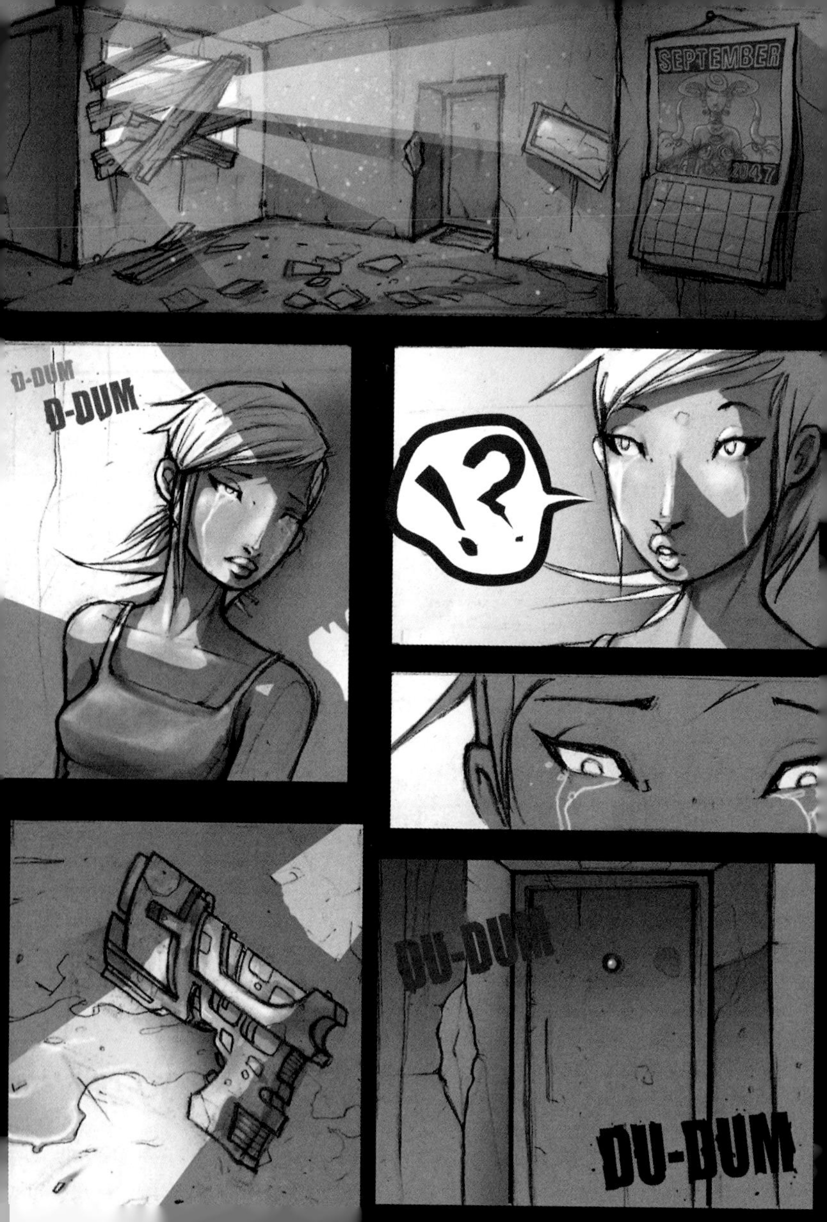
SEPTEMBER
2047
D-DUM
D-DUM
!?
DU-DUM
DU-DUM

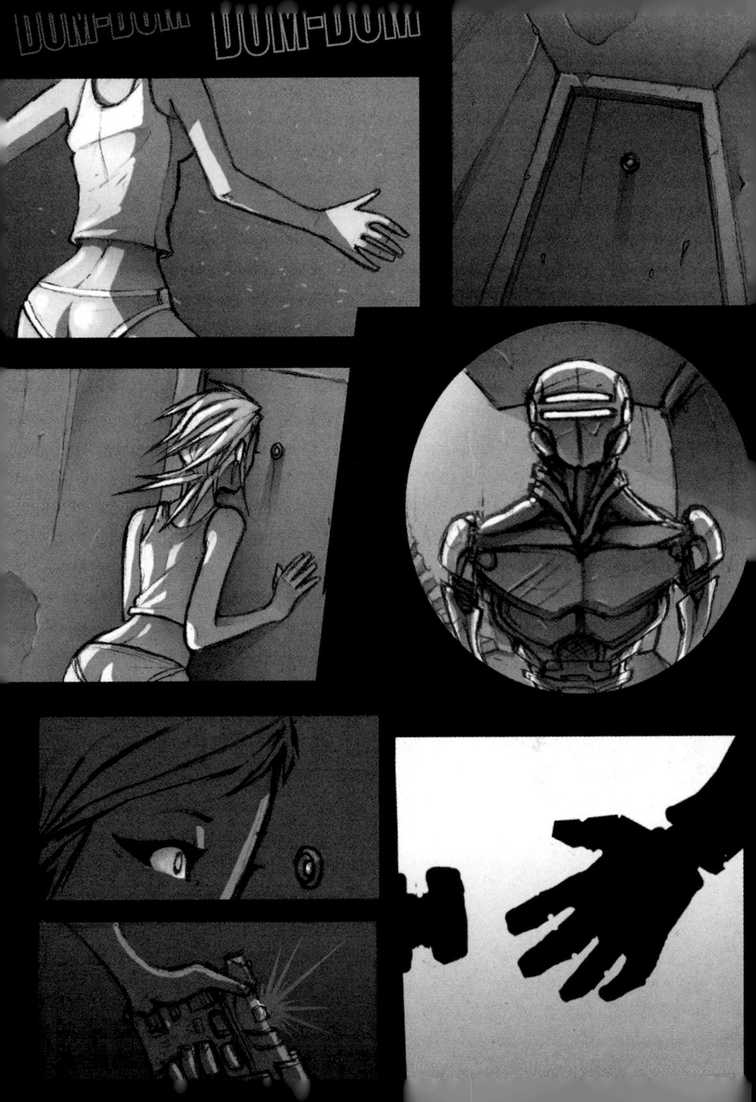
DUM-DUM
DUM-DUM

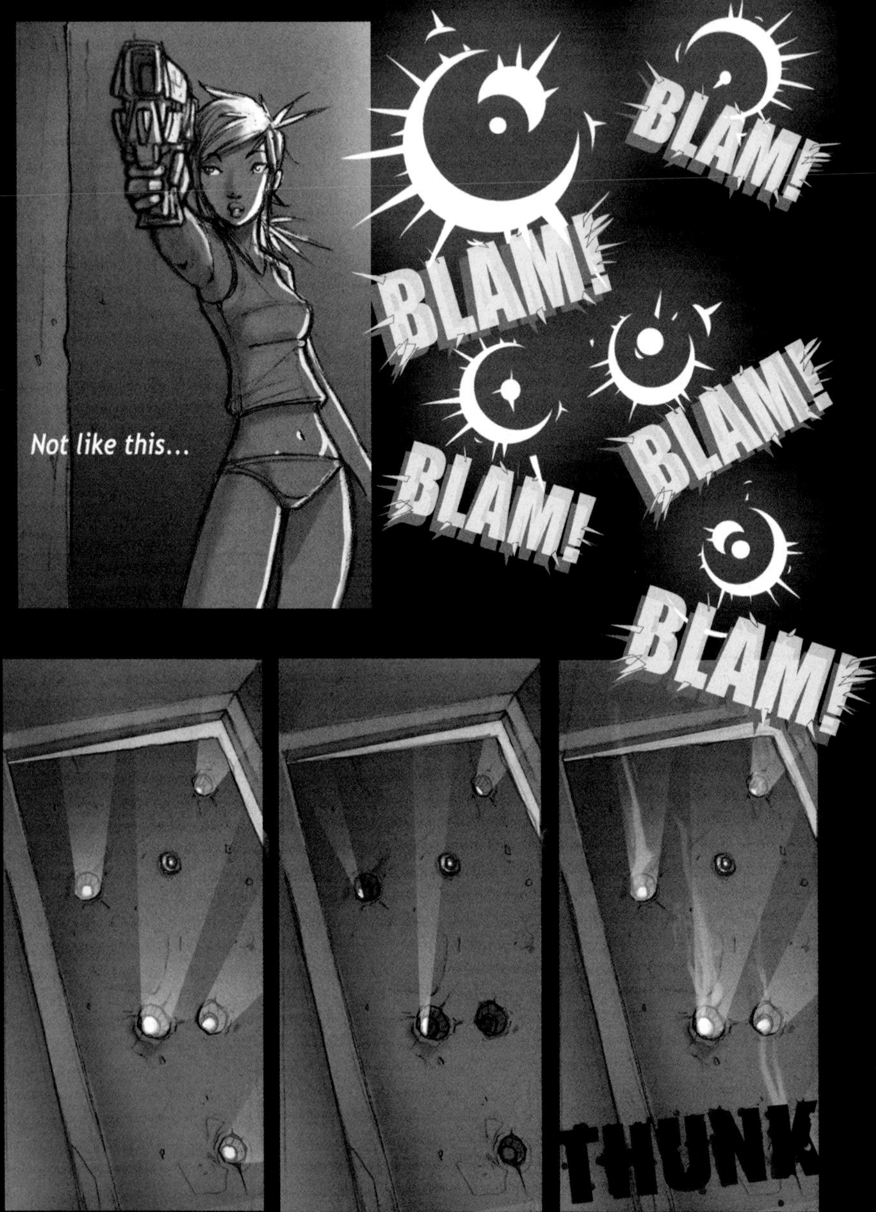
Not like this...
BLAM!
BLAM!
BLAM!
BLAM!
BLAM!
THUNK

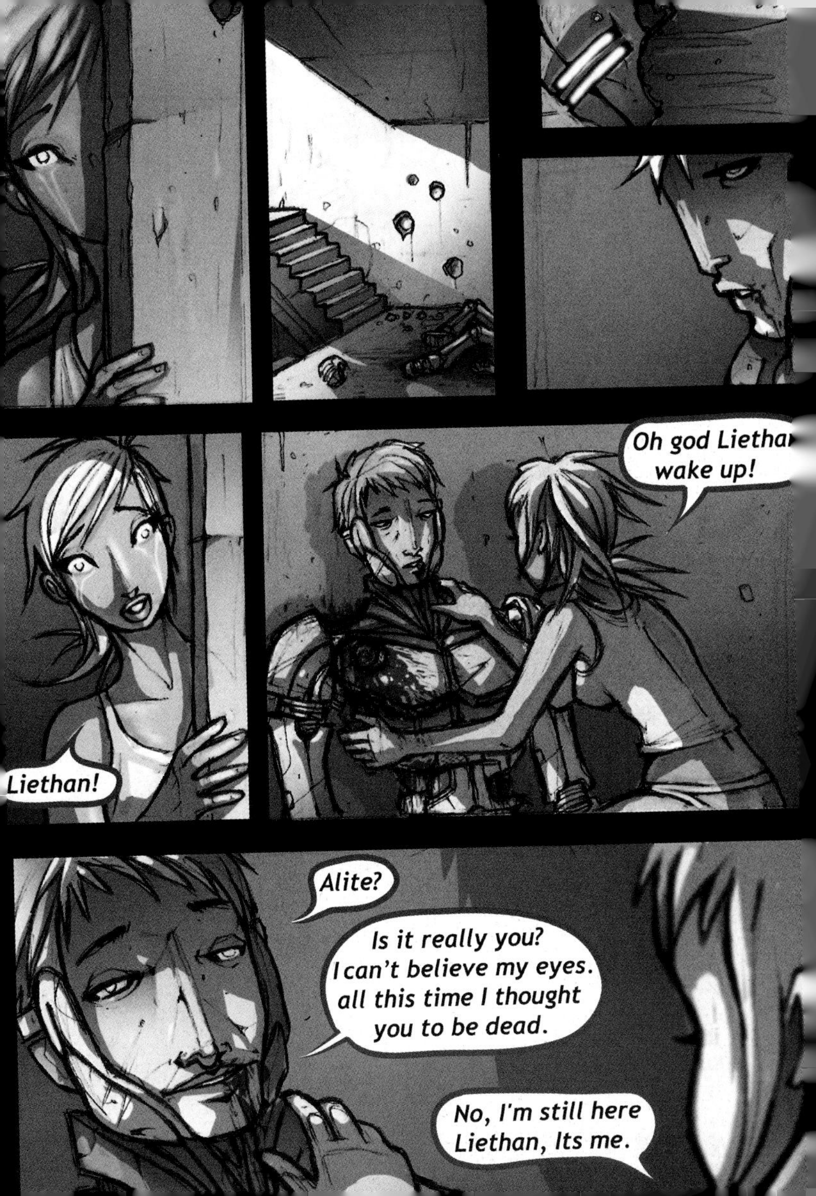
Liethan!
Oh god Liethan wake up!
Alite?
Is it really you? I can't believe my eyes. all this time I thought you to be dead.
No, I'm still here Liethan, Its me.

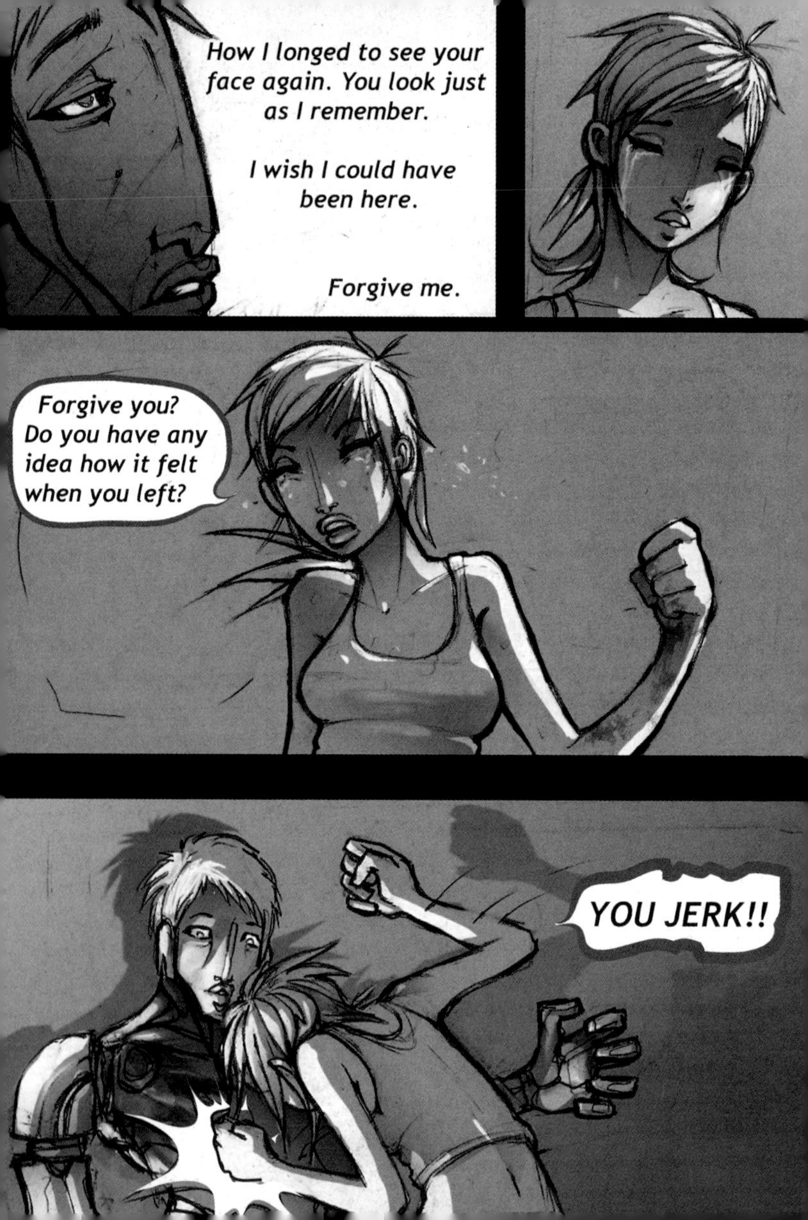
How I longed to see your face again. You look just as I remember.
I wish I could have been here.
Forgive me.
Forgive you? Do you have any idea how it felt when you left?
YOU JERK!!

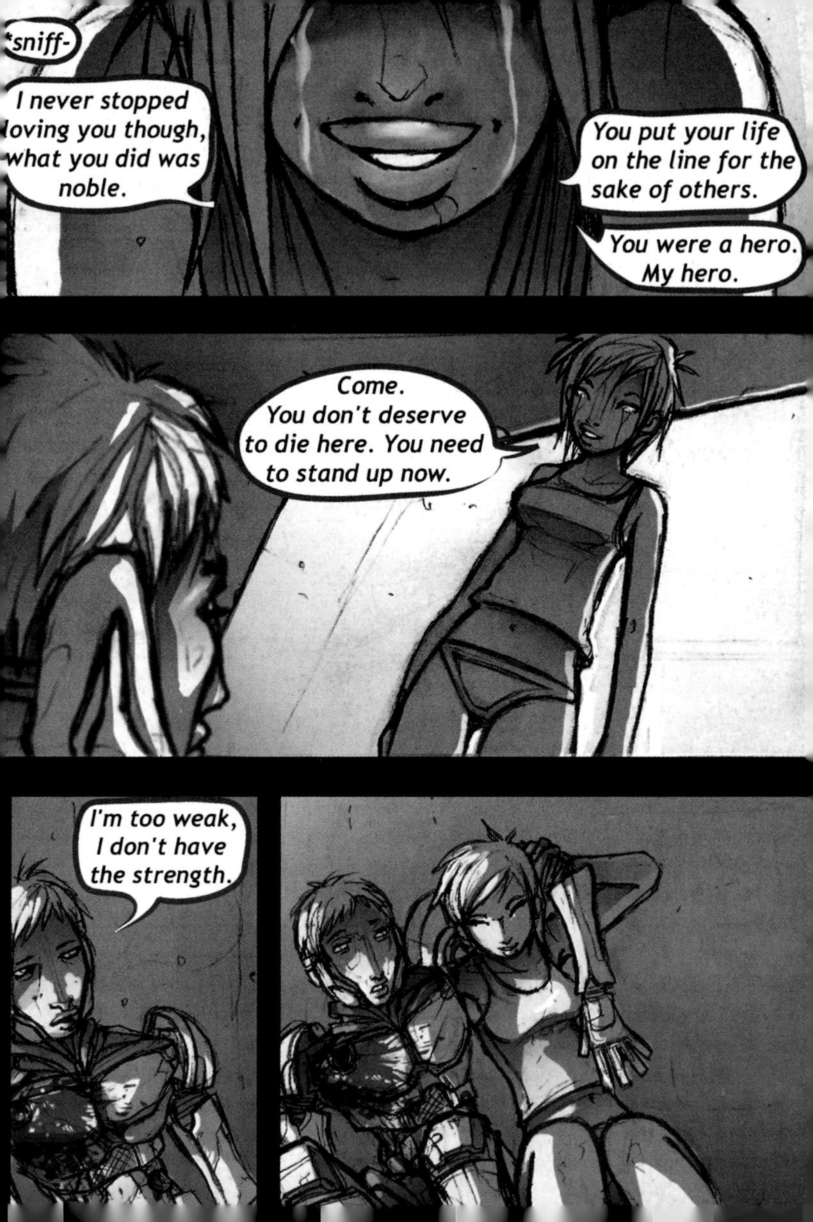
*sniff-
I never stopped loving you though, what you did was noble.
You put your life on the line for the sake of others.
You were a hero. My hero.
Come. You don't deserve to die here. You need to stand up now.
I'm too weak, I don't have the strength.

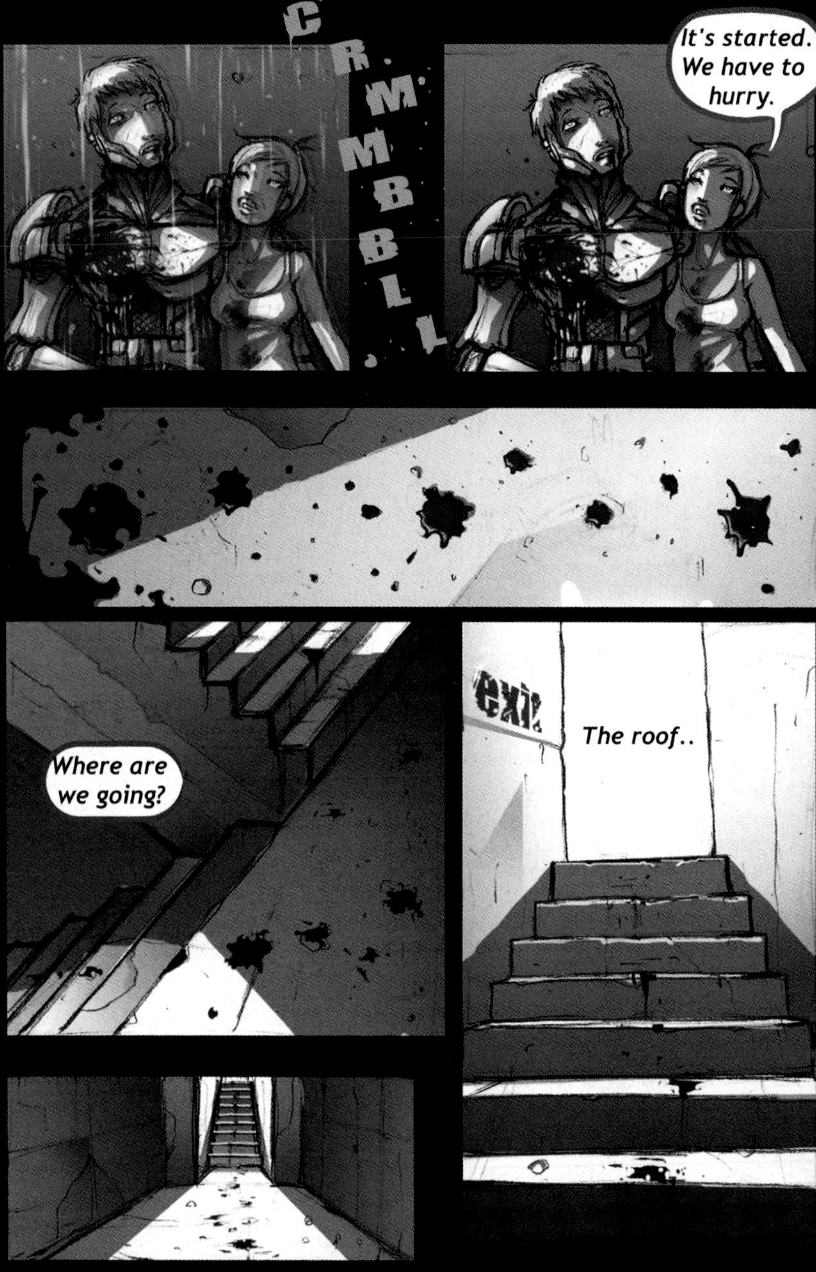
CRMMBBLL
It's started. We have to hurry.
Where are we going?
exit
The roof..

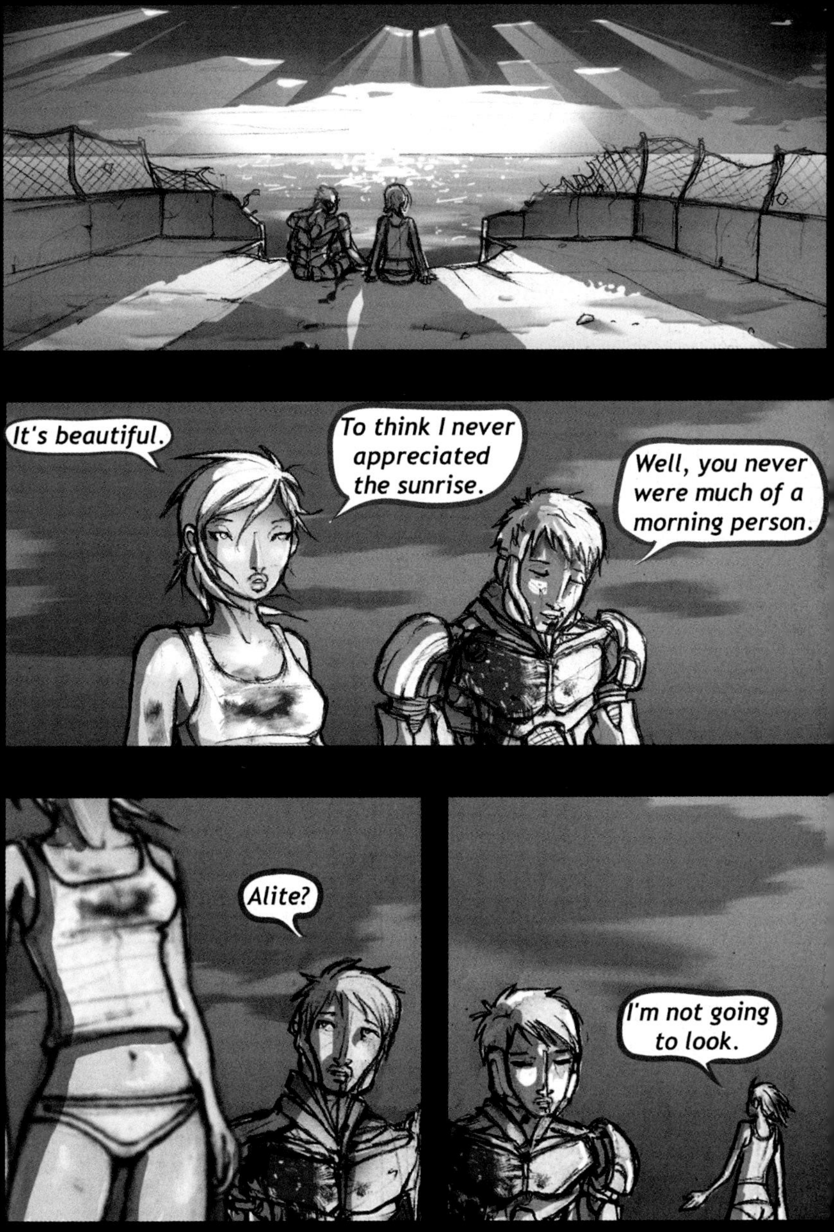
It's beautiful.
To think I never appreciated the sunrise.
Well, you never were much of a morning person.
Alite?
I'm not going to look.

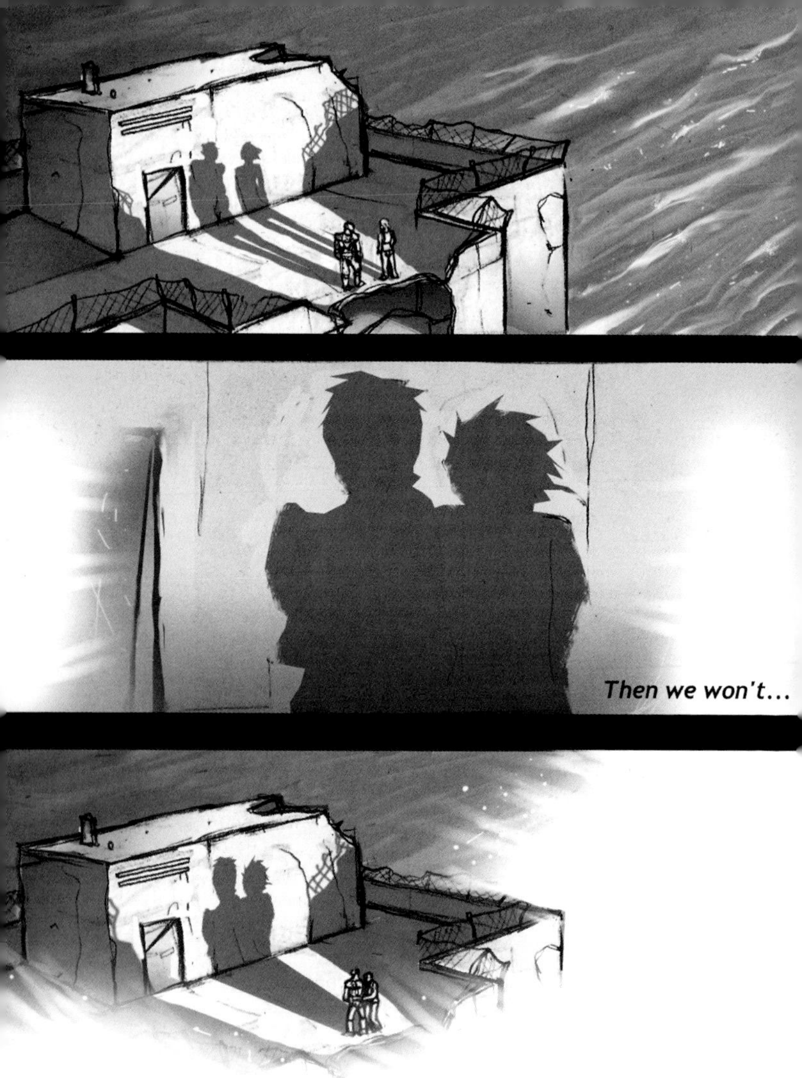
Then we won't...

Thank you

I'm no longer scared

We are together at last...

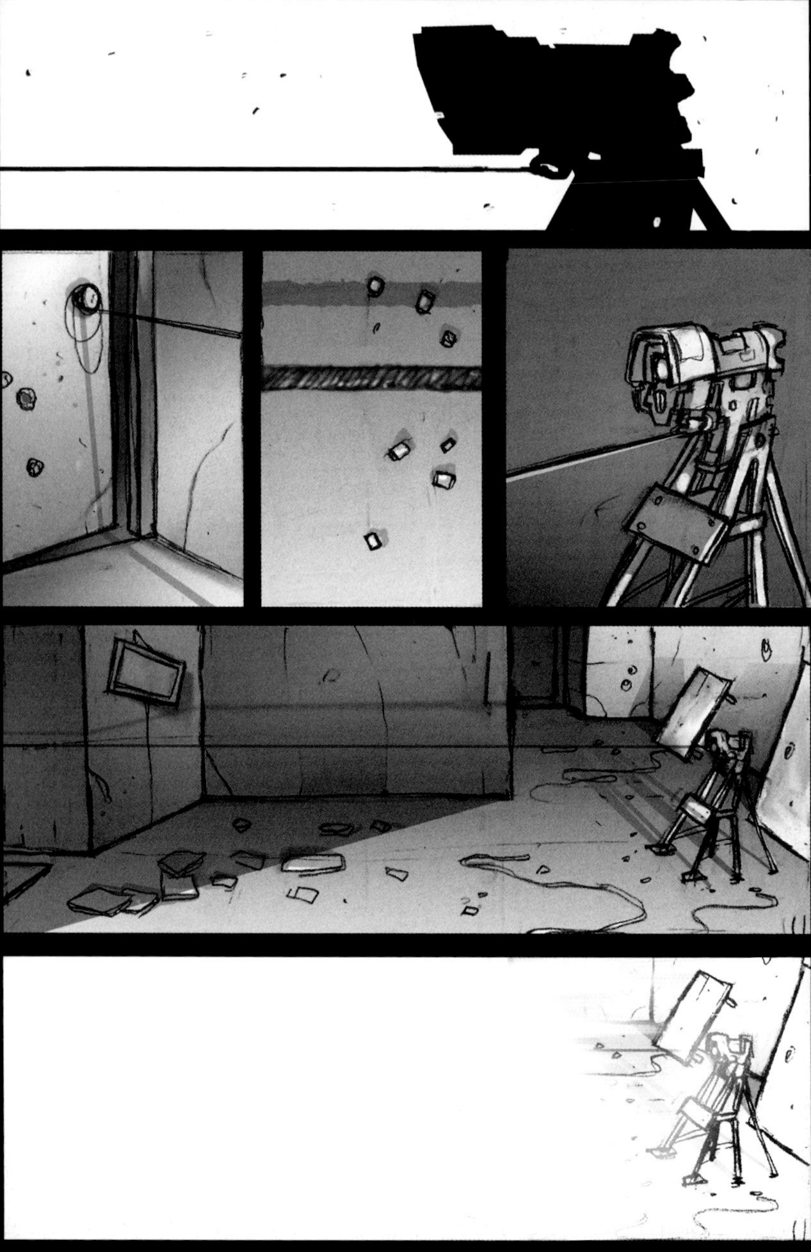

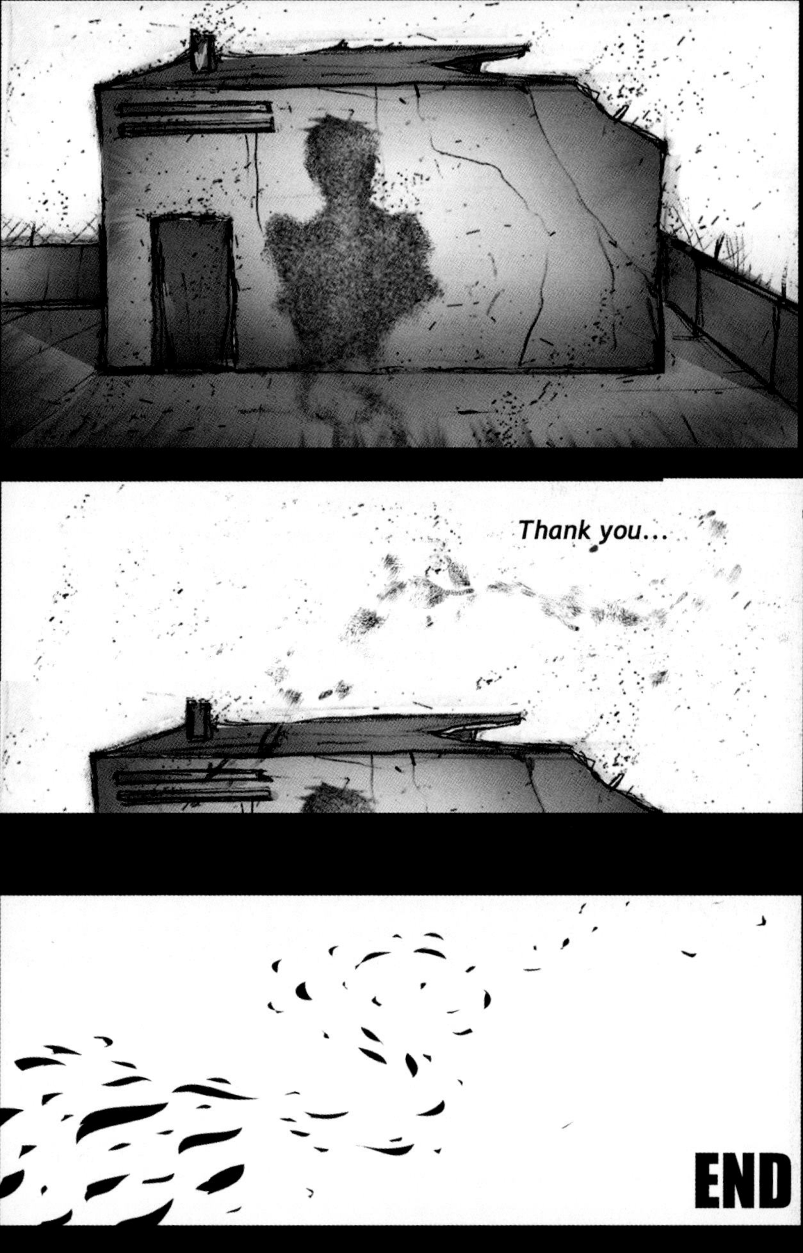
Thank you...
END

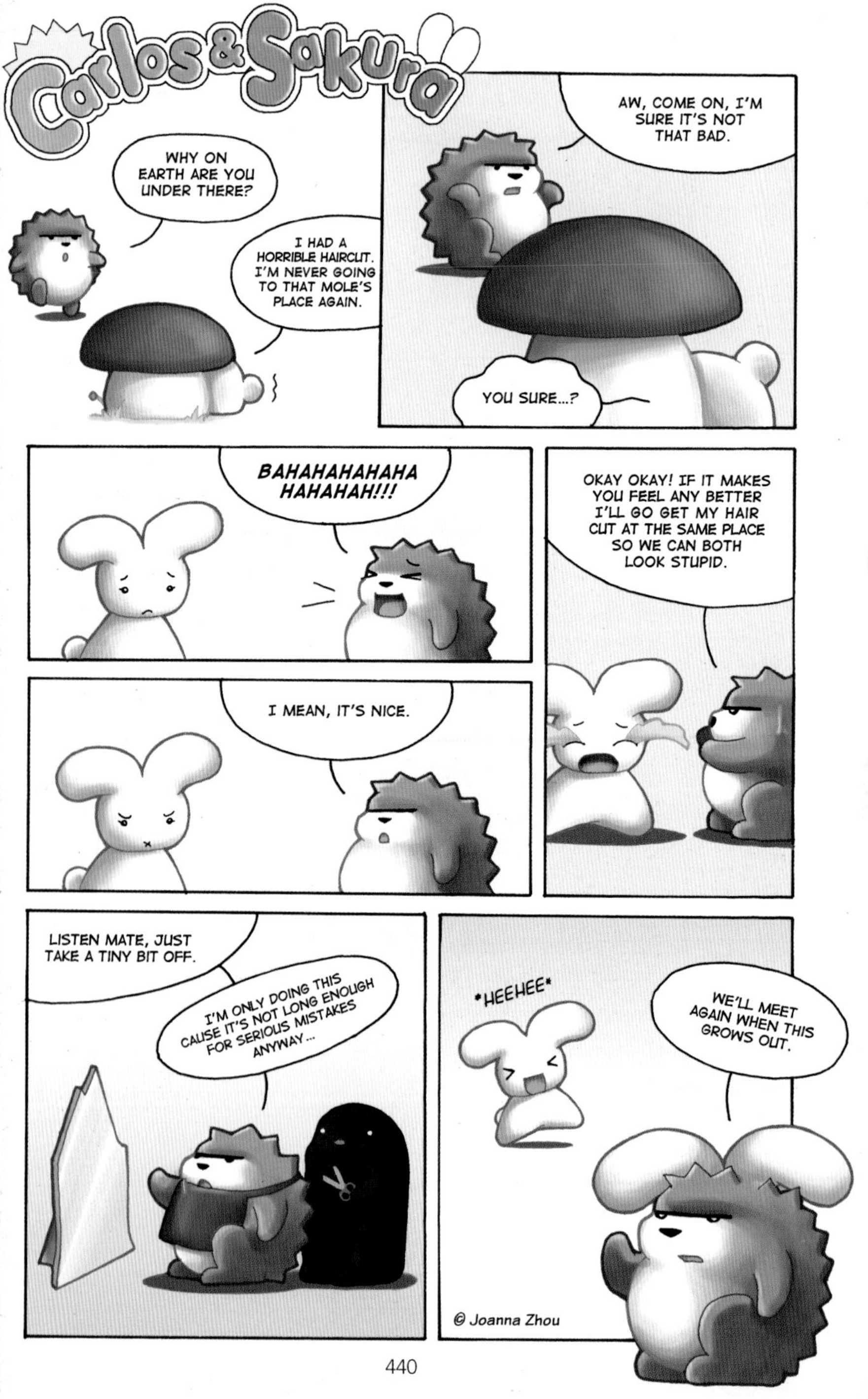
Carlos & Sakura
WHY ON EARTH ARE YOU UNDER THERE?
I HAD A HORRIBLE HAIRCUT. I'M NEVER GOING TO THAT MOLE'S PLACE AGAIN.
AW, COME ON, I'M SURE IT'S NOT THAT BAD.
YOU SURE...?
BAHAHAHAHAHA HAHAHAH!!!
I MEAN, IT'S NICE.
OKAY OKAY! IF IT MAKES YOU FEEL ANY BETTER I'LL GO GET MY HAIR CUT AT THE SAME PLACE SO WE CAN BOTH LOOK STUPID.
LISTEN MATE, JUST TAKE A TINY BIT OFF.
I'M ONLY DOING THIS CAUSE IT'S NOT LONG ENOUGH FOR SERIOUS MISTAKES ANYWAY...
HEEHEE
WE'LL MEET AGAIN WHEN THIS GROWS OUT.
© Joanna Zhou

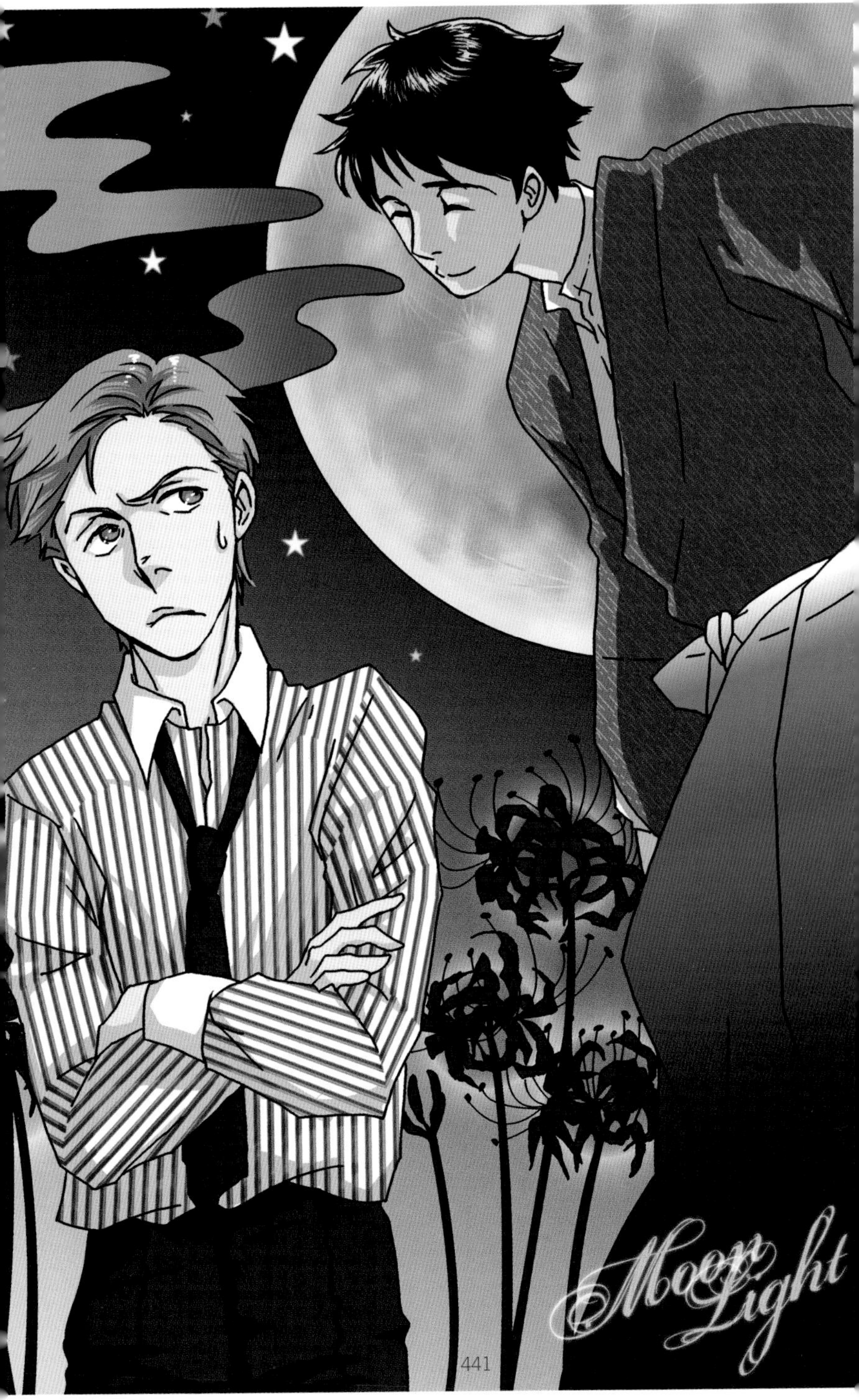
Moon Light

MOONLIGHT
Chi-Tan (Chie Kutsuwada)

To all things, an ending. The zero hour of midnight is of course but the start of a new day. How fitting a message for our last, yet far from final, manga, a ghost story that celebrates this medium where east meets west, and they come so gloriously together.

my soul

Chie Kutsuwada previously crafted one of our most unusual yet typically manga stories with her subtle and moving *King of a Miniature Garden* in *Volume Two*. A full 100 pages in length, that entry won an extended slot on its own merits and for its original vision – as neatly balanced as this new miniature is exquisite in six. Chie is currently busy working with William Shakespeare, a writer you might have heard of, adapting *As You Like It* for Self Made Hero. She is but one of many *BNM* alumni to do so – joining Kate Brown (*A Midsummer Night's Dream*), Rob Deas (*Macbeth*), and Mustashrik Mahbub (*Julius Caesar*).

www.umisen-yamasen.com

We hope you have enjoyed this latest batch of the best in new manga. Do feel free to write: editor@bestnewmanga.com. Congratulations or criticism, be sure to nominate your favourites. We can't guarantee to reply to everyone, but all of your comments will be taken on board.

Thank you, ILYA

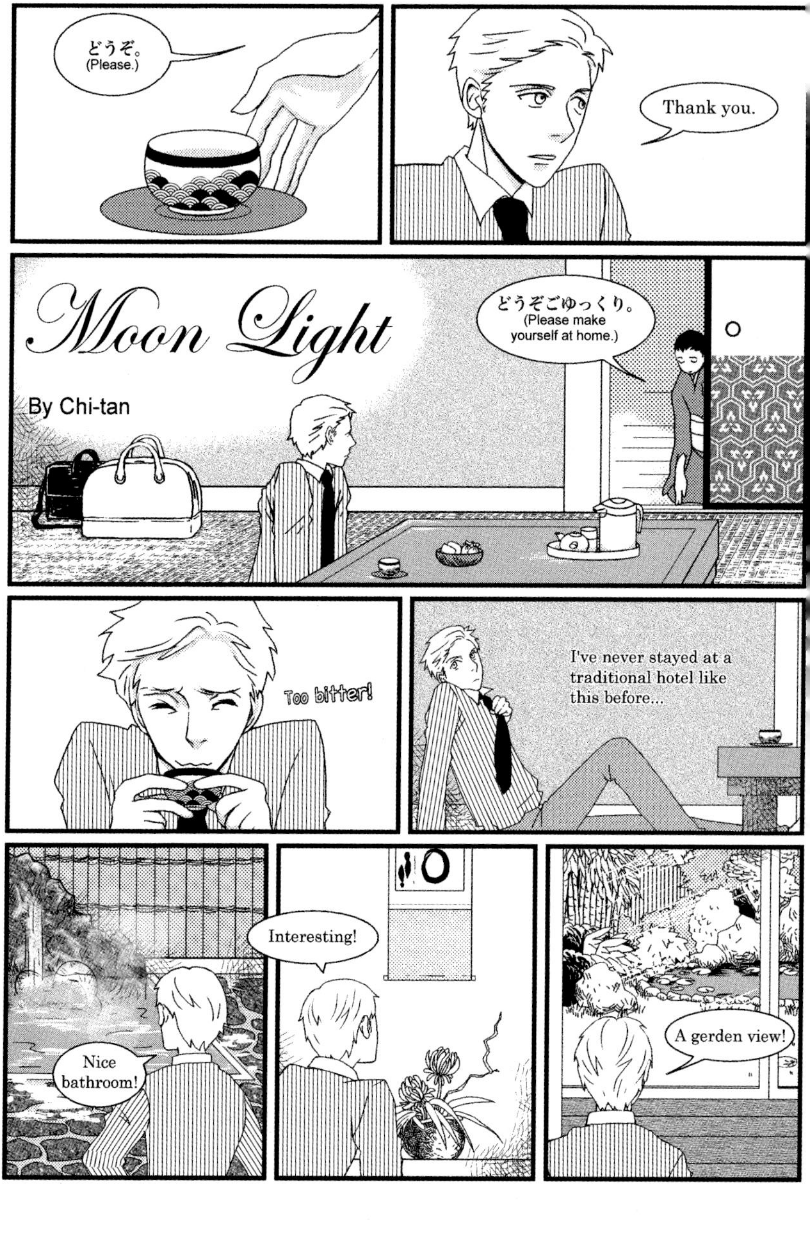
どうぞ。
(Please.)
Thank you.
Moon Light
By Chi-tan
どうぞごゆっくり。
(Please make yourself at home.)
Too bitter!
I've never stayed at a traditional hotel like this before...
Nice bathroom!
Interesting!
A gerden view!

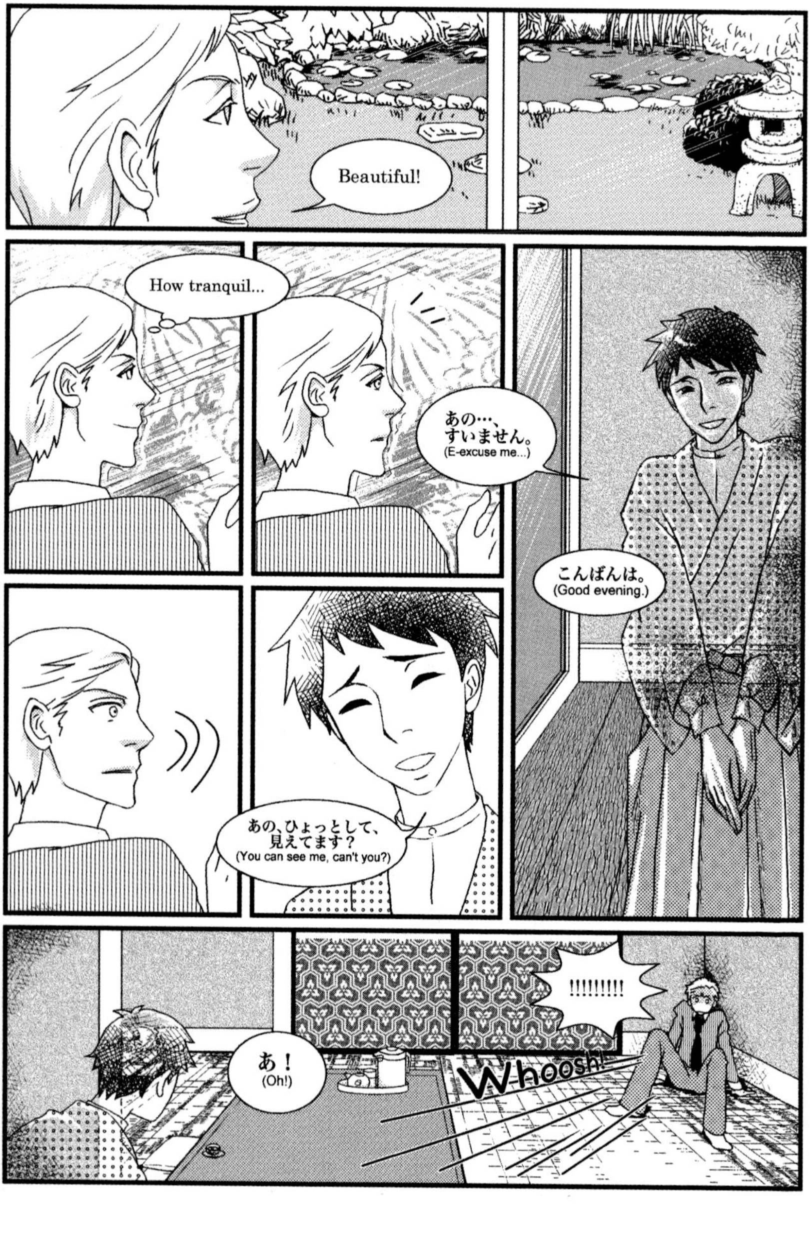
Beautiful!
How tranquil...
あの…、すいません。 (E-excuse me...)
こんばんは。 (Good evening.)
あの、ひょっとして、見えてます？ (You can see me, can't you?)
あ！ (Oh!)
Whoosh!
!!!!!!!!!

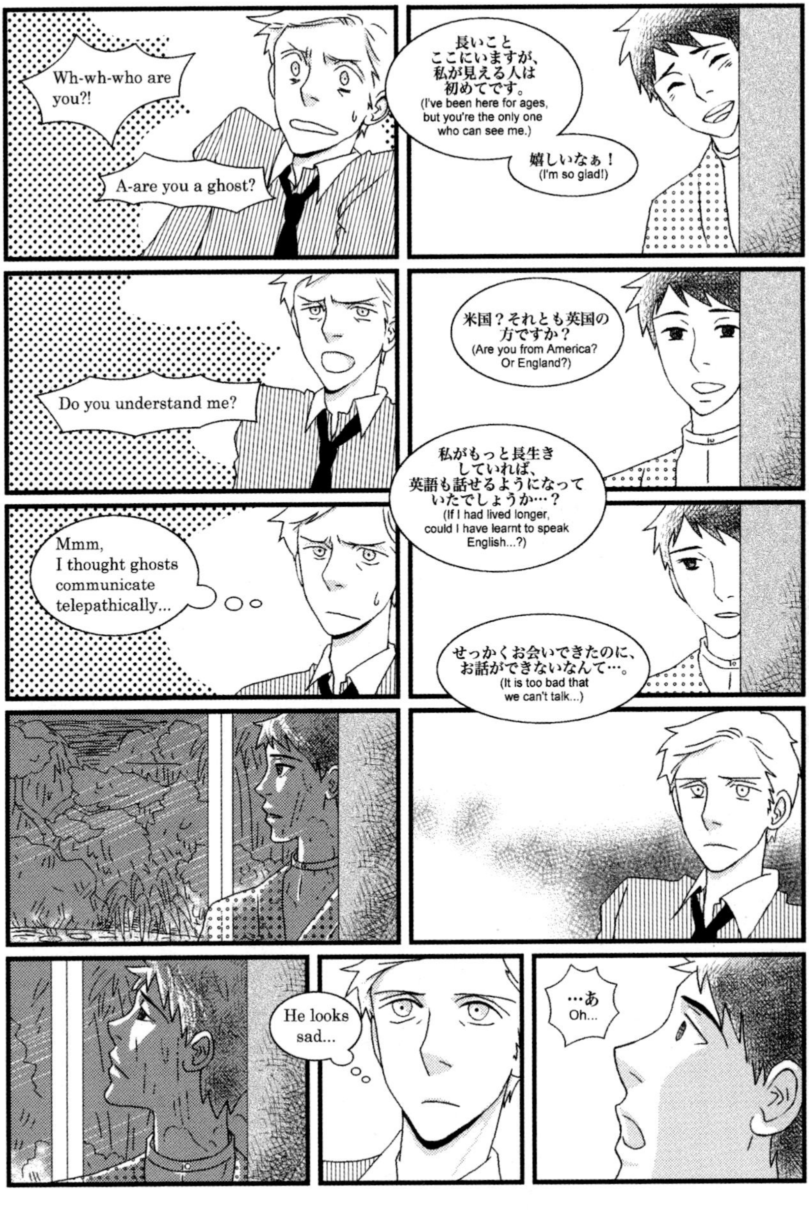
Wh-wh-who are you?!
A-are you a ghost?
長いこと ここにいますが、私が見える人は初めてです。 (I've been here for ages, but you're the only one who can see me.)
嬉しいなぁ！ (I'm so glad!)
Do you understand me?
米国？それとも英国の方ですか？ (Are you from America? Or England?)
Mmm, I thought ghosts communicate telepathically...
私がもっと長生きしていれば、英語も話せるようになっていたでしょうか…？ (If I had lived longer, could I have learnt to speak English...?)
せっかくお会いできたのに、お話ができないなんて…。 (It is too bad that we can't talk...)
He looks sad...
…あ Oh...

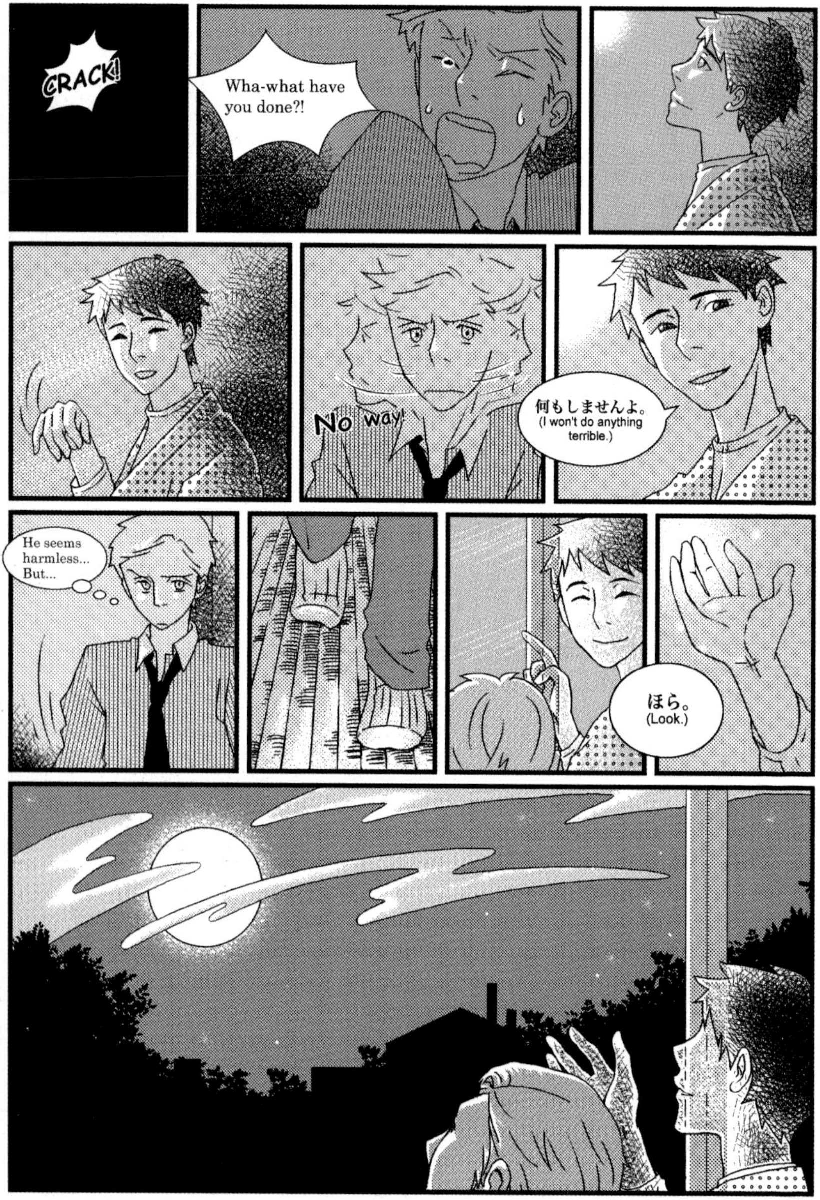
CRACK!
Wha-what have you done?!
No way!
何もしませんよ。
(I won't do anything terrible.)
He seems harmless... But...
ほら。
(Look.)

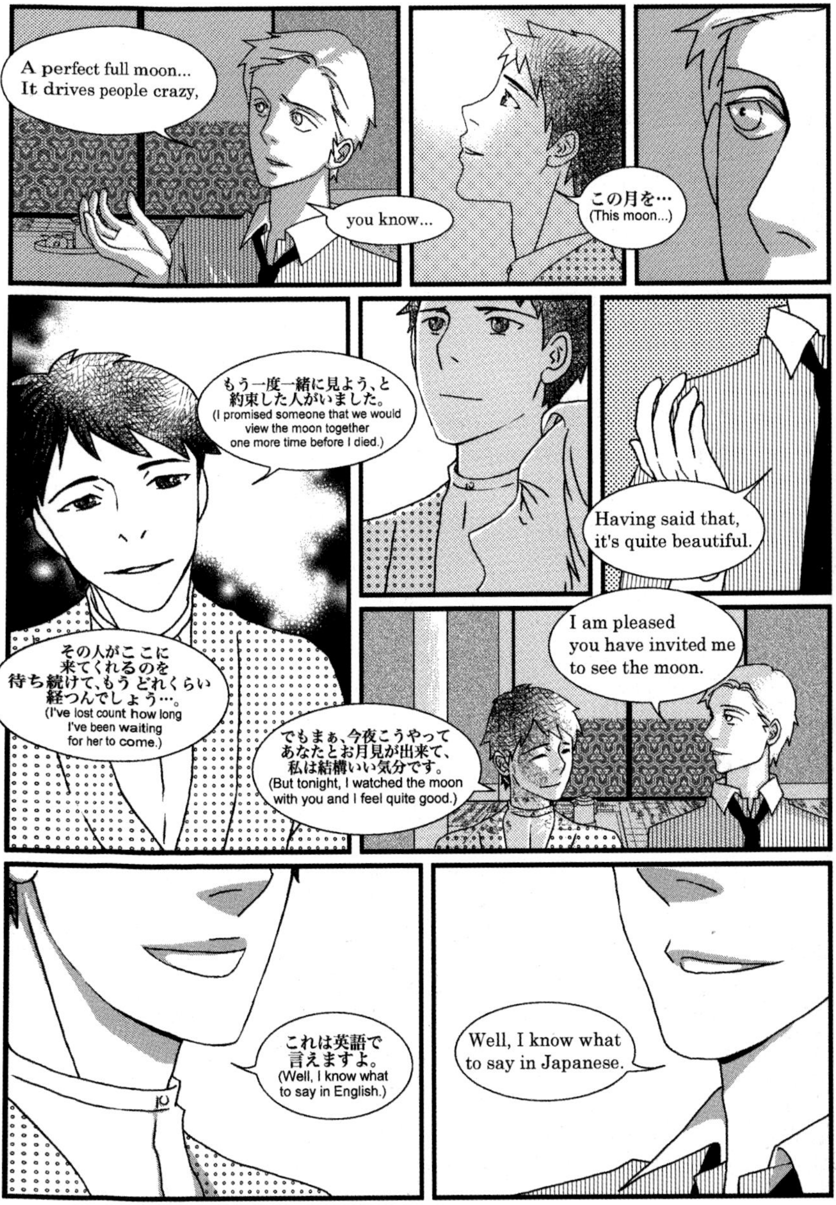
A perfect full moon... It drives people crazy,
you know...
この月を…
(This moon...)
もう一度一緒に見よう、と約束した人がいました。
(I promised someone that we would view the moon together one more time before I died.)
その人がここに来てくれるのを待ち続けて、もうどれくらい経つんでしょう…。
(I've lost count how long I've been waiting for her to come.)
Having said that, it's quite beautiful.
I am pleased you have invited me to see the moon.
でもまぁ、今夜こうやってあなたとお月見が出来て、私は結構いい気分です。
(But tonight, I watched the moon with you and I feel quite good.)
これは英語で言えますよ。
(Well, I know what to say in English.)
Well, I know what to say in Japanese.

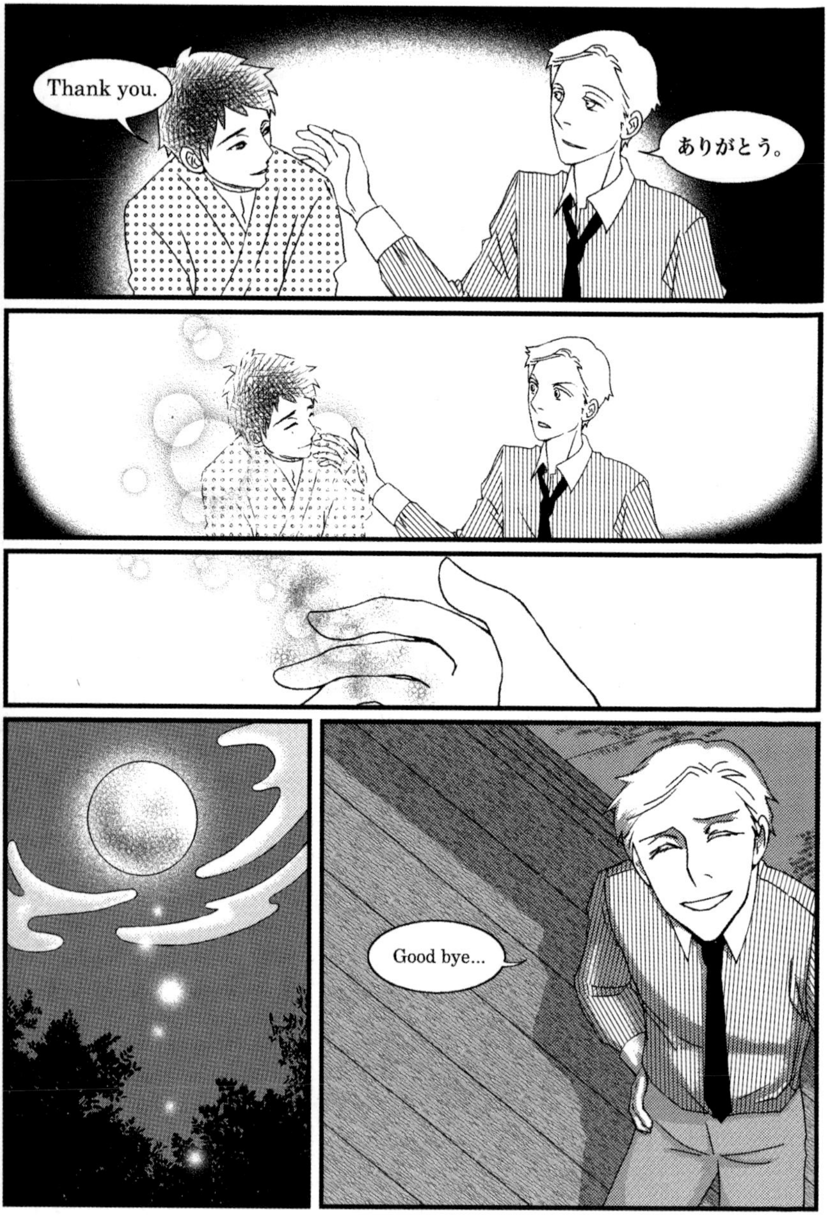
Thank you.
ありがとう。
Good bye...

End